Monographs in Theoretical Computer Science
An EATCS Series

T0137240

H. Ehrig · K. Ehrig
U. Prange · G. Taentzer

Fundamentals of Algebraic Graph Transformation

With 41 Figures

 Springer

Authors

Prof. Dr. Hartmut Ehrig
Dr. Karsten Ehrig
Ulrike Prange
Dr. Gabriele Taentzer

Technical University of Berlin
Institute for Software Engineering
and Theoretical Computer Science
Franklinstr. 28/29
10587 Berlin, Germany

ehrig@cs.tu-berlin.de
karstene@cs.tu-berlin.de
uprange@cs.tu-berlin.de
gabi@cs.tu-berlin.de

Series Editors

Prof. Dr. Wilfried Brauer
Institut für Informatik der TUM
Boltzmannstr. 3
85748 Garching, Germany
brauer@informatik.tu-muenchen.de

Prof. Dr. Grzegorz Rozenberg
Leiden Institute of Advanced
Computer Science
University of Leiden
Niels Bohrweg 1
2333 CA Leiden, The Netherlands
rozenber@liacs.nl

Prof. Dr. Arto Salomaa
Turku Centre of
Computer Science
Lemminkäisenkatu 14 A
20520 Turku, Finland
asalomaa@utu.fi

ACM Computing Classification (1998): D.1.7, D.2.1, D.3.1, F.4.2, F.4.3, G.2.2, I.1.

ISBN-13 978-3-642-06831-7   e-ISBN-13 978-3-540-31188-1

Springer is a part of Springer Science+Business Media
springer.com

© Springer-Verlag Berlin Heidelberg 2006
Softcover reprint of the hardcover 1st edition 2006

Cover Design: KünkelLopka, Heidelberg

Preface

In the late 1960s and early 1970s, the concepts of graph transformation and graph grammars started to become of interest in picture processing and computer science. The main idea was to generalize well-known rewriting techniques from strings and trees to graphs, leading to graph transformations and graph grammars. In particular, the concepts of algebraic graph transformation gained considerable importance in the early years and have done so even more in the last decade. Today, algebraic graph transformation techniques are playing a central role in theoretical computer science, as well as in several applied areas, such as software engineering, concurrent and distributed systems, and visual modeling techniques and model transformations.

The aim of this book is to present the fundamentals of algebraic graph transformation techniques for the purposes of teaching, research, and development, with respect to the following aspects:

1. Fundamentals in the sense of an introduction with a detailed motivation to algebraic graph transformation, including the main constructions and results, as well as their generalization to high-level replacement systems, with a wide range of applications in computer science and related areas.
2. Fundamentals in the sense of mathematical theories, which are the basis for precise definitions, constructions, and results, and for the implementation of algebraic graph transformation in a tool environment called AGG.
3. Fundamentals in the sense of the integration of data types and process specification techniques, where the concepts of algebraic data types are integrated with graph rewriting, leading to the concept of typed attributed graph transformation.

In accordance with these aims, the book is organized in four parts:

- *Part I: Introduction to Graph Transformation Systems*, where graph transformations based on classical graphs are introduced and the main constructions and results are motivated in detail.

- *Part II: Adhesive High-Level Replacement Categories and Systems*, where the theory is presented in a categorical framework with applications to a large variety of high-level structures, especially transformation systems for various kinds of graphs and Petri nets.
- *Part III: Typed Attributed Graph Transformation Systems*, where the concepts of typed attributed graphs are carefully introduced and the main results are obtained as instantiations of Part II.
- *Part IV: Case Study on Model Transformation, and Tool Support by AGG*, where the concepts of typed attributed graph transformation are applied in a separate case study to visual model transformation, and it is shown how the theory is implemented in the AGG tool.

The book is organized in such a way that the reader can switch, after the introduction in Part I, immediately to Part III; however, the concepts and results in both of these parts are instantiations of the categorical theory presented in Part II.

The material of this book is based on a theory of algebraic graph transformation developed at the Technical University of Berlin in cooperation with several international partners in the EU projects COMPUGRAPH, GET-GRATS, APPLIGRAPH and SEGRAVIS. This material can also be seen as being in the tradition of algebraic specification techniques, described in the EATCS series of Monographs in Theoretical Computer Science.

We are most thankful to Hans-Jörg Kreowski, Michael Pfender, Hans-Jürgen Schneider, Barry Rosen, and Grzegorz Rozenberg for creating the algebraic approach to graph transformation in fruitful cooperation with the first author in the 1970s. For the main contributions to the algebraic approach in subsequent years, we would like to thank in addition Paolo Baldan, Roswitha Bardohl, Paolo Bottoni, Andrea Corradini, Gregor Engels, Claudia Ermel, Ingrid Fischer, Annegret Habel, Reiko Heckel, Berthold Hoffmann, Manuel Koch, Barbara König, Martin Korff, Jochen Küster, Juan de Lara, Leen Lambers, Michael Löwe, Ugo Montanari, Mark Minas, Fernando Orejas, Julia Padberg, Karl-Heinz Pennemann, Francesco Parisi-Presicce, Detlef Plump, Leila Ribeiro, Francesca Rossi, Olga Runge, Andy Schürr, Pawel Sobociński, Daniel Varró, Szilvia Varró-Gyapay, Annika Wagner, and Dietmar Wolz.

We would especially like to thank Reiko Heckel for several useful comments concerning the overall structure of the book.

A draft version of the book was carefully studied by the participants of a compact seminar on "Fundamentals of Algebraic Graph Transformation" for advanced students and young researchers in the SEGRAVIS TMR network. We are most grateful to the following members of this seminar, whose comments led to several useful improvements in the final version of this book: Paolo Baldan, Enrico Biermann, Benjamin Braatz, Esther Guerra, Stefan Hänsgen, Frank Herrmann, Markus Klein, Barbara König, Sebastian Kuhnert, Juan de Lara, Tihamer Levendovsky, Katharina Mehner, Tony Modica,

Mattia Monga, Allesandra Raffaetta, Guilherme Rangel, Giovanni Toffetti Carughi, Daniel Varró, Szilvia Varró-Gyapay, and Jessica Winkelmann.

Finally, we thank Grzegorz Rozenberg and all the other editors of the EATCS monograph series, and those at Springer-Verlag, especially Ronan Nugent, for smooth publication.

Berlin, Summer 2005

Hartmut Ehrig
Karsten Ehrig
Ulrike Prange
Gabriele Taentzer

Contents

Part III Typed Attributed Graph Transformation Systems

Appendices

Introduction to Graph Transformation Systems

The first Part of this book provides a general introduction to graph transformation, graph transformation systems, and graph grammars. In Chapter 1, we start with an overview of various graph transformation approaches, especially the algebraic approach; we describe the organization of the chapters of the book; and we provide some bibliographic notes. In Chapter 2, we give a detailed introduction to the algebraic approach in the case of graphs, labeled graphs and typed graphs, leading to the basic notions and results of graph transformation systems described in Chapter 3.

The classical theory of labeled graph grammars and labeled graph transformation systems was mainly developed in the 1970s, particularly as a result of a cooperation between TU Berlin (H. Ehrig, M. Pfender, and H.J. Kreowski), the University of Erlangen (H.J. Schneider), and IBM Yorktown Heights (B. Rosen) (see [EPS73, ER76, Kre78, Ehr79]). The theory was extended in the 1980s and 1990s by groups in Bremen (H.J. Kreowski, A. Habel, D. Plump, and B. Hoffmann), Pisa (U. Montanari, A. Corradini, and P. Baldan), Rome (F. Parisi-Presicce and P. Bottoni), Leiden/Paderborn (G. Rozenberg and G. Engels) and Porto Allegre (L. Ribeiro and M. Korff), in cooperation with TU Berlin (H. Ehrig, G. Taentzer, M. Löwe, and R. Heckel); this is documented in the three volumes of the *Handbook of Graph Grammars and Computation by Graph Transformation* [Roz97, EEKR99, EKMR99]. The main work in the last five years has been on extensions of the theory to typed attributed graph transformation and adhesive high-level replacement systems, which are described in Parts II and III of this book.

For those readers who are interested mainly in the concepts and results of transformation systems for classical and typed attributed graphs, but not so much in the general theory and the proofs, it is advisable to read Part I, skip Part II, and continue after Part I with Parts III and IV.

1

General Introduction

The main idea of graph grammars and graph transformation is the rule-based modification of graphs, where each application of a graph rule leads to a graph transformation step. Graph grammars can be used to generate graph languages similar to Chomsky grammars in formal language theory. Moreover, graphs can be used to model the states of all kinds of systems, which allows one to use graph transformation to model state changes in these systems. This enables the user to apply graph grammars and graph transformation systems to a wide range of fields in computer science and other areas of science and engineering. A detailed presentation of various graph grammar approaches and application areas of graph transformation is given in the three volumes of the *Handbook of Graph Grammars and Computing by Graph Transformation* [Roz97, EEKR99, EKMR99].

1.1 General Overview of Graph Grammars and Graph Transformation

The research area of graph grammars or graph transformation is a discipline of computer science which dates back to the 1970s. Methods, techniques, and results from the area of graph transformation have already been studied and applied in many fields of computer science, such as formal language theory, pattern recognition and generation, compiler construction, software engineering, the modeling of concurrent and distributed systems, database design and theory, logical and functional programming, artificial intelligence, and visual modeling.

This wide applicability is due to the fact that graphs are a very natural way of explaining complex situations on an intuitive level. Hence, they are used in computer science almost everywhere, for example for data and control flow diagrams, for entity relationship and UML diagrams, for Petri nets, for visualization of software and hardware architectures, for evolution diagrams of nondeterministic processes, for SADT diagrams, and for many more purposes. Like the token game for Petri nets, graph transformation allows one to model the dynamics in all these descriptions, since it can describe the evolution of graphical structures. Therefore, graph transformations have become attractive as a modeling and programming paradigm for complex-structured software and graphical interfaces. In particular, graph rewriting is promising as a comprehensive framework in which the transformation of all these very different structures can be modeled and studied in a uniform way.

Before we go into more detail, we discuss the following basic question.

1.1.1 What Is Graph Transformation?

Graph transformation has at least three different roots:

- from Chomsky grammars on strings to graph grammars;
- from term rewriting to graph rewriting;
- from textual description to visual modeling.

We use the notion of graph transformation to comprise the concepts of graph grammars and graph rewriting. In any case, the main idea of graph transformation is the rule-based modification of graphs, as shown in Fig. 1.1.

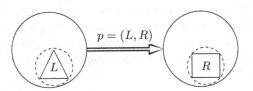

Fig. 1.1. Rule-based modification of graphs

The core of a rule or production, $p = (L, R)$ is a pair of graphs (L, R), called the left-hand side L and the right-hand side R. Applying the rule $p = (L, R)$ means finding a match of L in the source graph and replacing L by R, leading to the target graph of the graph transformation. The main technical problems are how to delete L and how to connect R with the context in the target graph. In fact, there are several different solutions to how to handle these problems, leading to several different graph transformation approaches, which are summarized below.

1.1.2 Aims and Paradigms of Graph Transformation

Computing was originally done on the level of the von Neumann Machine which is based on machine instructions and registers. This kind of low-level computing was considerably improved by assembler and high-level imperative languages. From the conceptual point of view – but not necessarily from the point of view of efficiency – these languages were further improved by functional and logical programming languages. This newer kind of computing is based mainly on term rewriting, which, by analogy with graphs and graph transformations, can be considered as a concept in the field of tree transformations. Trees, however, unlike graphs, do not allow sharing of common substructures, which was one of the main reasons for the efficiency problems concerning functional and logical programs. This motivates us to consider graphs rather than trees as the fundamental structures of computing.

The main idea is to advocate graph transformations for the whole range of computing. Our concept of computing by graph transformations is not focused only on programming but includes also specification and implementation by graph transformation, as well as graph algorithms and computational models, and computer architectures for graph transformations.

This concept of computing by graph transformations was developed as a basic paradigm in the ESPRIT Basic Research Actions COMPUGRAPH and APPLIGRAPH and in the TMR Network GETGRATS during the years 1990–2002. It can be summarized in the following way.

Computing by graph transformation is a fundamental concept for the following items:

- *Visual modeling and specification.* Graphs are a well-known, well-understood, and frequently used means to represent system states. Class and object diagrams, network graphs, entity-relationship diagrams, and Petri nets are common graphical representations of system states or classes of system states; there are also many other graphical representations. Rules have proved to be extremely useful for describing computations by local transformations of states. In object-oriented modeling, graphs occur at two levels: the type level (defined on the basis of class diagrams) and the instance level (given by all valid object diagrams). Modeling by graph transformation is visual, on the one hand, since it is very natural to use a visual representation of graphs; on the other hand, it is precise, owing to its formal foundation. Thus, graph transformation can also be used in formal specification techniques for state-based systems.

  The aspect of supporting visual modeling by graph transformation is one of the main intentions of the ESPRIT TMR Network SEGRAVIS (2002–2006). In fact, there are a wide range of applications in the support of visual modeling techniques, especially in the context of UML, by graph transformation techniques.

- *Model transformation.* In recent years, model-based software development processes (such as that proposed by the MDA [RFW+04]) have evolved. In this area, we are witnessing a paradigm shift, where models are no longer mere (passive) documentation, but are used for code generation, analysis, and simulation as well. An important question is how to specify such model transformations. Starting from visual models as discussed above, graph transformation is certainly a natural choice. On the basis of the underlying structure of such visual models, the abstract syntax graphs, the model transformation is defined. Owing to the formal foundation, the correctness of model transformations can be checked. More precisely, correctness can be formulated on a solid mathematical basis, and there is a good chance of verifying correctness using the theory of graph transformation. The first steps in this direction have been taken already (see Chapter 14).

- *Concurrency and distribution.* When graph transformation is used to describe a concurrent system, graphs are usually taken to describe static system structures. System behavior expressed by state changes is modeled by rule-based graph manipulations, i.e. graph transformation. The rules describe preconditions and postconditions of single transformation steps. In a pure graph transformation system, the order of the steps is determined by the causal dependency of actions only, i.e. independent rule applications can be executed in an arbitrary order. The concept of rules in graph transformation provides a clear concept for defining system behavior. In particular, for modeling the intrinsic concurrency of actions, graph rules provide a suitable means, because they explicate all structural interdependencies.

  If we stick to sequential execution, parallel transformations have to be modeled by interleaving their atomic actions arbitrarily. This interleaving leads to the same result if the atomic actions are independent of each other. Simultaneous execution of actions can be modeled if a parallel rule is composed from the actions.

  Parallel and distributed graph transformation both offer structured rule applications, in both temporal and spatial dimensions. Distributed graphs contain an additional structure on the graphs. Graphs are allowed to be split into local graphs and, after local transformations, local graphs are joined again to one global graph. Parallel graph transformation can be considered as a special case of distributed graph transformation, where the host graph is nondistributed.

- *Software development.* In software development, a large variety of different structures occur on different levels, which can be handled as graphs. We distinguish architectural and technical structures from administrative configurations and integration documents. All this structural information evolves, i.e. it changes during the software development process. This includes editing of documents, execution of operations, modification (optimization) of programs, analysis, configuration and revision control, etc. Graph transformation techniques have been used to describe this structural evolution in a rule-based way.

  For software development purposes, graphs have several advantages over trees. Graphs are a powerful description technique for any kind of structure. This means that all structural information can be expressed by graphs and does not have to be stored outside the structural part, as is done in the case of trees. Attributes are important for storing data information. In this way, structural information is separated from nonstructural.

Graph transformations are used to describe certain development processes. Thus, we can argue that we program on graphs. But we do so in a quite abstract form, since the class of structures is the class of graphs and is not specialized to a specific class. Furthermore, the elementary operations on graphs are rule applications. Mostly, the execution order of rule applications relies on structural dependencies only, i.e. it is just given implicitly. Alternatively, explicit control mechanisms for rule applications can be used.

A state-of-the-art report on applications, languages, and tools for graph transformation on the one hand and for concurrency, parallelism, and distribution on the other hand is given in Volumes 2 and 3 of the *Handbook of Graph Grammars and Computing by Graph Transformation* [EEKR99, EKMR99].

1.1.3 Overview of Various Approaches

From an operational point of view, a graph transformation from G to H, written $G \Rightarrow H$, usually contains the following main steps, as shown in Fig. 1.2:

1. *Choose* a production $p : L \Rightarrow R$ with a left-hand side L and a right-hand side R, and with an occurrence of L in G.
2. *Check* the application conditions of the production.
3. *Remove* from G that part of L which is not part of R. If edges dangle after deletion of L, either the production is not applied or the dangling edges are also deleted. The graph obtained is called D.
4. *Glue* the right-hand side R to the graph D at the part of L which still has an image in D. The part of R not coming from L is added disjointly to D. The resulting graph is E.
5. If the production p contains an additional embedding relation, then *embed* the right-hand side R further into the graph E according to this embedding relation. The end result is the graph H.

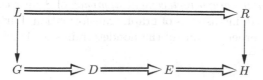

Fig. 1.2. Graph transformation from an operational point of view

Graph transformation systems can show two kinds of nondeterminism: first, several productions might be applicable and one of them is chosen arbitrarily; and second, given a certain production, several matches might be possible and one of them has to be chosen. There are techniques available to restrict both kinds of choice. Some kind of control flow on rules can be defined for applying them in a certain order or by using explicit control constructs, priorities, layers, etc. Moreover, the choice of matches can be restricted by specifying partial matches using input parameters.

The main graph grammar and graph transformation approaches developed in the literature so far are presented in Volume 1 of the *Handbook of Graph Grammars and Computing by Graph Transformation* [Roz97]:

1. The *node label replacement approach*, developed mainly by Rozenberg, Engelfriet, and Janssens, allows a single node, as the left-hand side L, to be replaced by an arbitrary graph R. The connection of R with the context is determined by an embedding relation depending on node labels. For each removed dangling edge incident with the image of a node n in L, and each node n' in R, a new edge (with the same label) incident with n' is established provided that (n, n') belongs to the embedding relation.

2. The *hyperedge replacement approach*, developed mainly by Habel, Kreowski, and Drewes, has as the left-hand side L a labeled hyperedge, which is replaced by an arbitrary hypergraph R with designated attachment nodes corresponding to the nodes of L. The gluing of R to the context at the corresponding attachment nodes leads to the target graph without using an additional embedding relation.

3. The *algebraic approach* is based on pushout constructions, where pushouts are used to model the gluing of graphs. In fact, there are two main variants of the algebraic approach, the double- and the single-pushout approach. The double-pushout approach, developed mainly by Ehrig, Schneider, and the Berlin and Pisa groups, is introduced in Section 1.2 and presented later in Part I of this book in more detail. In both cases, there is no additional embedding relation.

4. The *logical approach*, developed mainly by Courcelle and Bouderon, allows graph transformation and graph properties to be expressed in monadic second-order logic.

5. The *theory of 2-structures* was initiated by Rozenberg and Ehrenfeucht, as a framework for the decomposition and transformation of graphs.

6. The *programmed graph replacement approach* of Schürr combines the gluing and embedding aspects of graph transformation. Furthermore, it uses programs in order to control the nondeterministic choice of rule applications.

1.2 The Main Ideas of the Algebraic Graph Transformation Approach

As mentioned above, the algebraic graph transformation approach is based on pushout constructions, where pushouts are used to model the gluing of graphs. In the algebraic approach, initiated by Ehrig, Pfender, and Schneider in [EPS73], two gluing constructions are used to model a graph transformation step, as shown in Fig. 1.4. For this reason, this approach is also known as the double-pushout (DPO) approach, in contrast to the single-pushout (SPO) approach. Both of these approaches are briefly discussed below.

1.2.1 The DPO Approach

In the DPO approach, roughly speaking, a production is given by $p = (L, K, R)$, where L and R are the left- and right-hand side graphs and K is the common interface of L and R, i.e. their intersection. The left-hand side L represents the preconditions of the rule, while the right-hand side R describes the postconditions. K describes a graph part which has to exist to apply the rule, but which is not changed. $L \backslash K$ describes the part which is to be deleted, and $R \backslash K$ describes the part to be created.

A *direct graph transformation* with a production p is defined by first finding a match m of the left-hand side L in the current host graph G such that m is structure-preserving.

When a direct graph transformation with a production p and a match m is performed, all the vertices and edges which are matched by $L \backslash K$ are removed from G. The removed part is not a graph, in general, but the remaining structure $D := (G \backslash m(L)) \cup m(K)$ still has to be a legal graph, i.e., no edges should be left dangling. This means that the match m has to satisfy a suitable gluing condition, which makes sure that the gluing of $L \backslash K$ and D is equal to G (see (1) in Fig. 1.3). In the second step of a direct graph transformation, the graph D is glued together with $R \backslash K$ to obtain the derived graph H (see (2) in Fig. 1.3). Since L and R can overlap in K, the submatch occurs in the original graph G and is not deleted in the first step, i.e. it also occurs in the intermediate graph D. For gluing newly created vertices and edges into D, the graph K is used. This defines the gluing items at which R is inserted into D. A *graph transformation*, or, more precisely, a graph transformation sequence, consists of zero or more direct graph transformations.

More formally, a direct graph transformation with p and m is defined as follows. Given a production $p = (L \leftarrow K \rightarrow R)$ and a context graph D, which includes also the interface K, the source graph G of a graph transformation $G \Rightarrow H$ via p is given by the gluing of L and D via K, written $G = L +_K D$, and the target graph H is given by the gluing of R and D via K, written $H = R +_K D$. More precisely, we shall use graph morphisms $K \rightarrow L$, $K \rightarrow R$, and $K \rightarrow D$ to express how K is included in L, R, and D, respectively. This allows us to define the gluing constructions $G = L +_K D$ and $H = R +_K D$ as the pushout constructions (1) and (2) in Fig. 1.3, leading to a double pushout. The resulting graph morphism $R \rightarrow H$ is called the comatch of the graph transformation $G \Rightarrow H$.

In order to apply a production p with a match m of L in G, given by a graph morphism $m : L \rightarrow G$ as shown in Fig. 1.3, we first have to construct a context graph D such that the gluing $L+_K D$ of L and D via K is equal to G. In the second step, we construct the gluing $R+_K D$ of R and D via K, leading to the graph H and hence to a DPO graph transformation $G \Rightarrow H$ via p and m. For the construction of the first step, however, a *gluing condition* has to be satisfied, which allows us to construct D with $L +_K D = G$. In the case of an injective match m, the gluing condition states that all dangling points of L, i.e. the nodes x in L such that $m(x)$ is the source or target of an edge e in $G \setminus L$, must be gluing points x in K.

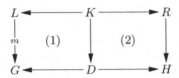

Fig. 1.3. DPO graph transformation

A simple example of a DPO graph transformation step is given in Fig. 1.4, corresponding to the general scheme in Fig. 1.3. Note that in the diagram (PO1), G is the gluing of the graphs L and D along K, where the numbering of the nodes indicates how the nodes are mapped by graph morphisms. The mapping of the edges can be uniquely deduced from the node mapping. Note that the gluing condition is satisfied in Fig. 1.4, because the dangling points (1) and (2) of L are also gluing points. Moreover, H is the gluing of R and D along K in (PO2), leading to a graph transformation $G \Rightarrow H$ via p. In fact, the diagrams (PO1) and (PO2) are pushouts in the category **Graphs** of graphs and graph morphisms (see Chapter 2).

For technical reasons, the morphisms $K \to L$ and $K \to R$ in the productions are usually restricted to injective graph morphisms. However, we allow noninjective matches $m : L \to G$ and comatches $n : R \to H$. This is especially useful when we consider a parallel production $p_1 + p_2 : L_1 + L_2 \leftarrow K_1 + K_2 \to R_1 + R_2$, where $+$ denotes the disjoint union. Even for injective matches $m_1 : L_1 \to G$ of p_1 and $m_2 : L_2 \to G$ of p_2, the resulting match $m : L_1 + L_2 \to G$ is noninjective if the matches $m_1(L_1)$ and $m_2(L_2)$ are overlapping in G.

1.2.2 The Algebraic Roots

In Chapter 2, we shall see that a graph $G = (V, E, s, t)$ is a special case of an algebra with two base sets V (vertices) and E (edges), and operations $s : E \to V$ (source) and $t : E \to V$ (target). Graph morphisms $f : G_1 \to G_2$ are special cases of algebra homomorphisms $f = (f_V : V_1 \to V_2, f_E : E_1 \to E_2)$. This means that f_V and f_E are required to be compatible with the operations, i.e. $f_V \circ s_1 = s_2 \circ f_E$ and $f_V \circ t_1 = t_2 \circ f_E$. In Fig. 1.4, all arrows

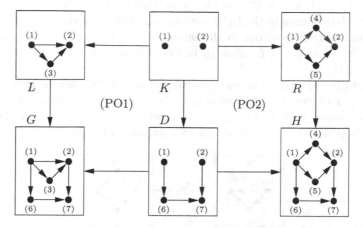

Fig. 1.4. Example of DPO graph transformation

between the boxes are graph morphisms. Moreover, the gluing construction of graphs can be considered as an algebraic quotient algebra construction. This algebraic view of graphs and graph transformations is one of the main ideas of the algebraic graph transformation approach introduced in [EPS73, Ehr79].

1.2.3 From the DPO to the SPO Approach

As pointed out already, the gluing constructions in the algebraic approach are pushouts in the category **Graphs** based on (total) graph morphisms. On the other hand, the production $p = (L \leftarrow K \rightarrow R)$ shown in Fig. 1.4 can also be considered as a partial graph morphism $p : L \rightarrow R$ with domain $dom(p) = K$. Moreover, the span $(G \leftarrow D \rightarrow H)$ can be considered as a partial graph morphism $s : G \rightarrow H$ with $dom(s) = D$. This leads to the diagram in Fig. 1.5, where the horizontal morphisms are partial and the vertical ones are total graph morphisms. In fact, Fig. 1.5 is a pushout in the category **PGraphs** of graphs and partial graph morphisms and shows that the graph transformation can be expressed by a single pushout in the category **PGraphs**. This approach was initiated by Raoult [Rao84] and fully worked out by Löwe [Löw90], leading to the single-pushout approach.

From the operational point of view, the SPO approach differs in one main respect from the DPO approach, which concerns the deletion of context graph elements during a graph transformation step. If the match $m : L \rightarrow G$ does not satisfy the gluing condition with respect to a production $p = (L \leftarrow K \rightarrow R)$, then the production is not applicable in the DPO approach. But it is applicable in the SPO approach, which allows dangling edges to occur after the deletion of $L \backslash K$ from G. However, the dangling edges in G are also deleted, leading to a well-defined graph H.

If, in Fig. 1.4, vertex (2) were to be deleted from K, the gluing condition would not be satisfied in the DPO approach. In the SPO approach, this would mean that vertex (2) is not in the domain of p, leading to a dangling edge e in G after deletion of $L \setminus dom(p)$ in Fig. 1.5. As a result, edge e would be deleted in H.

A detailed presentation and comparison of the two approaches is given in Volume 1 of the *Handbook of Graph Grammars and Computing by Graph Transformation* [Roz97]. In this book, however, we consider only the DPO approach as the algebraic graph transformation approach.

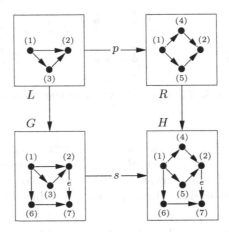

Fig. 1.5. Example of SPO graph transformation

1.2.4 From Graphs to High-Level Structures

The algebraic approach to graph transformation is not restricted to the graphs of the form $G = (V, E, s, t)$ considered above, but has been generalized to a large variety of different types of graphs and other kinds of high-level structures, such as labeled graphs, typed graphs, hypergraphs, attributed graphs, Petri nets, and algebraic specifications, which will be considered in later chapters of this book. This extension from graphs to high-level structures – in contrast to strings and trees, considered as low-level structures – was initiated in [EHKP91a, EHKP91b] leading to the theory of high-level replacement (HLR) systems. In [EHPP04], the concept of high-level replacement systems was joined to that of *adhesive categories* introduced by Lack and Sobociński in [LS04], leading to the concept of adhesive HLR categories and systems, which will be described in Chapters 4 and 5. The theory of adhesive HLR systems, developed in Part II of this book, can be instantiated in particular to typed attributed graph transformation systems, described in Part III, which are especially important for applications to visual languages and software engineering. In Part I of this book, we give an introduction to classical graph transformation systems, as considered in [Ehr79]. Hence the fundamentals of algebraic graph transformation are given in this book on three different levels: in Part I on the classical level, in Part II on the level of adhesive HLR systems, and in Part III on the level of typed attributed graph transformation systems. A more detailed overview of the four Parts is given below.

1.3 The Chapters of This Book and the Main Results

The chapters of this book are grouped into Parts I–IV and three appendices.

1.3.1 Part I: Introduction to Graph Transformation Systems

Part I of this book is an introduction to graph transformation systems in general and to the algebraic approach in the classical sense of [Ehr79] in particular. In Chapter 2, we introduce graphs, graph morphisms, typed graphs and the gluing construction for sets and graphs. In order to show that the gluing construction is a pushout in the sense of category theory, we also introduce some basic notions of category theory, including the categories **Sets** and **Graphs**, and pullbacks as dual constructions of pushouts.

This is the basis for introducing the basic notions of graph transformation systems in Chapter 3. As mentioned above, a direct graph transformation is defined by two gluing constructions, which are pushouts in the category **Graphs**. The first main results for graph transformations discussed in Chapter 3 are concerned with parallel and sequential independence of graph transformations. The Local Church–Rosser Theorem allows one to apply two graph transformations $G \Rightarrow H_1$ via p_1 and $G \Rightarrow H_2$ via p_2 in an arbitrary order, provided that they are *parallel independent*. In this case they can also be applied in parallel, leading to a parallel graph transformation $G \Rightarrow H$ via the *parallel production $p_1 + p_2$*. This second main result is called the Parallelism Theorem. In addition, in Chapter 3 we give a detailed description of the motivation for and an overview of some other main results including the Concurrency, Embedding, and Extension Theorems, as well as results related to critical pairs, confluence, termination, and the Local Confluence Theorem. Finally, we discuss graph constraints and application conditions for graph transformations. All these results are stated in Chapter 3 without proof, because they are special cases of corresponding results in Parts II and III.

1.3.2 Part II: Adhesive HLR Categories and Systems

In Part II, we introduce adhesive HLR categories and systems, as outlined in Subsection 1.2.4 above. In addition to pushouts, which correspond to the gluing of graphs, they are based on pullbacks, corresponding to the intersection and homomorphic preimages of graphs. The basic axioms of adhesive

HLR categories stated in Chapter 4 require construction and basic compatibility properties for pushouts and pullbacks. From these basic properties, several other results, called HLR properties, can be concluded, which allow us to prove the main results stated in Part I on the general level of high-level replacement systems. We are able to show that there are several interesting instantiations of adhesive HLR systems, including not only graph and typed graph transformation systems, but also hypergraph, Petri net, algebraic specification, and typed attributed graph transformation systems. The HLR properties allow us to prove, in Chapter 5, the Local Church–Rosser and Parallelism Theorems, concerning independent transformations, as well as the Concurrency Theorem, concerning the simultanous execution of causally dependent transformations.

Some further important results for transformation systems are the Embedding, Extension, and Local Confluence Theorems presented in Chapter 6. The first two allow us to embed transformations into larger contexts, and with the third one we are able to show local confluence of transformation systems on the basis of the confluence of critical pairs.

In Chapter 7, we define constraints and application conditions for adhesive HLR systems, which generalize the graph constraints and application conditions introduced in Chapter 3. We are able to show, as the main results, how to transform constraints into right application conditions and, further, how to transform right to left application conditions. A left or right application condition is a condition which has to be satisfied by the match $L \to G$ or the comatch $R \to H$, respectively, of a DPO transformation, as shown for graphs in Fig. 1.3.

1.3.3 Part III: Typed Attributed Graph Transformation Systems

In Part III, we apply the theory of Part II to the case of typed attributed graph transformation systems outlined in Subsection 1.2.4. In Chapter 8, we introduce attributed type graphs ATG, typed attributed graphs, and typed attributed graph morphisms leading to the category **AGraphs**$_{\mathbf{ATG}}$ of typed attributed graphs and the construction of pushouts and pullbacks in this category. In Chapter 9, we define the basic concepts of typed attributed graph transformations. Moreover, we extend some of the main results from the case of graphs considered in Chapter 3 to typed attributed graphs. In particular, this leads to the important result of local confluence for typed attributed graph transformation systems based on confluence of critical pairs. All the results suggested in Chapter 3 and presented in the general framework of Part II are instantiated for typed attributed graph transformation in Chapters 9 and 10. They are proven in Chapter 11 by showing that **AGraphs**$_{\mathbf{ATG}}$ is an adhesive HLR category with suitable additional properties, which allows us to apply the general results from Part II. In Chapter 12, we apply the categorical theory of constraints and application conditions to typed attributed graph transformation systems and discuss termination in addition. In Chapter 13, we introduce attributed type graphs with inheritance in order to model type inheritance in the sense of class inheritance in UML. The main result shows the equivalence of concrete transformations without inheritance and abstract transformations with inheritance. However, the use of inheritance leads to a much more efficient representation and computation of typed attributed graph transformations.

1.3.4 Part IV: Case Study and Tool Support

In Part IV, we show how the theory of Part III can be applied in a case study and what kind of tool support can be offered at present. A case study of model transformation from statecharts to Petri nets using typed attributed graph transformation systems is given in Chapter 14. In Chapter 15, we show how typed attributed graph transformation has been implemented in the AGG tool environment developed at TU Berlin [AGG, ERT99].

1.3.5 Appendices

In Appendix A, we give a short introduction to category theory summarizing the main categorical concepts introduced in Parts I–III together with some technical results. Since, on the one hand, typed attributed graphs as considered in Part III are based on algebraic signatures and algebras, and, on the other hand, algebraic specifications themselves and in connection with Petri nets are interesting instantiations of adhesive HLR systems, we review the corresponding algebraic concepts from [EM85] in Appendix B. Finally, we present in Appendix C all of the proofs that were postponed in Parts I–III.

1.3.6 Hints for Reading This Book

For those readers who are interested mainly in the concepts and results of transformation systems for classical and typed attributed graphs, but not so much in the general theory and in the proofs, it is advisable to read Part I but to skip Part II and continue immediately with Parts III and IV.

1.4 Bibliographic Notes and Further Topics

In this last section of the introduction, we present some bibliographic notes and an overview of further topics concerning concepts, applications, languages, and tools for graph transformation systems.

1.4.1 Concepts of Graph Grammars and Graph Transformation Systems

Graph transformation originally evolved in the late 1960s and early 1970s [PR69, Pra71, EPS73] as a reaction to shortcomings in the expressiveness of classical approaches to rewriting, such as Chomsky grammars and term rewriting, to deal with nonlinear structures. The main graph grammar and graph transformation approaches that are still popular today are presented in Volume 1 of the *Handbook of Graph Grammars and Computing by Graph Transformation* [Roz97] and have been mentioned in Subsection 1.1.2 already. In contrast to the algebraic approach, which is based on the concept of gluing (see Section 1.2), the NLC approach [JR80] and other ones such as that of Nagl in [Nag79] can be considered as embedding approaches. In this case, the embedding (of the right-hand side into the context graph) is realized by a disjoint union, with as many new edges as needed to connect the right-hand side with the context graph. Nagl's approach has been extended by Schürr to programmed graph replacement systems [Sch97], leading to the PROGRES approach in [SWZ99]. In the FUJABA approach [FUJ], graph transformations are used in order to define transformations from UML to Java and back again. Both approaches allow the replacement of substructures in an unknown context using the concept of *set nodes* or *multiobjects*.

Concerning the algebraic approach described in Parts I and II, most of the concepts in the classical case of graph transformation systems were developed in the 1970s [EPS73, Ehr79]. Application conditions were first considered in the 1980s [EH86], and negative application conditions together with graph constraints in the 1990s [HW95, HHT96], including the important result of transforming graph constraints into application conditions.

The main parts of the theory for the DPO and SPO approaches are presented in Volume 1 of the *Handbook of Graph Grammars and Computing by Graph Transformation* [Roz97]. In addition to our presentation in Part I, the presentation in the *Handbook* includes an abstract concurrent semantics of graph transformation systems in the DPO case. This is based on the shift equivalence of parallel graph transformations, developed by Kreowski in his Ph.D. thesis [Kre78]. Further concepts concerning parallelism, concurrency, and distribution for the algebraic and other approaches are presented in Baldan's Ph.D. thesis [Bal00] and in Volume 3 of the *Handbook of Graph Grammars and Computing by Graph Transformation* [EKMR99]. For the concepts of term graph rewriting, hierarchical graph transformation systems, graph transformation modules and units, and for the first approaches to the analysis, verification, and testing of graph transformation systems, we refer to the proceedings of the first and second International Conferences on Graph Transformation ICGT 2002 [CEKR02] and ICGT 2004 [EEPR04].

The first approach to HLR categories and systems, as presented in Part II, was described in [EHKP91b] and was joined to adhesive categories [LS04] in [EHPP04] and [EEHP04]. Attributed and typed attributed graph transformations, as described in Part III, were considered explicitly in the 1990s, especially in [LKW93, CL95, HKT02]. A fundamental theory for these important kinds of graph transformation systems was first developed in [EPT04] as an instantiation of adhesive HLR systems.

1.4.2 Application Areas of Graph Transformation Systems

At the very beginning, the main application areas of graph transformation systems were rule-based image recognition [PR69] and translation of diagram languages [Pra71]. Later on, graph transformations have been applied to several areas in computer science, biology, chemistry, and engineering, as documented in Volume 2 of the *Handbook of Graph Grammars and Computing by Graph Transformation* [EEKR99]. More recently, graph transformations have been applied most successfully to the following areas in software engineering, some part of which have been mentioned already in Subsection 1.1.2:

- model and program transformation;
- syntax and semantics of visual languages;
- visual modeling of behavior and programming;
- modeling, metamodeling, and model-driven architecture;
- software architectures and evolution;
- refactoring of programs and software systems;
- security policies.

Other important application areas have been term graph rewriting, DNA computing, Petri nets, process algebras and mobile systems, distributed algorithms and scheduling problems, graph theory, logic, and discrete structures. These application areas have been subject of the international conferences ICGT 2002 [CEKR02] and ICGT 2004 [EEPR04], together with the following satellite workshops and tutorials, most of which have been published in Electronic Notes in Theoretical Computer Science (see e.g. [GTV03, SET03]):

- Graph Transformation and Visual Modeling Techniques (GTVMT);
- Software Evolution through Transformations (SETRA);
- Petri Nets and Graph Transformations (PNGT);
- DNA Computing and Graph Transformation (DNAGT);
- Graphs, Logic and Discrete Structures;
- Term Graph Rewriting (TERMGRAPH).

1.4.3 Languages and Tools for Graph Transformation Systems

In Chapter 15, we discuss the implementation of typed attributed graph transformation using the AGG language and tool [AGG, ERT99]. A basic version of AGG was implemented by Löwe et al. in the early 1990s, and later a completely redesigned version was implemented and extended by Taentzer, Runge, and others. Another general-purpose graph transformation language and tool is PROGRES [Sch97, SWZ99]. Quite different support is offered by FUJABA [FUJ], an environment for round-trip engineering between UML and Java based on graph transformation.

Two examples of more application-specific tools are DIAGEN [Min97] and GenGed [BE00, Bar02]. These provide support for the generation of graphical editors based on the definition of visual languages using graph grammars. In addition, several model transformation tools based on graph transformation have been developed, e.g. ATOM^3 [dLV02a], MetaEnv [BP02], and Viatra [VP03]. More detailed presentations of languages and tools are given in Volume 2 of the *Handbook of Graph Grammars and Computing by Graph Transformation* [EEKR99] and in the proceedings [MST02, MST04] of the GraBats workshops on graph-based tools held as satellite events of ICGT 2002 and 2004 [CEKR02, EEPR04].

1.4.4 Future Work

The aim of this book is to present the fundamentals of algebraic graph transformation based on the double-pushout approach. As discussed above, there are several other topics within the DPO approach which have been published already, but are not presented in this book. There are also several interesting topics for future work. First of all, it would be interesting to have a similar fundamental theory for the single-pushout approach. A comparative study of the DPO and SPO approaches is presented in Volume 1 of the *Handbook of Graph Grammars and Computing by Graph Transformation* [Roz97]. Another important topic for future research is the DPO approach with borrowed context [EK04], motivated by process algebra and bigraphical reactive systems in the sense of Milner [Mil01] and Sobociński [Sob04]. Concerning the main topics of this book, it is open to extend the main results for graph transformations to the case of negative and general application conditions and also to study new kinds of constraints for graphs and typed attributed graphs. Concerning typed attributed graph transformation, we have introduced type inheritance, but it remains open to extend the theory in Chapters 9–12 to this case. Finally, the theory has to be extended to meet the needs of several interesting application domains. In particular, in the area of model transformations (Chapter 14), it remains open to develop new techniques in addition to the analysis of termination and confluence, to show the correctness of model transformations.

Graphs, Typed Graphs, and the Gluing Construction

This chapter is an introduction to graphs and typed graphs. Moreover, some basic notions of category theory are presented which are essential to the gluing construction of graphs. In Section 2.1, we define graphs, graph morphisms, and typed graphs. To analyze graphs with categorical methods, we introduce categories, and as special morphism types, monomorphisms, epimorphisms, and isomorphisms in Section 2.2. In Section 2.3, we present the gluing construction as the basis of graph transformation steps; it is a pushout in categorical terms. Pullbacks, which are the dual construction to pushouts in a category, are introduced in Section 2.4.

2.1 Graphs and Typed Graphs

A graph has nodes, and edges, which link two nodes. We consider directed graphs, i.e. every edge has a distinguished start node (its source) and end node (its target). We allow parallel edges, as well as loops.

Definition 2.1 (graph). *A graph* $G = (V, E, s, t)$ *consists of a set* V *of nodes (also called vertices), a set* E *of edges, and two functions* $s, t : E \to V$, *the source and target functions:*

$$E \underset{t}{\overset{s}{\rightrightarrows}} V$$

Remark 2.2. In the literature, a graph G is often represented by a set V of nodes and a set $E \subseteq V \times V$ of edges. This notion is almost the same as the one in Definition 2.1: for an element $(v, w) \in E$, v represents its source and w its target node, but parallel edges are not expressible.

To represent undirected graphs, for each undirected edge between two nodes v and w we add both directed edges (v, w) and (w, v) to the set E of edges.

Example 2.3 (graph). The graph $G_S = (V_S, E_S, s_S, t_S)$, with node set $V_S = \{u, v, x, y\}$, edge set $E_S = \{a, b\}$, source function $s_S : E_S \to V_S : a, b \mapsto u$ and target function $t_S : E_S \to V_S : a, b \mapsto v$, is visualized in the following:

$$G_S \qquad \boxed{\begin{array}{cc} u \bullet \mathrel{\overset{a}{\underset{b}{\rightleftarrows}}} \bullet v \\[1em] x \bullet \qquad \bullet y \end{array}}$$

□

Graphs are related by (total) graph morphisms, which map the nodes and edges of a graph to those of another one, preserving the source and target of each edge.

Definition 2.4 (graph morphism). *Given graphs G_1, G_2 with $G_i = (V_i, E_i, s_i, t_i)$ for $i = 1, 2$, a graph morphism $f : G_1 \to G_2$, $f = (f_V, f_E)$ consists of two functions $f_V : V_1 \to V_2$ and $f_E : E_1 \to E_2$ that preserve the source and target functions, i.e. $f_V \circ s_1 = s_2 \circ f_E$ and $f_V \circ t_1 = t_2 \circ f_E$:*

$$\begin{array}{ccc} E_1 & \overset{s_1}{\underset{t_1}{\rightrightarrows}} & V_1 \\[0.3em] \Big\downarrow f_E & = & \Big\downarrow f_V \\[0.3em] E_2 & \overset{s_2}{\underset{t_2}{\rightrightarrows}} & V_2 \end{array}$$

A graph morphism f is injective *(or* surjective*) if both functions f_V, f_E are injective (or surjective, respectively); f is called* isomorphic *if it is bijective, which means both injective and surjective.*

Fact 2.5 (composition of graph morphisms). *Given two graph morphisms $f = (f_V, f_E) : G_1 \to G_2$ and $g = (g_V, g_E) : G_2 \to G_3$, the composition $g \circ f = (g_V \circ f_V, g_E \circ f_E) : G_1 \to G_3$ is again a graph morphism.*

Proof. As compositions of functions, $g_V \circ f_V : V_1 \to V_3$ and $g_E \circ f_E : E_1 \to E_3$ are well defined. Using the associativity of the composition of functions and the fact that f and g, as graph morphisms, preserve the source and target functions, we conclude that

1. $g_V \circ f_V \circ s_1 = g_V \circ s_2 \circ f_E = s_3 \circ g_E \circ f_E$ and
2. $g_V \circ f_V \circ t_1 = g_V \circ t_2 \circ f_E = t_3 \circ g_E \circ f_E$.

Therefore $g \circ f$ also preserves the source and target functions.   □

A type graph defines a set of types, which can be used to assign a type to the nodes and edges of a graph. The typing itself is done by a graph morphism between the graph and the type graph.

Definition 2.6 (typed graph and typed graph morphism). *A type graph is a distinguished graph $TG = (V_{TG}, E_{TG}, s_{TG}, t_{TG})$. V_{TG} and E_{TG} are called the vertex and the edge type alphabets, respectively.*

*A tuple $(G, type)$ of a graph G together with a graph morphism $type : G \rightarrow$
TG is then called a* typed graph.

*Given typed graphs $G_1^T = (G_1, type_1)$ and $G_2^T = (G_2, type_2)$, a typed
graph morphism $f : G_1^T \rightarrow G_2^T$ is a graph morphism $f : G_1 \rightarrow G_2$ such that
$type_2 \circ f = type_1$:*

$$G_1 \xrightarrow{\quad f \quad} G_2$$
$$type_1 \searrow \underset{=}{} \swarrow type_2$$
$$TG$$

Example 2.7 (typed graph). Consider the following type graph $G_T = (V_T,$
$E_T, s_T, t_T)$ with $V_T = \{s, t\}$, $E_T = \{e\}$, $s_T : E_T \rightarrow V_T : e \mapsto s$, and $t_T : E_T \rightarrow$
$V_T : e \mapsto t$. This type graph ensures that all edges of a graph G typed over
G_T link from an s-typed node to a t-typed node, and each node is either a
source (with only outgoing edges) or a sink (with only incoming edges).

The graph G_S from Example 2.3, together with the morphism $type =$
$(type_V, type_E) : G_S \rightarrow G_T$ with $type_V : V_S \rightarrow V_T : u, x \mapsto s; v, y \mapsto t$ and
$type_E : E_S \rightarrow E_T : a, b \mapsto e$, is then a typed graph (typed over G_T). The
graph $G = (G_S, type)$ and its typing morphism are explicitly shown in the
left-hand side of the following diagram, and in a compact notation on the
right-hand side, where each node and edge is labeled with its type (we have
left out their names):

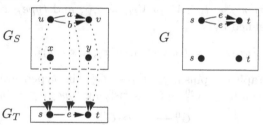

In addition to graphs and typed graphs, we now introduce labeled graphs,
which were originally considered as the main notion of graphs (see [EPS73,
Ehr79]). In fact, we can show that labeled graphs and labeled graph morphisms can be considered as special cases of typed graphs and typed graph
morphisms. For this reason, we present the theory in the following sections for
graphs and typed graphs only, but it can also be applied to labeled graphs.

Definition 2.8 (labeled graph and labeled graph morphism). *A* label
alphabet $L = (L_V, L_E)$ *consists of a set L_V of node labels and a set L_E
of edge labels.*

*A labeled graph $G = (V, E, s, t, l_V, l_E)$ consists of an underlying graph
$G^0 = (V, E, s, t)$ together with label functions*

$$l_V : V \rightarrow L_V \text{ and } l_E : E \rightarrow L_E.$$

A labeled graph morphism $f : G_1 \to G_2$ *is a graph morphism* $f : G_1^0 \to G_2^0$ *between the underlying graphs which is compatible with the label functions, i.e.* $l_{2,V} \circ f_V = l_{1,V}$ *and* $l_{2,E} \circ f_E = l_{1,E}$:

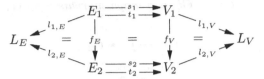

Fact 2.9 (labeled graphs as special typed graphs). *Given a label alphabet* $L = (L_V, L_E)$, *the type graph* $TG(L)$ *is defined by* $TG(L) = (V_{TG}, E_{TG}, s_{TG}, t_{TG})$ *with*

- $V_{TG} = L_V$,
- $E_{TG} = L_V \times L_E \times L_V$,
- $s_{TG} : E_{TG} \to V_{TG} : (a, x, b) \mapsto a$,
- $t_{TG} : E_{TG} \to V_{TG} : (a, x, b) \mapsto b$.

There is then a bijective correspondence between labeled graphs (and labeled graph morphisms) over the label alphabet L *and typed graphs (and typed graph morphisms) over the type graph* $TG(L)$.

Construction. Given a labeled graph $G = (V, E, s, t, l_V, l_E)$, the corresponding typed graph over $TG(L)$ is given by $G^T = (G^0, type : G^0 \to TG(L))$ with $G^0 = (V, E, s, t)$, $type_V = l_V : V \to V_{TG} = L_V$, and $type_E : E \to E_{TG} = L_V \times L_E \times L_V$, defined by

$$type_E(x) = (l_V \circ s(x), l_E(x), l_V \circ t(x)).$$

Given a labeled graph morphism $f : G_1 \to G_2$, the typed graph morphism $f : G_1^T \to G_2^T$ is given by $f : G_1^0 \to G_2^0$, satisfying $type_2 \circ f = type_1$:

$$
\begin{array}{ccc}
G_1^0 & \xrightarrow{\ f\ } & G_2^0 \\
 & \searrow \quad = \quad \swarrow & \\
 & {\scriptstyle type_1} \quad {\scriptstyle type_2} & \\
 & TG(L) &
\end{array}
$$

Vice versa, given $G^T = (G^0, type : G^0 \to TG(L))$, the corresponding labeled graph G is given by $G = (G^0, l_V, l_E)$, with $l_V = type_V : V \to L_V = V_{TG}$, and $l_E : E \to L_E$, defined by $l_E(e) = x$ with $type_E(e) = (a, x, b)$. Given a typed graph morphism $f : G_1^T \to G_2^T$ with a graph morphism $f : G_1^0 \to G_2^0$, then f is also a labeled graph morphism $f : G_1 \to G_2$.   □

Proof. It is easy to check that the commutativity of the diagrams (0) (separately for s and t), (1), and (2) below for labeled graph morphisms is equivalent to the commutativity of the diagrams (0), (2), (3), (4) for typed graph morphisms and that the constructions above are inverse to each other, with $type_{1,E}(x) = (l_{1,V} \circ s_1(x), l_{1,E}(x), l_{1,V} \circ t_1(x))$ and $type_{2,E}(x) = (l_{2,V} \circ s_2(x), l_{2,E}(x), l_{2,V} \circ t_2(x))$:

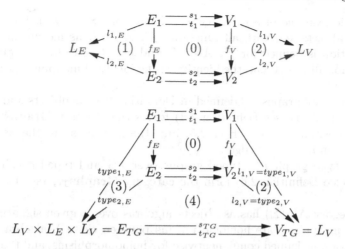

2.2 Introduction to Categories

In general, a category is a mathematical structure that has objects and morphisms, with a composition operation on the morphisms and an identity morphism for each object.

In particular, we shall show that sets, graphs, and typed graphs, together with functions, graph morphisms, and typed graph morphisms, lead to the categories **Sets**, **Graphs**, and **Graphs$_{TG}$**, respectively.

Definition 2.10 (category). *A category* $\mathbf{C} = (Ob_C, Mor_C, \circ, id)$ *is defined by*

- *a class Ob_C of objects;*
- *for each pair of objects $A, B \in Ob_C$, a set $Mor_C(A, B)$ of morphisms;*
- *for all objects $A, B, C \in Ob_C$, a composition operation $\circ_{(A,B,C)} : Mor_C(B, C) \times Mor_C(A, B) \rightarrow Mor_C(A, C);$ and*
- *for each object $A \in Ob_C$, an identity morphism $id_A \in Mor_C(A, A);$*

such that the following conditions hold:

1. *Associativity. For all objects $A, B, C, D \in Ob_C$ and morphisms $f : A \rightarrow B$, $g : B \rightarrow C$, and $h : C \rightarrow D$, it holds that $(h \circ g) \circ f = h \circ (g \circ f)$.*
2. *Identity. For all objects $A, B \in Ob_C$ and morphisms $f : A \rightarrow B$, it holds that $f \circ id_A = f$ and $id_B \circ f = f$.*

Remark 2.11. Instead of $f \in Mor_C(A, B)$, we write $f : A \rightarrow B$ and leave out the index for the composition operation, since it is clear which one to use. For such a morphism f, A is called its domain and B its codomain.

Example 2.12 (categories). In the following, we give examples of structures that are categories.

1. The basic example of a category is the category **Sets**, with the object class of all sets and with all functions $f : A \rightarrow B$ as morphisms. The composition is defined for $f : A \rightarrow B$ and $g : B \rightarrow C$ by $(g \circ f)(x) = g(f(x))$ for all $x \in A$, and the identity is the identical mapping $id_A : A \rightarrow A : x \mapsto x$.
2. The class of all graphs (as defined in Definition 2.1) as objects and of all graph morphisms (see Definition 2.4) forms the category **Graphs**, with the composition given in Fact 2.5, and the identities are the pairwise identities on nodes and edges.
3. Given a type graph TG, typed graphs over TG and typed graph morphisms (see Definition 2.6) form the category **Graphs$_{TG}$** (see Example A.6).
4. The category **Alg(Σ)** has as objects algebras over a given signature Σ, and the morphisms are homomorphisms between these Σ-algebras. The composition is defined componentwise for homomorphisms, and the identities are componentwise identities on the carrier sets (see Appendix B).

$\square$

In the categorical framework, the morphism classes of monomorphisms, epimorphisms, and isomorphisms are of special interest, because in our example categories they correspond to injective, surjective, and bijective functions or morphisms, respectively.

Definition 2.13 (monomorphism, epimorphism, and isomorphism).
Given a category **C**, *a morphism* $m : B \rightarrow C$ *is called a* monomorphism *if, for all morphisms* $f, g : A \rightarrow B \in Mor_C$, *it holds that* $m \circ f = m \circ g$ *implies* $f = g$:

$$A \underset{g}{\overset{f}{\rightrightarrows}} B \xrightarrow{\quad m \quad} C$$

A morphism $e : A \rightarrow B \in Mor_C$ *is called an* epimorphism *if, for all morphisms* $f, g : B \rightarrow C \in Mor_C$, *it holds that* $f \circ e = g \circ e$ *implies* $f = g$:

$$A \xrightarrow{\quad e \quad} B \underset{g}{\overset{f}{\rightrightarrows}} C$$

A morphism $i : A \rightarrow B$ *is called an* isomorphism *if there exists a morphism* $i^{-1} : B \rightarrow A$ *such that* $i \circ i^{-1} = id_B$ *and* $i^{-1} \circ i = id_A$:

$$A \underset{i}{\overset{i^{-1}}{\rightleftarrows}} B$$

Remark 2.14. Monomorphisms, epimorphisms, and isomorphisms are closed under composition: if $f : A \rightarrow B$ and $g : B \rightarrow C$ are monomorphisms (or epimorphisms or isomorphisms), so is $g \circ f$.

An isomorphism is also a monomorphism and an epimorphism. But the inverse conclusion does not hold: a morphism i that is both a monomorphism and an epimorphism need not be an isomorphism, since i^{-1} might not exist (in the category).

Fact 2.15 (monomorphisms, epimorphisms and isomorphisms). *In* Sets, Graphs, *and* Graphs$_{TG}$ *the monomorphisms (or epimorphisms or isomorphisms) are exactly those morphisms which are injective (or surjective or bijective, respectively).*

Proof. First we show this fact for the category **Sets**.

1. $m : B \rightarrow C$ is injective $\Leftrightarrow$ m is a monomorphism.

   "$\Rightarrow$". Given $f, g : A \rightarrow B$ with $m \circ f = m \circ g$, then we have, for all $a \in A$, $m(f(a)) = m(g(a))$, and since m is injective, $f(a) = g(a)$, i.e. $f = g$.

   "$\Leftarrow$". Suppose $\exists x \neq y \in B : m(x) = m(y)$. For $f, g : \{*\} \rightarrow B$ with $f(*) = x$ and $g(*) = y$, we have $m(f(*)) = m(x) = m(y) = m(g(*))$ and $f \neq g$, which is a contradiction.

2. $e : A \rightarrow B$ is surjective $\Leftrightarrow$ e is an epimorphism.

   "$\Rightarrow$". Given $f, g : B \rightarrow C$ with $f \circ e = g \circ e$, then we have, for all $a \in A$, $f(e(a)) = g(e(a))$, and since e is surjective, $f(b) = g(b)$, i.e. $f = g$.

   "$\Leftarrow$". Suppose $\exists x \in B : \forall a \in A : e(a) \neq x$. For $f, g : B \rightarrow \{*, 1, 2\}$ with

   $$f(b) = \begin{cases} 1 : & b = x \\ * : & \text{otherwise} \end{cases}, \quad g(b) = \begin{cases} 2 : & b = x \\ * : & \text{otherwise} \end{cases},$$

   we have $\forall a \in A : f(e(a)) = g(e(a))$. Therefore $f \circ e = g \circ e$, but $f \neq g$, which is a contradiction.

3. $i : A \rightarrow B$ is bijective iff the inverse function $i^{-1} : B \rightarrow A$ with $i^{-1} \circ i = id_A$ and $i \circ i^{-1} = id_B$ exists, i.e. i is an isomorphism.

In **Graphs** and **Graphs$_{TG}$**, a (typed) graph morphism f is injective (or surjective or bijective) if it is componentwise injective (or surjective or bijective, respectively), i.e. all components are monomorphisms (or epimorphisms or isomorphisms, respectively) in **Sets**, and then also f is a monomorphism (or an epimorphism or an isomorphism, respectively) in **Graphs** or **Graphs$_{TG}$**, respectively.

We still have to show that all monomorphisms (and epimorphisms and isomorphisms) are injective (and surjective and bijective, respectively).

1. Given a monomorphism $m : B \rightarrow C$ in **Graphs** or **Graphs$_{TG}$**, suppose that m is not injective.

   Case 1: m_V is not injective. Then we have $v_1 \neq v_2 \in V_B$ with $m_V(v_1) = m_V(v_2)$. Consider the graph A with a single node v (and the typing $type_A(v) = type_B(v_1) = type_B(v_2)$). We define morphisms $f, g : A \rightarrow B$ by $f_V(v) = v_1$ and $g_V(v) = v_2$; $m \circ f = m \circ g$, but $f \neq g$. Therefore m is not a monomorphism, which is a contradiction.

   Case 2: m_E is not injective. Then we have $e_1 \neq e_2 \in E_B$ with $m_E(e_1) = m_E(e_2)$. Consider the graph A with an edge e between the two nodes v and w (and the typing $type_A(v) = type_B(s_B(e_1)) = type_B(s_B(e_2))$, $type_A(w) = type_B(t_B(e_1)) = type_B(t_B(e_2))$, and

$type_A(e) = type_B(e_1) = type_B(e_2)$). We define morphisms $f, g : A \rightarrow B$ by $f_V(v) = s_B(e_1)$, $f_V(w) = t_B(e_1)$, $f_E(e) = e_1$, and $g_V(v) = s_B(e_2)$, $g_V(w) = t_B(e_2)$, $g_E(e) = e_2$; $m \circ f = m \circ g$, but $f \neq g$. Therefore m is not a monomorphism, which is a contradiction.

2. Given an epimorphism $e : A \rightarrow B$ in **Graphs** or **Graphs$_{TG}$**, suppose that e is not surjective.

   Case 1: e_V is not surjective, but e_E is. Then there exists a node $v \in V_B$ with $v \notin e_V(V_A)$, and v is isolated (otherwise e_E is not surjective). We construct the graph $C = (V_C, E_C, s_C, t_C)$ with the disjoint union $V_C = V_B \, \dot{\cup} \, \{\bar{v}\}$, $E_C = E_B$, $s_C = s_B$, $t_C = t_B$ (and the typing morphism $type_C : C \rightarrow TG$ with

   $$type_C(x) = \begin{cases} type_B(x) : x \in B \\ type_B(v) : x = \bar{v} \end{cases}).$$

   Now we define morphisms $f, g : B \rightarrow C$ with

   $$f(x) = x \text{ and } g(x) = \begin{cases} x : x \neq v \\ \bar{v} : x = v \end{cases}.$$

   These morphisms are well defined and we have $f \circ e = g \circ e$, but $f \neq g$. Therefore e is not an epimorphism, which is a contradiction.

   Case 2: e_E is not surjective. Then there exists an edge $e \in E_B$ with $e \notin e_E(E_A)$. We construct the graph $C = (V_C, E_C, s_C, t_C)$ with $V_C = V_B$, $E_C = E_B \, \dot{\cup} \, \{\bar{e}\}$,

   $$s_C = \begin{cases} s_B(x) : x \neq \bar{e} \\ s_B(e) : x = \bar{e} \end{cases}, \; t_C = \begin{cases} t_B(x) : x \neq \bar{e} \\ t_B(e) : x = \bar{e} \end{cases}$$

   (and the typing morphism $type_C : C \rightarrow TG$ with

   $$type_C(x) = \begin{cases} type_B(x) : x \in B \\ type_B(e) : x = \bar{e} \end{cases}).$$

   Finally, we define morphisms $f, g : B \rightarrow C$ with

   $$f(x) = x \text{ and } g(x) = \begin{cases} x : x \neq e \\ \bar{e} : x = e \end{cases}.$$

   These morphisms are well defined and we have $f \circ e = g \circ e$, but $f \neq g$. Therefore e is not an epimorphism, which is a contradiction.

3. Given an isomorphism i, then i is a monomorphism and an epimorphism, and therefore both injective and surjective, i.e. bijective.

$\square$

2.3 Pushouts as a Gluing Construction

For the application of a graph transformation rule to a graph, we need a technique to glue graphs together along a common subgraph. Intuitively, we use this common subgraph and add all other nodes and edges from both graphs. The idea of a pushout generalizes the gluing construction in the sense of category theory, i.e. a pushout object emerges from gluing two objects along a common subobject.

Definition 2.16 (pushout). *Given morphisms $f : A \to B$ and $g : A \to C$ in a category* $\mathbf{C}$, *a pushout* (D, f', g') *over f and g is defined by*

- *a pushout object D and*
- *morphisms $f' : C \to D$ and $g' : B \to D$ with $f' \circ g = g' \circ f$*

such that the following universal property is fulfilled: For all objects X and morphisms $h : B \to X$ and $k : C \to X$ with $k \circ g = h \circ f$, there is a unique morphism $x : D \to X$ such that $x \circ g' = h$ and $x \circ f' = k$:

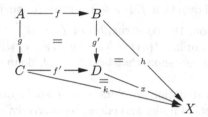

We shall often use the abbreviation "PO" for "pushout". We write $D = B +_A C$ for the pushout object D, where D is called the gluing of B and C via A, or, more precisely, via (A, f, g).

Fact 2.17 (POs in Sets, Graphs, and Graphs$_{\mathbf{TG}}$). *In* **Sets**, *the pushout object over the morphisms $f : A \to B$ and $g : A \to C$ can be constructed as the quotient $B \,\dot\cup\, C|_{\equiv}$, where $\equiv$ is the smallest equivalence relation with $(f(a), g(a)) \in \equiv$ for all $a \in A$. The morphisms f' and g' are defined by $f'(c) = [c]$ for all $c \in C$ and $g'(b) = [b]$ for all $b \in B$.*

Moreover, we have the following properties:

1. *If f is injective (or surjective), then f' is also injective (or surjective, respectively).*
2. *The pair (f', g') is jointly surjective, i.e. for each $x \in D$ there is a preimage $b \in B$ with $g'(b) = x$ or $c \in C$ with $f'(c) = x$.*
3. *If f is injective and $x \in D$ has preimages $b \in B$ and $c \in C$ with $g'(b) = f'(c) = x$, then there is a unique preimage $a \in A$ with $f(a) = b$ and $g(a) = c$.*
4. *If f and hence also f' is injective, then D is isomorphic to $D' = C \,\dot\cup\, B \setminus f(A)$.*

*In **Graphs** and **Graphs$_{TG}$**, pushouts can be constructed componentwise for nodes and edges in **Sets**. Moreover, the above properties 1–4 hold componentwise.*

Proof. In **Sets**, for a given object X with morphisms $h : B \to X$ and $k : C \to X$ such that $h \circ f = k \circ g$, we define

$$x([d]) = \begin{cases} h(b) & \text{if } \exists b \in B : b \in [d] \\ k(c) & \text{if } \exists c \in C : c \in [d] \end{cases}.$$

At least one of these two cases occurs, and if both occur, then the transitive closure of $\equiv$ implies the existence of $a_1, \ldots, a_n \in A$ with $f(a_1) = b$, $g(a_1) = g(a_2)$, $f(a_2) = f(a_3)$, $\ldots$, $g(a_{n-1}) = g(a_n) = c$, which implies $h(b) = k(c)$ using $h \circ f = k \circ g$. Similarly, $b_1, b_2 \in [d]$ implies $h(b_1) = h(b_2)$ and $c_1, c_2 \in [d]$ implies $k(c_1) = k(c_2)$. Therefore x is well defined and we have $x \circ f' = k$ and $x \circ g' = h$. The uniqueness of x follows from f' and g' being jointly surjective, i.e. for all $d \in D$ there is a $b \in B$ with $g'(b) = d$ or a $c \in C$ with $f'(c) = d$.

If f is injective (or surjective), using the properties of the equivalence relation $\equiv$ it can be shown that f' is also injective (or surjective, respectively).

Property 2 follows from the construction of $D = B \mathbin{\dot\cup} C|_\equiv$. If f is injective, the discussion above implies $f(a_1) = b$ and $g(a_1) = c$, which implies property 3. For property 4, we can show that $b : D' \to D$, defined by $b(x) = [x]$, is a bijection.

This pushout construction in **Sets** works analogously in **Graphs** and **Graphs$_{TG}$** for the sets of nodes and edges, respectively, of the pushout graph. The source and target functions of the pushout graph are uniquely determined by the pushout property of the node set of the pushout graph.   □

Remark 2.18. For the construction of pushout objects in **Sets** we consider the following steps:

1. Define the relation $\sim$ on the disjoint union $B \mathbin{\dot\cup} C$ as follows: For all $a \in A$ do $f(a) \sim g(a)$.

2. Let $[x] = \{y \in B \mathbin{\dot\cup} C \mid x \equiv y\}$, where $\equiv$ is the equivalence relation generated by $\sim$.

3. $D := \{[x] \mid x \in B \mathbin{\dot\cup} C\}$.

Note that the eqivalence relation $\equiv$ is the reflexive, symmetric, and transitive closure of $\sim$. In $\sim$, all those elements that are reached from the same $a \in A$ are identified. The result D is then the pushout object of f and g.

Example 2.19 (pushout). Given the sets $A = \{a, b, c, d\}$, $B = \{1, 2, 3, 4\}$, and $C = \{5, 6, 7, 8\}$ with morphisms $f : A \to B$, $f(a) = 1$, $f(b) = f(c) = 2$, $f(d) = 3$ and $g : A \to C$, $g(a) = g(b) = 5$, $g(c) = 6$, $g(d) = 7$, we use the construction in Remark 2.18:

1. $1 \sim 5$, $2 \sim 5$, $2 \sim 6$, $3 \sim 7$.

2. $1 \equiv 2 \equiv 5 \equiv 6$ and $3 \equiv 7$; therefore $[1] = [2] = [5] = [6] = \{1, 2, 5, 6\}$, $[3] = [7] = \{3, 7\}$, $[4] = \{4\}$, and $[8] = \{8\}$.

3. $D = \{[1], [3], [4], [8]\}$.

Altogether, we obtain the pushout object D and morphisms $f' : C \to D : x \mapsto [x]$ and $g' : B \to D : x \mapsto [x]$, as shown in the left-hand side of the following diagram. The analogous construction in **Graphs** leads to the pushout diagram over graphs on the right-hand side, where we have depicted the node mappings only:

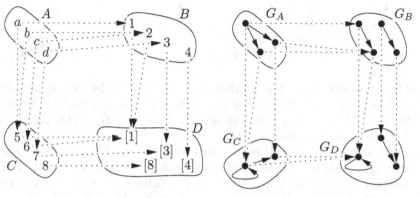

□

Finally, we show some important properties of pushouts which are essential for the theory of graph transformation.

Fact 2.20 (uniqueness, composition, and decomposition of POs).
Given a category **C**, *we have the following:*

(a) The pushout object D is unique up to isomorphism.

(b) The composition and decomposition of pushouts result again in a pushout, i.e., given the following commutative diagram, the statements below are valid:

$$
\begin{array}{ccccc}
A & \xrightarrow{\;f\;} & B & \xrightarrow{\;e\;} & E \\
\downarrow{\scriptstyle g} & (1) & \downarrow{\scriptstyle g'} & (2) & \downarrow{\scriptstyle e''} \\
C & \xrightarrow{\;f'\;} & D & \xrightarrow{\;e'\;} & F
\end{array}
$$

- *Pushout composition: if (1) and (2) are pushouts, then (1) + (2) is also a pushout.*
- *Pushout decomposition: if (1) and (1) + (2) are pushouts, then (2) is also a pushout.*

Proof.

(a) Given the pushout (1), suppose that there is another pushout (1″) with a pushout object D'' and morphisms $f'' : C \to D''$, $g'' : B \to D''$ such that $f'' \circ g = g'' \circ f$. Both of the squares (1) and (1″) below are pushouts; therefore we have morphisms $d : D \to D''$ with $d \circ f' = f''$ and $d \circ g' = g''$, and $d'' : D'' \to D$ with $d'' \circ f'' = f'$ and $d'' \circ g'' = g'$:

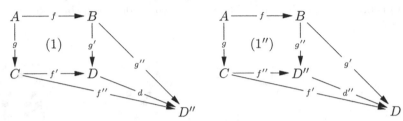

From pushout (1), it follows that $id_D : D \to D$ is the unique morphism with $id_D \circ f' = f'$ and $id_D \circ g' = g'$. The same holds for $d'' \circ d$; therefore we have $d'' \circ d = id_D$ and, analogously, $d \circ d'' = id_{D''}$. This means that $D \cong D''$ (see also Remark A.18).

(b) *Pushout composition.* Given the pushouts (1) and (2), in order to show that (1) + (2) is a pushout, we assume that we have an object X with morphisms $h : E \to X$ and $k : C \to X$ satisfying $h \circ e \circ f = k \circ g$. From pushout (1), we obtain a unique morphism $y : D \to X$ with $y \circ f' = k$ and $y \circ g' = h \circ e$. Pushout (2), in comparison with y and h, gives us a unique morphism $x : F \to X$ with $x \circ e'' = h$ and $x \circ e' = y$, which implies $x \circ e' \circ f' = y \circ f' = k$. Moreover, we can also show that x is unique with respect to the properties $x \circ e'' = h$ and $x \circ e' \circ f' = k$ using the uniqueness properties of the pushouts (1) and (2).

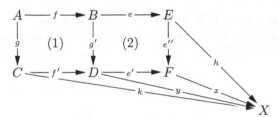

Pushout decomposition. Given the pushouts (1) and (1) + (2), in order to show that (2) is a pushout, we assume that we have an object X with morphisms $h : E \to X$ and $y : D \to X$ satisfying $h \circ e = y \circ g'$. From pushout (1) + (2), we obtain a unique morphism $x : F \to X$ with $x \circ e'' = h$ and $x \circ e' \circ f' = y \circ f'$. Since (1) is a pushout, the uniqueness of y with respect to (1) implies $x \circ e' = y$. Therefore x has the required properties $x \circ e'' = h$ and $x \circ e' = y$. Moreover, we can also show that x is unique with respect to these properties using the uniqueness properties of (1) + (2) and (1).   □

Example 2.21 (PO composition and decomposition). The following diagram illustrates the composition and decomposition of pushouts in **Graphs**. The squares (1) and (2) are pushouts, as well as the composed diagram (1) + (2):

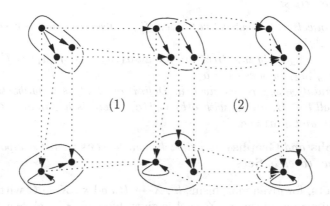

(1) (2)

□

2.4 Pullbacks as the Dual Construction of Pushouts

The dual construction of a pushout is a pullback. Pullbacks can be seen as a generalized intersection of objects over a common object.

Pushouts, pullbacks, and the stability of pushouts and pullbacks are essential for the concept and theory of (weak) adhesive HLR categories, which will be studied in Chapter 4.

Definition 2.22 (pullback). *Given morphisms $f : C \to D$ and $g : B \to D$ in a category* **C**, *a pullback (A, f', g') over f and g is defined by*

- *a pullback object A and*
- *morphisms $f' : A \to B$ and $g' : A \to C$ with $g \circ f' = f \circ g'$*

such that the following universal property is fulfilled: For all objects X with morphisms $h : X \to B$ and $k : X \to C$ with $f \circ k = g \circ h$, there is a unique morphism $x : X \to A$ such that $f' \circ x = h$ and $g' \circ x = k$:

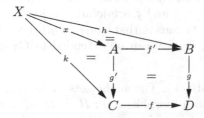

We shall often use the abbreviation "PB" for "pullback".

Fact 2.23 (PBs in Sets, Graphs, and Graphs$_\mathbf{TG}$). *In* **Sets**, *the pullback* $C \xleftarrow{g'} A \xrightarrow{f'} B$ *over the morphisms* $f : C \to D$ *and* $g : B \to D$ *is constructed by* $A = \bigcup_{d \in D} f^{-1}(d) \times g^{-1}(d) = \{(c, b) \mid f(c) = g(b)\} \subseteq C \times B$ *with morphisms* $f' : A \to B : (c, b) \mapsto b$ *and* $g' : A \to C : (c, b) \mapsto c$. *Moreover, we have the following properties:*

1. *If f is injective (or surjective), then f' is also injective (or surjective, respectively).*
2. *f' and g' are jointly injective, i.e. for all $a_1, a_2 \in A$, $f'(a_1) = f'(a_2)$ and $g'(a_1) = g'(a_2)$ implies $a_1 = a_2$.*
3. *A commutative square, as given in Definition 2.22, is a pullback in* **Sets** *iff, for all $b \in B$, $c \in C$ with $g(b) = f(c)$, there is a unique $a \in A$ with $f'(a) = b$ and $g'(a) = c$.*

In **Graphs** *and* **Graphs$_\mathbf{TG}$**, *pullbacks can be constructed componentwise for nodes and edges in* **Sets**.

Proof. In **Sets**, for given morphisms $h : X \to B$ and $k : X \to C$ with $f \circ k = g \circ h$, the unique morphism $x : X \to A$ is given by $x(p) = (k(p), h(p)) \in A$ for all $p \in X$. The required properties can be easily checked.

This pullback construction in **Sets** works analogously in **Graphs** and **Graphs$_\mathbf{TG}$** for the sets of nodes and edges, respectively, of the pullback graph. The source and target functions of the pullback graph are uniquely determined by the pullback property of the edge set of the pullback graph. □

Remark 2.24 (special cases of PBs). In **Sets**, if the given function $g : B \to D$ is an inclusion then the pullback object can be constructed as the preimage of B under f, i.e. $A = f^{-1}(B)$. If both given functions $g : B \to D$ and $f : C \to D$ are inclusions, then A can be constructed as the intersection of B and C, i.e. $A = B \cap C$. This interpretation works not only for **Sets**, but also for **Graphs** and **Graphs$_\mathbf{TG}$**.

Remark 2.25 (relationship between PBs and POs). In **Sets**, **Graphs**, and **Graphs$_\mathbf{TG}$** we have the interesting property that a pushout where at least one of the given morphisms is injective is also a pullback. This property will be shown for (weak) adhesive HLR categories in Section 4.3. For **Sets**, it is an easy consequence of the PO property 3 in Fact 2.17. Vice versa, given the pullback in Definition 2.22 in **Sets**, then this pullback is also a pushout if f and f' are injective, g and f are jointly surjective, and g is injective up to f'. The last property means that $g(b_1) = g(b_2)$ for $b_1 \neq b_2 \in B$ implies $b_1, b_2 \in f'(A)$. This property can be extended to **Graphs** and **Graphs$_\mathbf{GT}$** componentwise.

Example 2.26 (pullback). Given the sets $B = \{1, 2, 3, 4\}$, $C = \{5, 6, 7\}$, and $D = \{a, b, c, d\}$ with morphisms $g : B \to D$, $g(1) = g(2) = a$, $g(3) = b$, $g(4) = c$, and $f : C \to D$, $f(5) = a$, $f(6) = b$, $f(7) = d$, then the pullback object D is constructed as $D = \{(5, 1), (5, 2), (6, 3)\}$ with morphisms $f' : A \to$

$B : (x, y) \mapsto y$ and $g' : A \to C : (x, y) \mapsto x$, as shown in the left-hand side of the following diagram. The analogous construction in **Graphs** leads to the pullback diagram over graphs shown in the right-hand side, where we have depicted the node mappings only:

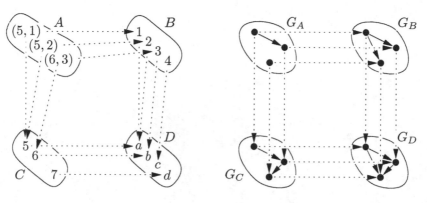

Dually to the uniqueness, composition, and decomposition of pushouts described in Fact 2.20, we have corresponding properties for pullbacks.

Fact 2.27 (uniqueness, composition, and decomposition of PBs).

(a) The pullback object A is unique up to isomorphism.
(b) The composition and decomposition of pullbacks result again in a pullback, i.e., given the following commutative diagram, the statements below are valid:

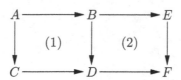

- *Pullback composition: if (1) and (2) are pullbacks, then (1) + (2) is also a pullback.*
- *Pullback decomposition: if (2) and (1) + (2) are pullbacks, then (1) is also a pullback.*

Proof. This fact follows by dualization from the corresponding Fact 2.20 for pushouts. □

3

Graph Transformation Systems

In this chapter, we introduce graph and typed graph transformation systems and grammars based on the constructions presented in Chapter 2. In Section 3.1, we present the basic definitions for graph transformation (GT) systems in the classical algebraic approach, based on double pushouts in the category **Graphs** of graphs. The construction of direct graph transformations in two steps is presented in Section 3.2. The first important results, concerning the independence of transformations, are presented in Section 3.3. In Section 3.4, we present an overview of the other main results for GT systems. The proofs of all these results are obtained by instantiation of corresponding results in the categorical framework of Chapter 5. Finally, we introduce graph constraints and application conditions in Section 3.5, and refer to the corresponding results in the general categorical framework in Chapter 7.

3.1 Basic Definitions for GT Systems

In this section, we introduce graph and typed graph transformation systems, or (typed) graph transformation systems, for short. In the following, we always use an abbreviated terminology of this kind to handle both cases simultaneously. Graph transformation is based on graph productions, which describe a general way how to transform graphs. The application of a production to a graph is called a *direct graph transformation*.

Definition 3.1 (graph production). *A (typed) graph production $p = (L \xleftarrow{l} K \xrightarrow{r} R)$ consists of (typed) graphs L, K, and R, called the left-hand side, gluing graph, and the right-hand side respectively, and two injective (typed) graph morphisms l and r.*

Given a (typed) graph production p, the inverse production *is defined by $p^{-1} = (R \xleftarrow{r} K \xrightarrow{l} L)$.*

Definition 3.2 (graph transformation). *Given a (typed) graph produc-tion $p = (L \xleftarrow{l} K \xrightarrow{r} R)$ and a (typed) graph G with a (typed) graph mor-phism $m : L \to G$, called the match, a direct (typed) graph transformation $G \xRightarrow{p,m} H$ from G to a (typed) graph H is given by the following double-pushout (DPO) diagram, where (1) and (2) are pushouts in the category* **Graphs** *(or* **Graphs**$_{TG}$, *respectively):*

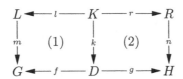

A sequence $G_0 \Rightarrow G_1 \Rightarrow \ldots \Rightarrow G_n$ of direct (typed) graph transformations is called a (typed) graph transformation and is denoted by $G_0 \xRightarrow{*} G_n$. For $n = 0$, we have the identical (typed) graph transformation $G_0 \xRightarrow{id} G_0$. Moreover, for $n = 0$ we allow also graph isomorphisms $G_0 \cong G_0'$, because pushouts and hence also direct graph transformations are only unique up to isomorphism.

In Section 3.2, we shall discuss how to construct a direct graph transfor-mation $G \xRightarrow{p,m} H$ from a given production p and match m.

The application of a production to a graph G can be reversed by its inverse production – the result is equal or at least isomorphic to the original graph G.

Fact 3.3 (inverse graph transformation). *Given a direct (typed) graph transformation $G \xRightarrow{p,m} H$ with a comatch morphism $n : R \to H$, then there is a direct (typed) graph transformation $H \xRightarrow{p^{-1},n} G$.*

Proof. This follows directly from Definitions 3.1 and 3.2.   □

Now we shall define (typed) graph transformation systems and (typed) graph grammars. The language of a (typed) graph grammar consists of those (typed) graphs that can be derived from the start graph.

Definition 3.4 (GT system, graph grammar, and language). *A graph transformation system $GTS = (P)$ consists of a set of graph productions P.*

A typed graph transformation system $GTS = (TG, P)$ consists of a type graph TG and a set of typed graph productions P.

A (typed) graph grammar $GG = (GTS, S)$ consists of a (typed) graph transformation system GTS and a (typed) start graph S.

The (typed) graph language L of GG is defined by

$$L = \{G \mid \exists \text{ (typed) graph transformation } S \xRightarrow{*} G\}.$$

We shall use the abbreviation "GT system" for "graph and typed graph transformations system".

Remark 3.5. A (typed) graph grammar without its start graph is a (typed) graph transformation system. In the context of (typed) graph grammars, (typed) graph transformations are often called (typed) graph derivations.

Similarly to Chomsky grammars, in the string case it is also possible to distinguish between terminal and nonterminal symbols for the productions in graph transformation systems and grammars. In the case of nonterminals, the language L would be restricted to graphs with terminal symbols only.

Example 3.6 (graph grammar *MutualExclusion***).** In the following, we show an example of a typed graph grammar, which is a variant of Dijkstra's algorithm for mutual exclusion (see [Lyn96]). Given two processes that compete for a resource used by both of them, the aim of the algorithm is to ensure that once one process is using the resource the other has to wait and cannot access it.

There is a global variable *turn* that assigns the resource to any of the processes initially. Each process i has a flag $f(i)$ with possible values 0, 1, 2, initially set to 0, and a state that is initially *non-active*. If the process wants to access the resource, its state changes to *active* and the flag value is set to 1. If the variable *turn* has assigned the resource already to the requesting process, the flag can be set to 2, which indicates that the process is accessing the resource. Then the process uses the resource and is in its critical section. Meanwhile, no other process can access the resource, because the turn variable cannot be changed in this stage of the process. After the critical section has been exited, the flag is set back to 0 and the state to *non-active*. Otherwise, if the resource is assigned to a nonactive process, it can be reassigned and then accessed analogously by the requesting process.

For our typed graph grammar, we have the following type graph TG and five typed graph productions, where all morphisms are inclusions:

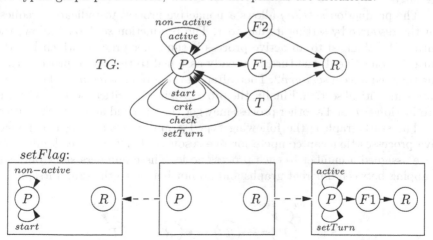

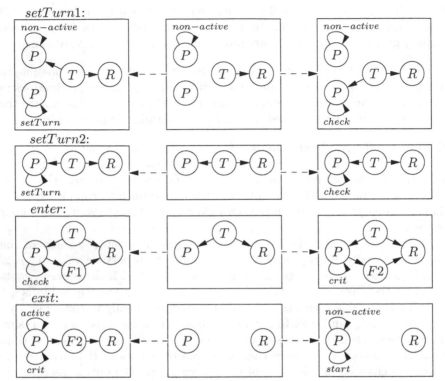

Each process is typed by P, a resource is typed by R, and T denotes the turn. If the flag of a process is set to 0, we do not depict it in the graph. The flag values 1 and 2 are shown by nodes typed with $F1$ or $F2$, respectively, with a link from the corresponding process to the node and a link to the required resource.

The production *setFlag* allows a nonactive process to indicate a request for the resource by setting its flag to 1. The production *setTurn1* allows the turn to be changed to an active process if the other process, which has the turn, is nonactive. If the turn is already assigned to the active process, then the turn remains in *setTurn2*. Thereafter, in the production *enter*, the process enters its critical section. Finally, the process exits the critical section with the production *exit* and another process may get the turn and access the resource.

The start graph is the following typed graph S, containing two nonactive processes that can compete for one resource. For better readability, we have assigned a number to each process node. These numbers show only the mapping between different graphs and do not belong to the graph itself:

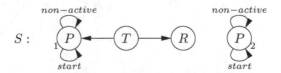

Altogether, we have the typed graph grammar $MutualExclusion = (P, S)$ with $P = \{setFlag, setTurn1, setTurn2, enter, exit\}$.

We can apply the typed graph production $setFlag$ to the start graph S with a match m, leading to the direct typed graph transformation $S \stackrel{setFlag,m}{\Longrightarrow} G_1$ shown in the following diagram:

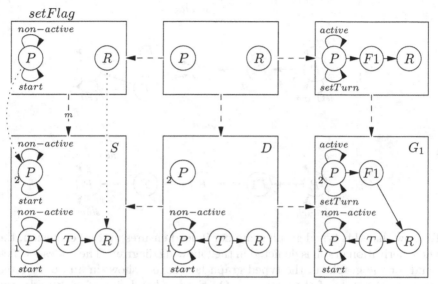

If we apply the typed graph productions $setTurn1$, $enter$, $setFlag$, and $exit$ to G_1, then we obtain the direct typed graph transformations $G_1 \stackrel{setTurn1,m_1}{\Longrightarrow} G_2$, $G_2 \stackrel{enter,m_2}{\Longrightarrow} G_3$, $G_3 \stackrel{setFlag,m_3}{\Longrightarrow} G_4$, and $G_4 \stackrel{exit,m_4}{\Longrightarrow} G_5$, where the graphs G_2, G_3, G_4, and G_5 are shown in the following, and a typed graph transformation $S \stackrel{*}{\Rightarrow} G_5$:

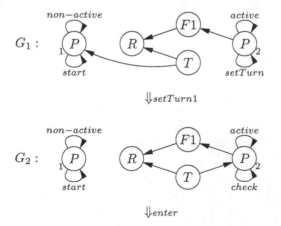

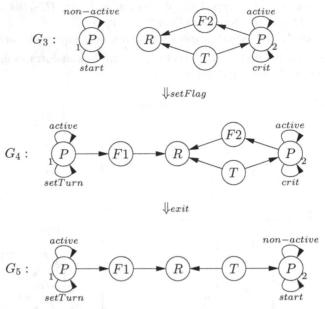

To show that this typed graph grammar indeed ensures mutual exclusion, the whole derivation graph is depicted in the following diagram. The nodes – which stand for the graphs in the typed graph language – show, in an abbreviated notation, the state of the processes. On the left-hand side of each node, the state of the first process is shown, and also its flag value and if the turn is assigned to that process. Analogously, this information for the second process is depicted on the right-hand side. The gray nodes are those nodes where the resource is actually accessed by a process – and only one process can access it at any one time.

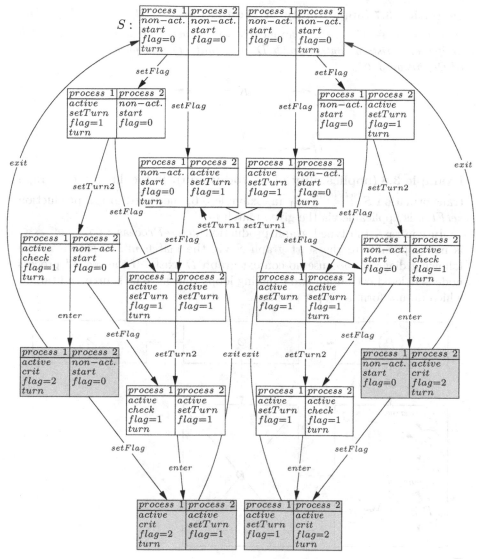

3.2 Construction of Graph Transformations

In this section, we analyze the question under what conditions a (typed) graph production $p = (L \leftarrow K \rightarrow R)$ can be applied to a (typed) graph G via a match m. In general, the existence of a context graph D that leads to a pushout is required. This allows us to construct a direct (typed) graph transformation $G \xrightarrow{p,m} H$, where, in a second step, the (typed) graph H is constructed as the gluing of D and R via K.

Definition 3.7 (applicability of productions). *A (typed) graph produc-tion* $p = (L \xleftarrow{l} K \xrightarrow{r} R)$ *is applicable to a (typed) graph G via the match m if there exists a context graph D such that (1) is a pushout in the sense of Definition 3.2:*

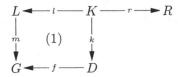

Example 3.8 (applicability of a production). In the direct typed graph transformation $S \overset{setFlag,m}{\Longrightarrow} G_1$ in Example 3.6, the typed graph production *setFlag* is applicable via the given match m.

In contrast, the typed graph production *deleteProcess* : $\circled{P} \leftarrow \varnothing \rightarrow \varnothing$ is not applicable to the start graph S via the match m', as shown in the following diagram, because no context graph D exists. If the second process node is deleted, we obtain two dangling loops that have no source and target, which do not form a proper graph.

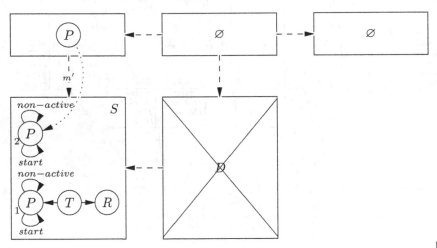

This definition does not formulate a syntactical criterion to decide whether a (typed) graph production is applicable or not. A more constructive approach is to check the following gluing condition. The two concepts are equivalent, as shown in Fact 3.11.

Definition 3.9 (gluing condition). *Given a (typed) graph production* $p = (L \xleftarrow{l} K \xrightarrow{r} R)$, *a (typed) graph G, and a match* $m : L \rightarrow G$ *with* $X = (V_X, E_X, s_X, t_X)$ *for all* $X \in \{L, K, R, G\}$, *we can state the following definitions:*

- *The* gluing points *GP* *are those nodes and edges in L that are not deleted by p, i.e.* $GP = l_V(V_K) \cup l_E(E_K) = l(K)$.
- *The* identification points *IP* *are those nodes and edges in L that are identified by m, i.e.* $IP = \{v \in V_L \mid \exists w \in V_L, w \neq v : m_V(v) = m_V(w)\} \cup \{e \in E_L \mid \exists f \in E_L, f \neq e : m_E(e) = m_E(f)\}$.
- *The* dangling points *DP* *are those nodes in L whose images under m are the source or target of an edge in G that does not belong to m(L), i.e.* $DP = \{v \in V_L \mid \exists e \in E_G \backslash m_E(E_L) : s_G(e) = m_V(v) \text{ or } t_G(e) = m_V(v)\}$.

p and m satisfy the gluing condition *if all identification points and all dangling points are also gluing points, i.e.* $IP \cup DP \subseteq GP$.

Note that in our terminology, a match $m : L \to G$ is a general graph morphism from the left-hand side L of a production to a graph G, but we still have to check the gluing condition in order to apply the production via the match m. If the gluing condition is not satisfied, the production p cannot be applied via the match m.

Example 3.10 (gluing condition). For the direct typed graph transformation $S \stackrel{setFlag,m}{\Longrightarrow} G_1$ in Example 3.6, we analyze the gluing, identification, and dangling points:

- $GP = l(K)$, which means that the gluing points in L are both nodes.
- $IP = \varnothing$, since m does not identify any nodes or edges.
- The resource node is the only dangling point: in S, there is an edge from the turn node T (which has no preimage in L) to the resource node R, but no edge from or to the upper process node P that is not already in L.

This means that $IP \cup DP \subseteq GP$, and the gluing condition is satisfied by m and $setFlag$.

If we look at the typed graph production *deleteProcess* from Example 3.8 with the match m', then we have:

- $GP = l(K)$, which means that there are no gluing points in L.
- $IP = \varnothing$, since m' does not identify any nodes or edges.
- The process node in L is a dangling point: in S, there are two loops at this node, which have no preimages in L.

This means that $DP \not\subseteq GP$, and the gluing condition is not satisfied by m' and *deleteProcess*. □

Fact 3.11 (existence and uniqueness of context graph). *For a (typed) graph production* $p = (L \stackrel{l}{\leftarrow} K \stackrel{r}{\to} R)$, *a (typed) graph G, and a match* $m : L \to G$, *the context graph D with the PO (1) exists iff the gluing condition is satisfied. If D exists, it is unique up to isomorphism.*

Remark 3.12. As usual, the word "iff" means "if and only if".

In categorical terms, the construction of D together with the morphisms $k : K \to D$ and $f : D \to G$ is called the pushout complement of $l : K \to L$ and $m : L \to G$ leading to the PO (1) below:

$$L \xleftarrow{\quad l \quad} K$$
$$\downarrow m \quad (1) \quad \downarrow k$$
$$G \xleftarrow{\quad f \quad} D$$

Proof. "⇒". Given the PO (1), then the properties of the gluing condition follow from the properties of pushouts in **Graphs** and **Graphs$_{TG}$**:

1. If $m(x) = m(y)$ for $x \neq y \in L$ and (1) is a pushout, then there exist $x' \neq y' \in K$ with $l(x') = x$ and $l(y') = y$. This means that $x, y \in l(K)$, i.e. $IP \subseteq GP$.
2. Consider $v \in DP$ with $e \in E_G \backslash m_E(E_L)$ and, without loss of generality $m_V(v) = s_G(e)$. From property 2 in Fact 2.17, f and m are jointly surjective, therefore there is an $e' \in E_D$ with $f_E(e') = e$ and $f_V(s_D(e')) = m_V(v)$. This means that, from property 3 in Fact 2.17, there is a $v' \in V_K$: $l(v') = v$ and $k_V(v') = s_D(e')$. This means that $v \in l(K)$, i.e. $DP \subseteq GP$.

"⇐". If the gluing condition is satisfied, we can construct $D = (V_D, E_D, s_D, t_D)$, k, and f (and $type_D : D \rightarrow TG$) as follows:

- $V_D = (V_G \backslash m_V(V_L)) \cup m_V(l_V(V_K))$;
- $E_D = (E_G \backslash m_E(E_L)) \cup m_E(l_E(E_K))$;
- $s_D = s_G|_{E_D}$, $t_D = t_G|_{E_D}$;
- $k_V(v) = m_V(l_V(v))$ for all $v \in V_K$, $k_E(e) = m_E(l_E(e))$ for all $e \in E_K$;
- f is an inclusion;
- in the case of typed graphs, $type_D = type_G|_D$.

The well-definedness of this construction and the pushout properties follow from Definition 3.9 and can be easily checked.

We omit the proof of the uniqueness of D. This can be shown explicitly, but it also follows from the properties of adhesive HLR categories, as shown in Theorem 4.26.   □

If a (typed) graph production is applicable to a (typed) graph via a match, i.e. the gluing condition is fulfilled, then we can construct the direct (typed) graph transformation as follows.

Fact 3.13 (construction of direct (typed) graph transformations).
Given a (typed) graph production $p = (L \xleftarrow{l} K \xrightarrow{r} R)$ and a match $m : L \rightarrow G$ such that p is applicable to a (typed) graph G via m, the direct (typed) graph transformation can be constructed in two steps:

1. *Delete those nodes and edges in G that are reached by the match m, but keep the image of K, i.e. $D = (G \backslash m(L)) \cup m(l(K))$. More precisely, construct the context graph D (see the proof of Fact 3.11) and pushout (1) such that $G = L +_K D$.*

2. *Add those nodes and edges that are newly created in R, i.e. $H = D \mathbin{\dot{\cup}}$*
   $(R \backslash r(K))$, where the disjoint union $\dot{\cup}$ is used to make sure that we add
   the elements of $R \backslash r(K)$ as new elements. More precisely, construct the
   pushout (2) of D and R via K such that $H = R +_K D$.

This construction is unique up to isomorphism.

$$
\begin{array}{ccccc}
L & \xleftarrow{\;l\;} & K & \xrightarrow{\;r\;} & R \\
\downarrow{\scriptstyle m} & (1) & \downarrow{\scriptstyle k} & (2) & \downarrow{\scriptstyle n} \\
G & \xleftarrow{\;f\;} & D & \xrightarrow{\;g\;} & H
\end{array}
$$

Proof. The first step corresponds to the construction of the pushout complement, as described in the proof of Fact 3.11.

The second step corresponds to the construction of the pushout, as shown in Fact 2.17.

The uniqueness of this construction follows from the uniqueness of D (see Fact 3.11) and the uniqueness of pushout objects (see Fact 2.20).   □

Example 3.14 (construction of a graph transformation). We follow this construction to analyze the typed graph transformation $S \overset{setFlag,m}{\Longrightarrow} G_1$ in Example 3.6:

1. The two loops at the match of the process node in L have no preimage in K; therefore they are deleted in D. The nodes have a preimage in K and therefore remain in D.
2. In R, we create the loops at the process node and the flag node with the label $F1$, and the corresponding edges. All these elements are added in G_1.

□

3.3 Local Church–Rosser and Parallelism Theorems for GT Systems

In this section, we study under what conditions two direct (typed) graph transformations applied to the same (typed) graph can be applied in arbitrary order, leading to the same result. This leads to the notions of parallel and sequential independence of direct (typed) graph transformations and to the Local Church–Rosser Theorem. Moreover, the corresponding (typed) graph productions can be applied in parallel in this case, leading to the Parallelism Theorem. Both results were shown in the 1970s [ER76, EK76, Ehr79].

Definition 3.15 (parallel and sequential independence). *Two direct (typed) graph transformations $G \overset{p_1,m_1}{\Longrightarrow} H_1$ and $G \overset{p_2,m_2}{\Longrightarrow} H_2$ are parallel independent if all nodes and edges in the intersection of the two matches are gluing items with respect to both transformations, i.e.*

$$m_1(L_1) \cap m_2(L_2) \subseteq m_1(l_1(K_1)) \cap m_2(l_2(K_2)).$$

Two direct (typed) graph transformations $G \overset{p_1,m_1}{\Longrightarrow} H_1 \overset{p_2,m_2}{\Longrightarrow} H_2$ *are sequentially independent if all nodes and edges in the intersection of the comatch* $n_1 : R_1 \to H_1$ *and the match* m_2 *are gluing items with respect to both transformations, i.e.*

$$n_1(R_1) \cap m_2(L_2) \subseteq n_1(r_1(K_1)) \cap m_2(l_2(K_2)).$$

Remark 3.16. $G_1 \overset{p_1}{\Rightarrow} G_2 \overset{p_2}{\Rightarrow} G_3$ are sequentially independent iff $G_1 \overset{p_1^{-1}}{\Leftarrow} G_2 \overset{p_2}{\Rightarrow} G_3$ are parallel independent.

Two direct (typed) graph transformations that are not parallel (or sequentially) independent are called *parallel (or sequentially) dependent.*

Example 3.17 (parallel and sequential independence). We apply the typed graph production *setFlag* from Example 3.6 twice to the start graph S, first with the match m, and the second time with a different match m' that maps the process node in L to the lower process node in S. These two direct typed graph transformations are parallel independent: in the intersection of the matches, there is only the resource node, which is a gluing point with respect to both transformations. In the diagram below, we show only the left-hand sides and the gluing graphs of the productions and, accordingly, the context graphs, but not the whole direct typed graph transformations:

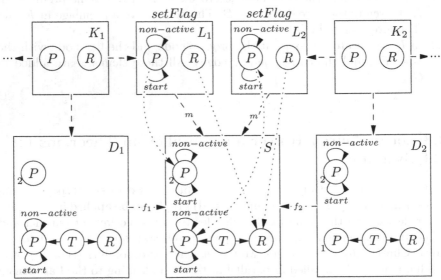

The two direct typed graph transformations $G_2 \overset{enter,m_2}{\Longrightarrow} G_3 \overset{setFlag,m_3}{\Longrightarrow} G_4$ of the typed graph transformation $S \Rightarrow G_5$ are sequentially independent: in the intersection of the first comatch n_2 and the second match m_3, there is only the resource node, which is a gluing point with respect to both transformations. In the diagram below, we show only the right-hand side and the gluing graph of the first typed graph production *enter*, and the left-hand side and the gluing graph of the second typed graph production *setFlag*. Accordingly, the context graphs, but not the whole direct typed graph transformations, are depicted:

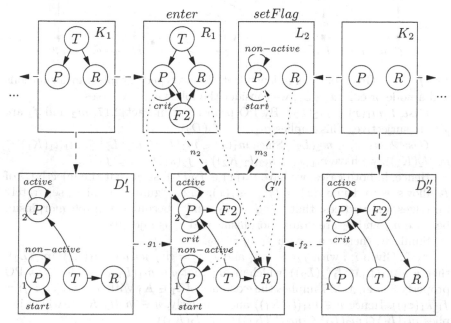

On the other hand, the first two direct typed graph transformations $S \overset{setFlag,m}{\Longrightarrow} G_1 \overset{setTurn1,m_1}{\Longrightarrow} G_5$ of the typed graph transformation $S \Rightarrow G_5$ in Example 3.6 are sequentially dependent: the *setTurn* loop at the process node is in the intersection of the first comatch and the second match, but it is not a gluing item, since it is deleted by the second transformation.   □

In order to show the Local Church–Rosser Theorem (Theorem 3.20), we need the following more categorical characterization of independence. This will be used as a definition of independence in Part II and allows us to prove Theorem 5.12, the categorical version of Theorem 3.20.

Fact 3.18 (characterization of parallel and sequential independence).
Two direct (typed) graph transformations $G \overset{p_1,m_1}{\Longrightarrow} H_1$ and $G \overset{p_2,m_2}{\Longrightarrow} H_2$ are parallel independent iff there exist morphisms $i : L_1 \to D_2$ and $j : L_2 \to D_1$ such that $f_2 \circ i = m_1$ and $f_1 \circ j = m_2$:

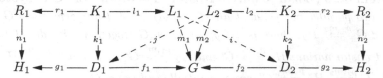

Two direct (typed) graph transformations $G \overset{p_1,m_1}{\Longrightarrow} H \overset{p_2,m_2}{\Longrightarrow} G'$ *are sequentially independent iff there exist morphisms* $i : R_1 \to D_2$ *and* $j : L_2 \to D_1$ *such that* $f_2 \circ i = n_1$ *and* $g_1 \circ j = m_2$:

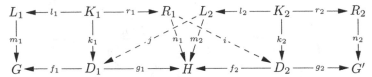

Proof. "$\Rightarrow$". Given parallel independent direct (typed) graph transformations and a node or edge $x \in L_1$, we consider the following two cases:

Case 1: $m_1(x) \notin m_2(L_2)$. By PO property 2 in Fact 2.17, m_2 and f_2 are jointly surjective. This implies $m_1(x) \in f_2(D_2)$.

Case 2: $m_1(x) \in m_2(L_2)$. Since $m_1(x) \in m_1(L_1) \cap m_2(L_2) \subseteq m_1(l_1(K_1)) \cap m_2(l_2(K_2))$, we have $m_1(x) \in m_2(l_2(K_2)) = f_2(k_2(K_2)) \subseteq f_2(D_2)$.

Hence, in both cases, we have $m_1(x) \in f_2(D_2)$, such that the injectivity of f_2 allows us to define $i(x) = f_2^{-1} \circ m_1(x)$. This argument implies, separately for edges and vertices, that $f_2 \circ i = m_1$, and i becomes a graph morphism, because m_1 and f_2 are graph morphisms and f_2 is injective.

Similarly, there is a j with $f_1 \circ j = m_2$.

"$\Leftarrow$". Given i, j with $f_2 \circ i = m_1$ and $f_1 \circ j = m_2$, let $y \in m_1(L_1) \cap m_2(L_2)$; then $y \in m_1(L_1) \cap f_1(j(L_2))$, which means that $y \in m_1(L_1) \cap f_1(D_1)$. Now PO property 3 in Fact 2.17 implies the existence of $z_1 \in K_1$ with $y = m_1(l_1(z_1)) = f_1(k_1(z_1))$. Hence $y \in m_1(l_1(K_1))$ and, similarly, $y \in m_2(l_2(K_2))$, which implies $m_1(L_1) \cap m_2(L_2) \subseteq m_1(l_1(K_1)) \cap m_2(l_2(K_2))$.

The characterization of sequential independence follows from Remark 3.16. □

Example 3.19 (characterization of independence). In the parallel independent typed graph transformations in Example 3.17, we have a graph morphism $i : L_1 \to D_2$ that maps the process node in L_1 to the second process node in D_2 such that $f_2 \circ i = m$, and a graph morphism $j : L_2 \to D_1$ that maps the process node in L_2 to the first process node in D_1 such that $f_1 \circ j = m'$.

Analogously, the sequential independence of the typed graph transformations $G_2 \overset{enter,m_2}{\Longrightarrow} G_3 \overset{setFlag,m_3}{\Longrightarrow} G_4$ implies the existence of graph morphisms $i : R_1 \to D_2''$ with $f_2 \circ i = n_2$ and $j : L_2 \to D_1'$ with $g_1 \circ j = m_3$; i maps the process node in R_1 to the second process in D_2'', while j maps the process node in L_2 to the first process node in D_1'. □

Theorem 3.20 (Local Church–Rosser Theorem for GT systems). *Given two parallel independent direct (typed) graph transformations* $G \overset{p_1,m_1}{\Longrightarrow} H_1$ *and* $G \overset{p_2,m_2}{\Longrightarrow} H_2$, *there is a (typed) graph* G' *together with direct (typed) graph transformations* $H_1 \overset{p_2,m_2'}{\Longrightarrow} G'$ *and* $H_2 \overset{p_1,m_1'}{\Longrightarrow} G'$ *such that* $G \overset{p_1,m_1}{\Longrightarrow} H_1 \overset{p_2,m_2'}{\Longrightarrow} G'$ *and* $G \overset{p_2,m_2}{\Longrightarrow} H_2 \overset{p_1,m_1'}{\Longrightarrow} G'$ *are sequentially independent.*

Given two sequentially independent direct (typed) graph transformations $G \overset{p_1,m_1}{\Longrightarrow} H_1 \overset{p_2,m_2'}{\Longrightarrow} G'$, there are a (typed) graph H_2 and direct (typed) graph transformations $G \overset{p_2,m_2}{\Longrightarrow} H_2 \overset{p_1,m_1'}{\Longrightarrow} G'$ such that $G \overset{p_1,m_1}{\Longrightarrow} H_1$ and $G \overset{p_2,m_2}{\Longrightarrow} H_2$ are parallel independent:

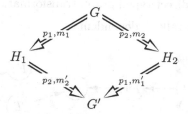

Proof. This follows from Theorem 5.12. □

Example 3.21 (Local Church–Rosser Theorem). We consider the two parallel independent direct typed graph transformations given in Example 3.17, $S \overset{setFlag,m}{\Longrightarrow} G$ and $S \overset{setFlag,m'}{\Longrightarrow} G'$, with G' as shown below:

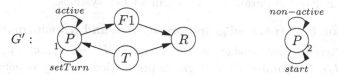

We can obviously apply the typed graph production *setFlag* with the opposite match to each of them, and obtain the following graph X:

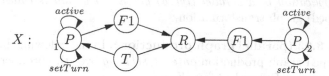

These transformations correspond to the following diagram, and Theorem 3.20 also implies that the typed graph transformations $S \overset{setFlag,m}{\Longrightarrow} G_1 \overset{setFlag,\overline{m'}}{\Longrightarrow} X$ and $S \overset{setFlag,m'}{\Longrightarrow} G' \overset{setFlag,\overline{m}}{\Longrightarrow} X$ are sequentially independent:

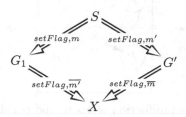

Given the sequentially independent direct typed graph transformations $G_2 \overset{enter,m_2}{\Longrightarrow} G_3 \overset{setFlag,m_3}{\Longrightarrow} G_4$, using Theorem 3.20 we can reverse the order of the typed graph productions, leading to a sequentially independent typed graph transformation $G_2 \overset{setFlag,m_3'}{\Longrightarrow} G_3' \overset{enter,m_2'}{\Longrightarrow} G_4$, with G_3' as depicted below, and the direct typed graph transformations $G_2 \overset{enter,m_2}{\Longrightarrow} G_3$ and $G_2 \overset{setFlag,m_3'}{\Longrightarrow} G_3'$ are parallel independent:

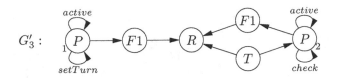

The Local Church–Rosser Theorem states that two parallel independent direct (typed) graph transformations can be applied in arbitrary order. Now we shall see that they can also be applied in parallel. For this purpose, we introduce parallel (typed) graph productions and transformations, which allow us to formulate the Parallelism Theorem for GT systems.

Definition 3.22 (parallel graph production and transformation). *Given two (typed) graph productions $p_1 = (L_1 \overset{l_1}{\leftarrow} K_1 \overset{r_1}{\rightarrow} R_1)$ and $p_2 = (L_2 \overset{l_2}{\leftarrow} K_2 \overset{r_2}{\rightarrow} R_2)$, the parallel (typed) graph production $p_1 + p_2$ is defined by the disjoint union of the corresponding objects and morphisms: $p_1 + p_2 = (L_1 \overset{.}{\cup} L_2 \overset{l_1 \overset{.}{\cup} l_2}{\leftarrow} K_1 \overset{.}{\cup} K_2 \overset{r_1 \overset{.}{\cup} r_2}{\longrightarrow} R_1 \overset{.}{\cup} R_2)$.*

The application of a parallel (typed) graph production is called a parallel direct (typed) graph transformation.

Example 3.23 (parallel graph production). In the following diagram, the parallel typed graph production *enter + setFlag* over the productions *enter* and *setFlag* from Example 3.6 is shown:

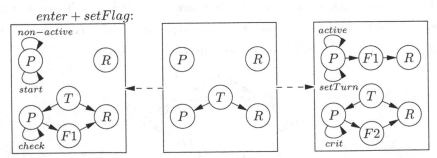

The application of this production leads to the parallel direct typed graph transformation $G_2 \overset{enter+setFlag,m_2+m_3}{\Longrightarrow} G_4$.

Theorem 3.24 (Parallelism Theorem for GT systems). *For a (typed) graph transformation system GTS, we have:*

1. Synthesis. *Given a sequentially independent direct (typed) graph transformation sequence $G \Rightarrow H_1 \Rightarrow G'$ via (typed) graph productions p_1 and p_2, then there is a parallel (typed) graph transformation $G \Rightarrow G'$ via the parallel (typed) graph production $p_1 + p_2$, called a* synthesis construction.
2. Analysis. *Given a parallel (typed) graph transformation $G \Rightarrow G'$ via $p_1 + p_2$, then there is a construction leading to two sequentially independent (typed) graph transformation sequences $G \Rightarrow H_1 \Rightarrow G'$ via p_1 and p_2 and $G \Rightarrow H_2 \Rightarrow G'$ via p_2 and p_1, called an* analysis construction.
3. Bijective correspondence. *The synthesis and analysis constructions are inverse to each other up to isomorphism.*

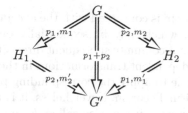

Proof. This follows from Theorem 5.18. □

The Parallelism Theorem is the basis of a shift construction which can be applied to a sequence of parallel (typed) graph transformations. This allows one to shift the application of a (typed) graph production p within a parallel (typed) graph transformation t to the left (i.e. toward the beginning), as long as p is sequentially independent in t from the previous productions, leading to a "canonical transformation". The construction and uniqueness of canonical transformations have been analyzed by Kreowski in [Kre78], leading to a concurrent semantics of algebraic graph transformation systems (see [Roz97]).

Example 3.25 (Parallelism Theorem). We can apply Theorem 3.24 to the sequentially independent direct typed graph transformation $G_2 \overset{enter,m_2}{\Rightarrow} G_3 \overset{setFlag,m_3}{\Rightarrow} G_4$ from Example 3.6, leading to the parallel graph production $enter + setFlag$ and the parallel direct graph transformation given in Example 3.23, and vice versa. □

3.4 Overview of Some Other Main Results for GT Systems

In the previous section, we have analyzed parallel and sequential independence of (typed) graph transformations, leading to the Local Church–Rosser and Parallelism Theorems. In this section, we shall give an overview of some other main results for (typed) graph transformation systems, which are presented in full detail in Part II on a categorical level and in Part III for the case of typed attributed graph transformation systems. In contrast to the previous section, we now study the properties of dependent transformations. As before, we present the main results with illustrative examples, but we shall give only an intuitive idea of some of the new notions used in these results. A formal definition of these notions and also the proofs of the results are given in Part II in the general framework of adhesive HLR categories.

This semiformal presentation is a compromise between completeness and symmetry between Parts I–III on the one hand and too much redundancy on the other hand.

3.4.1 Concurrency Theorem

The Concurrency Theorem is concerned with the execution of general (typed) graph transformations, which may be sequentially dependent. This means that, in general, we cannot commute subsequent direct (typed) graph transformations, as done for independent transformations in the Local Church–Rosser Theorem, nor are we able to apply the corresponding productions in parallel, as done in the Parallelism Theorem. Nevertheless, it is possible to apply both transformations concurrently using a so-called E-concurrent (typed) graph production $p_1 *_E p_2$. Given an arbitrary sequence $G \overset{p_1,m_1}{\Longrightarrow} H \overset{p_2,m_2}{\Longrightarrow} G'$ of direct (typed) graph transformations, it is possible to construct an E-concurrent (typed) graph production $p_1 *_E p_2$. The "epimorphic overlap graph" E can be constructed as a subgraph of H from $E = n_1(R_1) \cup m_2(L_2)$, where n_1 and m_2 are the first comatch and the second match, and R_1 and L_2 are the right- and the left-hand side of p_1 and p_2, respectively. Note that the restrictions $e_1 : R_1 \to E$ of n_1 and $e_2 : L_2 \to E$ of m_2 are jointly epimorphic (see Definition A.16), i.e. e_1 and e_2 are jointly surjective. The E-concurrent (typed) graph production $p_1 *_E p_2$ allows one to construct a direct (typed) graph transformation $G \overset{p_1 *_E p_2}{\Longrightarrow} G'$ from G to G' via $p_1 *_E p_2$. Vice versa, each direct (typed) graph transformation $G \overset{p_1 *_E p_2}{\Longrightarrow} G'$ via the E-concurrent (typed) graph production $p_1 *_E p_2$ can be sequentialized, leading to an E-related (typed) graph transformation sequence $G \overset{p_1,m_1}{\Longrightarrow} H \overset{p_2,m_2}{\Longrightarrow} G'$ of direct (typed) graph transformations via p_1 and p_2, where "E-related" means that n_1 and m_2 overlap in H as required by E. This leads to the following Concurrency Theorem for (typed) graph transformation systems, which is a special case of Theorem 5.23 in Part II.

Theorem 3.26 (Concurrency Theorem for GT systems). *Given two (typed) graph productions p_1 and p_2 and an E-concurrent (typed) graph production $p_1 *_E p_2$, we have:*

1. Synthesis. *Given an E-related (typed) graph transformation sequence $G \Rightarrow H \Rightarrow G'$ via p_1 and p_2, then there is a synthesis construction leading to a direct (typed) graph transformation $G \Rightarrow G'$ via $p_1 *_E p_2$.*

2. Analysis. *Given a direct (typed) graph transformation $G \Rightarrow G'$ via $p_1 *_E p_2$, then there is an analysis construction leading to an E-related (typed) graph transformation sequence $G \Rightarrow H \Rightarrow G'$ via p_1 and p_2.*

3. Bijective correspondence. *The synthesis and analysis constructions are inverse to each other up to isomorphism.*

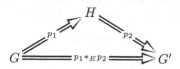

Proof. This follows from Theorem 5.23.   □

Note that the construction of E-concurrent (typed) graph productions can be iterated such that each (typed) graph transformation sequence $G \overset{*}{\Rightarrow} G'$ via $(p_1, \ldots, p_n)$ can be done in one direct (typed) graph transformation $G \Rightarrow G'$ via an iterated E-concurrent (typed) graph production $p_1 *_{E_1} p_2 *_{E_2} \cdots *_{E_{n-1}} p_n$.

Example 3.27 (E-concurrent production and E-related transformation). In Example 3.17, we showed that the direct typed graph transformations $S \overset{setFlag,m}{\Longrightarrow} G_1 \overset{setTurn1,m_1}{\Longrightarrow} G_2$ were sequentially dependent. This transformation sequence is E-related with respect to the following typed graph E:

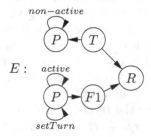

The corresponding E-concurrent typed graph production $setFlag *_E setTurn1$ is depicted in the following diagram and leads to the direct typed graph production $S \overset{setFlag *_E setTurn1}{\Longrightarrow} G_2$:

$setFlag *_E setTurn1$:

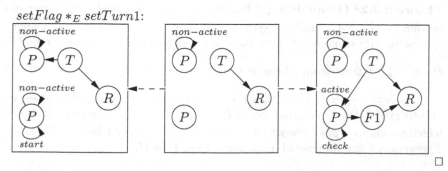

□

3.4.2 Embedding and Extension Theorems

In this subsection, we analyze the problem of under what conditions a (typed) graph transformation $t : G_0 \overset{*}{\Rightarrow} G_n$ can be extended to a graph transformation $t' : G_0' \overset{*}{\Rightarrow} G_n'$ via an extension morphism $k_0 : G_0 \to G_0'$. The idea is to obtain an extension diagram (1) as below, where the same (typed) graph productions $p_1, \ldots, p_n$ are applied in the same order in t and t':

$$
\begin{array}{ccc}
G_0 & \overset{*}{\underset{t}{\Longrightarrow}} & G_n \\
\downarrow{\scriptstyle k_0} & (1) & \downarrow{\scriptstyle k_n} \\
G_0' & \overset{*}{\underset{t'}{\Longrightarrow}} & G_n'
\end{array}
$$

Unfortunately, this is not always possible, but we are able to give a necessary and sufficient consistency condition to allow such an extension. This result is important for all kinds of applications where we have a large (typed) graph G_0', but only small subparts of G_0' have to be changed by the (typed) graph productions $p_1, \ldots, p_n$. In this case we choose a suitably small subgraph G_0 of G_0' and construct a (typed) graph transformation $t : G_0 \overset{*}{\Rightarrow} G_n$ via $p_1, \ldots, p_n$ first. In a second step, we extend $t : G_0 \overset{*}{\Rightarrow} G_n$ via the inclusion $k_0 : G_0 \to G_0'$ to a (typed) graph transformation $t' : G_0' \overset{*}{\Rightarrow} G_n'$ via the same (typed) graph productions $p_1, \ldots, p_n$.

Now we are going to formulate the consistency condition which allows us to extend $t : G_0 \overset{*}{\Rightarrow} G_n$ to $t' : G_0' \overset{*}{\Rightarrow} G_n'$ via $k_0 : G_0 \to G_0'$, leading to the extension diagram (1) above. The idea is to first construct a boundary graph B and a context graph C for $k_0 : G_0 \to G_0'$, such that G_0' is the gluing of G_0 and C along B, i.e. $G_0' = G_0 +_B C$. In fact, this boundary graph B is the smallest subgraph of G_0 which contains the identification points IP and the dangling points DP of $k_0 : G_0 \to G_0'$, considered as the match morphism in Definition 3.9. Now the (typed) graph morphism $k_0 : G_0 \to G_0'$ is said to be consistent with $t : G_0 \overset{*}{\Rightarrow} G_n$ if the boundary graph B is preserved by t. This means that none of the (typed) graph production $p_1, \ldots, p_n$ deletes any item of B. The following Embedding Theorem states that this consistency condition is sufficient; this is a special case of Theorem 6.14 in Part II.

Theorem 3.28 (Embedding Theorem). *Given a (typed) graph transformation $t : G_0 \overset{*}{\Rightarrow} G_n$ and a (typed) graph morphism $k_0 : G_0 \to G_0'$ which is consistent with respect to t, then there is an extension diagram over t and k_0.*

Proof. This follows from Theorem 6.14.   □

The next step is to show that the consistency condition is also necessary, and to give a direct construction of G_n' in the extension diagram (1) below, which avoids an explicit construction of $t' : G_0' \overset{*}{\Rightarrow} G_n'$. The following Extension Theorem is a special case of Theorem 6.16 in Part II.

Theorem 3.29 (Extension Theorem). *Given a (typed) graph transformation* $t : G_0 \overset{*}{\Rightarrow} G_n$ *with an extension diagram (1) and a pushout diagram (2), where B is the boundary and C is the context graph of $k_0 : G_0 \to G'_0$, then we have:*

1. *k_0 is consistent with respect to $t : G_0 \overset{*}{\Rightarrow} G_n$.*
2. *There is a (typed) graph production $der(t) = (G_0 \overset{d_0}{\leftarrow} D_n \overset{d_n}{\to} G_n)$, called the derived span of $t : G_0 \overset{*}{\Rightarrow} G_n$, a direct (typed) graph transformation $G'_0 \Rightarrow G'_n$ via $der(t)$, leading to pushouts (3) and (4), and an injective (typed) graph morphism $b : B \to D_n$.*
3. *There are pushouts (5) and (6), leading to a direct gluing construction of $D'_n = D_n +_B C$ and $G'_n = G_n +_B C$:*

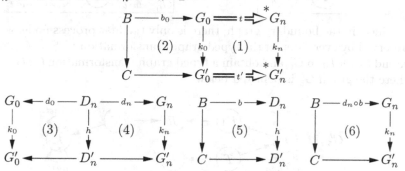

Proof. This follows from Theorem 6.16.   □

Note that the Embedding and Extension Theorems are, in a sense, inverse to each other. The Embedding Theorem allows one to embed a transformation $t : G_0 \overset{*}{\Rightarrow} G_n$ into a larger context given by $k_0 : G_0 \to G'_0$, by construction of an extension diagram. This is possible if k_0 is consistent with respect to t. Vice versa, the Extension Theorem shows that, for each extension diagram, we have consistency and a direct construction of G'_n.

Example 3.30 (Embedding and Extension Theorems). We embed the start graph S from Example 3.6, with the typed graph morphism k_0, into a larger context graph G'_0, where an additional resource is available that is also assigned to the first process. The boundary and context graphs for k_0 are shown in the following diagram:

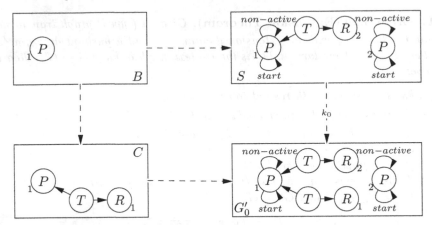

Since, in the boundary graph, there is only the first process node, which is preserved by every step of the typed graph transformation $t : S \overset{*}{\Rightarrow} G_5$, we can extend t over k_0 to G'_0 and obtain a typed graph transformation $t' : G'_0 \overset{*}{\Rightarrow} G'_5$, where the graph G'_5 is depicted below:

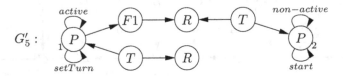

The embedding k'_0 of $S = G_0$ into a different typed graph G''_0 and the boundary and context graphs of k'_0 are shown in the following diagram. In this case, both process nodes and their loop edges are mapped together in G''_0 by k'_0. Since the typed graph transformation $t : S \overset{*}{\Rightarrow} G_5$ does not preserve the loop edges in the boundary graph, it cannot be extended to G''_0.

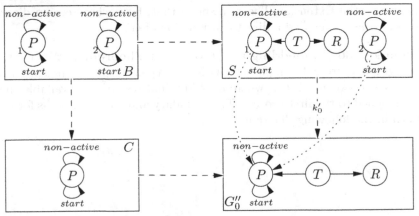

□

3.4.3 Confluence, Local Confluence, Termination, and Critical Pairs

The Local Church–Rosser Theorem shows that, for two parallel independent direct (typed) graph transformations $G \overset{p_1,m_1}{\Longrightarrow} H_1$ and $G \overset{p_2,m_2}{\Longrightarrow} H_2$, there is a (typed) graph G' together with direct (typed) graph transformations $H_1 \overset{p_2,m_2'}{\Longrightarrow} G'$ and $H_2 \overset{p_1,m_1'}{\Longrightarrow} G'$. This means that we can apply the (typed) graph productions p_1 and p_2 with given matches in an arbitrary order. If each pair of productions is parallel independent for all possible matches, then it can be shown that the corresponding (typed) graph transformation system (GTS) is confluent in the following sense: a GTS is called *confluent* if, for all (typed) graph transformations $G \overset{*}{\Rightarrow} H_1$ and $G \overset{*}{\Rightarrow} H_2$, there is a (typed) graph X together with (typed) graph transformations $H_1 \overset{*}{\Rightarrow} X$ and $H_2 \overset{*}{\Rightarrow} X$. *Local confluence* means that this property holds for all pairs of direct (typed) graph transformations $G \Rightarrow H_1$ and $G \Rightarrow H_2$:

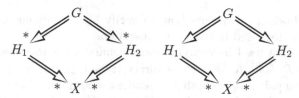

In the following, we discuss local confluence (and, similarly, confluence) for the general case in which $G \Rightarrow H_1$ and $G \Rightarrow H_2$ are not necessarily parallel independent.

Confluence is an important property of a GTS, because, in spite of local nondeterminism concerning the application of a (typed) graph production (see Subsection 1.1.3), we have global determinism for confluent (typed) graph transformation systems. *Global determinism* means that, for each pair of terminating (typed) graph transformations $G \overset{*}{\Rightarrow} H_1$ and $G \overset{*}{\Rightarrow} H_2$ with the same source graph, the target graphs H_1 and H_2 are equal or isomorphic. A (typed) graph transformation $G \overset{*}{\Rightarrow} H$ is called *terminating* if no (typed) graph production in the GTS is applicable to H anymore.

Lemma 3.31 (global determinism of a GTS). *Every confluent (typed) graph transformation system is globally deterministic.*

Proof. Given terminating (typed) graph transformations $G \overset{*}{\Rightarrow} H_1$ and $G \overset{*}{\Rightarrow} H_2$, confluence implies the existence of a (typed) graph X together with (typed) graph transformations $H_1 \overset{*}{\Rightarrow} X$ and $H_2 \overset{*}{\Rightarrow} X$. Since $G \overset{*}{\Rightarrow} H_1$ and $G \overset{*}{\Rightarrow} H_2$ are terminating, the (typed) graph transformations $H_1 \overset{*}{\Rightarrow} X$ and $H_2 \overset{*}{\Rightarrow} X$ must have length $n = 0$ such that $H_1 \cong X \cong H_2$.   □

As pointed out above, a sufficient condition for confluence of a GTS is the property that each pair of direct (typed) graph transformations $G \overset{*}{\Rightarrow} H_1$ and

$G \overset{*}{\Rightarrow} H_2$ is parallel independent. However, this condition is not necessary, and we shall now consider the general case including parallel dependence.

However, we only have to study the weak version of confluence, called local confluence, where the given (typed) graph transformations $G \overset{*}{\Rightarrow} H_1$ and $G \overset{*}{\Rightarrow} H_2$ are direct (typed) graph transformations, but $H_1 \overset{*}{\Rightarrow} X$ and $H_2 \overset{*}{\Rightarrow} X$ are still general. According to a general result for rewriting systems, it is sufficient to consider local confluence, provided that the GTS is terminating.

A GTS is defined to be *terminating* if there is no infinite sequence of graph transformations $(t_n : G \overset{n}{\Rightarrow} G_n)_{n \in \mathbb{N}}$ with $t_{n+1} = G \overset{t_n}{\Rightarrow} G_n \Rightarrow G_{n+1}$. This allows us to show the following result.

Lemma 3.32 (termination and local confluence imply confluence). *Every terminating and locally confluent (typed) graph transformation system is also confluent.*

Proof. This follows from Lemma 6.25.   □

In the following, we discuss how to verify local confluence; termination criteria will be discussed in the next subsection.

The main idea used in verifying local confluence is the study of critical pairs. A pair $P_1 \overset{p_1,o_1}{\Longleftarrow} K \overset{p_2,o_2}{\Longrightarrow} P_2$ of direct (typed) graph transformations is called a critical pair if it is parallel dependent, and minimal in the sense that the pair (o_1, o_2) of matches $o_1 : L_1 \to K$ and $o_2 : L_2 \to K$ is jointly surjective. This means that each item in K has a preimage in L_1 or L_2. In other words, K can be considered as a suitable gluing of L_1 and L_2.

The following lemma shows that every pair of parallel dependent direct (typed) graph transformations is an extension of a critical pair. This is a special case of Lemma 6.22 in Part II.

Lemma 3.33 (completeness of critical pairs). *For each pair of parallel dependent direct (typed) graph transformations $H_1 \overset{p_1,m_1}{\Longleftarrow} G \overset{p_2,m_2}{\Longrightarrow} H_2$, there is a critical pair $P_1 \overset{p_1,o_1}{\Longleftarrow} K \overset{p_2,o_2}{\Longrightarrow} P_2$ with extension diagrams (1) and (2) and an injective (typed) graph morphism m:*

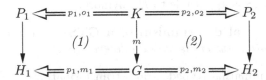

Proof. This follows from Lemma 6.22.   □

If the set of all critical pairs of a GTS is empty, this lemma implies already local confluence of the GTS. Otherwise, in order to show local confluence, it is sufficient to show strict confluence of all its critical pairs. As discussed above, confluence of a critical pair $P_1 \Leftarrow K \Rightarrow P_2$ means the existence of a (typed) graph K' together with (typed) graph transformations $P_1 \overset{*}{\Rightarrow} K'$ and $P_2 \overset{*}{\Rightarrow} K'$.

Strictness is a technical condition (see Definition 6.26 in Part II) which means, intuitively, that the largest subgraph N of K which is preserved by the critical pair $P_1 \Leftarrow K \Rightarrow P_2$ is also preserved by $P_1 \overset{*}{\Rightarrow} K'$ and $P_2 \overset{*}{\Rightarrow} K'$. In [Plu95], it has been shown that confluence of critical pairs without strictness is not sufficient to show local confluence.

This leads to the following Local Confluence Theorem, which is a special case of Theorem 6.28 in Part II.

Theorem 3.34 (Local Confluence Theorem and Critical Pair Lemma). *A (typed) graph transformation system is locally confluent if all its critical pairs are strictly confluent.*

Proof. This follows from Theorem 6.28.   □

Example 3.35 (critical pairs and local confluence). We analyze our typed graph grammar *MutualExclusion* from Example 3.6. We take a closer look at the typed graph productions *setFlag* and *setTurn1*. For a graph G that may lead to a critical pair, we have to consider overlappings of the left-hand sides L_1 of *setFlag* and L_2 of *setTurn1*. The typed graph transformations $G \overset{setFlag}{\Rightarrow} P_1$ and $G \overset{setTurn1}{\Rightarrow} P_2$ are parallel dependent if the loop in L_2 typed *non-active* is deleted by *setFlag*. This leads to the two critical overlappings G_1 and G_2, and we have the critical pairs $P_1 \overset{setFlag}{\Longleftarrow} G_1 \overset{setTurn1}{\Longrightarrow} P_2$ and $P_1' \overset{setFlag}{\Longleftarrow} G_2 \overset{setTurn1}{\Longrightarrow} P_2'$. We show only the corresponding graphs in the following diagram, not the complete typed graph transformations:

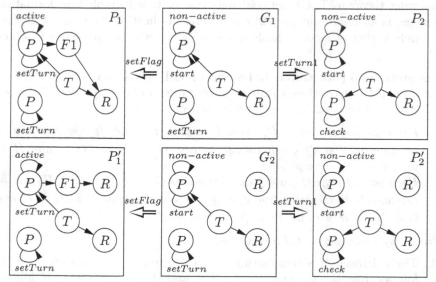

There are many more critical pairs for other pairs of typed graph transformations in our grammar. All these critical pairs are strictly confluent. Therefore the typed graph transformation system is locally confluent. However, as we can see in the derivation graph in Example 3.6, the typed graph grammar is not terminating; nevertheless, it is confluent. □

3.4.4 Functional Behavior of GT Systems and Termination Analysis

As pointed out in the Introduction, (typed) graph transformation systems can show two kinds of nondeterminism: first, several (typed) graph productions might be applicable to a given (typed) graph G and one of them is chosen arbitrarily, and, second, given a certain (typed) graph production, several matches might be possible and one of them has to be chosen. In addition to these two kinds of nondeterminism, a (typed) graph transformation system GTS is, in general, nonterminating (see Subsection 3.4.3).

If we consider a (typed) graph transformation system GTS as a computation device for (typed) graphs, where each (typed) graph transformation $G \overset{*}{\Rightarrow} H$ is a partial computation for G, then this computation device is, in general, nondeterministic and partial. If the (typed) graph transformation $G \overset{*}{\Rightarrow} H$ is terminating, i.e. no (typed) graph production in GTS is applicable to H anymore, then H can be considered as the result of G. But different terminating (typed) graph transformations $G \overset{*}{\Rightarrow} H_1$ and $G \overset{*}{\Rightarrow} H_2$ may lead to different, nonisomorphic results H_1 and H_2. This, however, can be avoided if the GTS is confluent (see Subsection 3.4.3). If the GTS is terminating and locally confluent, then the GTS has a functional behavior, as stated in the following theorem. The functional behavior of typed graph transformation systems is an important property in several application domains. A typical example is that of model transformations, which will be studied in Chapter 14.

Theorem 3.36 (functional behavior of GT systems). *Given a terminating and locally confluent (typed) graph transformation system GTS, then GTS has a functional behavior in the following sense:*

1. *For each (typed) graph G, there is a (typed) graph H together with a terminating (typed) graph transformation $G \overset{*}{\Rightarrow} H$ in GTS, and H is unique up to isomorphism.*
2. *Each pair of (typed) graph transformations $G \overset{*}{\Rightarrow} H_1$ and $G \overset{*}{\Rightarrow} H_2$ can be extended to terminating (typed) graph transformations $G \overset{*}{\Rightarrow} H_1 \overset{*}{\Rightarrow} H$ and $G \overset{*}{\Rightarrow} H_2 \overset{*}{\Rightarrow} H$ with the same (typed) graph H.*

Proof. By Lemma 3.32, GTS is also confluent.

1. The existence of a terminating (typed) graph transformation $G \overset{*}{\Rightarrow} H$ follows from the termination of GTS, and the uniqueness of H follows from the confluence of GTS.

2. This follows from the confluence of GTS.

□

In order to analyze the termination of typed graph transformation systems, let us consider the following kind of layered typed graph grammar. A layered typed graph grammar is a finite typed graph grammar where the typed graph productions are distributed over different layers. In each layer, the typed graph productions are applied for as long as possible before going to the next layer. Moreover, it makes sense to distinguish between deletion and nondeletion layers. All typed graph productions in a deletion layer delete at least one item. The typed graph productions in nondeletion layers do not delete any items, but they have negative application conditions to prohibit an infinite number of applications of the same typed graph production (see Section 3.5 for negative application conditions). Finally, a layered typed graph grammar has a number of deletion and nondeletion layer conditions which have to be satisfied by the typed graph productions. For a precise definition of layered typed graph grammars, see Definition 12.15 in Part III, where we use typed attributed graphs and grammars instead of typed graphs and grammars, and the condition "finitary" instead of "finite". A typed graph grammar $GG = (TG, P, G_0)$ is called "finite" if the graphs TG and G_0, the graphs in each typed graph production $p \in P$, and the set P are all finite. As a special case of Theorem 12.26 in Part III, we obtain the following theorem.

Theorem 3.37 (termination of layered typed graph grammars). *Every layered typed graph grammar $GG = (TG, P, G_0)$ with injective matches terminates, provided that it is layered in the following sense:*

1. *P is* layered, *i.e. for each $p \in P$ there is a production layer $pl(p)$ with $0 \le pl(p) \le k_0$ $(pl(p), k_0 \in \mathbb{N})$, where $k_0 + 1$ is the number of layers of GG, and each typed graph production $p \in P$ has a set NAC_p of negative application conditions $\mathrm{NAC}(n : L \to N)$ (see Definition 3.47); the latter is abbreviated as $n \in \mathrm{NAC}_p$.*
2. *The* type set *$TYPE$ of GG is given by all graph nodes and edges of the type graph TG, i.e. $TYPE = V_{TG} \dot\cup E_{TG}$.*
3. *GG is* finite.
4. *For each type $t \in TYPE$ there is a creation layer $cl(t) \in \mathbb{N}$ and a deletion layer $dl(t) \in \mathbb{N}$, and each production layer k is either a deletion layer or a nondeletion layer, satisfying the following layer conditions for all $p \in P_k$:*

Deletion layer conditions	Nondeletion layer conditions
1. p deletes at least one item.	1. p is nondeleting, i.e. $K = L$ such that p is given by $r : L \to R$ injective.
2. $0 \leq cl(t) \leq dl(t) \leq k_0$ for all $t \in TYPE$.	2. p has $n \in NAC_p$ with $n : L \to N$, and there is an injective $n' : N \to R$ with $n' \circ n = r$.
3. p deletes an item of type t $\Rightarrow dl(t) \leq pl(p)$.	3. $x \in L$ with $type(x) = t$ $\Rightarrow cl(t) \leq pl(p)$.
4. p creates an item of type t $\Rightarrow cl(t) > pl(p)$.	4. p creates an item of type t $\Rightarrow cl(t) > pl(p)$.

Proof. This follows from Theorem 12.26. □

Example 3.38 (nontermination). The derivation graph in Example 3.6 shows that the typed graph grammar *MutualExclusion* is not terminating. Therefore the termination criterion stated in Theorem 3.37 is not fulfilled.

Indeed, we cannot find a set of layers for our typed graph productions such that all the conditions are fulfilled. If we analyze the productions of our grammar, we see that all typed graph productions are deleting, i.e. have to belong to a deletion layer. However, each typed graph production also creates an item – at least a loop at a process node. Now the deletion layer conditions imply the following inequalities:

$$dl(start) \leq pl(setFlag) < cl(setTurn) \leq dl(setTurn) \leq$$
$$pl(setTurn1) < cl(check) \leq dl(check) \leq pl(enter) <$$
$$cl(crit) \leq dl(crit) \leq pl(exit) < cl(start) \leq dl(start),$$

which cannot be fulfilled. □

3.5 Graph Constraints and Application Conditions

Now we are going to extend the theory by introducing graph constraints and application conditions. Graph constraints allow us to formulate properties for graphs. In particular, we are able to formulate the condition that a graph G must (or must not) contain a certain subgraph G'. Beyond that, we can require that G contains C (conclusion) if it contains P (premise). Application conditions, similarly to the gluing condition in Definition 3.9, allow us to restrict the application of productions. Both concepts are important for increasing the expressive power of graph transformation systems.

Application conditions for graph productions were introduced in [EH86]. In a subsequent paper [HHT96], special kinds of application conditions were considered which can be represented in a graphical way. In particular, contextual conditions such as the existence or nonexistence of certain nodes and edges or certain subgraphs in the given graph can be expressed. Conditional application conditions were introduced in [HW95]. Our presentation is based on [EEHP04].

Definition 3.39 (graph constraint). *An atomic (typed) graph constraint is of the form* $PC(a)$, *where* $a : P \to C$ *is a (typed) graph morphism.*

A (typed) graph constraint is a Boolean formula over atomic (typed) graph constraints. This means that true and every atomic (typed) graph constraint are (typed) graph constraints, and, for (typed) graph constraints c *and* c_i *with* $i \in I$ *for some index set* I, $\neg c$, $\bigwedge_{i \in I} c_i$, *and* $\bigvee_{i \in I} c_i$ *are (typed) graph constraints:*

$$
\begin{array}{ccc}
P & \xrightarrow{\ a\ } & C \\
 & \searrow p \quad = \quad \swarrow q & \\
 & G &
\end{array}
$$

A (typed) graph G *satisfies a (typed) graph constraint* c, *written* $G \models c$, *if*

- $c = true$;
- $c = PC(a)$ *and, for every injective (typed) graph morphism* $p : P \to G$, *there exists an injective (typed) graph morphism* $q : C \to G$ *such that* $q \circ a = p$;
- $c = \neg c'$ *and* G *does not satisfy* c';
- $c = \bigwedge_{i \in I} c_i$ *and* G *satisfies all* c_i *with* $i \in I$;
- $c = \bigvee_{i \in I} c_i$ *and* G *satisfies some* c_i *with* $i \in I$.

Two (typed) graph constraints c *and* c' *are* equivalent, *denoted by* $c \equiv c'$, *if for all (typed) graphs* G, $G \models c$ *if and only if* $G \models c'$.

Remark 3.40. Note that we require injectivity for p and q in the definition of $G \models PC(a)$, but not for a. In fact, we can require a to be injective without changing the expressive power (see Remark 3.42).

On the other hand, we could instead drop the requirement that p and q must be injective, which would change the notion of satisfaction. This case is discussed in Chapter 7, where we require that p and q belong to a specific class $\mathcal{M}'$ of morphisms.

In the categories **Graphs** and **Graphs$_{\mathbf{TG}}$**, the empty (typed) graph $\varnothing$ is initial. This means that for each graph G, there is exactly one (typed) graph morphism $p : \varnothing \to G$. Hence $G \models PC(\varnothing \to C)$ means that G contains C as a subgraph (up to isomorphism). (Typed) graph constraints of the form $PC(\varnothing \to C)$ are abbreviated as $PC(C)$. The (typed) graph constraint of the form $PC(\varnothing)$ is equivalent to *true*, and $\neg true$ is abbreviated as *false*.

Example 3.41 (graph constraints). We consider the typed graph constraint $PC(a : P \to C)$, as shown below, for the typed graphs of the graph grammar in Example 3.6:

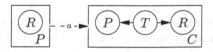

A typed graph G satisfies this constraint if, for each resource node R, there is a turn variable that connects it to a process. The start graph S obviously satisfies this constraint – there is only one resource, which is connected to the first process node.

Some more general examples of graph constraints are:

- $PC(\circ\,\circ \to \circ)$: There exists at most one node.
- $PC(\varnothing \to \text{⦵})$: There exists a node with a loop.
- $PC(\circ \to \text{⦵})$: Every node has a loop.
- $\neg PC(\varnothing \to \text{⦵})$: The graph is loop-free.
- $\neg PC(\circ \to \text{⦵})$: There exists a node without a loop.
- $\bigwedge_{k=1}^{\infty} \neg PC(\varnothing \to C_k)$: The graph is acyclic ($C_k$ denotes a cycle of length k).

Let us explain the first constraint $PC(a : P \to C)$, where P consists of two nodes, which are mapped by a to the one node in C. If the graph G contains two nodes, we shall have an injective morphism $p : P \to G$, but no injective $q : C \to G$ with $q \circ a = p$.

In the last graph constraint above, we use an infinite conjunction.

Analogously, given a type graph TG, typed graph constraints make statements about nodes or edges of a special type (where the label of the node or edge denotes its type):

- $PC(\textcircled{t}\,\textcircled{t} \to \textcircled{t})$: There exists at most one node of type t.
- $PC(\varnothing \to \overset{e}{\text{⦵}})$: There exists a node of type t with a loop of type e.
- $\bigwedge_{t \in V_{TG}} PC(\varnothing \to \textcircled{t})$: There is at least one node of each node type.
- $\bigvee_{t \in V_{TG}} PC(\varnothing \to \textcircled{t})$: There is at least one node (of any type).

$\square$

In most of our examples, the (typed) graph morphism $a : P \to C$ of a graph constraint $PC(a)$ is injective. Actually, concerning the expressive power, it is sufficient to use an injective a, as shown in the next Remark.

Remark 3.42. In Definition 3.39, we have not required that a in $PC(a)$ is injective. But (typed) graph constraints with noninjective (typed) graph morphisms do not give additional expressive power. For every (typed) graph constraint, there is an equivalent (typed) graph constraint with injective (typed) graph morphisms. In particular, for a noninjective a, $PC(P \overset{a}{\to} C) \equiv \neg PC(P)$: if there exists an injective $p : P \to G$, then there does not exist an injective $q : C \to G$ with $q \circ a = p$, otherwise a would have to be injective, since injective morphisms are closed under decomposition. This means that $G \not\models PC(a)$ and $G \models PC(P)$. If there does not exist an injective $p : P \to G$, then $G \models PC(a)$ and $G \not\models PC(P)$.

Let us now consider negative atomic graph constraints in order to express the absence of C in G. A *negative atomic graph constraint* is of the form

NC(a), where $a : P \rightarrow C$ is a graph morphism. A graph G satisfies NC(a) if, for every injective morphism $p : P \rightarrow G$, there *does not* exist an injective morphism $q : C \rightarrow G$ with $q \circ a = p$.

Remark 3.43. Negative atomic graph constraints do not give more expressive power. For every negative atomic graph constraint, there is an equivalent constraint: if a is injective, then NC($P \xrightarrow{a} C$) $\equiv \neg$PC(C); otherwise NC($P \xrightarrow{a}$ C) $\equiv true$ (see Fact 7.5).

Example 3.44 (negative graph constraint). For valid graphs of the typed graph grammar in Example 3.6, each resource node should be connected to exactly one process node. We have expressed the property that the node is connected by means of a graph constraint in Example 3.41. The following negative atomic graph constraint NC($a' : \varnothing \rightarrow C'$) is satisfied by a graph G if each resource node in G is connected to at most one process node:

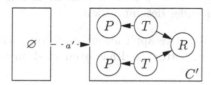

□

Now we introduce application conditions for a match $m : L \rightarrow G$, where L is the left-hand side of a (typed) graph production p. The idea is that the production cannot be applied at m if m violates the application condition.

Definition 3.45 (application condition). *An atomic application condition over a (typed) graph L is of the form $P(x, \vee_{i \in I} x_i)$, where $x : L \rightarrow X$ and $x_i : X \rightarrow C_i$ with $i \in I$ for some index set I are (typed) graph morphisms.*

An application condition over L is a Boolean formula over atomic application conditions over L. This means that true and every atomic application condition are application conditions, and, for application conditions acc and acc_i with $i \in I$, $\neg acc$, $\wedge_{i \in I} acc_i$, and $\vee_{i \in I} acc_i$ are application conditions:

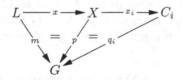

A (typed) graph morphism $m : L \rightarrow G$ satisfies an application condition acc, written $m \models acc$, if

- *acc = true;*
- *acc = $P(x, \vee_{i \in I} x_i)$ and, for all injective (typed) graph morphisms $p : X \rightarrow G$ with $p \circ x = m$, there exists an $i \in I$ and an injective (typed) graph morphism $q_i : C_i \rightarrow G$ with $q_i \circ x_i = p$;*

- $acc = \neg acc'$ and m does not satisfy acc';
- $acc = \wedge_{i \in I} acc_i$ and m satisfies all acc_i with $i \in I$;
- $acc = \vee_{i \in I} acc_i$ and m satisfies some acc_i with $i \in I$.

Two application conditions acc and acc' over a (typed) graph L are equivalent, denoted by $acc \equiv acc'$, if for all (typed) graph morphisms $m : L \to G$ for some G, $m \models acc$ if and only if $m \models acc'$.

The application condition $\neg true$ is abbreviated as $false$.

Remark 3.46. Application conditions with noninjective (typed) graph morphisms in the second component of the atomic application condition do not give more expressive power. For every application condition, there is an equivalent application condition with injective (typed) graph morphisms in the second component: $P(x, \vee_{i \in I} x_i) \equiv P(x, \vee_{i \in I'} x_i)$ with $I' = \{i \in I \mid x_i \text{ injective}\}$. For an injective $p : X \to G$ and an $i \in I$, the existence of an injective $q_i : C_i \to G$ with $q_i \circ x_i = p$ implies that x_i is injective, since injective morphisms are closed under decomposition.

Now we consider negative application conditions, where the simple form $NAC(x)$ is especially important and has been used already to deal with termination in Theorem 3.37.

Definition 3.47 (negative application condition). *A simple negative application condition is of the form $NAC(x)$, where $x : L \to X$ is a (typed) graph morphism. A (typed) graph morphism $m : L \to G$ satisfies $NAC(x)$ if there does not exist an injective (typed) graph morphism $p : X \to G$ with $p \circ x = m$:*

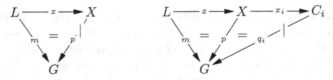

An atomic negative application condition is of the form $N(x, \wedge_{i \in I} x_i)$, where $x : L \to X$ and $x_i : X \to C_i$, with $i \in I$, are (typed) graph morphisms. A (typed) graph morphism $m : L \to G$ satisfies $N(x, \wedge_{i \in I} x_i)$ if, for all injective (typed) graph morphisms $p : X \to G$ with $p \circ x = m$, there does not exist an $i \in I$ and an injective (typed) graph morphism $q_i : C_i \to G$ with $q_i \circ x_i = p$.

Remark 3.48. The notation $N(x, \wedge_{i \in I} x_i)$ expresses the condition that, for all p with $p \circ x = m$ and for all $i \in I$, there is no q_i with $q_i \circ x_i = p$. Negative application conditions do not give more expressive power. A simple negative application condition $NAC(x)$ is equivalent to an application condition of the form $P(x, \vee_{i \in I} x_i)$ with an empty index set I: if a (typed) graph morphism m does not satisfy $NAC(x)$, then there is a morphism $p : X \to G$ with $p \circ x = m$, but no index $i \in I$ to obtain the required (typed) graph morphism q_i, i.e. m does not satisfy $P(x, \vee_{i \in I} x_i)$. If m satisfies $NAC(x)$, then there does not exist an injective (typed) graph morphism $p : X \to G$ with $p \circ x = m$, and for $P(x, \vee_{i \in I} x_i)$ there is nothing to show.

For every atomic negative application condition, there is an equivalent application condition: $N(x, \wedge_{i \in I} x_i) \equiv \wedge_{i \in I} P(x_i \circ x, e)$, where e is an expression with an empty index set (see Fact 7.9).

In analogy to $NAC(x) \equiv P(x, e)$, we write $PAC(x)$ (positive application condition) for an application condition $\neg P(x, e)$, i.e. $PAC(x) = \neg P(x, e) = \neg NAC(x)$. According to Definition 3.45, we have, for $m : L \to G$ and $x : L \to X$, that $m \models PAC(x)$ iff there exists an injective (typed) graph morphism $p : X \to G$ with $p \circ x = m$.

Example 3.49 (application conditions). Some examples of application conditions of graphs and their meanings for an injective match morphism m are given below:

- $PAC(\underset{1\ 2}{\circ\ \circ} \to \underset{1\ 2}{\circ\text{-}\circ})$: There is some edge from $m(1)$ to $m(2)$.
- $NAC(\underset{1\ 2}{\circ\ \circ} \to \underset{1\ 2}{\circ\text{-}\circ})$: There is no edge from $m(1)$ to $m(2)$.
- $PAC(\underset{1}{\circ} \to \underset{1}{\circ\text{-}\circ}) \vee PAC(\underset{1}{\circ} \to \underset{1}{\circ\text{-}\circ})$: $m(1)$ is not isolated.
- $NAC(\underset{1}{\circ} \to \underset{1}{\circ\text{-}\circ}) \wedge NAC(\underset{1}{\circ} \to \underset{1}{\circ\text{-}\circ})$: $m(1)$ is isolated.
- $P(\underset{1\ 2}{\circ\ \circ} \to \underset{1\ 2}{\circ\text{-}\circ}, \underset{1\ 2}{\circ\text{-}\circ} \to \underset{1\ 2}{\circ\rightleftarrows\circ})$: If there is an edge from $m(1)$ to $m(2)$, then there is an edge from $m(2)$ to $m(1)$.
- $P(\underset{1}{\circ} \to \underset{1\ 2}{\circ\ \circ}, \underset{1\ 2}{\circ\ \circ} \to \underset{1\ 2}{\circ\text{-}\circ} \vee \underset{1\ 2}{\circ\ \circ} \to \underset{1\ 2}{\circ\text{-}\circ})$: $m(1)$ is connected directly to all other nodes.
- $\bigwedge_{k=1}^{\infty} NAC(\underset{1\ 2}{\circ\ \circ} \to P_k)$: There is no path connecting $m(1)$ and $m(2)$ (P_k denotes a path of length k connecting 1 and 2).

$\square$

Up to now, we have considered application conditions over L, where L is the left-hand side of a production. Similarly, we can consider application conditions over R, where R is the right-hand side of a production. In the following, we combine both concepts.

Definition 3.50 (application condition for a production). *Given a (typed) graph production $p = (L \xleftarrow{l} K \xrightarrow{r} R)$, an application condition $A(p) = (A_L, A_R)$ for p consists of a left application condition A_L over L and a right application condition A_R over R.*

A direct (typed) graph transformation $G \overset{p,m}{\Rightarrow} H$ with a comatch $n : R \to H$ satisfies the application condition $A(p) = (A_L, A_R)$ if $m \models A_L$ and $n \models A_R$.

Example 3.51 (graph production with application condition). We add a new production *addResource* to our typed graph grammar *MutualExclusion* from Example 3.6, as shown in the following diagram. This production inserts a new resource node and a new turn node, connected to this resource and a given process:

addResource:

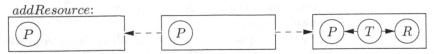

For the application of this production, we define an application condition $A(addResource)$. The left application condition NAC(x) and the right application condition P(x_1, y_1) are depicted below. With NAC(x), we forbid the possibility that the process that the turn will be connected to is already active. P(x_1, y_1) makes sure that after the application of *addResource*, only one turn is assigned to the process. Note that y_1 is not injective, but instead maps both turn nodes together.

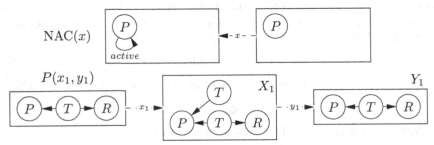

To apply the production *addResource* to the start graph S, there are two possible matches: the process node in the left-hand side may be mapped to the first process node in S, leading to the match m_1, or to the second process node in S, leading to the match m_2. Both matches satisfy the left application condition NAC(x), because both processes are nonactive.

The application of *addResource* to S via m_2 leads to the following typed graph H_2 with a comatch n_2; n_2 satisfies P(x_1, x_2), because there is no injective morphism $p : X_1 \to H_2$:

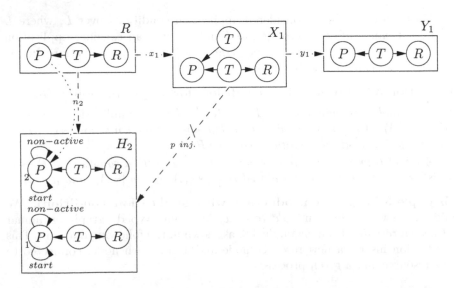

If we apply the production *addResource* to S via the match m_1, we obtain the typed graph H_1 with a comatch n_1; n_1 does not satisfy the right application condition $P(x_1, y_1)$, because there is an injective morphism $p : X_1 \rightarrow H_1$ such that $p \circ x_1 = n_1$, as depicted below, but there is no injective morphism $q : Y_1 \rightarrow H_1$ such that $q \circ y_1 = p$. Therefore the direct transformation $S \overset{addResource, m_1}{\Longrightarrow} H_1$ does not satisfy the application condition $A(addResource)$.

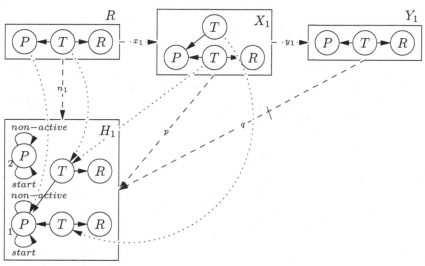

□

In Chapter 7, we shall extend graph constraints and application conditions to the framework of adhesive HLR categories and systems. In this framework, we shall show how to construct an equivalent right application condition for each graph constraint and an equivalent left application condition for each right application condition. This allows us to make sure that the derived graph H satisfies a given graph constraint $PC(a)$, provided that the match $m : L \rightarrow G$ of the direct graph transformation $G \overset{p,m}{\Longrightarrow} H$ satisfies the corresponding left application condition *acc*.

For an even more general concept of graph constraints and application conditions, we refer to [HP05], where nested constraints and application conditions are used in the sense of [Ren04]. A typical nested example is the following: "For all nodes, there exists an outgoing edge such that, for all edges outgoing from the target, the target has a loop".

Part II

Adhesive High-Level Replacement Categories and Systems

In the second Part of this book, we generalize the algebraic approach of graph transformation from classical graphs to high-level structures. This allows us to apply the concepts and results of graph transformation to high-level structures such as hypergraphs, Petri nets, algebraic signatures and specifications and, especially, typed attributed graphs, as is done in Part III. The concepts of graph grammars and transformations presented in Chapters 2 and 3 are now formulated in the categorical framework of adhesive high-level replacement (HLR) categories and systems in Chapters 4 and 5. Together with several instantiations of the categorical framework, we present some more advanced concepts and results in Chapters 6 and 7. The proofs of the basic and advanced results are presented in the framework of adhesive HLR categories. This implies the validity of the basic results in Chapter 3 for the classical case of graph transformations.

The theory of HLR systems was started in [EHKP91a, EHKP91b] in order to have a common framework for different types of graph and Petri net transformation systems. The theory of transformation systems for Petri nets extends the classical theory of Petri nets based on the token game by allowing also a rule-based modification of the structures of Petri nets (see [PER95, Pad96]). The HLR framework has also been applied to algebraic specifications (see [EM85, EM90]), where the interface of an algebraic module specification can be considered as a production of an algebraic specification transformation system (see [EGP99]). More recently, the concept of adhesive categories developed by Lack and Sobociński [LS04] has been combined with HLR categories and systems in [EHPP04], leading to the new concept of adhesive HLR categories and systems. The concepts and results in the present Part II are based on [EHPP04, Pra04] and [EEHP04] concerning Chapters 4–6 and Chapter 7, respectively.

For those readers who are interested mainly in the concepts and results of transformation systems for classical and typed attributed graphs, but not so much in the general theory and in the proofs, it is advisable to skip Part II and continue immediately with Parts III and IV after Part I.

4

Adhesive High-Level Replacement Categories

In this chapter, we generalize the basic concepts of the algebraic approach from graphs to high-level structures and instantiate them with various kinds of graphs, Petri nets, algebraic specifications, and typed attributed graphs. The concepts of adhesive categories and adhesive high-level replacement (HLR) categories are introduced as a suitable categorical framework for graph transformation in this more general sense. The necessary axioms for this generalization are stated. They rely on the concepts of pushouts and pullbacks and their compatibility which are essential for the Van Kampen squares and adhesive categories described in Section 4.1 and introduced by Lack and Sobociński in [LS04]. While adhesive categories are based on the class $\mathcal{M}$ of all monomorphisms, we introduce adhesive and weak adhesive HLR categories $(\mathbf{C}, \mathcal{M})$ in Section 4.2 based on a suitable subclass $\mathcal{M}$ of all monomorphisms. This more flexible class $\mathcal{M}$ is essential for the typed attributed graphs considered in Part III to be an adhesive HLR category. An important result in Section 4.2 shows how to construct new (weak) adhesive HLR categories from given ones. Finally, in Section 4.3, we show that (weak) adhesive HLR categories satisfy several HLR properties, originally considered in [EHKP91a] to prove the main results for graph transformation systems in a categorical framework. The concepts of adhesive HLR categories and systems were introduced in [EHPP04]. In this chapter, we also introduce the slightly weaker concept of weak HLR categories, because some interesting examples such as place/transition nets satisfy only the weaker version.

4.1 Van Kampen Squares and Adhesive Categories

The intuitive idea of adhesive categories is that of categories with suitable pushouts and pullbacks which are compatible with each other. More precisely, the definition is based on van Kampen squares.

The idea of a van Kampen (VK) square is that of a pushout which is stable under pullbacks, and, vice versa, that pullbacks are stable under combined pushouts and pullbacks. The name "van Kampen" is derived from the relationship between these squares and the Van Kampen Theorem in topology (see [BJ97]).

Definition 4.1 (van Kampen square). *A pushout (1) is a van Kampen square if, for any commutative cube (2) with (1) in the bottom and where the back faces are pullbacks, the following statement holds: the top face is a pushout iff the front faces are pullbacks:*

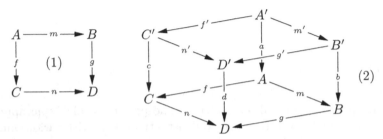

It might be expected that, at least in the category **Sets**, every pushout is a van Kampen square. Unfortunately, this is not true (see Ex. 4.4). However, at least pushouts along monomorphisms (injective functions) are VK squares.

Fact 4.2 (VK squares in Sets). *In **Sets**, every pushout along a monomorphism is a VK square. Pushout (1) above is called a pushout along a monomorphism if m (or, symmetrically, f) is a monomorphism.*

Proof. Consider the pushout (1) above, where m is a monomorphism, i.e. injective. We have to show that, given a commutative cube (2) as above with (1) in the bottom, where the back faces are pullbacks, the following holds:

the top face is a pushout $\Leftrightarrow$ the front faces are pullbacks.

If m is a monomorphism, we also have the result that n, m', and n' are monomorphisms, since monomorphisms in **Sets** are closed under pushouts and pullbacks (see Facts 2.17 and 2.23). Now we show the statement.

Part 1 ("$\Rightarrow$"). Assume that the top face in (2) is a pushout. Since pullbacks are unique up to isomorphism, it is sufficient to prove that B' and C' are isomorphic to the corresponding pullback objects.

We have to show that:

1. $B' \cong PB_1 := \bigcup_{d_1 \in D} d^{-1}(d_1) \times g^{-1}(d_1)$.
2. $C' \cong PB_2 := \bigcup_{d_1 \in D} d^{-1}(d_1) \times n^{-1}(d_1)$.

1. Since PB_1 is the pullback object over d and g and $d \circ g' = g \circ b$, there is an induced morphism $i : B' \to PB_1$ with $i(b') = (g'(b'), b(b'))$ for all $b' \in B'$.

- i is injective.

  Suppose that there are $b'_1 \neq b'_2 \in B'$ with $i(b'_1) = i(b'_2)$. Then we have $g'(b'_1) = g'(b'_2)$ and $b(b'_1) = b(b'_2)$.

  - Since the top is a pushout and m' is injective, there exist $a'_1 \neq a'_2 \in A'$ with $m'(a'_1) = b'_1$, $m'(a'_2) = b'_2$, and $f'(a'_1) = f'(a'_2)$ (property 1).
  - The back right face commutes, and, since m is injective, it follows that $a(a'_1) = a(a'_2)$ (property 2).
  - The back left face is a pullback, and therefore we have the result that $a(a'_1) \neq a(a'_2)$ or $f'(a'_1) \neq f'(a'_2)$.

  This is a contradiction of properties 1 and 2.

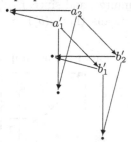

- i is surjective.

  Suppose that i is not surjective. Then there exist $d'_1 \in D'$ and $b_1 \in B$ with $d(d'_1) = g(b_1)$; therefore $(d'_1, b_1) \in PB_1$, but $i(b') = (g'(b'), b(b')) \neq (d'_1, b_1)$ for all $b' \in B'$.

  We consider the following case distinctions:

  Case 1. For all $b' \in B'$, it holds that $g'(b') \neq d'_1$.

  - Then there exists a $c'_1 \in C'$ such that $n'(c'_1) = d'_1$, and for all $a' \in A'$ we have $f'(a') \neq c'_1$, because the top is a pushout.
  - Since the back left face is a pullback, we have $f(a_1) \neq c(c'_1)$ for all $a_1 \in A$ (property 3).
  - The front left face commutes, which means that $n(c(c'_1)) = d(n'(c'_1)) = d(d'_1) = g(b_1)$.
  - Since the bottom is a pushout, there exists an $a_1 \in A$ with $m(a_1) = b_1$ and $f(a_1) = c(c'_1)$.

  This is a contradiction of property 3.

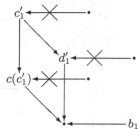

Case 2. There is a $b_2' \in B'$ with $g'(b_2') = d_1'$, but $b(b_2') = b_2 \neq b_1$.

- The front right face commutes, and therefore $g(b_2) = d(d_1') = g(b_1)$.
- Since the bottom is a pushout and m and n are injective, we have $a_1 \neq a_2 \in A$ with $m(a_1) = b_1$, $m(a_2) = b_2$ and $f(a_1) = f(a_2)$.
- The back right face is a pullback with $m(a_2) = b_2 = b(b_2')$, which means that there is an $a_2' \in A'$ with $a(a_2') = a_2$ and $m'(a_2') = b_2'$.
- The back left face is a pullback, and since $c(f'(a_2')) = f(a_2) = f(a_1)$, there is an $a_1' \in A'$ with $a(a_1') = a_1$ and $f'(a_1') = f'(a_2')$.
- Since the back right face is a pullback, we obtain a $b_1' \in B'$ with $m'(a_1') = b_1'$ and $b(b_1') = m(a_1) = b_1$.
- The top commutes, and since $f'(a_1') = f'(a_2')$, we obtain $g'(b_1') = g'(b_2')$. This means that $i(b_1') = (g'(b_1'), b(b_1')) = (g'(b_2'), b_1) = (d_1', b_1)$.

This is a contradiction of the assumption that i is not surjective.

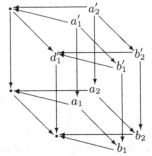

- We have shown that i is both injective and surjective, i.e. isomorphic; therefore the front right face of the cube (2) is a pullback.

2. Since PB_2 is the pullback object over d and n and $d \circ n' = n \circ c$, there is an induced morphism $j : C' \to PB_2$ with $j(c') = (n'(c'), c(c'))$ for all $c' \in C'$.

- j is injective.

   Monomorphisms, i.e. injective functions, are closed under pullbacks and decomposition. Since n is injective, $\hat{n} : PB_2 \to D'$ is also injective. Since $\hat{n} \circ j = n'$ and n' is injective, so is j:

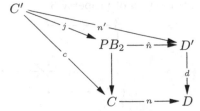

- j is surjective.

    Suppose that there exist $d_1' \in D'$ and $c_1 \in C$ with $d(d_1') = n(c_1)$; therefore $(d_1', c_1) \in PB_2$, but $j(c') = (n'(c'), c(c')) \neq (d_1', c_1)$ for all $c' \in C'$.

    We consider the following case distinctions:

    Case 1. For all $c' \in C'$, it holds that $n'(c') \neq d_1'$.

    - Since the top is a pushout, there exists a $b_1' \in B'$ with $g'(b_1') = d_1'$ and $m'(a') \neq b_1'$ for all $a' \in A'$.
    - Since the back right face is a pullback, we have $m(a_1) \neq b(b_1')$ for all $a_1 \in A$ (property 4).
    - The front right face commutes, which means that $g(b(b_1')) = d(g'(b_1')) = d(d_1') = n(c_1)$, where the last equality holds by assumption.
    - The bottom is a pushout with an injective m and hence is a pullback. Therefore there exists an $a_1 \in A$ with $f(a_1) = c_1$ and $m(a_1) = b(b_1')$.

    This is a contradiction of property 4.

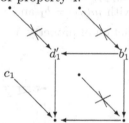

    Case 2. There is a $c_2' \in C'$ with $n'(c_2') = d_1'$, but $c(c_2') = c_2 \neq c_1$.

    - The front left commutes; therefore $n(c_1) = d(d_1') = d(n'(c_2')) = n(c(c_2')) = n(c_2)$.

    This is a contradiction of the fact that n is injective.

- j is both injective and surjective, i.e. isomorphic, and therefore the front left face of the cube (2) is a pullback.

Part 2 ("$\Leftarrow$"). Assume that the front faces of cube (2) are pullbacks. Pushouts are unique up to isomorphism. Since m' is injective, we can assume, from property 4 of Fact 2.17, that PO is given by $PO := C' \mathbin{\dot\cup} B' \backslash m'(A')$, and it remains to show that:

3. $D' \cong PO$.

3. Since PO is the pushout object over f' and m', and $g' \circ m' = n' \circ f'$, there is an induced morphism $k : PO \to D'$ with

$$k(p) = \begin{cases} n'(p) & \text{if } p \in C' \\ g'(p) & \text{otherwise} \end{cases}.$$

- k is injective.

  Let $p_1, p_2 \in C' \stackrel{.}{\cup} B' \backslash m'(A')$ with $k(p_1) = k(p_2)$; we have to show that $p_1 = p_2$. Assume that $p_1 \neq p_2$, and then we have the following case distinctions:

  Case 1. For $p_1 \neq p_2 \in C'$, we have $n'(p_1) \neq n'(p_2)$ because n' is injective, which contradicts $n'(p_1) = k(p_1) = k(p_2) = n'(p_2)$.

  Case 2. For $p_1 \neq p_2 \in B' \backslash m'(A')$, we have $g'(p_1) = k(p_1) = k(p_2) = g'(p_2)$.

  - For all $a' \in A'$, we have $m'(a') \neq p_1$ and $m'(a') \neq p_2$.
  - Since the front right face is a pullback with $d(g'(p_1)) = d(g'(p_2))$, there are $b_1 \neq b_2 \in B$ with $b(p_1) = b_1$, $b(p_2) = b_2$, and $g(b_1) = g(b_2)$.
  - The back right face is a pullback with $m'(a') \neq p_1$ and $m(a') \neq p_2$ for all $a' \in A$, and therefore $m(a_1) \neq b_1$ and $m(a_2) \neq b_2$ for all a_1, $a_2 \in A$ (property 5).
  - The bottom is a pushout, and since $g(b_1) = g(b(p_1)) = d(g'(p_1)) = d(g'(p_2)) = g(b(p_2)) = g(b_2)$ and m is injective, there have to exist $a_1 \neq a_2 \in A$ with $m(a_1) = b_1$ and $m(a_2) = b_2$.

  This is a contradiction of property 5.

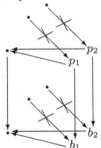

  Case 3. For $p_1 \in C'$, $p_2 \in B' \backslash m'(A')$, we have $n'(p_1) = k(p_1) = k(p_2) = g'(p_2)$.

  - For all $a' \in A'$, we have $m'(a') \neq p_2$ (property 6).
  - The front right and the front left face commute; therefore $n(c(p_1)) = d(n'(p_1)) = d(g'(p_2)) = g(b(p_2))$.
  - Since the bottom is a pushout with m injective and hence is a pullback, we obtain an $a_1 \in A$ with $f(a_1) = c(p_1)$ and $m(a_1) = b(p_2)$.
  - Since the back right face is a pullback, there exists an $a_1' \in A'$ with $a(a_1') = a_1$ and $m'(a_1') = p_2$.

  This is a contradiction of property 6.

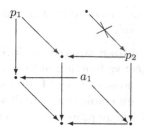

- k is surjective.

    Suppose that there exists a $d_1' \in D'$ with $k(p) \neq d_1'$ for all $p \in PO$, which means that $n'(c') \neq d_1'$ for all $c' \in C'$ and $g'(b') \neq d_1'$ for all $b' \in B'$. If there were a $b_1' \in m'(A')$ with $g'(b_1') = d_1'$, then there would also be a $c_1' \in C'$ and an $a_1' \in A$ with $n'(c_1') = n'(f'(a_1')) = g'(m'(a_1')) = g'(b_1') = d_1'$, which would contradict $n'(c') \neq d_1'$ for all $c' \in C'$.

    – The front faces are pullbacks; therefore $n(c_1) \neq d(d_1')$ for all $c_1 \in C$ and $g(b_1) \neq d(d_1')$ for all $b_1 \in B$ (property 7).
    – The bottom is a pushout; therefore there exists, for $d(d_1') \in D$, a $c_1 \in C$ with $n(c_1) = d(d_1')$ or a $b_1 \in B$ with $g(b_1) = d(d_1')$.

    This is a contradiction of property 7.

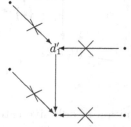

- k is both injective and surjective, i.e. isomorphic, and therefore the top face of the cube (2) is a pushout. □

Remark 4.3 (proof techniques for Fact 4.2). The proof of Fact 4.2 looks quite complicated, and it raises the question of the possibility of a simpler proof. The first idea would be to use only the composition and decomposition properties of POs (Fact 2.20) and of PBs (Fact 2.27). If the top face is a PO, then the top and bottom are POs and PBs by Remark 2.25. This implies that all faces in the cube (2) except for the front faces are PBs. However, Fact 2.27 cannot be applied to conclude that the front faces are also PBs.

An alternative way to show part 1 of the proof would be to use the properties of PBs in **Sets** in Fact 2.23 directly to show that the front faces are PBs. Concerning part 2, an alternative would be to show first that the top diagram in (2) is a PB using the fact that the bottom PO, with an injective m, is also a PB. In this case, Fact 2.27 could be applied to show that the top is a PB. In a second step, Remark 2.25 could be used to show that the top is also a PO. It would remain to show that m' and that g' are jointly surjective and g' is injective up to m'.

Example 4.4 (van Kampen square in Sets). In the following diagram a VK square along an injective function in **Sets** is shown on the left-hand side. All morphisms are inclusions, or 0 and 1 are mapped to $*$ and 3 to 2.

Arbitrary pushouts are stable under pullbacks in **Sets**. This means that one direction of the VK square property is also valid for arbitrary morphisms. However, the other direction is not necessarily valid. The cube on the right-hand side is such a counterexample, for arbitrary functions: all faces commute, the bottom and the top are pushouts, and the back faces are pullbacks. But, obviously, the front faces are not pullbacks, and therefore the pushout in the bottom fails to be a VK square.

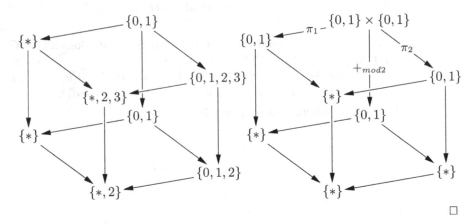

In the following definition of adhesive categories, only those VK squares (as defined in Definition 4.1) where m is a monomorphism are considered. Following Lack and Sobociński [LS04], we define an adhesive category as below.

Definition 4.5 (adhesive category). *A category* **C** *is an* adhesive category *if:*

1. **C** *has pushouts along monomorphisms (i.e. pushouts where at least one of the given morphisms is a monomorphism).*
2. **C** *has pullbacks.*
3. *Pushouts along monomorphisms are VK squares.*

In [Sob04] and related work, adhesive categories are used as the categorical framework for deriving process congruences from reaction rules. This is closely related to deriving bisimulation congruences in the DPO approach with a borrowed context, introduced in [EK04]. We shall not discuss these applications in this book, where adhesive categories are used only as a first step towards adhesive HLR categories in Section 4.2.

Let us first consider some basic examples and counterexamples of adhesive categories.

Theorem 4.6 (Sets, Graphs, and Graphs$_{TG}$ as adhesive categories).
Sets, Graphs, *and* Graphs$_{TG}$ *are adhesive categories.*

Proof. As shown in Facts 2.17 and 2.23, **Sets** has pushouts and pullbacks over arbitrary morphisms. In Fact 4.2, we have shown that pushouts along monomorphisms are VK squares. Therefore **Sets** is an adhesive category.

The result that **Graphs** and **Graphs$_{TG}$** are adhesive categories follows from Theorem 4.15 and is shown in Fact 4.16. □

Counterexample 4.7 (nonadhesive categories). The category **Posets** of partially ordered sets (see Example A.3) and the category **Top** of topological spaces and continuous functions are not adhesive categories. In the following diagram, a cube in **Posets** is shown that fails to be a van Kampen square. The bottom is a pushout with injective functions (monomorphisms) and all lateral faces are pullbacks, but the top square is not a pushout in **Posets**. The proper pushout over the corresponding morphisms is the square (1):

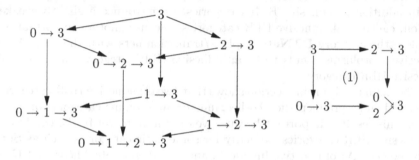

□

Remark 4.8 (quasiadhesive categories). In [LS05], Lack and Sobociński have also introduced a variant of adhesive categories, called quasiadhesive categories, where the class of monomorphisms in Definition 4.5 is replaced by regular monomorphisms. A monomorphism is called "regular" if it is the equalizer of two morphisms. For adhesive and also quasiadhesive categories, Lack and Sobociński have shown that all of the HLR properties shown for adhesive HLR categories in Thm. 4.26 (see below) are valid. This allows one to prove several important results for graph transformation systems, presented in Chapter 3, in the framework of both adhesive and quasiadhesive categories. On the other hand, adhesive and quasiadhesive categories are special cases of the adhesive HLR categories $(\mathbf{C}, \mathcal{M})$ (see Def. 4.9 below), where the class $\mathcal{M}$ is specialized to the class of all monomorphisms and of all regular monomorphisms, respectively. For this reason, we shall not develop the theory of adhesive and quasiadhesive categories in this section, but instead continue with adhesive HLR categories in the next section.

4.2 Adhesive HLR Categories

In this section, we consider high-level structures, including, especially, various kinds of graphs and Petri nets, as objects of a suitable high-level replacement category of the kind introduced in [EHKP91a, EHKP91b]. By combining these structures with the concept of adhesive categories described in Section 4.1 we obtain adhesive HLR categories.

The main difference between adhesive HLR categories and adhesive categories is that a distinguished class $\mathcal{M}$ of monomorphisms is considered instead of all monomorphisms, so that only pushouts along $\mathcal{M}$-morphisms have to be VK squares. Moreover, only pullbacks along $\mathcal{M}$-morphisms, not over arbitrary morphisms, are required.

The step from adhesive to adhesive HLR categories is justified by the fact that there are some important examples – such as algebraic specifications and typed attributed graphs – which are not adhesive categories. However, they are adhesive HLR categories for a suitable subclass $\mathcal{M}$ of monomorphisms.

In addition to adhesive HLR categories, we introduce a slightly weaker notion, called weak adhesive HLR categories, because another important example – the category **PTNets** of place/transition nets with the class $\mathcal{M}$ of injective morphisms – fails to be an adhesive HLR category, but is a weak adhesive HLR category.

The main result in this section shows that (weak) adhesive HLR categories are closed under product, slice, coslice, functor, and comma category constructions. This result is important because we only have to verify the conditions of adhesive HLR categories explicitly for some basic categories such as **Sets** with the class $\mathcal{M}$ of injective functions, and can then apply Theorem 4.15 to show that several other important categories are also (weak) adhesive HLR categories.

Definition 4.9 (adhesive HLR category). *A category* **C** *with a morphism class* $\mathcal{M}$ *is called an* adhesive HLR category *if:*

1. $\mathcal{M}$ *is a class of monomorphisms closed under isomorphisms, composition $(f : A \to B \in \mathcal{M}, g : B \to C \in \mathcal{M} \Rightarrow g \circ f \in \mathcal{M})$, and decomposition $(g \circ f \in \mathcal{M}, g \in \mathcal{M} \Rightarrow f \in \mathcal{M})$.*
2. **C** *has pushouts and pullbacks along $\mathcal{M}$-morphisms, and $\mathcal{M}$-morphisms are closed under pushouts and pullbacks.*
3. *Pushouts in* **C** *along $\mathcal{M}$-morphisms are VK squares.*

Remark 4.10. A pushout *along* an $\mathcal{M}$-morphism is a pushout where at least one of the given morphisms is in $\mathcal{M}$. Pushouts are closed under $\mathcal{M}$-morphisms if, for a given pushout (1), $m \in \mathcal{M}$ implies that $n \in \mathcal{M}$. Analogously, pullbacks are closed under $\mathcal{M}$-morphisms if, for a pullback (1), $n \in \mathcal{M}$ implies that $m \in \mathcal{M}$:

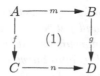

Note that the decomposition property of $\mathcal{M}$ is a consequence of the closure of $\mathcal{M}$ under pullbacks. In fact, the following diagram (2) with $g \circ f \in \mathcal{M}$ and $g \in \mathcal{M}$ is a pullback, because g is a monomorphism. Hence the closure of $\mathcal{M}$ under pullbacks implies $f \in \mathcal{M}$:

$$
\begin{array}{ccc}
A & \xrightarrow{\ f\ } & B \\
{\scriptstyle id_A}\downarrow & (2) & \downarrow{\scriptstyle g} \\
A & \xrightarrow{\ g \circ f\ } & C
\end{array}
$$

Example 4.11 (adhesive HLR categories).

- All adhesive categories (see Section 4.1) are adhesive HLR categories for the class $\mathcal{M}$ of all monomorphisms.
- The category (**HyperGraphs**, $\mathcal{M}$) of hypergraphs for the class $\mathcal{M}$ of injective hypergraph morphisms is an adhesive HLR category (see Fact 4.17).
- Another example of an adhesive HLR category is the category (**Sig**, $\mathcal{M}$) of algebraic signatures for the class $\mathcal{M}$ of all injective signature morphisms (see Fact 4.19).
- The category (**ElemNets**, $\mathcal{M}$) of elementary Petri nets for the class $\mathcal{M}$ of all injective Petri net morphisms is an adhesive HLR category (see Fact 4.20).
- An important example is the category (**AGraphs$_{ATG}$**, $\mathcal{M}$) of typed attributed graphs with a type graph ATG, where $\mathcal{M}$ is the class of all injective morphisms with isomorphisms on the data part. We introduce this category and show that it has the properties of an adhesive HLR category explicitly in Chapter 8.

$\square$

Counterexample 4.12 (nonadhesive HLR categories). The categories (**PTNets**, $\mathcal{M}$) and (**Spec**, $\mathcal{M}$), where $\mathcal{M}$ is the class of all monomorphisms, fail to be adhesive HLR categories (see Example 4.23 and Fact 4.24). $\square$

For a weak adhesive HLR category, we soften only item 3 in Definition 4.9, so that only special cubes are considered for the VK square property.

Definition 4.13 (weak adhesive HLR category). *A category* $\mathbf{C}$ *with a morphism class* $\mathcal{M}$ *is called a* weak adhesive HLR category *if:*

1. *$\mathcal{M}$ is a class of monomorphisms closed under isomorphisms, composition ($f : A \to B \in \mathcal{M}, g : B \to C \in \mathcal{M} \Rightarrow g \circ f \in \mathcal{M}$), and decomposition ($g \circ f \in \mathcal{M}, g \in \mathcal{M} \Rightarrow f \in \mathcal{M}$).*

2. **C** *has pushouts and pullbacks along* $\mathcal{M}$-*morphisms, and* $\mathcal{M}$-*morphisms are closed under pushouts and pullbacks.*

3. *Pushouts in* **C** *along* $\mathcal{M}$-*morphisms are weak VK squares, i.e. the VK square property holds for all commutative cubes with* $m \in \mathcal{M}$ *and* ($f \in \mathcal{M}$ *or* $b, c, d \in \mathcal{M}$) *(see Definition 4.1).*

Example 4.14 (weak adhesive HLR categories).

- The category (**PTNets**, $\mathcal{M}$) of Petri nets for the class $\mathcal{M}$ of all monomorphisms is a weak adhesive HLR category (see Fact 4.21).

- An interesting example of high-level structures that are not graph-like is that of algebraic specifications (see [EM85]). The category (**Spec**, $\mathcal{M}_{strict}$) of algebraic specifications, where $\mathcal{M}_{strict}$ is the class of all strict injective specification morphisms, is a weak adhesive HLR category (see Fact 4.24).

- Similarly, the category **AHLNets**(*SP*, **A**) of algebraic high-level nets with a fixed specification *SP* and algebra *A*, considered with the class $\mathcal{M}$ of injective morphisms, is a weak adhesive HLR category (see Fact 4.25).

□

By definition, every adhesive HLR category is also a weak adhesive HLR category, but not vice versa. In our main results (Theorems 4.15 and 4.26), it makes no difference whether we consider adhesive or weak adhesive HLR categories. Hence, for our present purposes, it would have been sufficient to consider only weak adhesive HLR categories. However, our idea of adhesive HLR categories is closer to that of the adhesive categories introduced in [LS04]. In the following, the phrase "(weak) adhesive HLR category" means that we can take either an adhesive or a weak adhesive HLR category.

(Weak) adhesive HLR categories are closed under product, slice, coslice, functor, and comma category constructions (see Sections A.2 and A.6). This means that we can construct new (weak) adhesive HLR categories from given ones.

Theorem 4.15 (construction of (weak) adhesive HLR categories).

(Weak) adhesive HLR categories can be constructed as follows:

1. *If* (**C**, $\mathcal{M}_1$) *and* (**D**, $\mathcal{M}_2$) *are (weak) adhesive HLR categories, then the product category* (**C** × **D**, $\mathcal{M}_1 \times \mathcal{M}_2$) *is a (weak) adhesive HLR category.*

2. *If* (**C**, $\mathcal{M}$) *is a (weak) adhesive HLR category, so are the slice category* (**C**\$X$, $\mathcal{M} \cap$ **C**\$X$) *and the coslice category* (X**C**, $\mathcal{M} \cap X$**C**) *for any object* X *in* **C**.

3. *If* (**C**, $\mathcal{M}$) *is a (weak) adhesive HLR category, then for every category* **X** *the functor category* ([**X**, **C**], $\mathcal{M} - functortransformations$) *is a (weak) adhesive HLR category. An* $\mathcal{M}$-*functor transformation is a natural transformation* $t : F \to G$, *where all morphisms* $t_X : F(X) \to G(X)$ *are in* $\mathcal{M}$.

4. *If* (**A**, $\mathcal{M}_1$) *and* (**B**, $\mathcal{M}_2$) *are (weak) adhesive HLR categories and* $F :$ **A** → **C**, $G :$ **B** → **C** *are functors, where* F *preserves pushouts along*

$\mathcal{M}_1$-morphisms and G preserves pullbacks (along $\mathcal{M}_2$-morphisms), then the comma category $(ComCat(F,G;\mathcal{I}), \mathcal{M})$ with $\mathcal{M} = (\mathcal{M}_1 \times \mathcal{M}_2) \cap Mor_{ComCat(F,G;\mathcal{I})}$ is a (weak) adhesive HLR category.

Proof.

1. The product category $(\mathbf{C} \times \mathbf{D}, \mathcal{M}_1 \times \mathcal{M}_2)$ is a (weak) adhesive category under the given assumptions, because $\mathcal{M}_1 \times \mathcal{M}_2$ inherits the required monomorphism composition and decomposition properties from $\mathcal{M}_1$ and $\mathcal{M}_2$. Moreover, pushouts and pullbacks along $\mathcal{M}_1 \times \mathcal{M}_2$-morphisms can be constructed componentwise according to Facts A.19 and A.23. In order to show that pushouts in $\mathbf{C} \times \mathbf{D}$ along $\mathcal{M}_1 \times \mathcal{M}_2$-morphisms are VK squares, we note that general pullbacks, which are used in the VK cube of Definition 4.1, can also be constructed componentwise in a product category.

2. The same is true for the slice category $(\mathbf{C} \backslash X, \mathcal{M} \cap \mathbf{C} \backslash X)$ and the coslice category $(X \backslash \mathbf{C}, \mathcal{M} \cap X \backslash \mathbf{C})$, where $\mathcal{M} \cap \mathbf{C} \backslash X$ and $\mathcal{M} \cap X \backslash \mathbf{C}$ are monomorphisms in $\mathbf{C} \backslash X$ and $X \backslash \mathbf{C}$, respectively. Note that monomorphisms in $\mathbf{C}$ are also monomorphisms in $\mathbf{C} \backslash X$ and $X \backslash \mathbf{C}$, but monomorphisms in $X \backslash \mathbf{C}$ are not necessarily monomorphisms in $\mathbf{C}$.

3. The functor category $([\mathbf{X}, \mathbf{C}], \mathcal{M}$-functor transformations) is a (weak) adhesive HLR category, provided that $(\mathbf{C}, \mathcal{M})$ is a (weak) adhesive HLR category. By Fact A.37, $\mathcal{M}$-functor transformations are monomorphisms in $[\mathbf{X}, \mathbf{C}]$, and the required monomorphism composition and decomposition properties are inherited from $\mathcal{M}$. Moreover, pushouts and pullbacks along $\mathcal{M}$-functor transformations, and general pullbacks are constructed pointwise (i.e. for each object $X \in Ob_{\mathbf{X}}$) in $[\mathbf{X}, \mathbf{C}]$.

4. The comma category $(ComCat(F,G;\mathcal{I}), \mathcal{M})$ is a (weak) adhesive HLR category under the given assumptions, using Fact A.43. In the case of general adhesive HLR categories, we require that F preserves pushouts along $\mathcal{M}_1$-morphisms, but for G we require that general pullbacks are preserved. This makes sure that in the VK cube of Definition 4.1, the general pullbacks can also be constructed componentwise, which allows us to inherit the VK properties of $(ComCat(F,G;\mathcal{I}), \mathcal{M})$ from $(\mathbf{A}, \mathcal{M}_1)$ and $(\mathbf{B}, \mathcal{M}_2)$. In the case of weak adhesive HLR categories, it is sufficient to require that F preserves pushouts along $\mathcal{M}_1$-morphisms and G preserves pullbacks along $\mathcal{M}_2$-morphisms.

$\square$

In the following, we use Theorem 4.15 in order to verify that **Graphs** and **Graphs$_{\mathbf{TG}}$** are adhesive categories and that the examples given in Examples 4.11 and 4.14 are (weak) adhesive HLR categories.

Fact 4.16 (Graphs and Graphs$_{\mathbf{TG}}$ are adhesive categories). *The categories* **Graphs** *and* **Graphs$_{\mathbf{TG}}$** *are adhesive categories, where the monomorphisms in* **Graphs** *and* **Graphs$_{\mathbf{TG}}$** *are exactly the injective graph morphisms and typed graph morphisms, respectively.*

Proof. The characterization of monomorphisms follows from Fact 2.15. According to Fact A.46, the category **Graphs** of graphs is isomorphic to the functor category $[\mathcal{S}, \textbf{Sets}]$. Now, $(\textbf{Sets}, \mathcal{M})$ for the class $\mathcal{M}$ of all injective functions, i.e. monomorphisms, is an adhesive HLR category, because **Sets** is an adhesive category by Theorem 4.6. This implies that $(\textbf{Graphs}, \mathcal{M}')$ for the class $\mathcal{M}'$ of all injective graph morphisms, i.e. monomorphisms, is an adhesive HLR category by Theorem 4.15, part 3. Since **Graphs** has general pullbacks, it is an adhesive category.

A similar argument using Theorem 4.15, part 2, implies that the slice category $\textbf{Graphs}_{\textbf{TG}} = (\textbf{Graphs}\backslash TG)$ over **Graphs** is an adhesive category. $\square$

As a variant of graphs, we now consider hypergraphs, where each edge no longer has one source and one target, but an arbitrary sequence of vertices used as attachment points.

Fact 4.17 (HyperGraphs is an adhesive HLR category). *The category* **(HyperGraphs,** $\mathcal{M}$**)** *of hypergraphs is an adhesive HLR category.*

A hypergraph G is given by $G = (V, E, s, t)$, with source and target functions $s, t : E \rightarrow V^*$, and a hypergraph morphism $f : G \rightarrow G'$ is given by $f = (f_V : V \rightarrow V', f_E : E \rightarrow E')$, compatible with the source and target functions, i.e. $s' \circ f_E = f_V^* \circ s$ and $t' \circ f_E = f_V^* \circ t$. Here, $\mathcal{M}$ is the class of all injective hypergraph morphisms (i.e. f_V and f_E are injective).

Proof. The category **HyperGraphs** is isomorphic to the comma category $ComCat(ID_{\textbf{Sets}}, \square^*; \mathcal{I})$, where $\square^* : \textbf{Sets} \rightarrow \textbf{Sets}$ assigns to each set A and function f the free monoid A^* and the free monoid morphism f^*, respectively, and $\mathcal{I} = \{1, 2\}$. According to Theorem 4.15, part 4, it suffices to note that $G = \square^* : \textbf{Sets} \rightarrow \textbf{Sets}$ preserves pullbacks (see Lemma A.38), using the fact that $(\textbf{Sets}, \mathcal{M})$ is an adhesive HLR category. $\square$

Graphs, typed graphs or hypergraphs can also be used to construct triple graphs $G_1 \leftarrow G_0 \rightarrow G_2$, where graphs G_1 and G_2 of different languages L_1 and L_2 are linked by an intermediate graph $G_0 \in L_0$ and graph morphisms $G_0 \rightarrow G_1$ and $G_0 \rightarrow G_2$. The concept of triple graph grammars for another graph grammar approach was introduced by Schürr in [Sch94] in order to specify graph translators.

The category **TripleGraphs** is the base category to define triple graph grammars in the DPO approach; it can be defined as the functor category $[\mathcal{S}_3, \textbf{Graphs}]$, where the "schema category" $\mathcal{S}_3$ is given by the schema $\mathcal{S}_3 :$ $\cdot \leftarrow \cdot \rightarrow \cdot$, which consists only of three objects and two morphisms.

Fact 4.18 (TripleGraphs is an adhesive HLR category). *The functor categories* **TripleGraphs** $= [\mathcal{S}_3, \textbf{Graphs}]$, **TripleGraphs**$_{\textbf{TG}}$ $= [\mathcal{S}_3, \textbf{Graphs}_{\textbf{TG}}]$ *and* **TripleHyperGraphs** $= [\mathcal{S}_3, \textbf{HyperGraphs}]$ *of triple graphs, triple typed graphs and triple hypergraphs, respectively, together with the class $\mathcal{M}$ of morphisms which are componentwise injective, are adhesive HLR categories.*

Proof. This is a direct consequence of Facts 4.16, 4.17 and Fact 4.15 item 3.

Next, we consider algebraic signatures in the framework of algebraic specifications (see [EM85] and Fact 4.24).

Fact 4.19 (algebraic signatures are an adhesive HLR category). *The category* (**Sig**, $\mathcal{M}$) *of algebraic signatures is an adhesive HLR category.*

An algebraic signature is given by $SIG = (S, OP, dom : OP \to S^*, cod : OP \to S)$ with a set S of sorts, a set OP of operation symbols, and domain and codomain functions dom and cod; $op \in OP$, with $dom(op) = s_1 \ldots s_n$ and $cod(op) = s$, is usually written $op : s_1 \ldots s_n \to s$ (see [EM85]). An algebraic signature morphism $f : SIG \to SIG'$ is given by a pair of functions $f = (f_S : S \to S', f_{OP} : OP \to OP')$ compatible with dom and cod, i.e. $f_S^* \circ dom = dom' \circ f_{OP}$ and $f_S \circ cod = cod' \circ f_{OP}$, and $\mathcal{M}$ is the class of all injective morphisms.

Proof. The category **Sig** is isomorphic to a variant of the comma category $ComCat(F, G; \mathcal{I})$ with $\mathcal{I} = \{1, 2\}$, $F = ID_{\mathbf{Sets}}$, and with G replaced by $G_1 = \square^* : \mathbf{Sets} \to \mathbf{Sets}$ as in Fact 4.17, and $G_2 = ID_{\mathbf{Sets}}$. Similarly to Fact 4.17, it is sufficient to note that $G_1 = \square^*$ and $G_2 = ID_{\mathbf{Sets}}$ preserve pullbacks. $\square$

In the following, we consider two kinds of Petri nets. Elementary Petri nets, also called condition/event nets, have arc weights restricted to one, while place/transition nets allow arbitrary finite arc weights. Instead of the original set-theoretical notations used in [Rei85, NRT92], we use a more algebraic version based on a power set or monoid construction, as introduced in [MM90].

Fact 4.20 (elementary Petri nets are an adhesive HLR category). *The category* (**ElemNets**, $\mathcal{M}$) *of elementary Petri nets is an adhesive HLR category.*

*An elementary Petri net is given by $N = (P, T, pre, post : T \to \mathcal{P}(P))$ with a set P of places, a set T of transitions, and predomain and postdomain functions $pre, post : T \to \mathcal{P}(P)$, where $\mathcal{P}(P)$ is the power set of P. A morphism $f : N \to N'$ in **ElemNets** is given by $f = (f_P : P \to P', f_T : T \to T')$ compatible with the predomain and postdomain functions, i.e. $pre' \circ f_T = \mathcal{P}(f_P) \circ pre$ and $post' \circ f_T = \mathcal{P}(f_P) \circ post$, and $\mathcal{M}$ is the class of all injective morphisms.*

Proof. The category **ElemNets** is isomorphic to the comma category $ComCat(ID_{\mathbf{Sets}}, \mathcal{P}; \mathcal{I})$, where $\mathcal{P} : \mathbf{Sets} \to \mathbf{Sets}$ is the power set functor and $\mathcal{I} = \{1, 2\}$. According to Theorem 4.15, part 4, it suffices to note that $\mathcal{P} : \mathbf{Sets} \to \mathbf{Sets}$ preserves pullbacks (see Lemma A.39), using the fact that (**Sets**, $\mathcal{M}$) is an adhesive HLR category. $\square$

As pointed out in Counterexample 4.12, the categories (**PTNet**, $\mathcal{M}$) of place/transition nets and (**Spec**, $\mathcal{M}$) of algebraic specifications, where $\mathcal{M}$ is the class of injective morphisms in both cases, are not adhesive HLR categories, but we can obtain the following weak adhesive HLR categories (**PTNets**, $\mathcal{M}$) and (**Spec**, $\mathcal{M}_{strict}$) defined below.

Fact 4.21 (place/transition nets are a weak adhesive HLR category).
The category (**PTNets**, $\mathcal{M}$) *of place/transition nets is a weak adhesive HLR category, but not an adhesive HLR category.*

According to [MM90], a place/transition net $N = (P, T, pre, post : T \to P^{\oplus})$ is given by a set P of places, a set T of transitions, and the predomain and postdomain functions $pre, post : T \to P^{\oplus}$, where $P^{\oplus}$ is the free commutative monoid over P. A morphism $f : N \to N'$ in **PTNets** *is given by $f = (f_P : P \to P', f_T : T \to T')$, compatible with the predomain and postdomain functions, i.e. $pre' \circ f_T = f_P^{\oplus} \circ pre$ and $post' \circ f_T = f_P^{\oplus} \circ post$, and $\mathcal{M}$ is the class of all injective morphisms.*

Proof. The category **PTNets** is isomorphic to the comma category $ComCat(ID_{\mathbf{Sets}}, \square^{\oplus}; \mathcal{I})$ with $\mathcal{I} = \{1, 2\}$, where $\square^{\oplus} : \mathbf{Sets} \to \mathbf{Sets}$ is the free commutative monoid functor. According to Theorem 4.15, part 4, it suffices to note that $\square^{\oplus} : \mathbf{Sets} \to \mathbf{Sets}$ preserves pullbacks along injective morphisms (see Lemma A.40), using the fact that (**Sets**, $\mathcal{M}$) is a (weak) adhesive HLR category. This implies that (**PTNets**, $\mathcal{M}$) is a weak adhesive HLR category.

It remains to show that (**PTNets**, $\mathcal{M}$) is not an adhesive HLR category. This is due to the fact that $\square^{\oplus} : \mathbf{Sets} \to \mathbf{Sets}$ does not preserve general pullbacks. This would imply that pullbacks in **PTNets** are constructed componentwise for places and transitions. In fact, in Example 4.23 we present a noninjective pullback in **PTNets**, where the transition component is not a pullback in **Sets**, and a cube which violates the VK properties of adhesive HLR categories. □

Remark 4.22 (pullbacks in comma categories). The category **PTNets** in Fact 4.21 is an example of a comma category $ComCat(F, G; \mathcal{I})$ where the functor $G : \mathbf{B} \to \mathbf{C}$ does not preserve general pullbacks. This means that we cannot conclude from Fact A.43 that pullbacks in $ComCat(F, G; \mathcal{I})$ are constructed componentwise.

However, it is interesting to note that in the case where $\mathbf{A}$ has an initial object I_A and $F : \mathbf{A} \to \mathbf{C}$ preserves initial objects, we can conclude that every pullback in the comma category is also a pullback in the $\mathbf{B}$-component. In fact, given a pullback (1) in $ComCat(F, G; \mathcal{I})$ with $C_j = (A_j, B_j; op_j)$ for $j = 0, \ldots, 3$, we are able to show that the $\mathbf{B}$-component of (1) is a pullback in $\mathbf{B}$. Given B, with morphisms $h_{1B} : B \to B_1$ and $h_{2B} : B \to B_2$ in $\mathbf{B}$, and $g_{1B} \circ \circ h_{1B} = g_{2B} \circ h_{2B}$, we consider the object $C = (I_A, B; op)$ with initial morphisms $op_i : F(I_A) \to G(B)$ in $\mathbf{C}$, using the fact that $F(I_A)$ is initial in $\mathbf{C}$. We then have morphisms $h_1 : C \to C_1$ and $h_2 : C \to C_2$ in $ComCat(F, G; \mathcal{I})$, where $h_{1A} : I_A \to A_1$ and $h_{2A} : I_A \to A_2$ are the initial morphisms in $\mathbf{A}$, and h_{1B}, h_{2B} as above satisfy $g_1 \circ h_1 = g_2 \circ h_2$:

$$
\begin{array}{ccc}
C_0 & \xrightarrow{\ f_1\ } & C_1 \\
\downarrow{\scriptstyle f_2} & (1) & \downarrow{\scriptstyle g_1} \\
C_2 & \xrightarrow{\ g_2\ } & C_3
\end{array}
$$

The pullback property of (1) in $ComCat(F, G; \mathcal{I})$ implies a unique $h : C \rightarrow C_1$ with $f_1 \circ h = h_1$ and $f_2 \circ h = h_2$. But this also implies that $h_B : B \rightarrow B_0$ in $\mathbf{B}$ is unique, with $f_{1B} \circ h_B = h_{1B}$ and $f_{2B} \circ h_B = h_{2B}$, using again the initialiy of I_A and $F(I_A)$.

This general result can be applied to show that pullbacks in **PTNets** have pullbacks in the P-component, because $F = ID_{\mathbf{Sets}}$ preserves the initial object $\varnothing$ in **Sets**. An example of a pullback in **PTNets** with this property is shown in Example 4.23, where the P-component is a pullback in **Sets**, but not the T-component.

Example 4.23 (non-VK square in PTNets). The following diagram (1), with noninjective morphisms g_1, g_2, p_1, p_2, is a pullback in the category **PTNets** (see Fact A.24), where the transition component is not a pullback in **Sets**:

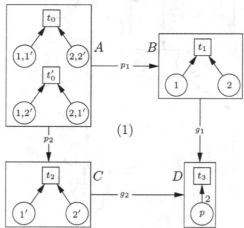

For the construction of the pullback over g_1 and g_2 in **PTNets** according to the general construction in Fact A.24, we first construct the pullback over the places in **Sets** and obtain the places $P_A = \{(1, 1'), (2, 2'), (1, 2'), (2, 1')\}$ and the morphisms $p_{1,P} : P_A \rightarrow P_B$ with $p_{1,P}(x, y) = x$ and $p_{2,P} : P_A \rightarrow P_C$ with $p_{2,P}(x, y) = y$.

We have only one transition $t_3 \in T_D$, with $pre_D(t_3) = 2p$ and $post_D(t_3) = \lambda$, and the tuple $(t_1, t_2) \in T_B \times T_C$ of transitions that are mapped to t. So the set $L_{(t_1, t_2)}$ is given by

$$L_{(t_1, t_2)} = \{((1, 1'), (2, 2')), ((2, 2'), (1, 1')), ((1, 2'), (2, 1')), ((2, 1'), (1, 2'))\}.$$

By the definition of the relation $\sim_{(t_1, t_2)}$, we have the result that

$$((1, 1'), (2, 2')) \sim_{(t_1, t_2)} ((2, 2'), (1, 1')) \text{ and}$$
$$((1, 2'), (2, 1')) \sim_{(t_1, t_2)} ((2, 1'), (1, 2'));$$

therefore we define $t_0 = t^{(t_1, t_2)}_{[((1,1'),(2,2'))]}$, $t'_0 = t^{(t_1, t_2)}_{[((1,2'),(2,1'))]}$, and $T_A = \{t_0, t'_0\}$.

In the following cube the bottom square is a pushout in **PTNets** along an injective morphism $m \in \mathcal{M}$, all side squares are pullbacks, but the top square is not a pushout in **PTNets**. Hence we have a counterexample for the VK property.

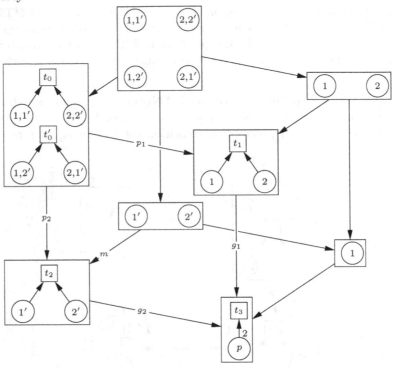

$\square$

The next example is the category of algebraic specifications in the sense of [EM85].

Fact 4.24 (algebraic specifications are a weak adhesive HLR category). *The category (**Spec**, $\mathcal{M}_{strict}$) of algebraic specifications, for the class $\mathcal{M}_{strict}$ of strict morphisms, is a weak adhesive HLR category. However, (**Spec**, $\mathcal{M}$), for the class $\mathcal{M}$ of all injective morphisms, is not a weak adhesive HLR category.*

An algebraic specification $SP = (SIG, E)$ consists of a signature $SIG = (S, OP)$ (see Fact 4.19) and a set E of equations $e = (X, L, R)$ over SIG with $L, R \in T_{SIG}(X)_s$ for some $s \in S$ (see [EM85]). A morphism $f : SP \rightarrow SP'$ in **Spec** *is a signature morphism $f : SIG \rightarrow SIG'$ (see Fact 4.19) with $f^{\#}(E) \subseteq E'$, where $f^{\#}(E)$ are the translated equations. A morphism $f : SP \rightarrow SP'$ in* **Spec** *is strict if it is injective and $f^{\#-1}(E') \subseteq E$.*

Proof. According to Fact 4.19, pushouts and pullbacks can be constructed componentwise for the signature part of an algebraic specification. Given f_1

and f_2 in diagram (1) below in **Spec**, the pushout object (SIG_3, E_3) is given by SIG_3, as the pushout object in **Sig**, and $E_3 = g_1^{\#}(E_1) \cup g_2^{\#}(E_2)$:

$$
\begin{array}{ccc}
(SIG_0, E_0) & \xrightarrow{\ f_1\ } & (SIG_1, E_1) \\
\downarrow{\scriptstyle f_2} & (1) & \downarrow{\scriptstyle g_1} \\
(SIG_2, E_2) & \xrightarrow{\ g_2\ } & (SIG_3, E_3)
\end{array}
$$

Vice versa, given g_1 and g_2 in diagram (1), the pullback object (SIG_0, E_0) is given by SIG_0, as the pullback object in **Sig**, and $E_0 = f_1^{\#-1}(E_1) \cap f_2^{\#-1}(E_2)$.

Moreover, it can be shown that pushouts and pullbacks in **Spec** preserve strict morphisms and that pushouts in **Spec** along strict morphisms are weak VK squares in the sense of Definition 4.13 (see Section C.1). This implies that (**Spec**, $\mathcal{M}_{strict}$) is a weak adhesive HLR category.

However, this is not true for (**Spec**, $\mathcal{M}$), where $\mathcal{M}$ is the class of all injective morphisms. In fact, the following pushout (2) in **Spec**, with $E \neq \varnothing$ and all morphisms in $\mathcal{M}$, is not a pullback. By Theorem 4.26, this implies that (**Spec**, $\mathcal{M}$) is not a weak adhesive HLR category.

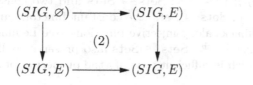

$$
\begin{array}{ccc}
(SIG, \varnothing) & \longrightarrow & (SIG, E) \\
\downarrow & (2) & \downarrow \\
(SIG, E) & \longrightarrow & (SIG, E)
\end{array}
$$

$\square$

In the following, we combine algebraic specifications with Petri nets, leading to algebraic high-level (AHL) nets (see [PER95]). For simplicity, we fix the corresponding algebraic specification SP and the SP-algebra A. For the more general case, where morphisms between different specifications and algebras are also allowed, we refer to [PER95]. Under suitable restrictions on the morphisms, we also obtain a weak adhesive HLR category in the more general case (see [Pad96] for the HLR properties of high-level abstract Petri nets).

Fact 4.25 (AHL nets are a weak adhesive HLR category). *Given an algebraic specification SP and an SP-algebra A, the category* (**AHLNets(SP, A)**, $\mathcal{M}$) *of algebraic high-level nets over (SP, A) is a weak adhesive HLR category.*

An AHL net over (SP, A), where $SP = (SIG, E, X)$ has additional variables X and $SIG = (S, OP)$, is given by $N = (SP, P, T, pre, post, cond, type, A)$, where P and T are the sets of places and transitions; $pre, post : T \to (T_{SIG}(X) \otimes P)^{\oplus}$ are the predomain and postdomain functions; $cond : T \to \mathcal{P}_{fin}(Eqns(SIG, X))$ assigns to each $t \in T$ a finite set $cond(t)$ of equations over SIG and X; $type : P \to S$ is a type function; and A is an SP-algebra.

Note that $T_{SIG}(X)$ is the SIG-term algebra with variables X, $(T_{SIG}(X) \otimes P) = \{(term, p) \mid term \in T_{SIG}(X)_{type(p)}, p \in P\}$, and $\square^{\oplus}$ is the free commutative monoid functor.

*A morphism $f : N \to N'$ in **AHLNets(SP, A)** is given by a pair of functions $f = (f_P : P \to P', f_T : T \to T')$ which are compatible with the functions pre, post, cond, and type as shown below. $\mathcal{M}$ is the class of all injective morphisms f, i.e. f_P and f_T are injective.*

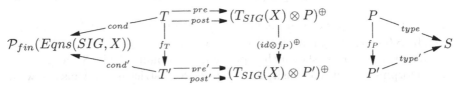

Proof. From the fact that (SP, A) is fixed, the construction of pushouts and pullbacks in **AHLNets(SP, A)** is essentially the same as in **PTNets**, which is also a weak adhesive HLR category. We can apply the idea of comma categories $ComCat(F, G; \mathcal{I})$, where in our case the source functor of the operations pre, post, cond, and type is always the identity $ID_{\mathbf{Sets}}$, and the target functors are $(T_{SIG}(X) \otimes \_)^{\oplus} : \mathbf{Sets} \to \mathbf{Sets}$ and two constant functors. In fact $(T_{SIG}(X) \otimes \_) : \mathbf{Sets} \to \mathbf{Sets}$, the constant functors, and $\square^{\oplus} : \mathbf{Sets} \to \mathbf{Sets}$ preserve pullbacks along injective functions (see Lemma A.40). This implies that $(T_{SIG}(X) \otimes \_)^{\oplus} : \mathbf{Sets} \to \mathbf{Sets}$ also preserves pullbacks along injective functions, which is sufficient to verify the properties of a weak adhesive HLR category. $\square$

4.3 HLR Properties of Adhesive HLR Categories

In this section, we show several important properties of (weak) adhesive HLR categories, which are essential to prove the main results in the following chapters. These properties were required as HLR properties in [EHKP91a, EHKP91b] to show the classical results for HLR systems. In [LS04], it was shown that these HLR properties are valid for adhesive categories. These properties were extended to adhesive HLR categories in [EHPP04]; we now extend them to weak adhesive HLR categories also.

Theorem 4.26 (properties of (weak) adhesive HLR categories). *Given a (weak) adhesive HLR category $(\mathbf{C}, \mathcal{M})$, then the following properties hold:*

1. *Pushouts along $\mathcal{M}$-morphisms are pullbacks. Given the following pushout (1) with $k \in \mathcal{M}$, then (1) is also a pullback.*
2. *$\mathcal{M}$ pushout–pullback decomposition lemma. Given the following commutative diagram, where (1) + (2) is a pushout, (2) is a pullback, $w \in \mathcal{M}$, and ($l \in \mathcal{M}$ or $k \in \mathcal{M}$), then (1) and (2) are pushouts and also pullbacks.*

3. Cube pushout–pullback lemma. *Given the following commutative cube (3), where all morphisms in the top and in the bottom are in $\mathcal{M}$, the top is a pullback, and the front faces are pushouts, then the bottom is a pullback iff the back faces of the cube are pushouts:*

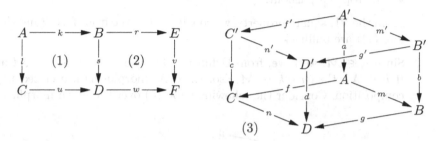

4. Uniqueness of pushout complements. *Given $k : A \to B \in \mathcal{M}$ and $s : B \to D$, then there is, up to isomorphism, at most one C with $l : A \to C$ and $u : C \to D$ such that (1) is a pushout.*

For the proofs, we need the following fact.

Fact 4.27. *For any morphism $f : A \to B$, the square (PO) below is a pushout and a pullback, and for any monomorphism $m : A \to B$, (PB) is a pullback. Since in a (weak) adhesive HLR category $\mathcal{M}$ is a class of monomorphisms, this holds in particular for $\mathcal{M}$-morphisms.*

$$
\begin{array}{ccc}
A & \xrightarrow{\ f\ } & B \\
{\scriptstyle id_A}\downarrow & (PO) & \downarrow{\scriptstyle id_B} \\
A & \xrightarrow{\ f\ } & B
\end{array}
\qquad
\begin{array}{ccc}
A & \xrightarrow{\ id_A\ } & A \\
{\scriptstyle id_A}\downarrow & (PB) & \downarrow{\scriptstyle m} \\
A & \xrightarrow{\ m\ } & B
\end{array}
$$

Proof. This follows from standard category theory. □

Proof (Theorem 4.26). We shall show these properties for weak adhesive HLR categories. In the nonweak case, we have to verify fewer of the $\mathcal{M}$-morphisms.

1. Consider the following cube (4):

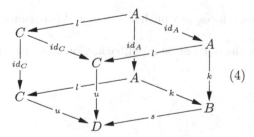

Since the bottom is the pushout (1) along the $\mathcal{M}$-morphism k, it is a weak VK square with $k, u, id_c \in \mathcal{M}$. From Fact 4.27, we have the result that:

- the back left face is a pullback;
- the back right face is a pullback;
- the top is a pushout.

From the VK square property, we conclude that the front faces (and therefore (1)) are pullbacks.

2. Since $w \in \mathcal{M}$, we have, from Definition 4.9, the result that $r \in \mathcal{M}$ also. If $k \in \mathcal{M}$, then $r \circ k \in \mathcal{M}$ also, since $\mathcal{M}$-morphisms are closed under composition. Consider the following cube (5) over the given morphisms:

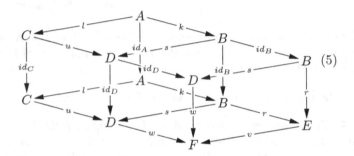

Since the bottom is a pushout along the $\mathcal{M}$-morphism l or along the $\mathcal{M}$-morphism $r \circ k$, it is a weak VK square with $w, r, id_B, id_C, id_D \in \mathcal{M}$. We then have:

- the back left face is a pullback;
- the back right face, since it is a composition of pullbacks (since $r \in \mathcal{M}$), is a pullback;
- the front left face, since it is a composition of pullbacks (since $w \in \mathcal{M}$), is a pullback;
- the front right face is a pullback, by assumption.

From the VK square property, we conclude that the top, corresponding to square (1), is a pushout, and the pushout decomposition gives us the result that (2) is also a pushout. 1 implies that both (1) and (2) are pullbacks.

3. Since the front faces are pushouts along $\mathcal{M}$-morphisms, they are also pullbacks.
   "$\Rightarrow$". Let the bottom be a pullback. Consider the turned cube (6):

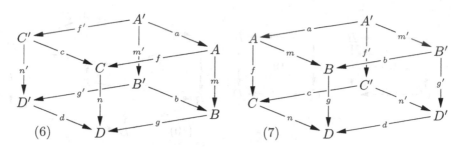

(6)   (7)

The following properties then apply:

- the bottom is a pushout along the $\mathcal{M}$-morphism g', and therefore a weak VK square with $n', n, m \in \mathcal{M}$;
- the front right face is a pullback;
- the front left face is a pushout along the $\mathcal{M}$-morphism n', and therefore a pullback;
- the back left face is a pullback;
- the back right face is a pullback (by composition and decomposition of pullbacks).

From the VK square property, it follows that the top is a pushout; this means that the back left face in the original cube (3) is a pushout.

By turning the cube once more, we obtain the same result for the back right face of the original cube (3). Hence the back faces are pushouts.

"⇐". Let the back faces be pushouts in the original cube (3). By turning the cube again, we obtain cube (7), where the bottom, top, back left face, and front right face are pushouts along $\mathcal{M}$-morphisms, and the back right face is a pullback.

Since the bottom is a weak VK square with $f, g, g' \in \mathcal{M}$ and the top is a pushout, the front faces must be pullbacks; this means that the bottom of the original cube is a pullback.

4. Suppose that (8) and (9) below are pushouts with $k \in \mathcal{M}$. It follows that $u, u' \in \mathcal{M}$. Consider the cube (10), where $C' \xleftarrow{x} U \xrightarrow{y} C$ is the pullback over $C' \xrightarrow{u'} D \xleftarrow{u} C$ with $x, y \in \mathcal{M}$. h is the resulting morphism for this pullback in comparison with the object A and the morphisms l and l', and it holds that $x \circ h = l'$ and $y \circ h = l$.

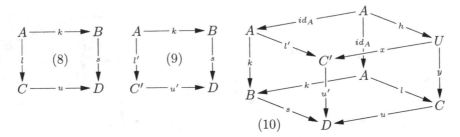

Pullbacks are closed under composition and decomposition, and since the left faces and the front right face are pullbacks and $y \circ h = l$, the back right face is a pullback.

The following properties then apply:

- the bottom is a pushout along the $\mathcal{M}$-morphism k, and therefore a weak VK square with $k, u', y \in \mathcal{M}$;
- the back left face is a pullback (with $k \in \mathcal{M}$);
- the front left face is a pushout along the $\mathcal{M}$-morphism k, and therefore a pullback;
- the front right face is a pullback by construction;
- the back right face is a pullback.

Hence it follows from the VK square property that the top is a pushout.

Since id_A is an isomorphism and pushouts preserve isomorphisms x is also an isomorphism. For similar reasons we can conclude by exchanging the roles of C and C' that y is an isomorphism. This means that C and C' are isomorphic.   □

5

Adhesive High-Level Replacement Systems

Adhesive high-level replacement (HLR) systems can be considered as abstract graph transformation systems based on the adhesive or weak adhesive HLR categories introduced in Chapter 4. More precisely, this chapter is an abstract categorical version of Sections 3.1–3.3 in Part I, which dealt with the case of (typed) graphs. The motivation behind the concepts of adhesive HLR systems is essentially the same as that behind the concepts of (typed) graph transformation systems considered in Part I. Hence there is little description of our motivation in this chapter, but we present the proofs of all our results.

In Section 5.1, we introduce the basic concepts of adhesive HLR systems, similarly to Section 3.1 for the classical case of graph transformation systems. Various kinds of graph and Petri net transformation systems are introduced as instantiations in Section 5.2. The Local Church–Rosser and Parallelism Theorems introduced for the graph case in Section 3.3 are formulated and proven for adhesive HLR systems in Section 5.3. Finally, we present in Section 5.4 another classical result mentioned in Section 3.4, the Concurrency Theorem, where the construction of dependent transformation sequences is based on the concept of pair factorization introduced in [EHPP04] for critical pair analysis.

5.1 Basic Concepts of Adhesive HLR Systems

In general, an adhesive HLR system is based on productions, also called rules, that describe in an abstract way how objects in the system can be transformed. The main difference from the graph productions considered in Definition 3.1 is the fact that graphs and injective graph morphisms are replaced by objects in a category $\mathbf{C}$ and by morphisms in the class $\mathcal{M}$ of (weak) adhesive HLR categories defined in Definitions 4.9 and 4.13.

Definition 5.1 (production). *Given a (weak) adhesive HLR category* $(\mathbf{C}, \mathcal{M})$*, a production* $p = (L \xleftarrow{l} K \xrightarrow{r} R)$ *(also called a rule) consists of three* *objects L, K, and R, called the left-hand side, gluing object, and right-hand side, respectively, and morphisms $l : K \to L$ and $r : K \to R$ with $l, r \in \mathcal{M}$.*

Given a production $p = (L \xleftarrow{l} K \xrightarrow{r} R)$, the inverse production p^{-1} is given by $p^{-1} = (R \xleftarrow{r} K \xrightarrow{l} L)$.

Similarly to the graph case in Definition 3.2, an application of a production is called a *direct transformation* and describes how an object is actually changed by the production. A sequence of these applications yields *a transformation*.

Definition 5.2 (transformation). *Given a production $p = (L \xleftarrow{l} K \xrightarrow{r} R)$ and an object G with a morphism $m : L \to G$, called the match, a direct transformation $G \xRightarrow{p,m} H$ from G to an object H is given by the following diagram, where (1) and (2) are pushouts:*

$$
\begin{array}{ccccc}
L & \xleftarrow{\;\;l\;\;} & K & \xrightarrow{\;\;r\;\;} & R \\
\downarrow{\scriptstyle m} & (1) & \downarrow{\scriptstyle k} & (2) & \downarrow{\scriptstyle n} \\
G & \xleftarrow{\;\;f\;\;} & D & \xrightarrow{\;\;g\;\;} & H
\end{array}
$$

A sequence $G_0 \Rightarrow G_1 \Rightarrow \ldots \Rightarrow G_n$ of direct transformations is called a transformation and is denoted by $G_0 \xRightarrow{*} G_n$. For $n = 0$, we have the identical transformation $G_0 \xRightarrow{id} G_0$, i.e. $f = g = id_{G_0}$. Moreover, for $n = 0$ we allow also isomorphisms $G_0 \cong G_0'$, because pushouts and hence also direct transformations are only unique up to isomorphism.

Remark 5.3. Similarly to the graph case considered in Section 3.2, we discuss below under what conditions a production p can be applied to G with a match $m : L \to G$ (see Definitions 5.6 and 6.3, Fact 5.8, and Theorem 6.4).

As stated in Fact 3.3 for the graph case, there is, for each direct transformation $G \xRightarrow{p,m} H$ with a comatch morphism $n : R \to H$, a direct transformation $H \xRightarrow{p^{-1},n} G$ over the inverse production.

If, in Definition 3.4 for GT systems, we replace the category **Graphs** with injective morphisms by a (weak) adhesive HLR category $(\mathbf{C}, \mathcal{M})$, we obtain a definition of adhesive HLR systems. Note that we do not distinguish between adhesive and weak adhesive HLR systems, because, for all our results, we need only the properties of weak adhesive HLR categories (see Theorem 4.26).

Definition 5.4 (adhesive HLR system, grammar, and language). *An adhesive HLR system $AHS = (\mathbf{C}, \mathcal{M}, P)$ consists of a (weak) adhesive HLR category $(\mathbf{C}, \mathcal{M})$ and a set of productions P.*

An adhesive HLR grammar $AHG = (AHS, S)$ is an adhesive HLR system together with a distinguished start object S.

The language L of an adhesive HLR grammar is defined by

$$L = \{G \mid \exists \text{ transformation } S \xRightarrow{*} G\}.$$

Example 5.5 (adhesive HLR grammar *ExAHG* and transformations).
In the following, we introduce as an example the adhesive HLR grammar *ExAHG* based on graphs (see Section 2.1). We define *ExAHG* =
(**Graphs**, $\mathcal{M}, P, S$). $\mathcal{M}$ is the class of all injective graph morphisms, and S is
the following start graph:

S

$P = \{addVertex, addEdge, deleteVertex, del1of2Edges\}$ is defined by the
following productions, where all morphisms are inclusions (and therefore are
in $\mathcal{M}$):

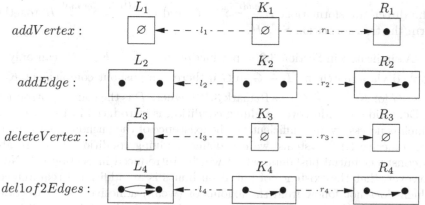

The production *addVertex* adds a single vertex to a graph, and with *addEdge*,
a directed edge between two vertices can be inserted. On the other hand,
deleteVertex deletes a single vertex, and *del1of2Edges* deletes one of two
parallel edges.

There are various options for transforming our start graph S by applying
one of the given productions. For example, we can use the production *addEdge*
to insert an additional edge, as shown in the following diagram. The node
labels indicate the mapping m between L_2 and S, and the graph marked by
a bold outline is the source for the transformation:

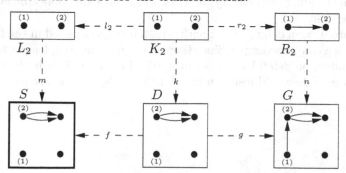

In the resulting graph G, we delete one of the two edges between the upper nodes by applying the production $del1of2Edges$:

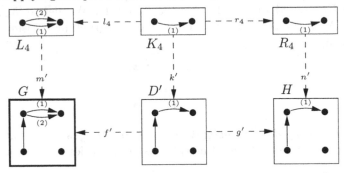

The direct transformations $S \stackrel{addEdge,m}{\Longrightarrow} G$ and $G \stackrel{del1of2Edges,m'}{\Longrightarrow} H$ together form the transformation $S \stackrel{*}{\Rightarrow} H$.   □

As indicated in Section 3.2, a production $p = (L \stackrel{l}{\leftarrow} K \stackrel{r}{\rightarrow} R)$ can only be applied via a match $m : L \rightarrow G$ to G if there is a pushout complement $K \stackrel{k}{\rightarrow} D \stackrel{f}{\rightarrow} G$ for $K \stackrel{l}{\rightarrow} L \stackrel{m}{\rightarrow} G$ (see Remark 3.12), where D is the context introduced in Definition 3.7. Moreover, a gluing condition is introduced in Definition 3.9 which is necessary and sufficient for the existence of the pushout complement. For adhesive HLR systems, we can define a gluing condition if we are able to construct initial pushouts, which will be introduced in Section 6.1. Note, however, that the existence of initial pushouts is an additional requirement, which does not follow from the axioms of (weak) adhesive HLR categories. The construction of initial pushouts, together with the gluing condition in Definition 6.3, leads in Theorem 6.4 directly to a construction of the context D and the pushout complement discussed above.

Definition 5.6 (applicability of productions). *Let $p = (L \stackrel{l}{\leftarrow} K \stackrel{r}{\rightarrow} R)$ be a production. For an object G and a match $m : L \rightarrow G$, p is applicable via m if the pushout complement for $K \stackrel{l}{\rightarrow} L \stackrel{m}{\rightarrow} G$ exists.*

Example 5.7 (nonapplicability of a production in $ExAHG$). In Example 5.5, the productions $addEdge$ and $del1of2Edges$ are applicable via m and m', respectively.

The production $deleteVertex$ with a match n, as depicted in the following diagram, is a counterexample. Since there is no pushout complement for l_3 and n, the production $deleteVertex$ is not applicable via n. This is clear because deleting the node would result in two dangling edges without a source node.

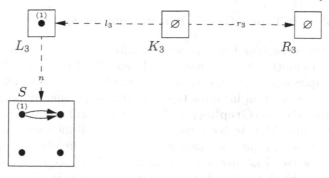

Similarly to Fact 3.13 for the graph case, we now obtain a fact about how to construct direct transformations.

Fact 5.8 (construction of direct transformations). *Given a production* $p = (L \xleftarrow{l} K \xrightarrow{r} R)$ *and a match* $m : L \to G$ *such that* p *is applicable to* G *via* m, *then a direct transformation can be constructed in two steps:*

1. *Construct the pushout complement* $K \xrightarrow{k} D \xrightarrow{f} G$ *of* $K \xrightarrow{l} L \xrightarrow{m} G$ *in diagram (1) below.*

2. *Construct the pushout* $D \xrightarrow{g} H \xleftarrow{n} R$ *of* $D \xleftarrow{k} K \xrightarrow{r} R$ *in diagram (2).*

This construction is unique up to isomorphism.

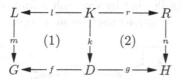

Proof. Since we have $l, r \in \mathcal{M}$, the construction of a pushout complement (1) and of a pushout (2) is unique up to isomorphism (see Theorem 4.26, part 4, and Remark A.18). □

5.2 Instantiation of Adhesive HLR Systems

In Chapter 4, we presented several examples of adhesive and weak adhesive HLR categrories. For each of these examples, we can obtain an instantiation of the adhesive HLR systems introduced in Section 5.1. In particular, we can obtain the graph and typed graph transformation systems introduced in Part I, and typed attributed graph transformation systems, which will be studied in Part III in more detail. In the following, we discuss some other interesting instantiations.

5.2.1 Graph and Typed Graph Transformation Systems

In order to obtain graph and typed graph transformation systems in the sense of Part I (see Definition 3.4), we use the adhesive HLR categories (**Graphs**, $\mathcal{M}$) and (**Graphs$_{\mathbf{TG}}$**, $\mathcal{M}$), respectively, where $\mathcal{M}$ is the class of all injective graph morphisms or of all injective typed graph morphisms, respectively. In fact, (**Graphs**, $\mathcal{M}$) and (**Graphs$_{\mathbf{TG}}$**, $\mathcal{M}$) are already adhesive categories (see Fact 4.16), because $\mathcal{M}$ is in both cases the class of all monomorphisms. An example of a typed graph grammar has been given already in Part I as a running example (see Example 3.6), and in Example 5.5 we have presented a graph grammar, which will be used as a running example in the present Part II.

5.2.2 Hypergraph Transformation Systems

The category (**HyperGraphs**, $\mathcal{M}$) is an adhesive HLR category (see Fact 4.17). The corresponding instantiation of adhesive HLR systems and grammars leads to hypergraph transformation systems. As a specific example, we shall consider a simple hypergraph grammar HGG from [BK02]. In fact, this hypergraph grammar is edge-labeled (and hence also typed, as in the graph case). However, typed hypergraph grammars are also adhesive HLR grammars, because (**HyperGraphs$_{\mathbf{TG}}$**, $\mathcal{M}$) is a slice category of (**Hypergraphs**, $\mathcal{M}$) and hence also an adhesive HLR category (see Theorem 4.15).

Let us consider the following hypergraph grammar HGG, with the start graph S and the two productions $useCon$ and $createCon$ depicted below:

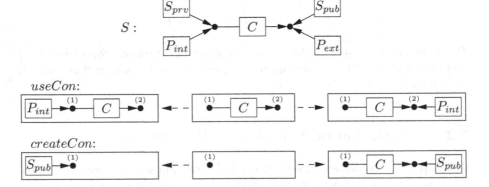

The edge labels have the following meanings: C, connection; S_{pub}, public server; S_{prv}, private server; P_{int}, internal process; and P_{ext}, external process. Using the production $useCon$, internal processes can move around the network. With $createCon$, public servers can extend the network by creating new connections. The aim of the paper [BK02] was to present verification techniques. For this example, it is possible to verify with these techniques that the external process is never connected to a private server and thus never has access to classified data. Note that in this example all hyperedges have arity 1, except for those of type C, which have arity 2.

For other examples of hypergraph transformation systems in the area of term graph rewriting, we refer to [Plu93, Plu95].

5.2.3 Petri Net Transformation Systems

Petri net transformation systems were introduced in [EHKP91a, EHKP91b] for the case of low-level nets and in [PER95] for the case of high-level nets. The main idea is to extend the well-known theory of Petri nets based on the token game by general techniques which allow one to change also the net structure of Petri nets. In [Pad96], a systematic study of Petri net transformation systems was presented in the categorical framework of abstract Petri nets, which can be instantiated to different kinds of low-level and high-level Petri nets. In Chapter 4, we have shown that the category (**ElemNets**, $\mathcal{M}$) of elementary Petri nets is an adhesive HLR category (see Fact 4.20) and that the categories (**PTNets**, $\mathcal{M}$) of place/transition nets and (**AHLNets(SP, A)**, $\mathcal{M}$) of algebraic high-level nets over (SP, A) are weak adhesive HLR categories (see Facts 4.21 and 4.25). The corresponding instantiations of adhesive HLR systems lead to various kinds of Petri net transformation systems, as discussed above.

In the following, we present a simple grammar $ENGG$ for elementary Petri nets, which allows one to generate all elementary nets. The start net S of $ENGG$ is empty. Note that we have to restrict the matches to injective morphisms to ensure the creation of valid elementary nets. We have a production $addPlace$ to create a new place p, and productions $addTrans(n, m)$ for $n, m \in \mathbb{N}$ to create a transition with n input and m output places:

$addPlace$:

$addTrans(n, m)$:

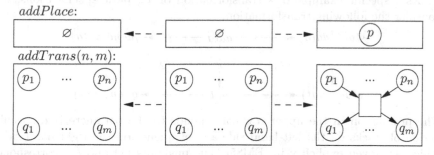

The grammar $ENGG$ can be modified to a grammar $PTGG$ for place/transition nets if we replace the productions $addTrans(n, m)$ by productions $addTrans(n, m)(i_1, \ldots, i_n, o_1, \ldots, o_m)$, where $i_1, \ldots, i_n$ and $o_1, \ldots, o_m$ correspond to the arc weights of the input places $p_1, \ldots, p_n$ and the output places $q_1, \ldots, q_m$, respectively.

For a more interesting example, we refer to [BEU03]. In this paper, a rule-based stepwise development of a simple communication-based system is constructed as an interconnection of three components: a buffer with two tasks, a printer, and a communication network between the buffer and the printer. All these components are represented by marked place/transition nets, which satisfy suitable safety and liveness properties. In addition, four productions are given, which allow one to transform the basic components to a more detailed final model. It can be shown that the final model inherits the safety and liveness properties of the initial model, because the productions can be shown to be safety- and liveness-preserving. In fact, the productions are Q-productions in the sense of [Pad96], where Q-productions were introduced to preserve certain properties.

Concerning examples of algebraic high-level net transformation systems, we refer to [PER95, EKMR99, EGP99].

5.2.4 Algebraic Specification Transformation Systems

Transformation systems for algebraic specifications have been considered especially in connection with algebraic module specification (see [EM90]). The import and export interfaces IMP and EXP, with a common parameter part PAR, of an algebraic module specification can be considered as a production $IMP \leftarrow PAR \rightarrow EXP$. This was the motivation for presenting algebraic specifications as an HLR category in [EHKP91a, EHKP91b]. In Chapter 4, we have shown that algebraic signatures (**Sig**, $\mathcal{M}$) and algebraic specifications (**Spec**, $\mathcal{M}_{strict}$) are adhesive and weak adhesive HLR categories, respectively. The corresponding instantiations are signature and algebraic specification transformation systems, respectively, as considered in [EHKP91a, EHKP91b, EGP99]. In [EGP99], a detailed example is presented of how to transform a modular airport schedule system (see [EM90]) into a library system using an algebraic transformation system.

As a specific example of a transformation of algebraic specifications, we consider the following transformation:

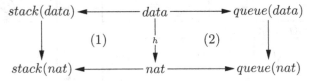

The production in the upper row corresponds to the parameterized specification of stacks on the left-hand side and of queues on the right-hand side, which are given explicitly in [EM85]. The pushouts (1) and (2) correspond to parameter-passing diagrams in the sense of algebraic specifications, where the formal parameter $data$ is replaced by the actual parameter nat using the parameter-passing morphism $h : data \rightarrow nat$ (see [EM85] for more detail).

5.2.5 Typed Attributed Graph Transformation Systems

In Example 4.11, we have mentioned that there is a category (**AGraphs**$_{\mathbf{ATG}}$, $\mathcal{M}$) of typed attributed graphs which is an adhesive HLR category. This will be shown in full detail in Part III where also a detailed introduction to the concepts and theory of typed attributed graph transformation systems and some examples are given. In particular, we present detailed examples concerning modeling and model transformations as running examples in Part III and Part IV, respectively.

5.3 The Local Church–Rosser and Parallelism Theorems

In this section, we study the parallel and sequential independence of direct transformations, leading to the Local Church–Rosser and Parallelism Theorems mentioned in Section 3.3 in Part I.

Intuitively, independence means that the intersection of the corresponding matches or the intersection of comatch and match consists of common gluing points (see Definition 3.15). In our categorical framework, however, we use the characterization via morphisms (see Fact 3.18) as definition.

Definition 5.9 (parallel and sequential independence). *Two direct transformations* $G \stackrel{p_1,m_1}{\Longrightarrow} H_1$ *and* $G \stackrel{p_2,m_2}{\Longrightarrow} H_2$ *are parallel independent if there exist morphisms* $i : L_1 \to D_2$ *and* $j : L_2 \to D_1$ *such that* $f_2 \circ i = m_1$ *and* $f_1 \circ j = m_2$:

$$
\begin{array}{ccccccccccc}
R_1 & \xleftarrow{\ r_1\ } & K_1 & \xrightarrow{\ l_1\ } & L_1 & & L_2 & \xleftarrow{\ l_2\ } & K_2 & \xrightarrow{\ r_2\ } & R_2 \\
\downarrow{\scriptstyle n_1} & & \downarrow{\scriptstyle k_1} & & {\scriptstyle j}\diagdown\ {\scriptstyle m_1}\ {\scriptstyle m_2}\ \diagdown{\scriptstyle i} & & & & \downarrow{\scriptstyle k_2} & & \downarrow{\scriptstyle n_2} \\
H_1 & \xleftarrow{\ g_1\ } & D_1 & \xrightarrow{\ f_1\ } & & G & & \xleftarrow{\ f_2\ } & D_2 & \xrightarrow{\ g_2\ } & H_2
\end{array}
$$

Two direct transformations $G \stackrel{p_1,m_1}{\Longrightarrow} H \stackrel{p_2,m_2}{\Longrightarrow} G'$ *are sequentially independent if there exist morphisms* $i : R_1 \to D_2$ *and* $j : L_2 \to D_1$ *such that* $f_2 \circ i = n_1$ *and* $g_1 \circ j = m_2$:

$$
\begin{array}{ccccccccccc}
L_1 & \xleftarrow{\ l_1\ } & K_1 & \xrightarrow{\ r_1\ } & R_1 & & L_2 & \xleftarrow{\ l_2\ } & K_2 & \xrightarrow{\ r_2\ } & R_2 \\
\downarrow{\scriptstyle m_1} & & \downarrow{\scriptstyle k_1} & & {\scriptstyle j}\diagdown\ {\scriptstyle n_1}\ {\scriptstyle m_2}\ \diagdown{\scriptstyle i} & & & & \downarrow{\scriptstyle k_2} & & \downarrow{\scriptstyle n_2} \\
G & \xleftarrow{\ f_1\ } & D_1 & \xrightarrow{\ g_1\ } & & H & & \xleftarrow{\ f_2\ } & D_2 & \xrightarrow{\ g_2\ } & G'
\end{array}
$$

Remark 5.10. $G_1 \stackrel{p_1}{\Rightarrow} G_2 \stackrel{p_2}{\Rightarrow} G_3$ are sequentially independent iff $G_1 \stackrel{p_1^{-1}}{\Leftarrow} G_2 \stackrel{p_2}{\Rightarrow} G_3$ are parallel independent.

Two direct transformations that are not parallel (or sequentially) independent, are called parallel (or sequentially) dependent.

Example 5.11 (parallel and sequential independence in $ExAHG$). In our adhesive HLR grammar $ExAHG$, we consider the two direct transformations $S \stackrel{addEdge,m}{\Longrightarrow} G$ and $S \stackrel{deleteVertex,m'}{\Longrightarrow} G'$. The left part of the diagram below depicts the application of the production $addEdge$, and the right part shows the application of the production *deleteVertex*. The two direct transformations are parallel independent. The matches m and m' and the required morphisms i and j are again indicated by the node labels. In this case, the intersection of m and m' is empty, and therefore no common gluing points have to be preserved:

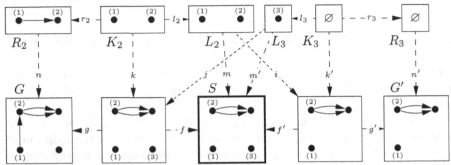

An example of parallel dependence is shown in the following diagram. We have used the same productions *addEdge* and *deleteVertex*, but have changed the match from m' to m'':

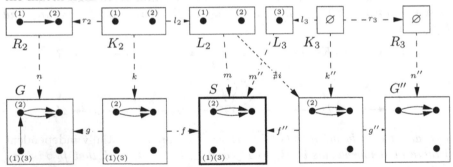

The common gluing point is the node labeled with (1) and (3). This node is necessary for adding the edge with the production *addEdge*, but it is deleted by applying the production *deleteVertex*. Thus no suitable i can be found such that $f'' \circ i = m$. Therefore the transformations are parallel dependent.

In the next diagram, we show two sequentially independent direct transformations. We look at the graph G', which is similar to our start graph S except for one missing node. First, we apply the production *addVertex* to obtain the start graph S. In a second step, we add another edge to derive the graph G. The direct transformations $G' \overset{addVertex,m}{\Longrightarrow} S \overset{addEdge,m'}{\Longrightarrow} G$ are sequentially independent:

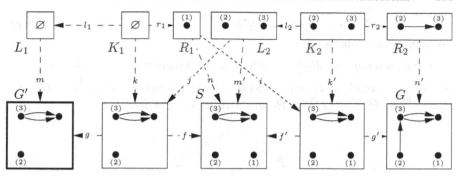

An example of sequentially dependent transformations can be found by choosing the match m'' instead of m'. Again we apply the productions *addVertex* and *addEdge*:

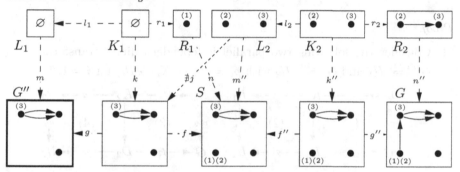

In this case, the direct transformations are sequentially dependent. No j can be found with $f \circ j = m''$, because *addVertex* creates one of the vertices required to apply *addEdge* with the given match m''. □

The Local Church–Rosser Theorem states that the productions of parallel independent direct transformations $G \Rightarrow H_1$ and $G \Rightarrow H_2$ can be applied in any order to G to obtain sequentially independent direct transformations $G \Rightarrow H_1 \Rightarrow X$ and $G \Rightarrow H_2 \Rightarrow X$ that lead to the same object X. For sequentially independent direct transformations $G \Rightarrow H_1 \Rightarrow X$, there is a transformation $G \Rightarrow H_2 \Rightarrow X$ over the same productions applied in the opposite order.

The following version of the Local Church–Rosser Theorem for adhesive HLR systems can be obtained from Theorem 3.20 for GT systems by abstraction, i.e. by replacing graphs and graph transformations by high-level structures, called objects, and corresponding transformations. Vice versa, Theorem 3.20 can be obtained from Theorem 5.12 by instantiation to the adhesive HLR categories (**Graphs**, $\mathcal{M}$) and (**Graphs**$_{\mathbf{TG}}$, $\mathcal{M}$) (see Subsection 5.2.1).

Theorem 5.12 (Local Church–Rosser Theorem). *Given an adhesive HLR system AHS and two parallel independent direct transformations $G \xRightarrow{p_1,m_1} H_1$ and $G \xRightarrow{p_2,m_2} H_2$, there are an object G' and direct transformations $H_1 \xRightarrow{p_2,m_2'}$*

G' and $H_2 \overset{p_1,m_1'}{\Longrightarrow} G'$ such that $G \overset{p_1,m_1}{\Longrightarrow} H_1 \overset{p_2,m_2'}{\Longrightarrow} G'$ and $G \overset{p_2,m_2}{\Longrightarrow} H_2 \overset{p_1,m_1'}{\Longrightarrow} G'$ are sequentially independent.

Given two sequentially independent direct transformations $G \overset{p_1,m_1}{\Longrightarrow} H_1 \overset{p_2,m_2'}{\Longrightarrow}$ G', there are an object H_2 and direct transformations $G \overset{p_2,m_2}{\Longrightarrow} H_2 \overset{p_1,m_1'}{\Longrightarrow} G'$ such that $G \overset{p_1,m_1}{\Longrightarrow} H_1$ and $G \overset{p_2,m_2}{\Longrightarrow} H_2$ are parallel independent:

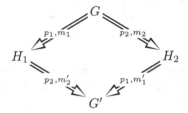

Proof.

1. Consider the following two parallel independent direct transformations $G \overset{p_1,m_1}{\Longrightarrow} H_1$ and $G \overset{p_2,m_2}{\Longrightarrow} H_2$ with $p_i = (L_i \overset{l_i}{\leftarrow} K_i \overset{r_i}{\rightarrow} R_i)$ for $i = 1, 2$:

$$
\begin{array}{ccccc}
L_1 \xleftarrow{l_1} K_1 \xrightarrow{r_1} R_1 & & L_2 \xleftarrow{l_2} K_2 \xrightarrow{r_2} R_2 \\
\downarrow{m_1} \quad (1) \quad \downarrow \quad (2) \quad \downarrow{n_1} & & \downarrow{m_2} \quad (3) \quad \downarrow \quad (4) \quad \downarrow{n_2} \\
G \xleftarrow{f_1} D_1 \xrightarrow{g_1} H_1 & & G \xleftarrow{f_2} D_2 \xrightarrow{g_2} H_2
\end{array}
$$

Combining the pushouts (1) and (3), we obtain the following diagram on the left-hand side, where i_1 and i_2 are the morphisms obtained by parallel independence. Since $f_1, f_2 \in \mathcal{M}$, we can construct the pullback (5) and obtain morphisms $j_1 : K_1 \to D$ and $j_2 : K_2 \to D$. Since (1) = (6) + (5) and $f_2, l_1 \in \mathcal{M}$, Theorem 4.26, item 2, implies that (6) and (5) are pushouts and, analogously, that (7) is a pushout. Note that Theorem 4.26 requires us to have a (weak) adhesive HLR category, while all other constructions are valid in any category with suitable pushouts and pullbacks.

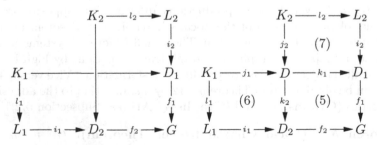

Now we construct the pushout (8) over j_1 and $r_1 \in \mathcal{M}$, the pushout (9) over j_2 and $r_2 \in \mathcal{M}$, and, finally, the pushout (10) over $h_1, h_2 \in \mathcal{M}$:

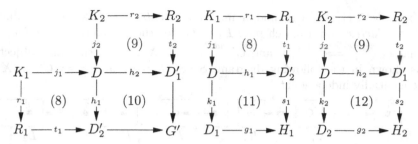

From pushout (8), we obtain a morphism $s_1 : D_2' \to H_1$ such that (11) commutes and $(2) = (8) + (11)$. From pushout decomposition, (11) is also a pushout. An analogous construction leads to the pushout (12). Combining all these pushouts, we obtain the direct transformations $H_1 \overset{p_2}{\Rightarrow} G'$ and $H_2 \overset{p_1}{\Rightarrow} G'$:

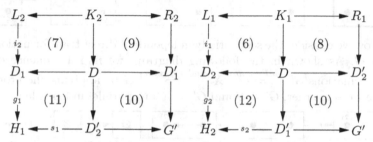

Since $s_1 \circ t_1 = n_1$ and $s_2 \circ t_2 = n_2$, the transformations $G \Rightarrow H_1 \Rightarrow G'$ and $G \Rightarrow H_2 \Rightarrow G'$ are sequentially independent.

2. Given sequentially independent direct transformations $G \overset{p_1,m_1}{\Longrightarrow} H_1 \overset{p_2,m_2'}{\Longrightarrow} G'$ with comatches n_1 and n_2', respectively, from Remark 5.10 we obtain parallel independent direct transformations $G \overset{p_1^{-1},n_1}{\Longleftarrow} H_1 \overset{p_2,m_2'}{\Longrightarrow} G'$. Now part 1 of the proof gives us sequentially independent direct transformations $H_1 \overset{p_1^{-1},n_1}{\Longrightarrow} G \overset{p_2,m_2}{\Longrightarrow} H_2$ and $H_1 \overset{p_2,m_2'}{\Longrightarrow} G' \overset{p_1^{-1},n_1'}{\Longrightarrow} H_2$, as shown in the diagram below. Applying Remark 5.10 to the first transformation means that $H_1 \overset{p_1,m_1}{\Longleftarrow} G \overset{p_2,m_2}{\Longrightarrow} H_2$ are the required parallel independent direct transformations.

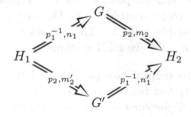

□

Example 5.13 (Local Church–Rosser Theorem in $ExAHG$). Consider the parallel independent direct transformations $S \Rightarrow G$ and $S \Rightarrow G'$ from

Example 5.11. We can find a match $m_1 : L_3 \to G$ for the production *deleteVertex* and a match $m_2 : L_2 \to G'$ for the production *addEdge*, such that $G \overset{deleteVertex,m_1}{\Longrightarrow} X$ and $G' \overset{addEdge,m_2}{\Longrightarrow} X$ lead to the same object X, as shown in the following diagram. $S \Rightarrow G \Rightarrow X$ and $S \Rightarrow G' \Rightarrow X$ are sequentially independent.

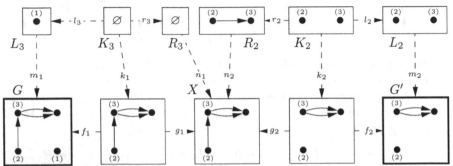

Now we consider the sequentially independent direct transformations $G' \Rightarrow S \Rightarrow G$. As shown in the following diagram, we find a sequence of direct transformations $G' \overset{addEdge,m_1}{\Longrightarrow} X \overset{addVertex,m_2}{\Longrightarrow} G$ by applying the productions in the reverse order. $G' \Rightarrow S$ and $G' \Rightarrow X$ are parallel independent.

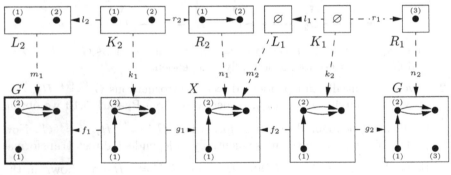

□

In analogy to Part I, we now present the Parallelism Theorem for adhesive HLR systems. For this purpose, we have to replace the disjoint unions of graphs and injective graph morphisms in Definition 3.22 by binary coproducts which are compatible with $\mathcal{M}$. This allows us to construct the parallel production $p_1 + p_2$ for adhesive HLR systems.

Definition 5.14 (coproduct compatible with $\mathcal{M}$). *A (weak) adhesive HLR category* $(\mathbf{C}, \mathcal{M})$ *has binary coproducts compatible with* $\mathcal{M}$ *if* $\mathbf{C}$ *has binary coproducts and, for each pair of morphisms* $f : A \to A'$, $g : B \to B'$ *with* $f, g \in \mathcal{M}$, *the coproduct morphism is also an* $\mathcal{M}$-*morphism, i.e.* $f + g : A + B \to A' + B' \in \mathcal{M}$.

Example 5.15 (coproducts compatible with $\mathcal{M}$). In **Sets**, **Graphs**, and **Graphs$_{TG}$**, binary coproduct objects are the disjoint unions of the elements of the sets or of the nodes and edges, respectively. If f and g are injective, then so is the coproduct morphism $f + g$.   □

On the basis of the compatibility of binary coproducts with $\mathcal{M}$, we can define parallel productions. These are well defined because the coproduct morphisms are also in $\mathcal{M}$.

Definition 5.16 (parallel production and transformation). *Let $AHS = (\mathbf{C}, \mathcal{M}, P)$ be an adhesive HLR system, where $(\mathbf{C}, \mathcal{M})$ has binary coproducts compatible with $\mathcal{M}$. Given two productions $p_1 = (L_1 \xleftarrow{l_1} K_1 \xrightarrow{r_1} R_1)$ and $p_2 = (L_2 \xleftarrow{l_2} K_2 \xrightarrow{r_2} R_2)$, the parallel production $p_1 + p_2$ is defined by the coproduct constructions over the corresponding objects and morphisms: $p_1 + p_2 = (L_1 + L_2 \xleftarrow{l_1+l_2} K_1 + K_2 \xrightarrow{r_1+r_2} R_1 + R_2)$.*

The application of a parallel production is called a parallel direct transformation, *or* parallel transformation, *for short.*

Example 5.17 (parallel production in $ExAHG$). In our example adhesive HLR grammar $ExAHG$, the parallel production of two productions p_1 and p_2 is the componentwise coproduct of the objects and morphisms. For example, combining the productions $addVertex$ and $addEdge$ results in the following parallel production; it inserts an edge between two given nodes and a new node at the same time:

□

Now we are able to prove the Parallelism Theorem for adhesive HLR systems, which is obtained from the graph case considered in Theorem 3.24 by abstraction. Vice versa, Theorem 3.24 is an instantiation of Theorem 5.18.

Theorem 5.18 (Parallelism Theorem). *Let $AHS = (\mathbf{C}, \mathcal{M}, P)$ be an adhesive HLR system, where $(\mathbf{C}, \mathcal{M})$ has binary coproducts compatible with $\mathcal{M}$.*

1. Synthesis. *Given a sequentially independent direct transformation sequence $G \Rightarrow H_1 \Rightarrow G'$ via productions p_1 and p_2, then there is a construction leading to a parallel transformation $G \Rightarrow G'$ via the parallel production $p_1 + p_2$, called a* synthesis construction.

2. Analysis. *Given a parallel transformation $G \Rightarrow G'$ via $p_1 + p_2$, then there is a construction leading to two sequentially independent transformation sequences $G \Rightarrow H_1 \Rightarrow G'$ via p_1 and p_2 and $G \Rightarrow H_2 \Rightarrow G'$ via p_2 and p_1, called an* analysis construction.

3. Bijective correspondence. *The synthesis and analysis constructions are inverse to each other up to isomorphism:*

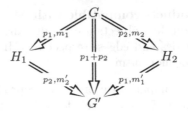

Proof.

1. Given the sequentially independent direct transformations $G \stackrel{p_1,m_1}{\Rightarrow} H_1 \stackrel{p_2,m_2}{\Rightarrow} G'$, using Theorem 5.12, we obtain parallel independent direct transformations $H_2 \stackrel{p_2,m_2'}{\Leftarrow} G \stackrel{p_1,m_1}{\Rightarrow} H_1$ and obtain morphisms i and j as shown in the following diagram:

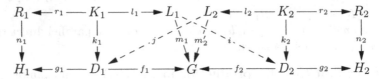

As in the proof of Theorem 5.12, we obtain the following diagrams, where all squares are pushouts:

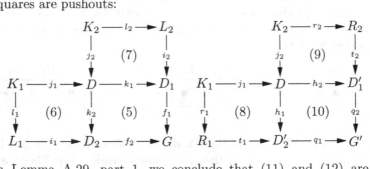

From Lemma A.29, part 1, we conclude that (11) and (12) are also pushouts; therefore we have a parallel transformation $G \stackrel{p_1+p_2,[f_2 \circ i_1, f_1 \circ i_2]}{\Rightarrow} G'$ via the parallel production:

$$
\begin{array}{ccccc}
L_1 + L_2 & \xleftarrow{\ l_1+l_2\ } & K_1 + K_2 & \xrightarrow{\ r_1+r_2\ } & R_1 + R_2 \\
\downarrow {\scriptstyle [f_2 \circ i_1, f_1 \circ i_2]} & (11) & \downarrow {\scriptstyle [j_1,j_2]} & (12) & \downarrow {\scriptstyle [q_1 \circ t_1, q_2 \circ t_2]} \\
G & \xleftarrow{\ f_1 \circ k_1\ } & D & \xrightarrow{\ q_1 \circ h_1\ } & G'
\end{array}
$$

2. Given the parallel direct transformation $G \stackrel{p_1+p_2,[m_1,m_2]}{\Rightarrow} G'$ via the parallel production p_1+p_2 as shown in diagrams (13) and (14), by applying Lemma A.29 we obtain the pushouts (5)–(7) and (8)–(10) with $m_1 = f_2 \circ i_1$, $m_2 = f_1 \circ i_2$, $n_1 = q_1 \circ t_1$, $n_2 = q_2 \circ t_2$, $f_1 \circ k_1 = d$ and $q_1 \circ h_1 = e$:

$$L_1 + L_2 \xleftarrow{l_1 + l_2} K_1 + K_2 \xrightarrow{r_1 + r_2} R_1 + R_2$$

$$\begin{array}{ccccc} \downarrow & & \downarrow & & \downarrow \\ {\scriptstyle [m_1, m_2]} & (13) & {\scriptstyle [j_1, j_2]} & (14) & {\scriptstyle [n_1, n_2]} \\ \downarrow & & \downarrow & & \downarrow \\ G & \xleftarrow{\quad d \quad} & D & \xrightarrow{\quad e \quad} & G' \end{array}$$

By applying p_1 to G via the match m_1 with the pushout complement (6) + (5), we obtain a direct transformation $G \overset{p_1, m_1}{\Longrightarrow} H_1$. Analogously, using p_2 and the match m_2 with the pushout complement (7) + (5), we obtain the direct transformation $G \overset{p_2, m_2}{\Longrightarrow} H_2$. $G \Rightarrow H_1$ and $G \Rightarrow H_2$ are parallel independent; therefore we can apply Theorem 5.12, leading to the sequentially independent transformations $G \Rightarrow H_1 \Rightarrow G''$ and $G \Rightarrow H_2 \Rightarrow G''$. By applying part 1 of the proof to this transformation, and using the uniqueness of pushouts and pushout complements, we have $G'' \cong G'$.

3. Because of the uniqueness of pushouts and pushout complements, the above constructions are inverse to each other up to isomorphism. □

Example 5.19 (Parallelism Theorem). We can apply Theorem 5.18 to the sequentially independent direct transformations $G' \overset{addVertex, m}{\Longrightarrow} S \overset{addEdge, m'}{\Longrightarrow} G$ of Example 5.11, leading to the parallel production $addVertex + addEdge$ that we have constructed already in Example 5.17, and the parallel direct transformation $G' \Rightarrow G$ via this parallel production. □

5.4 Concurrency Theorem and Pair Factorization

The Concurrency Theorem handles general transformations, which may be sequentially dependent. Roughly speaking, for a sequence $G \overset{p_1, m_1}{\Longrightarrow}$ $H \overset{p_2, m'_2}{\Longrightarrow} G'$ there is a production $p_1 *_E p_2$, called a concurrent production, which allows one to construct a corresponding direct transformation $G \overset{p_1 *_E p_2}{\Longrightarrow} G'$, and vice versa (see Section 3.4 for more detailed discussion).

In contrast to the version of the Concurrency Theorem presented in [EHKP91a, EHKP91b], where an explicit dependency relation $R_1 \leftarrow D \rightarrow L_2$ between productions p_1 and p_2 is considered, we use an E-dependency relation $R_1 \overset{e_1}{\rightarrow} E \overset{e_2}{\leftarrow} L_2$, which, in most examples, will be a jointly epimorphic pair (e_1, e_2) (see Definition A.16). This makes an essential difference to the construction of an E-related transformation sequence in Fact 5.29, in contrast to the D-related transformation sequences in [EHKP91a, EHKP91b]. We use only an $\mathcal{E}'$–$\mathcal{M}'$ pair factorization, which will also be used for critical pairs in Section 6.3, in contrast to [EHKP91a, EHKP91b], where general POs and PBs and a complicated triple PO–PB lemma are needed.

Definition 5.20 (E-dependency relation). *Given a class $\mathcal{E}'$ of morphism pairs with the same codomain, and two productions p_1 and p_2 with $p_i = (L_i \overset{l_i}{\leftarrow} K_i \overset{r_i}{\rightarrow} R_i)$ for $i = 1, 2$, an object E with morphisms $e_1 : R_1 \rightarrow E$ and $e_2 :$*

$L_2 \to E$ is an E-dependency relation *for p_1 and p_2 if $(e_1, e_2) \in \mathcal{E}'$ and the pushout complements (1) and (2) over $K_1 \xrightarrow{r_1} R_1 \xrightarrow{e_1} E$ and $K_2 \xrightarrow{l_2} L_2 \xrightarrow{e_2} E$ exist:*

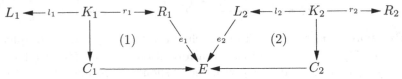

Definition 5.21 (E-concurrent production and E-related transformation). *Given an E-dependency relation $(e_1, e_2) \in \mathcal{E}'$ for the productions p_1 and p_2, the E-concurrent production $p_1 *_E p_2$ is defined by $p_1 *_E p_2 = (L \xleftarrow{lok_1} K \xrightarrow{rok_2} R)$ as shown in the following diagram, where (3) and (4) are pushouts and (5) is a pullback:*

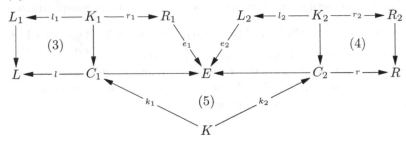

A transformation sequence $G \xRightarrow{p_1, m_1} H_1 \xRightarrow{p_2, m_2} G'$ is called E-related if there exists $h : E \to H_1$ with $h \circ e_1 = n_1$ and $h \circ e_2 = m_2$ and there are morphisms $c_1 : C_1 \to D_1$ and $c_2 : C_2 \to D_2$ such that (6) and (7) commute and (8) and (9) are pushouts:

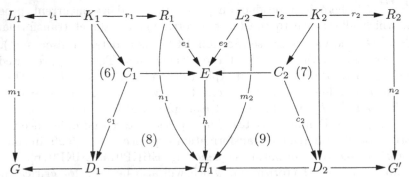

Example 5.22 (E-concurrent production and E-related transformation). Consider the sequentially dependent direct transformations $G'' \Rightarrow S \Rightarrow G$ in Example 5.11. The following diagram shows the construction of the E-concurrent production $addVertex *_E addEdge = (L \xleftarrow{lok_1} K \xrightarrow{rok_2} R)$ for the given dependency relation $R_1 \xrightarrow{e_1} E \xleftarrow{e_2} L_2$:

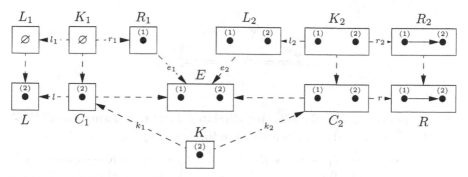

It can be verified that $G'' \Rightarrow G$ is an E-related transformation. In the following diagram, the transformation of G'' over the E-concurrent production $addVertex *_E addEdge$ is depicted:

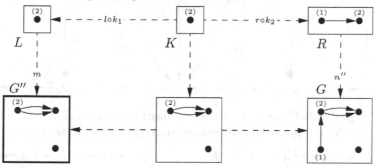

The following Concurrency Theorem for adhesive HLR systems is an abstraction from Theorem 3.26 for the graph case. Vice versa, Theorem 3.26 can be obtained from Theorem 5.23 by instantiation, where $(\mathbf{C}, \mathcal{M})$ and $\mathcal{E}'$ (see Definition 5.20) are specialized to $(\mathbf{Graphs}, \mathcal{M})$ and $(\mathbf{Graphs_{TG}}, \mathcal{M})$, respectively, where $\mathcal{M}$ is the class of injective (typed) graph morphisms and $\mathcal{E}'$ is the class of pairs of jointly surjective (typed) graph morphisms.

Theorem 5.23 (Concurrency Theorem). *Let $AHS = (\mathbf{C}, \mathcal{M}, P, S)$ be an adhesive HLR system, $R_1 \xrightarrow{e_1} E \xleftarrow{e_2} L_2$ an E-dependency relation for the productions p_1 and p_2 for a given class $\mathcal{E}'$ of morphism pairs, and $p_1 *_E p_2$ the corresponding E-concurrent production.*

1. Synthesis. *Given an E-related transformation sequence $G \Rightarrow H \Rightarrow G'$ via p_1 and p_2, then there is a synthesis construction leading to a direct transformation $G \Rightarrow G'$ via $p_1 *_E p_2$.*
2. Analysis. *Given a direct transformation $G \Rightarrow G'$ via $p_1 *_E p_2$, then there is an analysis construction leading to an E-related transformation sequence $G \Rightarrow H \Rightarrow G'$ via p_1 and p_2.*
3. Bijective correspondence. *The synthesis and analysis constructions are inverse to each other up to isomorphism, provided that every $(e_1, e_2) \in \mathcal{E}'$ is an epimorphic pair (see Definition A.16):*

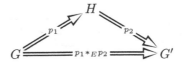

Proof.

1. *Synthesis.* Consider the following E-related direct transformations $G \stackrel{p_1,m_1}{\Longrightarrow}$ $H \stackrel{p_2,m_2}{\Longrightarrow} G'$ and the E-concurrent production $p_1 *_E p_2$:

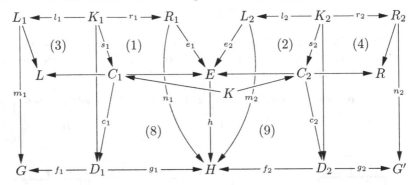

From pushouts (3) and (4), we obtain morphisms $L \to G$ and $R \to G'$, respectively, and by pushout decomposition, (10) and (11) are also pushouts:

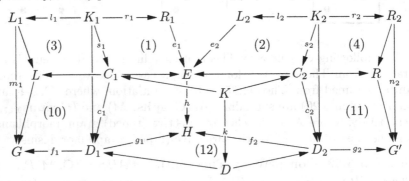

Now we construct the pullback (12) and obtain a morphism $k : K \to D$. Applying the cube PO–PB lemma in Theorem 4.26 to the cube in the diagram, where the top and bottom are pullbacks and the back faces are pushouts, it follows that the front faces are also pushouts, which leads to the direct transformation $G \Rightarrow G'$ via $p_1 *_E p_2$.

2. *Analysis.* Consider an E-dependency relation E and the E-related transformation $G \Rightarrow G'$ via the E-concurrent production $p_1 *_E p_2$:

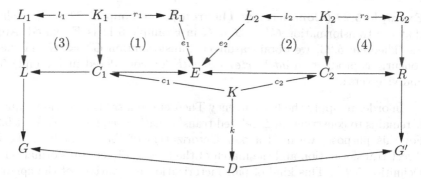

First we construct the pushouts (13) and (14) over c_1, k and c_2, k, respectively, and obtain the induced morphisms $D_1 \to G$ and $D_2 \to G'$; by pushout decomposition, (10) and (11) are also pushouts:

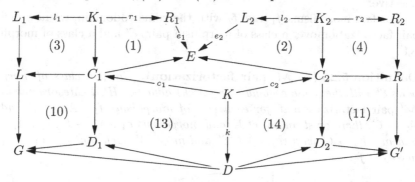

Now we construct pushout (8), leading to the object H, and obtain from pushout (14) the induced morphism $D_2 \to H$; by pushout composition and decomposition applied to the resulting cube, (9) is also a pushout.

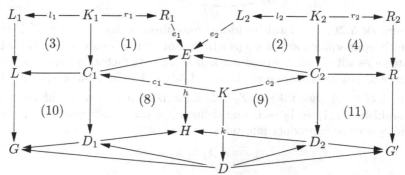

3. The *bijective correspondence* follows from the fact that pushout and pullback constructions are unique up to isomorphism and that the pair $(e_1, e_2) \in \mathcal{E}'$ is jointly epimorphic, leading to a unique h in Definition 5.21. □

Example 5.24 (Concurrency Theorem). In Example 5.22, we have shown that the transformation $G'' \Rightarrow S \Rightarrow G$ in Example 5.11 is E-related. Applying Theorem 5.23, we obtain a direct transformation $G'' \Rightarrow G$ via the E-concurrent production $addVertex *_E addEdge$ considered in Example 5.22, and vice versa.   □

In order to apply the Concurrency Theorem to a transformation sequence, it remains to construct an E-related transformation sequence (see Fact 5.29). For this purpose, we need a pair factorization of the comatch of the first direct transformation and the match of the second direct transformation (see Definition 5.27). This kind of pair factorization is a variant of the epi–mono factorization (see Definition A.15), which is well known from set theory: each function $f : A \to B$ can be decomposed, uniquely up to bijection, as $f = m \circ e$, where e is an epimorphism, i.e. surjective, and m is a monomorphism, i.e. injective.

For two morphisms f_1 and f_2 with the same codomain, we now define a pair factorization over a class of morphism pairs $\mathcal{E}'$ and a class of morphisms $\mathcal{M}'$.

Definition 5.25 ($\mathcal{E}'$–$\mathcal{M}'$ pair factorization). *Given a class of morphism pairs $\mathcal{E}'$ with the same codomain, a (weak) adhesive HLR category has an $\mathcal{E}'$–$\mathcal{M}'$ pair factorization if, for each pair of morphisms $f_1 : A_1 \to C$ and $f_2 : A_2 \to C$, there exist an object K and morphisms $e_1 : A_1 \to K$, $e_2 : A_2 \to K$, and $m : K \to C$ with $(e_1, e_2) \in \mathcal{E}'$ and $m \in \mathcal{M}'$ such that $m \circ e_1 = f_1$ and $m \circ e_2 = f_2$:*

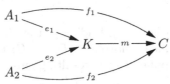

Remark 5.26. The intuitive idea of morphism pairs $(e_1, e_2) \in \mathcal{E}'$ is that of jointly epimorphic morphisms (see Definition A.16). This can be established in categories with binary coproducts and an $\mathcal{E}_0$–$\mathcal{M}_0$ factorization of morphisms, where $\mathcal{E}_0$ is a class of epimorphisms and $\mathcal{M}_0$ a class of monomorphisms. Given $A_1 \xrightarrow{f_1} C \xleftarrow{f_2} A_2$, we take an $\mathcal{E}_0$–$\mathcal{M}_0$ factorization $f = m \circ e$ of the induced morphism $f : A_1 + A_2 \to C$ and define $e_1 = e \circ \iota_1$ and $e_2 = e \circ \iota_2$, where ι_1 and ι_2 are the coproduct injections:

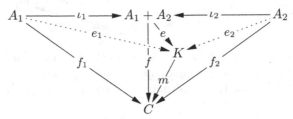

Similarly to the pushout–pullback decomposition (see Theorem 4.26, item 2), we need a decomposition property for pushouts that consist of a pullback and special morphisms in $\mathcal{M}$ and $\mathcal{M}'$. This property is necessary for proving the construction of E-related transformation sequences below and the completeness of the critical pairs in Section 6.3.

Definition 5.27 ($\mathcal{M}$–$\mathcal{M}'$ PO–PB decomposition property). *A (weak) adhesive HLR category* $(\mathbf{C}, \mathcal{M})$ *with a morphism class* $\mathcal{M}'$ *has the* $\mathcal{M}$–$\mathcal{M}'$ *pushout–pullback decomposition property if the following property holds. Given the following commutative diagram with $l \in \mathcal{M}$ and $w \in \mathcal{M}'$, and where (1)+(2) is a pushout and (2) a pullback, then (1) and (2) are pushouts and also pullbacks:*

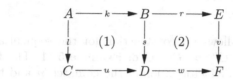

Remark 5.28. If $\mathcal{M}' \subseteq \mathcal{M}$, this property follows from Theorem 4.26, item 2. This means that for the case of (typed) graphs with $\mathcal{M} = \mathcal{M}'$, this property is satisfied. The $\mathcal{E}'$–$\mathcal{M}'$ pair factorization in the (typed) graph case is obtained when $\mathcal{E}'$ is the class of pairs of jointly surjective (typed) graph morphisms and $\mathcal{M} = \mathcal{M}'$ is the class of all injective (typed) graph morphisms. This allows us to apply the following construction of an E-related transformation sequence in the (typed) graph case.

Fact 5.29 (construction of E-related transformations). *Consider a (weak) adhesive HLR category* $(\mathbf{C}, \mathcal{M})$ *with an* $\mathcal{E}'$–$\mathcal{M}'$ *pair factorization such that the* $\mathcal{M}$–$\mathcal{M}'$ *PO–PB decomposition property holds. We then have, for each pair of direct transformations* $G \overset{p_1, m_1}{\Longrightarrow} H_1 \overset{p_2, m_2}{\Longrightarrow} G'$*, an E-dependency relation E such that* $G \overset{p_1, m_1}{\Longrightarrow} H_1 \overset{p_2, m_2}{\Longrightarrow} G'$ *is E-related.*

Proof. Given the direct transformations $G \overset{p_1, m_1}{\Longrightarrow} H_1$ with comatch $n_1 : R_1 \to H_1$ and $H_1 \overset{p_2, m_2}{\Longrightarrow} G'$, let $(e_1, e_2) \in \mathcal{E}'$, $h \in \mathcal{M}'$ be an $\mathcal{E}'$–$\mathcal{M}'$ pair factorization of n_1 and m_2 with $h \circ e_1 = n_1$ and $h \circ e_2 = m_2$.

Now we construct the pullbacks (8) and (9) over g_1, h and f_2, h, respectively. Since $h \circ e_1 \circ r_1 = n_1 \circ r_1 = g_1 \circ k_1$, we obtain from pullback (8) a morphism $s_1 : K_1 \to C_1$ such that (1) and (6) commute. Since $h \in \mathcal{M}'$, $r_1 \in \mathcal{M}$, (8) is a pullback and (1) + (8) is a pushout, from the $\mathcal{M}$–$\mathcal{M}'$ PO–PB decomposition property (1) and (8) are pushouts. Analogously, we obtain from pullback (9) a morphism s_2 with $c_2 \circ s_2 = k_2$, i.e. (7) commutes, and (2) and (9) are pushouts:

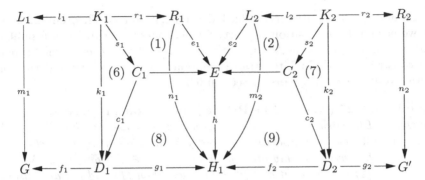

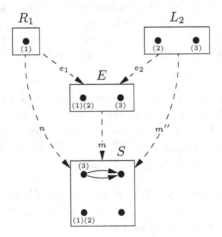

Altogether, E with $(e_1, e_2) \in \mathcal{E}'$ is an E-dependency relation, and $G \overset{p_1, m_1}{\Longrightarrow} H_1 \overset{p_2, m_2}{\Longrightarrow} G'$ is E-related. □

Example 5.30. We follow this construction for the sequentially dependent direct transformations $G'' \Rightarrow S \Rightarrow G$ of Example 5.11. The first step is to construct an $\mathcal{E}'$–$\mathcal{M}'$ pair factorization of the comatch n and the match m'', leading to the E-dependency relation (E, e_1, e_2). In this case $\mathcal{E}'$ consists of pairs of jointly surjective graph morphisms and $\mathcal{M}'$ consists of injective graph morphisms.

Constructing the pullbacks (8) and (9) as in the proof of Fact 5.29 leads to the pullback objects C_1 and C_2 in Example 5.22, which means that the transformation $G'' \Rightarrow S \Rightarrow G$ is indeed E-related. □

6

Embedding and Local Confluence

In this chapter, we continue to present important results for adhesive HLR systems which have been introduced in Section 3.4 of Part I already. The Embedding Theorem is one of the classical results for the graph case presented in [Ehr79]. For the categorical presentation of most of the results in this chapter, we introduce in Section 6.1 the concept of initial pushouts, which is a universal characterization of the boundary and the context, discussed in Section 3.2 for the graph case. This allows us to present the Embedding and Extension Theorems in Section 6.2, which characterize under what conditions a transformation sequence can be embedded into a larger context. The main ideas of the Embedding and Extension Theorems and of the other results in this chapter have been explained already in Section 3.4.

The concepts of critical pairs and local confluence were motivated originally by term rewriting systems, and were studied for hypergraph rewriting systems in [Plu93] and for typed attributed graph transformation systems in [HKT02]. The general theory of critical pairs and local confluence for adhesive HLR systems according to [EHPP04] is presented in Sections 6.3 and 6.4.

We start this chapter with the concept of initial pushouts in Section 6.1, because they are needed in the Extension Theorem. Initial pushouts and the Extension Theorem are both needed in the proof of the Local Confluence Theorem, which is the most important result in this chapter, because it has a large number of applications in various domains.

6.1 Initial Pushouts and the Gluing Condition

An initial pushout formalizes the construction of the boundary and the context which were mentioned earlier in Subsection 3.4.2. For a morphism $f : A \to A'$, we want to construct a boundary $b : B \to A$, a boundary object B, and a context object C, leading to a pushout. Roughly speaking, A' is the gluing of A and the context object C along the boundary object B.

Definition 6.1 (initial pushout). *Given a morphism* $f : A \to A'$ *in a (weak) adhesive HLR category, a morphism* $b : B \to A$ *with* $b \in \mathcal{M}$ *is called the* boundary *over* f *if there is a pushout complement of* f *and* b *such that (1) is a pushout which is* initial *over* f. *Initiality of (1) over* f *means, that for every pushout (2) with* $b' \in \mathcal{M}$ *there exist unique morphisms* $b^* : B \to D$ *and* $c^* : C \to E$ *with* b^*, $c^* \in \mathcal{M}$ *such that* $b' \circ b^* = b$, $c' \circ c^* = c$ *and (3) is a pushout.* B *is then called the* boundary object *and* C *the* context *with respect to* f.

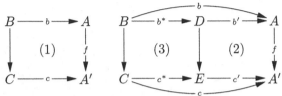

Example 6.2 (initial pushouts in Graphs). The boundary object B of an injective graph morphism $f : A \to A'$ consists of all nodes $a \in A$ such that $f(a)$ is adjacent to an edge in $A' \backslash f(A)$. These nodes are needed to glue A to the context graph $C = A' \backslash f(A) \cup f(b(B))$ in order to obtain A' as the gluing of A and C via B in the initial pushout.

Consider the following morphism $f : A \to A'$ induced by the node labels. Node (3) is the only node adjacent to an edge in $A' \backslash f(A)$ and therefore has to be in the boundary object B. The context object C contains the nodes (3) and (4) and the edge between them. All morphisms are inclusions.

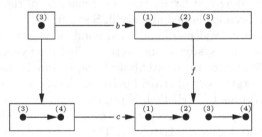

In **Graphs**, initial pushouts over arbitrary morphisms exist. If the given graph morphism $f : A \to A'$ is not injective, we have to add to the boundary object B all nodes and edges $x, y \in A$ with $f(x) = f(y)$ and those nodes that are the source or target of two edges that are equally mapped by f.   □

The concept of initial pushouts allows us to formulate a gluing condition analogous to that in the graph case (see Definition 3.9), leading to the existence and uniqueness of contexts in Theorem 6.4, which generalizes the graph case considered in Fact 3.11.

Definition 6.3 (gluing condition in adhesive HLR systems). *Given an adhesive HLR system* AHS *over a (weak) adhesive HLR category with initial pushouts, then a match* $m : L \to G$ *satisfies the* gluing condition *with respect* *to a production* $p = (L \xleftarrow{l} K \xrightarrow{r} R)$ *if, for the inital pushout (1) over m, there is a morphism* $b^* : B \to K$ *such that* $l \circ b^* = b$:

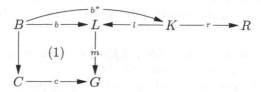

In this case $b, l \in \mathcal{M}$ *implies* $b^* \in \mathcal{M}$ *by the decomposition property of* $\mathcal{M}$.

Theorem 6.4 (existence and uniqueness of contexts). *Given an adhesive HLR system AHS over a (weak) adhesive HLR category with initial pushouts, a match* $m : L \to G$ *satisfies the gluing condition with respect to a production* $p = (L \xleftarrow{l} K \xrightarrow{r} R)$ *if and only if the context object D exists, i.e. there is a pushout complement (2) of l and m:*

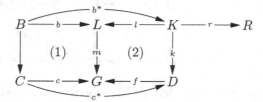

If it exists, the context object D is unique up to isomorphism.

Proof. If the gluing condition is fulfilled, then we can construct from $b^* \in \mathcal{M}$ and $B \to C$ a pushout (3) with the pushout object D and the morphisms k and c^*, where (3) is hidden behind (1) and (2). This new pushout (3), together with the morphisms c and $m \circ l$, implies a unique morphism f with $f \circ c^* = c$ and $m \circ l = f \circ k$, and by pushout decomposition of (3), (2) is also a pushout, leading to the context object D.

If the context object D with the pushout (2) exists, the initiality of pushout (1) implies the existence of b^* with $l \circ b^* = b$.

The uniqueness of D follows from the uniqueness of pushout complements shown in Theorem 4.26. $\square$

We shall now show an interesting closure property of initial pushouts, which we need for technical reasons (see the proof of Theorem 6.16). The closure property shows that initial pushouts over $\mathcal{M}'$-morphisms are closed under composition with double pushouts along $\mathcal{M}$-morphisms. In the (typed) graph case, we can take as $\mathcal{M}'$ the class of all (typed) graph morphisms or the class of all injective (typed) graph morphisms.

Lemma 6.5 (closure property of initial POs). *Let* $\mathcal{M}'$ *be a class of morphisms closed under pushouts and pullbacks along* $\mathcal{M}$-*morphisms (see Remark*

6.6), with initial pushouts over $\mathcal{M}'$-morphisms. Then initial pushouts over $\mathcal{M}'$-morphisms are closed under double pushouts along $\mathcal{M}$-morphisms.

This means that, given an initial pushout (1) over $h_0 \in \mathcal{M}'$ and a double-pushout diagram (2) with pushouts (2a) and (2b) and d_0, $d_1 \in \mathcal{M}$, we have the following:

1. The composition of (1) with (2a), defined as pushout (3) by the initiality of (1), is an initial pushout over $d \in \mathcal{M}'$.
2. The composition of the initial pushout (3) with pushout (2b), leading to pushout (4), is an initial pushout over $h_1 \in \mathcal{M}'$.

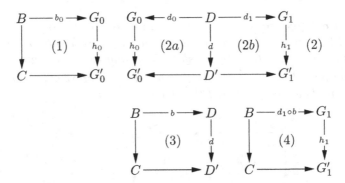

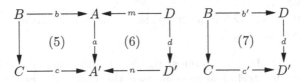

Remark 6.6. The statement that $\mathcal{M}'$ is closed under pushouts along $\mathcal{M}$-morphisms means that, for a pushout $C \xrightarrow{n} D \xleftarrow{g} B$ over $C \xleftarrow{f} A \xrightarrow{m} B$ with $m, n \in \mathcal{M}$ and $f \in \mathcal{M}'$, it holds also that $g \in \mathcal{M}'$. There is an analogous definition for pullbacks.

Proof. We prove this lemma in three steps.

Step I. Initial pushouts are closed under pushouts (in the opposite direction) in the following sense.

Given an initial pushout (5) over $a \in \mathcal{M}'$ and a pushout (6) with $m \in \mathcal{M}$, then there is an initial pushout (7) over $d \in \mathcal{M}'$ with $m \circ b' = b$ and $n \circ c' = c$:

$$
\begin{array}{ccccc}
B & \xrightarrow{\;b\;} & A & \xleftarrow{\;m\;} & D \\
\downarrow & (5) & \downarrow{\scriptstyle a} & (6) & \downarrow{\scriptstyle d} \\
C & \xrightarrow{\;c\;} & A' & \xleftarrow{\;n\;} & D'
\end{array}
\qquad
\begin{array}{ccc}
B & \xrightarrow{\;b'\;} & D \\
\downarrow & (7) & \downarrow{\scriptstyle d} \\
C & \xrightarrow{\;c'\;} & D'
\end{array}
$$

Since (5) is an initial pushout, there are unique morphisms b' and c' with $b', c' \in \mathcal{M}$ such that (7) is a pushout. It remains to show the initiality and that $d \in \mathcal{M}'$.

For any pushout (8) with $m' \in \mathcal{M}$, we have the result that the composition (8) + (6) is a pushout, with $m \circ m' \in \mathcal{M}$. Since (5) is an initial pushout, there are morphisms $b^* : B \to E$ and $c^* : C \to E' \in \mathcal{M}$ with $m \circ m' \circ b^* = b = m \circ b'$ and $n \circ n' \circ c^* = c = n \circ c'$, and (9) is a pushout:

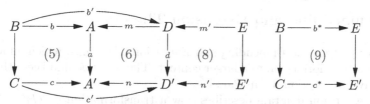

Since m and n are monomorphisms, it holds that $b' = m' \circ b^*$ and $c' = n' \circ c^*$. Therefore (7) is an initial pushout. Finally, pushout (6) is also a pullback by Theorem 4.26, part 1, with $a \in \mathcal{M}'$ such that the closure property of $\mathcal{M}'$ implies $d \in \mathcal{M}'$.

Step II. Initial pushouts are closed under pushouts (in the same direction) in the following sense.

Given an initial pushout (5) over $a \in \mathcal{M}'$ and a pushout (10) with $m \in \mathcal{M}$, then the composition (5) + (10) is an initial pushout over $d \in \mathcal{M}'$:

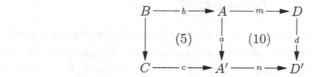

Since $\mathcal{M}'$-morphisms are closed under pushouts along $\mathcal{M}$-morphisms, we have $d \in \mathcal{M}'$. The initial pushout (11) over d then exists. Comparing (5) + (10) with (11), we obtain unique morphisms $l' : B' \to B$ and $k' : C' \to C \in \mathcal{M}$ with $m \circ b \circ l' = b'$ and $n \circ c \circ k' = c'$, and (12) is a pushout:

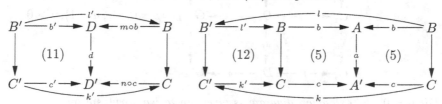

(12) + (5) is then also a pushout and, from the initial pushout (5), we obtain unique morphisms $l : B \to B'$ and $k : C \to C' \in \mathcal{M}$ with $b \circ l' \circ l = b$ and $c \circ k' \circ k = c$. Since b and c are monomorphisms, we obtain $l' \circ l = id_B$ and $k' \circ k = id_C$, and since l' and k' are monomorphisms they are also isomorphisms. This means that (5) + (10) and (11) are isomorphic, and (5) + (10) is an initial pushout over $d \in \mathcal{M}'$.then also

Step III. Initial pushouts are closed under double pushouts.

Square (3) is an initial pushout over $d \in \mathcal{M}'$, which follows directly from Step I.

(1) is a pushout along the $\mathcal{M}$-morphism b_0 and therefore a pullback by Theorem 4.26, part 1, and since $\mathcal{M}'$ is closed under pullbacks, we have $B \to C \in \mathcal{M}'$. We then have $d \in \mathcal{M}'$ and $h_1 \in \mathcal{M}'$ with $\mathcal{M}'$ closed under pushouts, and by applying Step II we also have the result that (4) is an initial pushout over $h_1 \in \mathcal{M}'$.   □

6.2 Embedding and Extension Theorems

We now present the Embedding and Extension Theorems, which allow us to extend a transformation to a larger context. The ideas behind these theorems were given in Section 3.4 in Part I.

An extension diagram describes how a transformation $t : G_0 \overset{*}{\Rightarrow} G_n$ can be extended to a transformation $t' : G'_0 \overset{*}{\Rightarrow} G'_n$ via an extension morphism $k_0 : G_0 \to G'_0$ that maps G_0 to G'_0.

Definition 6.7 (extension diagram). *An extension diagram is a diagram (1), as shown below,*

$$
\begin{array}{ccc}
G_0 & =\!t\!\overset{*}{\Rightarrow} & G_n \\
\Big| & & \Big| \\
k_0 & (1) & k_n \\
\downarrow & & \downarrow \\
G'_0 & =\!t'\!\overset{*}{\Rightarrow} & G'_n
\end{array}
$$

where $k_0 : G_0 \to G'_0$ is a morphism, called an extension morphism, and $t : G_0 \overset{*}{\Rightarrow} G_n$ and $t' : G'_0 \overset{*}{\Rightarrow} G'_n$ are transformations via the same productions $(p_0, \ldots, p_{n-1})$ and matches $(m_0, \ldots, m_{n-1})$ and $(k_0 \circ m_0, \ldots, k_{n-1} \circ m_{n-1})$ respectively, defined by the following DPO diagrams:

$$
\begin{array}{ccccc}
p_i: & L_i & \xleftarrow{\;l_i\;} K_i \xrightarrow{\;r_i\;} & R_i & \\
& \Big\downarrow{m_i} & \Big\downarrow{j_i} \qquad \Big\downarrow{n_i} & & \\
& G_i & \xleftarrow{\;f_i\;} D_i \xrightarrow{\;g_i\;} & G_{i+1} & (i = 0, \ldots, n-1), n > 0 \\
& \Big\downarrow{k_i} & \Big\downarrow{d_i} \qquad \Big\downarrow{k_{i+1}} & & \\
& G'_i & \xleftarrow{\;f'_i\;} D'_i \xrightarrow{\;g'_i\;} & G'_{i+1} &
\end{array}
$$

For $n = 0$, the extension diagram is given up to isomorphism by

$$
\begin{array}{ccccc}
G_0 & \xleftarrow{id_{G_0}} G_0 \xrightarrow{id_{G_0}} & G_0 \\
\Big\downarrow{k_0} & \Big\downarrow{k_0} \qquad \Big\downarrow{k_0} & \\
G'_0 & \xleftarrow{id_{G'_0}} G'_0 \xrightarrow{id'_{G_0}} & G'_0
\end{array}
$$

Example 6.8 (extension diagram). Consider the transformation sequence $t : S \Rightarrow G \Rightarrow H$ from Example 5.5 and the extension morphism $k : S \to S'$ as shown in the following diagram. The complete diagram is an extension diagram over t and k.

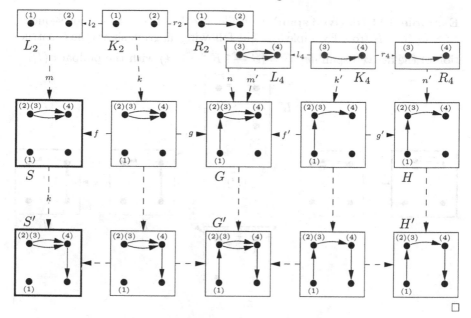

The consistency condition given in Definition 6.12 for a transformation $t : G_0 \stackrel{*}{\Rightarrow} G_n$ and an extension morphism $k_0 : G_0 \to G_0'$ means intuitively that the boundary object B of k_0 is preserved by t. In order to formulate this property, we use the notion of a derived span $der(t) = (G_0 \leftarrow D \to G_n)$ of the transformation t, which connects the first and the last object.

Definition 6.9 (derived span). *The* derived span *of an identical transformation* $t : G \stackrel{id}{\Rightarrow} G$ *is defined by* $der(t) = (G \leftarrow G \to G)$ *with identical morphisms.*

The derived span of a direct transformation $G \stackrel{p,m}{\Longrightarrow} H$ *is the span* $(G \leftarrow D \to H)$ *(see Def. 5.2).*

For a transformation $t : G_0 \stackrel{*}{\Rightarrow} G_n \Rightarrow G_{n+1}$, *the derived span is the composition via the pullback (P) of the derived spans* $der(G_0 \stackrel{*}{\Rightarrow} G_n) = (G_0 \stackrel{d_0}{\leftarrow} D' \stackrel{d_1}{\to} G_n)$ *and* $der(G_n \Rightarrow G_{n+1}) = (G_n \stackrel{f_n}{\leftarrow} D_n \stackrel{g_n}{\to} G_{n+1})$. *This construction leads to the derived span* $der(t) = (G_0 \stackrel{d_0 \circ d_2}{\longleftarrow} D \stackrel{g_n \circ d_3}{\longrightarrow} G_{n+1})$:

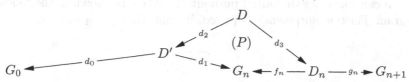

In the case $t : G_0 \Rightarrow^* G_n$ *where* $n = 0$, *we have either* $G_0 = G_n$ *and* $t : G_0 \stackrel{id}{\Rightarrow} G_0$ *(see above) or* $G_0 \cong G_0'$ *with* $der(t) = (G_0 \stackrel{id}{\leftarrow} G_0 \to G_0')$.

Remark 6.10. The derived span of a transformation is unique up to isomorphism and does not depend on the order of the pullback constructions.

Example 6.11 (derived span). Consider the direct transformation sequence $t : S \Rightarrow G \Rightarrow H$ from Example 5.5. The following diagram shows the construction of the derived span $der(t) = (S \xleftarrow{f \circ k_1} K \xrightarrow{g' \circ k_2} H)$ with the pullback (P):

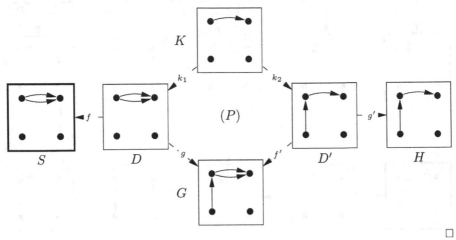

□

Definition 6.12 (consistency). *Given a transformation $t : G_0 \overset{*}{\Rightarrow} G_n$ with a derived span $der(t) = (G_0 \xleftarrow{d_0} D \xrightarrow{d_n} G_n)$, a morphism $k_0 : G_0 \to G_0'$ is called consistent with respect to t if there exist an initial pushout (1) over k_0 and a morphism $b \in \mathcal{M}$ with $d_0 \circ b = b_0$:*

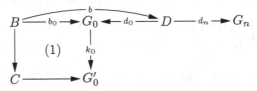

Example 6.13 (consistency). Consider the direct transformation sequence $t : S \Rightarrow G \Rightarrow H$ from Example 5.5 with the derived span $der(t) = (S \xleftarrow{f \circ k_1} K \xrightarrow{g' \circ k_2} H)$ as constructed in Example 6.11. The extension morphism $k : S \to S'$ given in Example 6.8 is then consistent with respect to t.

We can construct the initial pushout (1) over k as shown in the following diagram. For the morphism b depicted, it holds that $f \circ k_1 \circ b = b_0$:

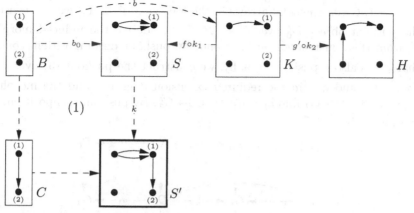

Using the following Embedding and Extension Theorems, we can show that consistency is both sufficient and necessary for the construction of extension diagrams. Both theorems are abstractions of the corresponding Theorems 3.28 and 3.29 for the graph case.

Theorem 6.14 (Embedding Theorem). *Given a transformation* $t : G_0 \overset{*}{\Rightarrow} G_n$ *and a morphism* $k_0 : G_0 \to G_0'$ *which is consistent with respect to* t, *then there is an extension diagram over* t *and* k_0.

Proof. We prove this theorem by induction over the number of direct transformation steps n.

Consider a transformation $t : G_0 \overset{n}{\Rightarrow} G_n$ with a derived span $(G_0 \overset{d_0}{\leftarrow} D_n \overset{d_n}{\to} G_n)$, the initial pushout (1) over $k_0 : G_0 \to G_0'$, and a morphism $b : B \to D_n$ with $d_0 \circ b = b_0$. We show that there is a suitable extension diagram and suitable morphisms $b_n = d_n \circ b : B \to G_n$ and $c_n : C \to G_n'$, such that (P_n) is a pushout:

$$
\begin{array}{ccc}
B \overset{b_0}{\longrightarrow} G_0 & \qquad & B \overset{b_n}{\longrightarrow} G_n \\
\downarrow \quad (1) \quad \downarrow {\scriptstyle k_0} & \qquad & \downarrow \quad (P_n) \quad \downarrow {\scriptstyle k_n} \\
C \overset{c_0}{\longrightarrow} G_0' & \qquad & C \overset{c_n}{\longrightarrow} G_n'
\end{array}
$$

Basis. $n = 0$. Consider the transformation $t : G_0 \overset{id}{\Rightarrow} G_0$ with the derived span $(G_0 \leftarrow G_0 \to G_0)$ and the morphism $k_0 : G_0 \to G_0'$, consistent with respect to t. There is then the initial pushout (1) over k_0 and a morphism $b = b_0 : B \to G_0$, and we have the following extension diagram:

$$
\begin{array}{ccccccc}
B & \overset{b_0}{\longrightarrow} & G_0 & \overset{id_{G_0}}{\longleftarrow} & G_0 & \overset{id_{G_0}}{\longrightarrow} & G_0 \\
\downarrow & (1) & \downarrow {\scriptstyle k_0} & & \downarrow {\scriptstyle k_0} & & \downarrow {\scriptstyle k_0} \\
C & \overset{c_0}{\longrightarrow} & G_0' & \overset{id_{G_0'}}{\longleftarrow} & G_0' & \overset{id_{G_0'}}{\longrightarrow} & G_0'
\end{array}
$$

$n = 1$. Given the solid arrows in the following diagram, we can construct the pushout object D_0' over $C \leftarrow B \xrightarrow{b} D_0$, derive the induced morphism d_0' from this constructed pushout and, by pushout decomposition, conclude that (2) is also a pushout. Finally, we construct the pushout (3) over $D_0' \xleftarrow{h_0} D_0 \xrightarrow{d_1} G_1$ and obtain the required extension diagram, and the morphisms $b_1 = d_1 \circ b : B \to G_1$ and $c_1 = d_1' \circ c : C \to G_1'$. By pushout composition, (P_1) is a pushout.

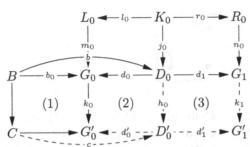

Induction step. Consider the transformation $t : G_0 \xRightarrow{n} G_n \xRightarrow{p_n, m_n} G_{n+1}$ with a derived span $der(t) = (G_0 \xleftarrow{d_0} D_{n+1} \xrightarrow{d_{n+1}} G_{n+1})$. There is then a transformation $t' : G_0 \xRightarrow{n} G_n$ with $der(t') = (G_0 \xleftarrow{d_0'} D_n \xrightarrow{d_n} G_n)$ such that (P) is the pullback obtained from the construction of the derived span, and we have the result that $d_0' \circ d_1' = d_0$ and $g_n \circ d_2' = d_{n+1}$:

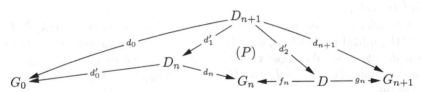

Since $k_0 : G_0 \to G_0'$ is consistent with respect to t, we have an initial pushout (1) over k_0 and a morphism $b : B \to D_{n+1}$ with $b_0 = d_0 \circ b = d_0' \circ d_1' \circ b$. This means that k_0 is also consistent with respect to t', using the morphism $b' = d_1' \circ b$. We can apply the induction assumption, obtaining an extension diagram for t' and k_0 and morphisms $b_n = d_n \circ b' : B \to G_n$ and $c_n : C \to G_n'$ such that (P_n) is a pushout. This is denoted by the dotted arrows in the following diagram:

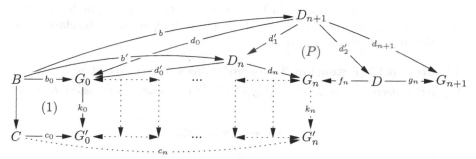

Now we construct the pushout object D' over $C \leftarrow B \xrightarrow{d'_2 \circ b} D$ and derive the induced morphism f'_n by applying $k_n \circ f_n$ and c_n to this constructed pushout. Since (P_n) is a pushout and it holds that $f_n \circ d'_2 \circ b = d_n \circ d'_1 \circ b = d_n \circ b' = b_n$, it follows by pushout decomposition that (2) is also a pushout. Finally, we construct the pushout (3) over $D' \xleftarrow{h} D \xrightarrow{g_n} G_{n+1}$ and obtain the required extension diagram and the morphisms $b_{n+1} = d_{n+1} \circ b : B \rightarrow G_{n+1}$ and $c_{n+1} = g'_n \circ c : C \rightarrow G'_{n+1}$. By pushout composition, (P_{n+1}) is a pushout.

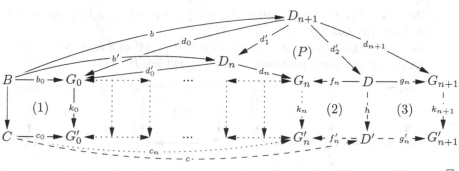

Example 6.15 (Embedding Theorem in $ExAHS$). Consider the transformation sequence $t : S \Rightarrow G \Rightarrow H$ in Example 5.5 and the extension morphism $k : S \rightarrow S'$ given in Example 6.8. In Example 6.13, we have verified that k is consistent with respect to t. We can conclude, from the Embedding Theorem, that there is an extension diagram over k and t. Indeed, this is the diagram presented in Example 6.8.   □

Similarly to the graph case considered in Section 3.4, the next step is to show, in the following Extension Theorem, that the consistency condition is also necessary for the construction of extension diagrams, provided that we have initial pushouts over $\mathcal{M}'$-morphisms. Moreover, we are able to give a direct construction of G'_n in the extension diagram (1) below. This avoids the need to give an explicit construction of $t' : G'_0 \xRightarrow{*} G'_n$.

For technical reasons, we consider again, in addition to the class $\mathcal{M}$ of the (weak) adhesive HLR category, a class $\mathcal{M}'$ with suitable properties; such a class has already been used in Lemma 6.5. In the (typed) graph case, we can take $\mathcal{M}'$ as the class of all (typed) graph morphisms or as the class of all injective (typed) graph morphisms.

Theorem 6.16 (Extension Theorem). *Given a transformation* $t : G_0 \overset{*}{\Rightarrow} G_n$ *with a derived span* $der(t) = (G_0 \overset{d_0}{\leftarrow} D_n \overset{d_n}{\rightarrow} G_n)$ *and an extension diagram* *(1),*

$$
\begin{array}{ccccc}
B & \xrightarrow{\;b_0\;} & G_0 & \overset{*}{=\!=\!t\!\Rightarrow} & G_n \\
\downarrow & & \downarrow k_0 & & \downarrow k_n \\
& (2) & & (1) & \\
C & \longrightarrow & G_0' & \overset{*}{=\!=\!t'\!\Rightarrow} & G_n'
\end{array}
$$

with an initial pushout (2) over $k_0 \in \mathcal{M}'$ *for some class* $\mathcal{M}'$, *closed under pushouts and pullbacks along* $\mathcal{M}$*-morphisms and with initial pushouts over* $\mathcal{M}'$*-morphisms, then we have the following, shown in the diagram below:*

1. k_0 *is consistent with respect to* $t : G_0 \overset{*}{\Rightarrow} G_n$, *with the morphism* $b : B \to D_n$.
2. *There is a direct transformation* $G_0' \Rightarrow G_n'$ *via* $der(t)$ *and* k_0 *given by the pushouts (3) and (4) with* $h, k_n \in \mathcal{M}'$.
3. *There are initial pushouts (5) and (6) over* $h \in \mathcal{M}'$ *and* $k_n \in \mathcal{M}'$, *respectively, with the same boundary–context morphism* $B \to C$.

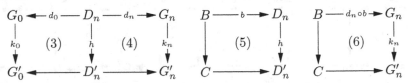

Proof. We prove this theorem by induction over the number of direct transformation steps n.

Basis. $n = 0$, $n = 1$. Given the solid arrows in the following diagram, for $n = 1$ and $t : G_0 \overset{p_0, m_0}{\Longrightarrow} G_1$ with $der(t) = (G_0 \overset{d_0}{\leftarrow} D_0 \overset{d_1}{\rightarrow} G_1)$, we conclude that:

1. k_0 is consistent with respect to t, since (1) is an initial pushout over k_0, and, since (7) is a pushout, we have $b : B \to D_0$ with $d_0 \circ b = b_0$.
2. (7) and (8) correspond to the required pushouts (3) and (4). In fact, (7) is a pushout along the $\mathcal{M}$-morphism d_0 and therefore a pullback. Since $\mathcal{M}'$ is closed under pullbacks along $\mathcal{M}$-morphisms, with $k_0 \in \mathcal{M}'$, it follows that $h_0 \in \mathcal{M}'$ also. (8) is a pushout along the $\mathcal{M}$-morphism d_1, and since $\mathcal{M}'$ is closed under pushouts along $\mathcal{M}$-morphisms, $k_1 \in \mathcal{M}'$ follows.
3. The initial pushouts corresponding to (5) and (6) follow directly from Lemma 6.5, where $d_0 \circ b = b_0$ has already been shown in item 1.

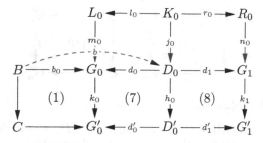

The case $n = 0$ can be dealt with analogously by substituting D_0 and G_1 by G_0, and d_0 and d_1 by id_{G_0}.

Induction step. Consider the transformation $t : G_0 \overset{n}{\Rightarrow} G_n \overset{p_n, m_n}{\Longrightarrow} G_{n+1}$ with a derived span $der(t) = (G_0 \overset{d_0}{\longleftarrow} D_{n+1} \overset{d_{n+1}}{\longrightarrow} G_{n+1})$, the following extension diagram, and the initial pushout (1) over $k_0 : G_0 \to G_0'$. There is then a transformation $t' : G_0 \overset{n}{\Rightarrow} G_n$ with $der(t') = (G_0 \overset{d_0'}{\longleftarrow} D_n \overset{d_n}{\to} G_n)$ such that (P) is the pullback obtained from the construction of the derived span, and we have the result that $d_0' \circ d_1' = d_0$ and $g_n \circ d_2' = d_{n+1}$:

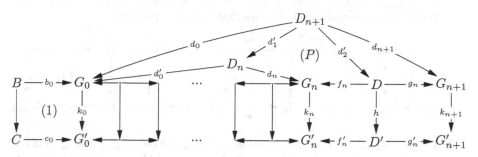

By the induction assumption, k_0 is consistent with respect to t', with a morphism $b' : B \to D_n$ such that $d_0' \circ b' = b_0$, and there exists a transformation $G_0' \Rightarrow G_n'$ via $der(t')$ with initial pushouts (9) over $h_n \in \mathcal{M}'$ and (10) over $k_n \in \mathcal{M}'$:

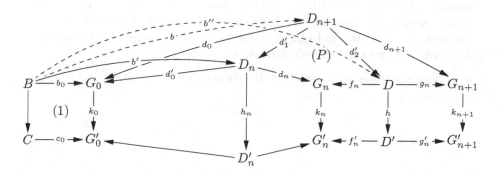

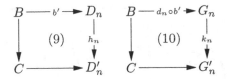

We then have the following:

1. The initiality of (10) implies a morphism $b'' : B \to D$ with $f_n \circ b'' = d_n \circ b'$. Since (P) is a pullback, there is an induced morphism $b : B \to D_{n+1}$ with $d_2' \circ b = b''$ and $d_1' \circ b = b'$. We then have the result that $d_0' \circ d_1' \circ b = d_0' \circ b' = b_0$. Thus k_0 is consistent with respect to t.

2. Since k_0 is consistent with respect to t we can easily construct the transformation $G_0' \Rightarrow G_{n+1}'$ via $der(t)$. First we construct the pushout (13) and obtain the induced morphism $h : D_{n+1}' \to G_0'$. By pushout decomposition, (11) is also a pushout. Lemma 6.5, with the initial pushout (10) over $k_n \in \mathcal{M}'$, implies that there is an initial pushout (14). Since $g_n \circ b'' = g_n \circ d_2' \circ b = d_{n+1} \circ b$ (see item 1), we obtain from the pushout (13), in comparison with the object G_{n+1}', a unique morphism $h' : D_{n+1}' \to G_{n+1}'$, with $h' \circ c = c'$ and $h' \circ h_{n+1} = k_{n+1} \circ d_{n+1}$. By pushout decomposition, it follows that (12) is a pushout.

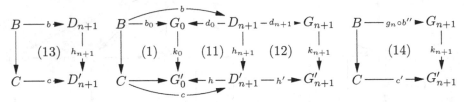

3. Lemma 6.5 states that (13) is an initial pushout over h_{n+1} and (14) is an initial pushout over k_{n+1} with $g_n \circ d_2' \circ b = g_n \circ b''$ (as shown in items 1 and 2).

$\qquad\qquad\qquad\qquad\qquad\qquad\qquad\qquad\qquad\qquad\qquad\qquad\qquad\square$

Example 6.17 (Extension Theorem in $ExAHS$). For the extension diagram in Example 6.8 with the derived span $der(t) = (S \xleftarrow{f \circ k_1} K \xrightarrow{g' \circ k_2} H)$ constructed in Example 6.11, we have shown in Example 6.13 that an initial pushout over k exists and that k is consistent with respect to t. Applying Theorem 6.16, we can conclude further that:

- There is a transformation $S' \Rightarrow H'$ via $der(t)$ and k, with d and k' being injective:

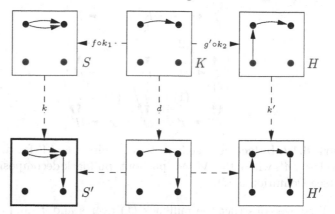

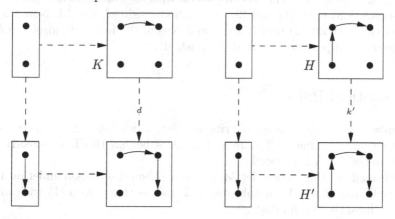

- There are initial pushouts over d and k':

□

In the following, we present a restriction construction which is in some sense inverse to the embedding construction in the Embedding Theorem (Theorem 6.14). The Restriction Theorem, however, is formulated only for direct transformations, in contrast to Theorem 6.14, which is formulated for general transformations. In [Ehr79], it was shown for the graph case that there is a corresponding theorem for the restriction of general graph transformations; however, this requires a consistency condition similar to Definition 6.12. It is most likely that such a general Restriction Theorem can also be formulated for adhesive HLR systems. However, in the following we need only the Restriction Theorem for direct transformations.

Theorem 6.18 (Restriction Theorem). *Given a direct transformation* $G' \overset{p,m'}{\Longrightarrow} H'$, *a morphism* $s : G \to G' \in \mathcal{M}$, *and a match* $m : L \to G$ *such that* $s \circ m = m'$, *then there is a direct transformation* $G \overset{p,m}{\Rightarrow} H$ *leading to the following extension diagram:*

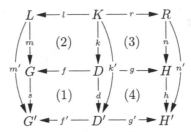

Remark 6.19. In fact, it is sufficient to require $s \in \mathcal{M}'$ for a suitable morphism class $\mathcal{M}'$, where the $\mathcal{M}$–$\mathcal{M}'$ pushout–pullback decomposition property holds (see Definition 5.27).

Proof. First we construct the pullback (1) over s and f' and obtain the induced morphism k from (1) in comparison with $m \circ l$ and k'. From the PO–PB decomposition, both (1) and (2) are pushouts using $l, s \in \mathcal{M}$. Now we construct the pushout (3) over k and r and obtain the induced morphism h; by pushout decomposition, (4) is also a pushout.   □

6.3 Critical Pairs

We now present the concept of critical pairs, which leads in the next section to the Local Confluence Theorem. The ideas behind this have already been given in Section 3.4 of Part I.

Throughout this section, let $\mathcal{M}'$ be a morphism class closed under pushouts and pullbacks along $\mathcal{M}$-morphisms. This means that, given (1) with $m, n \in \mathcal{M}$, we have the results that:

- if (1) is a pushout and $f \in \mathcal{M}'$, then $g \in \mathcal{M}'$ also and
- if (1) is a pullback and $g \in \mathcal{M}'$, then $f \in \mathcal{M}'$ also:

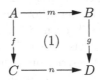

For the completeness of critical pairs considered in Lemma 6.22 and the Local Confluence Theorem given in Theorem 6.28, we need in addition the $\mathcal{M}$–$\mathcal{M}'$ pushout–pullback decomposition property (see Definition 5.27). In the (typed) graph case we take $\mathcal{M}' = \mathcal{M}$ as the class of all injective (typed) graph morphisms, but in Part III, for typed attributed graphs, we shall consider different morphism classes $\mathcal{M}$ and $\mathcal{M}'$.

On the basis of the $\mathcal{E}'$–$\mathcal{M}'$ pair factorization in Definition 5.25, we can define a critical pair as a pair of parallel dependent direct transformations, where both matches are a pair in $\mathcal{E}'$.

Definition 6.20 (critical pair). *Given an $\mathcal{E}'-\mathcal{M}'$ pair factorization, a criti-cal pair is a pair of parallel dependent direct transformations $P_1 \overset{p_1,o_1}{\Longleftarrow} K \overset{p_2,o_2}{\Longrightarrow} P_2$ such that $(o_1, o_2) \in \mathcal{E}'$ for the corresponding matches o_1 and o_2.*

Example 6.21 (critical pairs in $ExAHS$). Consider the adhesive HLR sys-tem $ExAHS$ introduced in Example 5.5. We use an $\mathcal{E}'-\mathcal{M}'$ pair factorization, where there are pairs of jointly epimorphic morphisms in $\mathcal{E}'$, and $\mathcal{M}'$ is the class of all monomorphisms. We then have the following five critical pairs (up to isomorphism).

The first critical pair consists of the productions *addEdge* and *deleteVertex*, where *deleteVertex* deletes the souce node of the edge inserted by *addEdge*. Therefore these transformations are parallel dependent. The choice of the matches and their codomain object makes sure that they are jointly surjective:

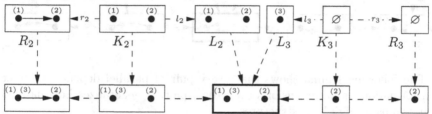

The second critical pair has the same productions *addEdge* and *deleteVertex*, but *deleteVertex* deletes the target node of the edge inserted by *addEdge*:

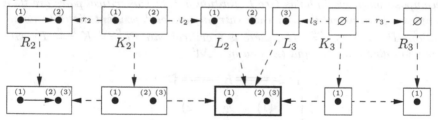

The third critical pair contains the production *deleteVertex* twice: the same vertex is deleted by both transformations:

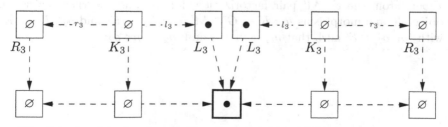

The fourth critical pair contains the production *del1of2edges* twice. The same edge is deleted by both transformations:

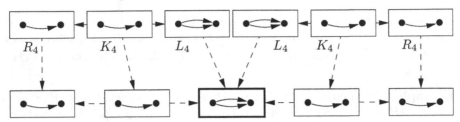

R_4 K_4 L_4 L_4 K_4 R_4

The last critical pair consists also of the production *del1of2edges* twice. In this case, different edges are deleted by the transformations. However, to apply *del1of2edges*, both edges are necessary:

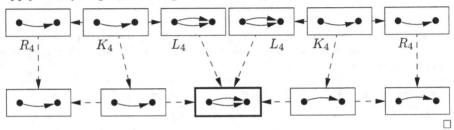

R_4 K_4 L_4 L_4 K_4 R_4

☐

The following lemma shows that every pair of parallel dependent direct transformations is an extension of a critical pair. It generalizes Lemma 3.33 from graphs to high-level structures.

Lemma 6.22 (completeness of critical pairs). *Consider an adhesive HLR system with an $\mathcal{E}'$–$\mathcal{M}'$ pair factorization, where the $\mathcal{M}$–$\mathcal{M}'$ pushout–pullback decomposition property holds (see Definition 5.27). The critical pairs are then complete. This means that for each pair of parallel dependent direct transformations $H_1 \overset{p_1,m_1}{\Longleftarrow} G \overset{p_2,m_2}{\Longrightarrow} H_2$, there is a critical pair $P_1 \overset{p_1,o_1}{\Longleftarrow} K \overset{p_2,o_2}{\Longrightarrow} P_2$ with extension diagrams (1) and (2) and $m \in \mathcal{M}'$:*

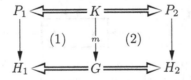

Proof. From the $\mathcal{E}'$–$\mathcal{M}'$ pair factorization, for m_1 and m_2 there exists an object K and morphisms $m : K \to G \in \mathcal{M}'$, $o_1 : L_1 \to K$, and $o_2 : L_2 \to K$, with $(o_1, o_2) \in \mathcal{E}'$ such that $m_1 = m \circ o_1$ and $m_2 = m \circ o_2$:

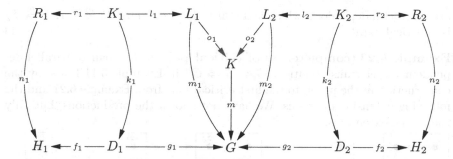

We can construct the required extension diagram. First we construct the pullback (1) over g_1 and m and derive the induced morphism t_1. By applying the $\mathcal{M}$–$\mathcal{M}'$ pushout–pullback decomposition property, we find that both squares (1) and (2) are pushouts, because $l_1 \in \mathcal{M}$ and $m \in \mathcal{M}'$:

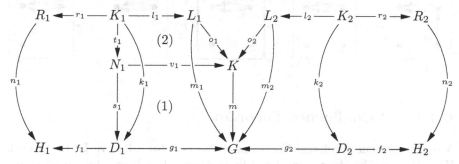

We then construct the pushout (3) over r_1 and t_1 and derive the induced morphism z_1. By pushout decomposition, the square (4) is a pushout. The same construction is applied to the second transformation. This results in the following extension diagrams, where the lower part corresponds to the required extension diagrams (1) and (2) with $m \in \mathcal{M}'$:

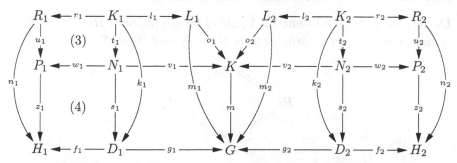

Now we show that $P_1 \Leftarrow K \Rightarrow P_2$ is a critical pair. We know that $(o_1, o_2) \in \mathcal{E}'$, by construction. It remains to show that the pair $P_1 \overset{p_1, o_1}{\Longleftarrow} K \overset{p_2, o_2}{\Longrightarrow} P_2$ is parallel dependent. Otherwise, there are morphisms $i : L_1 \to N_2$ and $j : L_2 \to N_1$ with $v_2 \circ i = o_1$ and $v_1 \circ j = o_2$. Then $g_2 \circ s_2 \circ i = m \circ v_2 \circ i = m \circ o_1 = m_1$ and $g_1 \circ s_1 \circ j = m \circ v_1 \circ j = m \circ o_2 = m_2$, which means that $H_1 \overset{p_1, m_1}{\Longleftarrow} G \overset{p_2, m_2}{\Longrightarrow} H_2$

are parallel independent, which is a contradiction. Thus, $P_1 \overset{p_1,o_1}{\Longleftarrow} K \overset{p_2,o_2}{\Longrightarrow} P_2$ is a critical pair.   □

Example 6.23 (completeness of critical pairs). The pair of parallel dependent direct transformations $G \Leftarrow S \Rightarrow G''$ in Example 5.11 leads, by the construction in the proof, to the first critical pair from Example 6.21 and the following extension diagrams. We have not shown the productions, but only the actual extensions.

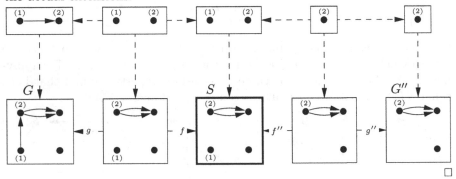

□

6.4 Local Confluence Theorem

We now present the Local Confluence Theorem for adhesive HLR systems. This theorem has been considered in Section 3.4 in Part I for graph transformation systems. As shown in Section 3.4 for graphs and in the following for adhesive HLR systems, local confluence and termination imply confluence, which is the main property of interest. Termination is discussed for the case of graphs in Section 3.4 and analyzed in more detail for the case of typed attributed graph transformation systems in Chapter 12 in Part III.

Definition 6.24 (confluence). *A pair of transformations $H_1 \overset{*}{\Leftarrow} G \overset{*}{\Rightarrow} H_2$ is confluent if there are transformations $H_1 \overset{*}{\Rightarrow} X$ and $H_2 \overset{*}{\Rightarrow} X$:*

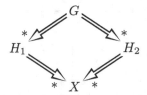

An adhesive HLR system is locally confluent *if this property holds for each pair of direct transformations. The system is* confluent *if this holds for all pairs of transformations.*

Lemma 6.25 (termination and local confluence imply confluence). *Every terminating and locally confluent adhesive HLR system is confluent.*

Proof. See Section C.2.   □

It remains to show local confluence. Roughly speaking, we have to require that all critical pairs are confluent. Unfortunately, however, confluence
of critical pairs is not sufficient to show local confluence. As discussed in Subsection 3.4.3, we need strict confluence of critical pairs, which is defined in
the following.

Definition 6.26 (strict confluence of critical pairs). *A critical pair*
$K \overset{p_1,o_1}{\Longrightarrow} P_1$, $K \overset{p_2,o_2}{\Longrightarrow} P_2$ *is called* strictly confluent, *if we have the following:*

1. Confluence.*: the critical pair is confluent, i.e. there are transformations*
   $P_1 \overset{*}{\Rightarrow} K'$, $P_2 \overset{*}{\Rightarrow} K'$ *with derived spans* $der(P_i \overset{*}{\Rightarrow} K') = (P_i \overset{v_{i+2}}{\leftarrow} N_{i+2} \overset{w_{i+2}}{\rightarrow} K')$ *for* $i = 1, 2$.
2. Strictness. *Let* $der(K \overset{p_i,o_i}{\Longrightarrow} P_i) = (K \overset{v_i}{\leftarrow} N_i \overset{w_i}{\rightarrow} P_i)$ *for* $i = 1, 2$, *and let* N
   be the pullback object of the pullback (1). There are then morphisms z_3
   and z_4 *such that (2), (3), and (4) commute:*

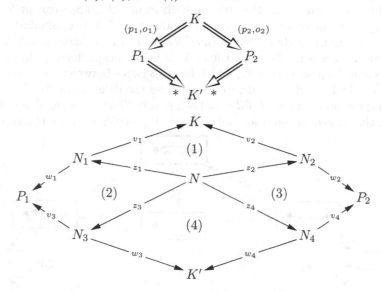

Example 6.27 (strict confluence in *ExAHS*). In our adhesive HLR system *ExAHS*, all critical pairs defined in Example 6.21 are strictly confluent.
The confluence of the first and the second critical pair is established by applying no further transformation to the first graph and applying *addVertex* and
addEdge to the second graph. This is shown in the following diagram for the
first critical pair, and works analogously for the second pair. The strictness
condition holds for the morphisms z_3 and z_4 shown:

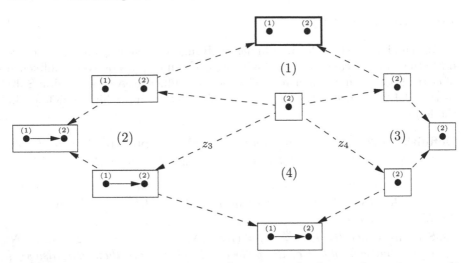

The third critical pair is also confluent, since both transformations result in the empty graph. In the strictness diagram, all graphs except for K are empty, and therefore the strictness condition is fulfilled. Similarly, for the fourth critical pair, both transformations result in the same graph, with two nodes and one edge between them. This is the graph for all objects in the strictness diagram except K, which has two edges between the two nodes.

For the last critical pair, we can reverse the deletion of the edges by applying the production *addEdge* to both graphs. The following diagram shows that the strictness condition holds, since all morphisms are inclusions:

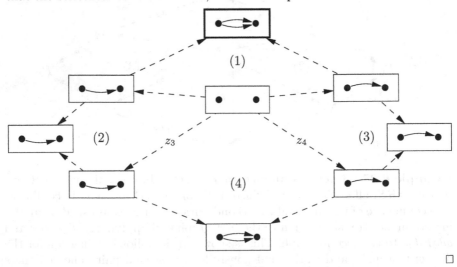

Now we are able to prove the following Local Confluence Theorem for adhesive HLR systems, which generalizes Theorem 3.34 for the graph case. In the special case of graphs, $\mathcal{E}'$ is the class of pairs of jointly surjective (typed)

graph morphisms and $\mathcal{M}' = \mathcal{M}$ is the class of all injective (typed) graph morphisms. In the case of typed attributed graphs considered in Part III, we shall consider different choices for $\mathcal{E}'$, $\mathcal{M}'$, and $\mathcal{M}$.

Theorem 6.28 (Local Confluence Theorem and Critical Pair Lemma). *Given an adhesive HLR system AHS with an $\mathcal{E}'$–$\mathcal{M}'$ pair factorization, let $\mathcal{M}'$ be a morphism class closed under pushouts and pullbacks along $\mathcal{M}$-morphisms, with initial pushouts over $\mathcal{M}'$-morphisms and where the $\mathcal{M}$–$\mathcal{M}'$ pushout–pullback decomposition property is fulfilled. AHS is then locally confluent if all its critical pairs are strictly confluent.*

Proof. For a given pair of direct transformations $H_1 \overset{p_1, m_2}{\Longleftarrow} G \overset{p_2, m_2}{\Longrightarrow} H_2$, we have to show the existence of transformations $t_1' : H_1 \overset{*}{\Rightarrow} G'$ and $t_2' : H_2 \overset{*}{\Rightarrow} G'$.

If the given pair is parallel independent, this follows from Theorem 5.12.

If the given pair is parallel dependent, Lemma 6.22 implies the existence of a critical pair $P_1 \overset{p_1, o_1}{\Longleftarrow} K \overset{p_2, o_2}{\Longrightarrow} P_2$ with the extension diagrams (5) and (6) below, and $m \in \mathcal{M}'$. By assumption, this critical pair is strictly confluent, leading to transformations $t_1 : P_1 \overset{*}{\Rightarrow} K'$, $t_2 : P_2 \overset{*}{\Rightarrow} K'$ and the following diagrams:

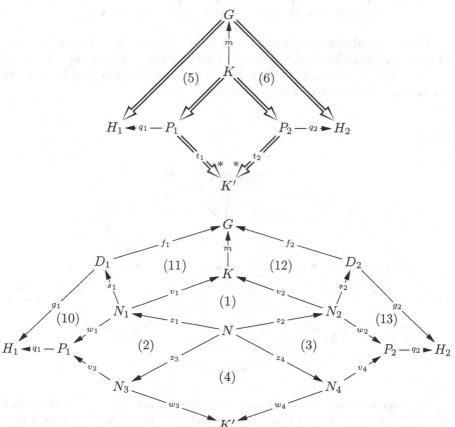

Since $v_1, v_2 \in \mathcal{M}$, (1) is a pullback, and $\mathcal{M}$ is closed under pullbacks, we have the result that $z_1, z_2 \in \mathcal{M}$. The fact that $w_1, w_2, v_3, v_4 \in \mathcal{M}$, (2) and (3) are commutative, and $\mathcal{M}$ is closed under decomposition gives us $z_3, z_4 \in \mathcal{M}$.

Now let (7) be an initial pushout over $m \in \mathcal{M}'$, and consider the double pushouts (10) and (11) corresponding to the extension diagram (5):

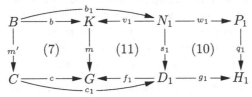

The initiality of (7), applied to the pushout (11), leads to unique morphisms $b_1, c_1 \in \mathcal{M}$ such that $v_1 \circ b_1 = b$, $f_1 \circ c_1 = c$, and (14) is a pushout. By Lemma 6.5, (14) is an initial pushout over s_1 and (15) is an initial pushout over q_1:

$$
\begin{array}{ccccc}
B & \xrightarrow{\;b_1\;} & N_1 & \xrightarrow{\;w_1\;} & P_1 \\
{\scriptstyle m'}\downarrow & (14) & {\scriptstyle s_1}\downarrow & (10) & {\scriptstyle q_1}\downarrow \\
C & \xrightarrow{\;c_1\;} & D_1 & \xrightarrow{\;g_1\;} & H_1
\end{array}
\qquad
\begin{array}{ccc}
B & \xrightarrow{\;w_1 \circ b_1\;} & P_1 \\
{\scriptstyle m'}\downarrow & (15) & {\scriptstyle q_1}\downarrow \\
C & \xrightarrow{\;g_1 \circ c_1\;} & H_1
\end{array}
$$

Dually, we obtain morphisms $b_2, c_2 \in \mathcal{M}$ with $v_2 \circ b_2 = b$ from (12) and (13). Using the pullback property of (1) with $v_1 \circ b_1 = b = v_2 \circ b_2$, we obtain a unique $b_3 : B \to N$ with $z_1 \circ b_3 = b_1$ and $z_2 \circ b_3 = b_2$. Moreover, $b_1, z_1 \in \mathcal{M}$ implies $b_3 \in \mathcal{M}$ by the decomposition property of $\mathcal{M}$:

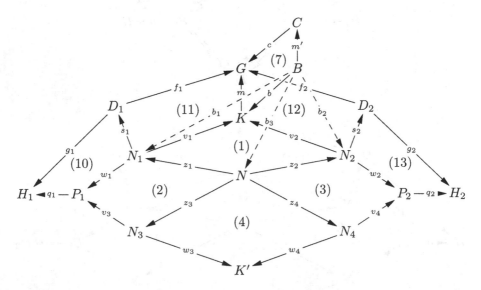

In order to show the consistency of q_1 with respect to t_1, with the initial pushout (15) over q_1, we have to construct $b_3' : B \to N_3 \in \mathcal{M}$ such that

$v_3 \circ b_3' = w_1 \circ b_1$. This holds for $b_3' = z_3 \circ b_3$, since then $v_3 \circ b_3' = v_3 \circ z_3 \circ b_3 \stackrel{(2)}{=} w_1 \circ z_1 \circ b_3 = w_1 \circ b_1$. It holds that $b_3' \in \mathcal{M}$, by the composition of $\mathcal{M}$-morphisms.

Dually, q_2 is consistent with respect to t_2, using $b_4' = z_4 \circ b_3 \in \mathcal{M}$ and the commutativity of (3). By Theorem 6.14, we obtain extension the diagrams (8) and (9), where the morphism $q : K' \to G'$ is the same in both cases:

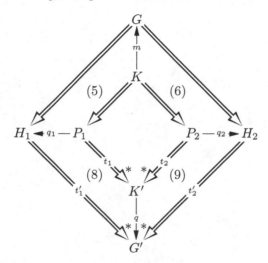

This equality can be shown using part 3 of Theorem 6.16, where q is determined by an initial pushout of $m' : B \to C$ and $w_3 \circ b_3' : B \to K'$ in the first case and $w_4 \circ b_4' : B \to K'$ in the second case, and we have $w_3 \circ b_3' = w_4 \circ b_4'$ given by the commutativity of (4).   □

Example 6.29 (local confluence of $ExAHS$). In $ExAHS$, we have $\mathcal{M}' = \mathcal{M}$ and initial pushouts over injective graph morphisms. Therefore all preconditions for the Local Confluence Theorem are fulfilled. Since all critical pairs in $ExAHS$ are strictly confluent, as shown in Example 6.27, $ExAHS$ is locally confluent.   □

7

Constraints and Application Conditions

Similarly to the graph constraints considered in Part I, we now consider constraints for high-level structures. In particular, we are able to formulate the condition that an object in a (weak) adhesive HLR category must (or must not) contain a certain subobject. We also introduce application conditions for productions in adhesive HLR systems which allow one to restrict the application of productions, similarly to the gluing condition described in Section 6.1.

Constraints and application conditions have already been considered for the graph case in Section 3.5. In this chapter, we present the corresponding abstract version for adhesive HLR systems in Section 7.1. In Sections 7.2 and 7.3, we prove two main results which show how to construct, for each constraint, an equivalent application condition, and for each right application condition an equivalent left application condition. Similar results have been presented for the graph case in [HW95] and for high-level structures in [EEHP04]. In Section 7.4, we combine these results to show the guaranteeing and preservation of constraints.

General Assumptions for Chapter 7

In this chapter, we assume that we have an adhesive HLR system based on a (weak) adhesive HLR category $(\mathbf{C}, \mathcal{M})$. In view of the applications to typed attributed graphs considered in Part III, we also consider an additional class $\mathcal{M}'$ of morphisms in $\mathbf{C}$ corresponding to the injective graph morphisms in Section 3.5 (and to various choices of typed attributed graph morphisms in Chapter 12) in order to define satisfiability.

For the results in this chapter, we need the following properties:

1. $\mathbf{C}$ has binary coproducts (see Definition A.26).
2. $\mathbf{C}$ has a (weak) epi–$\mathcal{M}'$ factorization (see Definition A.15).
3. $\mathcal{M}'$ is closed under composition and decomposition, i.e. $f : A \to B \in \mathcal{M}'$, $g : B \to C \in \mathcal{M}' \Rightarrow g \circ f \in \mathcal{M}'$, and $g \circ f \in \mathcal{M}', g \in \mathcal{M}' \Rightarrow f \in \mathcal{M}'$.

4. $\mathcal{M}'$ is closed under pushouts and pullbacks along $\mathcal{M}$-morphisms, i.e., given a pushout or a pullback (1) with $m \in \mathcal{M}$, $f \in \mathcal{M}'$ or $n \in \mathcal{M}$, $g \in \mathcal{M}'$, respectively, then we also have $g \in \mathcal{M}'$ or $f \in \mathcal{M}'$, respectively:

5. The $\mathcal{M}$–$\mathcal{M}'$ PO–PB decomposition property (see Definition 5.27).

More precisely, we need only the following:

- in Section 7.1, property 3;
- in Section 7.2, properties 1–4;
- in Section 7.3, properties 3–5;
- in Section 7.4, properties 1–5.

Remark 7.1. Note that all of these properties 1–5 are satisfied for the categories of graphs (**Graphs**, $\mathcal{M}$) and typed graphs (**Graphs**$_{\mathbf{TG}}$, $\mathcal{M}$) considered in Part I, where $\mathcal{M} = \mathcal{M}'$ is the class of all injective (typed) graph morphisms. Moreover, for any (weak) adhesive HLR category (**C**, $\mathcal{M}$), properties 3–5 are satisfied for $\mathcal{M}' = \mathcal{M}$.

Alternatively, we can take $\mathcal{M}'$ to be the class of all **C**-morphisms in Sections 7.1 and 7.2, because properties 2–4 are satisfied for arbitrary morphisms. This choice allows us to express satisfiability not only via injective but also via arbitrary morphisms. In Sections 7.3 and 7.4, this does not work, because in general the $\mathcal{M}$–$\mathcal{M}'$ PO–PB decomposition property is not fulfilled for arbitrary morphisms.

7.1 Definition of Constraints and Application Conditions

In this section, we consider structural constraints and application conditions in our general framework. Structural constraints, or "constraints" for short, correspond to the graph constraints in Definition 3.39. While injective graph morphisms were used in Definition 3.39 to define satisfiability we now use $\mathcal{M}'$-morphisms. In this section, we assume property 3 of the general assumptions for this chapter.

Definition 7.2 (constraint). *An* atomic constraint *is of the form* $PC(a)$, *where* $a : P \to C$ *is a morphism.*

A constraint *is a Boolean formula over atomic constraints. This means that* true *and every atomic constraint are constraints, and, for constraints* c *and* c_i *with* $i \in I$ *for some index set* I, *$\neg c$, $\wedge_{i \in I} c_i$, and $\vee_{i \in I} c_i$ are constraints:*

Similarly to Definition 3.39 for graphs, the satisfiability of arbitrary constraints is defined as follows: an object G satisfies a constraint c, written $G \models c$, if

- $c = true$;
- $c = PC(a)$ *and, for every morphism $p : P \to G$ in $\mathcal{M}'$, there exists a morphism $q : C \to G$ in $\mathcal{M}'$ such that $q \circ a = p$;*
- $c = \neg c'$ *and G does not satisfy c';*
- $c = \wedge_{i \in I} c_i$ *and G satisfies all c_i with $i \in I$;*
- $c = \vee_{i \in I} c_i$ *and G satisfies some c_i with $i \in I$.*

Two constraints c and c' are equivalent, denoted by $c \equiv c'$, if for all objects G, $G \models c$ if and only if $G \models c'$.

The constraint $\neg true$ is abbreviated as $false$.

For examples of constraints in the case of (typed) graphs, we refer to Example 3.41.

For a (weak) adhesive HLR category with an initial object O (see Definition A.30), corresponding to the empty graph $\varnothing$ in **Graphs**, constraints of the form $PC(O \to C)$ are abbreviated as $PC(C)$. They ensure the existence of a subobject C in G. In this case $PC(O)$ is equivalent to true.

Remark 7.3. In Definition 7.2 we have required that p and q are in $\mathcal{M}'$, but the morphism a in $PC(a)$ is arbitrary. However, in the case $q \circ a = p$, we can conclude from property 3 of the general assumptions for this chapter that we also have $a \in \mathcal{M}'$. This implies that, for $a \notin \mathcal{M}'$, we have $PC(a : P \to C) \equiv \neg PC(P)$, provided that we have an initial object O and that the initial morphisms $p : O \to G$ are in $\mathcal{M}'$ (see Remark 3.42). In this case atomic constraints $PC(a)$ with $a \notin \mathcal{M}'$ do not give additional expressive power.

In order to express the property that a certain structure C is not in G, although a structure P is in G, we introduce negative atomic constraints. In Fact 7.5, however, we shall see that in most cases negative constraints can be expressed by negation of positive constraints.

Definition 7.4 (negative atomic constraints). *A negative atomic constraint is of the form $NC(a)$, where $a : P \to C$ is a morphism. G satisfies $NC(a)$ if, for every morphism $p : P \to G$ in $\mathcal{M}'$, there does not exist a morphism $q : C \to G$ in $\mathcal{M}'$ with $q \circ a = p$.*

Fact 7.5 (negative atomic constraints). *Consider a (weak) adhesive HLR category with an initial object such that the initial morphisms are in $\mathcal{M}'$.*

Then negative atomic constraints do not give more expressive power. For every negative atomic constraint $NC(a)$, there is an equivalent constraint: $NC(P \xrightarrow{a} C) \equiv \neg PC(C)$, if a is in $\mathcal{M}'$, and $NC(P \xrightarrow{a} C) \equiv true$ otherwise.

Proof. If a is in $\mathcal{M}'$, $G \models NC(a)$ iff for all $p : P \to G$ in $\mathcal{M}'$ there does not exist $q : C \to G$ in $\mathcal{M}'$ such that $q \circ a = p$. This means that there does not exist a $q : C \to G$ in $\mathcal{M}'$, otherwise we would have $p := q \circ a \in \mathcal{M}'$, i.e. $G \not\models NC(a)$. There does not exist a $q : C \to G \in \mathcal{M}'$ iff $G \models \neg PC(C)$.

If a is not in $\mathcal{M}'$, assume that $G \not\models NC(a)$ for some G. Then there exist morphisms $p : P \to G$ in $\mathcal{M}'$ and $q : C \to G$ in $\mathcal{M}'$ with $q \circ a = p$. Now $p \in \mathcal{M}'$ implies $a \in \mathcal{M}'$ by the decomposition property of $\mathcal{M}'$, which is a contradiction. □

Application conditions in the general framework correspond to the application conditions in Definition 3.45. The general definition may be obtained from Definition 3.45 by replacing "graph" by "object" and "injective morphism" by "morphism in $\mathcal{M}'$". In the following, L can be considered as the left-hand side of a production, and $m : L \to G$ as a match. Similarly, L and m can be replaced by R and a comatch $n : R \to H$.

Definition 7.6 (application conditions). *An atomic application condition over an object L is of the form $P(x, \vee_{i \in I} x_i)$, where $x : L \to X$ and $x_i : X \to C_i$, with $i \in I$ for some index set I, are morphisms.*

An application condition over L is a Boolean formula over atomic application conditions over L. This means that true and every atomic application condition are application conditions, and, for application conditions acc and acc_i with $i \in I$, $\neg acc$, $\wedge_{i \in I} acc_i$, and $\vee_{i \in I} acc_i$ are application conditions:

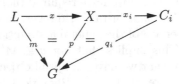

Similarly to Definition 3.45 for graphs, the satisfiability of arbitrary constraints is defined as follows: a morphism $m : L \to G$ satisfies an application condition acc, written $m \models acc$, if

- $acc = true$;
- $acc = P(x, \vee_{i \in I} x_i)$ *and, for all morphisms $p : X \to G \in \mathcal{M}'$ with $p \circ x = m$, there exist an $i \in I$ and a morphism $q_i : C_i \to G \in \mathcal{M}''$ with $q_i \circ x_i = p$;*
- $acc = \neg acc'$ *and m does not satisfy acc';*
- $acc = \wedge_{i \in I} acc_i$ *and m satisfies all acc_i with $i \in I$;*
- $acc = \vee_{i \in I} acc_i$ *and m satisfies some acc_i with $i \in I$.*

Two application conditions acc and acc' over L are equivalent, *denoted by $acc \equiv acc'$, if, for all morphisms m, $m \models acc$ if and only if $m \models acc'$.*

The application condition $\neg true$ is abbreviated as $false$.

Remark 7.7. Application conditions of the form $P(x, \vee_{i \in I} x_i)$ with an empty index set I are equivalent to negative application conditions in the sense of Definition 7.8 (see Fact 7.9).

Examples of application conditions in the case of graphs are given in Example 3.49.

In analogy to the negative application conditions in Definition 3.47 for the graph case, we now introduce negative application conditions in our general framework, where the simple version $NAC(x)$ is especially important. Again, $\mathcal{M}'$-morphisms correspond to injective (typed) graph morphisms.

Definition 7.8 (negative application condition). *A simple negative application condition is of the form $NAC(x)$, where $x : L \to X$ is a morphism. A morphism $m : L \to G$ satisfies $NAC(x)$ if there does not exist a morphism $p : X \to G$ in $\mathcal{M}'$ with $p \circ x = m$:*

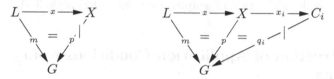

A negative atomic application condition *is of the form $N(x, \wedge_{i \in I} x_i)$, where $x : L \to X$ and $x_i : X \to C_i$, with $i \in I$, are morphisms. A morphism $m : L \to G$ satisfies $N(x, \wedge_{i \in I} x_i)$ if, for all morphisms $p : X \to G$ in $\mathcal{M}'$ with $p \circ x = m$, there does not exist an $i \in I$ and a morphism $q_i : C_i \to G$ in $\mathcal{M}'$ with $q_i \circ x_i = p$.*

Fact 7.9 (negative application condition). *Negative application conditions do not give more expressive power. For every negative application condition, there is an equivalent application condition. For $NAC(x)$ and negative atomic application conditions, we have*

$$NAC(x) \equiv P(x, e) \text{ and } N(x, \wedge_{i \in I} x_i) \equiv \wedge_{i \in I'} NAC(x_i \circ x),$$

where e is an expression with an empty index set and $I' = \{i \in I \mid x_i \in \mathcal{M}'\}$.

Proof. For every $m : L \to G$, $m \models NAC(x)$ iff there does not exist $p : X \to G$ in $\mathcal{M}'$ with $m = p \circ x$. This means that for all $p : X \to G$ in $\mathcal{M}'$, $m = p \circ x$ implies the existence of $i \in \varnothing$, i.e. $m \models P(x, \vee_{i \in I} x_i)$ with $I = \varnothing$.

For the second statement, we show that $N(x, \wedge_{i \in I} x_i) \equiv \wedge_{i \in I'} NAC(x_i \circ x)$ with $I' = \{i \in I \mid x_i \in \mathcal{M}'\}$. From the first statement, we obtain the desired property. For every $m : L \to G$, $m \models N(x, \wedge_{i \in I} x_i)$ iff for all $p : X \to G$ in $\mathcal{M}'$ with $p \circ x = m$ there does not exist an $i \in I$ and $q_i : C_i \to G$ in $\mathcal{M}'$ with $q_i \circ x_i = p$. This means that for all $p : X \to G$ in $\mathcal{M}'$, we have the result that $p \circ x \neq m$ or there do not exist an $i \in I$ and $q_i : C_i \to G$ in $\mathcal{M}'$ with $q_i \circ x_i = p$. This is equivalent to the statement that there do not exist an $i \in I$ and $p : X \to G$ in $\mathcal{M}'$ with $p \circ x = m$, and $q_i : C_i \to G$ in $\mathcal{M}'$ with

$q_i \circ x_i = p$. This means, using the decomposition property of $\mathcal{M}'$, that there do not exist an $i \in I'$ and $q_i : C_i \to G$ in $\mathcal{M}'$ with $q_i \circ x_i \circ x = m$. Therefore, for all $i \in I'$, there does not exist a $q_i : C_i \to G$ in $\mathcal{M}'$ with $q_i \circ x_i \circ x = m$, i.e. $m \models \wedge_{i \in I'} NAC(x_i \circ x)$.   □

Similarly to Definition 3.50, we now define application conditions for productions.

Definition 7.10 (application condition for a production). *Given a production* $p = (L \xleftarrow{l} K \xrightarrow{r} R)$, *an application condition* $A(p) = (A_L, A_R)$ *for p consists of a left application condition* A_L *over L and a right application condition* A_R *over R.*

A direct transformation $G \overset{p,m}{\Rightarrow} H$ *with comatch* $n : R \to H$ *satisfies the application condition* $A(p) = (A_L, A_R)$ *if* $m \models A_L$ *and* $n \models A_R$.

For an example in the case of graphs, we refer to Example 3.51.

7.2 Construction of Application Conditions from Constraints

In this section, we shall show that for each atomic constraint $PC(a)$ with $a : P \to C \in \mathcal{M}$, there is an equivalent application condition. If $G \overset{p,m}{\Longrightarrow} H$ is a direct transformation and $PC(a)$ is an atomic constraint for H with $a \in \mathcal{M}$, then we are able to construct a right application condition $Acc(PC(a))$ such that the comatch n satisfies $Acc(PC(a))$ if and only if H satisfies $PC(a)$. Taking this together with the main result of the next section, we can construct a left application condition $L_p(Acc(PC(a)))$ such that the match $m : L \to G$ satisfies $L_p(Acc(PC(a)))$ if and only if H satisfies $PC(a)$. This result is most important for all kinds of applications.

In this section, we assume properties 1–4 of the general assumptions for this chapter.

First, we describe the construction of application conditions from constraints. In our terminology, R corresponds to the right-hand side of a production and $PC(a)$ is intended to be a constraint for H, where $G \overset{p,m}{\Longrightarrow} H$ is a direct transformation with comatch n. $Acc(PC(a))$ is intended to be the equivalent right application condition for the comatch n. However, by replacing R by L, H by G, and n by m, we can also consider the construction as a left application condition corresponding to a constraint for G.

Definition 7.11 (construction of application conditions from constraints). *For atomic constraints* $PC(a)$ *with a morphism* $a : P \to C \in \mathcal{M}$ *and an object R, we define*

$$Acc(PC(a)) = \wedge_S P(R \xrightarrow{s} S, \vee_{i \in I} S \overset{t_i \circ t}{\Rightarrow} T_i),$$

where $P(R \xrightarrow{s} S, \vee_{i \in I} S \xrightarrow{t_i \circ t} T_i)$ *is an atomic application condition over* R *(see Definition 7.6) and* I *depends on the choice of* S:

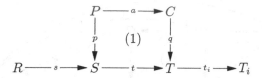

- *The conjunction* $\wedge_S$ *ranges over all "gluings"* S *of* R *and* P. *More precisely, it ranges over all triples* $\langle S, s, p \rangle$ *with arbitrary* $s\colon R \to S$ *and* $p\colon P \to S$ *in* $\mathcal{M}'$ *such that the pair* (s, p) *is jointly epimorphic (see Definition A.16). For each such triple* $\langle S, s, p \rangle$, *we construct the pushout (1) of* p *and* a, *leading to* $t\colon S \to T \in \mathcal{M}$ *and* $q\colon C \to T \in \mathcal{M}'$.
- *For each* S, *the disjunction* $\vee_{i \in I}$ *ranges over all* $S \xrightarrow{t_i \circ t} T_i$ *with an epimorphism* t_i *such that* $t_i \circ t$ *and* $t_i \circ q$ *are in* $\mathcal{M}'$. *For* $I = \varnothing$, *we have* $P(R \xrightarrow{s} S, \vee_{i \in I} S \xrightarrow{t_i \circ t} T_i) = \mathrm{NAC}(R \xrightarrow{s} S)$.

The construction can be extended to Boolean formulas over atomic constraints: $\mathrm{Acc}(true) = true$ *and for constraints* c, c_j *with* $j \in J$, $\mathrm{Acc}(\neg c) = \neg \mathrm{Acc}(c)$, $\mathrm{Acc}(\wedge_{j \in J} c_j) = \wedge_{j \in J} \mathrm{Acc}(c_j)$, *and* $\mathrm{Acc}(\vee_{j \in J} c_j) = \vee_{j \in J} \mathrm{Acc}(c_j)$.

Remark 7.12. In the special case of (typed) graphs in the sense of Section 3.5, we have $\mathcal{M} = \mathcal{M}'$ as the class of all injective (typed) graph morphisms and "jointly epimorphic" means "jointly surjective".

The requirement $a \in \mathcal{M}$ makes sure that the pushout (1) exists. It can be avoided if the existence of pushout (1) can be guaranteed by other means, for example in the case $\mathcal{M}' = \mathcal{M}$, because we have $p \in \mathcal{M}'$.

Theorem 7.13 (construction of application conditions from constraints). *There is a construction* Acc *such that for every constraint* c *built up from atomic constraints* $a : P \to C \in \mathcal{M}$ *and every object* R, $\mathrm{Acc}(c)$ *is an application condition over* R *with the property that, for all morphisms* $n\colon R \to H$,

$$n \models \mathrm{Acc}(c) \quad \Longleftrightarrow \quad H \models c.$$

Proof. The main part of the proof is to show that the statement holds for atomic constraints.

If. Let $n \models \mathrm{Acc}(\mathrm{PC}(a))$. We have to show that $H \models \mathrm{PC}(a)$, i.e., for all morphisms $p'\colon P \to H$ in $\mathcal{M}'$, there is a morphism $q'\colon C \to H$ in $\mathcal{M}'$ with $q' \circ a = p'$.

We have $n \models \mathrm{Acc}(\mathrm{PC}(a)) = \wedge_S P(R \xrightarrow{s} S, \vee_{i \in I} S \xrightarrow{t_i \circ t} T_i)$, and therefore for each gluing S of R and P we have $n \models P(R \xrightarrow{s} S, \vee_{i \in I} S \xrightarrow{t_i \circ t} T_i)$.

First we construct the coproduct $R + P$ with injections in_R and in_P in the following diagram. From the universal property of coproducts, for a given morphism $p'\colon P \to H$ in $\mathcal{M}'$ and n there is a unique morphism $f\colon R + P \to H$

with $f \circ in_R = n$ and $f \circ in_P = p'$. Now let $f = p'' \circ e$ be an epi–$\mathcal{M}'$ factorization of f with an epimorphism e and $p'' \in \mathcal{M}'$.

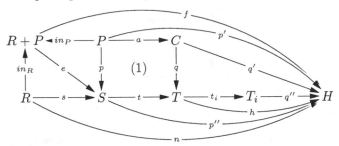

We define $s = e \circ in_R$ and $p = e \circ in_P$. The pair (s, p) is then jointly epimorphic, because e is an epimorphism, and p is in $\mathcal{M}'$, because $p'' \circ p = p'' \circ e \circ in_P = f \circ in_P = p'$ is in $\mathcal{M}'$ and $\mathcal{M}'$-morphisms are closed under decomposition.

Hence $\langle S, s, p \rangle$ belongs to the conjunction $\wedge_S$ of $Acc(PC(a))$, and we construct the pushout (1) with pushout object T and morphisms $t \in \mathcal{M}$ and $q \in \mathcal{M}'$. Moreover, we have $p'' \circ s = p'' \circ e \circ in_R = f \circ in_R = n$.

In the case $I \neq \varnothing$, $n \models Acc(PC(a))$ implies the existence of $i \in I$ and $q'' : T_i \to H \in \mathcal{M}'$ with $q'' \circ t_i \circ t = p''$. Now let $q' = q'' \circ t_i \circ q$. Then q' is in $\mathcal{M}'$, because $q'' \in \mathcal{M}'$ by construction, $t_i \circ q \in \mathcal{M}'$ by step 2 in the construction, and $\mathcal{M}'$-morphisms are closed under composition. Finally, we have $H \models PC(a)$, because $q' \circ a = q'' \circ t_i \circ q \circ a = q'' \circ t_i \circ t \circ p = p'' \circ p = p'$.

In the case $I = \varnothing$, the existence of $p'' \in \mathcal{M}'$ with $p'' \circ s = n$ contradicts $n \models Acc(PC(a)) = \wedge_S NAC(s)$. Hence our assumption that we have a $p' : P \to H \in \mathcal{M}'$ is false, which implies $H \models PC(a)$.

Only if. Let $H \models PC(a)$. We have to show that $n \models Acc(PC(a))$, i.e., for all triples $\langle S, s, p \rangle$ constructed in the first step of Definition 7.11 and all $p'' : S \to H \in \mathcal{M}'$ with $p'' \circ s = n$, we have to find an $i \in I$ and a morphism $q'' : T_i \to H \in \mathcal{M}'$ with $q'' \circ t_i \circ t = p''$.

Given $\langle S, s, p \rangle$ and p'' in $\mathcal{M}'$ as above, we define $p' = p'' \circ p : P \to H$. Then $p' \in \mathcal{M}'$, because p and p'' are $\mathcal{M}'$-morphisms and $\mathcal{M}'$ is closed under composition.

$H \models PC(a)$ implies the existence of $q' : C \to H \in \mathcal{M}'$ with $q' \circ a = p'$. Hence $p'' \circ p = p' = q' \circ a$. The universal property of pushout (1) implies the existence of a unique morphism $h : T \to H$ with $h \circ t = p''$ and $h \circ q = q'$.

Now let $h = q'' \circ e'$ be an epi–$\mathcal{M}'$ factorization of h with an epimorphism e' and $q'' \in \mathcal{M}'$. The decomposition property of $\mathcal{M}'$ and $q'' \circ e' \circ t = h \circ t = p'' \in \mathcal{M}'$ then imply that $e' \circ t \in \mathcal{M}'$, and $q'' \circ e' \circ q = h \circ q = q' \in \mathcal{M}'$ implies $e' \circ q \in \mathcal{M}'$. Hence, according to the second step of the construction in Definition 7.11, $e' \circ t$ belongs to the family $(S \overset{t_i \circ t}{\to} T_i)_{i \in I}$ of $Acc(PC(a))$ such that $e' = t_i : T \to T_i$ for some $i \in I$.

In the case $I \neq \varnothing$, we have $q'' \in \mathcal{M}'$, and $q'' \circ t_i \circ t = q'' \circ e' \circ t = h \circ t = p''$ implies $n \models Acc(PC(a))$.

In the case $I = \varnothing$, we have a contradiction. This means that our assumption that we have $p'' \in \mathcal{M}'$ with $p'' \circ s = n$ is false. This implies $n \models \wedge_S \mathrm{NAC}(s) = \mathrm{Acc}(\mathrm{PC}(a))$.

Thus, the statement holds for atomic constraints. For arbitrary constraints, the proof of the statement is straightforward. □

Example 7.14 (construction of application conditions for graphs). In the category **Graphs** of graphs, we take $\mathcal{M} = \mathcal{M}'$ as the class of all monomorphisms. Now consider the atomic graph constraint $c = \mathrm{PC}(\mathsf{o} \to \mathsf{8})$ and the right-hand side of the production $p = \langle \mathsf{o\,o} \leftarrow \mathsf{o\,o} \to \mathsf{o\text{-}o} \rangle$. According to Definition 7.11, the graph constraint c can be transformed into the following conjunction of five atomic application conditions:

$$\mathrm{Acc}(c) = \wedge_{j=1}^{4} \mathrm{P}(\mathsf{o\text{-}o} \to S_j, S_j \to T_j) \wedge \mathrm{P}(\mathsf{o\text{-}o} \to S_5, \vee_{i=1}^{2} S_5 \to T_{5i}),$$

where S_j, T_j, T_{5i} are shown below, and the set I in the disjunction of Definition 7.11 has cardinality 1 for $j = 1, \ldots, 4$ and cardinality 2 for $j = 5$. Note that $S_1, \ldots, S_5$ are all possible gluings of R and P, and $T_1, \ldots, T_5$ are the corresponding gluings of S_1 and C via P. For $j = 1, \ldots, 4$, the identical morphism $t_i = id_{T_i} : T_i \to T_i$ is the only possible epimorphism t_i such that $t_i \circ t$ and $t_i \circ q$ are injective. For $j = 5$, we have $t_{5i} : T_5 \to T_{5i}$ $(i = 1, 2)$, with the corresponding property.

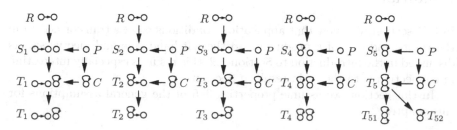

This condition expresses the application condition "Every node outside (see T_1, T_4) and inside (see T_2, T_3, T_{51}, T_{52}) the morphism must have a loop", where S_1, S_2, S_3 correspond to injective and S_4, S_5 to noninjective morphisms. This means that, for every morphism $n : R \to H$, every node of H must have a loop, which is equivalent to $H \models \mathrm{PC}(\mathsf{o} \to \mathsf{8})$. □

Example 7.15 (construction of application conditions for Petri nets). In the category **PTNets** of place/transition nets, we take $\mathcal{M}' = \mathcal{M}$ as the class of all injective morphisms in **PTNets** (see Fact 4.21). Now consider the net constraint $c = \neg\mathrm{PC}(\varnothing \to \mathsf{o\text{-}\square})$, where $\varnothing$ is the empty net, and the right-hand side of a production $p = \langle \mathsf{o\text{-}\square\text{-}o} \leftarrow \mathsf{o\,o} \to \mathsf{o\text{-}\square\text{-}o} \rangle$. A net H satisfies the constraint c if the net H does not contain a subnet of the form $\mathsf{o\text{-}\square}$; we call such a place a "sink place". According to Definition 7.11, the net constraint c can be transformed into the application condition

$$\mathrm{Acc}(c) = \neg(\ \mathrm{P}(R \to S_1, \vee_{i=1}^{3} S_1 \to T_{1i}\ ) \wedge \mathrm{P}(R \to S_2, \vee_{i=1}^{2} S_2 \to T_{2i})),$$

where R, S_1, S_2, and T_{ij} are given below. This condition means "No sink place is allowed to be outside or inside the morphism, i.e. no sink place is allowed in H"; here S_1 takes care of injective and S_2 of noninjective morphisms $n\colon R \to H$.

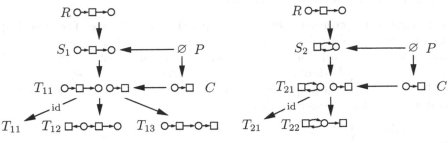

An example with $\mathcal{M}' \neq \mathcal{M}$ will be discussed for typed attributed graphs in Example 12.10.

7.3 Construction of Left from Right Application Conditions

In this section, we show that application conditions can be transformed from the right-hand side of a production to the left-hand side and vice versa. As discussed in the introduction to Section 7.2, this result is especially interesting in connection with the main result in Section 7.2.

In this section, we assume properties 3–5 of the general assumptions for this chapter.

Definition 7.16 (construction of left from right application conditions). *For each right atomic application condition* acc $= \mathrm{P}(R \xrightarrow{x} X,$ $\vee_{i \in I} X \xrightarrow{x_i} C_i)$ *of a production* $p = (L \leftarrow K \to R)$, *let*

$$\mathrm{L}_p(\mathrm{acc}) = \mathrm{P}(L \xrightarrow{y} Y, \vee_{i \in I'} Y \xrightarrow{y_i} D_i) \text{ with } I' \subseteq I \text{ or } \mathrm{L}_p(\mathrm{acc}) = true,$$

where y, y_i, and I are constructed as follows:

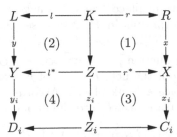

- If the pair $(K \xrightarrow{r} R, R \xrightarrow{x} X)$ has a pushout complement, we define $(K \rightarrow Z, Z \xrightarrow{r^*} X)$ as the pushout complement (1). We then construct pushout (2) with the morphism $y \colon L \rightarrow Y$. Otherwise, $L_p(\mathrm{acc}) = true$.

- For each $i \in I$, if the pair $(Z \xrightarrow{r^*} X, X \xrightarrow{x_i} C_i)$ has a pushout complement, then $i \in I'$, and we define $(Z \xrightarrow{z_i} Z_i, Z_i \rightarrow C_i)$ as the pushout complement (3). We then construct pushout (4) with morphism $y_i \colon Y \rightarrow D_i$. Otherwise, $i \notin I'$.

According to Chapter 4, pushout complements of $\mathcal{M}$-morphisms (if they exist) are unique up to isomorphism. Therefore, the construction of a left application condition is unique up to isomorphism. The transformation can be extended to arbitrary right application conditions as follows: $L_p(true) = true$, $L_p(\neg \mathrm{acc}) = \neg L_p(\mathrm{acc})$, $L_p(\wedge_{i \in I} \mathrm{acc}_i) = \wedge_{i \in I} L_p(\mathrm{acc}_i)$, and $L_p(\vee_{i \in I} \mathrm{acc}_i) = \vee_{i \in I} L_p(\mathrm{acc}_i)$.

Theorem 7.17 (construction of left from right application conditions). *For every production p, and for every right application condition acc for p, $L_p(\mathrm{acc})$ as defined in Definition 7.16 is a left application condition for p with the property that, for all direct transformations $G \xRightarrow{p,m} H$ with comatch n,*

$$m \models L_p(\mathrm{acc}) \Leftrightarrow n \models \mathrm{acc}.$$

Proof. The main part of the proof is to prove the statement for right atomic application conditions. Let $G \xRightarrow{p,m} H$ be any direct transformation with co-match n. We then have the following cases:

Case 1. The pair $(r \colon K \rightarrow R, x \colon R \rightarrow X)$ has no pushout complement. Then $L_p(\mathrm{acc}) = true$ and $m \models L_p(\mathrm{acc})$. We have to show that $n \models \mathrm{acc}$. This is true because there is no $p \colon X \rightarrow H$ with $p \in \mathcal{M}'$ and $p \circ x = n$.

Otherwise, since the pair (r, n) has a pushout complement, the pair (r, x) would have a pushout complement ($\mathcal{M}$–$\mathcal{M}'$ pushout–pullback decomposition, with $r \in \mathcal{M}$ and $p \in \mathcal{M}'$). This is a contradiction.

Case 2. The pair $(r \colon K \rightarrow R, x \colon R \rightarrow X)$ has a pushout complement and $I \neq \varnothing$.

Case 2.1. $m \models L_p(\mathrm{acc})$. We have to show that $n \models \mathrm{acc}$, i.e., given a morphism $p \colon X \rightarrow H \in \mathcal{M}'$ with $p \circ x = n$, we have to find an $i \in I$ and a morphism $q \colon C_i \rightarrow H \in \mathcal{M}'$ with $q \circ x_i = p$.

Using Theorem 6.18, we obtain from the double pushout for $G \xRightarrow{p,m} H$ (more precisely, from the inverse transformation) with $p \circ x = n$ a decomposition into pushouts (1), (2), (5), and (6) shown below with $r, r^*, d_1, l, l^*, d_2 \in \mathcal{M}$ and $p, z, p' \in \mathcal{M}'$. (1) and (2) are the same pushouts as in the construction in Definition 7.16 because of the uniqueness of pushouts and pushout complements.

In the case $I' = \varnothing$, we have no $p \colon X \rightarrow H$ with $p \in \mathcal{M}'$ and $p \circ x = n$, because this would imply the existence of a $p' \colon Y \rightarrow G$ with $p' \in \mathcal{M}'$ and

$p' \circ y = m$, violating $m \models L_p(\text{acc})$. Having no p with $p \circ x = n$, however, implies that $n \models \text{acc}$.

In the case $I' \neq \varnothing$, the assumption $m \models L_p(\text{acc})$ implies the existence of an $i \in I' \subseteq I$ with a morphism $y_i \colon Y \to D_i$, and $q' \colon D_i \to G$ in $\mathcal{M}'$ with $q' \circ y_i = p'$. Now we are able to decompose pushouts (6) and (5) into pushouts (4) + (8) and (3) + (7), respectively, using Theorem 6.18 again and interpreting $(Y \xleftarrow{l^*} Z \xrightarrow{r^*} X)$ as a production. This leads to a morphism $q \colon C_i \to H \in \mathcal{M}'$ with $q \circ x_i = p$, and therefore $n \models \text{acc}$.

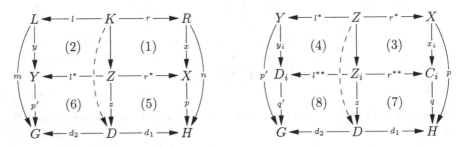

Case 2.2. $n \models \text{acc}$. We have to show that $m \models L_p(\text{acc})$. From the statement above that defines Case 2, we have $L_p(\text{acc}) \neq true$. Hence, for each morphism $p' \colon Y \to G \in \mathcal{M}'$ with $p' \circ y = m$, we have to find an $i \in I'$ and a morphism $q' \colon D_i \to G \in \mathcal{M}'$ with $q' \circ y_i = p'$.

Given a morphism $p' \in \mathcal{M}'$ with $p' \circ y = m$, we can construct the pushouts (1), (2), (5), and (6) as above using Theorem 6.18, leading to a morphism $p \colon X \to H \in \mathcal{M}$ with $p \circ x = n$. Now $n \models \text{acc}$ implies the existence of $i \in I$ and morphisms $q \colon C_i \to H \in \mathcal{M}'$ and $x_i \colon X \to C_i$ with $q \circ x_i = p$. Owing to pushout (5), the pair (r^*, p) has a pushout complement, so that this is also true for (r^*, x_i) by decomposition. Hence we have an $i \in I'$ and can decompose the pushouts (5) and (6) into the pushouts (3) + (7) and (4) + (8) from right to left, leading to a morphism $q' \colon D_i \to G \in \mathcal{M}'$ with $q' \circ y_i = p'$. This implies that $m \models L_p(\text{acc})$.

Case 3. The pair (r, x) has a pushout complement, but $I = \varnothing$. Then $n \not\models \text{acc} = \text{NAC}(x)$ implies that $p \in \mathcal{M}$ with $p \circ x = n$. As shown for Case 2.1, we obtain $p' \in \mathcal{M}'$ with $p' \circ y = m$, which implies that $m \not\models \text{NAC}(y)$. Vice versa, $m \not\models L_p(\text{acc}) = \text{NAC}(y)$ implies in a similar way that $n \not\models \text{NAC}(x)$, using the construction in Case 2.2.

Thus, the statement holds for right atomic application conditions. For arbitrary right application conditions, the proof of the statement is straightforward. $\qquad\square$

Example 7.18 (construction of left from right application conditions). For the adhesive HLR category **Graphs** of graphs, where $\mathcal{M} = \mathcal{M}'$ is the class of all injective graph morphisms, consider the right application condition acc = NAC($\bigcirc\,\bigcirc \atop {\scriptstyle 1\ \ 2}$ → $\bigcirc\!\!\!-\!\!\!\bigcirc \atop {\scriptstyle 1\ \ 2}$) for the production $p = (\bigcirc\!\!-\!\!\bigcirc \leftarrow \bigcirc\,\bigcirc \atop {\scriptstyle 1\ \ 2} \to \bigcirc\,\bigcirc \atop {\scriptstyle 1\ \ 2})$, meaning that an edge between the nodes in the comatch must not exist. We have $NAC(R \to X) \equiv P(R \to X, e)$, where e has an empty index set $I = \varnothing$.

Now we construct Z and the pushout complement (1), and then construct Y as the pushout object of pushout (2) as shown below. In accordance with Definition 7.16, acc is transformed into the left atomic application condition $L_p(\text{acc}) = P(L \to Y, e) \equiv NAC(\bigcirc\!\!-\!\!\bigcirc \atop {\scriptstyle 1\ \ 2} \to \bigcirc\!\!\!\supset\!\!\!\subset\!\!\!\bigcirc \atop {\scriptstyle 1\ \ 2})$ with $I' = \varnothing$, meaning that two parallel edges between the nodes in the match must not exist.

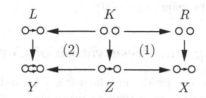

Example 7.19 (construction of left from right application conditions for Petri nets). For the weak adhesive HLR category **PTNets** of place/transition nets, where $\mathcal{M} = \mathcal{M}'$ is the class of all injective morphisms in **PTNets**, consider the right application condition acc $= \neg P(R \to X, X \to C)$ for the production $p = (\bigcirc\!\!\Leftarrow\!\!\square\!\!\Rightarrow\!\!\bigcirc \leftarrow \bigcirc\,\bigcirc \to \bigcirc\!\!-\!\!\square\!\!-\!\!\bigcirc)$ in Example 7.15, where $R \to X = R \to S_2$ and $X \to C = S_2 \to T_{22}$. This means that we consider only a subcase of the right application condition constructed in Example 7.15.

$H \models$ acc means that for each noninjective comatch $n \colon R \to H$, the place in $n(R)$ must not be a sink place. In accordance with Definition 7.16, we obtain the left application condition $L_p(\text{acc}) = \neg P(L \to Y, Y \to D)$ shown below. $G \models L_p(\text{acc})$ means that for each noninjective match $m \colon L \to G$, the place in $m(L)$ must not be a sink place. Note that a noninjective match $m \colon L \to G$ can only identify the places, because otherwise the gluing condition would be violated.

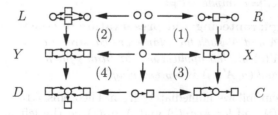

Remark 7.20. For the double-pushout approach with match and comatch morphisms in $\mathcal{M}'$, there is a result similar to Theorem 7.17: for every production p, there is a construction L_p, as given in Definition 7.16, such that for every right application condition acc for p, $L_p(\text{acc})$ is a left application condition for p. For all direct transformations $G \stackrel{p,m}{\Longrightarrow} H$ with $m \in \mathcal{M}'$ and a comatch $n \in \mathcal{M}'$, we have

$$m \models \mathrm{L}_p(\mathrm{acc}) \quad \Longleftrightarrow \quad n \models \mathrm{acc}.$$

Remark 7.21. For every production p, there is also a transformation $\mathrm{L}_{p^{-1}}$ such that for every left application condition acc for p, $\mathrm{L}_{p^{-1}}(\mathrm{acc})$ is a right application condition for p with the property that, for all direct transformations $G \stackrel{p,m}{\Longrightarrow} H$ with comatch n, $n \models \mathrm{L}_{p^{-1}}(\mathrm{acc}) \Leftrightarrow m \models \mathrm{acc}$. A left application condition acc of p is the right application condition of the inverse rule $p^{-1} = (R \leftarrow K \rightarrow L)$ of p. By Theorem 7.17, acc can be transformed into a left application condition $\mathrm{L}_{p^{-1}}(\mathrm{acc})$ of p^{-1}, being a right application condition of p. Then $\mathrm{L}_{p^{-1}}$ has the wanted property.

7.4 Guaranteeing and Preservation of Constraints

In this section, we use the results in Theorems 7.13 and 7.17 for integrating constraints into application conditions of productions such that every direct transformation satisfying the application condition is constraint-guaranteeing and constraint-preserving, respectively. We consider productions with integrated application conditions. Every production in the sense of Definition 5.1 is a production. If p is a production and A an application condition for p, then (p, A) is an extended production. A direct transformation $G \stackrel{(p,A),m}{\Longrightarrow} H$ is a direct transformation $G \stackrel{p,m}{\Longrightarrow} H$ that satisfies the application condition A.

In this section, we assume properties 1–5 of the general assumptions for this chapter.

Definition 7.22 (guaranteeing and preservation of constraints). *Given a constraint c, an extended production (p, A) is*

- *c-guaranteeing if, for all direct transformations $G \stackrel{(p,A),m}{\Longrightarrow} H$, it holds that $H \models c$; and*
- *c-preserving if, for all direct transformations $G \stackrel{(p,A),m}{\Longrightarrow} H$, we have the condition that $G \models c$ implies $H \models c$.*

Theorem 7.23 (guaranteeing and preservation of constraints). *There are constructions A and A' such that, for every constraint c and every production p, $A(c)$ and $A'(c)$ are left application conditions for p such that $(p, A(c))$ is c-guaranteeing and $(p, A'(c))$ is c-preserving.*

Proof. This theorem follows immediately from Theorems 7.13 and 7.17. Let $p = (L \leftarrow K \rightarrow R)$ and let $\mathrm{Acc}_L(c)$ and $\mathrm{Acc}_R(c)$ be the left and the right application condition, respectively, of c, where $\mathrm{Acc}_R(c) = \mathrm{Acc}(c)$ as given in Definition 7.11 and $\mathrm{Acc}_L(c)$ is defined similarly with R replaced by L.

Now let $\mathrm{L}_p(\mathrm{Acc}_R(c))$ be the left application condition corresponding to $\mathrm{Acc}_R(c)$, as given in Definition 7.16. Let $A(c) = \mathrm{L}_p(\mathrm{Acc}_R(c))$ and $A'(c) = (\mathrm{Acc}_L(c) \Rightarrow \mathrm{L}_p(\mathrm{Acc}_R(c)))$, where $A \Rightarrow B$ denotes $\neg A \vee B$. Then the left application conditions $A(c)$ and $A'(c)$ have the required properties, from Theorems 7.13 and 7.17:

- Given $G \overset{(p,A(c)),m}{\Longrightarrow} H$ with a comatch n, we have $H \models c$ iff $n \models \mathrm{Acc}_R(c)$ iff $m \models \mathrm{L}_p(\mathrm{Acc}_R(c))$ iff $m \models A(c)$, which is *true* by assumption.

- Given $G \overset{(p,A'(c)),m}{\Longrightarrow} H$ with a comatch n, $G \models c$ implies that $H \models c$ is equivalent to $\neg(G \models c) \lor H \models c$. This is true iff $\neg(m \models \mathrm{Acc}_L(c)) \lor n \models \mathrm{Acc}_R(c)$, which means that $\neg(m \models \mathrm{Acc}_L(c)) \lor m \models \mathrm{L}_p(\mathrm{Acc}_R(c))$, i.e. $m \models \neg\mathrm{Acc}_L(c) \lor \mathrm{L}_p(\mathrm{Acc}_R(c))$. This is equivalent to $m \models A'(c)$, which is *true* by assumption. $\qquad \square$

Typed Attributed Graph Transformation
Systems

In Parts I and II, we have presented an introduction to the classical case of graph and typed graph transformation systems and a general categorical theory based on adhesive high-level replacement (HLR) categories and systems, respectively. This categorical theory can be instantiated not only to the classical case, but also to graph transformations based on several other kinds of graphs, such as hypergraphs and attributed graphs, and various kinds of Petri nets. Several of these instantiations have been discussed in Section 5.2.

In the present Part, we study typed attributed graph transformation systems in full detail. The concept of typed attributed graph transformation is most significant for modeling and metamodeling in software engineering and visual languages. Hence it is important to have an adequate theory for this approach to graph transformation.

The main purpose of Part III is to provide the basic concepts and results of graph transformation for typed attributed graphs; these concepts and results correspond to those already known for the case of graphs [Ehr79]. The straightforward way would be to extend the classical theory in Part I step by step, first to attributed graphs and then to typed attributed graphs. Following [EPT04], however, we propose the more elegant solution of obtaining the theory of typed attributed graph transformation as an instantiation of the "adhesive HLR categories and systems" presented in Part II.

In Chapter 8, we give a formalization of typed attributed graphs, which allows node and edge attribution, and we show how to construct pushouts and pullbacks in the corresponding category **AGraphs$_{\mathbf{ATG}}$** of typed attributed graphs. In Chapters 9 and 10, we present the main concepts of typed attributed graph transformation, providing as fundamental results the Local Church–Rosser, Parallelism, Concurrency, Embedding, and Extension Theorems and a Local Confluence Theorem known as the Critical Pair Lemma in the literature. These results are presented without explicit proofs, because they can be obtained as special cases of the corresponding results in Part II. For this purpose, we show in Chapter 11 that the category **AGraphs$_{\mathbf{ATG}}$** is isomorphic to the category of algebras over a specific kind of attributed graph structure signature. This allows us to show that the category of typed attributed graphs is an instance of an adhesive HLR category in the sense of Part II and that the corresponding results can be specialized to those of Chapters 9 and 10.

In Chapter 12, we extend the concept of constraints and application conditions from the graph case presented in Chapter 3 to typed attributed graph transformation, by instantiation of the general theory presented in Chapter 7. In Chapter 13, we study attributed type graphs with inheritance, motivated by the concept of class inheritance in object-oriented modeling. The concepts and results in Chapters 8–11 are based on [HKT02, EPT04], and Chapters 12 and 13 are based on the papers [EEHP04] and [BEdLT04, EEPT05], respectively.

Hints for reading:
For those readers who are interested mainly in the concepts and results of typed attributed graph transformation, we advise them to start with Part I and continue directly to Parts III and IV. The main part of the theory of typed attributed graphs and graph transformation is presented independently of Part II in Chapters 8–10, while Chapter 11 bridges the gap between Parts II and III. Chapters 12 and 13 can be read independently of each other, directly after Chapter 8.

8

Typed Attributed Graphs

Within the last decade, graph transformation has been used as a modeling technique in software engineering and as a metalanguage to specify and implement visual modeling techniques such as UML. Especially for those applications, it is important to use not only labeled graphs, as considered in the classical approach presented in Part I, but also typed and attributed graphs. In fact, there are already several different concepts for typed and attributed graph transformations in the literature (see e.g. [LKW93, HKT02, BFK00, EPT04]). However, for a long period there was no adequate theory for this important branch of graph transformation.

The key idea in [HKT02] is to model an attributed graph with node attribution as a pair $AG = (G, A)$ of a graph G and a data type algebra A. In this chapter, we follow the approach of [EPT04], where this idea is used to model attributed graphs with node and edge attribution. However, G is now a new kind of graph, called an E-graph, which allows edges from edges to attribute nodes also. This new kind of attributed graph, combined with the concept of typing, leads to a category **AGraphs**$_\mathbf{ATG}$ of attributed graphs typed over an attributed type graph ATG. This category seems to be an adequate formal model not only for various applications in software engineering and visual languages but also for the internal representation of attributed graphs in our graph transformation tool AGG [ERT99].

In this chapter, we introduce typed attributed graphs and the corresponding graph morphisms, leading to the category **AGraphs**$_\mathbf{ATG}$. In analogy to Chapter 2 for the case of graphs, we show how to construct pushouts and pullbacks for typed attributed graphs, which are the basis for typed attributed graph transformations and transformation systems described in Chapter 9.

Throughout Chapters 8 and 9, we use a simple running example from the area of model transformation to illustrate the main concepts and results. We have selected a small set of model elements that is basic for all kinds of object-oriented models. It describes the abstract syntax, i.e. the structure of the method signatures. These structures are naturally represented by node- and edge-attributed graphs, where node attributes store names, for example, while edge attributes are useful, for example, for keeping the order of parameters belonging to one method. Typed attributed graph transformation is used in Chapter 9 to specify simple refactorings such as adding a parameter or exchanging two parameters.

8.1 Attributed Graphs and Typing

In order to model attributed graphs with attributes for nodes and edges, we have to extend the classical notion of graphs (see Definition 2.1) to E-graphs.

An E-graph has two different kinds of nodes, representing the graph and data nodes, and three kinds of edges, the usual graph edges and special edges used for the node and edge attribution. The differences between E-graphs, graphs, and labeled graphs are discussed below.

Definition 8.1 (E-graph and E-graph morphism). *An E-graph G with $G = (V_G, V_D, E_G, E_{NA}, E_{EA}, (source_j, target_j)_{j \in \{G,NA,EA\}})$ consists of the sets*

- V_G *and* V_D, *called the graph and data nodes (or vertices), respectively;*
- E_G, E_{NA}, *and* E_{EA} *called the graph, node attribute, and edge attribute edges, respectively;*

and the source and target functions

- $source_G : E_G \to V_G$, $target_G : E_G \to V_G$ *for graph edges;*
- $source_{NA} : E_{NA} \to V_G$, $target_{NA} : E_{NA} \to V_D$ *for node attribute edges; and*
- $source_{EA} : E_{EA} \to E_G$, $target_{EA} : E_{EA} \to V_D$ *for edge attribute edges:*

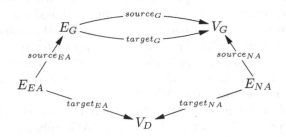

Consider the E-graphs G^1 and G^2 with $G^k = (V_G^k, V_D^k, E_G^k, E_{NA}^k, E_{EA}^k, (source_j^k, target_j^k)_{j \in \{G,NA,EA\}})$ for $k = 1, 2$. An E-graph morphism $f : G^1 \to G^2$ is a tuple $(f_{V_G}, f_{V_D}, f_{E_G}, f_{E_{NA}}, f_{E_{EA}})$ with $f_{V_i} : V_i^1 \to V_i^2$ and $f_{E_j} : E_j^1 \to E_j^2$ for $i \in \{G, D\}$, $j \in \{G, NA, EA\}$ such that f commutes with all source and target functions, for example $f_{V_G} \circ source_G^1 = source_G^2 \circ f_{E_G}$.

Remark 8.2. The main difference between E-graphs and graphs is that we allow edge attribute edges, where the source of these edges is not a graph node but a graph edge. The main difference between E-graphs and labeled graphs (see Definition 2.8) is the fact that we use node and edge attribute edges instead of labeling functions $l_V : V_G \rightarrow V_D$ and $l_E : E_G \rightarrow V_D$. This allows us to change attributes in going from the left- to the right-hand side of a production, whereas, in the case of labeled graphs, the labels of common items in the left- and right-hand sides are preserved.

Definition 8.3 (category EGraphs). *E-graphs and E-graph morphisms form the category* **EGraphs**.

An attributed graph is an E-graph combined with an algebra over a data signature $DSIG$. In the signature, we distinguish a set of attribute value sorts. The corresponding carrier sets in the algebra can be used for the attribution.

Definition 8.4 (attributed graph and attributed graph morphism). *Let $DSIG = (S_D, OP_D)$ be a data signature with attribute value sorts $S'_D \subseteq S_D$. An attributed graph $AG = (G, D)$ consists of an E-graph G together with a DSIG-algebra D such that $\dot{\bigcup}_{s \in S'_D} D_s = V_D$.*

For two attributed graphs $AG^1 = (G^1, D^1)$ and $AG^2 = (G^2, D^2)$, an attributed graph morphism $f : AG^1 \rightarrow AG^2$ is a pair $f = (f_G, f_D)$ with an E-graph morphism $f_G : G^1 \rightarrow G^2$ and an algebra homomorphism $f_D : D^1 \rightarrow D^2$ such that (1) commutes for all $s \in S'_D$, where the vertical arrows below are inclusions:

$$
\begin{array}{ccc}
D^1_s & \xrightarrow{\ f_{D,s}\ } & D^2_s \\
\cup\ \uparrow & (1) & \uparrow\ \cup \\
V^1_D & \xrightarrow{\ f_{G,V_D}\ } & V^2_D
\end{array}
$$

Example 8.5 (attributed graphs). Given suitable signatures $CHAR$, $STRING$, and NAT (see Example B.3), we define the data signature $DSIG$ by

$$DSIG = CHAR + STRING + NAT +$$
$$sorts : parameter DirectionKind$$
$$opns : in, out, inout, return :\rightarrow parameter DirectionKind$$

with attribute value sorts $S'_D = \{string, nat, parameter DirectionKind\}$.

Now we consider as the $DSIG$-algebra D the standard algebras for characters, strings, and natural numbers (see Example B.10), together with the set $D_{parameterDirectionKind} = \{in, out, inout, return\}$ and constants $in_D = in$, $out_D = out$, $inout_D = inout$, and $return_D = return$. The graph $AG = (G, D)$ is then an attributed graph, with G defined as follows:

- $V_G = \{m, c, par_1, par_2, par_3\}$,

- $V_D = D_{nat} \mathbin{\dot{\cup}} D_{string} \mathbin{\dot{\cup}} D_{parameterDirectionKind}$,
- $E_G = \{mpar_1, mpar_2, mpar_3, par_1c, par_2c, par_3c\}$,
- $E_{NA} = \{mname, noOfPars, cname, pname_1, pname_2, kind_1, kind_2, kind_3\}$,
- $E_{EA} = \{order_1, order_2, order_3\}$,
- $source_G : E_G \to V_G : x \mapsto \begin{cases} m & : \quad x = mpar_1, mpar_2, mpar_3 \\ par_i & : \quad x = par_ic, i = 1,2,3 \end{cases}$,
- $target_G : E_G \to V_G : x \mapsto \begin{cases} par_i & : \quad x = mpar_i, i = 1,2,3 \\ c & : \quad x = par_1c, par_2c, par_3c \end{cases}$,
- $source_{NA} : E_{NA} \to V_G : x \mapsto \begin{cases} m & : \quad x = mname, noOfPars \\ c & : \quad x = cname \\ par_i & : \quad x = pname_i, i = 1,2 \\ par_i & : \quad x = kind_i, i = 1,2,3 \end{cases}$,
- $target_{NA} : E_{NA} \to V_D : x \mapsto \begin{cases} add & : \quad x = mname \\ 3 & : \quad x = noOfPars \\ Nat & : \quad x = cname \\ pi & : \quad x = pname_i, i = 1,2 \\ in & : \quad x = kind_1, kind_2 \\ return & : \quad x = kind_3 \end{cases}$,
- $source_{EA} : E_{EA} \to E_G : order_i \mapsto mpar_i, i = 1,2,3$,
- $target_{EA} : E_{EA} \to V_D : order_i \mapsto i, i = 1,2,3$.

In the diagram below, we have omitted the edge names and all unreachable data nodes (*inout*, *out*, 0, numbers greater than 3, and all unused string representations) for clarity. The solid nodes and arrows are the graph nodes V_G and edges E_G, respectively. The dashed nodes are the (used) data nodes V_D, and dashed and dotted arrows represent node and edge attribute edges E_{NA} and E_{EA}, respectively:

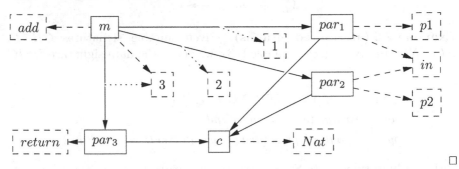

Definition 8.6 (category AGraphs). *Given a data signature DSIG as above, attributed graphs and attributed graph morphisms form the category* **AGraphs**.

For the typing of attributed graphs, we use a distinguished graph attributed over the final *DSIG*-algebra Z (see Definition B.11). This graph defines the set of all possible types.

Definition 8.7 (typed attributed graph and typed attributed graph morphism). *Given a data signature DSIG, an attributed type graph is an attributed graph $ATG = (TG, Z)$, where Z is the final DSIG-algebra.*

A typed attributed graph (AG, t) over ATG consists of an attributed graph AG together with an attributed graph morphism $t : AG \to ATG$.

A typed attributed graph morphism $f : (AG^1, t^1) \to (AG^2, t^2)$ is an attributed graph morphism $f : AG^1 \to AG^2$ such that $t^2 \circ f = t^1$:

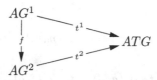

Definition 8.8 (category AGraphs_ATG). *Typed attributed graphs over an attributed type graph ATG and typed attributed graph morphisms form the category $\mathbf{AGraphs_{ATG}}$.*

Example 8.9 (typed attributed graphs). We extend Example 8.5 by the following type graph ATG with the data algebra Z. We have the graph nodes $Method$, $Parameter$, and $Class$ and the data nodes $parameterDirectionKind$, $string$, and nat:

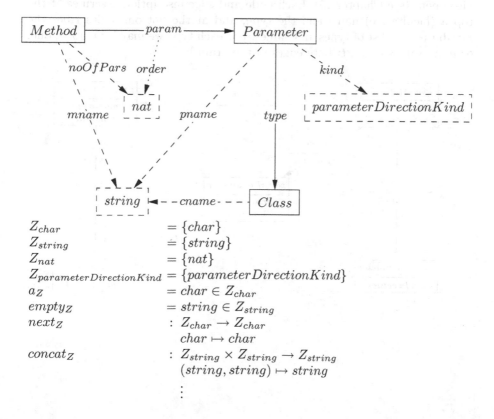

$$
\begin{aligned}
Z_{char} &= \{char\} \\
Z_{string} &= \{string\} \\
Z_{nat} &= \{nat\} \\
Z_{parameterDirectionKind} &= \{parameterDirectionKind\} \\
a_Z &= char \in Z_{char} \\
empty_Z &= string \in Z_{string} \\
next_Z &: Z_{char} \to Z_{char} \\
&\quad char \mapsto char \\
concat_Z &: Z_{string} \times Z_{string} \to Z_{string} \\
&\quad (string, string) \mapsto string
\end{aligned}
$$

$\vdots$

Each data node is named after its corresponding sort, owing to the fact that the final $DSIG$-algebra Z has carrier sets $Z_s = \{s\}$ for all $s \in S_D$. The nodes and edges in ATG represent the types that can be used for the typing of an attributed graph.

The graph AG given in Example 8.5 is typed over ATG by the attributed graph morphism $t : AG \to ATG$ with $t = (t_{G,V_G}, t_{G,V_D}, t_{G,E_G}, t_{G,E_{NA}}, t_{G,E_{EA}}, t_D)$, defined by

$t_{D,s}(x) = s$ for all $s \in S_D$,

$t_{G,V_G}(m) = Method, t_{G,V_G}(par_1) = t_{G,V_G}(par_2) = t_{G,V_G}(par_3) = Parameter,$

$t_{G,V_G}(c) = Class,$

$t_{G,V_D}(p1) = t_{G,V_D}(p2) = t_{G,V_D}(add) = t_{G,V_D}(Nat) = string,$

$t_{G,V_D}(return) = t_{G,V_D}(in) = parameterDirectionKind,$

$t_{G,V_D}(1) = t_{G,V_D}(2) = t_{G,V_D}(3) = nat,$

and analogously for all unused data nodes and t_{G,E_G}, $t_{G,E_{NA}}$, and $t_{G,E_{EA}}$ defined by the induced edge morphisms.

In the following we use a more compact notation for typed attributed graphs, as depicted in the following diagram and used in the AGG tool environment (see Chapter 15). Each node and edge inscription describes at the top a (facultative) name and the type, and at the bottom it describes the attributes as a list of types and values. For each type we may have none, one, or more values (i.e. attribute edges in the graph):

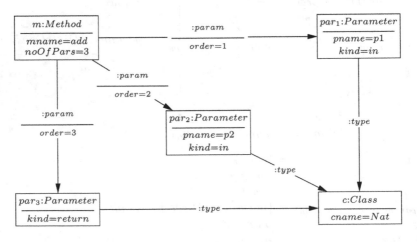

8.2 Pushouts as a Gluing Construction of Attributed Graphs

Similarly to the gluing of graphs in Section 2.3, we now study the gluing of attributed and typed attributed graphs. This is needed for the construction of typed attributed graph transformations in the next chapter and is defined via pushouts in the categories **AGraphs** and **AGraphs$_{ATG}$**, respectively. In fact, we need only pushouts where one of the given morphisms belongs to a special class $\mathcal{M}$ of monomorphisms, which are injective on the graph part and isomorphisms on the data type part.

Definition 8.10 (class $\mathcal{M}$). *An attributed graph morphism $f : AG^1 \rightarrow AG^2$ with $f = (f_G, f_D)$ belongs to the class $\mathcal{M}$ if f_G is an injective E-graph morphism, i.e. injective in each component, and f_D is an isomorphism of DSIG-algebras. This implies also that f_{V_D} is bijective.*

A typed attributed graph morphism $f : (AG^1, t^1) \rightarrow (AG^2, t^2)$ belongs to the class $\mathcal{M}$ if $f : AG^1 \rightarrow AG^2$ belongs to $\mathcal{M}$.

Remark 8.11. The class $\mathcal{M}$ is a class of monomorphisms in **AGraphs** or **AGraphs$_{ATG}$**, which is closed under composition ($g \circ f$ with $f, g \in \mathcal{M}$ implies $g \circ f \in \mathcal{M}$). For $f \in \mathcal{M}$ with f_G bijective, f is an isomorphism in **AGraphs** or **AGraphs$_{ATG}$**, respectively.

The following pushout construction in **AGraphs** and **AGraphs$_{ATG}$** is based on Fact 2.17. The main difference is in the pushout construction for the corresponding $DSIG$-algebras. In general, a pushout of $DSIG$-algebras cannot be constructed componentwise. However, since $\mathcal{M}$-morphisms are isomorphisms on the $DSIG$-algebras, we can avoid this problem by preserving the $DSIG$-algebra in the morphism opposite to the given $\mathcal{M}$-morphism.

Fact 8.12 (pushouts along $\mathcal{M}$-morphisms in AGraphs and AGraphs$_{ATG}$).

1. *Given attributed graph morphisms $f : AG^0 \rightarrow AG^1$ and $g : AG^0 \rightarrow AG^2$ with $f \in \mathcal{M}$, the pushout (1) in **AGraphs** with the pushout object (AG^3, f', g') can be constructed as follows, where $AG^k = (G^k, D^k)$, and $G^k = (V_G^k, V_D^k, E_G^k, E_{NA}^k, E_{EA}^k, (source_j^k, target_j^k)_{j \in \{G, NA, EA\}})$ for ($k = 0, 1, 2, 3$):*

$$AG^0 = (G^0, D^0) \xrightarrow{\quad f = (f_G, f_D) \in \mathcal{M} \quad} (G^1, D^1) = AG^1$$

$$\downarrow{\scriptstyle g = (g_G, g_D)} \qquad\qquad (1) \qquad\qquad \downarrow{\scriptstyle g = (g'_G, g'_D)}$$

$$AG^2 = (G^2, D^2) \xrightarrow{\quad f' = (f'_G, f'_D) \in \mathcal{M} \quad} (G^3, D^3) = AG^3$$

   *a) (X^3, f'_X, g'_X) is a pushout of (X^0, f_X, g_X) in **Sets** for $X \in \{V_G, E_G, E_{NA}, E_{EA}\}$.*

   b) $(V_D^3, f'_{V_D}, g'_{V_D}) = (V_D^2, id, g'_{V_D})$ with $g'_{V_D} = g_{V_D} \circ f_{V_D}^{-1} : V_D^1 \rightarrow V_D^3$.

c) $(D^3, f'_D, g'_D) = (D^2, id, g'_D)$ with $g'_D = g_D \circ f_D^{-1} : D^1 \to D^3$.

d) The source and target functions of G^3 are uniquely determined by the pushouts in a).

AG^3 is unique up to isomorphism and $f' \in \mathcal{M}$.

2. Given typed attributed graph morphisms $f : (AG^0, t^0) \to (AG^1, t^1)$ and $g : (AG^0, t^0) \to (AG^2, t^2)$ with $f \in \mathcal{M}$, then the pushout $((AG^3, t^3), f', g')$ in **AGraphs**$_{\mathbf{ATG}}$ can be constructed as a pushout (AG^3, f', g') of $f : AG^0 \to AG^1$ and $g : AG^0 \to AG^2$ with $f \in \mathcal{M}$ in **AGraphs**, and $t^3 : AG^3 \to ATG$ is uniquely induced by t_1 and t_2, using the pushout properties of (AG^3, f', g') in **AGraphs**.

Proof.

1. The componentwise construction leads to a well-defined $AG^3 = (G^3, D^3)$ and to morphisms f', g' in **AGraphs**, where $f' \in \mathcal{M}$ and (1) is commutative. The universal pushout property follows from the PO constructions in **Sets** for each component, where the constructions in the V_D and D components are also pushouts in **Sets** and **DSIG-Alg**, respectively.

2. This follows from the construction of pushouts in slice categories (see Fact A.19, item 5).

$\square$

Example 8.13 (pushout in AGraphs$_{\mathbf{ATG}}$). The diagram in Fig. 8.1 is a pushout in **AGraphs**$_{\mathbf{ATG}}$. The graph $AG^1 = AG$ has been shown in Example 8.5. All four typed attributed graphs have the same data algebra and therefore also the same data nodes. Since f_G and g_G are injective, both of the morphisms f and g are $\mathcal{M}$-morphisms. Therefore the pushout object AG^3 can be constructed componentwise. $\square$

8.3 Pullbacks of Attributed Graphs

In analogy to the pullbacks of graphs described in Section 2.4, we now study pullbacks of attributed and typed attributed graphs. The universal property of pullbacks is dual to that of pushouts, and in fact, pushouts along $\mathcal{M}$-morphisms are also pullbacks in **AGraphs** and **AGraphs**$_{\mathbf{ATG}}$. In contrast to pushouts, which are essential for the definition of direct transformations, pullbacks are needed mainly for technical reasons in connection with the statements and proofs of several of the main results, especially for the properties of adhesive and weak adhesive HLR categories.

The following pullback construction in **AGraphs** and **AGraphs**$_{\mathbf{ATG}}$ is based on Fact 2.23. Similarly to the pushout construction, the main difference is in the pullback construction for the corresponding $DSIG$-algebras. In contrast to pushouts, a pullback of $DSIG$-algebras can be constructed componentwise. However, we do not need this property, because one of the given morphisms is an $\mathcal{M}$-morphism such that the opposite morphism can be defined to preserve the $DSIG$-algebra.

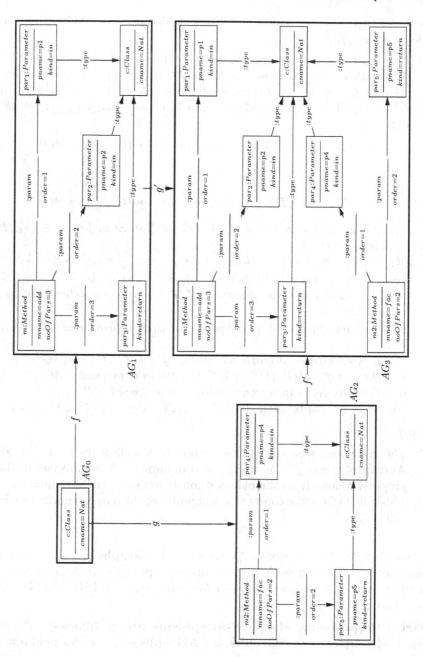

Fig. 8.1. Pushout and Pullback in **AGraphs**ATG

Fact 8.14 (pullbacks along $\mathcal{M}$-morphisms in AGraphs and AGraphs$_{\text{ATG}}$).

1. *Given attributed graph morphisms $f' : AG^2 \to AG^3$ and $g' : AG^1 \to AG^3$ with $f' \in \mathcal{M}$, the pullback (1) in AGraphs with the pullback object (AG^0, f, g) can be constructed as follows, where $AG^k = (G^k, D^k)$ and $G^k = (V_G^k, V_D^k, E_G^k, E_{NA}^k, E_{EA}^k, (source_j^k, target_j^k)_{j \in \{G, NA, EA\}})$ for $(k = 0, 1, 2, 3)$:*

$$AG^0 = (G^0, D^0) \xrightarrow{\quad f = (f_G, f_D) \in \mathcal{M} \quad} (G^1, D^1) = AG^1$$

$$g = (g_G, g_D) \downarrow \qquad\qquad (1) \qquad\qquad \downarrow g = (g_G', g_D')$$

$$AG^2 = (G^2, D^2) \xrightarrow{\quad f' = (f_G', f_D') \in \mathcal{M} \quad} (G^3, D^3) = AG^3$$

   a) *(X^0, f_X, g_X) is pullback of (X^3, f_X', g_X') in **Sets** for $X \in \{V_G, E_G, E_{NA}, E_{EA}\}$.*
   b) *$(V_D^0, f_{V_D}, g_{V_D}) = (V_D^1, id, g_{V_D})$ with $g_{V_D} = f_{V_D}'^{-1} \circ g_{V_D}' : V_D^0 \to V_D^2$.*
   c) *$(D^0, f_D, g_D) = (D^1, id, g_D)$ with $g_D = f_D'^{-1} \circ g_D' : D^0 \to D^2$.*
   d) *The source and target functions of G^0 are uniquely determined by the pullbacks in a).*
   The pullback object AG^0 is unique up to isomorphism, and we have $f \in \mathcal{M}$.

2. *Given typed attributed graph morphisms $f' : (AG^2, t^2) \to (AG^3, t^3)$ with $f' \in \mathcal{M}$ and $g' : (AG^1, t^1) \to (AG^3, t^3)$, then the pullback $((AG^0, t^0), f, g)$ in AGraphs$_{\text{ATG}}$ can be constructed as a pullback (AG^0, f, g) of f, g with $f \in \mathcal{M}$ in AGraphs, and $t^0 : AG^0 \to ATG$ is given by $t^0 = t^1 \circ f = t^2 \circ g$.*

Proof.

1. The componentwise construction leads to a well-defined (AG^0, f, g) in **AGraphs**, where $f \in \mathcal{M}$ and (1) is commutative. The universal pullback property follows from the pullback constructions in each component.
2. This follows from the construction of pullbacks in slice categories (see Fact A.23, item 4).

$\square$

Remark 8.15. The categories **AGraphs** and **AGraphs$_{\text{ATG}}$** also have general pullbacks. This follows from the existence of pullbacks in $\mathbf{Alg}(\Sigma)$ (see Fact A.19, item 3) and the isomorphism $\mathbf{AGraphs_{ATG}} \cong \mathbf{AGSIG(ATG)} - \mathbf{Alg}$ (see Theorem 11.3).

Fact 8.16 (pushouts along $\mathcal{M}$-morphisms are pullbacks). *Pushouts along $\mathcal{M}$-morphisms in AGraphs and AGraphs$_{\text{ATG}}$ are also pullbacks.*

Proof. This follows from the fact that pushouts along injective functions in **Sets** are also pullbacks. See also Theorem 4.26 and 11.11. $\square$

Example 8.17. Fact 8.16 implies that the pushout in Fig. 8.1 is also an example of a pullback in **AGraphs$_{\text{ATG}}$**. $\square$

9

Typed Attributed Graph Transformation Systems

On the basis of the concepts of attributed graphs and typing introduced in Chapter 8, we present the theory of typed attributed graph transformation (AGT) systems in this chapter. The main idea used to obtain this theory is to instantiate the general theory for adhesive HLR systems given in Part II with the category $(\mathbf{AGraphs_{ATG}}, \mathcal{M})$ of typed attributed graphs, which will be shown to be an adhesive HLR category in Chapter 11. On the other hand, we consider it to be important that the concepts and results presented in this chapter also make sense for readers not interested in the general categorical theory of Part II. For this purpose, we follow the style of Part I and introduce directly the basic concepts and results for typed attributed graph transformation in this and the next chapter. We postpone the verification of the main results to Chapter 11.

9.1 Basic Concepts for Typed AGT Systems

In this section, we define typed attributed graph transformation systems on the basis of the concepts of attributed graphs and typing described in Section 8.1.

For a typed attributed graph transformation system, we fix a category $\mathbf{AGraphs_{ATG}}$ over an attributed type graph ATG and the class $\mathcal{M}$, as defined in the last chapter. The productions are restricted to graphs attributed over a term algebra with variables.

The example of typed attributed graphs introduced in Chapter 8 is extended to a typed attributed graph transformation system called *Method-Modeling*.

A typed attributed graph production is a typed graph production (see Definition 3.1) where typed graphs are replaced by typed attributed graphs which share the same termalgebra $T_{DSIG}(X)$ with variables X (see Def. B.15) as algebra.

Definition 9.1 (typed attributed graph production). *Given an attributed type graph ATG with a data signature DSIG, a typed attributed graph production, or "production" for short, $p = (L \xleftarrow{l} K \xrightarrow{r} R)$ consists of typed attributed graphs L, K, and R with a common DSIG-algebra $T_{DSIG}(X)$, the DSIG-termalgebra with variables X, and $l, r \in \mathcal{M}$. This means that we have injective typed attributed graph morphisms $l : K \to L$, $r : K \to R$, where the DSIG-part of l and r is the identity on $T_{DSIG}(X)$.*

A typed attributed graph transformation is a typed graph transformation (see Definition 3.2) where pushouts in the category **Graphs$_{TG}$** are replaced by pushouts in **AGraphs$_{ATG}$**.

Definition 9.2 (typed attributed graph transformation). *Given a production $p = (L \xleftarrow{l} K \xrightarrow{r} R)$ as defined above and a typed attributed graph G with a typed attributed graph morphism $m : L \to G$, called match, a direct typed attributed graph transformation, or "direct graph transformation" for short, $G \xLongrightarrow{p,m} H$ from G to a typed attributed graph H is given by the following double pushout (DPO) diagram in the category **AGraphs$_{ATG}$**, where (1) and (2) are pushouts:*

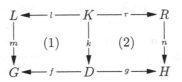

A sequence $G_0 \Rightarrow G_1 \Rightarrow ... \Rightarrow G_n$ of direct graph transformations is called a typed attributed graph transformation, or "graph transformation" for short, and is denoted by $G_0 \overset{*}{\Rightarrow} G_n$. In the case $n = 0$, we have an identical transformation on G_0 or an isomorphism $G_0 \cong G_0'$, because direct graph transformations are only unique up to isomorphism.

Notation. *We shall use the short form "(typed) AGT system" for "(typed) attributed graph transformation system".*

Remark 9.3. Similarly to the construction of graph transformations in Section 3.2, the construction of typed attributed graph transformations is also based on the construction of two pushouts, but now in the category **AGraphs$_{ATG}$**.

In Section 9.2, we analyze the construction of a direct typed attributed graph transformation in more detail.

At this point, let us discuss the difference concerning match morphisms in the attributed case compared with the classical case. The match morphism $m : L \to G$ has an E-graph part m_G – which corresponds to the classical case – and also a data type part $m_D : T_{DSIG}(X) \to D^G$. In fact, the DSIG homomorphism m_D is completely determined by an assignment $asg : X \to D^G$ of variables (see Section B.3 and [EM85]). Since l_D and r_D are the identities on $T_{DSIG}(X)$, we can assume without loss of generality that f_D and g_D are the identities of the data algebra D^G of G. This implies that the data algebras D^G, D^D, and D^H of G, D, and H are all equal, i.e. $D^G = D^D = D^H$, and that the data type parts k_D and n_D of k and n in (1) and (2) are equal to m_D, i.e. $m_D = k_D = n_D$.

At first glance this may seem strange, because the variables $var(L)$ occurring in the terms of the node and edge attributes of L may not coincide with $var(K)$ of K and $var(R)$ of R. We only have $var(K) \subseteq var(L) \subseteq X$ and $var(K) \subseteq var(R) \subseteq X$. But the definition of the match $m_D : T_{DSIG}(X) \to D^G$ already requires an assignment for all variables X, and not only for $var(L) \subseteq X$.

From the practical point of view, to find a match $m : L \to G$ we first have to find an assignment for the variables $var(L)$ such that the corresponding term evaluation matches the corresponding attributes of G. In a second step, we can choose an appropriate assignment for $var(R) \setminus var(L)$ which determines the corresponding attributes of H. In general it makes sense to have $X = var(L) \cup var(R)$, but this is not necessarily required for arbitrary productions.

Finally, we define typed attributed graph transformation systems, grammars, and languages by analogy with the corresponding concepts in the graph case (see Definition 3.4).

Definition 9.4 (typed AGT system, grammar and language). *A typed attributed graph transformation system (or "graph transformation system" for short) $GTS = (DSIG, ATG, P)$ consists of a data type signature $DSIG$, an attributed type graph ATG, and a set P of typed attributed graph productions.*

$GG = (GTS, S)$, with a typed attributed start graph S, is called a typed attributed graph grammar. The language L generated by GG is given as usual by $L = \{G \mid S \Rightarrow^* G\}$.

Remark 9.5. A typed attributed graph transformation system is an adhesive HLR system in the sense of Definition 5.4, based on the adhesive HLR category $(\mathbf{AGraphs_{ATG}}, \mathcal{M})$. The category $\mathbf{AGraphs_{ATG}}$ is determined by the data signature $DSIG$ and the attributed type graph ATG, the morphism class $\mathcal{M}$, as defined in Definition 8.10, is fixed.

To illustrate this definition, we present an example that comes from the area of model transformation. It describes the signatures of method declarations.

Example 9.6 (graph grammar *MethodModeling***).** In the following, we define the typed attributed graph grammar *MethodModeling*.

We use the data signature $DSIG$ presented in Example 8.5 and the attributed type graph from Example 8.9. The start graph S is the empty graph.

All graphs occurring in the productions are attributed over the term algebra $T_{DSIG}(X)$ with variables $X = X_{int} \cup X_{String} \cup X_{ParameterDirectionKind}$, where $X_{int} = \{n, x, y\}$, $X_{String} = \{m, p, ptype, P1, P2\}$, and $X_{ParameterDirectionKind} = \{k\}$.

We present the productions in a shorter notation showing only the left-hand and the right-hand side of each production. The gluing object is the intersection of both graphs, where a partial mapping is given by the names of the nodes.

Using the productions *addMethod* and *addClass* with an empty left-hand side and a single method or class, respectively, on the right-hand side, new methods and classes can be inserted:

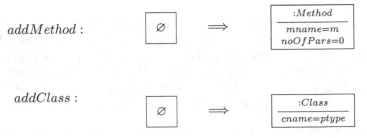

The production *addParameter* adds a parameter of a special type to a method. It is inserted as the last element in the list of parameters for this method:

addParameter :

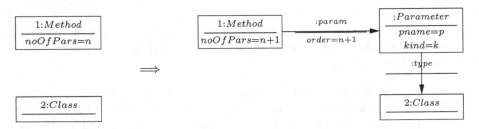

With *checkNewParameter*, we can delete the last parameter if it is already in the list of parameters. The name, kind, and type of the last parameter have to match with those of the parameter that is used for the comparison:

checkNewParameter :

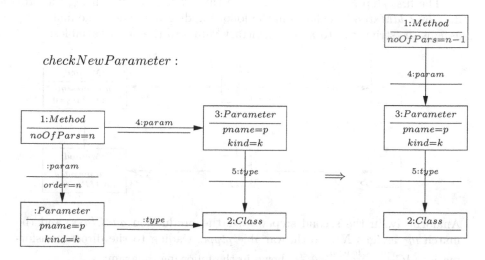

The production *exchangeParameter* exchanges the order of two parameters:

exchangeParameter :

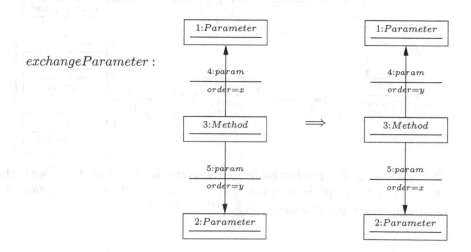

Altogether, the typed attributed graph grammar is given by $MethodModeling = (DSIG, ATG, S, P)$, where $P = \{addMethod, addClass, addParameter, exchangeParameter, checkNewParameter\}$.

The typed attributed graph AG in Example 8.9 can be derived from the empty start graph S by applying first the productions *addMethod* and *addClass* and then the production *addParameter* three times. The matches have to assign the corresponding value to each variable.

The first step $S \overset{addMethod,m_1}{\Longrightarrow} AG_1$ of this transformation, using the production $addMethod$, is shown in the following diagram, where the match m_1 assigns the string add to m and arbitrary values to the other variables:

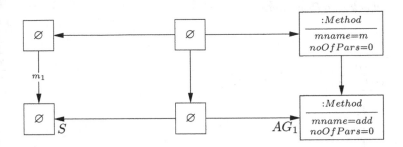

Analogously, in the second step we use the production $addClass$, and the match m_2 assigns Nat to the variable $ptype$, leading to the direct transformation $AG_1 \overset{addClass,m_2}{\Longrightarrow} AG_2$ shown in the following diagram:

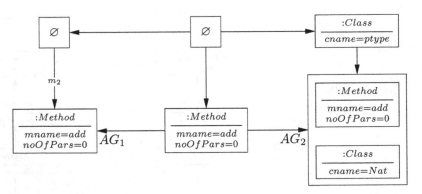

Now, applying the production $addParameter$ for the first time, with the match m_3, where $p1$ is assigned to p, in to k, and 0 to n, we obtain the following direct transformation $AG_2 \overset{addParameter,m_3}{\Longrightarrow} AG_3$:

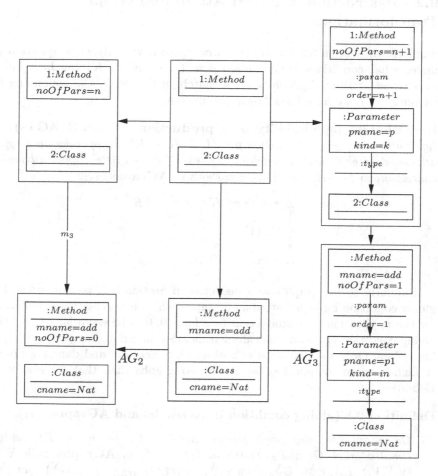

We apply *addParameter* two more times similarly, and obtain the graph *AG*:

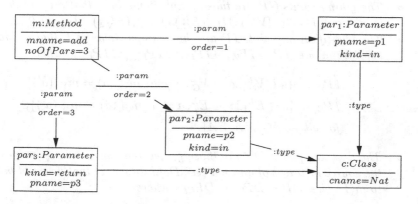

9.2 Construction of Typed Attributed Graph Transformations

Similarly to Section 3.2 for the graph case, we now analyze the question of under what conditions a production $p = (L \leftarrow K \rightarrow K)$ can be applied to a typed attributed graph G via a match $m : L \rightarrow G$. Corresponding to Definition 3.7, we have the following definition:

Definition 9.7 (applicability of a production for typed AGTs). *A typed attributed graph production $p = (L \leftarrow K \rightarrow K)$ is applicable to a typed attributed graph G with a match $m : L \rightarrow G$ if there exists a typed attributed context graph D such that (1) is a pushout in $\mathbf{AGraphs_{ATG}}$:*

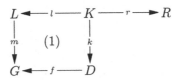

Similarly to the graph case considered in Section 3.2, we now present a gluing condition for typed attributed graphs which is necessary and sufficient for the application of a production (see Fact 9.9). The essential part of the gluing condition is, again, that all identification and dangling points are gluing points. Only the definition of gluing, identification, and dangling points is slightly more complicated for attributed graphs than that for graphs in Definition 3.9.

Definition 9.8 (gluing condition in AGraphs and AGraphs_{ATG}).

1. *Given an attributed graph production $p = (L \leftarrow K \rightarrow R)$, an attributed graph G, and a match $m : L \rightarrow G$ in $\mathbf{AGraphs}$ with $X = (V_G^X, V_D^X, E_G^X, E_{NA}^X, E_{EA}^X, (source_j^X, target_j^X)_{j \in \{G, NA, EA\}}, D^X)$ for all $X \in \{L, K, R, G\}$, we can state the following definitions:*
   - *The gluing points GP are those graph items in L that are not deleted by p, i.e. $GP = l_{V_G}(V_G^K) \cup l_{E_G}(E_G^K) \cup l_{E_{NA}}(E_{NA}^K) \cup l_{E_{EA}}(E_{EA}^K)$.*
   - *The identification points IP are those graph items in L that are identified by m, i.e. $IP = IP_{V_G} \cup IP_{E_G} \cup IP_{E_{NA}} \cup IP_{E_{EA}}$, where*

   $$IP_{V_G} = \{a \in V_G^L | \exists a' \in V_G^L, a \neq a', m_{V_G}(a) = m_{V_G}(a')\},$$
   $$IP_{E_j} = \{a \in E_j^L | \exists a' \in E_j^L, a \neq a', m_{E_j}(a) = m_{E_j}(a')\},$$
   for all $j \in \{G, NA, EA\}$.

   - *The dangling points DP are those graph items in L, whose images are the source or target of an item (see Definition 8.1) that does not belong to $m(L)$, i.e. $DP = DP_{V_G} \cup DP_{E_G}$, where*

$$DP_{V_G} = \{a \in V_G^L | (\exists a' \in E_{NA}^G \setminus m_{E_{NA}}(E_{NA}^L),$$
$$m_{E_{NA}}(a) = source_{NA}^G(a')) \vee (\exists a' \in E_G^G \setminus m_{E_G}(E_G^L),$$
$$m_{E_G}(a) = source_G^G(a') \text{ or } m_{E_G}(a) = target_G^G(a'))\},$$
$$DP_{E_G} = \{a \in E_G^L | (\exists a' \in E_{EA}^G \setminus m_{E_{EA}}(E_{EA}^L),$$
$$m_{E_{EA}}(a) = source_{EA}^G(a')\};$$

p *and* m *satisfy the gluing condition in* **AGraphs** *if all identification and all dangling points are also gluing points, i.e.* $IP \cup DP \subseteq GP$.

2. *Given* p *and* m *in* **AGraphs**$_{\mathbf{ATG}}$, *they satisfy the gluing condition in* **AGraphs**$_{\mathbf{ATG}}$ *if* p *and* m, *considered in* **AGraphs**, *satisfy the gluing condition in* **AGraphs**.

Fact 9.9 (existence and uniqueness of typed attributed context graphs). *For a typed attributed graph production* p, *a typed attributed graph* G, *and a match* $m : L \to G$, *the typed attributed context graph* D *with the PO (1) exists in* **AGraphs**$_{\mathbf{ATG}}$ *iff* p *and* m *satisfy the gluing condition in* **AGraphs**$_{\mathbf{ATG}}$. *If* D *exists, it is unique up to isomorphism:*

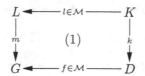

Proof. "⇒". Given the PO (1), then the properties of the gluing condition follow from the properties of pushouts along $\mathcal{M}$-morphisms in **AGraphs** and **AGraphs**$_{\mathbf{ATG}}$ (see Fact 8.12; this is similar to the proof of Fact 3.11).

"⇐". If the gluing condition is satisfied, we can construct
$D = (V_G^D, V_D^D, E_G^D, E_{NA}^D, E_{EA}^D, (source_j^D, target_j^D)_{j \in \{G, NA, EA\}}, D^D)$, k, f, and $type_D : D \to ATG$ as follows:

- $V_G^D = (V_G^G \setminus m_{V_G}(V_G^L)) \cup m_{V_G} \circ l_{V_G}(V_G^K);$
- $V_D^D = V_D^G;$
- $E_j^D = (E_j^G \setminus m_{E_j}(E_j^L)) \cup m_{E_j} \circ l_{E_j}(E_j^K), \quad j \in \{G, NA, EA\};$
- $source_j^D = source_j^G|_D, target_j^D = target_j^G|_D \quad j \in \{G, NA, EA\};$
- $D^D = D^G;$
- $k(x) = m(l(x))$ for all items x in $K;$
- f is an inclusion;
- $type_D = type_G|_D.$

$\square$

Remark 9.10. This fact corresponds to Theorem 6.4 in the general theory given in Part II. This implies that the context graph D can be constructed as the gluing $D = C +_B K$ of C and K along B, where B and C are the boundary and context objects of m, as defined in Definition 10.5.

Similarly to the graph case considered in Section 3.2, we now have the following result:

If a typed attributed production is applicable to a typed attributed graph via a match, i.e. the gluing condition is satisfied, then we can construct a direct transformation as follows.

Fact 9.11 (construction of direct typed attributed graph transformation). *Given a typed attributed graph production p and a match $m : L \to G$ such that p is applicable to G via m, then a direct typed attributed graph transformation can be constructed in two steps:*

1. *Delete all graph items from G that are reached by the match m, but keep those which come from K. More precisely, construct the typed attributed context graph D and the pushout (1) below in $\mathbf{AGraphs_{ATG}}$ such that $G = L +_K D$.*
2. *Add new graph items to D that are newly created in R. More precisely, construct the pushout (2) of D and R via K such that $H = R +_K D$.*

This construction is unique up to isomorphism.

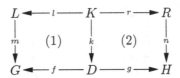

Proof. Since p is applicable to G via m, we have the existence of the context graph D, leading to pushout (1), where D is also called the pushout complement. Pushout (2) exists according to the construction in Fact 8.12. Moreover, the construction of pushout complements in (1) and pushouts in (2) in $\mathbf{AGraphs_{ATG}}$ is unique up to isomorphism. For pushouts, this is true in any category, for pushout complements with $l \in \mathcal{M}$, because $\mathbf{AGraphs_{ATG}}$ is an adhesive HLR category. $\square$

9.3 Local Church–Rosser and Parallelism Theorem for Typed AGT Systems

In this section we present the Local Church–Rosser and Parallelism Theorems for typed attributed graph transformation systems as defined in Definition 9.4.

In order to present the Local Church–Rosser Theorem similarly to the classical graph case considered in Section 3.3 we first have to define parallel and sequential independence of two direct typed attributed graph transformations. We use the categorical version of independence defined by the existence of suitable morphisms as the definition, which corresponds to the characterization that we have given in the classical graph case (see Fact 3.18).

Here, we use the short forms "graph" and "graph transformation" introduced in Section 9.1 to mean "typed attributed graphs" and "typed attributed graph transformation", respectively. When we speak of morphisms, we always mean morphisms in the category $\mathbf{AGraphs_{ATG}}$.

Definition 9.12 (parallel and sequential independence). *Two direct graph transformations* $G \stackrel{p_1,m_1}{\Longrightarrow} H_1$ *and* $G \stackrel{p_2,m_2}{\Longrightarrow} H_2$ *are parallel independent if there exist morphisms* $i : L_1 \to D_2$ *and* $j : L_2 \to D_1$ *such that* $f_2 \circ i = m_1$ *and* $f_1 \circ j = m_2$:

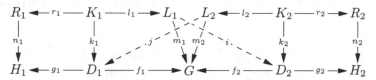

Two direct graph transformations $G \stackrel{p_1,m_1}{\Longrightarrow} H \stackrel{p_2,m_2}{\Longrightarrow} G'$ *are sequentially independent if there exist morphisms* $i : R_1 \to D_2$ *and* $j : L_2 \to D_1$ *such that* $f_2 \circ i = n_1$ *and* $g_1 \circ j = m_2$:

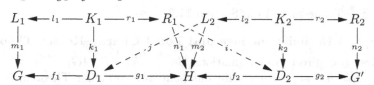

Remark 9.13 (characterization of parallel and sequential independence). Two direct transformations that are not parallel or sequentially independent are called parallel or sequentially dependent, respectively.

Intuitively speaking, parallel independence means that the intersection of the match $m_1(L_1)$ and the match $m_2(L_2)$ in G consists of common gluing points only, i.e. it is included in $m_1 \circ l_1(K_1) \cap m_2 \circ l_2(K_2)$ (see Section 3.3 for the classical graph case, where the set theoretical version is used as a definition and the categorical version as a characterization).

Similarly, sequential independence means that the first rule does not produce anything needed by the second one.

Note that this condition is trivially satisfied for the algebras of attributed graphs, because K_i and L_i have the same algebra $T_{DSIG}(X_i)$, which is preserved by $l_i : K_i \to L_i$ for $i = 1, 2$.

This implies that the condition is also trivially satisfied for the V_D component. For the components V_G, E_G, E_{NA}, and E_{EA}, independence means, more precisely:

- $m_1(L_1) \cap m_2(L_2) \subseteq l_1 \circ m_1(K_1) \cap l_2 \circ m_2(K_2)$ (parallel independence);
- $n_1(R_1) \cap m_2(L_2) \subseteq r_1 \circ n_1(K_1) \cap l_2 \circ m_2(K_2)$ (sequential independence).

Similarly to Theorem 3.20 for the classical case, we are now able to present the Local Church–Rosser Theorem for typed AGT systems.

Theorem 9.14 (Local Church–Rosser Theorem for typed AGT systems). *Given two parallel independent direct graph transformations $G \overset{p_1,m_1}{\Longrightarrow} H_1$ and $G \overset{p_2,m_2}{\Longrightarrow} H_2$, there are a graph G' and direct graph transformations $H_1 \overset{p_2,m_2'}{\Longrightarrow} G'$ and $H_2 \overset{p_1,m_1'}{\Longrightarrow} G'$ such that $G \overset{p_1,m_1}{\Longrightarrow} H_1 \overset{p_2,m_2'}{\Longrightarrow} G'$ and $G \overset{p_2,m_2}{\Longrightarrow} H_2 \overset{p_1,m_1'}{\Longrightarrow} G'$ are sequentially independent.*

Given two sequentially independent direct graph transformations $G \overset{p_1,m_1}{\Longrightarrow} H_1 \overset{p_2,m_2'}{\Longrightarrow} G'$, there are a graph H_2 and direct graph transformations $G \overset{p_2,m_2}{\Longrightarrow} H_2 \overset{p_1,m_1'}{\Longrightarrow} G'$ such that $G \overset{p_1,m_1}{\Longrightarrow} H_1$ and $G \overset{p_2,m_2}{\Longrightarrow} H_2$ are parallel independent:

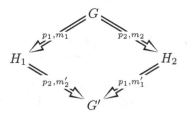

Proof. See Theorem 11.14 in Section 11.3.   □

Example 9.15 (independence and Local Church–Rosser Theorem). The first two direct transformations $S \overset{addMethod,m_1}{\Longrightarrow} AG_1 \overset{addClass,m_2}{\Longrightarrow} AG_2$ in Example 9.6 are sequentially independent. Applying Theorem 9.14, we can change the order of the application of the two productions, leading to a transformation $S \overset{addClass,m_2'}{\Longrightarrow} AG_1' \overset{addMethod,m_1'}{\Longrightarrow} AG_2$, where AG_1' contains only the class node with the attribute $cname = Nat$. Furthermore, the direct transformations $S \Rightarrow AG_1$ and $S \Rightarrow AG_1'$ are parallel independent.

The second direct transformation $AG_1 \overset{addClass,m_2}{\Longrightarrow} AG_2$ and the third one $AG_2 \overset{addParameter,m_3}{\Longrightarrow} AG_3$ are sequentially dependent. In the first step, we create the class that is needed in the second step. Therefore we cannot change the order in which we apply the productions $addClass$ and $addParameter$.   □

Similarly to the classical graph case considered in Section 3.3, we now define parallel productions and transformations in order to formulate the Parallelism Theorem for typed AGT systems.

Definition 9.16 (parallel production and transformation). *Given two productions $p_1 = (L_1 \overset{l_1}{\leftarrow} K_1 \overset{r_1}{\rightarrow} R_1)$ and $p_2 = (L_2 \overset{l_2}{\leftarrow} K_2 \overset{r_2}{\rightarrow} R_2)$, the parallel production $p_1 + p_2$ is defined by the coproduct constructions over the corresponding objects and morphisms: $p_1 + p_2 = (L_1 + L_2 \overset{l_1+l_2}{\longleftarrow} K_1 + K_2 \overset{r_1+r_2}{\longrightarrow} R_1 + R_2)$ (see Remark 9.17).*

The application of a parallel production is called a parallel direct transformation, or parallel transformation for short.

Remark 9.17. The coproduct $L_1 + L_2$ (and similarly for $K_1 + K_2$ and $R_1 + R_2$) in **AGraphs** with $L_i = (L_i^E, T_{DSIG}(X_i))$ $(i = 1, 2)$, where L_i^E is the *E-graph* for L_i, is given by $L_1 + L_2 = ((L_1 + L_2)^E, T_{DSIG}(X_1 + X_2))$, where

- $(L_1 + L_2)_j^E = L_{1,j}^E \mathbin{\dot{\cup}} L_{2,j}^E$ for the components $j = V_G, E_G, E_{NA}$, and E_{EA};
- $(L_1 + L_2)_{V_D}^E = \dot{\cup}_{s \in S_D'} T_{DSIG}(X_1 + X_2)_s$.

Note that $T_{DSIG}(X_1 + X_2)$ is the coproduct of $T_{DSIG}(X_1)$ and $T_{DSIG}(X_2)$ in **Alg(DSIG)**, because $T_{DSIG}(X)$ is a free construction which preserves coproducts. For the V_D-component, we have $(L_1 + L_2)_{V_D}^E \neq L_{1,V_D}^E \mathbin{\dot{\cup}} L_{2,V_D}^E$ in general, but the compatibility with the $DSIG$-component $T_{DSIG}(X_1 + X_2)$ leads to the equation stated above for attributed graphs in **AGraphs**. For $l_i : K_i \to L_i \in \mathcal{M}$ for $(i = 1, 2)$, we have $(l_1 + l_2) \in \mathcal{M}$ and, similarly $(r_1 + r_2) \in \mathcal{M}$.

The coproduct $L_1 + L_2$ in **AGraphs_ATG** for typed attributed graphs L_1 with $type_1 : L_1 \to ATG$ and L_2 with $type_2 : L_2 \to ATG$ is constructed like the coproduct $L_1 + L_2$ in **AGraphs** as above, where the coproduct property of $L_1 + L_2$ in **AGraphs** leads to a unique typing morphism $type : L_1 + L_2 \to ATG$, with $type \circ i_1 = type_1$ and $type \circ i_2 = type_2$ for the coproduct injections $i_1 : L_1 \to L_1 + L_2$ and $i_2 : L_2 \to L_1 + L_2$.

The following Parallelism Theorem for typed AGT systems corresponds to Theorem 3.24 for the typed graph case, where direct transformations are now direct typed attributed graph transformations (see Definition 9.2).

Theorem 9.18 (Parallelism Theorem for typed AGT systems).

1. Synthesis. *Given a sequentially independent direct transformation sequence $G \Rightarrow H_1 \Rightarrow G'$ via productions p_1 and p_2, then there is a construction leading to a parallel transformation $G \Rightarrow G'$ via the parallel production $p_1 + p_2$, called a* synthesis construction.
2. Analysis. *Given a parallel transformation $G \Rightarrow G'$ via $p_1 + p_2$, then there is a construction leading to two sequentially independent transformation sequences, $G \Rightarrow H_1 \Rightarrow G'$ via p_1 and p_2 and $G \Rightarrow H_2 \Rightarrow G'$ via p_2 and p_1, called an* analysis construction.
3. Bijective correspondence. *The synthesis and analysis constructions are inverse to each other up to isomorphism.*

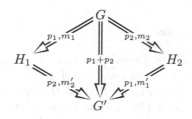

Proof. See Theorem 11.14 in Section 11.3. □

Example 9.19 (Parallelism Theorem). We have shown in Example 9.15 that the direct transformations $S \overset{addMethod,m_1}{\Longrightarrow} AG_1$ and $S \overset{addClass,m_2}{\Longrightarrow} AG_1'$ are parallel independent. In the following diagram, we show the parallel production $addMethod + addClass$. Note that we use the term algebra over the disjoint union $X \overset{\cdot}{\cup} X$ for the data part, because both productions have data algebras $T_{DSIG}(X)$. We use the following representation of the disjoint union:

$$X \overset{\cdot}{\cup} X = X \times \{1\} \cup X \times \{2\} \text{ (see Example A.28).}$$

$$addMethod + addClass :$$

The application of the parallel production $addMethod + addClass$ to the start graph S with the match $m_1 + m_2'$, where add is assigned to $(m, 1)$ and Nat to $(ptype, 2)$, leads to the parallel direct transformation

$$S \overset{addMethod+addClass,m_1+m_2'}{\Longrightarrow} AG_2.$$

$\square$

9.4 Concurrency Theorem and Pair Factorization for Typed AGT Systems

In this section, we present the Concurrency Theorem for typed AGT systems, as discussed for the graph case in Subsection 3.4.1. For technical reasons, we start by considering pair factorizations which will be used later for the Concurrency Theorem in this section and for the consideration of critical pairs and local confluence for typed AGT systems in the next chapter.

9.4.1 Pair Factorizations

In this subsection, we define $\mathcal{E}'$–$\mathcal{M}'$ pair factorizations of two morphisms in **AGraphs$_{\mathbf{ATG}}$** with the same codomain and give several examples. The idea of a pair factorization is similar to that of the epi–mono factorization of a morphism (see Definition A.15). On the basis of this pair factorization, we define E-related transformation sequences in this section and critical pairs over $\mathcal{E}'$-morphisms for parallel dependent direct transformations in the next chapter, and show that these critical pairs are complete.

Throughout this section, let $\mathcal{M}'$ be a morphism class closed under pushouts and pullbacks along $\mathcal{M}$-morphisms. This means, given (1) with $m, n \in \mathcal{M}$, that:

- if (1) is a pushout and $f \in \mathcal{M}'$, then $g \in \mathcal{M}'$, and
- if (1) is a pullback and $g \in \mathcal{M}'$, then $f \in \mathcal{M}'$:

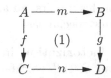

For two morphisms f_1 and f_2 with the same codomain, we now define a pair factorization over a class of morphism pairs $\mathcal{E}'$ and over $\mathcal{M}'$.

Definition 9.20 ($\mathcal{E}'$–$\mathcal{M}'$ pair factorization in AGraphs$_{\mathbf{ATG}}$). *Given a class of morphism pairs $\mathcal{E}'$ with the same codomain and a class $\mathcal{M}'$ in* **AGraphs$_{\mathbf{ATG}}$** *as considered above, then* **AGraphs$_{\mathbf{ATG}}$** *has an $\mathcal{E}'$–$\mathcal{M}'$ pair factorization if, for each pair of morphisms $f_1 : A_1 \to C$, $f_2 : A_2 \to C$, there exist a graph K and morphisms $e_1 : A_1 \to K$, $e_2 : A_2 \to K$, $m : K \to C$ with $(e_1, e_2) \in \mathcal{E}'$, $m \in \mathcal{M}'$ such that $m \circ e_1 = f_1$ and $m \circ e_2 = f_2$:*

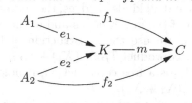

Remark 9.21. The intuitive idea of morphism pairs $(e_1, e_2) \in \mathcal{E}'$ is that of jointly epimorphic morphisms (see Definition A.16). This can be established for categories with binary coproducts and an $\mathcal{E}_0$–$\mathcal{M}_0$ factorization of morphisms, where $\mathcal{E}_0$ is a class of epimorphisms and $\mathcal{M}_0$ a class of monomorphisms. Given $A_1 \xrightarrow{f_1} C \xleftarrow{f_2} A_2$, we take an $\mathcal{E}_0$–$\mathcal{M}_0$ factorization $f = m \circ e$ of the induced morphism $f : A_1 + A_2 \to C$ and define $e_1 = e \circ \iota_1$ and $e_2 = e \circ \iota_2$, where ι_1 and ι_2 are the coproduct injections:

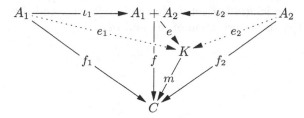

An $\mathcal{E}_0$–$\mathcal{M}_0$ factorization in **AGraphs$_{\mathbf{ATG}}$** is given by the classes $\mathcal{E}_0$ of surjective morphisms and $\mathcal{M}_0$ of injective morphisms.

For the construction of E-dependency relations in the next subsection and for the definition of critical pairs for typed AGT systems in Section 10.2, we need a suitable $\mathcal{E}'$–$\mathcal{M}'$ pair factorization in **AGraphs$_{\mathbf{ATG}}$**. There are several options for the choice of this factorization. For the completeness of critical pairs only those morphisms are relevant whose domain is attributed over the term algebra with variables, owing to the restriction of the attribution of the rule objects. For other morphism pairs, an arbitrary choice can be made. Therefore we concentrate on this special case.

Example 9.22 ($\mathcal{E}'$–$\mathcal{M}'$ pair factorization in AGraphs$_{\mathbf{ATG}}$). There are various options for defining an $\mathcal{E}'$–$\mathcal{M}'$ pair factorization of matches $m_1 : AG^1 \rightarrow AG^3$ and $m_2 : AG^2 \rightarrow AG^3$ in **AGraphs$_{\mathbf{ATG}}$**, with $AG^i = (G^i, T_{DSIG}(X_i), t^i : G^i \rightarrow ATG)$ for $i = 1, 2$. In the following, we introduce some of them.

1. $\mathcal{E}'_1$–$\mathcal{M}'_1$ pair factorization.
   For the first pair factorization, we use the construction in Remark 9.21 for an epi–mono factorization (see Definition A.15). Let $\mathcal{E}'_1$ be the class of jointly surjective morphisms in **AGraphs$_{\mathbf{ATG}}$** with the same codomain, and $\mathcal{M}'_1$ the class of all monomorphisms.

   We construct the binary coproduct of AG_1 and AG_2 (see Lemma 11.15). For the graph nodes and all kinds of edges, the coproduct of AG_1 and AG_2 is the disjoint union of the graph nodes and of the edges, respectively.

   On the data part, we use the construction of binary coproducts to obtain the data part coproduct $T_{DSIG}(X_1) + T_{DSIG}(X_2)$. Since the term algebra with variables is a free construction, it holds that $T_{DSIG}(X_1) + T_{DSIG}(X_2) \cong T_{DSIG}(X_1 + X_2)$.

   For the matches m_1 and m_2, there is an induced morphism $[m_1, m_2] : AG^1 + AG^2 \rightarrow AG^3$ such that $[m_1, m_2] \circ \iota_{AG^1} = m_1$ and $[m_1, m_2] \circ \iota_{AG^2} = m_2$.

   Now we factorize the morphism $[m_1, m_2]$ with an epi–mono factorization and obtain an object K, an epimorphism $e : AG^1 + AG^2 \rightarrow K$, and a monomorphism $m : K \rightarrow AG^3$ such that $m \circ e = [m_1, m_2]$. We then define $e_1 = e \circ \iota_{AG^1}$ and $e_2 = e \circ \iota_{AG^2}$. It holds that $m \circ e_1 = m \circ e \circ \iota_{AG^1} = [m_1, m_2] \circ \iota_{AG^1} = m_1$ and $m \circ e_2 = m \circ e \circ \iota_{AG^2} = [m_1, m_2] \circ \iota_{AG^2} = m_2$. e_1 and e_2 are jointly surjective and m is injective, and therefore we have an $\mathcal{E}'_1$–$\mathcal{M}'_1$ pair factorization of m_1 and m_2:

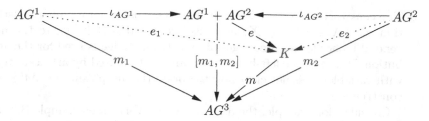

$[m_1, m_2]$ maps the variables in X_1 and X_2 as specified by m_1 and m_2, and all terms to their evaluation in AG^3. In general, there are different terms with the same evaluation, which means the data part of K must be a quotient term algebra $T_{DSIG}(X_1 + X_2)|_{\equiv}$.

2. $\mathcal{E}'_2$–$\mathcal{M}'_2$ *pair factorization*. We consider another case, where the left-hand sides of the rules are attributed only by variables, which is a very common case. This leads to the $\mathcal{E}'_2$–$\mathcal{M}'_2$ pair factorization, where $(e_1, e_2) \in \mathcal{E}'_2$ are jointly surjective for the graph nodes and all kinds of edges, and $m \in \mathcal{M}'_2$ is injective for the graph nodes and all kinds of edges.

For the graph nodes and edges of the object K and the morphisms e_1, e_2 and m on the graph part, we use the construction above over the coproducts and an epi–mono factorization.

On the data part, the construction is different, as follows. The data algebra of K is $T_{DSIG}(X_1 + X_2)$, which implies that the V_D-component of K, also consists of terms with variables over $X_1 + X_2$. For each d in D^3, the data algebra of AG^3, we define X_d to be the set of all variables x in $X_1 + X_2$ which are evaluated by m_1 or m_2 to d, i.e. $m_1(x) = d$ for $x \in X_1$ and $m_2(x) = d$ for $x \in X_2$. Now we choose, for each $X_d \neq \varnothing$, exactly one $x_d \in X_d$, and each variable $x \in X_i$ with $m_i(x) = d$ is mapped by e_i to x_d and x_d is mapped by m to d, i.e. $e_i(x) = x_d$ and $m(x_d) = d$. This is shown in the following example, where m_i maps a_i and a'_i to a_3 and a'_3, respectively, for $i = 1, 2$. The well-definedness of this construction is shown in Fact 9.23.

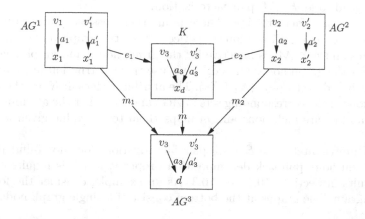

3. The construction in item 2 is similar to the most general unifier construction $\sigma_n : X \rightarrow T_{DSIG}(X)$ as considered in [HKT02]. There the most general unifier for all preimages of an attribute edge is used for the attribution. However, the left-hand sides can be attributed by arbitrary terms with variables. It is not clear how to obtain the morphism $m \in \mathcal{M}'$ in this construction.

Consider, for example, the data signature NAT (see Example B.3) and the graphs and morphisms in the following diagram. The graphs AG^1 and AG^2 are attributed over the term algebra $T_{NAT}(\{x, y\})$, and AG^3 is attributed over the algebra A, as in Example B.10.

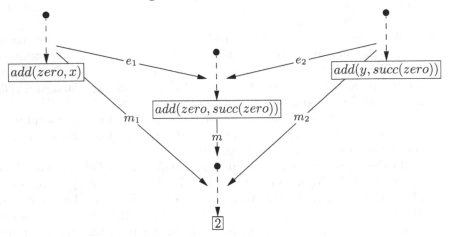

Here m_1 assigns the value 2 to x, and m_2 assigns the value 1 to y. This means that $add(zero, x)$ and $add(y, succ(zero))$ are evaluated to 2 by m_1 and m_2 respectively. The most general unifier of the terms $add(zero, x)$ and $add(y, succ(zero))$ is the term $add(zero, succ(zero))$. However there is no morphism $m : K \rightarrow AG^3$ (which has to be the evaluation) such that $m(add(zero, succ(zero))) = 2$. Hence, unfortunately, this construction does not lead to an $\mathcal{E}'$–$\mathcal{M}'$ pair factorization.

4. $\mathcal{E}'_3$–$\mathcal{M}'_3$ pair factorization. There is another possible pair factorization, where $(e_1, e_2) \in \mathcal{E}'_2$ are jointly surjective for the graph nodes and graph edges and $m \in \mathcal{M}'_2$ is injective for the graph nodes and graph edges.

For the graph nodes and edges, we use the construction in item 1. K is attributed over $T_{DSIG}(X_1 + X_2)$. The attribute edges in K are the disjoint unions of the corresponding sets in AG^1 and AG^2. For the attribute edges, e_1 and e_2 are inclusions and m maps them to the value given by m_1 or m_2.

Unfortunately, the $\mathcal{E}'_3$–$\mathcal{M}'_3$ pair factorization does not fulfill the $\mathcal{M}$–$\mathcal{M}'$ pushout–pullback decomposition property, which is required for our results in Sections 10.2 and 10.3. As an example, consider the following diagram. The graphs at the bottom consist of a single graph node that is attributed once or twice by the same type. We have the result that (1) + (2) is a pushout and (2) is a pullback, but neither (1) nor (2) is a pushout:

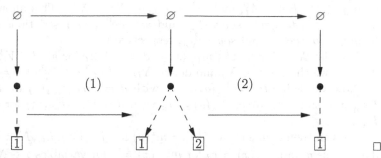

For the completeness of critical pairs and the Local Confluence Theorem, we need in addition the condition that the class $\mathcal{M}'$ is closed under pushouts and pullbacks along $\mathcal{M}$-morphisms and that the $\mathcal{M}$–$\mathcal{M}'$ pushout–pullback decomposition property (see Definition 5.27) holds.

In the $\mathcal{E}'_1$–$\mathcal{M}'_1$ pair factorization, $\mathcal{M}'_1$ is the class of all injective graph morphisms. For this morphism class, the required properties are fulfilled.

For the $\mathcal{E}'_2$–$\mathcal{M}'_2$ pair factorization, the morphism class $\mathcal{M}'_2$ is defined as the class of graph morphisms that are injective on the non data part. We show in Lemma 11.16 that the required properties are already fulfilled in the category **AGSIG-Alg** over an attributed graph structure signature $AGSIG$ for the corresponding morphism class. Therefore these properties hold for our class $\mathcal{M}'_2$ in **AGraphs$_{\mathbf{ATG}}$** in particular.

Fact 9.23 ($\mathcal{E}'_2$–$\mathcal{M}'_2$ pair factorization). *Given $AG^i = (G^i, D^i)$ for $i = 1, 2, 3$, where $D^i = T_{DSIG}(X^i)$ for $i = 1, 2$ and $m^1 : AG^1 \rightarrow AG^3$, and $m^2 : AG^2 \rightarrow AG^3$ in **AGraphs** (or **AGraphs$_{\mathbf{ATG}}$**), where AG^1 and AG^2 are attributed by variables only, i.e.*

$$target^i_{EA}(E^i_{EA}) \subseteq X^i \text{ and } target^i_{NA}(E^i_{NA}) \subseteq X^i \text{ for } i = 1, 2.$$

then there is an $\mathcal{E}'_2$–$\mathcal{M}'_2$ pair factorization $m^1 = m \circ e^1$, $m^2 = m \circ e^2$

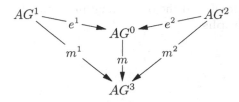

of m^1 and m^2 with $(e^1, e^2) \in \mathcal{E}'_2$ and $m \in \mathcal{M}'_2$.

Construction. Let $AG^0 = (G^0, D^0)$ with $V_G^0 = m^1(V_G^1) \cup m^2(V_G^2)$ and $V_D^0 = \cup_{s \in S_D'} T_{DSIG}(X^1 + X^2)_s$. For the edges, we define $E_j^0 = m^1(E_j^1) \cup m^2(E_j^2)$ with $j \in \{G, EA, NA\}$, and $D^0 = T_{DSIG}(X^1 + X^2)$. This allows us to define $source_G^0$, $target_G^0$, $source_{EA}^0$, and $source_{NA}^0$ as restrictions of $source_G^3$, $target_G^3$, $source_{EA}^3$, and $source_{NA}^3$, respectively.

Now let $X_d = \{x \in X^i \mid m_{V_D}^i(x) = d,\ i = 1, 2\}$ for all $d \in V_D^3$ and for all $X_d \neq \varnothing$ we choose $x_d \in X_d$ and define $X_D = \{x_d \mid d \in V_D^3, X_d \neq \varnothing\}$.

Now we define $target_{EA}^0(a) = x_d$ with $d = target_{EA}^3(a)$ for $a \in E_{EA}^0 \subseteq E_{EA}^3$ and similarly, $target_{NA}^0(a) = x_d$ with $d = target_{NA}^3(a)$ for $a \in E_{NA}^0 \subseteq E_{NA}^3$.

We can then define e^i by $e_j^i(a) = m_j^i(a)$ for $j \in \{V_G, E_G, NA, EA\}$ on non data items a and $e_{V_D}^i(x) = x_d$ for $m_{V_D}^i(x) = d$ for variables $x \in X_i$ ($i = 1, 2$). We define m by $m_j(a) = a$ for $j \in \{V_G, E_G, NA, EA\}$ on non data items a, for variables $m_{V_D} = (x_d) = d$ and $m_{V_D}(x) = m_{V_D}^i(x)$ for $x \in X^i \setminus X_D$ ($i = 1, 2$).

This leads to unique homomorphisms $e_D^i : T_{DSIG}(X^i) \to T_{DSIG}(X^1 + X^2)$ defined by $e_D^i(x) = e_{V_D}^i(x)$, and $m_D : T_{DSIG}(X^1 + X^2) \to D^3$ defined by $m_D(x) = m_{V_D}(x)$. $\square$

Proof. We have to show the following:

1. $m \circ e^1 = m^1$ and $m \circ e^2 = m^2$ with $(e^1, e^2) \in \mathcal{E}_2'$ and $m \in \mathcal{M}_2'$;
2. e^1, e^2, and m are well-defined morphisms in **AGraphs**;
3. e^1, e^2, and m are morphisms in **AGraphs$_{\text{ATG}}$**.

1. For $j \in \{V_G, E_G, E_{NA}, E_{EA}\}$, we have $m_j \circ e_j^i(a) = m_j(m_j^i(a)) = m_j^i(a)$ for $i = 1, 2$. Furthermore, $m_{V_D} \circ e_{V_D}^i(x) = m_{V_D}(x_d) = d$ for $m_{V_D}^i(x) = d$ ($i = 1, 2$), and for $x_d \in X_d$ we have $m_{V_D}(x_d) = d$. This implies that $m_{V_D} \circ e_{V_D}^i = m_{V_D}^i$. For the D-components, we have $m_D \circ e_D^i(x) = m_D(x_d) = d = m_D^i(x)$ ($i = 1, 2$), for $x \in X^i$ with $m_D^i(x) = d$.

   Moreover, $(e^1, e^2) \in \mathcal{E}_2'$ and $m \in \mathcal{M}_2'$, because, except for the data nodes, (e^1, e^2) are jointly surjective and m is injective.

2. For the well-definedness of e^i ($i = 1, 2$) and m, we have to show, for the EA-component (and similarly for the NA-component), that (1) and (2) in the following diagram commute. In this diagram, (3) and (4) commute, by item 1 of the proof, and the outer diagram commutes because m^i is a morphism in **AGraphs**:

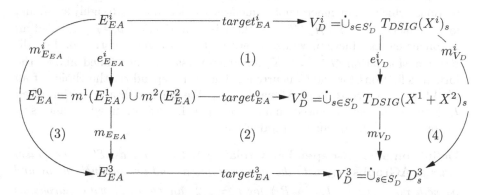

(1) commutes, because for $a \in E^i_{EA}$, we have:
$target^0_{EA} \circ e^i_{E_{EA}}(a) = target^0_{EA}(m^i_{E_{EA}}(a)) = x_d$ for $d = target^3_{EA} \circ m^i_{E_{EA}}(a)$, and $e^i_{V_D} \circ target^i_{EA}(a) = x_{d'}$ for $m^i_{V_D}(target^i_{EA}(a)) = d'$. Now we have $d = d'$, because $target^3_{EA} \circ m^i_{E_{EA}} = m^i_{V_D} \circ target^i_{EA}$ (outer diagram).

The commutativity of (2) follows from that of (1), (3), and (4) and the fact that $e^1_{E_{EA}}$ and $e^2_{E_{EA}}$ are jointly surjective.

3. In **AGraphs$_{ATG}$**, we have typing morphisms $type^i : AG^i \to ATG$ for $i = 1, 2, 3$ by assumption, and we can define $type^0 = type^3 \circ m$, which implies that e_1, e_2, and m are type-preserving, by tem 1:

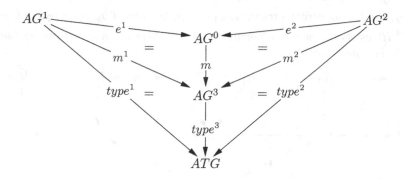

9.4.2 Concurrency Theorem

In the following, we extend the discussion of the Concurrency Theorem from the graph case considered in Subsection 3.4.1 to typed attributed graphs. The following constructions can also be seen as an instantiation of the categorical theory in Section 5.4. In fact, the notation is almost identical to that in Section 5.4. However, Section 5.4 is based on an adhesive HLR system AHS, while this section is based on a typed attributed graph transformation system GTS.

The Concurrency Theorem handles direct typed attributed graph transformations, which are in general not sequentially independent. Roughly speaking, for a sequence $G \overset{p_1,m_1}{\Rightarrow} H_1 \overset{p_2,m_2}{\Rightarrow} X$ there is a production $p_1 *_E p_2$, called an E-concurrent production, which allows us to construct a corresponding direct transformation $G \overset{p_1 *_E p_2}{\Rightarrow} X$, and vice versa. As mentioned above, the formal definitions for the Concurrency Theorem depend on the choice of an $\mathcal{E}'-\mathcal{M}'$ pair factorization in $\mathbf{AGraphs_{ATG}}$. We start with a definition of an E-dependency relation based on an $\mathcal{E}'-\mathcal{M}'$ pair factorization, which allows us to construct an E-concurrent production.

Definition 9.24 (E-dependency relation). *Given a class $\mathcal{E}'$ of morphism pairs in $\mathbf{AGraphs_{ATG}}$ with the same codomain, and two productions p_1 and p_2 with $p_i = (L_i \overset{l_i}{\leftarrow} K_i \overset{r_i}{\rightarrow} R_i)$ for $i = 1, 2$, an object E with morphisms $e_1 : R_1 \rightarrow E$ and $e_2 : L_2 \rightarrow E$ is an E-dependency relation for p_1 and p_2, if $(e_1, e_2) \in \mathcal{E}'$ and the pushout complements (1) and (2) over $K_1 \overset{r_1}{\rightarrow} R_1 \overset{e_1}{\rightarrow} E$ and $K_2 \overset{l_2}{\rightarrow} L_2 \overset{e_2}{\rightarrow} E$ exist:*

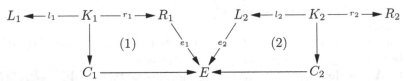

Definition 9.25 (E-concurrent production and E-related transformation). *Given an E-dependency relation $(e_1, e_2) \in \mathcal{E}'$ for the productions p_1 and p_2, the E-concurrent production $p_1 *_E p_2$ is defined by $p_1 *_E p_2 = (L \overset{lok_1}{\leftarrow} K \overset{rok_2}{\rightarrow} R)$ as shown in the following diagram, where (3) and (4) are pushouts and (5) is a pullback:*

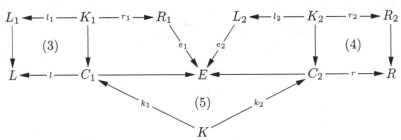

A transformation sequence $G \overset{p_1,m_1}{\Rightarrow} H_1 \overset{p_2,m_2}{\Rightarrow} G'$ is called E-related if there exists $h : E \rightarrow H_1$ with $h \circ e_1 = n_1$ and $h \circ e_2 = m_2$ and there are morphisms $c_1 : C_1 \rightarrow D_1$ and $c_2 : C_2 \rightarrow D_2$ such that (6) and (7) commute and (8) and (9) are pushouts:

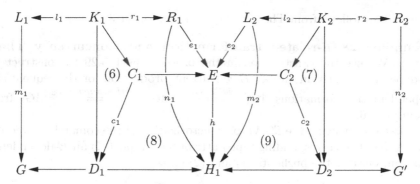

The following Concurrency Theorem for typed AGT systems corresponds to Theorem 3.26 for the graph case, where the transformations are now typed attributed graph transformations (see Definition 9.2).

Theorem 9.26 (Concurrency Theorem for typed AGT systems). *Let GTS be a typed attributed graph transformation system, let $R_1 \overset{e_1}{\to} E \overset{e_2}{\leftarrow} L_2$ be an E-dependency relation for the productions p_1 and p_2 for a given class $\mathcal{E}'$ of morphism pairs, and let $p_1 *_E p_2$ be the corresponding E-concurrent production.*

1. *Synthesis. Given a E-related transformation sequence $G \Rightarrow H \Rightarrow G'$ via p_1 and p_2, then there is a synthesis construction leading to a direct transformation $G \Rightarrow G'$ via $p_1 *_E p_2$.*
2. *Analysis. Given a direct transformation $G \Rightarrow G'$ via $p_1 *_E p_2$, then there is an analysis construction leading to a E-related transformation sequence $G \Rightarrow H \Rightarrow G'$ via p_1 and p_2.*
3. *Bijective correspondence. The synthesis and analysis constructions are inverse to each other up to isomorphism, provided that $\mathcal{E}'$ consists of epimorphic pairs only (see Definition A.16).*

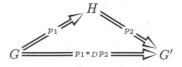

Proof. See Theorem 11.14 in Section 11.3.   □

Finally, we show, as instantiation of Fact 5.29, how to construct E-related transformations.

Fact 9.27 (construction of E–related transformations). *Given an $\mathcal{E}'$-$\mathcal{M}'$ pair factorization in $\mathbf{AGraphs_{ATG}}$, then for each pair of direct transformations $G \overset{p_1,m_1}{\Longrightarrow} H_1 \overset{p_2,m_2}{\Longrightarrow} G'$, we have an E-dependency relation E such that $G \overset{p_1,m_1}{\Longrightarrow} H_1 \overset{p_2,m_2}{\Longrightarrow} G'$ is E-related provided that $\mathcal{M}'$ is equal to $\mathcal{M}'_1$ or $\mathcal{M}'_2$ (see Example 9.22).*

Proof. This follows from Theorem 11.14 in Section 11.3.   □

Example 9.28 (*E*-related transformation and Concurrency Theorem). We use the construction in the proof of Fact 5.29 to construct an *E*-dependency relation and an *E*-concurrent production for the sequentially dependent transformations $AG_1 \overset{addClass,m_2}{\Longrightarrow} AG_2 \overset{addParameter,m_3}{\Longrightarrow} AG_3$ from Example 9.6.

First we construct the $\mathcal{E}'$–$\mathcal{M}'$ pair factorization of the comatch n_2 and the match m_3. The corresponding typed attributed graph E is an *E*-dependency relation, because the pushouts (1) and (2) exist:

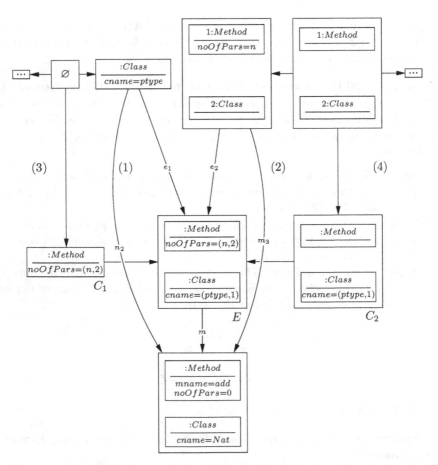

Now we construct the pushouts (3) and (4) with the pushout objects L^* and R^* and construct the pullback over $C_1 \to E \leftarrow C_2$ with the pullback object K^*, and obtain the following *E*-concurrent production $addClass *_E addParameter = (L^* \leftarrow K^* \to R^*)$, where K^* (not shown explicitly) consists of a node of type *Method* without attributes:

$$addClass *_E \ addParameter:$$

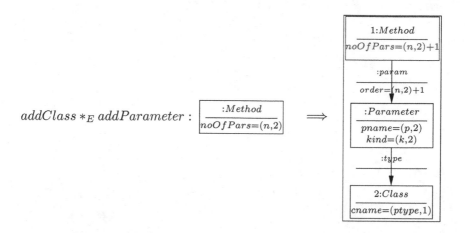

This construction makes sure that the transformation

$$AG_1 \stackrel{addClass, m_2}{\Longrightarrow} AG_2 \stackrel{addParameter, m_3}{\Longrightarrow} AG_3$$

is E-related. Applying Theorem 9.26, we obtain a direct transformation $AG_1 \Rightarrow AG_3$ using the constructed E-concurrent production $addClass *_E$ $addParameter$.   □

10

Embedding and Local Confluence for Typed AGT Systems

In this chapter, we continue the theory of typed attributed graph transformation systems by describing the Embedding and Extension Theorems, critical pairs and local confluence in Sections 10.1, 10.2, and 10.3, respectively. The constructions have been considered for the graph case in Subsections 3.4.2 and 3.4.3 in Part I.

The notation for the main constructions and results in this chapter is almost identical to that in Chapter 6. However, Chapter 6 is based on an adhesive HLR system AHS, while the present chapter is based on a typed attributed graph transformation system GTS.

10.1 Embedding and Extension Theorems for Typed AGT Systems

In this section, we study the problem of under what conditions a graph transformation $t : G_0 \Rightarrow^* G_n$ can be embedded into a larger context given by a graph morphism $k_0 : G_0 \to G'_0$. In fact, an extension of $t : G_0 \Rightarrow^* G_n$ to a graph transformation $t' : G'_0 \Rightarrow^* G'_n$ is possible only if the extension morphism k_0 is consistent with the given graph transformation $t : G_0 \Rightarrow^* G_n$. This will be shown in the Embedding and Extension Theorems for typed AGT systems below.

This problem has been discussed for the graph case in Part I and presented in the categorical framework in Part II (see Sections 6.1 and 6.2).

First of all we introduce the notion of an extension diagram. An extension diagram describes how a graph transformation $t : G_0 \Rightarrow^* G_n$ can be extended to a transformation $t' : G'_0 \Rightarrow G'_n$ via an extension morphism $k_0 : G_0 \to G'_0$.

Definition 10.1 (extension diagram for typed AGT system). *An extension diagram is a diagram (1),*

$$G_0 = t \stackrel{*}{\Longrightarrow} G_n$$

$$\downarrow k_0 \quad (1) \quad \downarrow k_n$$

$$G_0' = t' \stackrel{*}{\Longrightarrow} G_n'$$

where $k_0 : G_0 \to G_0'$ is a morphism, called an extension morphism, and $t : G_0 \stackrel{*}{\Rightarrow} G_n$ and $t' : G_0' \stackrel{*}{\Rightarrow} G_n'$ are graph transformations via the same productions $(p_0, ..., p_{n-1})$ and via the matches $(m_0, ..., m_{n-1})$ and $(k_0 \circ m_0, ..., k_{n-1} \circ m_{n-1})$, respectively, defined by the following DPO diagrams in $\mathbf{AGraphs_{ATG}}$:

$$p_i: \quad L_i \stackrel{l_i}{\longleftarrow} K_i \stackrel{r_i}{\longrightarrow} R_i$$

$$\downarrow m_i \qquad \downarrow j_i \qquad \downarrow n_i$$

$$G_i \stackrel{f_i}{\longleftarrow} D_i \stackrel{g_i}{\longrightarrow} G_{i+1} \quad (i = 0, ..., n-1), n > 0$$

$$\downarrow k_i \qquad \downarrow d_i \qquad \downarrow k_{i+1}$$

$$G_i' \stackrel{f_i'}{\longleftarrow} D_i' \stackrel{g_i'}{\longrightarrow} G_{i+1}'$$

For $n = 0$ (see Definition 6.7) the extension diagram is given up to isomorphism by

$$G_0 \stackrel{id_{G_0}}{\longleftarrow} G_0 \stackrel{id_{G_0}}{\longrightarrow} G_0$$

$$\downarrow k_0 \qquad \downarrow k_0 \qquad \downarrow k_0$$

$$G_0' \stackrel{id_{G_0'}}{\longleftarrow} G_0' \stackrel{id'_{G_0}}{\longrightarrow} G_0'$$

The following condition for a graph transformation $t : G_0 \stackrel{*}{\Rightarrow} G_n$ and an extension morphism $k_0 : G_0 \to G_0'$ means intuitively that the boundary graph B of k_0 is preserved by t. In order to formulate this property, we first introduce the notion of a derived span $der(t) = (G_0 \leftarrow D \to G_n)$ of the graph transformation t, which connects the first and the last graph, and later the notion of a boundary graph B for k_0.

Definition 10.2 (derived span). *The derived span of an identical graph transformation $t : G \stackrel{id}{\Rightarrow} G$ is defined by $der(t) = (G \leftarrow G \to G)$ with identical morphisms.*

The derived span of a direct graph transformation $G \stackrel{p,m}{\Longrightarrow} H$ is the span $(G \leftarrow D \to H)$ (see Definition 9.4).

For a graph transformation $t : G_0 \stackrel{*}{\Rightarrow} G_n \Rightarrow G_{n+1}$, the derived span is the composition via the pullback (P) in the category $\mathbf{AGraph_{ATG}}$ (see below) of the derived spans $der(G_0 \stackrel{*}{\Rightarrow} G_n) = (G_0 \stackrel{d_0}{\leftarrow} D' \stackrel{d_1}{\to} G_n)$ and $der(G_n \Rightarrow G_{n+1}) = (G_n \stackrel{f_n}{\leftarrow} D_n \stackrel{g_n}{\to} G_{n+1})$. This construction leads (uniquely up to isomorphism) to the derived span $der(t) = (G_0 \stackrel{d_0 \circ d_2}{\longleftarrow} D \stackrel{g_n \circ d_3}{\longrightarrow} G_{n+1})$.

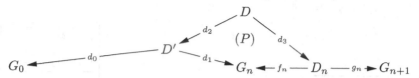

In the case $t : G_0 \Rightarrow^* G_n$ with $n = 0$, we have either $G_0 = G_n$ and $t : G_0 \stackrel{id}{\Rightarrow} G_0$ (see above), or $G_0 \cong G_0'$ with $der(t) = (G_0 \stackrel{id}{\leftarrow} G_0 \stackrel{\sim}{\to} G_0')$.

Remark 10.3. According to Section 8.3, we know that pullbacks in **AGraphs$_{\textbf{ATG}}$** exist and that they are constructed componentwise in **Sets**. For the construction in **Sets**, we refer to Fact 2.23. In our construction of derived spans above, the given graph morphisms d_1 and f_n are in $\mathcal{M}$ such that the resulting graph morphisms d_2 and d_3 are also in $\mathcal{M}$. This means that the graph D is the intersection of D' and D_n. Altogether, D can be considered as the largest subgraph of G_0 which is preserved by the graph transformation $t : G_0 \Rightarrow^* G_n$, leading to a derived span $(G_0 \leftarrow D \to G_n)$ with subgraph embeddings $D \to G_0$ and $D \to G_n$.

Example 10.4 (derived span). Here, we construct the derived spans of some of the transformations presented in Example 9.6.

The derived span of the direct transformation $S \stackrel{addMethod, m_1}{\Longrightarrow} AG_1$ is given by the span of this transformation, as shown below:

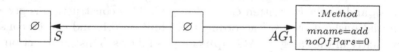

For the transformation $S \stackrel{addMethod, m_1}{\Longrightarrow} AG_1 \stackrel{addClass, m_2}{\Longrightarrow} AG_2$, the derived span is depicted in the following, where the pullback object is the empty graph:

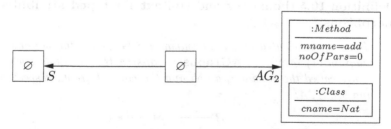

For the transformation $AG_1 \stackrel{addClass, m_2}{\Longrightarrow} AG_2 \stackrel{addParameter, m_3}{\Longrightarrow} AG_3$ with $m_3(n) = 0$, $m_3(p) = p1$, and $m_3(k) = in$, we have the following derived span:

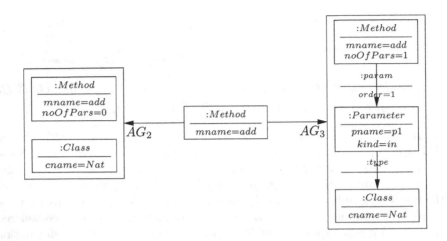

The derived span for the complete transformation $S \overset{*}{\Rightarrow} AG_3$ is the span $\varnothing \leftarrow \varnothing \rightarrow AG_3$. □

In order to define consistency of the extension morphism $k_0 : G_0 \rightarrow G_0'$ with respect to the graph transformation $t : G_0 \Rightarrow^* G_n$, we have to define the boundary graph B and, later, also the context graph C for k_0. Intuitively, the boundary B is the minimal interface graph that we need in order to be able to construct a context graph C such that G_0' can be considered as a pushout of G_0 and C via B, written $G_0' = G_0 +_B C$. This construction is given by an "initial pushout over k_0" according to Definition 6.1, and can be constructed explicitly in the category **AGraphs$_{\mathbf{ATG}}$** as follows. This construction is given by the initial pushout over k_0 in **AGraphs$_{\mathbf{ATG}}$** as defined in Fact 10.7.

The main idea of the construction is similar to that of initial pushouts in the graph case (see Section 6.2).

Definition 10.5 (boundary and context for typed attributed graph morphisms).

1. *Given an attributed graph morphism $f : G \rightarrow H$, the boundary–context diagram (1) over f in **AGraphs** is constructed as follows, where B and C are called the boundary graph and the context graph, respectively, of f, and $b, c \in \mathcal{M}$:*

$$
\begin{array}{ccc}
B & \xrightarrow{\quad c\in\mathcal{M} \quad} & G \\
\downarrow{\scriptstyle f} & (1) & \downarrow{\scriptstyle g} \\
C & \xrightarrow{\quad b\in\mathcal{M} \quad} & H
\end{array}
$$

2. *Given a typed attributed graph morphism $f : (G, t^G) \rightarrow (H, t^H)$, the boundary–context diagram (2) over f in **AGraphs$_{\mathbf{ATG}}$** is given by the*

boundary–context diagram (1) *over f in* **AGraphs**, *where* $t^B = t^G \circ b$ *and* $t^C = t^H \circ c$:

$$
\begin{array}{ccc}
(B, t^B) & \xrightarrow{\ c \in \mathcal{M}\ } & (G, t^G) \\
\downarrow f & (1) & \downarrow g \\
(C, t^C) & \xrightarrow{\ b \in \mathcal{M}\ } & (H, t^H)
\end{array}
$$

Construction (boundary–context diagram (1)*).* In the following, we denote an attributed graph X by

$$
X = (V_G^X, V_D^X, E_G^X, E_{NA}^X, E_{EA}^X, (source_j^X, target_j^X)_{j \in \{G, NA, EA\}}, D^X),
$$

where D^X is the *DSIG*-algebra of X, and we denote an attributed graph morphism f by $f = (f_{V_G}, f_{V_D}, f_{E_G}, f_{E_{NA}}, f_{E_{EA}}, f_D)$, where f_D is the *DSIG*-homomorphism of f with $f_{V_D} = \dot{\cup}_{s \in S_D'} f_{D_s}$.

In order to clarify the construction of the boundary graph B, let us recall the signature of an *E-graph* (see Definition 8.1):

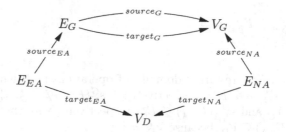

The boundary graph B is the intersection of suitable attributed subgraphs B' of G,

$$
B = \cap \{ B' \subseteq G \,|\, D^G = D^{B'}, V_D^G = V_D^{B'}, V_G^* \subseteq V_G^{B'}, E_G^* \subseteq E_G^{B'},
$$
$$
E_{NA}^* \subseteq E_{NA}^{B'}, E_{EA}^* \subseteq E_{EA}^{B'} \},
$$

where the sets V_G^*, E_G^*, E_{NA}^*, and E_{EA}^* built up by the dangling and identification points (see Definition 9.8) are defined as follows:

- $V_G^* = \{ a \in V_G^G \,|\, \exists a' \in E_G^H \setminus f_{E_G}(E_G^G)$ with $f_{E_G}(a) = source_G^H(a')$ or $f_{E_G}(a) = target_G^H(a') \}$
  $\cup \{ a \in V_G^G \,|\, \exists a' \in E_{NA}^H \setminus f_{E_{NA}}(E_{NA}^G)$ with $f_{E_{NA}}(a) = source_{NA}^H(a') \}$
  $\cup \{ a \in V_G^G \,|\, \exists a' \in V_G^G$ with $a \neq a'$ and $f_{V_G}(a) = f_{V_G}(a') \}$;
- $E_G^* = \{ a \in E_G^G \,|\, \exists a' \in E_{EA}^H \setminus f_{E_{EA}}(E_{EA}^G)$ with $f_{E_{EA}}(a) = source_{EA}^H(a') \}$
  $\cup \{ a \in E_G^G \,|\, \exists a' \in E_G^G$ with $a \neq a'$ and $f_{E_G}(a) = f_{E_G}(a') \}$;
- $E_{NA}^* = \{ a \in E_{NA}^G \,|\, \exists a' \in E_{NA}^G$ with $a \neq a'$ and $f_{E_{NA}}(a) = f_{E_{NA}}(a') \}$;
- $E_{EA}^* = \{ a \in E_{EA}^G \,|\, \exists a' \in E_{EA}^G$ with $a \neq a'$ and $f_{E_{EA}}(a) = f_{E_{EA}}(a') \}$.

The context graph C is the attributed subgraph of H defined by

- $V_G^C = (V_G^H \setminus f_{V_G}(V_G^G)) \cup f_{V_G}(V_G^B)$;
- $V_D^C = V_D^H$;
- $E_j^C = (E_j^H \setminus f_{E_j}(E_j^G)) \cup f_{E_j}(E_j^B)$, $j \in \{G, NA, EA\}$;
- $D^C = D^H$.

The attributed graph morphisms $b, c \in \mathcal{M}$, and g are given by

- $b : B \to G$, inclusion with $b_{V_D} = id$ and $b_D = id$;
- $c : C \to H$, inclusion with $c_{V_D} = id$ and $c_D = id$;
- $g : B \to C$, by $g_j(x) = f_j \circ b_j(x)$, $j \in \{V_G, V_D, E_G, E_{NA}, E_{EA}, D\}$.

$\square$

Remark 10.6. Note that $B^* = (V_G^*, V_D^G, E_G^*, E_{NA}^*, E_{EA}^*, (s_j^*, t_j^*)_{j \in \{G, NA, EA\}}, D^G)$ with restrictions $s_j^*(t_j^*)$ of $s_j^G(t_j^G)$, where s and t are abbreviations for *source* and *target*, respectively, is in general not an attributed subgraph of G, such that the subgraph B has to be constructed as the intersection of all subgraphs $B' \subseteq G$ defined above. However, we have the following for B:

- $V_G^* \subseteq V_G^B \subseteq V_G^G$,
- $V_D^B = V_D^G$,
- $E_G^* \subseteq E_G^B \subseteq E_G^G$,
- $E_{NA}^* \subseteq E_{NA}^B \subseteq E_{NA}^G$,
- $E_{EA}^* \subseteq E_{EA}^B \subseteq E_{EA}^G$,
- $D^B = D^G$.

In fact, V_G^B and E_G^B are target domains of operations in B which are proper extensions of V_G^* and E_G^*, respectively, if $s_G^G(E_G^*) \not\subseteq V_G^*$, $t_G^G(E_G^*) \not\subseteq V_G^*$, $s_{NA}^G(E_{NA}^*) \not\subseteq V_G^*$ and $s_{EA}^G(E_{EA}^*) \not\subseteq E_G^*$, respectively. Note that $t_{NA}^G(E_{NA}^*) \subseteq V_D^B$ and $t_{EA}^G(E_{EA}^*) \subseteq V_D^B$ because $V_D^B = V_D^G$.

The above constructions are all well defined, leading to an initial pushout over f in **AGraphs$_{\text{ATG}}$** (see Definition 6.1).

Fact 10.7 (initial pushouts in AGraphs and AGraphs$_{\text{ATG}}$).

1. *Given an attributed graph morphism* $f : G \to H$*, the boundary–context diagram* (1) *over* f *in Definition 10.5 is well defined and is an initial pushout over* f *in* (**AGraphs**, $\mathcal{M}$).
2. *Given a typed attributed graph morphism* $f : (G, t^G) \to (H, t^H)$*, the boundary–context diagram* (2) *over* f *is well-defined and is an initial pushout over* f *in* (**AGraphs$_{\text{ATG}}$**, $\mathcal{M}$).

Proof. The construction of the boundary–context diagrams in **AGraphs** and **AGraphs$_{\text{ATG}}$** is a special case of the initial-pushout construction in the category **AGSIG-Alg** (see Lemma 11.17) using the isomorphism **AGSIG(ATG)-Alg** $\cong$ **AGraphs$_{\text{ATG}}$** of categories, which will be shown in Chapter 11. Note that an explicit proof of initial pushouts for (**AGraphs$_{\text{ATG}}$**, $\mathcal{M}$) is more difficult than the general proof for (**AGSIG-Alg**, $\mathcal{M}$). $\square$

Example 10.8 (initial pushout). In the following diagram, the boundary–context diagram of the match morphism m_3 in Example 10.4 is depicted. We have no identification points, but the boundary object B consists of the two dangling points – the *Method* and the *Class* node – because in both cases a node attribute edge is added in AG_2.

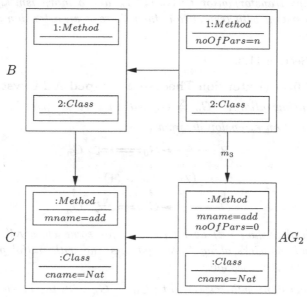

Now we are able to define the consistency of a morphism k_0 with respect to a graph transformation t. The main idea is that the boundary B of k_0, defined by the initial pushout over k_0, is preserved by the transformation t. This means that there is a suitable morphism $b : B \to D$, where D, defined by the derived span of t, is the largest subgraph of G_0 which is preserved by $t : G_0 \Rightarrow^* G_n$.

Definition 10.9 (consistency). *Given a graph transformation* $t : G_0 \overset{*}{\Rightarrow} G_n$ *with a derived span* $der(t) = (G_0 \overset{d_0}{\leftarrow} D \overset{d_n}{\to} G_n)$, *a morphism* $k_0 : G_0 \to G_0'$ *in* **AGraphs**$_{\mathbf{ATG}}$ *with the initial PO (1) over* k_0 *is called* consistent *with respect to* t *if there exists a morphism* $b \in \mathcal{M}$ *with* $d_0 \circ b = b_0$:

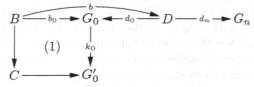

With the following Embedding and Extension Theorems, we can show that consistency is both necessary and sufficient for the construction of extension diagrams. These theorems correspond exactly to the corresponding Theorems 3.28 and 3.29 for the graph case and to Theorems 6.14 and 6.16 for the general case.

Theorem 10.10 (Embedding Theorem for typed AGT systems).
Given a graph transformation $t : G_0 \overset{*}{\Rightarrow} G_n$ *and a morphism* $k_0 : G_0 \to G_0'$ *which is consistent with respect to* t, *then there is an extension diagram over* t *and* k_0.

Proof. See Section 11.3.   □

Theorem 10.11 (Extension Theorem for typed AGT systems). *Given a graph transformation* $t : G_0 \overset{*}{\Rightarrow} G_n$ *with a derived span* $der(t) = (G_0 \overset{d_0}{\leftarrow} D_n \overset{d_n}{\to} G_n)$ *and an extension diagram (1),*

$$
\begin{array}{ccccc}
B & \overset{b_0}{\longrightarrow} & G_0 & \overset{*}{=\!\!=\!\!{}_t\!\!\Rightarrow} & G_n \\
\downarrow & & \downarrow {\scriptstyle k_0} & & \downarrow {\scriptstyle k_n} \\
& (2) & & (1) & \\
C & \longrightarrow & G_0' & \overset{*}{=\!\!=\!\!{}_{t'}\!\!\Rightarrow} & G_n'
\end{array}
$$

with an initial pushout (2) over $k_0 \in \mathcal{M}'$ *for some class* $\mathcal{M}'$ *closed under pushouts and pullbacks along* $\mathcal{M}$-*morphisms and with initial pushouts over* $\mathcal{M}'$-*morphisms, then we have:*

1. k_0 *is consistent with respect to* $t : G_0 \overset{*}{\Rightarrow} G_n$ *with the morphism* $b : B \to D_n$.
2. *There is a graph transformation* $G_0' \Rightarrow G_n'$ *via* $der(t)$ *and* k_0 *given by the pushouts (3) and (4) below with* $h, k_n \in \mathcal{M}'$.
3. *There are initial pushouts (5) and (6) over* $h \in \mathcal{M}'$ *and* $k_n \in \mathcal{M}'$, *respectively, with the same boundary–context morphism* $B \to C$:

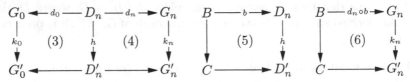

Proof. See Section 11.3.   □

Example 10.12 (Embedding and Extension Theorems). If we embed the start graph S from Example 10.4 via a morphism k_0 into a larger context H, k_0 is consistent with respect to the transformation $t : S \overset{*}{\Rightarrow} AG_3$. This is due to the fact that S is the empty graph, and therefore the boundary graph is also empty and no items have to be preserved by the transformation. Applying Theorem 10.10 allows us to embed the transformation $S \overset{*}{\Rightarrow} AG_3$, leading to an extension diagram over t and k_0. From Theorem 10.11, we conclude that there is a direct transformation $H \Rightarrow H'$ via the derived span $der(t)$ shown in Example 10.4. The resulting graph H' is the disjoint union of H and AG_3.   □

10.2 Critical Pairs for Typed AGT Systems

In order to study local confluence in Section 10.3, we now introduce critical pairs, as discussed in Section 3.4 and used for adhesive HLR systems in Chapter 6.

For the definition of critical pairs, we need the concept of an $\mathcal{E}'$–$\mathcal{M}'$ pair factorization introduced in Section 9.3.

Definition 10.13 (critical pair). *Given an $\mathcal{E}'$–$\mathcal{M}'$ pair factorization in* **AGraphs$_{ATG}$**, *a critical pair is a pair of parallel dependent direct transformations $P_1 \overset{p_1,o_1}{\Longleftarrow} K \overset{p_2,o_2}{\Longrightarrow} P_2$ such that $(o_1, o_2) \in \mathcal{E}'$ for the corresponding matches o_1 and o_2.*

In analogy to the graph case considered in Lemma 3.33 and the general case considered in Lemma 6.22, we now show the completeness of critical pairs in **AGraphs$_{ATG}$**.

Lemma 10.14 (completeness of critical pairs in AGraphs$_{ATG}$). *Given an $\mathcal{E}'$–$\mathcal{M}'$ pair factorization where the $\mathcal{M}$–$\mathcal{M}'$ pushout–pullback decomposition property holds (see Definition 5.27), then the critical pairs in* **AGraphs$_{ATG}$** *are complete. This means that for each pair of parallel dependent direct transformations $H_1 \overset{p_1,m_1}{\Longleftarrow} G \overset{p_2,m_2}{\Longrightarrow} H_2$, there is a critical pair $P_1 \overset{p_1,o_1}{\Longleftarrow} K \overset{p_2,o_2}{\Longrightarrow} P_2$ with extension diagrams (1) and (2) and $m \in \mathcal{M}'$:*

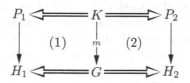

Remark 10.15. The requirements above are valid in particular for the $\mathcal{E}'_1$–$\mathcal{M}'_1$ and $\mathcal{E}'_2$–$\mathcal{M}'_2$ pair factorizations given in Definition 9.20.

Example 10.16 (critical pairs in *MethodModeling*). In the following, we analyze the critical pairs in our graph grammar *MethodModeling* from Example 9.6. We use the $\mathcal{E}'_2$–$\mathcal{M}'_2$ pair factorization given in Definition 9.20.

For the underlying category **AGraphs$_{ATG}$** with the given type graph *ATG* (see Example 8.9), there is a large number of critical pairs. We have counted 88 different possibilities for only the application of the production *checkNewParameter* in two different ways that lead to a critical pair.

If we analyze all these pairs, we see that most of them are strange in some way and do not meet our intentions for the graph grammar *MethodModeling*. We have aimed at modeling the signatures of method declarations, and our productions reflect this. However, in the critical pairs, often graph nodes have multiple occurrences of the same attribute, or parameters have multiple types or belong to more than one method. All these things are allowed in our general theory of typed attributed graphs, but they do not lead to a consistent method declaration, and cause a high number of critical pairs.

Therefore we analyze only those critical pairs which are of interest for the language of $MethodModeling$, which means that we consider only those graphs that can be derived from the empty graph by applying our productions.

With this restriction, we obtain the following critical pairs $P_1 \overset{p_1,m_1}{\Longleftarrow} K \overset{p_2,m_2}{\Longrightarrow} P_2$:

1. $p_1 = p_2 = addParameter$: 2 critical pairs. In this case, two parameters are added to the same method, which increases the number of parameters in the method, i.e. changes the attribute $noOfPars$ and causes a conflict. There are two possible cases: the classes of the two new parameters are the same or different.

2. $p_1 = addParameter$, $p_2 = checkNewParameter$: 2 critical pairs. One parameter is added to a method, and another one is deleted. Adding a parameter increases the value of $noOfPars$ and the deletion decreases this value, which leads to a conflict. Again there are two possible cases: the classes of the new and deleted parameters are the same or different.

3. $p_1 = p_2 = checkNewParameter$: 2 critical pairs. We delete the last parameter with both transformations. There are then two cases: the parameters that we use for the comparison (which means checking that the last parameter is already in the list) are the same or different.

4. $p_1 = checkNewParameter$, $p_2 = exchangeParameter$: 5 critical pairs. The last parameter of a method is deleted by one transformation, but the other transformation exchanges it with another parameter. There are several different ways in which the parameters involed can be matched.

   If one of the exchanged parameters is deleted, the other one can be the same as or different from the parameter we use for the comparison in $checkNewParameter$. This leads to four critical pairs. The fifth critical pair is obtained if both exchanged parameters are mapped together with the deleted one. This is possible, since matches do not have to be injective.

5. $p_1 = p_2 = exchangeParameter$: 11 critical pairs. If the same parameter is exchanged by both transformations, this leads to a conflict. There are 11 cases of how to map at least one parameter of one left-hand side to one parameter of the other left-hand side (including the cases where the matches are not injective).

Other combinations of productions do not result in critical pairs with overlapping graphs being generated by our productions; therefore, altogether, there are 22 critical pairs.

In the following diagram, the two critical pairs $P_1 \Leftarrow K \Rightarrow P_2$ and $P_1' \Leftarrow K' \Rightarrow P_2'$ for the case $p_1 = p_2 = addParameter$ are represented. In the top part of the diagram, we show only the left-hand sides of the productions, and the graphs K and K'. In the bottom part, the resulting direct transformations are depicted. The matches are shown by the names of the nodes. The value of the attribute $noOfPars$ is changed, which means that in the gluing object (not shown explicitly) of the direct transformations $P_1 \Leftarrow K \Rightarrow P_2$ and $P_1' \Leftarrow K' \Rightarrow P_2'$, there is no node attribute edge between the method and the variable n. Therefore these transformations are parallel dependent. The matches are jointly surjective on the graph part, and both transformation pairs are critical pairs.

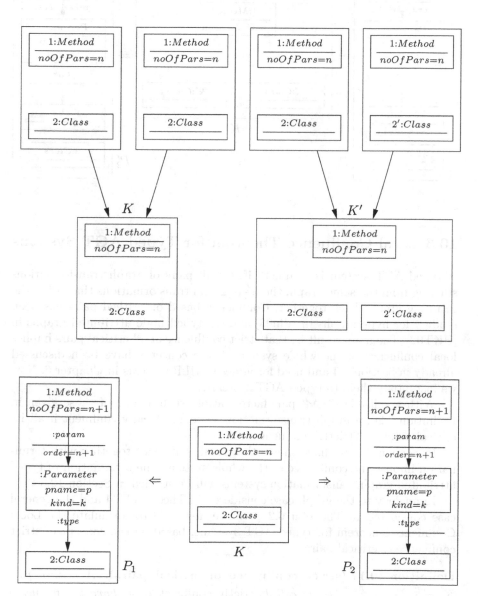

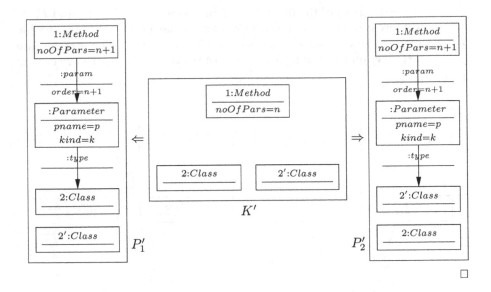

10.3 Local Confluence Theorem for Typed AGT Systems

A typed AGT system is confluent if, for all pairs of graph transformations starting from the same graph, there are graph transformations that bring the resulting graphs back together. Confluence based on critical pairs has been studied for hypergraphs in [Plu93] and for typed node attributed graphs in [HKT02]. The main result is, that strict confluence of all critical pairs implies local confluence of the whole system. These concepts have been discussed already in Section 3.4 and used for adhesive HLR systems in Chapter 6. Now we instantiate them to typed AGT systems.

With a suitable $\mathcal{E}'$–$\mathcal{M}'$ pair factorization, such as one of those given in Definition 9.20, a graph transformation system is locally confluent if all its critical pairs are strictly confluent.

In Section 3.4, we have shown that local confluence together with termination implies the confluence of the whole system. The termination of typed attributed graph transformation systems will be studied in Section 12.3.

In analogy to the graph case considered in Theorem 3.34 and the general case considered in Theorem 6.28, we are now able to formulate the Local Confluence Theorem for typed AGT systems, based on the concept of strict confluence of critical pairs.

Definition 10.17 (strict confluence of critical pairs). *A critical pair* $K \overset{p_1,o_1}{\Longrightarrow} P_1$, $K \overset{p_2,o_2}{\Longrightarrow} P_2$ *is called* strictly confluent *if we have the following conditions:*

1. Confluence. *the critical pair is confluent, i.e. there are transformations* $P_1 \overset{*}{\Rightarrow} K'$, $P_2 \overset{*}{\Rightarrow} K'$ *with derived spans* $der(P_i \overset{*}{\Rightarrow} K') = (P_i \overset{v_{i+2}}{\leftarrow} N_{i+2} \overset{w_{i+2}}{\rightarrow} K')$ *for* $i = 1, 2$.

2. Strictness. *Let* $der(K \overset{p_i, o_i}{\Longrightarrow} P_i) = (K \overset{v_i}{\leftarrow} N_i \overset{w_i}{\rightarrow} P_i)$ *for* $i = 1, 2$, *and let* N *be the pullback object of the pullback (1). There are then morphisms* z_3 *and* z_4 *such that (2), (3), and (4) commute:*

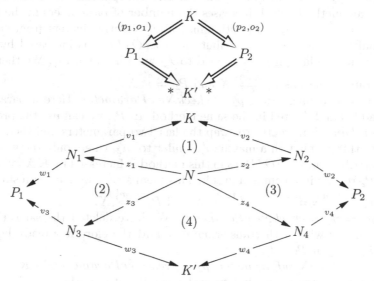

Theorem 10.18 (Local Confluence Theorem for typed AGT systems). *Given a graph transformation system* GTS *based on* (**AGraphs**$_{\mathbf{ATG}}$, $\mathcal{M}$) *with an* $\mathcal{E}'$–$\mathcal{M}'$ *pair factorization such that* $\mathcal{M}'$ *is closed under pushouts and pullbacks along* $\mathcal{M}$-*morphisms and the* $\mathcal{M}$–$\mathcal{M}'$ *pushout–pullback decomposition property holds, then* GTS *is locally confluent if all its critical pairs are strictly confluent.*

Proof. See Theorem 11.14 in Section 11.3. □

Remark 10.19. The language L of a graph transformation system GTS is locally confluent if we consider only those critical pairs $P_1 \Leftarrow K \Rightarrow P_2$, where K is an $\mathcal{M}'$-subgraph of a graph G which can be derived from the start graph S. "K is $\mathcal{M}'$-subgraph of G" means that there is an $\mathcal{M}'$-morphism $m : K \to G$.

In Section 11.3, we show that the Local Confluence Theorem is valid for a typed AGT system over the category **AGSIG-Alg** with a well-structured $AGSIG$ and a suitable $\mathcal{E}'$–$\mathcal{M}'$ pair factorization. This implies Theorem 10.18. The requirements for $\mathcal{M}'$ are valid for $\mathcal{M}' = \mathcal{M}'_1$ and $\mathcal{M}' = \mathcal{M}'_2$ as considered in Example 9.22.

Example 10.20 (local confluence in *MethodModeling***).** The task of analyzing the local confluence of our graph grammar *MethodModeling* is extensive owing to the fact that there are so many critical pairs, even if we consider only the language of *MethodModeling* (see Example 10.16). Therefore we only give arguments for local confluence here, and do not prove it.

The confluence of the critical pairs can be shown relatively easily. In the following we describe how to find suitable productions and matches for a critical pair $P_1 \overset{p_1,m_1}{\Longleftarrow} K \overset{p_2,m_2}{\Longrightarrow} P_2$ that lead to confluence.

1. $p_1 = p_2 = addParameter$. In this case two parameters are added to the same method, which increases the number of parameters in the method. We can apply p_2 to P_1 with a match m_2' slightly different from m_2, where only the value of the attribute $numberOfPars$ is increased by 1. This works similarly if p_1 is applied to P_2 with a match m_1'. We then obtain transformations $P_1 \overset{p_2,m_2'}{\Longrightarrow} X$ and $P_2 \overset{p_1,m_1'}{\Longrightarrow} X$.

2. $p_1 = addParameter$, $p_2 = checkNewParameter$. Here a parameter is added and deleted in the same method. In P_1, we can use the production $exchangeParameter$ to swap the last two parameters and then apply p_2 to this graph with a match m_2' similar to m_2, where only the value of the attribute $numberOfPars$ in this method is increased by 1. Applying p_1 to P_2 results in a common graph. This means that we have transformations $P_1 \overset{exchangeParameter}{\Longrightarrow} X' \overset{p_2,m_2'}{\Longrightarrow} X$ and $P_2 \overset{p_1,m_1'}{\Longrightarrow} X$.

3. $p_1 = p_2 = checkNewParameter$. We have deleted the same (last) parameter with both transformations, and therefore it already holds that $P_1 = P_2$ or $P_1 \cong P_2$.

4. $p_1 = checkNewParameter$, $p_2 = exchangeParameter$. In K, a parameter is deleted by p_1, but p_2 exchanges it with another one. In this case, we can restore the old order by applying p_2 once again to P_2, resulting in the graph K. Applying p_1 with the match m_1 leads to a common object. Altogether, we obtain the transformations $P_1 \overset{id}{\Rightarrow} P_1$ and $P_2 \overset{exchangeParameter}{\Longrightarrow} K \overset{p_1,m_1}{\Longrightarrow} P_1$.

5. $p_1 = p_2 = exchangeParameter$. Exchanging parameters can be reversed, so there are transformations $P_1 \overset{p_2}{\Longrightarrow} K$ and $P_2 \overset{p_1}{\Longrightarrow} K$.

In all these cases, the common part of K that is preserved by applying p_1 and p_2 is also preserved by the further transformations and mapped equally to the resulting common object. Therefore the critical pairs are strictly confluent.

By Theorem 10.18, this means that the graph grammar *MethodModeling* is locally confluent.   □

Adhesive HLR Categories for Typed Attributed Graphs

In Chapters 8–10, we have presented the main concepts and results for typed attributed graph transformation systems. However, we have postponed most of the proofs, because they have been given already for adhesive HLR systems in Part II. It remains to instantiate them for typed attributed graph transformation systems.

For this purpose, we have to show that the category **AGraphs$_{ATG}$** of typed attributed graphs is an adhesive HLR category. In Theorem 11.3, we show that the category **AGraphs$_{ATG}$** is isomorphic to a category of algebras over a suitable signature $AGSIG(ATG)$, which is uniquely defined by the attributed type graph ATG. In fact, it is much easier to verify the categorical properties of adhesive HLR categories for the category of algebras **AGSIG(ATG)-Alg** and to show the isomorphism between **AGSIG(ATG)-Alg** and **AGraphs$_{ATG}$** than to show the categorical properties directly for the category **AGraphs$_{ATG}$**.

In Theorem 11.11, we show that **AGSIG(ATG)-Alg**, and hence also **AGraphs$_{ATG}$**, is an adhesive HLR category. In fact, we show this result for the category **AGSIG-Alg**, where $AGSIG$ is a more general kind of attributed graph structure signatures in the sense of [LKW93, CL95, FKTV99]. This allows us to obtain the results of our theory for other kinds of attributed graphs, also. However, we shall not discuss these other instantiations in more detail. By combining the results given in Sections 11.1 and 11.2 with those in Part II, we are able to verify in Section 11.3 that the following basic results stated in Chapters 9 and 10 are valid for typed attributed graph transformations:

1. The Local Church–Rosser, Parallelism, and Concurrency Theorems.
2. The Embedding and Extension Theorems.
3. The completeness of critical pairs and the Local Confluence Theorem.

An alternative way to show that **AGraphs$_{ATG}$** is an adhesive HLR category is given at the end of Section 11.2, where **AGraphs** is represented as a subcategory of a comma category and **AGraphs$_{ATG}$** as a slice category of

AGraphs. However, for showing the existence of initial pushouts, it is easier to give the corresponding construction in the more general context of the category **AGSIG-Alg**. Moreover, this allows us to apply the results to the general attributed graph structure signatures mentioned above.

11.1 Attributed Graph Structure Signatures and Typed Attributed Graphs

Attributed graph structure signatures were introduced in [LKW93] to model attributed graphs and the corresponding transformations. In fact, this concept is general enough to model various kinds of attributed graphs, especially attributed graphs with node attributes only, as presented in [HKT02], and our concept with node and edge attributes introduced in Chapter 8.

In this section, we review attributed graph structure signatures and show that, for each type graph ATG, there is a graph structure signature $AGSIG(ATG)$ such that the category **AGraphs$_{ATG}$** of attributed graphs typed over ATG and the category **AGSIG(ATG)-Alg** of $AGSIG(ATG)$-algebras are isomorphic.

We start with the definition of attributed graph structure signatures.

Definition 11.1 (attributed graph structure signature). *A graph structure signature* $GSIG = (S_G, OP_G)$ *is an algebraic signature with unary operations* $op : s \rightarrow s'$ *in* OP_G *only.*

An attributed graph structure signature $AGSIG = (GSIG, DSIG)$ *consists of a graph structure signature* $GSIG$ *and a data signature* $DSIG = (S_D, OP_D)$ *with attribute value sorts* $S'_D \subseteq S_D$ *such that* $S'_D = S_D \cap S_G$ *and* $OP_D \cap OP_G = \varnothing$.

AGSIG is called well structured *if, for each* $op : s \rightarrow s'$ *in* OP_G, *we have* $s \notin S_D$.

The next steps are to introduce the category **AGSIG-Alg** of attributed graph structure signatures and the special case **AGSIG(ATG)-Alg**, which allows us to construct an isomorphism with the category **AGraphs$_{ATG}$**. In Example 11.4, we construct an explicit attributed graph structure signature $AGSIG(ATG)$ for the attributed type graph in Example 8.9.

Definition 11.2 (category AGSIG-Alg). *Given an attributed graph structure signature* $AGSIG = (GSIG, DSIG)$, *the category of all* $AGSIG$-algebras *and* $AGSIG$-homomorphisms *is denoted by* **AGSIG-Alg**, *where* **AGSIG-Alg** *corresponds to the category* **Alg(Σ)** *(see Definition B.9) with*

$$\Sigma = GSIG \cup DSIG.$$

Theorem 11.3 (isomorphism AGraphs$_{\text{ATG}}$ $\cong$ AGSIG(ATG)-Alg). *For each attributed type graph ATG, there is a well-structured attributed graph structure signature $AGSIG(ATG)$ such that the category* **AGraphs$_{\text{ATG}}$** *is isomorphic to the category* **AGSIG(ATG)-Alg***:*
AGraphs$_{\text{ATG}}$ $\cong$ AGSIG(ATG)-Alg.

Proof. For a given attributed type graph ATG, we suppose that $S_D \cap V_G^{TG} = \varnothing$ and $S_D \cap E_j^{TG} = \varnothing$ for all $j \in \{G, NA, EA\}$. This means that data sorts cannot be graph node types or the type of any kind of edge. Otherwise, we would rename them accordingly.

We first construct the corresponding attributed graph structure signature $AGSIG(ATG)$. Then we find a functor $F : \textbf{AGraphs}_{\textbf{ATG}} \to \textbf{AGSIG(ATG)-}$ **Alg** and an inverse functor $F^{-1}: \textbf{AGSIG(ATG)-Alg} \to \textbf{AGraphs}_{\textbf{ATG}}$ that show the isomorphism.

For an attributed type graph $ATG = (TG, Z)$ with a final $DSIG$-algebra Z, a type graph $TG = (V_G^{TG}, V_D^{TG}, E_G^{TG}, E_{NA}^{TG}, E_{EA}^{TG}, (source_j^{TG}, target_j^{TG})_{j \in \{G, NA, EA\}})$ and $S'_D \subseteq S_D$, we define $AGSIG(ATG) = (GSIG, DSIG)$, where $GSIG = (S_G, OP_G)$, $S_G = S_V \,\dot\cup\, S_E$, $S_V = V_G^{TG} \,\dot\cup\, V_D^{TG}$, $S_E = E_G^{TG} \,\dot\cup\, E_{NA}^{TG} \,\dot\cup\, E_{EA}^{TG}$, and $OP_G = \dot\cup_{e \in S_E} OP_e$, with $OP_e = \{src_e, tar_e\}$ defined by

- $src_e : e \to v(e)$ for $e \in E_G^{TG}$ with $v(e) = source_G^{TG}(e) \in V_G^{TG}$,
- $tar_e : e \to v'(e)$ for $e \in E_G^{TG}$ with $v'(e) = target_G^{TG}(e) \in V_G^{TG}$,
- src_e, tar_e for $e \in E_{NA}^{TG}$ and $e \in E_{EA}^{TG}$ are defined analogously.

$AGSIG(ATG)$ is a well-structured attributed graph structure signature, since we have only unary operations and, from $V_D^{TG} = \dot\cup_{s \in S'_D} Z_s = S'_D$, $V_G^{TG} \cap S_D = \varnothing$ and $E_j^{TG} \cap S_D = \varnothing$ for all $j \in \{G, NA, EA\}$, we have $S_D \cap S_G = S_D \cap V_D^{TG} = S'_D$ and the well-structuredness follows.

The functor $F : \textbf{AGraphs}_{\textbf{ATG}} \to \textbf{AGSIG(ATG)-Alg}$ is defined, for objects $(AG, t : AG \to ATG)$ with $AG = (G, D)$, $t_G : G \to TG$ and $t_D : D \to Z$, by $F(AG, t) = A$, with the following $AGSIG(ATG)$-algebra A:

- $A_s = t_{G,V_i}^{-1}(s) \subseteq V_i$ for $s \in V_i^{TG} \subseteq S_V$, $i \in \{G, D\}$;
- $A_e = t_{G,E_j}^{-1}(e) \subseteq E_j$ for $e \in E_j^{TG} \subseteq S_E$, $j \in \{G, NA, EA\}$;
- $A_s = t_{D_s}^{-1}(s) = D_s$ for $s \in S_D$;
- $src_e^A(a) = source_G(a)$ for $e \in E_G^{TG} \subseteq S_E$, $a \in t_{G,E_G}^{-1}(e) = A_e \subseteq E_G$;
- $tar_e^A(a) = target_G(a)$ for $e \in E_G^{TG}$, $a \in t_{G,E_G}^{-1}(e) = A_e \subseteq E_G$;
- analogously for $src_e^A(a)$, $tar_e^A(a)$, with $e \in E_j^{TG}$, $a \in t_{G,E_j}^{-1}(e)$, $j \in \{NA, EA\}$;
- $op^A = op^D$ for all $op \in OP_D$.

For a typed attributed graph morphism $f : (AG^1, t^1) \to (AG^2, t^2)$, we have $F(f) = h : F(AG^1, t^1) = A \to F(AG^2, t^2) = B$; h is an algebra homomorphism defined by

- $h_s(a) = f_{G,V_i}(a)$ for $s \in V_i^{TG} \subseteq S_V$, $a \in A_s$, $i \in \{G, D\}$,
- $h_e(a) = f_{G,E_j}(a)$ for $e \in E_j^{TG} \subset S_E$, $a \in A_e$, $j \in \{G, NA, EA\}$,
- $h_s = f_{D,s}$ for $s \in S_D$.

In the other direction, the functor F^{-1} is defined for an $AGSIG(ATG)$-algebra A by $F^{-1}(A) = (AG = (G, D), t : AG \to ATG)$, with

- $V_i = \dot{\cup}_{s \in V_i^{TG}} A_s$, $E_j = \dot{\cup}_{e \in E_j^{TG}} A_e$ for $i \in \{G, D\}$, $j \in \{G, NA, EA\}$;
- $source_j(a) = src_e^A(a)$ for $e \in E_j^{TG}$, $a \in A_e$, $j \in \{G, NA, EA\}$;
- $target_j(a) = tar_e^A(a)$ for $e \in E_j^{TG}$, $a \in A_e$, $j \in \{G, NA, EA\}$;
- $t_{G,V_i}(a) = s$ for $a \in A_s$, $s \in V_i^{TG}$, $i \in \{G, D\}$;
- $t_{G,E_j}(a) = e$ for $a \in A_e$, $e \in E_j^{TG}$, $j \in \{G, NA, EA\}$;
- $D = A|_{DSIG}$;
- $t_{D,s}(a) = s$ for $a \in A_s$, $s \in S_D$.

For a homomorphism $h : A \to B$, we define $F^{-1}(h) = f : F^{-1}(A) \to F^{-1}(B)$ by

- $f_{G,V_i}(a) = h_s(a)$ for $a \in A_s$, $s \in V_i^{TG}$, $i \in \{G, D\}$;
- $f_{G,E_j}(a) = h_e(a)$ for $a \in A_e$, $e \in E_j^{TG}$, $j \in \{G, NA, EA\}$;
- $f_D = h|_{DSIG}$.

The constructed morphisms F and F^{-1} are well defined; they are actually functors and isomorphisms (as proven in Section C.3).   □

Example 11.4 (corresponding $AGSIG(ATG)$ and algebra). We present the corresponding signature $AGSIG(ATG)$ for the the type graph ATG defined in Example 8.9 and the resulting $AGSIG(ATG)$-algebra for the typed attributed graph (AG, t).

$AGSIG(ATG) = (GSIG, DSIG)$ for type graph $ATG = (TG, Z)$ has the same data signature $DSIG$. $GSIG$ has the following structure:

$$
\begin{aligned}
GSIG : \quad sorts : \quad & Method, Parameter, Class, \\
& string, nat, parameterDirectionKind, \\
& param, type, noOfPars, mname, pname, cname, \\
& kind, order \\
opns : \quad & src_{param} : param \to Method \\
& tar_{param} : param \to Parameter \\
& src_{type} : type \to Parameter \\
& tar_{type} : type \to Class \\
& \quad \vdots \\
& src_{order} : order \to param \\
& tar_{order} : order \to nat
\end{aligned}
$$

All node and edge types in the type graph correspond to a sort, and for all edge types we define operation symbols that describe the types of the source and target.

The corresponding $AGSIG(ATG)$-algebra A for $AG = (G, D)$ is defined as follows:

$$
\begin{aligned}
A: \quad & A_{Method} && = \{m\} \\
& A_{Parameter} && = \{par_1, par_2, par_3\} \\
& A_{Class} && = \{c\} \\
& A_{nat} && = D_{nat} \\
& \quad\vdots \\
& A_{param} && = \{mpar_1, mpar_2, mpar_3\} \\
& A_{type} && = \{par_1c, par_2c, par_3c\} \\
& \quad\vdots \\
& A_{order} && = \{order_1, order_2, order_3\} \\
& A_s && = D_s \text{ for all } s \in S_D \\[4pt]
& src^A_{param} && : A_{param} \to A_{Method} \; : \; mpar_i \mapsto m \\
& tar^A_{param} && : A_{param} \to A_{Parameter} \; : \; mpar_i \mapsto par_i \\
& src^A_{type} && : A_{type} \to A_{Parameter} \; : \; par_ic \mapsto par_i \\
& tar^A_{type} && : A_{type} \to A_{Class} \; : \; par_ic \mapsto c \\
& \quad\vdots \\
& src^A_{order} && : A_{order} \to A_{param} \; : \; order_i \mapsto mpar_i \\
& tar^A_{order} && : A_{order} \to A_{nat} \; : \; order_i \mapsto i \\
& op_A && = op_D \text{ for all } op \in OP_D
\end{aligned}
$$

$\square$

11.2 Definition of Concrete Adhesive HLR Categories

In this section, we consider a fixed attributed graph structure signature $AGSIG = (GSIG, DSIG)$. We prove that the category **AGSIG-Alg** over $AGSIG$ with a distinguished class $\mathcal{M}$ (defined in the following) fulfills all properties of an adhesive HLR category. By Theorem 11.3, **AGraphs$_{ATG}$** is also an adhesive HLR category.

Finally, we sketch an alternative way to show that **AGraphs$_{ATG}$** is an adhesive HLR category using comma categories.

Definition 11.5 (class $\mathcal{M}$ in AGSIG-Alg and AGraphs$_{ATG}$). *The class $\mathcal{M}$ in **AGSIG-Alg** is the class of all algebra homomorphisms $f = (f_{GSIG}, f_{DSIG})$, where f_{GSIG} is injective and f_{DSIG} is an isomorphism. The notation $f = (f_{GSIG}, f_{DSIG})$ means that f_{GSIG} and f_{DSIG} are the restrictions of f to $GSIG$ and $DSIG$, respectively, where the two restrictions coincide on $S'_D = S_D \cap S_G$.*

*In **AGraphs$_{ATG}$**, the morphism class $\mathcal{M}$ is the class of all morphisms $f = (f_G, f_D)$, where f_G is injective and f_D is an isomorphism on the data part (see Definition 8.10).*

Remark 11.6. We use the same notation for the morphism classes $\mathcal{M}$ in **AGraphs$_\mathbf{ATG}$** and in **AGSIG(ATG)-Alg** because they correspond to each other, owing to the construction of the functors F and F^{-1} in the proof of Theorem 11.3.

We prove step by step the properties necessary for an adhesive HLR category. First we check the closure properties of $\mathcal{M}$.

Lemma 11.7 (properties of $\mathcal{M}$). *The class $\mathcal{M}$ in* **AGSIG-Alg** *as defined in Definition 11.5 is closed under isomorphisms, composition, and decomposition.*

Proof. An algebra homomorphism is injective or isomorphic if all its components are injective or isomorphic, respectively, in **Sets**. In **Sets**, the class of injective morphisms and the class of isomorphic morphisms are closed under isomorphism, composition and decomposition. Therefore this property holds for the class $\mathcal{M}$ of injective homorphisms with an isomorphic data part. $\square$

For the second property, we need to the prove existence and closedness of pushouts and pullbacks along $\mathcal{M}$-morphisms. This is done with the following lemmas, where we show that pushouts along $\mathcal{M}$-morphisms and pullbacks can be constructed componentwise in **Sets**. Note that general pushouts in **AGSIG-Alg** exist, but in general cannot be constructed componentwise, which is essential for the proof of the VK property in Lemma 11.10. On the other hand, general pullbacks in **AGSIG-Alg** can be constructed componentwise.

Lemma 11.8 (POs in AGSIG-Alg along $\mathcal{M}$-morphisms). *For given morphisms $m : A \to B \in \mathcal{M}$ and $f : A \to C$, there is a pushout (1) in* **AGSIG-Alg** *with $n \in \mathcal{M}$:*

$$
\begin{array}{ccc}
A & \xrightarrow{\ m\ } & B \\
\downarrow{\scriptstyle f} & (1) & \downarrow{\scriptstyle g} \\
C & \xrightarrow{\ n\ } & D
\end{array}
$$

Moreover, given that (1) is commutative with $m \in \mathcal{M}$, then (1) is a pushout in **AGSIG-Alg** *iff (1) is a componentwise pushout in* **Sets**. *Then $m \in \mathcal{M}$ implies $n \in \mathcal{M}$.*

Proof. **Part 1.** If (1) is commutative, $m \in \mathcal{M}$, and (1)$_s$ are componentwise pushouts in **Sets**, we can show that (1) is a pushout in **AGSIG-Alg**. Consider an object X with morphisms $k : B \to X$ and $l : C \to X$ such that $k \circ m = l \circ f$:

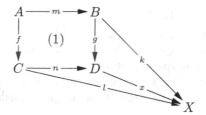

Then, for each $s \in S_G \cup S_D$, there exists a unique $x_s : D_s \to X_s$ such that $x_s \circ g_s = k_s$ and $x_s \circ n_s = l_s$.

We show that $x = (x_s)_{s \in S_G \cup S_D}$ is a homomorphism as follows:

1. $op \in OP_D$. For $s \in S_D$, m_s being an isomorphism implies that n_s is an isomorphism. This gives the compatibility of x with $op \in OP_D$, because l is a homomorphism.

2. $op \in OP_G$. Since $(1)_s$ is a pushout, n_s and g_s are jointly surjective. This means that for every $d \in D_S$ there is a $b \in B_s$ with $g_s(b) = d$ or a $c \in C_s$ with $n_s(c) = d$. Then, for $op : s \to s' \in OP_G$ it holds that $op_X(x_s(d)) = op_X(x_s(g_s(b))) = op_X(k_s(b)) = k_{s'}(op_B(b)) = x_{s'}(g_{s'}(op_B(b))) = x_{s'}(op_D(g_s(b))) = x_{s'}(op_D(d))$ or $op_X(x_s(d)) = op_X(x_s(n_s(c))) = op_X(l_s(c)) = l_{s'}(op_C(c)) = x_{s'}(n_{s'}(op_C(c))) = x_{s'}(op_D(n_s(c))) = x_{s'}(op_D(d))$.

x is unique, since all its components are unique, and therefore (1) is a pushout in **AGSIG-Alg**.

Part 2. Now we construct a pushout object D with morphisms n and g for given objects and morphisms $C \xleftarrow{f} A \xrightarrow{m} B$, with $m \in \mathcal{M}$. For all $s \in S_D$, let $D_s = C_s$, $g_s = f_s \circ m_s^{-1}$, and $n_s = id_{C_s}$. For $op \in OP_D$, we define $op_D = op_C$. Since m_s is an isomorphism and n_s is the identity, $(1)_s$ is obviously a pushout in **Sets**.

For $s \in S_G \backslash S_D$, let $B_s \xrightarrow{g_s} D_s \xleftarrow{n_s} C_s$ be the pushout over $C_s \xleftarrow{f_s} A_s \xrightarrow{m_s} B_s$ in **Sets**, and for $op : s \to s' \in OP_G$ we define

$$op_D(d) = \begin{cases} n_{s'} \circ f_{s'}(op_A(a)) & : \quad \exists a \in A_s : n_s(f_s(a)) = d \\ g_{s'}(op_B(b)) & : \quad \exists b \in B_s \backslash m_s(A_s) : g_s(b) = d \\ n_{s'}(op_C(c)) & : \quad \exists c \in C_s \backslash f_s(A_s) : n_s(c) = d \end{cases}$$

We have to show that these operations are well defined. Since $(1)_s$ is a pushout, exactly one of the cases above applies. In the second or the third case b or c, respectively, must be unique. In the first case we have the result that m_s being injective implies that n_s is injective. For $a_1, a_2 \in A_s$ with $n_s(f_s(a_1)) = n_s(f_s(a_2)) = d$, it holds that $f_s(a_1) = f_s(a_2)$. Then $n_{s'} \circ f_{s'}(op_A(a_1)) = n_{s'}(op_C(f_s(a_1))) = n_{s'}(op_C(f_s(a_2))) = n_{s'} \circ f_{s'}(op_A(a_2))$ follows.

$n = (n_s)_{s \in S_G \cup S_D}$ is a homomorphism. This is clear for all $op \in OP_D$. Consider an operation $op : s \to s' \in OP_G$. Then, for all $c \in C_s$, it holds that $op_D(n_s(c)) = n_{s'}(op_C(c))$: if $c \in C_s \backslash f_s(A_s)$, then $op_D(n_s(c)) = n_{s'}(op_C(c))$ by definition. Otherwise, $c \in f_s(A_s)$. There then exists an $a \in A_s$ with $f_s(a) = c$, and it holds that $op_D(n_s(c)) = op_D(n_s(f_s(a))) \stackrel{Def.}{=} n_{s'}(f_{s'}(op_A(a))) = n_{s'}(op_C(f_s(a))) = n_{s'}(op_C(c))$. Obviously, we have $n \in \mathcal{M}$. That $g = (g_s)_{s \in S_G \cup S_D}$ is a homomorphism follows analogously.

Since $g \circ m = n \circ f$ and we have componentwise pushouts, it follows by part 1 that (1) with the constructed D, n, and g is a pushout in **AGSIG-Alg**.

Part 3. Let (1) be a pushout in **AGSIG-Alg** with $m \in \mathcal{M}$. By the construction in part 2 and the uniqueness of pushouts up to isomorphism, it follows directly that $n \in \mathcal{M}$ and that (1) is a componentwise pushout in **Sets**. $\square$

Lemma 11.9 (PBs in AGSIG-Alg). *Given $g : B \to D$ and $n : C \to D$, then there is a pullback (1) in* **AGSIG-Alg**:

$$
\begin{array}{ccc}
A & \xrightarrow{\;\;m\;\;} & B \\
\downarrow{\scriptstyle f} & (1) & \downarrow{\scriptstyle g} \\
C & \xrightarrow{\;\;n\;\;} & D
\end{array}
$$

Moreover, given that (1) is commutative, then (1) is a pullback in **AGSIG-Alg** *iff (1) is a componentwise pullback in* **Sets**. *If $n \in \mathcal{M}$, then $m \in \mathcal{M}$ also.*

Proof. **Part 1.** If (1) is commutative and $(1)_s$ are componentwise pullbacks in **Sets**, we can show that (1) is a pullback in **AGSIG-Alg**. Consider an object X with morphisms $k : X \to B$ and $l : X \to C$ such that $n \circ l = g \circ k$:

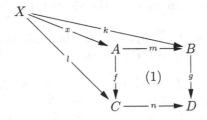

Then, for each $s \in S_G \cup S_D$, there exists a unique $x_s : X_s \to A_s$ such that $m_s \circ x_s = k_s$ and $f_s \circ x_s = l_s$.

We show that $x = (x_s)_{s \in S_G \cup S_D}$ is a homomorphism. For each operation $op : s_1 \ldots s_n \to s \in OP_G \cup OP_D$ and $y_i \in X_{s_i}$, it holds that

- $f_s(x_s(op_X(y_1, \ldots, y_n))) = l_s(op_X(y_1, \ldots, y_n)) = op_C(l_{s_1}(y_1), \ldots, l_{s_n}(y_n)) = op_C(f_{s_1}(x_{s_1}(y_1)), \ldots, f_{s_n}(x_{s_n}(y_n))) = f_s(op_A(x_{s_1}(y_1), \ldots, x_{s_n}(y_n)))$ and
- $m_s(x_s(op_X(y_1, \ldots, y_n))) = k_s(op_X(y_1, \ldots, y_n)) = op_B(k_{s_1}(y_1), \ldots, k_{s_n}(y_n)) = op_B(m_{s_1}(x_{s_1}(y_1)), \ldots, m_{s_n}(x_{s_n}(y_n))) = m_s(op_A(x_{s_1}(y_1), \ldots, x_{s_n}(y_n)))$.

Since $(1)_s$ is a pullback in **Sets**, m_s and f_s are jointly injective (see Fact 2.23). This means that if $m_s(a_1) = m_s(a_2)$ and $f_s(a_1) = f_s(a_2)$, it follows that $a_1 = a_2$. Therefore $x_s(op_X(y_1, ..., y_n)) = op_A(x_{s_1}(y_1), ..., x_{s_n}(y_n))$, and x is a homomorphism.

x is unique, since all its components are unique. Therefore (1) is a pullback in **AGSIG-Alg**.

Part 2. Now we construct a pullback object A with morphisms f and m for given objects and morphisms $C \xrightarrow{n} D \xleftarrow{g} B$.

For $s \in S_G \cup S_D$, let $B_s \xleftarrow{m_s} A_s \xrightarrow{f_s} C_s$ be the pullback over $C_s \xrightarrow{n_s} D_s \xleftarrow{g_s} B_s$ in **Sets**. For $op : s_1...s_n \rightarrow s \in OP_G \cup OP_D$, we define $op_A(a_1, ..., a_n) = a$, with $op_B(m_{s_1}(a_1), ..., m_{s_n}(a_n)) = m_s(a)$ and $op_C(f_{s_1}(a_1), ..., f_{s_n}(a_n)) = f_s(a)$. This a exists and is unique, since $(1)_s$ is a pullback in **Sets**.

$f = (f_s)_{s \in S_G \cup S_D}$ and $m = (m_s)_{s \in S_G \cup S_D}$ are homomorphisms by construction. Since $g \circ m = n \circ f$ and we have componentwise pullbacks, it follows by part 1 that (1), with the constructed object A and morphisms f and m is a pullback in **AGSIG-Alg**.

Part 3. Let (1) be a pullback in **AGSIG-Alg**. By the construction in part 2 and the uniqueness of pullbacks up to isomorphism, it follows directly that (1) is a componentwise pullback in **Sets**.

Part 4. If $n \in \mathcal{M}$, we have the result that n_s is injective for all $s \in S_G$, and it is an isomorphism for $s \in S_D$. Since pullbacks in **Sets** are closed under monomorphisms and isomorphisms, it follows that m_s is injective for $s \in S_G$ and is an isomorphism for $s \in S_D$, which means that $m \in \mathcal{M}$.   □

Lemma 11.10 (VK property of POs along $\mathcal{M}$-morphisms). *A pushout in* **AGSIG-Alg** *along an $\mathcal{M}$-morphism is a VK square.*

Proof. Consider the pushout (1) below with $m \in \mathcal{M}$, and the commutative cube (2), where (1) is in the bottom and the back faces are pullbacks.

Part 1. If the front faces are pullbacks, then the top is a pushout.

Let the front faces be pullbacks. By applying Lemmas 11.8 and 11.9, we can decompose the cube for every component $s \in S_G \cup S_D$ such that the bottom is a pushout with $m_s \in \mathcal{M}$, and the front and back faces are pullbacks in **Sets**. Then $(1)_s$ is a VK square in **Sets**. From the VK square property, we obtain the top as a componentwise pushout. The fact that $m \in \mathcal{M}$ and the back right square is a pullback implies that $m' \in \mathcal{M}$, owing to Lemma 11.9. By Lemma 11.8, the top of cube (2) is a pushout in **AGSIG-Alg**.

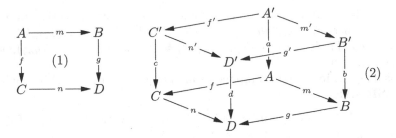

Part 2. If the top is a pushout, then the front faces are pullbacks.

Let the top be a pushout. The fact that $m \in \mathcal{M}$ and the back right is a pullback implies, from Lemma 11.9, that $m' \in \mathcal{M}$. By applying Lemmas 11.8 and 11.9, we can decompose the cube for every component $s \in S_G \cup S_D$ such that the bottom and the top are pushouts, $m_s \in \mathcal{M}$ and the back faces are pullbacks in **Sets**. Then $(1)_s$ is a VK square in **Sets**. From the VK square property, we obtain the result that the front faces are componentwise pullbacks. By Lemma 11.9, the front faces of cube (2) are pullbacks in **AGSIG-Alg**. □

Theorem 11.11 (AGSIG-Alg and AGraphs$_{\text{ATG}}$ are adhesive HLR categories). *The categories* (**AGSIG-Alg**, $\mathcal{M}$) *and* (**AGraphs$_{\text{ATG}}$**, $\mathcal{M}$) *with morphism classes $\mathcal{M}$ as defined in Definition 11.5 are adhesive HLR categories.*

Proof. In **AGSIG-Alg**, $\mathcal{M}$ is a class of monomorphisms since monomorphisms in **AGSIG-Alg** are componentwise monomorphisms in **Sets**, which means that they are componentwise injective (and isomorphisms are both injective and surjective). The closure properties of $\mathcal{M}$ are explicitly proven in Lemma 11.7.

The existence and closedness of pushouts and pullbacks along $\mathcal{M}$-morphisms follow from Lemmas 11.8 and 11.9.

In Lemma 11.10, it is shown that pushouts along $\mathcal{M}$-morphisms are VK squares.

Therefore (**AGSIG-Alg**, $\mathcal{M}$) is an adhesive HLR category.

For each attributed type graph ATG there is by Theorem 11.3, a corresponding graph structure signature $AGSIG(ATG)$ such that **AGraphs$_{\text{ATG}}$** is isomorphic to **AGSIG(ATG)-Alg**. The morphism classes $\mathcal{M}$ in **AGraphs$_{\text{ATG}}$** and **AGSIG(ATG)-Alg** are isomorphic. Therefore (**AGraphs$_{\text{ATG}}$**, $\mathcal{M}$) is also an adhesive HLR category. □

Finally, let us sketch an alternative way to show that (**AGraphs**, $\mathcal{M}$) and (**AGraphs$_{\text{ATG}}$**, $\mathcal{M}$) are adhesive HLR categories. First we use a comma category construction to show this for **AGraphs**, and then we use a slice category construction for **AGraphs$_{\text{ATG}}$**.

Fact 11.12 (comma category construction for AGraphs). *The category* **AGraphs** *is isomorphic to a subcategory* **ComCat($\mathbf{V_1}, \mathbf{V_2}; \mathbf{Id}$)** *of the comma* *category* **ComCat**$(\mathbf{V_1}, \mathbf{V_2}; \mathbf{I})$ *defined below, where* $I = \{1\}$, *which implies that* (**AGraphs**, $\mathcal{M}$) *with* $\mathcal{M}$ *as defined in Definition 8.10 is an adhesive HLR category.*

Construction. Let V_1 and V_2 be the forgetful functors defined by

- $V_1 : \mathbf{E\text{-}Graphs} \to \mathbf{Sets}$ with $V_1(G) = V_D^G$ and $V_1(f_G) = f_{G,V_D}$;
- $V_2 : \mathbf{DSIG\text{-}Alg} \to \mathbf{Sets}$ with $V_2(D) = \dot{\cup}_{s \in S'_D} D_s$ and $V_2(f_D) = \dot{\cup}_{s \in S'_D} f_{D_s}$.

ComCat$(\mathbf{V_1}, \mathbf{V_2}; \mathbf{Id})$ is the subcategory of **ComCat**$(\mathbf{V_1}, \mathbf{V_2}; \mathbf{I})$ where $I = \{1\}$ and the objects $(G, D, op : V_1(G) \to V_2(D))$ satisfy $V_1(G) = V_2(D)$ and $op = id$. $\qquad\square$

Proof. For attributed graphs $AG = (G, D)$, we have, by Definition 8.10, $\dot{\cup}_{s \in S'_D} D_s = V_D^G$, and for morphisms $f = (f_G, f_D) : AG^1 \to AG^2$, we have commutativity of (1) for all $s \in S'_D$, which is equivalent to commutativity of (2):

$$
\begin{array}{ccc}
D_s^1 \xrightarrow{\ f_{D_s}\ } D_s^2 & \qquad & \dot{\cup}_{s \in S'_D} D_s^1 \xrightarrow{\ \dot{\cup} f_{D_s}\ } \dot{\cup}_{s \in S'_D} D_s^2 \\
\Big\cap \quad (1) \quad \Big\cap & & \Big\downarrow{\scriptstyle id} \quad (2) \quad \Big\downarrow{\scriptstyle id} \\
V_D^1 \xrightarrow{\ f_{G,V_D}\ } V_D^2 & & V_D^1 \xrightarrow{\qquad f_{G,V_D} \qquad} V_D^2
\end{array}
$$

Using $V_1(G) = V_2(D)$, we have $V_D^i = \dot{\cup}_{s \in S'_D} D_s^i$ for $i = 1, 2$, and (2) expresses exactly the compatibility of the morphisms f_G and f_D in **ComCat**$(\mathbf{V_1}, \mathbf{V_2}; \mathbf{ID})$, because $V_1(f_G) = f_{G,V_D}$ and $V_2(f_D) = \dot{\cup}_{s \in S'_D} f_{D_1}$. This implies that
AGraphs $\cong$ **ComCat**$(\mathbf{V_1}, \mathbf{V_2}; \mathbf{ID})$.

Let $\mathcal{M}_1$ be the class of injective E-graph morphisms and $\mathcal{M}_2$ the class of $DSIG$-isomorphisms. Then (**E-Graphs**, $\mathcal{M}_1$) is a functor category over (**Sets**, $\mathcal{M}_1$) and hence an adhesive HLR category by Theorem 4.15, item 3. Moreover, each category (**C**, $\mathcal{M}_{iso}$) with the class $\mathcal{M}_{iso}$ of all isomorphisms is an adhesive HLR category; hence, so is (**DSIG-Alg**, $\mathcal{M}_2$). This implies, by Theorem 4.15 item 4, that **ComCat**$(\mathbf{V_1}, \mathbf{V_2}; \mathbf{I})$ with $I = \{1\}$ and $\mathcal{M} = (\mathcal{M}_1 \times \mathcal{M}_2) \cap Mor_{\mathbf{ComCat}(\mathbf{V_1}, \mathbf{V_2}; \mathbf{I})}$ is an adhesive HLR category, provided that V_1 preserves pushouts along $\mathcal{M}_1$-morphisms and V_2 preserves pullbacks. But pushouts in **E-graphs** are constructed componentwise in **Sets**; hence V_1 preserves pushouts. Also, pullbacks in **DSIG-Alg** are constructed componentwise, and the disjoint union functor $\dot{\cup}_{s \in S'_D} : \mathbf{Sets}^{S'_D} \to \mathbf{Sets}$ preserves pullbacks; therefore V_2 preserves pullbacks. This implies that **ComCat**$(\mathbf{V_1}, \mathbf{V_2}; \mathbf{I})$ with $I = \{1\}$ and $\mathcal{M}$ as above, which corresponds to $\mathcal{M}$ in **AGraphs**, is an adhesive HLR category. Finally, it can be shown that a special choice of pushouts and pullbacks in **E-graphs** and **DSIG-Alg** leads also to pushouts and pullbacks in the subcategory **ComCat**$(\mathbf{V_1}, \mathbf{V_2}; \mathbf{ID})$, which allows us to conclude that $(\textbf{ComCat}(\textbf{V}_1, \textbf{V}_2; \textbf{ID}), \mathcal{M})$ and hence also $(\textbf{AGraphs}, \mathcal{M})$ are adhesive HLR categories. □

Fact 11.13 (slice category construction for AGraphs$_{\textbf{ATG}}$). *The category (***AGraphs$_{\textbf{ATG}}$**, $\mathcal{M}$) is a slice category of (***AGraphs**, $\mathcal{M}$) with $\mathcal{M}$ as defined in Definition 8.10, and hence it is an adhesive HLR category.*

Proof. This is a direct consequence of Theorem 4.15, item 2, and Fact 11.12.

□

11.3 Verification of the Main Results for Typed AGT Systems

In this section, we give proofs for the results in Chapters 9 and 10 based on the corresponding results for adhesive HLR categories and systems in Part II. In Section 11.2, we have shown that the categories (**AGSIG-Alg**, $\mathcal{M}$) (see Definition 11.2) and (**AGraphs$_{\textbf{ATG}}$**, $\mathcal{M}$) are adhesive HLR categories with a morphism class $\mathcal{M}$ as defined in Definition 11.5.

This is already sufficient to prove the Local Church–Rosser and Embedding Theorems. For the Parallelism Theorem, we need binary coproducts compatible with $\mathcal{M}$ in addition. For the construction of the boundary and context and the Extension Theorem, we also use initial pushouts. Finally, we need an $\mathcal{E}'$–$\mathcal{M}'$ pair factorization for the Concurrency Theorem, the completeness of critical pairs, and the Local Confluence Theorem. We show all these properties for the category **AGSIG-Alg**, where in some cases we need to require that $AGSIG$ is well structured. By Theorem 11.3, the results are also true for the category **AGraphs$_{\textbf{ATG}}$**.

Theorem 11.14 (main results for typed AGT systems). *Given a typed attributed graph transformation system $GTS = (DSIG, ATG, P)$, we have the following results:*

1. *Local Church–Rosser Theorem (Theorem 9.14);*
2. *Parallelism Theorem (Theorem 9.18);*
3. *Concurrency Theorem (Theorem 9.26);*
4. *E-related transformations (Fact 9.27);*
5. *Embedding Theorem (Theorem 10.10);*
6. *Extension Theorem (Theorem 10.11);*
7. *completeness of critical pairs (Theorem 10.14);*
8. *Local Confluence Theorem (Theorem 10.18).*

Proof.

1. This follows from Theorems 5.12 and 11.11.
2. This follows from Theorems 5.18 and 11.11 and Lemma 11.15 below.
3. This follows from Theorems 5.23 and 11.11.

4. This follows from Fact 5.29, Theorem 11.11, and Lemma 11.16 below.
5. This follows from Theorems 6.14 and 11.11.
6. This follows from Theorems 6.16 and 11.11 and Lemma 11.17 below.
7. This follows from Lemma 6.22 and Theorem 11.11.
8. This follows from Theorems 6.28 and 11.11 and Lemma 11.17.

□

It remains to state and prove all the lemmas which are needed in the proof of Theorem 11.14 above.

Lemma 11.15 (binary coproducts compatible with $\mathcal{M}$). *Given a well-structured attributed graph structure signature $AGSIG$, then the categories* **AGSIG-Alg** *and* **AGraphs$_{\mathbf{ATG}}$** *have binary coproducts compatible with $\mathcal{M}$. This means that f, $g \in \mathcal{M}$ implies $f + g \in \mathcal{M}$.*

Proof. By Theorem 11.3, it suffices to show the property for **AGSIG-Alg**. Given algebras A and B in (**AGSIG-Alg**, $\mathcal{M}$) with a well-structured attributed graph structure signature $AGSIG$, for all sorts $s \in S_G \backslash S_D$ we construct the componentwise coproduct $(A + B)_s = A_s + B_s$ with coproduct injections $\iota_{A,s}$ and $\iota_{B,s}$ in **Sets**. For the data part, we construct the algebra coproduct $(A + B)_D = A|_{DSIG} + B|_{DSIG}$ with coproduct injections $\iota_{A,D}$ and $\iota_{B,D}$.

For the coproduct $A + B$, we combine these components into the coproduct object $A + B = (((A + B)_s)_{s \in S_G \backslash S_D}, (A + B)_D)$ with morphisms $\iota_i = ((\iota_{i,s})_{s \in S_G \backslash S_D}, \iota_{i,D})$ for $i = A, B$. For $op : s \to s' \in OP_G$ the operation op_{A+B} is defined by

$$op_{A+B} : (A + B)_s \to (A + B)_{s'} : x \mapsto$$
$$\begin{cases} \iota_{A,s'}(op_A(y)) & : \quad \exists y \in A_s : \iota_{A,s}(y) = x \\ \iota_{B,s'}(op_B(y)) & : \quad \exists y \in B_s : \iota_{B,s}(y) = x \end{cases}$$

This is well defined, since $AGSIG$ is well structured and therefore it holds that $s \in S_G \backslash S_D$ and $(A + B)_s = A_s \mathbin{\dot{\cup}} B_s$. If $s' \in S_D$, we know that $A_{s'} \dot{\cup} B_{s'} \subseteq (A+B)_{D,s'}$; otherwise, $s' \in S_G \backslash S_D$ and we have $(A+B)_{s'} = A_{s'} \dot{\cup} B_{s'}$.

We have to show that the constructed object $A + B$ is indeed a coproduct. Consider morphisms $f : A \to X$ and $g : B \to X$ as in the following diagram. There then has to be a unique morphism $[f, g] : A + B \to X$ such that $[f, g] \circ \iota_A = f$ and $[f, g] \circ \iota_B = g$:

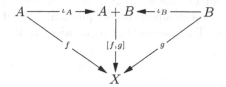

Since $(A+B)_D$ is the coproduct for the data part, there is a morphism $[f,g]_D :$ $(A+B)_D \to X|_{DSIG}$ with $[f,g]_D \circ \iota_{A,D} = f|_{DSIG}$ and $[f,g]_D \circ \iota_{B,D} = g|_{DSIG}$. Similarly, we have for each $s \in S_G \backslash S_D$ a morphism $[f,g]_s : (A+B)_s \to X_s$ such that $[f,g]_s \circ \iota_{A,s} = f_s$ and $[f,g]_s \circ \iota_{B,s} = g_s$.

For the data operations, it is clear that $[f,g]_D$ is a homomorphism. Consider an operation $op : s \to s' \in OP_G$. Since $s \in S_G \backslash S_D$, it holds that $(A+B)_s = A_s \dot\cup B_s$. For an $x \in (A+B)_s$, suppose without loss of generality that there is a $y \in A_s$ with $\iota_{A,s}(y) = x$. We then have the result that $[f,g]_{s'}(op_{A+B}(x)) = [f,g]_{s'}(\iota_{A,s'}(op_A(y))) = f_{s'}(op_A(y)) = op_X(f_s(y)) = op_X([f,g]_s(\iota_{A,s}(y))) = op_X([f,g]_s(x))$. Therefore $[f,g] = (([f,g]_s)_{s\in S_G\backslash S_D}, [f,g]_D)$ is a homomorphism.

The result that $[f,g] \circ \iota_A = f$ and $[f,g] \circ \iota_B = g$ follows by definition, and $[f,g]$ is unique, since all its components are unique. Therefore $[f,g]$ is the required morphism, and $A+B$ is the coproduct of A and B in **AGSIG-Alg**.

It remains to show the compatibility with $\mathcal{M}$. Given $f : A \to A'$ and $g : B \to B'$ with $f, g \in \mathcal{M}$, we construct the coproduct morphism $f+g : A+B \to A'+B'$. In **Sets**, binary coproducts are compatible with monomorphisms, and therefore $(f+g)_s = [\iota_{A',s} \circ f_s, \iota_{B',s} \circ g_s]$ is injective for all $s \in S_G \backslash S_D$.

The coproduct can be considered as a functor and hence preserves isomorphisms. Therefore, if $f|_{DSIG}$ and $g|_{DSIG}$ are isomorphisms, $(f+g)|_{DSIG} = [(\iota_{A'} \circ f)|_{DSIG}, (\iota_{B'} \circ g)|_{DSIG}] = f|_{DSIG} + g|_{DSIG}$ is also an isomorphism.

If $AGSIG$ is not well structured, we still have binary coproducts in **AGSIG-Alg**, but they may not be compatible with $\mathcal{M}$. □

Lemma 11.16 (closure properties of $\mathcal{M}$–$\mathcal{M}'$ and PO–PB decompositions). *Let $\mathcal{M}' = \mathcal{M}'_1$ or $\mathcal{M}' = \mathcal{M}'_2$ in* **AGraphs$_{ATG}$** *as given in Example 9.22 or consider the corresponding morphism classes in* **AGSIG-Alg**. *We then have:*

1. *$\mathcal{M}'$ is closed under pushouts and pullbacks along $\mathcal{M}$-morphisms in* **AGSIG-Alg** *and* **AGraphs$_{ATG}$**.
2. *The $\mathcal{M}$–$\mathcal{M}'$ pushout–pullback decomposition property holds in the categories* **AGSIG-Alg** *and* **AGraphs$_{ATG}$**.
3. *$\mathcal{M}'$ is closed under composition and decomposition.*

Proof. It suffices to prove the lemma for **AGSIG-Alg** with the class $\mathcal{M}'_2$. For the class $\mathcal{M}'_1 = \mathcal{M}$ of all monomorphisms, the lemma follows from the properties of adhesive HLR categories.

1. Given the pushout (1) below, with $m, n \in \mathcal{M}$ and $f \in \mathcal{M}'_2$, Lemma 11.8 implies that (1) is a componentwise pushout in **Sets**. In **Sets**, if f_s is injective, so is g_s. This means that g_s is injective for all $s \in S_G \backslash S_D$, and therefore $g \in \mathcal{M}'_2$.

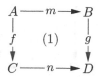

It follows analogously, by Lemma 11.9, that if (1) is a pullback with $m, n \in \mathcal{M}$ and $g \in \mathcal{M}'_2$, then $f \in \mathcal{M}'_2$ also.

2. Consider the following diagram, where $l \in \mathcal{M}$, $w \in \mathcal{M}'_2$, (1) + (2) is a pushout, and (2) is a pullback. It follows that $v, s \in \mathcal{M}$ and $r \in \mathcal{M}'_2$, since $\mathcal{M}$ is closed under pushouts and pullbacks and $\mathcal{M}'_2$ is closed under pullbacks along $\mathcal{M}$-morphisms.

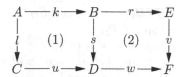

We have to show that (1) and (2) are pushouts in **AGSIG-Alg**.

Using Lemmas 11.8 and 11.9, we can split up this diagram componen-twise and obtain a pushout $(1)_s + (2)_s$ and a pullback $(2)_s$ in **Sets** for each $s \in S_G \cup S_D$.

a) For $s \in S_D$, l is an isomorphism. In **Sets**, a commmutative square along an isomorphism is a pushout. Therefore $(1)_s$ is a pushout.

b) For $s \in S_G \backslash S_D$, we have the fact that l, s, v, w, and r are injective. Since **Sets** is an adhesive HLR category, we can conclude from Theorem 4.26 that $(1)_s$ is a pushout in **Sets**.

By Lemma 11.8, (1) is a pushout in **AGSIG-Alg**. By pushout decomposition, (2) is also a pushout.

3. By the definition of $\mathcal{M}' = \mathcal{M}'_2$, we have the result that $f : A \to B \in \mathcal{M}'$, and $g : B \to C \in \mathcal{M}'$ implies $g \circ f \in \mathcal{M}'$ and $g \circ f, g \in \mathcal{M}'$ implies $f \in \mathcal{M}'$, since injectivity is preserved componentwise.

$\square$

Lemma 11.17 (initial POs in AGSIG-Alg). *The categories* (**AGSIG-Alg**, $\mathcal{M}$)*, where AGSIG and* (**AGraphs$_{\mathbf{ATG}}$**, $\mathcal{M}$) *are well structured, have initial pushouts over general morphisms.*

Construction. *By Theorem 11.3, it suffices to show the construction and property for* (**AGSIG-Alg**, $\mathcal{M}$)*. For an explicit construction in* (**AGraphs$_{\mathbf{ATG}}$**, $\mathcal{M}$)*, see Definition 10.5 and Fact 10.7.*

Consider a well-structured AGSIG, which means that for all op : $s' \to s$ in OP_G we have $s' \notin S_D$. Given $f : A \to A'$, the initial pushout over f is constructed by the following diagram:

$$B \xrightarrow{\quad b \quad} A$$

$$g \downarrow \qquad (1) \qquad \downarrow f$$

$$C \xrightarrow{\quad c \quad} A'$$

Here, the objects B, and C and the morphisms b, c, and g are defined as follows:

- $B = \cap\{B' \subseteq A \mid B'_{DSIG} = A_{DSIG}$ and $A^*_s \subseteq B'_s$ for all $s \in S_G \backslash S_D\}$ with
  $A^*_s = \{a \in A_s \mid \exists op : s' \to s \in OP_G \; \exists a' \in A'_{s'} \backslash f_{s'}(A_{s'}) : f_s(a) = op_{A'}(a')\}$
  $\cup \{a \in A_s \mid \exists a' \in A_s, a \neq a' : f_s(a) = f_s(a')\}$,

- $C_s = \begin{cases} A'_s & : \quad s \in S_D \\ A'_s \backslash f_s(A_s) \cup f_s(B_s) & : \quad s \in S_G \backslash S_D \end{cases}$,

  $op_C = \begin{cases} op_{A'} & : \quad op \in OP_D \\ op_{A'}|_{C_s} & : \quad op : s \to s' \in OP_G \end{cases}$,

- $b : B \to A$, $c : C \to A'$ are inclusions with identical data type parts and hence $b, c \in \mathcal{M}$. $g : B \to C$ is defined by $g_s = f_s|_{B_s}$ for all $s \in S_G \cup S_D$.

Initial pushouts are closed under double pushouts (see Lemma 6.5).

Proof. It can be shown that this construction is well defined and is indeed an initial pushout over f (see the proof in Section C.4). $\square$

Constraints, Application Conditions and Termination for Typed AGT Systems

In this chapter we make a first attempt to extend the theory of typed attributed graph transformation (AGT) systems by considering various kinds of execution control for AGT systems, such as graph constraints, application conditions, and application layers for productions, and also termination criteria.

In Section 12.1, we present the basic concepts of constraints and application conditions for typed AGT systems. The corresponding idea in the classical case of graphs was introduced in Section 3.4 and considered in the framework of adhesive HLR systems in Chapter 7. We instantiate the main results of Chapter 7 concerning equivalence of constraints and application conditions in Section 12.2. Finally, we present termination criteria for layered graph grammars based on typed AGT systems in Section 12.3; these criteria were introduced for the graph case in Section 3.4.

12.1 Constraints and Application Conditions for Typed AGT Systems

In this section, we extend graph constraints and application conditions from the case of classical graphs considered in Section 3.4 to typed attributed graphs, where the injective graph morphisms in Section 3.4 are replaced by a morphism class $\mathcal{M}'$ in **AGraphs$_{\mathbf{ATG}}$**, which has to be closed under composition and decomposition. In particular, we can take $\mathcal{M}'$ as the class of all typed attributed graph morphisms, i.e. $\mathcal{M}' = \mathcal{M}$ (see Definition 11.5), $\mathcal{M}' = \mathcal{M}'_1$, or $\mathcal{M}' = \mathcal{M}'_2$ (see Example 9.22), where $f \in \mathcal{M}'_1$ means that f is injective and $f \in \mathcal{M}'_2$ means that f is injective on graph nodes and all kinds of edges.

General Assumptions for Section 12.1

We consider the adhesive HLR category (**AGraphs$_{\mathbf{ATG}}$**, $\mathcal{M}$) of typed attributed graphs with an additional class $\mathcal{M}'$ of morphisms in **AGraphs$_{\mathbf{ATG}}$**, which is closed under composition and decomposition (see the general assumption 3 for Chapter 7). Graphs and graph morphisms are now – unlike the case in Section 3.4 – objects and morphisms in **AGraphs**$_\text{ATG}$.

First of all, we introduce graph constraints for **AGraphs**$_\text{ATG}$, in analogy to Definition 3.39 in Part I and Definition 7.2 in Part II.

Definition 12.1 (graph constraint for AGraphs$_\text{ATG}$). *An atomic graph constraint for* **AGraphs**$_\text{ATG}$ *is of the form* $\text{PC}(a)$*, where* $a\colon P \to C$ *is a morphism in* **AGraphs**$_\text{ATG}$*.*

A graph constraint for **AGraphs**$_\text{ATG}$ *is a Boolean formula over atomic graph constraints. This means that true and every atomic graph constraint for* **AGraphs**$_\text{ATG}$ *is a graph constraint for* **AGraphs**$_\text{ATG}$*, and given graph constraints* c *and* c_i *for* **AGraphs**$_\text{ATG}$ *with* $i \in I$ *for some index set* I*,* $\neg c$*,* $\wedge_{i \in I} c_i$*, and* $\vee_{i \in I} c_i$ *are graph constraints for* **AGraphs**$_\text{ATG}$*:*

A graph G *in* **AGraphs**$_\text{ATG}$ *satisfies a graph constraint* c*, written* $G \models c$*, if*

- $c = true;$
- $c = \text{PC}(a)$ *and, for every graph morphism* $p\colon P \to G$ *in* $\mathcal{M}'$*, there exists a graph morphism* $q\colon C \to G$ *in* $\mathcal{M}'$ *such that* $q \circ a = p;$
- $c = \neg c'$*, and* G *does not satisfy* $c';$
- $c = \wedge_{i \in I} c_i$*, and* G *satisfies all* c_i *with* $i \in I;$
- $c = \vee_{i \in I} c_i$*, and* G *satisfies some* c_i *with* $i \in I.$

Two graph constraints c *and* c' *are* equivalent*, denoted by* $c \equiv c'$*, if for all graphs* G*,* $G \models c$ *if and only if* $G \models c'$*.*

The constraint $\neg true$ *is abbreviated as* $false$*.*

Example 12.2 (graph constraint for AGraphs$_\text{ATG}$). We extend the graphs based on the type graph ATG in Example 8.9 by the following graph constraints $\text{PC}(a_1)$ and $\text{PC}(a_2)$:

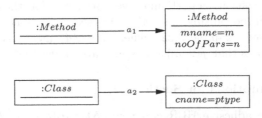

A graph G satisfies the first graph constraint, if every graph node of type *Method* has attributes of type *mname* and *noOfPars*. Analogously, the second graph constraint is fulfilled if each *Class* node has an attribute *cname*.

On the basis of the following graph constraint PC(a), we shall analyze the effects of the various choices of the class $\mathcal{M}'$. $\varnothing$ represents the initial graph, which means the graph that has the term algebra as its data part, but no graph nodes or any kinds of edges. The graph C looks strange at first sight because of the double attribute *mname*, but remember that we allow multiple attributes of the same type in the general theory. This means that we have two node attribute edges of type *mname* in C, one connecting the *Method* node to the data node m and one connecting it to the data node p. Note that the data part of the morphism a is the inclusion of the term algebra T_{DSIG} to the term algebra with variables $T_{DSIG}(X)$, which is the data part of C:

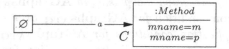

In the following, we discuss four different choices of the class $\mathcal{M}'$:

1. In the case where $\mathcal{M}' = \mathcal{M}'_1$ is the class of all monomorphisms, the morphism $\varnothing \rightarrow G$ is in general not in $\mathcal{M}'$, because the evaluation of terms is not necessarily injective. This means that a graph G satisfies PC(a) if the evaluation of the term algebra T_{DSIG} into the data part D^G of G is not injective. If $\varnothing \rightarrow G$ is injective, and there is also an injective morphism $q : T_{DSIG}(X) \rightarrow D^G$, then G satisfies PC(a) if there is a method with two different names, i.e. two node attribute edges *mname* linking the same method to different data nodes.

2. In the case $\mathcal{M}' = \mathcal{M}'_2$, a graph G satisfies the constraint PC(a) if G has a method with two node attribute edges *mname*, which may link to the same data node, because we allow non injectivity for the data part in $\mathcal{M}'$.

3. If $\mathcal{M}'$ is the class of all morphisms, G satisfies PC(a) if it contains a method with a name, because both data nodes m and m', as well as the node attribute edges, may be mapped together.

4. In the case $\mathcal{M}' = \mathcal{M}$, each graph G whose data part is not isomorphic to the term algebra satisfies the graph constraint, because we do not find a morphism $\varnothing \rightarrow G \in \mathcal{M}$. A graph G' whose data type is isomorphic to the term algebra does not satisfy PC(a), because $\varnothing \rightarrow G'$ is an $\mathcal{M}$-morphism, but we do not find a morphism $q : C \rightarrow G' \in \mathcal{M}$ since the data parts are not isomorphic.

$\square$

Remark 12.3. Similarly to Chapter 7, we can also consider negative atomic constraints of the form NC(a), with $a : P \rightarrow C$ as above. G satisfies NC(a) if, for every morphism $p : P \rightarrow G$ in $\mathcal{M}'$, there does not exist a morphism $q : C \rightarrow G$ in $\mathcal{M}'$ with $q \circ a = p$.

From Fact 7.5, we can conclude, in the case where $\mathcal{M}' = \mathcal{M}_2'$ or where $\mathcal{M}'$ is the class of all morphisms, that negative atomic constraints do not give more expressive power. In fact, we have $\mathrm{NC}(P \xrightarrow{a} C) \equiv \neg\mathrm{PC}(\varnothing \to C)$ for the initial graph $\varnothing$ in **AGraphs$_{\mathbf{ATG}}$** if $a \in \mathcal{M}'$, and $\mathrm{NC}(P \xrightarrow{a} C) \equiv true$ otherwise.

Now we shall introduce application conditions for **AGraphs$_{\mathbf{ATG}}$** in analogy to Definition 3.50 in Part I and Definition 7.6 in Part II. In the following, L can be seen as the left-hand side of a production and $m : L \to G$ as a match. Similarly, L and m can be replaced by R and a comatch $n : R \to H$.

Definition 12.4 (application condition for AGraphs$_{\mathbf{ATG}}$). *An atomic application condition for* **AGraphs$_{\mathbf{ATG}}$** *over a graph L in* **AGraphs$_{\mathbf{ATG}}$** *is of the form* $\mathrm{P}(x, \vee_{i \in I} x_i)$, *where* $x : L \to X$ *and* $x_i : X \to C_i$ *with* $i \in I$ *(for some index set I) are graph morphisms in* **AGraphs$_{\mathbf{ATG}}$**.

An application condition for **AGraphs$_{\mathbf{ATG}}$** *over L is a Boolean formula over atomic application conditions for* **AGraphs$_{\mathbf{ATG}}$** *over L. This means that true and every atomic application condition for* **AGraphs$_{\mathbf{ATG}}$** *is an application condition for* **AGraphs$_{\mathbf{ATG}}$** *and, for application conditions* acc *and* acc$_i$ *for* **AGraphs$_{\mathbf{ATG}}$** *with* $i \in I$, $\neg$acc, $\wedge_{i \in I}$acc$_i$, *and* $\vee_{i \in I}$acc$_i$ *are application conditions for* **AGraphs$_{\mathbf{ATG}}$**:

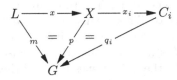

A graph morphism $m : L \to G$ in **AGraphs$_{\mathbf{ATG}}$** *satisfies an application condition* acc, *written* $m \models$ acc, *if*

- acc $= true$;
- acc $= P(x, \vee_{i \in I} x_i)$ *and, for all graph morphisms* $p : X \to G \in \mathcal{M}'$ *with* $p \circ x = m$, *there exist an* $i \in I$ *and a graph morphism* $q_i : C_i \to G \in \mathcal{M}''$ *such that* $q_i \circ x_i = p$;
- acc $= \neg$acc', *and m does not satisfy* acc';
- acc $= \wedge_{i \in I}$acc$_i$, *and m satisfies all* acc$_i$ *with* $i \in I$;
- acc $= \vee_{i \in I}$acc$_i$, *and m satisfies some* acc$_i$ *with* $i \in I$.

Two application conditions acc *and* acc' *over a graph L in* **AGraphs$_{\mathbf{ATG}}$** *are* equivalent, *denoted by* acc $\equiv$ acc', *if for all graph morphisms m, $m \models$ acc if and only if $m \models$ acc'.*

The application condition $\neg true$ is abbreviated as $false$.

An application condition $A(p) = (A_L, A_R)$ *for a production* $p = (L \leftarrow K \to R)$ *consists of a left application condition A_L over L and a right application condition A_R over R. A direct transformation $G \xRightarrow{p,m} H$ with a comatch n satisfies an application condition $A(p) = (A_L, A_R)$ if $m \models A_L$ and $n \models A_R$.*

A special kind of atomic application condition with an empty index set I is the negative application condition NAC(x). In fact, this kind of negative application condition is most important for modeling and metamodeling using typed AGT systems, especially to show termination (see Section 12.3).

Definition 12.5 (negative application condition NAC for AGraphs$_{\mathbf{ATG}}$). *A simple negative application condition NAC for* **AGraphs$_{\mathbf{ATG}}$** *is of the form* NAC(x)*, where* $x : L \to X$ *is a morphism in* **AGraphs$_{\mathbf{ATG}}$***. A (match) morphism* $m : L \to G$ *satisfies* NAC(x) *if there does not exist a morphism* $p : X \to G$ *in* $\mathcal{M}'$ *with* $p \circ x = m$:

Example 12.6 (negative application condition). We express negative application conditions here for some of the productions in Example 9.6.

The following negative application condition for the production *addClass* makes sure that we do not add a new class with the same name as an existing one; here $x_1 \in \mathcal{M}$, which means that the data part is preserved. Note that this interpretation is only valid for the choice $\mathcal{M}' = \mathcal{M}'_2$ or where $\mathcal{M}'$ is the class of all morphisms.

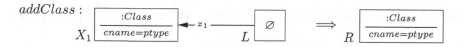

Analogously, the following negative application condition for the production
addParameter guarantees that each method has at most one return parameter. In this case the morphism $x_2 : L \to X_2$ is not an $\mathcal{M}$-morphism, but instead maps the data node p in L to the data node p, and maps k to *return* in X_2. This means that if we apply this production to a graph G via a match m and insert a parameter whose kind is not *return*, there is no morphism $q : X_2 \to G$ such that $q \circ x_2 = m$. Otherwise, the existence of a parameter of kind *return* prevents the production being applied.

$addParameter:$

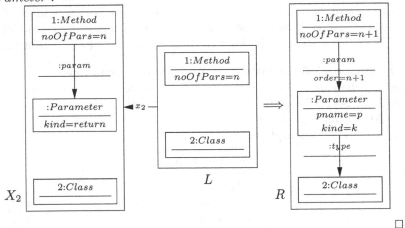

Remark 12.7 (negative application condition). A negative atomic application condition for $\mathbf{AGraphs_{ATG}}$ is of the form $N(x, \wedge_{i \in I} x_i)$, where $x : L \to X$ and $x_i : X \to C_i$ are morphisms in $\mathbf{AGraphs_{ATG}}$. Satisfaction is defined as in Definition 7.8. According to Fact 7.9, negative application conditions do not give more expressive power, because they are equivalent to application conditions for $\mathbf{AGraphs_{ATG}}$:

$$\mathrm{NAC}(x) \equiv \mathrm{P}(x, e) \text{ and } \mathrm{N}(x, \wedge_{i \in I} x_i) \equiv \wedge_{i \in I'} \mathrm{NAC}(x_i \circ x)$$

where e is an expression with an empty index set and $I' = \{i \in I \mid x_i \in \mathcal{M}'\}$.

12.2 Equivalence of Constraints and Application Conditions

In this section, we show two main results. The construction of (right) application conditions from graph constraints, and the construction of left from right application conditions for $\mathbf{AGraphs_{ATG}}$. The results are obtained as instantiations of the corresponding results for adhesive HLR systems in Sections 7.2 and 7.3, respectively. In addition to the general assumptions for Section 12.1, we have to satisfy the following general assumptions for Chapter 7:

1. $\mathbf{AGraphs_{ATG}}$ has binary coproducts (see Theorem 11.3 and Lemma 11.15).
2. $\mathbf{AGraphs_{ATG}}$ has a weak epi–$\mathcal{M}'$ factorization (see Definition A.15).
3. The additional class $\mathcal{M}'$ must be closed under composition and decomposition, and under pushouts and pullbacks along $\mathcal{M}$-morphisms, and we need the $\mathcal{M}$–$\mathcal{M}'$ PO–PB decomposition property (see Definition 5.27) in $\mathbf{AGraphs_{ATG}}$.

This means that we cannot take $\mathcal{M}' = \mathcal{M}$, because we have no epi–$\mathcal{M}$ factorization for all morphisms f in $\mathbf{AGraphs_{ATG}}$, but only such a factorization for f with a surjective data type part. However, all the conditions above are satisfied if we take $\mathcal{M}' = \mathcal{M}'_1$ or $\mathcal{M}' = \mathcal{M}'_2$, where $\mathcal{M}'_1$ is the class of injective morphisms in $\mathbf{AGraphs_{ATG}}$ and $f \in \mathcal{M}'_2$ is injective for graph nodes and all kinds of edges (see Example 9.22). In fact, we have an epi–$\mathcal{M}'_1$ and a weak epi–$\mathcal{M}'_2$ factorization in $\mathbf{AGraphs_{ATG}}$. The other properties for $\mathcal{M}'_1$ and $\mathcal{M}'_2$ are shown in Lemma 11.16.

According to the general assumptions for Section 7.2, we do not need the $\mathcal{M}$–$\mathcal{M}'$ PO–PB decomposition property for Theorem 7.13, which corresponds to Theorem 12.8 in our context. This means that Theorem 12.8 is also valid for the class $\mathcal{M}'$ of all morphisms in $\mathbf{AGraphs_{ATG}}$. For simplicity, however, we require $\mathcal{M}' = \mathcal{M}'_1$ or $\mathcal{M}' = \mathcal{M}'_2$ in the general assumptions for this section.

General Assumptions for Section 12.2

We consider the adhesive HLR category $(\mathbf{AGraphs_{ATG}}, \mathcal{M})$ with an additional class $\mathcal{M}' = \mathcal{M}'_1$ or $\mathcal{M}' = \mathcal{M}'_2$ (see above) and a graph transformation system GTS with a production p (see Definition 9.4). Graphs and graph morphisms are again objects and morphisms in $\mathbf{AGraphs_{ATG}}$.

First, we construct, as an instantiation of Definition 7.11 for each atomic constraint $\mathrm{PC}(a)$ with $a : P \to C \in \mathcal{M}$, an equivalent application condition.

Concerning the underlying ideas and the terminology, we refer to the introduction to Section 7.2 in Part II.

Definition 12.8 (construction of application conditions from graph constraints in $\mathbf{AGraphs_{ATG}}$). *For atomic graph constraints $\mathrm{PC}(a)$ with a morphism $a\colon P \to C \in \mathcal{M}$ and a graph R in $\mathbf{AGraphs_{ATG}}$, we define*

$$\mathrm{Acc}(\mathrm{PC}(a)) = \wedge_S \mathrm{P}(R \xrightarrow{s} S, \vee_{i \in I} S \xrightarrow{t_i \circ t} T_i),$$

where $\mathrm{P}(R \xrightarrow{s} S, \vee_{i \in I} S \xrightarrow{t_i \circ t} T_i)$ is an atomic application condition over R in $\mathbf{AGraphs_{ATG}}$ (see Definition 12.4), and I depends on S:

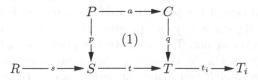

- *The conjunction $\wedge_S$ ranges over all "gluings" S of R and P, or, more precisely, over all triples $\langle S, s, p \rangle$ with arbitrary $s\colon R \to S$ and $p\colon P \to S$ in $\mathcal{M}'$ such that the pair (s, p) is jointly surjective. For each such triple $\langle S, s, p \rangle$ we construct the pushout (1) of p and a in $\mathbf{AGraphs_{ATG}}$, leading to $t\colon S \to T$ in $\mathcal{M}$ and $q\colon C \to T$.*

- *For each S, the disjunction $\vee_{i \in I}$ ranges over all $S \overset{t_i \circ t}{\hookrightarrow} T_i$ with epimorphisms t_i such that $t_i \circ t$ and $t_i \circ q$ are in $\mathcal{M}'$. For $I = \varnothing$, we have $\mathrm{Acc}(PC(a)) = \wedge_S \mathrm{NAC}(R \overset{s}{\to} S)$.*

The construction can be extended to Boolean formulas over atomic constraints in $\mathbf{AGraphs_{ATG}}$: $\mathrm{Acc}(true) = true$ and, for constraints c, c_j in $\mathbf{AGraphs_{ATG}}$ with $j \in J$, $\mathrm{Acc}(\neg c) = \neg\mathrm{Acc}(c)$, $\mathrm{Acc}(\wedge_{j \in J} c_j) = \wedge_{j \in J} \mathrm{Acc}(c_j)$, and $\mathrm{Acc}(\vee_{j \in J} c_j) = \vee_{j \in J} \mathrm{Acc}(c_j)$.

Note that the pushout (1) of p and a exists in $\mathbf{AGraphs_{ATG}}$, because we have $a \in \mathcal{M}$. Now we are able to show the first main result as an instantiation of Theorem 7.13.

Theorem 12.9 (construction of application conditions from graph constraints in $\mathbf{AGraphs_{ATG}}$). *For every graph constraint c for $\mathbf{AGraphs_{ATG}}$, where c is built up from atomic constraints $PC(a)$ with $a \in \mathcal{M}$, and every graph R and morphism $n : R \to H$, we have*

$$n \models \mathrm{Acc}(c) \Leftrightarrow H \models c.$$

Proof. This follows directly from Theorem 7.13 and the general assumptions for this section. $\square$

Example 12.10 (construction of application conditions from graph constraints in $\mathbf{AGraphs_{ATG}}$). We follow the construction of application conditions from constraints for the production *addParameter* and the graph constraint $\neg PC(a : P \to C)$, which forbids a method to have two parameters of kind *return*:

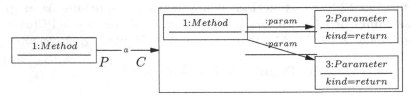

First we have to compute all gluings S of R and P with morphisms $s : R \to S$ and $p : P \to S \in \mathcal{M}'$ such that s and p are jointly surjective, where R is the right-hand side of the production *addParameter*. For the graph part, this means that there are only two possible gluings: both *Method* nodes can be mapped together or not. This leads to the graph gluings S_1 in Fig. 12.1, and S_2 (not shown). On the data part, the gluing depends on the choice of $\mathcal{M}'$. The data parts of R and P are the same, namely the term algebra with variables $T_{DSIG}(X)$. In the case where $\mathcal{M}' = \mathcal{M}'_1$, this means that we can glue together two copies of $T_{DSIG}(X)$ as long as p is injective. For $\mathcal{M}' = \mathcal{M}'_2$, an arbitrary gluing is allowed. For simplicity, we have shown only the graph part, but one should keep in mind that each graph represents all possible gluings of the data part.

Now we construct the pushout over a and p_1, and obtain the epimorphisms t_{11}, t_{12}, and t_{13}, which fulfill the required properties on the graph part. This leads to one component $acc_1 = P(R \xrightarrow{s} S_1, \vee_{i=1,..,5} S_1 \xrightarrow{t_{1i} \circ t} T_{1i})$ of the conjunction $\wedge_S$, which is shown in part in Fig. 12.1. The remaining objects T_{14} and T_{15} are similar to T_{12} and T_{13} but the *Parameter* node 6 has two attributes of type *kind*, one with the value k and one with the value *return*.

An analogous construction for the second gluing S_2 leads to an application condition $acc_2 = P(R \xrightarrow{s} S_2, \vee_{i=1,...,5} S_2 \xrightarrow{t_{2i} \circ t} T_{2i})$ that consists of five disjunctions; we shall not analyze it explicitly. Since the original constraint was a negation, the resulting right application condition is also negated and we have $Acc(\neg PC(a : P \to C)) = \neg(acc_1 \wedge acc_2)$.

If we choose $\mathcal{M}' = \mathcal{M}'_1$, $t_i \circ t$ and $t_i \circ q$ have to be monomorphisms, i.e. injective. This is only the case if S, T, and T_i have the same data part, which is preserved by the morphisms. Therefore, in the first construction the objects T_{12} and T_{13} do not fulfill the required properties, because the variable k and the value *return* are mapped together. For $\mathcal{M}' = \mathcal{M}'_2$, the data parts of these morphisms may be arbitrary, and therefore there are also different choices of the data part for each T_i in addition to those for S.

$\square$

As the second main result, we show that for each right application condition we can construct an equivalent left application condition in **AGraphs**$_{\mathbf{ATG}}$ (see Definition 7.16 and Theorem 7.17 for the general framework).

Definition 12.11 (construction of left from right application condition in AGraphs$_{\mathbf{ATG}}$). *For each right atomic application condition* $\text{acc} = P(R \xrightarrow{x} X, \vee_{i \in I} X \xrightarrow{x_i} C_i)$ *of a production* $p = \langle L \leftarrow K \to R \rangle$, *let*

$$L_p(\text{acc}) = P(L \xrightarrow{y} Y, \vee_{i \in I'} Y \xrightarrow{y_i} D_i) \text{ with } I' \subseteq I \text{ or } L_p(\text{acc}) = true,$$

where y, y_i *and* I' *are constructed as follows:*

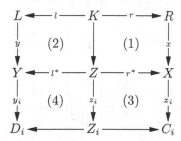

- *If the pair* $\langle K \xrightarrow{r} R, R \xrightarrow{x} X \rangle$ *has a pushout complement in* **AGraphs**$_{\mathbf{ATG}}$, *define* $y \colon L \to Y$ *by the two pushouts (1) and (2); otherwise,* $L_p(\text{acc}) = true$.

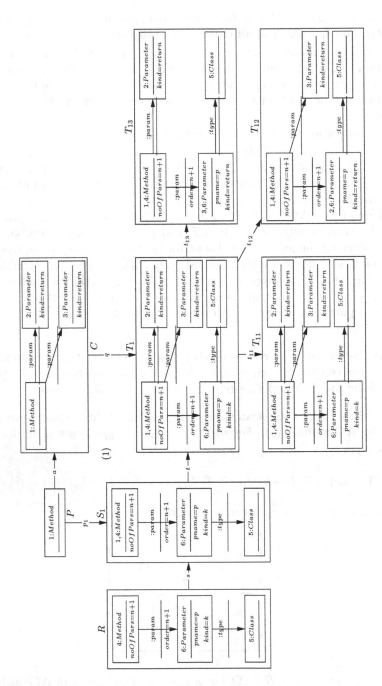

Fig. 12.1. Construction of application condition for the gluing S_1

- For each $i \in I$, if the pair $\langle Z \xrightarrow{r^*} X, X \xrightarrow{x_i} C_i \rangle$ has a pushout complement in **AGraphs$_{\mathbf{ATG}}$**, then $i \in I'$, and $y_i \colon Y \to D_i$ is defined by the two pushouts (3) and (4); otherwise, $i \notin I'$.

Since pushout complements of $\mathcal{M}$-morphisms (if they exist) are unique up to isomorphism (see Theorem 4.26), the construction of a left application condition is also unique up to isomorphism.

The transformation can be extended to arbitrary right application conditions as follows: $L_p(\mathrm{true}) = \mathrm{true}, L_p(\neg \mathrm{acc}) = \neg L_p(\mathrm{acc})$, $L_p(\wedge_{i \in I} \mathrm{acc}_i) = \wedge_{i \in I} L_p(\mathrm{acc}_i)$, and $L_p(\vee_{i \in I} \mathrm{acc}_i) = \vee_{i \in I} L_p(\mathrm{acc}_i)$.

Theorem 12.12 (construction of left from right application conditions in AGraphs$_{\mathbf{ATG}}$). *For every production p of a typed attributed graph transformation system and for every right application condition* acc *for p in* **AGraphs$_{\mathbf{ATG}}$**, $L_p(\mathrm{acc})$ *as defined in Definition 12.11 is a left application condition for p in* **AGraphs$_{\mathbf{ATG}}$**, *with the property that, for all direct transformations $G \xRightarrow{p,m} H$ with a comatch n,*

$$m \models L_p(\mathrm{acc}) \quad \Longleftrightarrow \quad n \models \mathrm{acc}.$$

Proof. This follows directly from Theorem 7.17 and the general assumptions for this section. □

Example 12.13 (construction of left from right application conditions in AGraphs$_{\mathbf{ATG}}$). Here, we construct a left application condition from the right application condition that we constructed in Example 12.10.

The first part of the conjunction $\wedge_S$ is the application condition $P(R \xrightarrow{s} S_1, \vee_{i=1,..,5} S_1 \xrightarrow{t_{1i} \circ t} T_{1i})$. The graph parts of R and S_1 are equal, and since the data parts of K and R are equal too, the pushout complement Z exists. Z consists of the graph part of K and the data part of S. Similarly, we can now construct the pushout object Y, which has the same data part, but its graph part is equal to L.

Now we have to analyze the disjunction $\vee_{i=1,...,5}$. For T_{14} and T_{15} there does not exist the pushout complement (3), because in T_{14} and T_{15} we add a node attribute edge of type *kind* to the *Parameter* node 6 in S_1 which is not in the interface Z. For T_{12} and T_{13}, the results are isomorphic and are shown in the following diagram, where we depict only the pushouts (3) and (4). Note that in the data parts of t_{12}, z_{12}, and y_{12} the variable k is mapped to the value *return*:

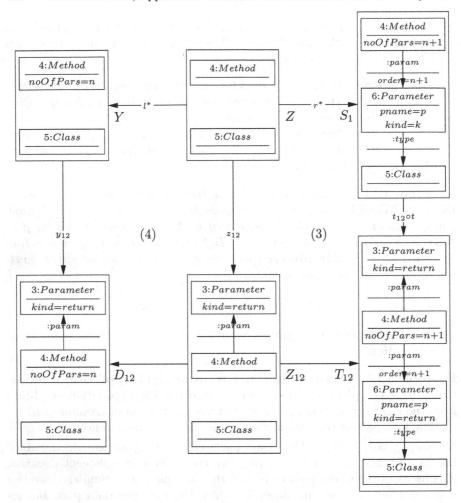

The analogous result for T_{11} is shown in the following, where the data parts of D_{11}, Z_{11}, and T_{11} are the same, and we show only the bottom line of the pushouts (3) and (4):

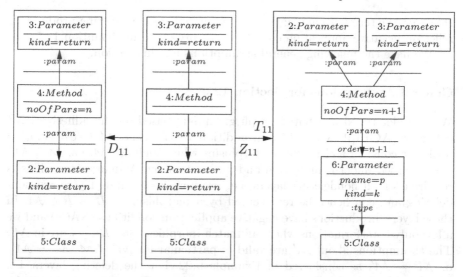

For the second part of the conjunction, concerning the gluing S_2, we have a very similar construction. Since the original right application condition is negated, we also have to negate the resulting left application condition.

Note that the part of the application condition constructed from T_{12} is very similar to the one that we presented in Example 12.6 for the same problem: it prohibits the addition of a second *return* parameter. The other parts of the left application condition $L_p(\neg(acc_1 \wedge acc_2))$ only make sure that the graph G does not already contain a method that violates this constraint.   □

Remark 12.14 (guaranteeing and preservation of constraints). Similarly to the general theory in Chapter 7, we can define the guaranteeing and preservation of constraints (see Definition 7.22) and show that for every constraint c in **AGraphs**$_{\mathbf{ATG}}$ (built up from atomic constraints $PC(a)$ with $a \in \mathcal{M}$) and every production p, there are left application conditions $A(c)$ and $A'(c)$ for p in **AGraphs**$_{\mathbf{ATG}}$ such that the extended production $(p, A(c))$ is c-guaranteeing and $(p, A'(c))$ is c-preserving (see Theorem 7.23).

12.3 Termination Criteria for Layered Typed Attributed Graph Grammars

In this section, we introduce and prove termination criteria for typed AGT systems, as presented in [EEdL$^+$05]; these criteria were introduced for the graph case in Section 3.4. For proving termination, the productions are distributed among different layers, and the productions in one layer are applied for as long as possible before going on to the next layer. The termination criteria for deletion layers are not specific to the algebraic approach. They are also applicable to all other kinds of graph grammars based on typed graphs.

However, the termination of layers consisting only of non deleting productions relies on negative application conditions, as presented in Definition 12.5.

We have the following general assumptions for this section.

General Assumptions for Section 12.3

We consider typed attributed graph grammars based on the adhesive HLR category ($\mathbf{AGraphs_{ATG}}$, $\mathcal{M}$). In addition to the class $\mathcal{M}$ (see Definition 8.10), we consider a class $\mathcal{M}'$ of morphisms which includes $\mathcal{M}$, i.e. $\mathcal{M} \subseteq \mathcal{M}'$, and is closed under composition and pushouts along $\mathcal{M}$-morphisms. This is required for all nondeleting layers, i.e. productions in these layers are nondeleting and can hence be represented by a morphism $r : L \rightarrow R \in \mathcal{M}$. In these layers, productions have negative application conditions (NACs) and we allow only transformations where all match morphisms $m : L \rightarrow G$ are in $\mathcal{M}'$. The assumptions about $\mathcal{M}'$ are valid in particular for $\mathcal{M}' = \mathcal{M}$, $\mathcal{M}' = \mathcal{M}'_1$, or $\mathcal{M}' = \mathcal{M}'_2$ as considered in Example 9.22. For the deleting layers, i.e. where productions in these layers delete at least one item, we have no restrictions concerning productions and matches. In fact, we could use any kind of graph transformation or high-level replacement system where at least one of the items in the left- and right-hand sides of the productions is typed by a set of types $TYPE$ in the traditional way or by a subset of types for typed attributed graphs.

First, we define layered graph grammars with deletion and nondeletion layers in analogy to the graph case considered in Theorem 3.37. Informally, the deletion layer conditions express the condition that the last creation of a node with a certain type should precede the first deletion of a node with the same type. On the other hand, the nondeletion layer conditions ensure that if an element of type t occurs in the left-hand side (LHS) of a production then all elements of the same type have already been created in previous layers.

Definition 12.15 (layered typed attributed graph grammar). *A typed attributed graph grammar* $GG = (DSIG, ATG, P, G_0)$ *with an attributed type graph* ATG, *a set of productions* P, *and a start graph* G_0 *is called a* layered typed attributed graph grammar *if:*

1. *P is layered, i.e. for each $p \in P$ there is a production layer $pl(p)$ with $0 \le pl(p) \le k_0$ ($pl(p), k_0 \in \mathbb{N}$), where $k_0 + 1$ is the number of layers in GG, and each production $p \in P$ has a set NAC_p of negative application conditions $NAC(n : L \rightarrow N)$ (see Definition 12.5), or $n \in NAC_p$ for short.*
2. *The type set $TYPE$ of GG is given by the graph nodes, graph edges, node attributes, and edge attributes of the type graph $ATG = (TG, Z)$, i.e. all items of TG except the data nodes, where Z is the final $DSIG$-algebra.*

3. *GG is finitary, i.e. G_0 and all graphs G derivable in layer k with productions $P_k = \{p \in P \mid pl(p) = k\}$ for $0 \le k \le k_0$ are finitary, which means that $card\{x \in G \mid type(x) \in TYPE\}$ is finite, and for each nondeletion layer k and $p \in P_k$ with left-hand side L, there is only a finite number of matches $m : L \to G$ with $m \models NAC_p$.*

4. *For each type $t \in TYPE$, there is a creation layer $cl(t) \in \mathbb{N}$, and a deletion layer $dl(t) \in \mathbb{N}$, and each production layer k is either a deletion layer or a nondeletion layer, satisfying the following conditions for all $p \in P_k$:*

If k is a deletion layer: deletion layer conditions	If k is a nondeletion layer: nondeletion layer conditions
1. p deletes at least one item x with $type(x) \in TYPE$ 2. $0 \le cl(t) \le dl(t) \le k_0$ for all $t \in TYPE$ 3. p deletes $t \Rightarrow dl(t) \le pl(p)$ 4. p creates $t \Rightarrow cl(t) > pl(p)$	1. p is nondeleting, i.e. $K = L$ such that p is given by $r : L \to R \in \mathcal{M}$ 2. p has $n \in NAC_p$ with $n : L \to N$ and there is an $n' : N \to R \in \mathcal{M}'$ with $n' \circ n = r$ 3. $x \in L$ with $type(x) \in TYPE$ $\Rightarrow cl(type(x)) \le pl(p)$ 4. p creates $t \Rightarrow cl(t) > pl(p)$

Remark 12.16.

1. Note that in the layer conditions above, the notation "p deletes (or creates) t" means that for productions $p = (L \leftarrow K \to R, NAC_p)$ there is an item x in L (or x in R, respectively) with $type(x) = t \in TYPE$, which is deleted (or created) by p. In addition, $x \in L$ means that x is an item of L with $type(x) \in TYPE$, i.e. a graph node, graph edge, node attribute, or edge attribute.

2. The deletion layer conditions 2–4 imply that a type $t \in TYPE$ cannot be created by some production p and deleted by some p' in the same layer k, because this would imply $cl(t) > pl(p) = k = pl(p') \ge dl(t)$, in contradiction to $cl(t) \le dl(t)$.

3. If GG is finite, i.e. $DSIG$, ATG, P, each $p \in P$, and G_0 are finite, then GG is finitary. In general, however, the term algebra $T_{DSIG}(X)$ of the productions and the algebra A of G_0 will not be finite. In this case we have to restrict the number of matches $m : L \to G$ with $n \models NAC_p$ to being finite in order to achieve termination. If X and the algebra A are finite, or at least all domains A_s are finite for all $s \in S$ with $X_s \ne \varnothing$, then we have only a finite number of homomorphisms $h : T_{DSIG}(X) \to A$. If in addition all graph nodes, graph edges, node attributes, and edge attributes of G_0 and all graphs within the productions are finite, then GG is finitary. An example which violates the condition of being finitary, and is in fact a non-terminating GG, is given below; however, it satisfies the nondeletion layer conditions above.

Example 12.17 (non-terminating typed attributed graph grammar).
We consider a graph grammar $GG = (DSIG, ATG, P, G_0)$, where

- $DSIG = NAT$ (see Example B.3);
- $ATG = (TG, Z)$ with $V_G^{TG} = \{v\}$, $E_G^{TG} = \varnothing$, $E_{NA}^{TG} = \{a\}$, and $E_{EA}^{TG} = \varnothing$;
- $P = \{p\}$, attributed over $T_{DSIG}(X)$ and the variables $X = \{x\}$, where p is the nondeleting production $p = (L \xrightarrow{r} R, NAC_p = \{n : L \to N\})$ shown in Fig. 12.2, with a data-type-preserving morphism n;
- $G_0 = (G, NAT)$, where G consists of one graph node only.

Note that L contains terms with variables as data nodes; however, in general, we only show explicitly those nodes which are the target of a node or edge attribute edge. As an exception, we have shown the data node with the variable x (by a dashed circle) in L in Fig. 12.2, to make it clear that this node is not only in N and R, but also in L.

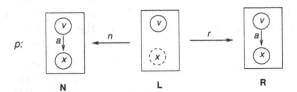

Fig. 12.2. Counterexample production

We then have the infinite transformation sequence shown in Fig. 12.3, where the match m_k in step k for $(k \geq 0)$ is given by $m_k(x) = k \in \mathbb{N}$.

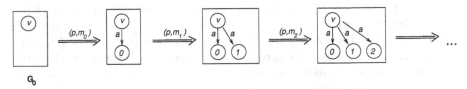

Fig. 12.3. Counterexample transformation sequence

Note that GG is almost a layered graph transformation system in the sense of Definition 12.15 ($k_0 = 0, pl(p) = 0, TYPE = \{v, a\}, cl(v) = 0, dl(v) = 0, cl(a) = 1, dl(a) = 0$), but it is not finitary and is non-terminating, owing to an infinite number of matches $m : L \to G_0$. $\square$

The assignment of the creation and deletion layers for the types $t \in TYPE$ is not fixed in Definition 12.15 above, but in several applications the following automatic assignment is useful; it leads to the reduced layer conditions in Lemma 12.19, which are sufficient to show termination.

Definition 12.18 (layer assignments). *Given a layered typed attributed graph grammar GG with a start graph G_0 and start types $T_0 \subseteq TYPE$, i.e. each typed item x in G_0 has $type(x) \in T_0$, then we can define for each $t \in TYPE$ the creation and deletion layers as follows:*

$cl(t) = \underline{if}\, t \in T_0 \,\underline{then}\, 0 \,\underline{else}\, max\{pl(p) \mid p \text{ creates } t\} + 1,$
$dl(t) = \underline{if}\, t \text{ is deleted by some } p \,\underline{then}\, min\{pl(p) \mid p \text{ deletes } t\} \,\underline{else}\, k_0 + 1.$

Lemma 12.19 (reduced conditions for layer assignment). *Consider a layered typed attributed graph grammar GG with the layer assignment of Definition 12.18 such that the following general layer conditions are satisfied:*

1. *p creates $t \Rightarrow t \notin T_0$.*
2. *$0 \leq cl(t) \leq dl(t) \leq k_0 + 1$ for all $t \in TYPE$.*

The following reduced deletion and nondeletion layer conditions then imply the deletion and nondeletion layer conditions given in Definition 12.15:

Reduced deletion layer conditions	Reduced nondeletion layer conditions
1. p deletes at least one item x with $type(x) \in TYPE$	1. p is nondeleting with $r : L \to R \in \mathcal{M}$ 2. p has NAC $n : L \to N$ with $n' : N \to R \in \mathcal{M}'$ and $n' \circ n = r$ 3. $x \in L$ with $type(x) \in TYPE$ $\Rightarrow cl(type(x)) \leq pl(p)$

Proof. It remains to show the deletion layer conditions 3 and 4 and the nondeletion layer condition 4.

Deletion layer condition 3: p deletes $t \Rightarrow dl(t) \leq pl(p)$, by the definition of $dl(t)$.

Deletion and nondeletion layer conditions 4: p creates $t \Rightarrow cl(t) > pl(p)$, by the definition of $cl(t)$. □

Remark 12.20. Note that, in order to show termination, in addition to ensuring that the reduced layer conditions are satisfied, we also have to make sure that GG is finitary. This means that, in particular, for each $p \in P_k$ for a nondeletion layer k, there is only a finite number of matches $m : L \to G$ (see Definition 12.15, item 3).

The termination of a layered graph grammar expresses the condition that no infinite derivation sequences exist starting from the start graph if productions are applied within layers as long as possible.

Definition 12.21 (termination of layered typed attributed graph grammars). *A layered typed attributed graph grammar as given in Definition 12.15 terminates if there is no infinite transformation sequence from G_0 via P, where, starting with the layer $k = 0$, productions $p \in P_k$ are applied for as long as possible before going on to the layer $k + 1 \leq k_0$.*

The termination of layered graph grammars will be shown separately for the deletion and the nondeletion layers.

Lemma 12.22 (termination of layered typed attributed graph grammars with deletion). *Every layered typed attributed graph grammar that contains only deletion layers terminates.*

Proof.
Step 0. Let $c_0 = card\{x \in G_0 \mid dl(type(x)) = 0\}$. c_0 is finite because GG is finitary.

By the deletion layer conditions 1 and 3, the application of a production p to G_0 with $pl(p) = 0$ deletes at least one item $x \in G_0$ with type $t = type(x) \in TYPE$ and $dl(t) = 0$.

Moreover, by the deletion layer condition 4, each of the productions p can create only items x with $type(x) = t$, where $cl(t) > 0$. This means, by using the deletion layer condition 2, that only items x with $type(x) = t$ and $dl(t) \geq cl(t) > 0$ can be created. Hence at most c_0 applications of productions $p \in P_0$ are possible in layer 0, leading to $G_0 \overset{*}{\Rightarrow} G_1$ via P_0.

Step k. Given a graph G_k as the result of step $(k-1)$ for $1 \leq k \leq k_0$, we define $c_k = card\{x \in G_k \mid dl(type(x)) \leq k\}$. Note that c_k is finitary because GG is finitary.

Using now a production p with $pl(p) = k$, each $p \in P_k$ deletes at least one item $x \in G_k$ with $dl(type(x)) \leq k$ by the deletion layer conditions 1 and 3, and creates at most items x with $cl(type(x)) > k$ by the deletion layer condition 4, which implies $dl(type(x)) \geq cl(type(x)) > k$ by the deletion layer condition 2. Hence at most c_k applications of productions $p \in P_k$ are possible in layer k, leading to $G_k \overset{*}{\Rightarrow} G_{k+1}$ via P_k.

After step n, we have at most $c = \sum_{k=0}^{k_0} c_k$ applications of productions $p \in P$, leading to $G_0 \overset{*}{\Rightarrow} G_{k_0+1}$, which implies termination. $\square$

Before proving termination for nondeletion layers, we need to define the notion of an essential match. Informally, an essential match m_0 of a match $m_1 : L \to H_1$ for a transformation $G_0 \overset{*}{\Rightarrow} H_1$ with $G_0 \subseteq H_1$ means that m_1 can be restricted to $m_0 : L \to G_0$.

Definition 12.23 (tracking morphism and essential match). *Given a nondeleting layered typed attributed graph grammar with matches $m \in \mathcal{M}'$, nondeleting production p given by a morphism $r : L \to R \in \mathcal{M}$ and a match $m : L \to G \in \mathcal{M}'$ lead to a direct transformation $G \overset{p,m}{\Longrightarrow} H$ via (p,m), defined by the pushout (1) of r and m, where $d : G \to H$ is called the* tracking *morphism of $G \overset{p,m}{\Longrightarrow} H$:*

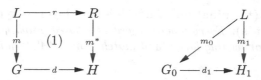

Since we have $r \in \mathcal{M}$ and $m \in \mathcal{M}'$, our general assumptions imply for the pushout (1) that $d \in \mathcal{M}$ and $m^* \in \mathcal{M}'$, also.

Given a transformation $G_0 \stackrel{*}{\Rightarrow} H_1$, i.e. a sequence of direct transformations with an induced tracking morphism $d_1 : G_0 \rightarrow H_1 \in \mathcal{M}$, a match $m_1 : L \rightarrow H_1$ of L in H_1 has an essential match $m_0 : L \rightarrow G_0$ of L in G_0 if we have $d_1 \circ m_0 = m_1$. Note that there is at most one essential match m_0 for m_1, because $d_1 \in \mathcal{M}$ is injective.

The following lemma states that productions can be applied at most once with the same essential match.

Lemma 12.24 (essential match). *In every transformation starting from G_0 of a nondeleting layered typed attributed graph grammar with matches $m \in \mathcal{M}'$, each production $p \in P_0$ with $r : L \rightarrow R$ can be applied at most once with the same essential match $m_0 : L \rightarrow G_0$ and where $m_0 \models NAC$.*

Proof. Assume that in $G_0 \stackrel{*}{\Rightarrow} H_1$, the production p has already been applied with the same essential match m_0. This means that we can decompose $G_0 \stackrel{*}{\Rightarrow} H_1$ into $G_0 \stackrel{*}{\Rightarrow} G \Rightarrow H \stackrel{*}{\Rightarrow} H_1$ with the pushout (1) and injective morphisms $G_0 \stackrel{g}{\rightarrow} G \stackrel{d}{\rightarrow} H \stackrel{h_1}{\rightarrow} H_1$ in $\mathcal{M}$ satisfying $d_1 = h_1 \circ d \circ g$ and $d_1 \circ m_0 = m_1$, as shown in the following diagram:

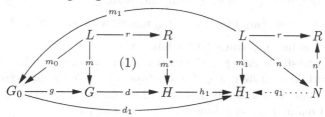

In order to prove the lemma, it is sufficient to show that $m_1 : L \rightarrow H_1$ does not satisfy the NAC of p, i.e. $m_1 \not\models NAC$, where the NAC is given by a morphism $n : L \rightarrow N \in \mathcal{M}'$ with $n' : N \rightarrow R \in \mathcal{M}'$ satisfying $n' \circ n = r$ by the nondeletion layer condition 2.

In fact, we are able to construct a morphism $q_1 : N \rightarrow H_1 \in \mathcal{M}'$ with $q_1 \circ n = m_1$, as follows. Let $q_1 = h_1 \circ m^* \circ n'$. Then $q_1 \in \mathcal{M}'$, because $\mathcal{M}'$ is closed under composition, $n', m^* \in \mathcal{M}'$, and $h_1 \in \mathcal{M} \subseteq \mathcal{M}'$ by our general assumptions; $m^* \in \mathcal{M}'$ follows from the match $m \in \mathcal{M}'$ and $\mathcal{M}'$ is closed under pushouts along $\mathcal{M}$-morphisms. Moreover, we have

$$q_1 \circ n = h_1 \circ m^* \circ n' \circ n = h_1 \circ m^* \circ r = h_1 \circ d \circ m = h_1 \circ d \circ g \circ m_0 = d_1 \circ m_0 = m_1$$

$\square$

Lemma 12.25 (termination of nondeleting layered typed attributed graph grammars). *Every layered typed attributed graph grammar GG that contains only nondeleting layers and matches $m \in \mathcal{M}'$ terminates.*

Proof.

Step 0. Given the start graph G_0, we count for each $p \in P_0$ with $r : L \to R$ and NAC the number of possible matches $m : L \to G_0$ with $m \models NAC$:

$$c_p^0 = card\{m_0 \mid m_0 : L \to G_0 \text{ match with } m_0 \models NAC\}.$$

Note that c_p^0 is finite, because GG is finitary.

The application of a production $p \in P_0$ creates, by the nondeletion layer condition 4, only new items x with $cl(type(x)) > pl(p) = 0$, while each item $x \in L$ with $type(x) \in TYPE$ for any production $p \in P_0$ has $cl(type(x)) \leq pl(p) = 0$, by the nondeletion layer condition 3. This means that for each transformation $G_0 \overset{*}{\Rightarrow} H_1$ via P_0 with matches $m \in \mathcal{M}'$ and morphism $d_1 : G_0 \to H_1 \in \mathcal{M}$, induced from $G_0 \overset{*}{\Rightarrow} H_1$ by the nondeletion layer condition 1, each match $m_1 : L \to H_1$ of a $p \in P_0$ must have an essential match $m_0 : L \to G_0$ with $d_1 \circ m_0 = m_1$.

From Lemma 12.24, we conclude that in step 0 we have at most

$$c_0 = \sum_{p \in P_0} c_p^0$$

applications of productions $p \in P_0$ leading to $G_0 \overset{*}{\Rightarrow} G_1$ via P_0, where c_p^0 is the number of different matches of p in G_0 as defined above.

Step k. Given a graph G_k as the result of step $(k-1)$ for $1 \leq k \leq k_0$, we define, for each $p \in P_k$ with $r : L \to R$ and NAC,

$$c_r^k = card\{m_k \mid m_k : L \to G_k \text{ match with } m \models NAC\}.$$

Note that c_r^k is finite, because GG is finitary.

Similarly to step 0, each $p \in P_k$ creates only new items x with $cl(type(x)) > pl(p) = k$, while each item $x \in L$ with $type(x) \in TYPE$ has $cl(type(x)) \leq pl(p) = k$. Now we can apply Lemma 12.24 for G_k, P_k, and m_k instead of G_0, P_0, and m_0 and can conclude that we have at most $c_k = \sum_{p \in P_k} c_r^k$ applications of productions leading to $G_k \overset{*}{\Rightarrow} G_{k+1}$ via P_k.

After step n, we have at most $c = \sum_{k=0}^{k_0} c_k$ applications of productions $p \in P$ leading to $G_0 \overset{*}{\Rightarrow} G_{k_0+1}$, which implies termination. $\square$

Combining Lemmas 12.22 and 12.25, we obtain the termination of layered typed attributed graph grammars, which generalizes Theorem 3.37 for the case of typed graph grammars.

Theorem 12.26 (termination of layered typed attributed graph grammars). *Every layered typed attributed graph grammar with matches $m \in \mathcal{M}'$ terminates.*

Proof. Starting with $k = 0$ we can apply the deletion layer conditions for each deletion layer (see Lemma 12.22) and the nondeletion layer conditions for each nondeletion layer (see Lemma 12.25), leading to termination in each layer $0 \leq k \leq k_0$ and hence to termination of the layered typed attributed graph grammar. □

For a detailed example for the termination of a layered typed attributed graph transformation system we refer to the termination analysis of the model transformation from statecharts to Petri nets in Subsection 14.2.4. Although the model transformation is a graph transformation system it can be considered as a family of grammars, where each statechart is the start graph of a corresponding grammar.

13

Typed Attributed Graph Transformation with Inheritance

The concepts of typed attributed graph transformation developed in Chapters 8 and 9 are most significant for modeling and metamodeling in software engineering. However, up to now we have not considered the concept of inheritance, which is especially important for the object-oriented approach to metamodeling. It can be combined with graph transformation, as shown in [BEd+03, BEdLT04]. In this chapter, we combine both concepts, leading to *attributed type graphs with inheritance (ATGIs)*.

The visual alphabet of a visual language corresponds roughly to the type graph of a graph grammar. While constraints describe additional requirements on this alphabet, productions formulate a constructive procedure. In the object-oriented approach, classes can be inherited, meaning that their fields and their associations are also present in all their descendants. In the approach of graph transformation, on the other hand, an additional type graph is used to ensure a certain kind of type safety on nodes and edges. Supporting node type inheritance in addition leads to a denser form of graph transformation system, since similar productions can be abstracted into one production. In [BEdLT04], this was shown for typed graph transformation, and in [EEPT05] this approach was extended to typed attributed graph transformation (typed AGT, for short). A solid formal framework for typed AGT with attributes for nodes and edges has been presented in Chapters 8 and 9. In this chapter, we show how to extend this approach to a formal integration of node type inheritance with typed AGT. For this purpose, we introduce AGT based on attributed type graphs with inheritance and show how this can be flattened to typed AGT without inheritance.

In this chapter, we focus on the formal framework concerning typed AGT with inheritance. The main results show that, for each graph transformation and grammar GG based on an attributed type graph with inheritance $ATGI$, there is an equivalent typed attributed graph transformation and grammar $\overline{GG}$ without inheritance. Hence there is a direct correspondence to typed attributed graph transformation without inheritance, for which some fundamental theory has already been presented in Chapters 9–12.

In Section 13.1, we introduce attributed type graphs with inheritance, and define ATGI-clan morphisms in Section 13.2. Abstract and concrete graph transformations as well as typed attributed graph transformation with inheritance are presented in Section 13.3. Finally, we show in Section 13.4 the main results concerning the equivalence of transformations and attributed graph grammars with and without inheritance.

13.1 Attributed Type Graphs with Inheritance

The concepts of node type inheritance [BEdLT04] and typed attributed graph transformation [EPT04, HKT02] are most significant for modeling and meta-modeling in software engineering and have been combined in [EEPT05].

In this section, we start by combining the two concepts, which results in a general concept of attributed type graphs with inheritance and a close relationship between typing with and without inheritance.

For clarity in this construction, we repeat the description of the signature of an E-graph and the definition of an attributed graph, both presented in Chapter 8.

Let G be an E-graph $G = (G_{V_G}, G_{V_D}, G_{E_G}, G_{E_{NA}}, G_{E_{EA}}, ((source_i), (target_i))_{i \in \{G, NA, EA\}})$, where G refers to the graph parts, NA to node attribution, and EA to edge attribution, according to the following signature:

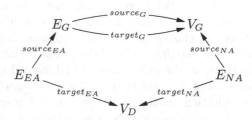

An attributed graph AG over a data signature $DSIG = (S_D, OP_D)$ with attribute value sorts $S'_D \subseteq S_D$ is given by $AG = (G, D)$, where G is an E-graph as described above and D is a $DSIG$-algebra such that $\dot{\bigcup}_{s \in S'_D} D_s = G_{V_D}$.

An attributed type graph with inheritance is an attributed type graph in the sense of Definition 8.7, with a distinguished set of abstract nodes and inheritance relations between the nodes. The inheritance clan of a node represents all its subnodes.

Definition 13.1 (attributed type graph with inheritance). *An attributed type graph with inheritance $ATGI = (TG, Z, I, A)$ consists of an attributed type graph $ATG = (TG, Z)$ (see Definition 8.7), where TG is an E-graph*

$$TG = (TG_{V_G}, TG_{V_D}, TG_{E_G}, TG_{E_{NA}}, TG_{E_{EA}}, (source_i, target_i)_{i \in \{G, NA, EA\}})$$

with $TG_{V_D} = S'_D$ and final DSIG-algebra Z; an inheritance graph I =
(I_V, I_E, s, t) with $I_V = TG_{V_G}$; and a set $A \subseteq I_V$, called the abstract nodes.
For each node $n \in I_V$, the inheritance clan is defined by

$$clan_I(n) = \{n' \in I_V \mid \exists\, path\ n' \xrightarrow{*} n\ in\ I\} \subseteq I_V\ with\ n \in clan_I(n).$$

The inheritance graph I could be defined to be acyclic, but this is not necessary for our theory.

Remark 13.2. $x \in clan_I(y)$ implies $clan_I(x) \subseteq clan_I(y)$.

Example 13.3 (attributed type graph with inheritance). The running example that will be used in this chapter is a very small section of a notational model for diagrams. We start with the presentation of an attributed type graph with inheritance. In Fig. 13.1 we show the compact notation and in Fig. 13.2 the explicit notation for an example of an attributed type graph with inheritance. The dashed and solid arrows represent the edges of the attributed graph, and the solid arrows with open heads belong to the inheritance graph. A *Screen* with a resolution (*width, height*) has geometrical *Figures*, which have a position and a visibility (*x, y, visible*). The *Figures* are abstract, i.e. before they can be used it has to be specified which kind of figure is to be used. Therefore there is an inheritance relation to the concrete figures *Circle*, *Rectangle*, and *Line*. A *Circle* has the additional attribute *radius*, a *Rectangle* the additional attributes *width* and *height*, and a *Line* has the end points (*endx, endy*) as additional attributes. The edge attribute *id* : *Nat* is added to demonstrate the behavior of edge attributes in attributed type graphs with inheritance.   □

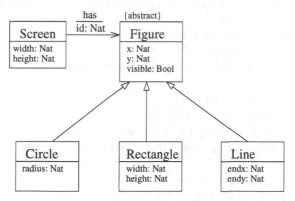

Fig. 13.1. Example of an attributed type graph with inheritance (compact notation).

In order to benefit from the well-founded theory of typed attributed graph transformation (see Chapters 8–12), we flatten attributed type graphs with

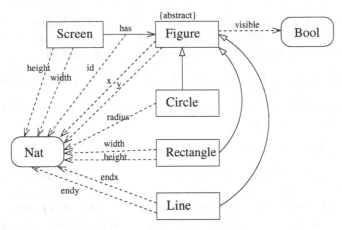

Fig. 13.2. Example of an attributed type graph with inheritance (explicit notation).

inheritance to ordinary attributed type graphs. We define the closure of an attributed type graph with inheritance, leading to an (explicit) attributed type graph, which allows us to define instances of attributed type graphs with inheritance.

Definition 13.4 (closure of attributed type graphs with inheritance).
Given an attributed type graph with inheritance $ATGI = (TG, Z, I, A)$ with $ATG = (TG, Z)$ as above, the abstract closure of $ATGI$ is the attributed type graph $\overline{ATG} = (\overline{TG}, Z)$, where $\overline{TG} = (TG_{V_G}, TG_{V_D}, \overline{TG_{E_G}}, \overline{TG_{E_{NA}}}, \overline{TG_{E_{EA}}}, (\overline{source_i}, \overline{target_i})_{i \in \{G, NA, EA\}})$. Here,

- $\overline{TG_{E_G}} = \{(n_1, e, n_2) \mid n_1 \in clan_I(source_1(e)), n_2 \in clan_I(target_1(e)), e \in TG_{E_G}\}$;
- $\overline{source_1}((n_1, e, n_2)) = n_1 \in TG_{V_G}$;
- $\overline{target_1}((n_1, e, n_2)) = n_2 \in TG_{V_G}$;
- $\overline{TG_{E_{NA}}} = \{(n_1, e, n_2) \mid n_1 \in clan_I(source_2(e)), n_2 = target_2(e), e \in TG_{E_{NA}}\}$;
- $\overline{source_2}((n_1, e, n_2)) = n_1 \in TG_{V_G}$;
- $\overline{target_2}((n_1, e, n_2)) = n_2 \in TG_{V_D}$;
- $\overline{TG_{E_{EA}}} = \{((n_{11}, e_1, n_{12}), e, n_2) \mid e_1 = source_3(e) \in TG_{E_G}, n_{11} \in clan_I(source_1(e_1)), n_{12} \in clan_I(target_1(e_1)), n_2 = target_3(e) \in TG_{V_D}, e \in TG_{E_{EA}}\}$;
- $\overline{source_3}((n_{11}, e_1, n_{12}), e, n_2) = (n_{11}, e_1, n_{12})$;
- $\overline{target_3}((n_{11}, e_1, n_{12}), e, n_2) = n_2$.

The attributed type graph $\widehat{ATG} = (\widehat{TG}, Z)$, where $\widehat{TG} = \overline{TG}|_{TG_{V_G} \setminus A} \subseteq \overline{TG}$, is called the concrete closure of $ATGI$, because all abstract nodes are removed: $\widehat{TG} = \overline{TG}|_{TG_{V_G} \setminus A}$ is the restriction of $\overline{TG}$ to $TG_{V_G} \setminus A$, given by

- $\widehat{TG_{V_G}} = TG_{V_G} \setminus A$, $\widehat{TG_{V_D}} = TG_{V_D}$,

- $\widehat{TG_{E_G}} = \{(n_1, e, n_2) \in \overline{TG_{E_G}} \mid n_1, n_2 \in TG_{V_G} \setminus A\}$,
- $\widehat{TG_{E_{NA}}} = \{(n_1, e, n_2) \in \overline{TG_{E_{NA}}} \mid n_1 \in TG_{V_G} \setminus A\}$,
- $\widehat{TG_{E_{EA}}} = \{(n_1, e, n_2) \in \overline{TG_{E_{EA}}} \mid n_1 \in \widehat{TG_{E_G}}\}$;

$\widehat{source_i}$ and $\widehat{target_i}$ are restrictions of $\overline{source_i}$ and $\overline{target_i}$, respectively, for $i \in \{G, NA, EA\}$.

The distinction between the abstract and the concrete closure of a type graph is necessary. The left-hand side and the right-hand side of the abstract productions considered in Section 13.3 are typed over the abstract closure, while the ordinary host graphs and concrete productions are typed over the concrete closure.

Remark 13.5.

1. We have $TG \subseteq \overline{TG}$ with TG_{V_i} for $i \in \{G, D\}$ and $TG_{E_i} \subseteq \overline{TG_{E_i}}$ if we identify $e \in TG_{E_i}$ with $(source_i(e), e, target_i(e)) \in \overline{TG_{E_i}}$ for $i \in \{G, NA, EA\}$. Owing to the existence of the canonical inclusion $TG \subseteq \overline{TG}$, all graphs typed over TG are also typed over $\overline{TG}$.
2. Note that there are no inheritance relations in the abstract and concrete closures of an $ATGI$, and hence no inheritance relations in the instance graphs defined below.

Instances of attributed type graphs with inheritance are attributed graphs. Here again, we can notice a direct correspondence to metamodeling, where models consisting of symbols and relations are instances of metamodels containing the correspondent classes and associations.

Now we are able to define instances of attributed type graphs with inheritance using the closure defined above, i.e. typing morphisms $type : AG \to \overline{ATG}$. In the next section, we show that such typing morphisms are equivalent to a new concept called clan-morphisms.

Definition 13.6 (instance of ATGI). *An abstract instance of an ATGI is an attributed graph typed over* $\overline{ATG}$, *i.e.* $(AG, type : AG \to \overline{ATG})$.
Similarly, a concrete instance of an ATGI is an instance of an attributed graph typed over $\widehat{ATG}$, *i.e.* $(AG, type : AG \to \widehat{ATG})$.

Example 13.7 (abstract and concrete closures of an ATGI). Fig. 13.3 shows the compact notation for the abstract and concrete closures of the ATGI example shown in Fig. 13.1, which follows from the explicit notation in Fig. 13.4. The node NAT is depicted twice for clarity.

Fig. 13.4 shows the explicit notation for the abstract closures of the ATGI example shown in Fig. 13.2, which can be calculated from Definition 13.4 as follows:

- $clan(Figure) = \{Figure, Circle, Rectangle, Line\}$,
- $clan(X) = \{X\}$, for $X = Circle, Rectangle, Line, Screen$,

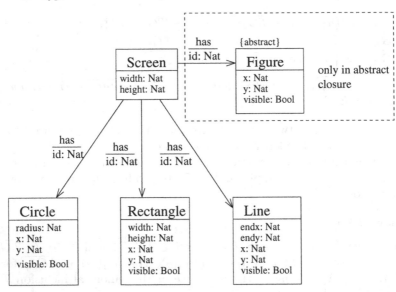

Fig. 13.3. Abstract and concrete closures of the ATGI example shown in Fig. 13.1 (compact notation)

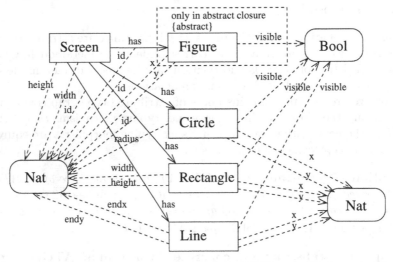

Fig. 13.4. Abstract and concrete closures of the ATGI example shown in Fig. 13.2 (explicit notation)

- $\overline{TG_{V_i}} = TG_{V_i}, (i \in \{G, D\})$,
- $TG_{E_G} = \{has\}$ implies $\overline{TG_{E_G}} = \{(Screen, has, Figure), (Screen, has, Circle), (Screen, has, Rectangle), (Screen, has, Line)\}$,
- $TG_{E_{NA}} = \{visible, height_1, width_1, x, y, radius, width_2, height_2, endx, endy\}$;

where the indices of *height* and *width* corresponding to different edges are dropped in the following. This implies

$$\overline{TG_{E_{NA}}} = \{(Figure, visible, Bool), (Circle, visible, Bool),$$
$$(Rectangle, visible, Bool), (Line, visible, Bool), (Screen, height, Nat),$$
$$(Screen, width, Nat), (Figure, x, Nat), (Circle, x, Nat),$$
$$(Rectangle, x, Nat), (Line, x, Nat), (Figure, y, Nat),$$
$$(Circle, y, Nat), (Rectangle, y, Nat), (Line, y, Nat),$$
$$(Circle, radius, Nat), (Rectangle, width, Nat), (Rectangle, height, Nat),$$
$$(Line, endx, Nat), (Line, endy, Nat)\}.$$

$TG_{E_{EA}} = \{id\}$ implies

$$\overline{TG_{E_{EA}}} = \{((Screen, has, Figure), id, Nat), ((Screen, has, Circle), id, Nat),$$
$$((Screen, has, Rectangle), id, Nat), ((Screen, has, Line), id, Nat)\}.$$

The explicit notation for the concrete closure, according to Definition 13.4, is given by:

- $\widehat{TG_{V_G}} = \overline{TG_{V_G}} \setminus \{Figure\}$,
- $\widehat{TG_{V_D}} = \overline{TG_{V_D}} = TG_{V_D}$,
- $\widehat{TG_{E_G}} = \overline{TG_{E_G}} \setminus \{(Screen, has, Figure)\}$,
- $\widehat{TG_{E_{NA}}} = \overline{TG_{E_{NA}}} \setminus \{(Figure, visible, Bool), (Figure, x, Nat), (Figure, y, Nat)\}$,
- $\widehat{TG_{E_{EA}}} = \overline{TG_{E_{EA}}} \setminus \{((Screen, has, Figure), id, Nat)\}$;

which leads to the compact notation for the concrete closure shown in Fig. 13.3.   □

13.2 Attributed Clan Morphisms

For the formal definition of the instance–type relation, we introduce attributed clan morphisms. The choice of triples for the edges of a type graph's closure described in the previous section allows one to express a typing property with respect to the type graph with inheritance. The instance graph can be typed over the type graph with inheritance (for convenience) by means of a pair of functions, one assigning a node type to each node and the other one assigning an edge type to each edge. Both are defined canonically. A graph morphism is not obtained in this way, but a similar mapping, called a *clan morphism*, uniquely characterizing the type morphism into the flattened type graph, is obtained.

We introduce ATGI-clan morphisms in this section. An ATGI-clan morphism $type : AG \to ATGI$, where $ATGI$ is an attributed type graph with inheritance, corresponds uniquely to a normal type morphism $\overline{type} : AG \to \overline{ATG}$, where $\overline{ATG}$ is the abstract closure of $ATGI$ as discussed in the previous section.

Definition 13.8 (ATGI-clan morphism). *Given an attributed type graph with inheritance* $ATGI = (TG, Z, I, A)$ *with* $TG_{V_D} = S'_D$ *and* $ATG = (TG, Z)$ *and an attributed graph* $AG = (G, D)$, *where*

$$G = ((G_{V_i})_{i \in \{G,D\}}, (G_{E_i}, s_{G_i}, t_{G_i})_{i \in \{G, NA, EA\}}) \text{ and } \dot{\bigcup}_{s \in S'_D} D_s = G_{V_D},$$

then $type : AG \to ATGI$, *where* $type = (type_{V_G}, type_{V_D}, type_{E_G}, type_{E_{NA}}, type_{E_{EA}}, type_D)$ *and*

- $type_{V_i} : G_{V_i} \to TG_{V_i}$ $(i \in \{G, D\})$,
- $type_{E_i} : G_{E_i} \to TG_{E_i}$ $(i \in \{G, NA, EA\})$,
- $type_D : D \to Z$,   *unique final DSIG-homomorphism,*

is called an ATGI-clan morphism, *if*

1. $\forall s \in S'_D$ *the following diagram commutes;*

$$
\begin{array}{ccc}
D_s & \xrightarrow{\ type_{D,s}\ } & Z_s = \{s\} \\
\downarrow & = & \downarrow \\
G_{V_D} & \xrightarrow{\ type_{V_D}\ } & TG_{V_D} = S'_D
\end{array}
$$

   i.e. $type_{V_D}(d) = s$ *for* $d \in D_s$ *and* $s \in S'_D$.
2. $type_{V_G} \circ s_{G_G}(e_1) \in clan_I(src_G \circ type_{E_G}(e_1))$ $\forall e_1 \in G_{E_G}$.
3. $type_{V_G} \circ t_{G_G}(e_1) \in clan_I(tar_G \circ type_{E_G}(e_1))$ $\forall e_1 \in G_{E_G}$.
4. $type_{V_G} \circ s_{G_{NA}}(e_2) \in clan_I(src_{NA} \circ type_{E_{NA}}(e_2))$ $\forall e_2 \in G_{E_{NA}}$.
5. $type_{V_D} \circ t_{G_{NA}}(e_2) = tar_{NA} \circ type_{E_{NA}}(e_2)$ $\forall e_2 \in G_{E_{NA}}$.
6. $type_{E_G} \circ s_{G_{EA}}(e_3) = src_{EA} \circ type_{E_{EA}}(e_3)$ $\forall e_3 \in G_{E_{EA}}$.
7. $type_{V_D} \circ t_{G_{EA}}(e_3) = tar_{EA} \circ type_{E_{EA}}(e_3)$ $\forall e_3 \in G_{E_{EA}}$.

In the above, we have used the abbreviations "src" and "tar" for "source" and "target", respectively.

   An ATGI-clan *morphism type* $: AG \to ATG$ *is called* concrete *if* $type_{V_G}(n) \notin A$ *for all* $n \in G_{V_G}$.

The following technical properties of ATGI-clan morphisms are needed to show the results in Section 13.3, which are based on double-pushout transformations in the category **AGraphs** of attributed graphs and morphisms in the sense of Definition 8.6.

   In order to show the bijective correspondence between ATGI-clan morphisms and normal type morphisms $\overline{type} : AG \to \overline{ATG}$, we first define a universal ATGI-clan morphism.

Definition 13.9 (universal ATGI-clan morphism). *Given an attributed type graph with inheritance $ATGI = (TG, Z, I, A)$, then the universal ATGI-clan morphism $u_{ATG} : \overline{ATG} \to ATGI$ with $\overline{ATG} = (\overline{TG}, Z)$ is defined by*

- $u_{ATG,V_G} = id_1 : \overline{TG_{V_G}} \to TG_{V_G}$;
- $u_{ATG,V_D} = id_2 : \overline{TG_{V_D}} \to TG_{V_D}$;
- $u_{ATG,E_G} : \overline{TG_{E_G}} \to TG_{E_G}$, $u_{ATG,E_G}[(n_1, e, n_2)] = e \in TG_{E_G}$;
- $u_{ATG,E_{NA}} : \overline{TG_{E_{NA}}} \to TG_{E_{NA}}$, $u_{ATG,E_{NA}}[(n_1, e, n_2)] = e \in TG_{E_{NA}}$;
- $u_{ATG,E_{EA}} : \overline{TG_{E_{EA}}} \to TG_{E_{EA}}$, $u_{ATG,E_{EA}}[((n_{11}, e_1, n_{12}), e, n_2)] = e \in TG_{E_{EA}}$;
- $u_{ATG,D} = id_Z : Z \to Z$.

Below, we prove a universal ATGI-clan property in Theorem 13.12. For that theorem, we need the following facts, where we show that u_{ATG} is an ATGI-clan morphism and that ATGI-clan morphisms are closed under composition with attributed graph morphisms.

Fact 13.10 (universal ATGI-clan morphism). *The universal morphism $u_{ATG} : \overline{ATG} \to ATGI$ is an ATGI-clan morphism.*

Proof. We check conditions 1–7 of Definition 13.8 for u_{ATG}:

1. This is clear because u_{ATG,V_D} and $u_{ATG,D}$ are identities.
2. $u_{ATG,V_G} \circ \overline{src_G}[(n_1, e, n_2)] = u_{ATG,V_G}(n_1) = n_1 \in clan_I(src_G(e)).$
   $= clan_I(src_G \circ u_{ATG,E_G}[(n_1, e, n_2)]).$
3. $u_{ATG,V_G} \circ \overline{tar_G}[(n_1, e, n_2)] = u_{ATG,V_G}(n_2) = n_2 \in clan_I(tar_G(e)), = clan_I(tar_G \circ u_{ATG,E_G}[(n_1, e, n_2)]).$
4. $u_{ATG,V_G} \circ \overline{src_{NA}}[(n_1, e, n_2)] = u_{ATG,V_G}(n_1) = n_1 \in clan_I(src_{NA}(e)), = clan_I(src_{NA} \circ u_{ATG,E_{NA}}[(n_1, e, n_2)]).$
5. $u_{ATG,V_D} \circ \overline{tar_{NA}}[(n_1, e, n_2)] = u_{ATG,V_{NA}}(n_2) = n_2 = tar_{NA}(e), = tar_{NA} \circ u_{ATG,E_{NA}}[(n_1, e, n_2)].$
6. $u_{ATG,E_G} \circ \overline{src_{EA}}[((n_{11}, e_1, n_{12}), e, n_2)] = u_{ATG,E_G}((n_{11}, e_1, n_{12})) = e_1,$
   $src_{EA} \circ u_{ATG,E_{EA}}[((n_{11}, e_1, n_{12}), e, n_2)]) = src_{EA}(e) = e_1.$
7. $u_{ATG,V_D} \circ \overline{tar_{EA}}[((n_{11}, e_1, n_{12}), e, n_2)] = u_{ATG,V_D}(n_2) = n_2,$
   $tar_{EA} \circ u_{ATG,E_{EA}}[((n_{11}, e_1, n_{12}), e, n_2)]) = tar_3(e) = n_2.$

$\square$

Fact 13.11 (composition). *Given an attributed graph morphism, or AG-morphism for short, $f : AG' \to AG$, and an ATGI-clan morphism $f' : AG \to ATGI$, then $f' \circ f : AG' \to ATGI$ is an ATGI-clan-morphism.*
  If f' is concrete, so is $f' \circ f$.

Proof. We check conditions 1–7 of Definition 13.8 for $f' \circ f$ with $AG' = (G', D')$, $AG = (G, D)$ and $ATGI = (TG, Z, I, A)$:

1. $(f' \circ f)_{V_D}(d') = f'_{V_D}(f_{V_D}(d')) = f'_{V_D}(d) = s,$
   because $d' \in D'_s$, $s \in S'_D$ implies $d = f_{V_D}(d') = f_{D_s}(d') \in D_s$.

2. $(f' \circ f)_{V_G} \circ s_{G'_G}(e'_1) = f'_{V_G}[f_{V_G} \circ s_{G'_G}(e'_1)] = f'_{V_G}[s_{G_G} \circ f_{E_G}(e'_1)]$
$= f'_{V_G} \circ s_{G_G}(f_{E_G}(e'_1)) \in clan_I[src_G \circ f'_{E_G}(f_{E_G}(e'_1))]$
$= clan_I(src_G \circ (f' \circ f)_{E_G}(e'_1)).$

3. $(f' \circ f)_{V_G} \circ t_{G'_G}(e'_1) = f'_{V_G}[f_{V_G} \circ t_{G'_G}(e'_1)] = f'_{V_G}[t_{G_G} \circ f_{E_G}(e'_1)]$
$= f'_{V_G} \circ t_{G_G}(f_{E_G}(e'_1)) \in clan_I[tar_G \circ f'_{E_G}(f_{E_G}(e'_1))]$
$= clan_I(tar_G \circ (f' \circ f)_{E_G}(e'_1)).$

4. $(f' \circ f)_{V_G} \circ s_{G'_{NA}}(e'_2) = f'_{V_G}[f_{V_G} \circ s_{G'_{NA}}(e'_2)] = f'_{V_G}[s_{G_{NA}} \circ f_{E_{NA}}(e'_2)]$
$= f'_{V_G} \circ s_{G_{NA}}(f_{E_{NA}}(e'_2)) \in clan_I[src_{NA} \circ f'_{E_{NA}}(f_{E_{NA}}(e'_2))]$
$= clan_I(src_{NA} \circ (f' \circ f)_{E_{NA}}(e'_2)).$

5. $(f' \circ f)_{V_D} \circ t_{G'_{NA}}(e'_2) = f'_{V_D}[f_{V_D} \circ t_{G'_{NA}}(e'_2)] = f'_{V_D}[t_{G_{NA}} \circ f_{E_{NA}}(e'_2)]$
$= f'_{V_D} \circ t_{G_{NA}}(f_{E_{NA}}(e'_2)) = tar_{NA} \circ f'_{E_{NA}}(f_{E_{NA}}(e'_2))$
$= tar_{NA} \circ (f' \circ f)_{E_{NA}}(e'_2).$

6. $(f' \circ f)_{E_G} \circ s_{G'_{EA}}(e'_3) = f'_{E_G}[f_{E_G} \circ s_{G'_{EA}}(e'_3)] = f'_{E_G}[s_{G_{EA}} \circ f_{E_{EA}}(e'_3)]$
$= f'_{E_G} \circ s_{G_{EA}}(f_{E_{EA}}(e'_3)) = src_{EA} \circ f'_{E_{EA}}(f_{E_{EA}}(e'_3))$
$= src_{EA} \circ (f' \circ f)_{E_{EA}}(e'_3).$

7. $(f' \circ f)_{V_D} \circ t_{G'_{EA}}(e'_3) = f'_{V_D}[f_{V_D} \circ t_{G'_{EA}}(e'_3)] = f'_{V_D}[t_{G_{EA}} \circ f_{E_{EA}}(e'_3)]$
$= f'_{V_D} \circ t_{G_{EA}}(f_{E_{EA}}(e'_3)) = tar_{EA} \circ f'_{E_{EA}}(f_{E_{EA}}(e'_3))$
$= tar_{EA} \circ (f' \circ f)_{E_{EA}}(e'_3).$

If f' is concrete, then $f'_{V_G}(n) \notin A$ for all $n \in G_{V_G}$ and also $f'_{V_G}(f_{V_G}(n)) \notin A$ for all $n \in G'_{V_G}$.   □

The following theorem is the key property relating ATGI-clan morphisms and AG-morphisms, and is essential for showing the main results in this chapter.

Theorem 13.12 (universal ATGI-clan property). *For each ATGI-clan morphism* $type : AG \to ATGI$, *there is a unique AG-morphism* $\overline{type} : AG \to \overline{ATG}$ *such that* $u_{ATG} \circ \overline{type} = type$:

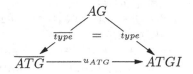

Construction. Given $type : AG \to ATGI$ with $AG = (G, D)$, we construct $\overline{type} : AG \to \overline{ATG}$ as follows (see Fig. 13.5):

- $\overline{type}_{V_G} = type_{V_G} : G_{V_G} \to TG_{V_G} = \overline{TG}_{V_G}$;
- $\overline{type}_{V_D} = type_{V_D} : G_{V_D} \to TG_{V_D} = \overline{TG}_{V_D}$;
- $\overline{type}_{E_G} : G_{E_G} \to \overline{TG}_{E_G}$, $\overline{type}_{E_G}(e_1) = (n_1, e'_1, n_2)$ with $e'_1 = type_{E_G}(e_1) \in TG_{E_G}$, $n_1 = \overline{type}_{V_G}(s_{G_G}(e_1)) \in TG_{V_G}$, $n_2 = \overline{type}_{V_G}(t_{G_G}(e_1)) \in TG_{V_G}$;
- $\overline{type}_{E_{NA}} : G_{E_{NA}} \to \overline{TG}_{E_{NA}}$, $\overline{type}_{E_{NA}}(e_2) = (n_1, e'_2, n_2)$ with $e'_2 = type_{E_{NA}}(e_2) \in TG_{E_{NA}}$, $n_1 = \overline{type}_{V_G}(s_{G_{NA}}(e_2)) \in TG_{V_G}$, $n_2 = \overline{type}_{V_D}(t_{G_{NA}}(e_2)) \in TG_{V_D}$;
- $\overline{type}_{E_{EA}} : G_{E_{EA}} \to \overline{TG}_{E_{EA}}$, $\overline{type}_{E_{EA}}(e_3) = ((n_{11}, e''_3, n_{12}), e'_3, n_2)$ with $e'_3 = type_{E_{EA}}(e_3) \in TG_{E_{EA}}$, $(n_{11}, e''_3, n_{12}) = \overline{type}_{E_G}(s_{G_{EA}}(e_3)) \in \overline{TG}_{E_G}$, $n_2 = \overline{type}_{V_D}(t_{G_{EA}}(e_3)) \in TG_{V_D}$;

- $\overline{type_D} = type_D : D \to Z$.

Fact 13.11 implies that the composition $u_{ATG} \circ type$ is an ATGI-clan-morphism.   □

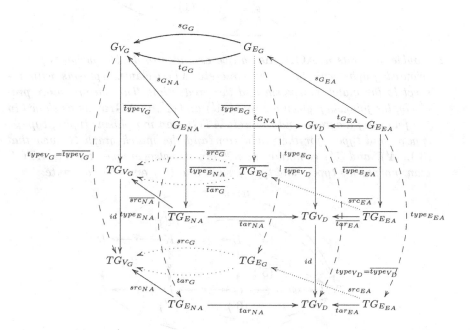

Fig. 13.5. Construction of the universal ATGI-clan property

Proof. See Section C.5.   □

The univeral property shown above allows us to prove important properties of pushouts for $ATGI$-clan morphisms.

Lemma 13.13 (PO property of ATGI-clan morphisms).

1. *A pushout in* **AGraphs** *is also a pushout with respect to (concrete) clan morphisms. This means, more precisely, the following: given a pushout PO in* **AGraphs** *as shown in the following diagram with AG-morphisms g_1, g_2, g'_1, g'_2 and ATGI-clan morphisms f_1, f_2 with $f_1 \circ g_1 = f_2 \circ g_2$, then there is a unique ATGI-clan morphism $f : G_3 \to ATGI$ with $f \circ g'_1 = f_1$ and $f \circ g'_2 = f_2$:*

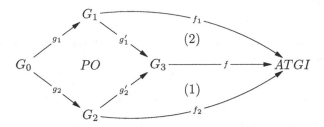

2. *Double pushouts in* **AGraphs** *can be extended to double pushouts for attributed graphs with typing by concrete ATGI-clan-morphisms with respect to the match morphism and the production. This means, more precisely, the following: given pushouts* (1′) *and* (2′) *in* **AGraphs** *as shown in the following diagram, and concrete ATGI-clan morphisms* $type_L$, $type_K$, $type_R$, *and* $type_G$ *for the production and the match graph* G *such that* (3′), (4′), *and* (5′) *commute, then there are also unique concrete ATGI-clan morphisms* $type_D$ *and* $type_H$ *such that* (6′) *and* (7′) *commute:*

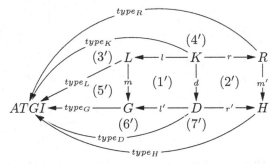

Proof.

1. Given a pushout in **AGraphs** of $g_1 : G_0 \to G_1$, $g_2 : G_0 \to G_2$ with $g'_1 : G_1 \to G_3$ and $g'_2 : G_2 \to G_3$, we shall show that, for each pair of ATGI-clan morphisms $f_1 : G_1 \to ATGI$ and $f_2 : G_2 \to ATGI$ with $f_1 \circ g_1 = f_2 \circ g_2$, there is a unique ATGI-clan morphism $f : G_3 \to ATGI$ such that (1) and (2) in the following diagram commute:

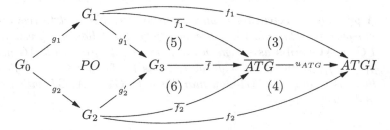

Using Theorem 13.12, we have unique graph morphisms $\overline{f_1}, \overline{f_2}$ such that (3) and (4) commute. Moreover, $f_1 \circ g_1 = f_2 \circ g_2$ implies $u_{ATG} \circ \overline{f_1} \circ g_1 =$

$u_{ATG} \circ \overline{f_2} \circ g_2$ and hence $\overline{f_1} \circ g_1 = \overline{f_2} \circ g_2$ by the uniqueness described in Theorem 13.12. Now the PO property of G_3 in **AGraphs** implies a unique $\overline{f} : G_3 \to \overline{ATG}$ such that (5) and (6) commute. We define $f = u_{ATG} \circ \overline{f} : G_3 \to ATG$, where commutativity of (3)–(6) implies that of (1) and (2).

The uniqueness of f in (1) and (2) can be shown using the existence and uniqueness described in Theorem 13.12 and the uniqueness of $\overline{f}$ in (5) and (6) according to the PO property of G_3 in **AGraphs**.

Finally, let us discuss the case of concrete ATGI-clan morphisms. If f_1, f_2 are concrete, then $f : G_3 \to ATG$ is also concrete. In fact, for each $x \in G_{3,V_G}$ we have $x_1 \in G_{1,V_G}$ with $f_{V_G}(x) = f_{1_{V_G}}(x_1) \notin A$, or $x_2 \in G_{2,V_G}$ with $f_{V_G}(x) = f_{2_{V_G}}(x_2) \notin A$.

2. Given a double pushout $(1')$, $(2')$ in **AGraphs** and concrete ATGI-clan morphisms $type_L, type_K, type_R$, and $type_G$ such that the diagrams $(3')$–$(5')$ commute, we need concrete clan morphisms $type_D : D \to ATGI$ with $type_D = type_G \circ l'$ and $type_H : H \to ATGI$, where

$$(8') \quad type_H \circ r' = type_D \text{ and } type_H \circ m' = type_R.$$

In fact, we define $type_D$ as the composition $type_G \circ l'$. This implies $type_D \circ d = type_R \circ r$ using the commutativity of $(1')$ and $(3')$–$(6')$. Now Theorem 13.12 can be applied to the pushout $(2')$, yielding a unique $type_H$ with the property $(8')$.

$\square$

13.3 Productions and Attributed Graph Transformation with Inheritance

In this section, we show how to adapt the concept of inheritance to the concepts of typed attributed graph transformation, graph grammars and graph languages. The use of abstract types in graph transformation is helpful in formulating concise graph productions.

Our goal is to allow abstract typed nodes in productions, such that these abstract productions actually represent a set of structurally similar productions, which we call *concrete productions*. To obtain all concrete productions for an abstract production, all combinations of node types of the corresponding clans in the production's left-hand side (LHS) (whether of concrete or abstract type) must be considered. Nodes which are preserved by the production have to keep their type. Nodes which are created in the right-hand side (RHS) have to have a concrete type, since abstract types should not be instantiated.

We define abstract and concrete transformations for abstract and concrete productions based on attributed type graphs with inheritance. The first main result shows the equivalence of abstract and concrete transformations. This allows us to use safely the more efficient presentation of abstract transformations with abstract productions, because they are equivalent to the corresponding concrete transformations with concrete productions. The second main result, presented in the next section, shows the equivalence of attributed graph grammars with and without inheritance.

In the following, we consider productions and graph transformations in the sense of Chapter 9, i.e. typed attributed graph transformation extended by negative application conditions (NACs) (see Definition 12.5).

As we have done for type graphs with inheritance, we define a flattening of abstract productions to concrete ones. The concrete productions are structurally equal to the abstract production, but their typing morphisms are finer than those of the abstract production and are concrete clan morphisms. A typing morphism is said to be finer than another one if it is distinguished from the other one only by the presence of more concrete types in corresponding clans.

First we introduce the notion of type refinement in order to formalize the relationship between abstract and concrete productions, to be defined below.

Definition 13.14 (ATGI-type refinement). *Given an attributed graph* $AG = (G, D)$ *and ATGI-clan morphisms type* : $AG \to ATGI$ *and* $type'$: $AG \to ATGI$, *then* $type'$ *is called an* **ATGI**-type refinement *of type, written* $type' \leq type$, *if*

- $type'_{V_G}(n) \in clan_I(type_{V_G}(n))$ $\forall n \in G_{V_G}$,
- $type'_X = type_X$ *for* $X \in \{V_D, E_G, E_{NA}, E_{EA}, D\}$.

Remark 13.15. Given ATGI-clan morphisms $type, type' : AG \to ATGI$ with $type' \leq type$ and an AG-morphism $g : AG' \to AG$, then $type' \circ g \leq type \circ g$ also. Note that "*AG-morphism*" means a morphism in the category **AGraphs**.

Definition 13.16 (abstract and concrete productions). *An abstract production typed over ATGI is given by* $p = (L \xleftarrow{l} K \xrightarrow{r} R, type, NAC)$, *where* l *and* r *are AG-morphisms, type is a triple of typing morphisms, i.e. ATGI-clan morphisms* $type = (type_L : L \to ATGI, type_K : K \to ATGI, type_R : R \to ATGI)$, *and NAC is a set of triples* $nac = (N, n, type_N)$ *with an attributed graph* N, *an AG-morphism* $n : L \to N$, *and a typing ATGI-clan morphism* $type_N : N \to ATGI$, *such that the following conditions hold:*

- $type_L \circ l = type_K = type_R \circ r$;
- $type_{R,V_G}(R'_{V_G}) \cap A = \varnothing$, *where* $R'_{V_G} := R_{V_G} - r_{V_G}(K_{V_G})$;
- $type_N \circ n \leq type_L$ *for all* $(N, n, type_N) \in NAC$;
- l, r, *and* n *are data-preserving, i.e.* l_D, r_D, *and* n_D *are identities*:

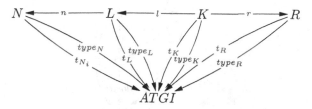

A concrete production p_t *with respect to an abstract production* p *is given by* $p_t = (L \xleftarrow{l} K \xrightarrow{r} R, t, \overline{NAC})$, *where* t *is a triple of concrete typing ATGI-clan morphisms* $t = (t_L : L \to ATGI, t_K : K \to ATGI, t_R : R \to ATGI)$, *such that*

- $t_L \circ l = t_K = t_R \circ r$;
- $t_L \le type_L$, $t_K \le type_K$, $t_R \le type_R$;
- $t_{R,V_G}(x) = type_{R,V_G}(x) \; \forall x \in R'_{V_G}$;
- *for each* $(N, n, type_N) \in NAC$, *we have all* $(N, n, t_N) \in \overline{NAC}$ *for concrete ATGI-clan morphisms* t_N *satisfying* $t_N \circ n = t_L$ *and* $t_N \le type_N$.

The set of all concrete productions p_t *with respect to an abstract production* p *is denoted by* $\widehat{p}$.

The application of an abstract production can be defined or expressed directly by using the idea of flattening, i.e. of applying one of its concrete productions. Both the host graph and the concrete production are typed by concrete clan morphisms such that we can define the application of a concrete production. Later, we shall also define the application of an abstract production directly and show the equivalence of the two.

Definition 13.17 (application of concrete production). *Let* $p_t = (L \xleftarrow{l} K \xrightarrow{r} R, t, \overline{NAC})$ *be a concrete production, let* $(G, type_G)$ *be a typed attributed graph with a concrete ATGI-clan morphism* $type_G : G \to ATGI$, *and let* $m : L \to G$ *be an AG-morphism. Then* m *is a* consistent match *with respect to* p_t *and* $(G, type_G)$ *if*

- m *satisfies the gluing condition (see Definition 9.8) with respect to the untyped production* $L \xleftarrow{l} K \xrightarrow{r} R$ *and the attributed graph* G;
- $type_G \circ m = t_L$; *and*
- m *satisfies the negative application conditions* $\overline{NAC}$, *i.e., for each* $(N, n, t_N) \in \overline{NAC}$, *there exists no AG-morphism* $o : N \to G$ *in* $\mathcal{M}'$ *such that* $o \circ n = m$ *and* $type_G \circ o = t_N$. $\mathcal{M}'$ *is a suitable class of morphisms for application conditions (see Section 12.1).*

Given a consistent match m, *the concrete production can be applied to the typed attributed graph* $(G, type_G)$, *yielding a typed attributed graph* $(H, type_H)$ *by constructing the DPO of* l, r, *and* m *and applying Lemma 13.13.2. We write* $(G, type_G) \overset{p_t, m}{\Longrightarrow} (H, type_H)$ *for such a direct transformation:*

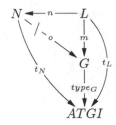

The classical theory of typed attributed graph transformations relies on typing morphisms which are normal graph morphisms, i.e. not clan morphisms. To show the equivalence of abstract and concrete graph transformations, we first have to consider the following statement: The application of a concrete production typed by concrete clan morphisms is equivalent to the application of the same production correspondingly typed over the concrete closure of the given type graph. This lemma is formulated and proven in Lemma 13.13 for productions without NACs.

Although the semantics of the application of an abstract production can be given by the application of its concrete productions, this solution is not efficient at all. Imagine a tool which implements graph transformation with node type inheritance; it would have to check all concrete productions of an abstract production to find the right one to apply to a given instance graph.

Thus, as the next step, we want to examine more direct ways to apply an abstract production. Since abstract and concrete productions differ only in this typing, but have the same structure, a match morphism from the left-hand side (LHS) of a concrete production into a given instance graph is also a match morphism for its abstract production. But, of course, the typing morphisms differ. Using the notion of type refinement, however, we can express a compatibility property.

Definition 13.18 (application of abstract production). *Let* $p = (L \xleftarrow{l} K \xrightarrow{r} R, type, NAC)$ *be an abstract production typed over an attributed type graph with inheritance ATGI, let* $(G, type_G)$ *be a typed attributed graph with a concrete ATGI-clan morphism* $type_G : G \to ATGI$, *and let* $m : L \to G$ *be an AG-morphism. Then* m *is called a* consistent match *with respect to* p *and* $(G, type_G)$ *if*

- m *satisfies the gluing condition (see Definition 9.8) with respect to the untyped production* $L \xleftarrow{l} K \xrightarrow{r} R$ *and the attributed graph* G, *i.e. the PO (1) in the following diagram exists;*
- $type_G \circ m \leq type_L$;
- $t_{K,V_G}(x_1) = t_{K,V_G}(x_2)$ *for* $t_K = type_G \circ m \circ l$ *and all* $x_1, x_2 \in K_{V_G}$ *with* $r_{V_G}(x_1) = r_{V_G}(x_2)$;
- m *satisfies* NAC, *i.e., for each* $nac = (N, n, type_N) \in NAC$, *exists no AG-morphism* $o : N \to G$ *in* $\mathcal{M}'$ *(see Definition 13.17) such that* $o \circ n = m$ *and* $type_G \circ o \leq type_N$.

Given a consistent match m, the abstract production can be applied to $(G, type_G)$, *yielding an* abstract direct transformation $(G, type_G) \overset{p,m}{\Longrightarrow}$ $(H, type_H)$ *with a concrete ATGI-clan morphism* $type_H$ *as follows:*

1. *Construct the (untyped) DPO of l, r, and m in* **AGraphs** *given by the pushouts (1) and (2) in the following diagram:*

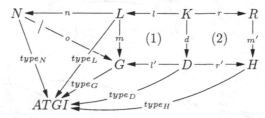

2. *Construct* $type_D$ *and* $type_H$ *as follows:*
   - $type_D = type_G \circ l'$;
   - $type_{H,X}(x) = \underline{if}\ x = r'_X(x')\ \underline{then}\ type_{D,X}(x')\ \underline{else}\ type_{R,X}(x'')$, *where* $m'(x'') = x$ *and* $X \in \{V_G, V_D, E_G, E_{NA}, E_{EA}, D\}$.

Remark 13.19. $type_H$ is a well-defined ATGI-clan morphism with $type_H \circ r' = type_D$ and $type_H \circ m' \leq type_R$. Moreover, we have $type_G \circ m \leq type_L$ (as required) and $type_D \circ d \leq type_K$ (see Lemma 13.20, item 3). The third match condition is not needed if r_{V_G} is injective (as is the case in most examples).

Now we are able to construct concrete and abstract transformations from an abstract production with a consistent match. This is the basis for the equivalence results in the next section.

Lemma 13.20 (construction of concrete and abstract transformations). *Given an abstract production* $p = (L \overset{l}{\leftarrow} K \overset{r}{\to} R, type, NAC)$, *where* $NAC = \{(N_i, n_i, type_{N_i}) \mid i \in I\}$, *a concrete typed attributed graph* $(G, type_G : G \to ATGI)$, *and a consistent match morphism* $m : L \to G$ *with respect to p and $(G, type_G)$, we have the following:*

1. *There is a unique concrete production* $p_t \in \hat{p}$ *with* $p_t = (L \overset{l}{\leftarrow} K \overset{r}{\to} R, t, \overline{NAC})$ *and* $t_L = type_G \circ m$. *In this case, t_K and t_R are defined by:*
   - $t_K = t_L \circ l$;
   - $t_{R,V_G}(x) = \underline{if}\ x = r_{V_G}(x')\ \underline{then}\ t_{K,V_G}(x')\ \underline{else}\ type_{R,V_G}(x)$ *for* $x \in R_{V_G}$;
   - $t_{R,X} = type_{R,X}$ *for* $X \in \{V_D, E_G, E_{NA}, E_{EA}, D\}$;
   - $\overline{NAC} = \cup_{i \in I}\{(N_i, n_i, t_{N_i}) \mid t_{N_i}$ *is a concrete ATGI-clan morphism with* $t_{N_i} \leq type_{N_i}$ *and* $t_{N_i} \circ n_i = t_L\}$.

2. *There is a concrete direct transformation* $(G, type_G) \overset{p_t,m}{\Longrightarrow} (H, type_H)$ *with a consistent match m with respect to p_t, where* $type_D = type_G \circ l'$ *and* $type_H$ *is uniquely defined by $type_D$, t_R, and the pushout properties of (2) below (see Lemma 13.13); $type_H : H \to ATGI$ is a concrete ATGI-clan morphism given explicitly by*

$$type_{H,X}(x) = \underline{if}\ x = r'_X(x')\ \underline{then}\ type_{D(,X}x')\ \underline{else}\ t_{R,X}(x'')$$

$$where\ m'(x'') = x\ and\ X \in \{V_G, V_D, E_G, E_{NA}, E_{EA}, D\}:$$

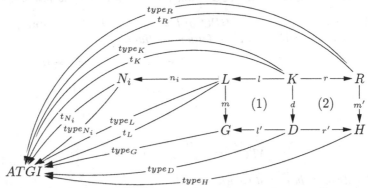

3. *The concrete direct transformation becomes an abstract direct transformation (see Definition 13.18):* $(G, type_G) \overset{p,m}{\Longrightarrow} (H, type_H)$ *with* $type_D = type_H \circ r'$, $type_G \circ m \leq type_L$, $type_D \circ d \leq type_K$, *and* $type_H \circ m' \leq type_R$, *where the typing* $t = (t_L, t_K, t_R)$ *of the concrete production* p_t *is replaced by* $type = (type_L, type_K, type_R)$ *of the abstract production* p.

Proof. See Section C.6. □

Example 13.21 (abstract and concrete productions and transformations). Fig. 13.6 shows sample productions for the ATGI example shown in Fig. 13.1. The production $moveFigure(dx, dy : Nat)$ is an example of an abstract production; for example, the production $moveFigure$ has to be defined only once and could be applied to the concrete graphical objects *Circle*, *Rectangle*, and *Line*. Owing to the positive values of dx and dy, the figures can only be moved up and to the right.

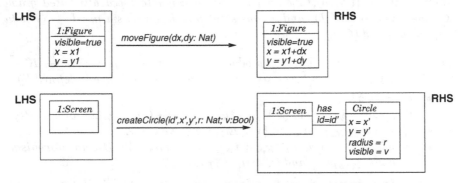

Fig. 13.6. Example productions for the ATGI example in Fig. 13.1

$createCircle(id', x', y', r : Nat; v : Bool)$ is an example of a concrete production and creates a *Circle* graphical object. Note that the production has to take care of the abstract attributes x, y, *visible* derived from the abstract class *Figure*, as well as the concrete attribute *radius* and the edge attribute *id*. A rule *createFigure* is not possible, because instances of abstract classes cannot be created. Fig. 13.7 shows the concrete production for moving a *Circle* graphical object derived from the abstract production *moveFigure* in Fig. 13.6.

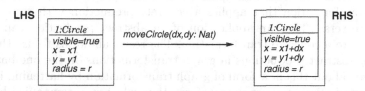

Fig. 13.7. Concrete Production *moveCircle* Derived from *moveFigure*.

Fig. 13.8 shows a sample transformation sequence for the productions *createCircle* and *moveCircle* starting with an empty *Screen* with a resolution *width* = 100 and *height* = 100. First a new circle is created at the position $(10, 10)$ by application of the production *createCircle*. Then the production *moveFigure*$(50, 0)$ instantiates the attributes $x1$ and $y1$ with values $x1 = 10$ and $y1 = 10$. After the results $x = x1 + dx$ and $y = y1 + dy$ have been calculated using the input parameters $dx = 50$ and $dy = 0$, the attributes x and y are assigned new values. Note that the abstract production *moveFigure* can be applied directly to the instance of the concrete class *Circle* derived from the abstract class *Figure*.

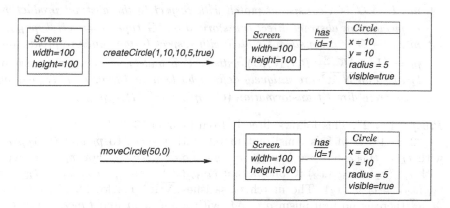

Fig. 13.8. Sample transformation sequence

□

13.4 Equivalence of Concepts with and without Inheritance

Now that we have defined concrete and abstract transformations, the question arises of how these two kinds of graph transformations are related to each other. Theorem 13.22 will answer this question by showing that for each abstract transformation that applies an abstract production p there is a concrete transformation that applies a concrete production with respect to p, and vice versa. Thus an application of an abstract production can also be flattened to a concrete transformation. The result allows us to use the dense form of abstract productions in graph transformations on the one hand, and to reason about this new form of graph transformation by flattening it to the usual typed attributed graph transformation, which is accompanied by a rich theory, on the other hand.

Furthermore, we show the equivalence of typed attributed graph grammars with and without inheritance.

In the following, all typing morphisms $type : AG \to ATGI$ are ATGI-clan morphisms, unless stated otherwise. We denote the corresponding graph morphism by $\overline{type} : AG \to \overline{ATG}$ (see Theorem 13.12).

Theorem 13.22 (equivalence of transformations). *Given an abstract production* $p = (L \xleftarrow{l} K \xrightarrow{r} R, type, NAC)$ *over an attributed type graph* $ATGI$ *with inheritance, a concrete typed attributed graph* $(G, type_G)$, *and a match morphism* $m : L \to G$ *which satisfies the gluing condition with respect to the untyped production* $(L \longleftarrow K \longrightarrow R)$, *then the following statements are equivalent, where* $(H, type_H)$ *is the same concrete typed graph in both cases:*

1. *$m : L \to G$ is a consistent match with respect to the abstract production p, yielding an abstract direct transformation $(G, type_G) \xRightarrow{p,m} (H, type_H)$.*
2. *$m : L \to G$ is a consistent match with respect to the concrete production $p_t = (L \xleftarrow{l} K \xrightarrow{r} R, t, \overline{NAC})$ with $p_t \in \hat{p}$ and $t_L = type_G \circ m$ (where t_K, t_R and $\overline{NAC}$ are uniquely defined by Lemma 13.20, item 1, yielding a concrete direct transformation $(G, type_G) \xRightarrow{p_t,m} (H, type_H)$.*

Proof. "1 ⇒ 2". This follows directly from Lemma 13.20.

"2 ⇒ 1". If m is a consistent match with respect to p_t and $(G, type_G)$ with $t_L = type_G \circ m$ we have $t_L = type_G \circ m \le type_L$. For $x_1, x_2 \in K_{V_G}$ with $r_{V_G}(x_1) = r_{V_G}(x_2)$ it follows that $t_{K,V_G}(x_1) = t_{R,V_G} \circ r_{V_G}(x_1) = t_{R,V_G} \circ r_{V_G}(x_2) = t_{L,V_G}(x_2)$. The match m satisfies $\overline{NAC}$, i.e. for all $(N, n, t_N) \in \overline{NAC}$ there is no morphism $o \in \mathcal{M}'$ with $o \circ n = m$ and $type_G \circ o = t_N$. It follows that m also satisfies NAC. Otherwise, there would exist an $nac = (N, n, type_N) \in NAC$, where $o \in \mathcal{M}'$ with $o \circ n = m$ and $type_G \circ o \le type_N$. This would contradict the requirement that m satisfies $\overline{nac} = (N, n, t_N) \in \overline{NAC}$ with $t_N = type_G \circ o \le type_N$. This means that m is a consistent match with respect to p and $(G, type_G)$.

Now we apply Lemma 13.20, where the induced concrete production in item 1 coincides with the given production, and obtain the abstract direct transformation $(G, type_G) \overset{p,m}{\Longrightarrow} (H, type_H)$.   □

Theorem 13.22 allows us to use the dense form of abstract productions for model manipulation instead of generating and holding all concrete rules, i.e. abstract derivations are much more efficient than concrete derivations. This means that, on the one hand, we have an efficient procedure and, on the other hand, we are sure that the result will be the same as that obtained using concrete rules. Moreover, as a consequence of Theorem 13.22, graph languages built over abstract productions and mechanisms are equivalent to graph languages that are built over a corresponding set of concrete productions. In addition, graph grammars with inheritance are equivalent to the corresponding grammars without inheritance, where, however, the type graph $ATGI$ has to be replaced by the closure $\overline{ATG}$. Before showing this main result, we define graph grammars and languages in our context.

Definition 13.23 (ATGI graph grammar and language). *Given an attributed type graph $ATGI$ and an attributed graph G typed over $ATGI$ with a concrete $ATGI$-clan morphism $type_G$, an $ATGI$-graph grammar is denoted by $GG = (ATGI, (G, type_G : G \to ATGI), P)$, where P is a set of abstract productions that are typed over $ATGI$.*

The corresponding graph language *is defined by the set of all concrete typed graphs which are generated by an abstract transformation (see Definitions 13.17 and 13.18):*

$$L(GG) = \{(H,\ type_H : H \to ATGI) \mid \exists \text{ abstract transformation } (G, type_G)$$
$$\overset{*}{\Rightarrow} (H, type_H)\},$$

where $type_H$ is always concrete, by Lemma 13.20, item 2.

Theorem 13.24 (equivalence of attributed graph grammars). *For each $ATGI$-graph grammar $GG = (ATGI, (G, type_G), P)$ with abstract productions P, there are:*

1. *An equivalent $ATGI$-graph grammar $\widehat{GG} = (ATGI, (G, type_G), \widehat{P})$ with concrete productions $\widehat{P}$, i.e. $L(GG) = L(\widehat{GG})$.*
2. *An equivalent typed attributed graph grammar without inheritance $\overline{GG} = (\overline{ATG}, (G, \overline{type_G}), \overline{P})$ typed over $\overline{ATG}$ where $\overline{ATG}$ is the closure of $ATGI$, and with productions $\overline{P}$, i.e. $L(GG) \overset{\sim}{=} L(\overline{GG})$, which means that $(G, type_G) \in L(GG) \Leftrightarrow (G, \overline{type_G}) \in L(\overline{GG})$.*

Construction.

1. The set $\widehat{P}$ is defined by $\widehat{P} = \cup_{p \in P} \widehat{p}$, where $\widehat{p}$ is the set of all concrete productions with respect to p.

2. $\overline{type_G} : G \to \overline{ATG}$ is the graph morphism corresponding to the ATGI-clan morphism $type_G$ (see Theorem 13.12). $\overline{P}$ is defined by $\overline{P} = \cup_{p \in P} \{\overline{p_t} \mid p_t \in \hat{p}\}$, where, for $p_t \in \hat{p}$ with $p_t = (p, t, \overline{NAC})$, we define $\overline{p_t} = (p, \overline{t}, \overline{NAC}')$ with $u_{ATG} \circ \overline{t_X} = t_X$ for $X \in \{L, K, R\}$, and $\overline{NAC}'$ is defined as follows: for each $(N, n, t_N) \in \overline{NAC}$, we have $(N, n, \overline{t_N}) \in \overline{NAC}'$ with $u_{ATG} \circ \overline{t_N} = t_N$.

$\square$

Remark 13.25. In the grammar $\overline{GG}$ of item 2 of Theorem 13.24 using the abstract closure $\overline{ATG}$ of $ATGI$, only graphs with concrete typing are generated. In fact, there is also an equivalent grammar $\widehat{GG}'$ over the type graph $\widehat{ATG}$, the concrete closure of $ATGI$.

Proof.

1. From Theorem 13.22, the abstract direct transformation $(G_1, type_{G_1}) \overset{p,m}{\Longrightarrow} (G_2, type_{G_2})$ and the concrete direct transformation $(G_1, type_{G_1}) \overset{p_t,m}{\Longrightarrow} (G_2, type_{G_2})$ with $t_L = type_G \circ m$ are equivalent, and if one exists, so does the other one. This means that, if $(G_1, type_{G_1}) \in L(GG) \cap L(\widehat{GG})$, then $(G_2, type_{G_2}) \in L(GG) \cap L(\widehat{GG})$. Since we start in both grammars with the same start graph, $L(GG) = L(\widehat{GG})$.

2. We show that (a) for a concrete direct transformation $(G_1, type_{G_1}) \overset{p_t,m}{\Longrightarrow} (G_2, type_{G_2})$ in $\widehat{GG}$, there is a corresponding direct transformation $(G_1, \overline{type_{G_1}}) \overset{\overline{p_t},m}{\Longrightarrow} (G_2, \overline{type_{G_2}}))$ in $\overline{GG}$ with $u_{ATG} \circ \overline{type_{G_i}} = type_{G_i}$ for $i = 1, 2$, and (b) if a production $\overline{p_t}$ can be applied to $(G_1, \overline{type_{G_1}})$ via m in $\overline{GG}$, then p_t can be applied to $(G_1, u_{ATG} \circ \overline{type_{G_1}})$ via m in $\widehat{GG}$.

   (a) For all objects $(X, type_X)$ in the DPO diagram corresponding to the concrete direct transformation $(G_1, type_{G_1}) \overset{p_t,m}{\Longrightarrow} (G_2, type_{G_2})$, Theorem 13.12 gives us a morphism $\overline{type_X} : X \to \overline{ATG}$. The DPO diagram with these new morphisms corresponds to the direct transformation $(G_1, \overline{type_{G_1}}) \overset{\overline{p_t},m}{\Longrightarrow} (G_2, \overline{type_{G_2}})$ in $\overline{GG}$.

   It remains to show that $\overline{p_t}$ can be applied to G_1 via m, i.e. m satisfies the negative application condition $\overline{NAC}'$. Suppose that this is not the case, and we have a negative application condition $(N, n, \overline{t_N}) \in \overline{NAC}'$ that is not satisfied by m and corresponds to $(N, n, t_N) \in \overline{NAC}$ with $u_{ATG} \circ \overline{t_N} = t_N$. There is then a morphism $o : N \to G_1$ with $o \circ n = m$, and since o is a typed attributed graph morphism, $\overline{type_{G_1}} \circ o = \overline{t_N}$. Then $type_{G_1} \circ o = u_{ATG} \circ \overline{type_{G_1}} \circ o = u_{ATG} \circ \overline{t_N} = t_N$. According to Definition 13.18, this means that m does not satisfy $\overline{NAC}$, which is a contradiction.

   (b) The application of $\overline{p_t}$ to G_1 via m leads to a direct transformation $(G_1, \overline{type_{G_1}}) \overset{\overline{p_t},m}{\Longrightarrow} (G_2, \overline{type_{G_2}})$. For all objects $(X, type_X)$ in the corresponding DPO diagram, we define $type_X = u_{ATG} \circ \overline{type_X}$ and obtain a new DPO diagram corresponding to the concrete direct transformation $(G_1, type_{G_1}) \overset{p_t, m}{\Longrightarrow} (G_2, type_{G_2})$.

We have to check that m satisfies $\overline{NAC}$. Suppose that is not the case; there is then a negative application condition $(N, n, t_N) \in \overline{NAC}$ and an AG-morphism $o : N \to G$ such that $o \circ n = m$ and $type_{G_1} \circ o = t_N$. Then the negative application condition $(N, n, \overline{t_N}) \in \overline{NAC}'$ with $t_N = type_{G_1} \circ o$ is not satisfied by m. This is a contradiction.

For a concrete transformation $(G, type_G) \overset{*}{\Rightarrow} (H, type_H)$ in $\widehat{GG}$, item (a) gives us the corresponding transformation $(G, \overline{type_G}) \overset{*}{\Rightarrow} (H, \overline{type_H})$ in $\overline{GG}$. Item (b) guarantees that, for a transformation $(G, \overline{type_G}) \overset{*}{\Rightarrow} (H, \overline{type_H})$ in $\overline{GG}$, there is a corresponding concrete transformation $(G, type_G) \overset{*}{\Rightarrow} (H, type_H)$ in $\widehat{GG}$. Combining (a) and (b), we have $L(\widehat{GG}) \cong L(\overline{GG})$. By part 1, we have $L(GG) = L(\widehat{GG})$, which implies $L(GG) \cong L(\overline{GG})$ as required.

$\square$

Part IV

Case Study on Model Transformation, and
Tool Support by AGG

In Parts I–III, we have presented the algebraic theory of graph transformations on the level of graphs and typed graphs, in adhesive HLR categories, and on the level of typed attributed graphs respectively. In each Part, we have illustrated the concepts and results with a specific running example. In this Part, we shall show, with a case study on model transformation in Chapter 14, how the concepts of typed attributed graph transformation can be applied in an important application area: model transformation between visual languages. In addition, it is most important, in all application domains, to have suitable tool support. For this purpose, we show in Chapter 15 how typed attributed graph transformation has been implemented at TU Berlin by means of the language and tool environment AGG in the last decade. The initial ideas concerning Chapters 14 and 15 were presented in [EEdL$^+$05] and [AGG, ERT99], respectively.

Case Study on Model Transformation

In this chapter, we show in a case study how typed attributed graph transformation can be used to define a model transformation from a simple version of UML statecharts to Petri nets. In Section 14.1, we introduce the general idea of model transformation by graph transformation, and we present the case study in Section 14.2. One of the main basic properties of model transformation is its functional behavior. A graph transformation system shows functional behavior if it is locally confluent and terminates. In this chapter, we show the termination of the corresponding layered graph transformation system. The local confluence is discussed in the following chapter. In Section 14.3, we briefly discuss two other case studies of model transformations presented in the literature using the same approach.

14.1 Model Transformation by Typed Attributed Graph Transformation

When a model transformation by typed attributed graph transformation is described, the source and target models have to be given as typed attributed graphs. This is not a restriction, since the underlying structure of any model, especially visual models, can be described by typed attributed graphs, owing to their multi-dimensional extension. Performing model transformation by typed attributed graph transformation means taking the underlying structure of a model as a typed attributed graph and transforming it according to certain transformation productions. The result is a typed attributed graph which shows the underlying structure of the target model.

A model transformation can be precisely defined by a typed attributed graph transformation system $GTS = (ATG, P)$ consisting of an attributed type graph ATG and a set of productions P for the model transformation. The abstract syntax graphs of the source models can be specified by all instance graphs (or a subset of them) over an attributed type graph ATG_S.

Correspondingly, the abstract syntax graphs of the target models are specified by all instance graphs (or a subset of them) over an attributed type graph ATG_T. Both type graphs ATG_S and ATG_T have to be subgraphs of the model transformation type graph ATG (see Fig. 14.1). Starting the model transformation with instance graph G_S typed over ATG_S, it is also typed over ATG. During the model transformation process, the intermediate graphs are typed over ATG. This type graph may contain not only ATG_S and ATG_T, but also additional types and relations which are needed for the transformation process only. The result graph G_T is automatically typed over ATG. If it is also typed over ATG_T, it fulfills one main requirement for being syntactically correct. Data types are preserved during the transformation process.

In general, the correctness of model transformation is an important issue. This includes syntactical correctness, functional behavior, and semantical correctness. As discussed in Subsection 3.4.4, functional behavior is based on local confluence and termination. We shall show termination in our case study in the next section, and confluence based on critical pair analysis will be discussed in Section 15.2. Note, however, that our criteria have only worked in simple cases up to now, and work will have to be done in the future to support all aspects of the correctness of model transformations in more general cases.

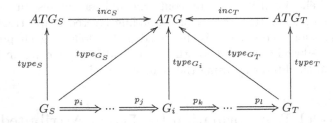

Fig. 14.1. Typing in the model transformation process

14.2 Model Transformation from Statecharts to Petri Nets

In order to illustrate the idea of model transformation by graph transformation, we introduce a model transformation from a simple version of UML statecharts into Petri nets. Similar transformations into various classes of Petri nets could be used to carry out dependability and performance analysis for the system model in the early stages of design, and the properties of UML statecharts could be validated by means of the model transformation and the corresponding analysis techniques for Petri nets.

14.2.1 Source Modeling Language: Simple Version of UML Statecharts

UML statecharts are an object-oriented variant of the classical Harel state-charts [Har87], which describe behavioral aspects of (any instance of) a class in the system under design. The statechart formalism is an extension of that of finite-state machines to allow a decomposition of states into a state hierarchy with parallel regions that greatly enhance the readability and scalability of state models.

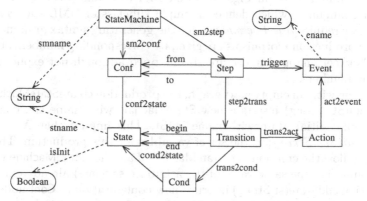

Fig. 14.2. Statechart type graph shown as an E-graph

The statechart type graph T_S is shown as an E-graph (see Definition 8.1) in Fig. 14.2, where the graph nodes are represented by rectangles, the data nodes by rounded rectangles, the graph edges by solid arrows with inscriptions, and the node attribute edges by dashed arrows with inscriptions. In this example, there are no edge attributes. The data type signature $DSIG = Sig(string) + Sig(boolean)$ is given by the signatures of strings and booleans, where only the sorts "String" and "Boolean" are shown in Fig. 14.2. The type graph T_S together with the final **DSIG**-algebra Z defines the attributed type graph $ATG_S = (T_S, Z)$.

This type graph has some similarities to the standard UML metamodel. The type graph explicitly introduces several ideas from the area of statecharts that are only implicitly present in the standard metamodel (such as state configurations). In fact, we consider a network of state machines StateMachine. A single state machine captures the behavior of any object of a specific class by flattening the state hierarchy into *state configurations* and grouping parallel transitions into *steps*. A Configuration is composed of a set of States that can be active at the same time.

A Step is composed of non conflicting Transitions (which are, in turn, binary relations between states) that can be fired in parallel. A step leads from a configuration from to a configuration to, and it is triggered by a common Event for all its transitions. The effect of a step is a set of Actions.

The Generating Syntax Graph Grammar for the Statecharts Source Modeling Language

The type graph of the statechart in Fig. 14.2 allows not only valid statecharts, but also other graphs. For example, a Step could be connected to two StateMachines by an edge sm2step. For this reason we use the generating syntax grammar given in Figs. 14.3 and 14.4 to define precisely the source modeling language, which defines a simple subclass of UML statecharts. In general, we require *injective matches* for the generating syntax grammar. Note that the production morphisms are given by corresponding numbers at nodes. Edges between mapped nodes are also mapped although not explicitly indicated by numbers.

Starting with an empty start graph, the production createStateMachine(sm: String, initSt: String) inserts a new StateMachine with name sm, containing exactly one initial State with name initSt. This implies that $X = \{sm : String, initSt : String\}$ is the set of variables for this production. The NAC does not allow the creation of a StateMachine if another StateMachine with the same name (i.e. the same value of the attribute smname) already exists. The production addState(st:String) inserts a new configuration (a Conf node with a State node) to an existing StateMachine if a configuration with the same name does not exist already. The production addStep() inserts a new Step with a Transition between two existing States. The Transition is connected to a new Step. addEvent(en: String) inserts a new Event with name en; addCond() inserts a condition Cond between a Transition and a State of two different StateMachines. In the same way, an Action can only be placed between two different StateMachines using the production addAction(), i.e. conditions and actions are used only for communication between different state machines here.

The syntax grammar productions given in Fig. 14.3 are sufficient to create the sample statechart shown in Fig. 14.8. They realize the generation of simplified statecharts.

Fig. 14.4 contains three additional syntax grammar productions addTransition(), addTransitionLeftState(), and addTransitionRightState(), which create Transitions to existing steps such that they are connected to additional States belonging to the configurations Conf related to the step. These productions allow us to generate some more general statecharts, which can be considered as the core subset of the statecharts defined in UML 2.0.

14.2.2 Target Modeling Language: Petri Nets

Petri nets are widely used to formally capture the dynamic semantics of concurrent systems, owing to their easy-to-understand visual notation and the wide range of analysis tools available.

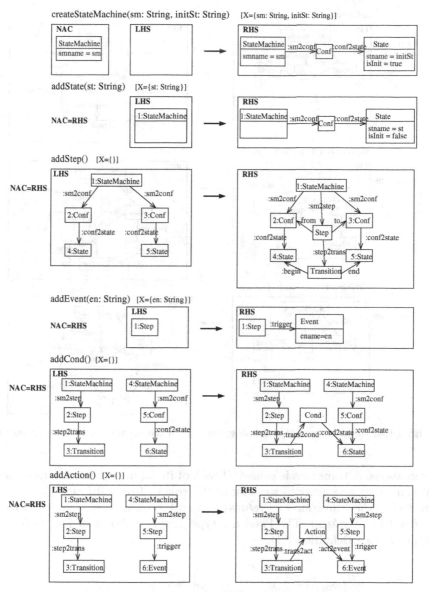

Fig. 14.3. Generating syntax graph grammar for the source modeling language (1)

In the following, we consider place/transition nets with initial marking, also called place/transition systems in the Petri net literature [NRT92, Rei85]. Roughly speaking, Petri nets are bipartite graphs, with two disjoint sets of nodes: Places and Transitions. In our case the initial marking allows each place to contain at most one **token**. A token distribution defines the state of the modeled system. The state of the net can be changed by firing enabled

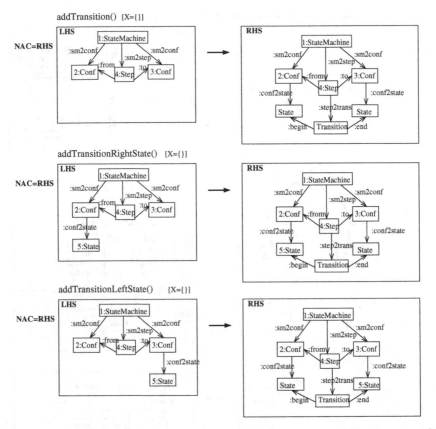

Fig. 14.4. Generating syntax graph grammar for the source modeling language (2)

transitions. A transition is *enabled* if each of its input places contains a token. When firing a transition, we remove the tokens from all input places (connected to the transition by PreArcs) and add a token to all output places (as defined by PostArcs). The Petri net type graph is shown in Fig. 14.5 as an E-graph (see Definition 8.1).

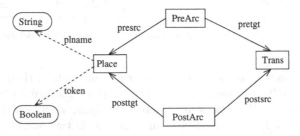

Fig. 14.5. Petri net type graph shown as an E-graph

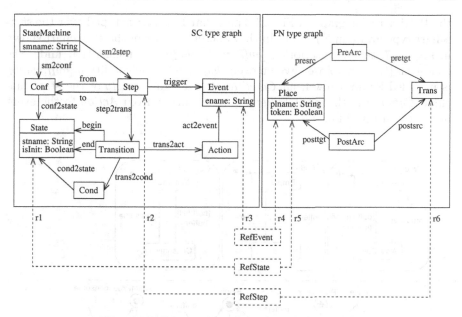

Fig. 14.6. Integration of attributed type graphs

14.2.3 Model Transformation

Integration of Attributed Type Graphs

In order to interrelate the source and target modeling languages, we use reference types [VVP02] to construct an integrated attributed type graph, as shown in Fig. 14.6. For instance, the reference node type RefState relates the source type State to the target type Place.

In the notation of Fig. 14.6, type graphs on the left- and right-hand sides correspond to Figs. 14.2 and 14.5, respectively; data node types and node attribute types are listed in a box below the corresponding graph node type, for example, the node attribute types *stname* and *isInit* of *State*, with targets *String* and *Boolean*, respectively, in Fig. 14.2 are given by the attributes *stname: String* and *isInit: Boolean* of *State* in Fig. 14.6.

Example Statechart: Producer–Consumer System

As an example, we shall apply our model transformation to a producer–consumer system. Fig. 14.7 shows the concrete syntax of the producer–consumer system statechart in the upper part and the concrete syntax of the transformed Petri net in the lower part. The abstract syntax graph of the corresponding statechart is shown in Fig. 14.8, and Fig. 14.9 shows the abstract syntax of the transformed Petri net. Note that Fig. 14.9 is typed over the Petri net type graph in Fig. 14.6 and that Fig. 14.8 is typed over the statechart type graph in Fig. 14.6. In the concrete syntax of the statechart shown in Fig. 14.7, the arc inscription [*buff.empty*]/*buffer++* means that under the condition [*buff.empty*] we have an event *buffer++*. The condition [*buff.empty*] is modeled by an arrow from *Condition* to the state *empty* of the state machine *Buffer*, and the event *buffer++* by the arrow from *Action* to the event *buffer++* in Fig. 14.8.

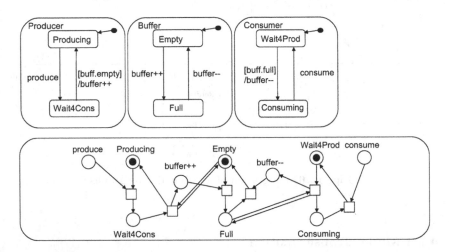

Fig. 14.7. Example statechart: concrete syntax graph of producer–consumer system (upper part) and concrete syntax graph of the transformed Petri net (lower part)

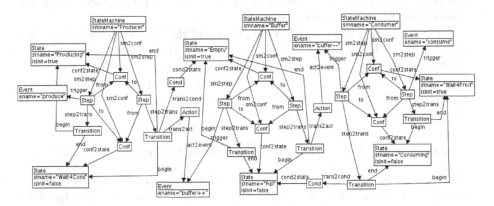

Fig. 14.8. Abstract syntax graph of producer–consumer system statechart

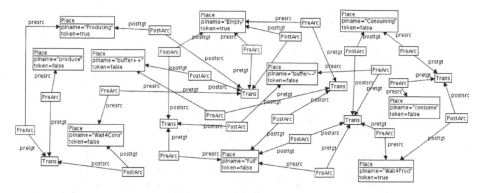

Fig. 14.9. Abstract syntax graph of the transformed producer–consumer system Petri net

Productions for Model Transformation

The model transformation from statecharts into Petri nets is mainly given by the transformation productions shown in Figs. 14.11–14.13. In order to obtain a target graph typed over the Petri net type graph, the abstract syntax graph of the statechart and the reference nodes and edges are deleted after applying these productions of the model transformation.

The model transformation is done in the following three steps. In our example, starting with the statechart graph in Fig. 14.8, we obtain the graph in Fig. 14.10 as an intermediate step, leading to the Petri net graph in Fig. 14.9. The productions are typed over $T_{DSIG}(X)$ with different sets X of variables and with $DSIG = Sig(Strings) + Sig(Boolean)$, as discussed above.

- Each state in the statechart is transformed to a corresponding place in the target Petri net model, where a token in such a place denotes that the corresponding state is active initially (productions InitState2Place and State2Place). A separate place is generated for each valid event Event2Place (see the graph in Fig. 14.10), after these productions have been applied for as long as possible to the sample statechart graph in Fig. 14.8.

- Each step in the statechart is transformed into a Petri net transition (Step2Trans). Naturally, the Petri net should simulate how to exit and enter the corresponding states in the statechart, and therefore input and output arcs of the transition have to be generated accordingly (see StepFrom2PreArc and StepTo2PostArc). Furthermore, firing a transition should consume the token of the trigger event (Trigger2PreArc), and should generate tokens to (the places related to) the target event indicated as the action (Action2PostArc).

- Finally, we clean up the joint model by removing all model elements from the source language and the reference types. This can be done either by restriction or by using another set of graph transformation productions.

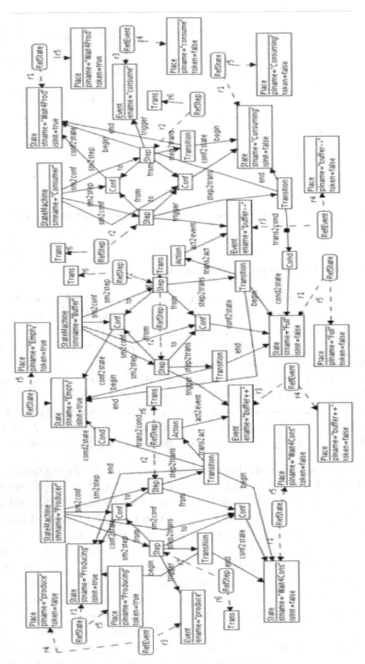

Fig. 14.10. Model Transformation after applying the productions of layer 0

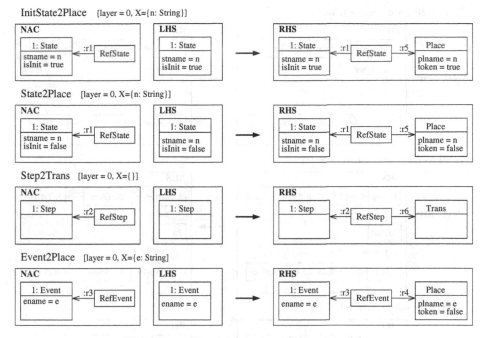

Fig. 14.11. Transformation productions (1)

In fact, there are general schemes for deletion productions as shown in Fig. 14.14:

- DeleteEA_attr deletes an edge attribute of type $attr \in E_{EA}^{ATG} \setminus E_{EA}^{ATG_T}$ of an edge with edge type $e \in E_G^{ATG}$, with $T_1 = src(e)$, $T_2 = tar(e)$, and $T_3 = tar(attr)$;
- Delete_e deletes an edge typed over $e \in E_G^{ATG} \setminus E_G^{ATG_T}$, and $T_1 = src(e)$, $T_2 = tar(e)$;
- DeleteNA_attr deletes a node attribute of type $attr \in V_{NA}^{ATG} \setminus V_{NA}^{ATG_T}$ of a node with node type $T_1 \in V_G^{ATG}$, with $T_2 = tar(attr)$;
- Delete_T deletes a node typed over $T \in V_G^{ATG} \setminus V_G^{ATG_T}$.

The set of deletion productions for a given model transformation consists of all possible productions DeleteEA_attr, Delete_e, DeleteNA_attr, and Delete_T in the schemes given above.

Fig. 14.15 shows three sample deletion productions derived from the schemes: Delete_sm2step corresponds to schema Delete_e, DeleteNA_smname corresponds to schema DeleteNA_attr, and Delete_StateMachine corresponds to schema Delete_T. In the type graph of our model transformation in Fig. 14.6 we do not have edge attribute edges, therefore we do not present an example production corresponding to schema DeleteEA_attr.

Restriction of a graph G typed over ATG by $type : G \rightarrow ATG$ to the type graph ATG_T shown in Fig. 14.1 with the inclusion $inc_T : ATG_T \rightarrow ATG$ means the construction of the pullback

Trigger2PreArc [layer = 1, X={}]

LHS	RHS

```
LHS
┌─────────┐ :r2 ┌──────────┐ :r6 ┌──────────┐
│ 1: Step │◄────┤ 2:RefStep├────►│ 3: Trans │
└─────────┘     └──────────┘     └──────────┘
     │ :trigger
     ▼
┌─────────┐ :r3 ┌──────────┐ :r4 ┌──────────┐
│ 4:Event │◄────┤ 5:RefEvent├───►│ 6:Place  │
└─────────┘     └──────────┘     └──────────┘
```

NAC=RHS

```
RHS
┌─────────┐ :r2 ┌──────────┐ :r6 ┌──────────┐
│ 1: Step │◄────┤ 2:RefStep├────►│ 3: Trans │
└─────────┘     └──────────┘     └──────────┘
     │ :trigger             ▲ :pretgt
     │                  ┌────────┐
     │                  │ PreArc │
     │                  └────────┘
     ▼                      │ :presrc
┌─────────┐ :r3 ┌──────────┐ :r4 ┌──────────┐
│ 4:Event │◄────┤ 5:RefEvent├───►│ 6:Place  │
└─────────┘     └──────────┘     └──────────┘
```

StepFrom2PreArc [layer = 1, X={}]

NAC=RHS

```
LHS
┌─────────┐ :r2 ┌──────────┐ :r6 ┌──────────┐
│ 1: Step │◄────┤ 2:RefStep├────►│ 3: Trans │
└─────────┘     └──────────┘     └──────────┘
     │ :from
     ▼
┌─────────┐
│ 7:Conf  │
└─────────┘
     │ :conf2state
     ▼
┌─────────┐ :r1 ┌──────────┐ :r5 ┌──────────┐
│ 4:State │◄────┤ 5:RefState├───►│ 6:Place  │
└─────────┘     └──────────┘     └──────────┘
```

```
RHS
┌─────────┐ :r2 ┌──────────┐ :r6 ┌──────────┐
│ 1: Step │◄────┤ 2:RefStep├────►│ 3: Trans │
└─────────┘     └──────────┘     └──────────┘
     │ :from                ▲ :pretgt
     ▼                  ┌────────┐
┌─────────┐             │ PreArc │
│ 7:Conf  │             └────────┘
└─────────┘                 │ :presrc
     │ :conf2state
     ▼
┌─────────┐ :r1 ┌──────────┐ :r5 ┌──────────┐
│ 4:State │◄────┤ 5:RefState├───►│ 6:Place  │
└─────────┘     └──────────┘     └──────────┘
```

StepTo2PostArc [layer = 1, X={}]

NAC=RHS

```
LHS
┌─────────┐ :r2 ┌──────────┐ :r6 ┌──────────┐
│ 1: Step │◄────┤ 2:RefStep├────►│ 3: Trans │
└─────────┘     └──────────┘     └──────────┘
     │ :to
     ▼
┌─────────┐
│ 7:Conf  │
└─────────┘
     │ :conf2state
     ▼
┌─────────┐ :r1 ┌──────────┐ :r5 ┌──────────┐
│ 4:State │◄────┤ 5:RefState├───►│ 6:Place  │
└─────────┘     └──────────┘     └──────────┘
```

```
RHS
┌─────────┐ :r2 ┌──────────┐ :r6 ┌──────────┐
│ 1: Step │◄────┤ 2:RefStep├────►│ 3: Trans │
└─────────┘     └──────────┘     └──────────┘
     │ :to                  ▲ :postsrc
     ▼                  ┌────────┐
┌─────────┐             │ PostArc│
│ 7:Conf  │             └────────┘
└─────────┘                 │ :posttgt
     │ :conf2state
     ▼
┌─────────┐ :r1 ┌──────────┐ :r5 ┌──────────┐
│ 4:State │◄────┤ 5:RefState├───►│ 6:Place  │
└─────────┘     └──────────┘     └──────────┘
```

Fig. 14.12. Transformation productions (2)

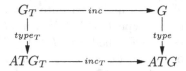

leading to a subgraph G_T of G, typed over ATG_T by $type_T : G_T \to ATG_T$.
After applying the restriction construction, or alternatively, applying all
deletion productions for as long as possible, we obtain the target graph
G_T shown in Fig. 14.9.

In the following diagram we show the alternative to Fig. 14.1 where the
deletion productions are replaced by a restriction construction:

Action2PostArc [layer=1, X={}]

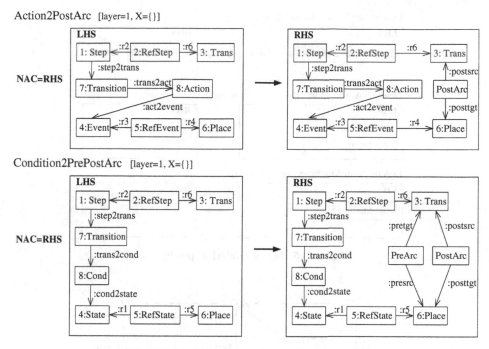

Fig. 14.13. Transformation productions (3)

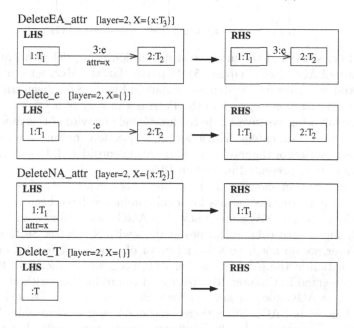

Fig. 14.14. Schemes for deletion productions

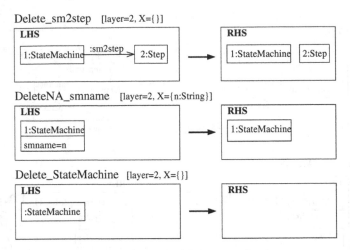

Fig. 14.15. Sample deletion productions

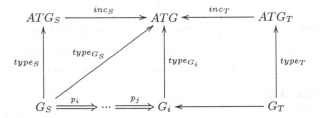

We have simulated the model transformation using deletion productions with our tool AGG (see Chapter 15). In particular, the abstract syntax graph of the producer–consumer system statechart in Fig. 14.8 has been transformed into the abstract syntax graph of the Petri net in Fig. 14.9.

In the following, we investigate the functional behavior of this model transformation to certain extent. The following subsection contains a formal proof of the termination of the model transformation considered, based on the termination criteria presented in Section 12.3.

The first step in showing local confluence is the analysis of critical pairs. Although the theoretical results for local confluence have been restricted to productions without NACs up to now, the AGG tool performs an initial step by analyzing the critical pairs for productions with NACs (see Section 15.2.2).

However, we do not have a formal proof of local confluence of our model transformation in the sense of Section 10.2, because the theory of local confluence presented in Chapter 10 is restricted to productions without NACs at present. The AGG tool, however, allows us to analyze the critical pairs for productions with NACs. Since there are no relevant critical pairs here, the model transformation is locally confluent (see Section 15.2). Together with termination (see below), this implies confluence and functional behavior (see Subsection 3.4.4).

Finally, let us note that the restriction construction discussed above, or alternatively using the general schemes of deletion productions, implies weak syntactical correctness by construction. Weak syntactical correctness means that the result graph is typed over the type graph in Fig. 14.5. In our example, however, syntactical correctness requires in addition that the result graph is a Petri net, which means that there is at most one PreArc and at most one PostArc between each pair of Place and Trans. This constraint is satisfied according to the NACs of the transformation productions in Figs. 14.12 and 14.13.

14.2.4 Termination Analysis of the Model Transformation

Now we shall apply the termination criteria of Section 12.3 to prove the termination of the model transformation from statecharts to Petri nets. Note that for each statechart the model transformation can be considered as a grammar with the statechart as its start graph. First, we assign the productions of Figs. 14.11–14.13 to two creation layers and the deletion productions derived from the schemes in Fig. 14.14 to one deletion layer. Then, the creation and deletion layers of the types contained in the type graph in Fig. 14.6 are set. Finally, a check of the conditions in Definition 12.15 yields the termination of the transformation according to Theorem 12.26.

Assigning Production Layers

Let us define three layers for the model transformation productions, as shown in Fig. 14.16. Productions in Fig. 14.11 are assigned to layer 0, productions in Figs. 14.12 and 14.13 to layer 1, and deletion productions corresponding to the schemes in Fig. 14.14 to layer 2. The type graph ATG is shown in Fig. 14.6; ATG_T is the Petri net part, shown as an E-graph in Fig. 14.5.

Assigning Layers to Types

According to Definition 12.15, the type set $TYPE$ is given by all graph nodes, graph edges, node attribute edges, and edge attribute edges of the type graph in Fig. 14.6, which are presented in Fig. 14.17. Note that we have no edge attributes in Fig. 14.6 and hence no edge attribute edges in $TYPE$.

According to Section 12.3, we can automatically assign creation and deletion layers to each type $t \in TYPE$ in the type graph on the basis of the previous layer definitions for productions. Let us recall the general procedure.

Since, initially, only the elements in the source language are present, exactly those types are included in the start types T_0. (Compare this with the start graph G_0 in Fig. 14.8.) The creation and deletion layers of types are now assigned as shown in Fig. 14.17, following the layer assignment in Definition 12.18 for $k_0 = 2$.

Layer 0	Layer 1	Layer 2
Nondeletion	Nondeletion	Deletion
$pl(p) = 0$	$pl(p) = 1$	$pl(p) = 2$
InitState2Place	Trigger2PreArc	DeleteEA_attr with
State2Place	StepFrom2PreArc	$attr \in E_{EA}^{ATG} \setminus E_{EA}^{ATG_T}$
Step2Trans	StepTo2PostArc	(not used in the example);
Event2Place	Action2PostArc	Delete_e with
	Condition2PrePostArc	$e \in E_G^{ATG} \setminus E_G^{ATG_T}$;
		DeleteNA_attr with
		$attr \in V_{NA}^{ATG} \setminus V_{NA}^{ATG_T}$;
		Delete_T with
		$T \in V_G^{ATG} \setminus V_G^{ATG_T}$.

Fig. 14.16. Production layers

Source type t_s	$cl(t)$	$dl(t)$	Reference type t_r	$cl(t)$	$dl(t)$	Target type t_t	$cl(t)$	$dl(t)$
StateMachine	0	2	RefState	1	2	Place	1	3
State	0	2	RefStep	1	2	Trans	1	3
Step	0	2	RefEvent	1	2	PreArc	2	3
Event	0	2	r1	1	2	PostArc	2	3
Conf	0	2	r2	1	2	presrc	2	3
Transition	0	2	r3	1	2	pretgt	2	3
Action	0	2	r4	1	2	postsrc	2	3
Cond	0	2	r5	1	2	posttgt	2	3
sm2step	0	2	r6	1	2	plname	1	3
sm2conf	0	2				token	1	3
conf2state	0	2						
cond2state	0	2						
step2trans	0	2						
trans2act	0	2						
trans2cond	0	2						
act2event	0	2						
smname	0	2						
stname	0	2						
ename	0	2						
isInit	0	2						
from	0	2						
to	0	2						
trigger	0	2						
begin	0	2						
end	0	2						

Fig. 14.17. Creation and deletion layers for types

Verification of Termination Criteria

First of all, we note that it is enough to verify the reduced layer conditions in Lemma 12.19, because the following conditions are satisfied:

1. p creates $t \Rightarrow t \notin T_0$;
2. $0 \leq cl(t) \leq dl(t) \leq k_0 + 1$ for all $t \in TYPE$.

Next, we observe that our graph transformation system GTS is finitary (see Definition 12.15, item 3), i.e., for $G = G_0$ and all graphs G derivable from G_0, the cardinality $card\{x \in G | type(x) \in TYPE\}$ is finite. Moreover, for all productions p of the non deleting layers 0 and 1, there is only a finite number of matches $m : L \to G$ with $m \models NAC_p$. For productions p with $X = \varnothing$ and $m : L \to G$, this is obvious because G is finitary. The remaining productions InitState2Place, State2Place, and Event2Place in Fig. 14.11 have one variable n or e of type $String$, and the domain of $String$ in the $DSIG$-algebra A is infinite. However, for each match $m : L \to G$, the node attribute edge e_{NA} of type $stname$ or $ename$ in G has $target_{NA}^G(e_{NA}) = w \in A_{String}$. This implies, for the variable n or e in an LHS in Fig. 14.11, that $m_D(n) = w$ or $m_D(e) = w$, respectively, showing also that the number of matches $m : L \to G$ is finite in these cases. Hence GTS is finitary.

Now it suffices to verify the reduced layer conditions in Lemma 12.19:

- *Reduced nondeletion layer conditions.* First, we notice that the corresponding conditions 1 and 2 in Lemma 12.19 are straightforwardly guaranteed by the construction (as NAC is isomorphic/identical to the right-hand side or a subgraph of the right-hand side). Now, we shall show the validity of condition 3 for a single production only, namely $p = $ StepFrom2PreArc (the rest of the productions can be checked similarly). In condition 3, for each graph element x in the left-hand side with $type(x) \in TYPE$, we need to check $cl(type(x)) \leq pl(p)$, which is valid because of the layer assignments above (since $max_{x \in L}\{cl(type(x))\} = 1$ and $pl(p) = 1$).
- *Reduced deletion layer conditions.* The reduced deletion layer condition is satisfied, because each deletion production derived from the schemes in Fig. 14.14 deletes at least one item x with $type(x) \in TYPE$.

14.3 Further Case Studies

In the following, we briefly discuss two other case studies of model transformations which have been described in the literature.

14.3.1 From the General Resource Model to Petri Nets

For the treatment of Petri-net-based simultaneous optimization and verification of resource allocation problems, we refer to [Var04], where an application-specific Petri net model was generated from a variant of the General Resource Modeling (GRM) framework (GRM) [Gro] using typed attributed graph transformation. The graph grammar (implemented in AGG [AGG]) for this model transformation consists of five production layers as follows (where layers 0 and 2 are nondeletion layers, and the others are deletion layers):

0. Target model elements are derived from core GRM elements such as resource types, activities, and control flow elements,
1. Petri net transitions and arcs are created between the transformed Petri net items according to the control flow in the source model,
2. The start and end points of the process are marked by auxiliary edges,
3. The quantitative attributes of the Petri net elements are set,
4. All the auxiliary edges and the source model elements are deleted.

14.3.2 From Process Interaction Diagrams to Timed Petri Nets

In [dLT04], a model transformation from a Process Interaction notation to Timed Transition Petri nets is specified using graph transformation. The source language is customized towards the area of manufacturing and allows the building and simulation of networks of machines and queues through which pieces can flow. In the mapping, timed transitions depict service times of machines, places are used to model queues and machine states, and, finally, pieces are mapped to tokens. The transformation is divided into four layers, the first one being non deleting, while the others are deleting. The first layer creates Petri net elements connected to the source elements. Productions in the second layer delete the pieces in the model, creating tokens in the appropriate places. In the third layer, we connect the Petri net elements, following the connectivity of the source language elements. In addition, the connectivity of the Process Interaction elements is deleted. Finally, the last layer deletes the Process Interaction elements. The languages and the transformation were defined with the AToM^3 tool [dLV02b], and then analyzed using AGG.

14.4 Conclusion

In this chapter, we have shown how typed attributed graph transformations can be used to define model transformations between models of different visual languages. It is interesting to note that typed attributed graph transformation systems can be used not only for the model transformation but also as generating grammars for the source and target languages. Moreover, in several cases an interpreter semantics for the source and/or target languages can be obtained from another typed attributed graph transformation system. For example, the token game of Petri nets can be modeled by graph transformations. As pointed out in Section 14.1, the theory of typed attributed graph transformation described in Part III provides a good basis for defining and verifying the correctness of model transformations. For a more detailed discussion of this problem, we refer to [EE05].

15

Implementation of Typed Attributed Graph Transformation by AGG

In the previous chapter, we showed how the comprehensive theory of typed attributed graph transformation can be used to describe and analyze visual model transformations. Now, we present an account of how this theory can be implemented in an integrated development tool for typed attributed graph transformation that supports the development of graph grammars, as well as their testing and analysis. The tool environment presented is called the Attributed Graph Grammar (AGG) system and is implemented in Java. Since the theoretical concepts are implemented as directly as possible – but, naturally, respecting necessary efficiency considerations – AGG offers clear concepts and sound behavior concerning the graph transformation part. The running example in this chapter is the model transformation example presented in the previous chapter, but here it is treated as an AGG graph grammar.

Since graph transformation can be applied on very different levels of abstraction, it can be non-attributed, attributed by simple computations, or attributed by complex processes, depending on the abstraction level. To reflect this wide application area for attributed graph transformation, we have decided to attribute AGG graphs by use of Java objects. On the one hand, this design decision certainly allows a large variety of applications to graph transformation, but on the other hand it is clear that the Java semantics is not covered by the formal foundation.

Owing to its formal foundation, AGG offers validation support in the form of graph parsing, consistency checking of graphs and graph transformation systems, critical pair analysis, and analysis of the termination of graph transformation systems.

15.1 Language Concepts of AGG

In the following, we step through the whole list of basic concepts for typed attributed graph transformation based on the adhesive HLR category

($\mathbf{AGraphs_{ATG}}, \mathcal{M}$), and present for each concept how it is defined in AGG and to what extent it conforms to the corresponding theoretical concept.

15.1.1 Graphs

A *graph* in AGG consists of two (disjoint) sets containing the *nodes* and the *edges* of the graph. Considered together, the nodes and edges are called the *objects* of a graph. Every edge represents a directed connection between two nodes, which are called the *source* and *target* nodes of the edge. Note that in our idea of a graph, we can have multiple edges between a single pair of nodes, because every edge has an identity of its own, just as a node does. This fact distinguishes our view from another popular idea of a graph, where an arc is described just as a relation between nodes. Our concept of a graph corresponds exactly to that in the theory (see Definition 8.7). Examples of AGG graphs have been given in Figs. 14.8 and 14.9 within the case study.

Note that in our idea of a graph, the position of a node or an edge in the plane does not store syntactic or semantic information, i.e. the layout of a graph is just a matter of presentation for the sake of readability to the user. Obviously, the layout of a graph may be considered as the equivalent of the indentation (or "pretty-printing") of a program in a conventional textual programming language such as C. It is a well-known fact that a program which is properly indented according to its logical structure is far more comprehensible to the human reader than the same program put into one line; whereas, to the compiler, both versions are equivalent. This experience is perfectly transferable to the layout aspect of a graph, and makes it clear that the layout is of considerable importance for a human user, even though it does not carry any relevant information itself. Unfortunately, the problem of automatically computing a reasonable layout of a graph is much more complex than that of pretty-printing a textual program, but it is solved in AGG in quite a simple way.

15.1.2 Typing Facilities

To allow for further classification of graph objects, each graph object is associated with exactly one *type* from a given type set. This type set is structured into two subsets: the set of node types and the set of edge types. Non-typed nodes or edges are not allowed in AGG. The type information is given by a type name (which may be empty) and a graphical representation that specifies the shape, color, and kind of line used to represent the node or edge. If two type names are equal but the graphical representations differ, the corresponding types are considered to be different.

AGG supports not only type sets, but also type graphs. As in the theory, nodes and edges of the type graph represent node and edge types. In addition, an AGG type graph may contain multiplicity constraints on edge types that constrain how many objects may be connected by an instance of a certain edge type. For each edge type, two multiplicity constraints can be given, one for the source and one for the target nodes. Moreover, a node type may have a multiplicity constraint, restricting the number of instances of this node type. In the theory, multiplicities can be expressed by graph constraints, as presented in Chapter 12. Upper bounds are expressed by negative constraints, and lower bounds by positive constraints.

Example: Transformation from Statecharts to Petri Nets

Taking up the case study from Chapter 14, we can create an AGG graph grammar from it. Here, we start with the type graph shown in Fig. 14.6. Note that in the corresponding AGG type graph (in Fig. 15.1), some of the edge type names have been shortened or omitted. Furthermore, owing to the possibility in AGG of adding multiplicities to node and edge types, the type graph has been extended by multiplicities at the source and target ends of type edges. Multiplicities of node types have not been used, i.e. all node types are marked with an asterisk at their upper right corner, allowing arbitrary numbers of instances.

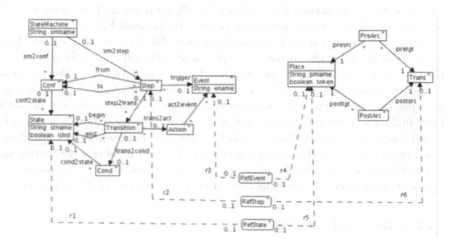

Fig. 15.1. Type graph of Fig. 14.6 extended by multiplicities

15.1.3 Node and Edge Attributes

In AGG, an attribute is declared just like a variable in a conventional programming language: we specify a *name* and a certain *type* for the attribute, and we may then assign any *value* of the specified type to it. As in the theory, all graph objects of the same type also share their attribute declarations, i.e.

the list of attribute types and names; only the values of the attributes may be chosen individually. From a conceptual point of view, attribute declarations have to be considered as an integral part of the definition of a type.

Slightly differently from the general definition of attributed graphs in Chapter 8, each attributed node and edge has exactly one value for each attribute declared in its type. Consequently, AGG allows neither graphs which are only partially attributed, nor several values for one attribute. This restriction is natural, since in many respects, the concept of a type with integral attribute declarations resembles the notion of a class with its member variables or class attributes in the paradigm of object-oriented programming. In the theory, this restriction can be expressed by adding positive graph constraints which require at least one value, and negative constraints forbidding more than one value.

A further important question that we have to deal with is the following: What types are actually available for the declaration of attributes? The answer is short and simple, but emphasizes the affinity of the graphical AGG approach to the object-oriented paradigm: the attributes may be typed with any valid Java type. This means that not only it is possible to annotate graph objects with simple types such as strings or integers, but we can also utilize arbitrary Java classes to gain maximal flexibility in attribution. Apart from the standard Java library JDK,[1] user-defined classes can also be used for attribution.

It is an open research issue to check how far this attribution by Java objects conforms to the formal concepts of attribution by algebras which is required in the definition of an attributed graph in Chapter 8. We use Java primitive types such as "int", "float", and "boolean", and Java classes as possible attribute types. Pre-defined operations and methods will be used later in Java expressions to compute new attribute values. Java is a strongly typed language, and thus the general attribution scheme, where each attribute has a type, a name, and a value, can be used. Further algebraic properties are not required in AGG. In the following, we shall discuss the consequences of this design decision whenever the theoretical concept of attribution is relevant.

15.1.4 Rules and Matches

First of all, it has to be noted that productions are called "rules" in AGG. Internally, AGG follows the single-pushout approach, and thus rules are represented by a left- (LHS) and a right-hand side (RHS), together with a partial graph morphism $r : LHS \rightarrow RHS$. However, this morphism can be considered as a span of two total graph morphisms with the morphism's domain as the gluing graph, i.e. $LHS \leftarrow dom(r) \rightarrow RHS$, the way DPO rules are denoted. AGG supports both approaches to graph transformation. The approach is chosen on the level of graph grammars, i.e. the approach is the same for all rules of one grammar.

---

[1] Java Development Kit.

The partial graph morphism $r : LHS \to RHS$ is not necessarily injective, i.e. non injective rules are also supported. Negative application conditions (NACs) can be added to a rule, as many as are needed. They are allowed to contain the LHS only partially. We shall discuss below the fact that this relaxation does not affect the satisfaction of NACs. Usually, we have considered NACs with injective mappings from the LHS to the NAC to express the context in which the rule must not be applied. However, there is a special situation where it is very useful that we are not restricted to injectivity: if we allow non injective matches for rules in general, the use of non injective NACs allows us to enforce injective matching just for particular objects. Recall this rule of thumb: by mapping two objects in the LHS to the same object in the NAC, we can specify that we do not allow this identification to happen in an actual match.

The rule's LHS or NACs may contain constants or variables as attribute values, but no Java expressions. This restriction allows attribute matching by simply comparing constant values or instantiating variables. However, the RHS of a graph rule may contain Java expressions in addition. NAC may use the variables declared in the LHS or new variables declared as an input parameters. The scope of a variable is its rule, i.e. each variable is globally known in its rule. The Java expressions occurring in the RHS may contain any variable declared within the LHS or as an input parameter. Multiple usage of the same variable is allowed and can be used to require equality of values.

Moreover, rules may have a set of attribute conditions which are Boolean Java expressions. These conditions can also be expressed by attributed graph rules that add a new Boolean attribute to some graph object which contains the conjunction of all these conditions as a value. Vice versa, attributed graph rules with expressions in the LHS can be converted into AGG rules by inventing new variables for each of the expressions in the LHS, replacing each expression by its corresponding variable, and adding new conditions which state the equality of each variable with its corresponding condition.

In general, we may find multiple matches of the LHS into the host graph, and, on the other hand, there may be no matches at all. In the later case, the rule is *not applicable* to the given graph. The same is true in the DPO approach, if the match does not satisfy the gluing condition (see Subsection 15.1.5). In the case of multiple matching possibilities, one match has to be chosen. It depends entirely on the application context whether this selection is done randomly or by preference, for example by user interaction.

Moreover, the rule matches may also be non injective, i.e. two or more graph objects in the LHS of a rule may be mapped to one single object in the host graph. Note that non injective matches may cause conflicts between deletion and preservation: we could have, for instance, two graph objects in the LHS, one to be deleted and one to be preserved, and both mapped to the same image object in the host graph. Conflicts such as this can be resolved either by giving deletion precedence over preservation (SPO approach) or by nonapplicability of the rule (DPO approach), since the gluing condition is not fulfilled.

When a match has been fixed, the rule's NACs have to be checked. A match satisfies an NAC if there exists no morphism from the NAC to the host graph that extends the match and maps objects not coming from the LHS injectively. This satisfaction relation differs slightly from that in the theory, where a NAC is satisfied if there is no injective morphisms from the NAC to the host graph.

Moreover, AGG allows NACs which contain their LHS only partially. The NAC is satisfied if there is a total graph morphism from the NAC to the host graph that extends the match. In the formal approach, NACs have to include their LHS completely. Clearly, every possible NAC n which contains its LHS only partially can be completed to some NAC n' such that the LHS is totally included. It is obvious that a match satisfies n if and only if it satisfies n'. Within AGG, the partial representation of NACs on one hand is more compact and intuitive, and hence is more user-friendly. On the other hand, it is equivalent to the theory in the DPO approach as discussed above.

Example: a Model Transformation Rule

Considering the case study in Chapter 14 again, we shall pick one of the rules in Fig. 14.11 and discuss how it can be defined in AGG. We take the rule *InitState2Place* for our small comparison. Except for the layout, the only difference is the attribute list of the "State" node in the NAC. This list does not have to contain the whole attribute list, but only those attributes that are interesting for the NAC. In our example, the attribute list is empty. The NAC is shown on the left, the LHS in the middle, and the RHS on the right in Fig. 15.2.

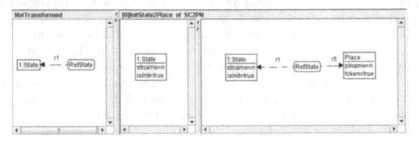

Fig. 15.2. Rule *InitState2Place* of Fig. 14.11, represented in AGG

15.1.5 Graph Transformations

The effect of applying a rule $r : LHS \rightarrow RHS$ in AGG with a given match is a graph transformation. The basic idea of what happens during a graph transformation in AGG is the following: the pattern found for the LHS is taken out of the host graph and replaced by the RHS of the rule. Since a match $m : LHS \rightarrow G$ is a total morphism, any object o in the LHS has a proper image object $m(o)$ in the host graph G. Now, if o also has an image $r(o)$ in the RHS, its corresponding object $m(o)$ in the host graph is *preserved* during the transformation; otherwise, it is *removed*. Objects appearing exclusively in the RHS without an original object in the LHS are *newly created* during the transformation. Finally, the objects of the host graph which are not covered by the match are not affected by the rule application at all; they form the *context*, which is always preserved during derivations. If the gluing condition is not set, AGG supports the SPO approach. In this case dangling arcs are implicitly removed by the transformation as well, even though they belong to the context which is normally to be preserved. On the other hand, if the gluing condition is set, AGG supports the DPO approach (see Subsection 1.2.3). AGG offers the possibility to set a number of transformation options: (1) matches can be arbitrary or restricted to injective ones, (2) the dangling condition can be active or not, (3) the identification condition can be active or not, and (4) the NACs can be active or not. Every combination of these options is possible. Choosing the dangling and the identification condition (or injective matches) corresponds to the DPO approach to graph transformation.

Besides manipulating the nodes and edges of a graph, a graph rule may also perform attribute computations. During rule application, expressions are evaluated with respect to the instantiation of variables induced by the current match. However, in AGG, we are not limited to applying simple arithmetic operations on attributes. In fact, we may call arbitrary Java methods in attribute expressions, as long as the overall type of the expression matches the type of the attribute whose value it represents. From interfacing databases to calling sophisticated mathematical libraries or invoking interactive dialogs, everything is possible. Actual invocation of a method occurs whenever the expression is evaluated, i.e. every time the corresponding rule is applied.

To summarize, the effect of the transformation is

- *complete:* any effect specified in the rule is actually performed in the concrete transformation;
- *minimal:* nothing more is done than what is specified in the rule;[2]
- *local:* only the fraction of the host graph covered by the match is actually affected by the transformation.[3]

In this way, AGG graph transformations with the gluing condition corresponds strongly to the typed attributed graph transformations defined in Chapter 9.

---

[2] With the well-defined exception of the implicit removal of dangling edges and conflicting objects, if the gluing condition is not set (SPO approach).

[3] In the SPO approach, the coverage has to be extended to include potentially dangling edges.

15.1.6 Graph Grammars

A graph grammar in AGG consists of a start graph and a rule set. Graph objects in the graphs and rules are classified by two type sets, one for nodes and one for edges. Optionally, a type graph with multiplicity constraints can be defined in addition.

AGG supports the possibility to set rule layers and thus to define layered graph grammars. The layers fix an order on how rules are applied. The interpretation process first has to apply all rules of layer 0 for as long as possible, then all rules of layer 1, etc. After the rules of the highest layer have been applied for as long as possible, the transformation process stops. To summarize, rule layers allow one to specify a *simple control flow* on graph transformation, and they correspond exactly to those defined in Section 12.3.

15.2 Analysis Techniques Implemented in AGG

Several analysis techniques have already been implemented in AGG. They rely on the language concepts of AGG. Not all theoretical constructions introduced in Part III have been implemented in AGG, but the main ones are available. On the other hand, the practical application of certain analysis techniques has led to new ideas for presenting the results of the analysis in a suitable way. Layout and filtering play important roles here.

15.2.1 Graph Constraints

AGG provides the possibility to formulate consistency conditions which can be tested on single graphs, but which can also be checked for a whole graph transformation system. Generally, *consistency conditions* describe basic (global) properties of graphs such as the existence or nonexistence of certain substructures, independent of a particular rule.

An *atomic graph constraint* in AGG is a total injective morphism $c : P \to C$, the left graph P is called the premise and the right graph C is called the conclusion. An *atomic graph constraint* is satisfied by a graph G if for all total injective morphisms $p : P \to G$ there is a total injective morphism $q : C \to G$ such that $q \circ c = p$. Here, we restrict the atomic graph constraints presented in Chapter 12 to injective ones. It is left to future work to extend AGG to general graph constraints.

While the default number of conclusions is equal to 1, an atomic graph constraint can also have more than one conclusion in AGG. The graph constraint is then defined by a set of total injective morphisms $\{c_i : P \to C_i | i \in I\}$. Such an extended atomic graph constraint is satisfied if at least one morphism c_i fulfills the above condition. This extension was not presented in Chapter 12, but has been introduced in [HW95] for labeled graphs and in [RT05] for typed graphs. It extends the expressiveness of atomic graph constraints. As presented in Chapter 12, we can build up formulas over atomic graph constraints, using the operators ¬, ∨, and ∧. Atomic graph constraints and formulas are called *graph constraints*.

If GC is a set of graph constraints, we say that G satisfies GC if G satisfies all constraints in GC.

It is possible to generate *postapplication conditions* for a rule from graph constraints such that the constraints are always ensured when the rule is applied. A rule extended in this way is applicable to a consistent graph if and only if the derived graph is also consistent. A graph grammar is *consistent* if the start graph satisfies all graph constraints and the rules preserve this property. Thus, AGG realizes the transformation of graph constraints to application conditions of rules, but the transformation from postconditions to preconditions (from right to left application conditions) is left for future work (see Section 12.2).

15.2.2 Critical Pair Analysis

AGG supports critical pair analysis, which is one of the main analysis techniques for rewrite systems. Critical pair analysis is known from term rewriting and is used there to check if a term rewriting system is locally confluent. It has been generalized to graph rewriting by Plump [Plu95]. Critical pairs formalize the idea of a minimal example of a conflicting situation. From the set of all critical pairs, we can extract the objects and links which cause conflicts or dependencies. Recall that two graph transformations $G \Rightarrow H_1$ and $G \Rightarrow H_2$ are in conflict if they are parallel dependent (see Definition 9.12).

A *critical pair* is a pair of transformations $G \stackrel{p_1,m_1}{\Longrightarrow} H_1$ and $G \stackrel{p_2,m_2}{\Longrightarrow} H_2$ which are in conflict, such that, roughly speaking (see Definition 10.13), the graph G is minimal, i.e., G is the gluing of the left-hand sides L_1 and L_2 of the rules p_1 and p_2. It can be computed by overlapping L_1 and L_2 in all possible ways, such that the intersection of L_1 and L_2 contains at least one item that is deleted or changed by one of the rules and that both rules are applicable to G at their respective occurrences.

The set of critical pairs represents precisely all *potential conflicts*. This means that a critical pair for rules p_1 and p_2 exists iff there is an application of p_1 which disables that of p_2 or vice versa.

There are three main reasons why rule applications can be conflicting. The first two are related to the structure of the graph, whereas the third concerns its attributes.

1. One rule application deletes a graph object which is in the match of another rule application (*delete–use conflict*).
2. One rule application generates graph objects in such a way that a graph structure would occur which is prohibited by a negative application condition of another rule application (*produce–forbid conflict*).

3. One rule application changes attributes that are in the match of another rule application (*change–attribute conflict*).

Two rule applications are in conflict if at least one of the conditions above is fulfilled. To find all conflicting rule applications, minimal critical graphs to which rules can be applied in a conflicting way are computed. Basically, we consider all overlapping graphs in the LHSs of two rules with the obvious matches and analyze these rule applications. All conflicting rule applications that we find are called critical pairs. This construction follows the definitions in Chapter 9, except of rules with NACs, which are not handled in the theory of critical pairs up to now. If one of the rules contains negative application conditions, the graphs of one LHS that overlap with a proper part of the NAC have to be considered in addition. We are currently extending the theoretical foundation to support this construction, which is already implemented in AGG.

Example: Critical Pairs for Sample Model Transformation

As an example of critical pair analysis, we consider the transformation rules in the case study, depicted in Fig. 14.11–14.13. In Fig. 15.3, a table is shown which gives an overview of all critical pairs for these rules, found by AGG separately for the rule layers 0 and 1; critical pairs of transformations with the same rule and the same match are not shown because they are isomorphic and hence locally confluent. Fig. 15.3 just shows the critical pairs of layers 0 and 1. Layer 2 contains all deletion rules schematically described in Fig. 14.14. Considering layer 2 containing the deletion rules, it is obvious that only trivial critical pairs exist, i.e. critical pairs using the same rule and the same match, which always lead to a confluent situation.

first \ second	1: InL	2: St_	3: St_	4: Ev_	5: Tri_	6: St_	7: St_	8: Ac_
1: InitState2Place	0	0	0	0	0	0	0	0
2: State2Place	0	0	0	0	0	0	0	0
3: Step2Trans	0	0	0	0	0	0	0	0
4: Event2Place	0	0	0	0	0	0	0	0
5: Trigger2PreArc	0	0	0	0	0	1	0	0
6: StepFrom2PreArc	0	0	0	0	1	0	0	0
7: StepTo2PostArc	0	0	0	0	0	0	0	1
8: Action2PostArc	0	0	0	0	0	0	1	0
9: Condition2PrePostArc	0	0	0	0	1	1	1	1

Fig. 15.3. Critical pairs of transformation rules in Figs. 14.11–14.13

Now we shall consider one pair of rules more closely: the rules *Trigger2PreArc* and *StepFrom2PreArc* (depicted in Fig. 14.12). The upper part of Fig. 15.4 shows the LHS of the rules involved. Below, the overlapping graph, is shown which causes a conflict of the following sort: both rules use the same *Place*. The first rule approaches it via a *RefEvent* node, while the second rule does so via a *RefState* node. This possible conflict situation cannot occur during the model transformation that we described in Chapter 14, since events and states are always translated to different places according to the rules *State2Place* and *Event2Place*, which generate a new *Place* in each case. Moreover, there are no rules which can identify different *Places*. If we were to add a graph constraint forbidding this situation, the critical pair analysis would not report this conflict anymore (see the extensions below).

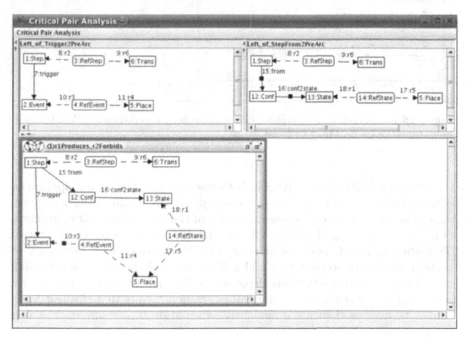

Fig. 15.4. Overlapping graph for the rules *Trigger2PreArc* and *StepFrom2Arc* in Fig. 14.12

As a second example, we consider the pair of rules *Condition2PrePostArc* (depicted in Fig. 14.13) and *StepFrom2PreArc* (depicted in Fig. 14.12). The upper part of Fig. 15.5 shows the LHS of the rules involved. Below, the overlapping graph is shown, which depicts a situation where both rules refer to the same *Trans* and *Place* nodes. Between the *Trans* and the *Place*, the first rule inserts a *PreArc* and a *PostArc*, while the second rule inserts a *PreArc* (see the RHS of the corresponding rules in Figs. 14.12 and 14.13). The NACs of

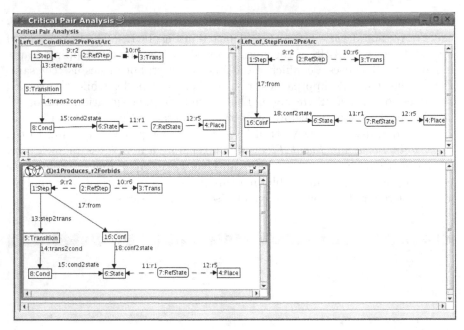

Fig. 15.5. Overlapping graph for the rules *Condition2PrePostArc* and *StepFrom2PreArc* in Fig. 14.12 and 14.13

the two rules (with NAC = RHS in both cases) forbid the second application of these rules owing to a *produce-forbid-conflict*. This conflict situation cannot appear in our case study, because the rules of the generating syntax grammar of the source language in Figs. 14.3 and 14.4 allow a condition *Cond* between *Transition* and *State* nodes of different *StateMachines* only. However, a *Conf* node is allowed between a *Step* and a *State* node of the same *StateMachine* only. Hence the two situations depicted in Fig. 15.5 cannot appear in the same host graph generated by the syntax grammar. Note that this restriction cannot be expressed with the model transformation type graph itself, shown in Fig. 14.6.

We have now shown for two of the critical pairs in Fig. 15.3 that they cannot occur during the model transformation, owing to the restriction of the source language given by the generating syntax grammar in Figs. 14.3 and 14.4. In fact, the same is true for the other critical pairs in Fig. 15.3. Since there are no critical pairs left, the model transformation is locally confluent. Together with the termination of the model transformation shown in Chapter 14, the implemented analysis techniques of AGG imply that the model transformation is also confluent and has functional behavior, as discussed in Section 3.4.2.

Extensions

Practical experience with critical pair analysis has shown that, often, critical situations which cannot occur in the system are shown. Moreover, often too many similar critical pairs are computed, which all show essentially the same conflicts. We have implemented the following additional filtering possibilities in AGG, which can reduce the number of critical pairs drastically:

- To rule out unwanted conflict situations, the user can enforce a check of multiplicity and graph constraints for all overlapping graphs. Only those constraints are taken into account which remain true for all possible embeddings of critical graphs into larger contexts. These are mainly those constraints which forbid certain parts of a graph.
- The set of critical pairs can be reduced by ruling out similar critical pairs that report essentially the same conflict. If one critical pair includes another one, only that with the smallest overlapping graph is kept.
- If the graph grammar is *layered*, critical pairs are sought for rules in the same layer only.

Automatic conflict resolution analysis in AGG is left to future work.

15.2.3 Graph Parsing

AGG provides a graph parser which is able to check if a given graph belongs to a particular graph language determined by a graph grammar. In formal language theory, this problem is known as the *membership problem*. Here, the membership problem is lifted to graphs. This problem is undecidable for graph grammars in general, but for restricted classes of graph grammars it is more or less efficiently solvable.

Usually, a graph grammar is given to generate all graphs of a graph language. For parsing, all rules of the graph grammar have to be inverted. By applying the inverted rules in the right way, all graphs of the corresponding graph language can be reduced to the start graph of the grammar.

In AGG not all kinds of rules can be automatically inverted. For this reason, the graph parser expects, instead of a generating grammar, a "parse grammar" containing reducing parsing rules and a stop graph. Given an arbitrary host graph, AGG tries to apply the parsing rules in such a way that the host graph is reduced to the stop graph. If this is possible, the host graph belongs to the graph language determined by the grammar, and there is a transformation sequence from the host graph to the stop graph; otherwise, this is not the case.

AGG offers three different parsing algorithms, all based on backtracking, i.e. the parser builds up a derivation tree of possible reductions of the host graph with dead ends, called leaf graphs (i.e. where no rule can be applied anymore), but the leaf graph is not isomorphic to the stop graph. Since simple backtracking has exponential time complexity, the simple backtracking parser is accompanied by two further parser variants exploiting critical pair analysis for rules.

Critical pair analysis can be used to make the parsing of graphs more efficient: decisions between conflicting rule applications are delayed as far as possible. This means that *nonconflicting* rules are applied first and the graph is reduced as much as possible. Afterwards, the *conflicting* rules are applied, first in noncritical situations and, when this is not possible, in critical ones. In general, this optimization reduces the derivation tree constructed, but does not change the worst-case complexity.

15.2.4 Termination

In AGG, termination criteria are implemented for layered graph transformation systems (see Chapter 12). In general, termination is undecidable for graph grammars. However, if graph grammars with negative application conditions meet suitable termination criteria, we can conclude that they are terminating. We have implemented the following termination criteria:

- *Deletion layer conditions (1).* If k is a deletion layer, then one of the following applies:
  1. Each rule decreases the number of graph items.
  2. Each rule decreases the number of graph items of one special type.

  The termination of attributed graph transformation systems using these termination criteria has been shown in [BKPT05].
- *Deletion layer conditions (2).* See Definition 12.15.
- *Nondeletion layer conditions.* See Definition 12.15.

In AGG, the rule layers can be set by the user or generated. The creation and deletion type layers will be generated automatically, such that for each layer one set of layer conditions is satisfied, if this is possible.

Example: Termination of Model Transformation

In Fig. 15.6, the termination dialog is shown for the case study in Chapter 12. For the given rule layers, creation and deletion layers of node and edge type are generated such that the termination criteria are fulfilled. As shown in Fig. 15.6, the termination criteria are fulfilled for the case study, i.e. the model transformation always terminates.

15.3 Tool Environment of AGG

AGG is an integrated development environment for graph transformation systems. It contains several visual editors for graph grammars, graphs and rules;

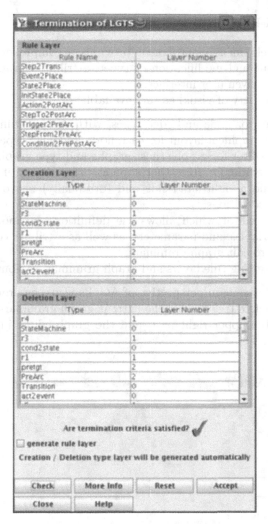

Fig. 15.6. Termination dialog

a visual interpreter that performs graph transformations step by step or for as long as possible; and a validation tool which supports the analysis techniques described in the previous section. The internal graph transformation engine can also be used by a Java API and thus can be integrated into other tool environments.

15.3.1 Visual Environment

The AGG development environment provides a comprehensive functionality for the input and modification of typed attributed graph grammars by a mouse/menu-driven user interface.

There is a variety of visual editors available:

- a type editor for node and edge types, with the possibility to name and set a simple graphical layout for each node and edge type,
- a graphical editor for graphs (host graphs and type graphs),
- a graphical editor for rules that supports the editing of rules consisting of a left- and a right-hand side and (optionally) one or more negative application conditions;
- an attribute editor which allows the definition and modification of attributes, variables, and parameters, as well as attribute conditions;
- a tree view to edit graph grammars;
- dialogs for setting rule layers and graph grammar attributes.

In Fig. 15.7, the main perspective of AGG's visual environment is shown. The figure depicts a tree view of the current graph grammars on the left, the rule editor in the upper right part, and the graph editor in the lower right part.

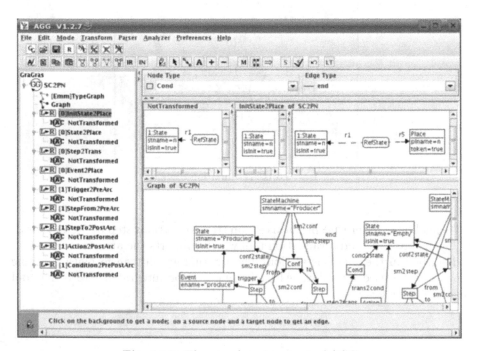

Fig. 15.7. The visual environment of AGG

Graph transformations are also performed in a visual manner. After a rule and a match have been chosen interactively, the result of the rule application is displayed using a simple layout algorithm which changes the given graph layout as little as possible. When the automatic selection of rules and matches is chosen and the rules are applied for as long as possible, the intermediate graphs can be optionally shown. It is also possible for a graph transformation sequence to be stopped by the user.

For a detailed description of the graphical user interface, see the user manual at the AGG home page [AGG].

AGG is designed according to the model–view–controller architecture. It distinguishes between graphs with a concrete layout and graphs without a layout. The model is formed by the graph transformation engine, which manipulates graphs without a layout.

15.3.2 Graph Transformation Engine

The graph transformation engine is the internal model of the AGG system, which is also usable without the visual environment. The engine's API directly reflects the concepts of graph transformation described in Section 15.1.

Rule applications can be performed in two different modes: an interaction mode and an interpreter mode. In the interaction mode, the rule selection and match definition can be done interactively. After a rule has been chosen, the match can either be given elementwise by clicking on LHS and host graph elements alternately, or be computed automatically. If several matches are possible, they are computed one after the other. A third possibility is the manual definition of a partial match, which is completed automatically afterwards. Again, if several completions exist, they are shown sequentially. The automatic match completion computes the possible matches in an arbitrary order, which will certainly differ from the order that will be used if the computation of all possible matches is repeated. After the rule and match have been fixed, the rule is applied to the current host graph.

To ensure compliance with the formal definition of graph transformation, AGG's transformation engine is based on a library designed to perform arbitrary colimit computations [Wol98], where pushouts fit in as a special case. Note, however, that AGG will never face you with an explicit pushout diagram, i.e. the rules modify the host graph directly. However, owing to the freedom to use arbitrary Java expressions for attribute computations, a graph transformation might yield unexpected results; for example, when a method throws an exception, it might happen that the attribute values are not set.

The second possible mode of rule application is the interpreter mode, where rules are applied for as long as possible. The selection orders for the rules and matches are nondeterministic, except for layered graph grammars or other kind of rule control such as by Java programs using the AGG API.

15.3.3 Tool Integration

Since graphs are a very general data structure which is used in various fields of computer science, a variety of graph-based tools exist. To increase their interoperability, GXL [GXL], a common exchange format for graphs, has been developed on the basis of XML. GXL allows one to store the logical structure of nearly all kinds of graphs, for example typed and attributed graphs with hyperedges, and also hierarchical graphs. GXL is used not only by graph transformation tools, but also by graph-drawing tools, reengineering tools, etc.

AGG supports the exchange of graphs by GXL, i.e. the current host graph of a graph grammar can be stored in GXL or a GXL graph can be read in and set as a new host graph in AGG. Input graphs which use graph concepts not supported by AGG, such as hyperedges, cannot yet be loaded. It is left to future work to support various kinds of style sheet transformations between GXL graphs and advanced graph concepts.

To support model transformation by AGG graph transformation, some CASE tool (with subsequent XSL transformation if needed) could produce a GXL graph, which would be the input graph for a model transformation in AGG. The resulting graph could be exported in GXL again and prepared for further processing.

Graph grammars are currently stored in a proprietary XML format of AGG. It is planned to replace this format by GTXL [Tae01, Lam04], the future exchange format for graph transformation systems, which is build on top of GXL. If graph transformation is to be used as a semantic model domain, it is intended that GTXL will be used as the target format for model transformations and thus as the input format for graph transformation tools that perform validations.

15.4 Conclusion

This chapter has given a short overview of the graph transformation environment AGG and its relation to the theory of graph transformation. AGG is an integrated development environment for graph transformation systems which supports standard validation techniques for graph transformation. The applications of AGG may have a large variety, because of its very flexible concept of attribution, which relies on Java objects and expressions.

AGG has become one of the standard development environments for graph transformation systems and has been applied in a variety of contexts. For example, the following applications of AGG have been considered:

- visual language parsing [BST00], implemented in GenGEd [Bar02];
- conflict detection in functional requirement specifications [HHT02];
- conflict detection in model refactorings [MTR04]; and
- termination checks for model transformations [EEdL+05].

The AGG development group at the Technical University of Berlin will continue implementing concepts and results concerning the validation and structuring of graph transformation systems in order to continue implementing concepts from the theory of graph transformation. AGG is available from the AGG Homebase [AGG].

Appendices

Appendices A and B are short introductions to category theory and to signatures and algebras, respectively, to the extent needed for understanding the main part (Parts I–IV) of the book. Appendix C contains selected proofs not presented in the main part of the book.

A

A Short Introduction to Category Theory

In this appendix, we give a short summary of the categorical terms used throughout this book. We introduce categories, show how to construct them, and present some basic constructions such as pushouts, pullbacks, and binary coproducts. In addition, we give some specific categorical results which are needed for the main part of the book. For a more detailed introduction to category theory see [Mac71, EM85, EM90, AHS90, EMC+01].

A.1 Categories

In general, a category is a mathematical structure that has objects and morphisms, with a composition operation on the morphisms and an identity morphism for each object.

Definition A.1 (category). *A category* $\mathbf{C} = (Ob_C, Mor_C, \circ, id)$ *is defined by*

- *a class Ob_C of objects;*
- *for each pair of objects $A, B \in Ob_C$, a set $Mor_C(A, B)$ of morphisms;*
- *for all objects $A, B, C \in Ob_C$, a composition operation $\circ_{(A,B,C)}$:* $Mor_C(B, C) \times Mor_C(A, B) \to Mor_C(A, C)$; *and*
- *for each object $A \in Ob_C$, an identity morphism $id_A \in Mor_C(A, A)$,*

such that the following conditions hold:

1. *Associativity. For all objects $A, B, C, D \in Ob_C$ and morphisms $f : A \to B$, $g : B \to C$ and $h : C \to D$, it holds that $(h \circ g) \circ f = h \circ (g \circ f)$.*
2. *Identity. For all objects $A, B \in Ob_C$ and morphisms $f : A \to B$, it holds that $f \circ id_A = f$ and $id_B \circ f = f$.*

Remark A.2. Instead of $f \in Mor_C(A, B)$, we write $f : A \to B$ and leave out the index for the composition operation, since it is clear which one to use. For such a morphism f, A is called its domain and B its codomain.

Example A.3 (categories).

1. The basic example of a category is the category **Sets**,, with the object class of all sets and with all functions $f : A \to B$ as morphisms. The composition is defined for $f : A \to B$ and $g : B \to C$ by $(g \circ f)(x) = g(f(x))$ for all $x \in A$, and the identity is the identical mapping $id_A : A \to A : x \mapsto x$.

2. Another category based on sets is the category **Rels**, where the objects are sets and the morphisms are relations $R \subseteq A \times B$ between two sets. The composition is defined for $R \subseteq A \times B$ and $Q \subseteq B \times C$ by $(a, c) \in Q \circ R \Leftrightarrow \exists b \in B : (a, b) \in R \wedge (b, c) \in Q$. The identity on a set A is the diagonal relation $\Delta_A = \{(a, a) \mid a \in A\}$.

3. The category **Posets** consists of partially ordered sets as objects, i.e. tuples (M, O) of a set M and a relation $O \subseteq M \times M$ that is reflexive, antisymmetric, and transitive; a morphism $f : (M_1, O_1) \to (M_2, O_2)$ is a mapping $f : M_1 \to M_2$ that is order-preserving, i.e. $(x, y) \in O_1 \Rightarrow (f(x), f(y)) \in O_2$. Composition and the identities are the same as in **Sets**.

4. The class of all graphs (as defined in Definition 2.1) as objects and the class of all graph morphisms (see Definition 2.4) form the category **Graphs**; the composition is given in Fact 2.5 and the identities are the pairwise identities on nodes and edges.

5. Typed graphs and typed graph morphisms (see Section 2.2) form the category **Graphs$_{TG}$** (see Example A.6).

6. The category **Alg(Σ)** has as its objects algebras over a given signature Σ, and the morphisms are homomorphisms between these Σ-algebras. The composition is defined componentwise for homomorphisms, and the identities are componentwise identities on the carrier sets (see Appendix B).

$\square$

A.2 Construction of Categories, and Duality

There are various ways to construct new categories from given ones. The first way that we describe here is the Cartesian product of two categories, which is defined by the Cartesian products of the class of objects and the sets of morphisms with componentwise composition and identities.

Definition A.4 (product category). *Given two categories* **C** *and* **D**, *the product category* **C** $\times$ **D** *is defined by*

- $Ob_{C \times D} = Ob_C \times Ob_D$;
- $Mor_{C \times D}((A, A'), (B, B')) = Mor_C(A, B) \times Mor_D(A', B')$;
- *for morphisms* $f : A \to B$, $g : B \to C \in Mor_C$ *and* $f' : A' \to B'$, $g' : B' \to C' \in Mor_D$, *we define* $(g, g') \circ (f, f') = (g \circ f, g' \circ f')$;

- $id_{(A,A')} = (id_A, id_{A'})$.

Another construction is that of a slice or a coslice category. Here the objects are morphisms of a category $\mathbf{C}$, to or from a distinguished object X, respectively. The morphisms are morphisms in $\mathbf{C}$ that connect the object morphisms so as to lead to commutative diagrams.

Definition A.5 (slice category). *Given a category $\mathbf{C}$ and an object $X \in Ob_C$, then the slice category $\mathbf{C}\backslash X$ is defined as follows:*

- $Ob_{C\backslash X} = \{f : A \to X \mid A \in Ob_C, f \in Mor_C(A, X)\}$,
- $Mor_{C\backslash X}(f : A \to X, g : B \to X) = \{m : A \to B \mid g \circ m = f\}$,
- *for morphisms $m \in Mor_{C\backslash X}(f : A \to X, g : B \to X)$ and $n \in Mor_{C\backslash X}(g : B \to X, h : C \to X)$, we have $n \circ m$ as defined in $\mathbf{C}$ for $m : A \to B$ and $n : B \to C$:*

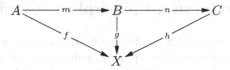

- $id_{f:A\to X} = id_A \in Mor_C$.

Example A.6 (slice category Graphs$_{\mathbf{TG}}$). *Given a type graph TG, the category $\mathbf{Graphs_{TG}}$ can be considered as the slice category $\mathbf{Graphs}\backslash TG$. Each typed graph is represented in this slice category by its typing morphism, and the typed graph morphisms are exactly the morphisms in the slice category.* □

Definition A.7 (coslice category). *Given a category $\mathbf{C}$ and an object $X \in Ob_C$, then the coslice category $X\backslash\mathbf{C}$ is defined as follows:*

- $Ob_{X\backslash C} = \{f : X \to A \mid A \in Ob_C, f \in Mor_C(X, A)\}$;
- $Mor_{X\backslash C}(f : X \to A, g : X \to B) = \{m : A \to B \mid g = m \circ f\}$;
- *for morphisms $m \in Mor_{X\backslash C}(f : X \to A, g : X \to B)$ and $n \in Mor_{X\backslash C}(g : X \to B, h : X \to C)$, we have $n \circ m$ as defined in $\mathbf{C}$ for $m : A \to B$ and $n : B \to C$:*

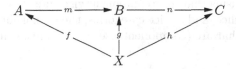

- $id_{f:X\to A} = id_A \in Mor_C$.

As the last construction in this section, we introduce the dual category. For the dual category, we use the objects of a given category, but reverse all arrows, i.e. morphisms.

Definition A.8 (dual category). *Given a category* **C***, the* dual category **C**^{op} *is defined by*

- $OB_{C^{op}} = Ob_C$;
- $Mor_{C^{op}}(A, B) = Mor_C(B, A)$;
- $f \circ^{C^{op}} g = g \circ^C f$ *for all* $f : A \to B$, $g : B \to C$;
- $id_A^{C^{op}} = id_A^C$ *for all* $A \in Ob_{C^{op}}$.

The *duality principle* asserts that for each construction (statement) there is a dual construction. If a statement holds in all categories, then the dual statement holds in all categories too. Some examples of dual constructions are monomorphisms and epimorphisms, pushouts and pullbacks, and initial and final objects, which will be described in the following sections.

A.3 Monomorphisms, Epimorphisms, and Isomorphisms

In this section, we consider a category **C** and analyze some important types of morphisms, namely monomorphisms, epimorphisms, and isomorphisms.

Intuitively speaking two objects are isomorphic if they have the same structure. Morphisms that preserve this structure are called isomorphisms.

Definition A.9 (isomorphism). *A morphism* $i : A \to B$ *is called an* isomorphism *if there exists a morphism* $i^{-1} : B \to A$ *such that* $i \circ i^{-1} = id_B$ *and* $i^{-1} \circ i = id_A$:

$$A \underset{i^{-1}}{\overset{i}{\rightleftarrows}} B$$

Two objects A *and* B *are isomorphic, written* $A \cong B$, *if there is an isomorphism* $i : A \to B$.

Remark A.10. If i is an isomorphism, then i is both a monomorphisms and an epimorphism. For every isomorphism i, the inverse morphism i^{-1} is unique.

Example A.11 (isomorphisms).

- In **Sets**, **Graphs**, **Graphs**_{TG}, and **Alg(Σ)**, the isomorphisms are exactly those morphisms that are (componentwise) injective and surjective.
- In product, slice, and coslice categories, the isomorphisms are exactly those morphisms that are (componentwise) isomorphisms in the underlying category.

□

Definition A.12 (monomorphism and epimorphism). *Given a category* **C***, a morphism* $m : B \to C$ *is called a* monomorphism *if, for all morphisms* $f, g : A \to B \in Mor_C$, *it holds that* $m \circ f = m \circ g \Rightarrow f = g$:

$$A \underset{g}{\overset{f}{\rightrightarrows}} B \xrightarrow{m} C$$

A morphism $e : A \to B \in Mor_C$ *is called an* epimorphism *if, for all morphisms* $f, g : B \to C \in Mor_C$, *it holds that* $f \circ e = g \circ e \Rightarrow f = g$:

$$A \xrightarrow{\quad e \quad} B \overset{f}{\underset{g}{\rightrightarrows}} C$$

Remark A.13. Monomorphisms and epimorphisms are dual notions, i.e. a monomorphism in a category $\mathbf{C}$ is an epimorphism in the dual category $\mathbf{C}^{\mathrm{op}}$ and vice versa.

Fact A.14 (monomorphisms and epimorphisms).

- *In* **Sets**, *the monomorphisms are all injective mappings, and the epimorphisms are all surjective mappings.*
- *In* **Graphs** *and* **Graphs$_{\mathbf{TG}}$**, *the monomorphisms and epimorphisms are exactly those morphisms that are injective and surjective, respectively.*
- *In* **Alg(Σ)**, *the monomorphisms are the injective homomorphisms. Injective homomorphisms are componentwise injective. Analogously, the epimorphisms are the surjective homomorphisms, which means that they are componentwise surjective.*
- *In a product category* $\mathbf{C} \times \mathbf{D}$, *monomorphisms and epimorphisms are componentwise monomorphisms and epimorphisms in* $\mathbf{C}$ *and* $\mathbf{D}$, *respectively.*
- *In a slice category, the monomorphisms are exactly the monomorphisms of the underlying category. The epimorphisms of the underlying category are epimorphisms in the slice category, but not necessarily vice versa.*
- *In a coslice category, the epimorphisms are exactly the epimorphisms of the underlying category. The monomorphisms of the underlying category are monomorphisms in the slice category, but not necessarily vice versa.*

Proof. For **Sets**, **Graphs**, and **Graphs$_{\mathbf{TG}}$**, the above characterization of monomorphisms, epimorphisms, and isomorphisms have been proven explicitly in Fact 2.15. These proofs can be extended to **Alg(Σ)**. For product, slice, and coslice categories, the results stated above can be shown directly from the definitions. However, the characterization of epimorphisms in slice categories and of monomorphisms in coslice categories is an open problem. □

In general, a factorization of a morphism decomposes it into morphisms with special properties. In an epi–mono factorization, these morphisms are an epimorphism and a monomorphism.

Definition A.15 (epi–mono and (weak) $\mathcal{E}$–$\mathcal{M}$ factorizations). *Given a category* $\mathbf{C}$ *and morphisms* $f : A \to B$, $e : A \to C$, *and* $m : C \to B$ *with* $m \circ e = f$, *if* e *is an epimorphism and* m *is a monomorphism then* e *and* m *are called an* epi–mono factorization *of* f:

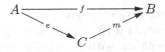

*If for every morphism f we can find such morphisms e and m, with f = m∘e, and this decomposition is unique up to isomorphism, then the category **C** is said to have an epi–mono factorization.*

*   **C** has an $\mathcal{E}$–$\mathcal{M}$ factorization for given morphism classes $\mathcal{E}$ and $\mathcal{M}$ if for each f there is a decomposition, unique up to isomorphism, f = m ∘ e with e ∈ $\mathcal{E}$ and m ∈ $\mathcal{M}$. Usually $\mathcal{E}$ is a subclass of epimorphisms and $\mathcal{M}$ is a subclass of monomorphisms.*

*   If we require only f = m ∘ e with e ∈ $\mathcal{E}$ and m ∈ $\mathcal{M}$, but not necessarily uniqueness up to isomorphism, we have a weak $\mathcal{E}$–$\mathcal{M}$ factorization.*

The categories **Sets**, **Graphs**, **Graphs$_{TG}$**, and **Alg(Σ)** have epi–mono factorizations.

Definition A.16 (jointly epimorphic). *A morphism pair (e_1, e_2) with e_i : $A_i \to B$ $(i = 1, 2)$ is called* jointly epimorphic *if, for all $g, h : B \to C$ with $g \circ e_i = h \circ e_i$ for $i = 1, 2$, we have $g = h$.*

In the categories **Sets**, **Graphs**, **Graphs$_{TG}$**, and **Alg(Σ)**, "jointly epimorphic" means "jointly surjective".

A.4 Pushouts and Pullbacks

Intuitively, a pushout is an object that emerges from gluing two objects along a common subobject. In addition, we introduce the dual concept of a pullback and the construction of both in specific categories.

Definition A.17 (pushout). *Given morphisms $f : A \to B$ and $g : A \to C \in Mor_C$, a* pushout (D, f', g') over f and g *is defined by*

- *a pushout object D and*
- *morphisms $f' : C \to D$ and $g' : B \to D$ with $f' \circ g = g' \circ f$,*

such that the following universal property is fulfilled: for all objects X with morphisms $h : B \to X$ and $k : C \to X$ with $k \circ g = h \circ f$, there is a unique morphism $x : D \to X$ such that $x \circ g' = h$ and $x \circ f' = k$:

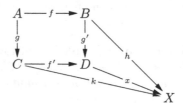

Remark A.18 (pushout object). The pushout object D is unique up to isomorphism. This means that if (X, k, h) is also a pushout over f and g, then $x : D \xrightarrow{\sim} X$ is an isomorphism with $x \circ g' = h$ and $x \circ f' = k$. Vice versa, if (D, f', g') is a pushout over f and g and $x : D \xrightarrow{\sim} X$ is an isomorphism, then (X, k, h) is also a pushout over f and g, where $k = x \circ f'$ and $h = x \circ g'$. Uniqueness up to isomorphism follows directly from the corresponding universal properties (see Fact 2.20).

Fact A.19 (pushout constructions).

1. In **Sets**, a pushout over morphisms $f : A \to B$ and $g : A \to C$ can be constructed as follows. Let

$$\sim_{f,g} = t(\{(a_1, a_2) \in A \times A \mid f(a_1) = f(a_2) \vee g(a_1) = g(a_2)\})$$

be the transitive closure of $Kern(f)$ and $Kern(g)$; $\sim_{f,g}$ is an equivalence relation. We define the object D and the morphisms as:

- $D = A|_{\sim_{f,g}} \dot{\cup} B \backslash f(A) \dot{\cup} C \backslash g(A)$,

- $f' : C \to D : x \mapsto \begin{cases} [a] & : & \exists a \in A : g(a) = x \\ x & : & otherwise \end{cases}$,

- $g' : B \to D : x \mapsto \begin{cases} [a] & : & \exists a \in A : f(a) = x \\ x & : & otherwise \end{cases}$.

2. In **Graphs** and **Graphs$_{\mathbf{TG}}$**, pushouts can be constructed componentwise in **Sets**.

3. In **Alg(Σ)**, pushouts over arbitrary morphisms exist. However, in general, the pushouts cannot be constructed componentwise.

4. If the categories **C** and **D** have pushouts, the pushouts in the product category can be constructed componentwise.

5. If the category **C** has pushouts, the pushouts in the slice category **C**$\backslash X$ can be constructed over the pushouts in **C**. Given objects $f : A \to X$, $g : B \to X$, and $h : C \to X$, and morphisms m and n in **C**$\backslash X$ as in (1) below, it holds that $g \circ m = f = h \circ n$ by the definition of morphisms in **C**$\backslash X$. We construct the pushout (2) in **C** over $C \xleftarrow{n} A \xrightarrow{m} B$. From (2), we obtain the induced morphism $d : D \to X$ as the pushout object, and morphisms s and t with $d \circ s = g$ and $d \circ t = h$, leading to the pushout (1) in **C**$\backslash X$:

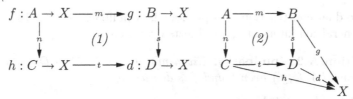

This construction works analogously for the coslice category $X \backslash \mathbf{C}$.

Proof idea. The construction of a pushout in **Sets** is equivalent to that given in Fact 2.17. For **Graphs** and **Graphs$_{\mathbf{TG}}$**, pushouts can be constructed componentwise in **Sets** for nodes and edges, respectively. The source and target functions are uniquely determined by the universal pushout properties. For more details concerning $\mathbf{Alg}(\Sigma)$, we refer to [EM85], but we do not give an explicit proof here. For product, slice, and coslice categories, the proofs can be obtained directly from the constructions. □

In various situations, we need a reverse construction of a pushout. This is called the pushout complement.

Definition A.20 (pushout complement). *Given morphisms $f : A \to B$ and $n : B \to D$, then $A \xrightarrow{m} C \xrightarrow{g} D$ is the pushout complement of f and n if (1) below is a pushout:*

$$
\begin{array}{ccc}
A & \xrightarrow{\ f\ } & B \\
\downarrow{\scriptstyle m} & (1) & \downarrow{\scriptstyle n} \\
C & \xrightarrow{\ g\ } & D
\end{array}
$$

Pushout squares can be decomposed if the first square is a pushout, and can be composed, preserving their pushout properties.

Lemma A.21 (pushout composition and decomposition). *Given the following commutative diagram,*

$$
\begin{array}{ccccc}
A & \longrightarrow & B & \longrightarrow & E \\
\downarrow & (1) & \downarrow & (2) & \downarrow \\
C & \longrightarrow & D & \longrightarrow & F
\end{array}
$$

then the following hold:

- Pushout composition. *If (1) and (2) are pushouts, then (1) + (2) is also a pushout.*
- Pushout decomposition. *If (1) and (1) + (2) are pushouts, then (2) is also a pushout.*

Proof. See Fact 2.20. □

The dual construction of a pushout is a pullback. Pullbacks can be seen as a generalized intersection of objects over a common object.

Definition A.22 (pullback). *Given morphisms $f : C \to D$ and $g : B \to D$, a pullback (A, f', g') over f and g is defined by*

- *a pullback object A and*
- *morphisms $f' : A \to B$ and $g' : A \to C$ with $g \circ f' = f \circ g'$,*

such that the following universal property is fulfilled: for all objects X with morphisms $h : X \to B$ and $k : X \to C$, with $f \circ k = g \circ h$, there is a unique morphism $x : X \to A$ such that $f' \circ x = h$ and $g' \circ x = k$:

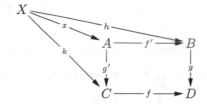

Fact A.23 (pullback constructions).

1. *In* **Sets***, the pullback* $C \xleftarrow{\pi_g} A \xrightarrow{\pi_f} B$ *over morphisms* $f : C \to D$ *and* $g : B \to D$ *is constructed by* $A = \bigcup_{d \in D} f^{-1}(d) \times g^{-1}(d)$ *with morphisms* $f' : A \to B : (x, y) \mapsto y$ *and* $g' : A \to C : (x, y) \mapsto x$.
2. *In* **Graphs** *and* **Graphs$_{TG}$***, pullbacks can be constructed componentwise in* **Sets***.*
3. *In* **Alg**(Σ)*, for given morphisms* $f : C \to D$ *and* $g : B \to D$*, the carrier sets of the pullback object* A *and the morphisms can be constructed componentwise for all* $s \in S$*. For an operation* $op : s_1 \ldots s_2 \to s \in OP$*, we define* $op_A((x_1, y_1), \ldots (x_n, y_n)) = (op_C(x_1, \ldots, x_n), op_B(y_1, \ldots, y_n))$*.*
4. *In a product, slice, or coslice category, the construction of pullbacks is dual to the construction of pushouts if the underlying categories have pullbacks.*

Proof idea. The proof for **Sets** is given in Fact 2.23 and can be extended componentwise to **Graphs** and **Graphs$_{TG}$**, where the source and target functions are uniquely determined by the universal pullback properties. For **Alg**(Σ), the componentwise construction described above can be shown to satisfy the pullback properties. The results for product, slice, and coslice categories follow by duality from Fact A.19.   □

In the following, we present a category where general pullbacks exist, but cannot be constructed componentwise.

Fact A.24 (pullbacks in PTNets). *The category* **PTNets** *has pullbacks.*

Construction. In contrast to pushouts, the construction of pullbacks in **PTNets** cannot be done componentwise for places and transitions in general (see Example 4.23). If, however, at least one of the given morphisms is injective, then the construction can be done componentwise (see Fact 4.21). If both morphisms are noninjective, the places of pullbacks for **PTNets** are constructed as pullbacks in **Sets** (see Remark 4.21), but the construction for the transitions is quite complicated, as shown below.

Given Petri nets B, C, D with $X = (P_X, T_X, pre_X, post_X)$ for $X = B, C, D$, we assume, without loss of generality, that $P_D = \{p_1, \ldots, p_d\}$ and define $p_i \leq p_j \Leftrightarrow i \leq j$. For given Petri net morphisms $f : B \to D$ and $g : C \to D$, we want to construct the pullback object $A = (P_A, T_A, pre_A, post_A)$ and morphisms $f' : A \to C$ and $g' : A \to B$.

We define $P_A := \{(i, j) \in P_B \times P_C \mid f(i) = g(j)\}$ as the pullback in **Sets** over the places.

Consider $t \in T_D$ and a tuple $(t_B, t_C) \in T_B \times T_C$ with $f(t_B) = t$ and $g(t_C) = t$.

Without loss of generality, let $pre_D(t) = \sum_{k=1}^{n} \bar{p}_k$ and $post_D(t) = \sum_{k=1}^{m} \bar{p}_{n+k}$ with $\bar{p}_k \in P_D$ for $k = 1, \ldots, m+n$, and $\bar{p}_k \leq \bar{p}_{k+1}$ for $k = 1, \ldots, n-1$ and $k = n+1, \ldots, m+n-1$.

We define a set of lists of possible matches for the preplaces and postplaces

$$L_{(t_B, t_C)} = \{((i_k, j_k)_{k=1,\ldots,n+m}) \subseteq P_A^{n+m} \mid f(i_k) = \bar{p}_k, \sum_{k=1}^{n} i_k = pre_B(t_B),$$

$$\sum_{k=1}^{n} j_k = pre_C(t_C), \sum_{k=1}^{m} i_{n+k} = post_B(t_B), \sum_{k=1}^{m} j_{n+k} = post_C(t_C)\}.$$

We define the relation $\sim_{(t_B, t_C)}$ on $L_{(t_B, t_C)}$ by $((i_k^1, j_k^1)) \sim_{(t_B, t_C)} ((i_k^2, j_k^2))$ if

1. for $l_1, l_2 \in \{1, \ldots, n\}$, we have $\bar{p}_{l_1} = \bar{p}_{l_2}$, $(i_{l_1}^1, j_{l_1}^1) = (i_{l_2}^2, j_{l_2}^2)$, $(i_{l_2}^1, j_{l_2}^1) = (i_{l_1}^2, j_{l_1}^2)$, and $(i_k^1, j_k^1) = (i_k^2, j_k^2)$ for $k \neq l_1, l_2$;
2. for $l_1, l_2 \in \{n+1, \ldots, n+m\}$, we have $\bar{p}_{l_1} = \bar{p}_{l_2}$, $(i_{l_1}^1, j_{l_1}^1) = (i_{l_2}^2, j_{l_2}^2)$, $(i_{l_2}^1, j_{l_2}^1) = (i_{l_1}^2, j_{l_1}^2)$, and $(i_k^1, j_k^1) = (i_k^2, j_k^2)$ for $k \neq l_1, l_2$;

and the equivalence relation $\equiv_{(t_B, t_C)}$ on $L_{(t_B, t_C)}$ is the transitive closure of $\sim_{(t_B, t_C)}$.

Now $T_A := \{t_{[l]}^{(t_B, t_C)} \mid t \in T_D, (t_B, t_C) \in T_B \times T_C, f(t_B) = g(t_C) = t, [l] \in L_{(t_B, t_C)}|_{\equiv_{(t_B, t_C)}}\}$, $pre_A(t_{[((i_k, j_k))]}^{(t_B, t_C)}) = \sum_{k=1}^{n} (i_k, j_k)$, and $post_A(t_{[((i_k, j_k))]}^{(t_B, t_C)}) = \sum_{k=1}^{m} (i_{n+k}, j_{n+k})$.

With this definition, the preplaces and postplaces of $t_{[l_1]}^{(t_B, t_C)}$ and $t_{[l_2]}^{(t_B, t_C)}$ are exactly the same iff $[l_1] = [l_2]$.

For the morphism f', we define $f_P'((i, j)) = j$ and $f_T'(t_{[l]}^{(t_B, t_C)}) = t_C$, and, analogously, $g_P'((i, j)) = i$ and $g_T'(t_{[l]}^{(t_B, t_C)}) = t_B$.   □

Proof. **1. Well-definedness and commutativity.** A is well defined, since pre_A and $post_A$ are well defined.

f' is well defined, because for all $t_{[((i_k, j_k))]}^{(t_B, t_C)} \in T_A$ we have:

- $f_P'^{\oplus}(pre_A(t_{[((i_k, j_k))]}^{(t_B, t_C)})) = f_P'^{\oplus}(\sum_{k=1}^{n} (i_k, j_k)) = \sum_{k=1}^{n} f_P'(i_k, j_k) = \sum_{k=1}^{n} j_k = prec(t_C) = prec(f_T'(t_{[((i_k, j_k))]}^{(t_B, t_C)}))$;

- $f_P'^{\oplus}(post_A(t_{[((i_k, j_k))]}^{(t_B, t_C)})) = f_P'^{\oplus}(\sum_{k=1}^{m} (i_{n+k}, j_{n+k})) = \sum_{k=1}^{m} f_P'(i_{n+k}, j_{n+k}) = \sum_{k=1}^{m} j_{n+k} = post_C(t_C) = post_C(f_T'(t_{[((i_k, j_k))]}^{(t_B, t_C)}))$.

The well-definedness of g' follows analogously.

Now we have, for all $(i,j) \in P_A$, the result that $g_P(f'_P(i,j)) = g_P(j) = f_P(i) = f_P(g'_P(i,j))$, and for all $t^{(t_B,t_C)}_{[((i_k,j_k))]} \in T_A$, $g_T(f'_T(t^{(t_B,t_C)}_{[((i_k,j_k))]})) = g_T(t_C) = t = f_T(t_B) = f_T(g'_T(t^{(t_B,t_C)}_{[((i_k,j_k))]}))$. Therefore the diagram commutes.

2. Pullback properties. Given a Petri net X and morphisms $h : X \to B$, $l : X \to C$ with $g \circ l = f \circ h$, we have to show that there exists a unique morphism $x : X \to A$ with $f' \circ x = l$ and $g' \circ x = h$.

Suppose that $P_X = \{q_1,\ldots,q_x\}$ such that $f_P(h_P(q_k)) \leq f_P(h_P(q_{k+1}))$ with respect to the order on P_D defined above, and we define $q_i \leq q_j \Leftrightarrow i \leq j$ analogously. This order is not unique if f or g is not injective.

Now we define $x_P(q) = (h_P(q), l_P(q))$; and, for $t_X \in T_X$, where $h_T(t_X) = t_B$, $l_T(t_X) = t_C$, $g(t_C) = T$, $pre_X(t_X) = \sum_{k=1}^{n} \bar{q}_k$, and $post_X(t_X) = \sum_{k=1}^{m} \bar{q}_{n+k}$, with $\bar{q}_k \in P_X$ for $k = 1,\ldots,m+n$ and $\bar{q}_k \leq \bar{q}_{k+1}$ for $k = 1,\ldots,n-1$ and $k = n+1,\ldots,m+n-1$, we define $x_T(t_X) = t^{(t_B,t_C)}_{[((h_P(\bar{q}_k),l_P(\bar{q}_k))]}$.

Then $x^{\oplus}_P(pre_X(t_X)) = x^{\oplus}_P(\sum_{k=1}^{n} \bar{q}_k) = \sum_{k=1}^{n} x_P(\bar{q}_k) = \sum_{k=1}^{n} (h_P(\bar{q}_k), l_P(\bar{q}_k)) = pre_A(t^{(t_B,t_C)}_{[((h_P(\bar{q}_k),l_P(\bar{q}_k))]}) = pre_A(x_T(t_X))$ and $x^{\oplus}_P(post_X(t_X)) = x^{\oplus}_P(\sum_{k=1}^{m} \bar{q}_{n+k}) = \sum_{k=1}^{m} x_P(\bar{q}_{n+k}) = \sum_{k=1}^{m} (h_P(\bar{q}_{n+k}), l_P(\bar{q}_{n+k})) = post_A(t^{(t_B,t_C)}_{[((h_P(\bar{q}_k),l_P(\bar{q}_k))]}) = post_A(x_T(t_X))$.

For the well-definedness of x, we have to show that $(h_P(\bar{q}_k), l_P(\bar{q}_k)) \in L_{(t_B,t_C)}$. We check the necessary properties:

- We know that $f^{\oplus}_P(h^{\oplus}_P(pre_X(t_X))) = \sum_{k=1}^{n} f_P(h_P(\bar{q}_k)) = \sum_{k=1}^{n} \bar{p}_k$. Since $\bar{p}_k \leq \bar{p}_{k+1}$, $\bar{q}_k \leq \bar{q}_{k+1}$, and $f_P(h_P(\bar{q}_k)) \leq f_P(h_P(\bar{q}_{k+1}))$, it follows that $f_P(h_P(\bar{q}_k)) = \bar{p}_k$ for $k = 1,\ldots,n$. Analogously, $f_P(h_P(\bar{q}_{n+k})) = \bar{p}_{n+k}$ for $k = 1,\ldots,m$.

- $\sum_{k=1}^{n} h_P(\bar{q}_k) = h^{\oplus}_P(\sum_{k=1}^{n} \bar{q}_k) = h^{\oplus}_P(pre_X(t_X)) = pre_B(h_T(t_X)) = pre_B(t_B)$.

- $\sum_{k=1}^{n} l_P(\bar{q}_k) = l^{\oplus}_P(\sum_{k=1}^{n} \bar{q}_k) = l^{\oplus}_P(pre_X(t_X)) = pre_C(l_T(t_X)) = pre_C(t_C)$.

- Analogously for $post$.

The equivalence class for t_X is independent of the chosen order on P_X, i.e. if $f_P(h_P(\bar{q}_k)) \leq f_P(h_P(\bar{q}_{k+1}))$, exchanging the roles of $\bar{q}_k$ and $\bar{q}_{k+1}$ leads to an exchange of $((h_P(\bar{q}_k), l_P(\bar{q}_k)))$ and $((h_P(\bar{q}_{k+1}), l_P(\bar{q}_{k+1})))$ and therefore to the same equivalence class.

We then have $f'_P(x_P(q)) = f'_P(h_P(q), l_P(q)) = l_P(q)$ and $f'_P(x_P(t_X)) = f'_P(t^{(h_T(tx),l_T(tx))}_{[l]}) = l_T(t_X)$, which means that $f' \circ x = l$. Analogously, $g'_P(x_P(q)) = g'_P(h_P(q), l_P(q)) = h_P(q)$ and $g'_P(x_P(t_X)) = g'_P(t^{(h_T(tx),l_T(tx))}_{[l]}) = h_T(t_X)$, and therefore $g' \circ x = h$.

Now we show that x is unique. For any $x' : X \to A$ with $f' \circ x' = l$ and $g' \circ x' = h$, we have the following:

- Let $x'_P(q) = (i, j)$. Since $l_P(q) = f'_P(x'_P(q)) = f'_P(i, j) = j$ and $h_P(q) = g'_P(x'_P(q)) = g'_P(i, j) = i$, we have $x'(q) = (i, j) = (h_P(q), l_P(q)) = x_P(q)$.
- For $x_T(t_X) = g_T(l_T(t_X))^{(h_T(t_X), l_T(t_X))}_{[((h_P(\bar{q}_k), l_P(\bar{q}_k)))]}$ and $x'(t_X) = t^{(t_B, t_C)}_{[s]}$, we have:

  1. $l_T(t_X) = f'_T(x'_T(t_X)) = f'(t^{(t_B, t_C)}_{[l]}) = t_C$.
  2. $h_T(t_X) = g'_T(x'_T(t_X)) = g'(t^{(t_B, t_C)}_{[l]}) = t_B$.
  3. $g_T(l_T(t_X)) = g_T(t_C) = t$.
  4. Suppose that $[s] \neq [((h_P(\bar{q}_k), l_P(\bar{q}_k)))]$; then $x(t_X) \neq x'(t_X)$, but we have the same preplaces and postplaces (defined by x_P), which is a contradiction.

It follows that $x = x'$.   □

Pullback squares can be decomposed if the last square is a pushout, and can be composed, preserving their pullback properties.

Lemma A.25 (pullback composition and decomposition). *Given the following commutative diagram,*

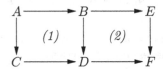

then the following hold:

- Pullback composition. *If (1) and (2) are pullbacks, then (1) + (2) is also a pullback.*
- Pullback decomposition. *If (2) and (1) + (2) are pullbacks, then (1) is also a pullback.*

Proof. See Fact 2.27.   □

A.5 Binary Coproducts and Initial Objects

Binary coproducts can be seen as a generalization of the disjoint union of sets and graphs in a categorical framework. Analogously, initial objects are the categorical representation of the empty set and the empty graph. Note, however, that the construction of binary coproducts and initial objects of algebras is much more difficult.

Definition A.26 (binary coproduct). *Given two objects $A, B \in Ob_C$, the binary coproduct $(A + B, i_A, i_B)$ is given by*

- *a coproduct object $A + B$ and*
- *morphisms $i_A : A \to A + B$ and $i_B : B \to A + B$,*

such that the following universal property is fulfilled: for all objects X with morphisms $f : A \to X$ and $g : B \to X$, there is a morphism $[f, g] : A + B \to X$ such that $[f, g] \circ i_A = f$ and $[f, g] \circ i_B = g$:

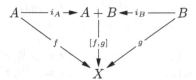

Remark A.27. Given two morphisms $f : A \to A'$ and $g : B \to B'$, there is a unique coproduct morphism $f + g : A + B \to A' + B'$, induced by the binary coproduct $A + B$ and the morphisms $i_{A'} \circ f$ and $i_{B'} \circ g$:

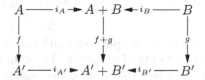

Example A.28 (binary coproduct constructions).

- In **Sets**, the coproduct object $A + B$ is the disjoint union $A \overset{\cdot}{\cup} B$ of A and B, and i_A and i_B are inclusions. For $A \cap B = \varnothing$, we use the representation $A \overset{\cdot}{\cup} B = A \cup B$, and for $A \cap B \neq \varnothing$, we use $A \overset{\cdot}{\cup} B = A \times \{1\} \cup B \times \{2\}$.
- In **Graphs** and **Graphs$_{\mathbf{TG}}$**, the coproduct can be constructed componentwise in **Sets**.
- In a product or slice category, coproducts can be constructed componentwise if the underlying categories have coproducts.
- In a coslice category, the coproduct of objects $f : X \to A$ and $g : X \to B$ is constructed as the pushout of f and g in the underlying category.

$\square$

In the following, we give an example where binary coproducts exist, but in general cannot be constructed componentwise in **Sets**.

Construction (binary coproducts in $\mathbf{Alg}(\Sigma)$). Given a signature $\Sigma = (S, OP)$ and objects $A, B \in \mathbf{Alg}(\Sigma)$, for the construction of the coproduct $A + B$ we extend Σ to a signature $\Sigma(A + B) = (S, OP \overset{\cdot}{\cup} OP_A \overset{\cdot}{\cup} OP_B)$, where $OP_A = \{x^A :\to s \mid s \in S, x \in A_s\}$ and $OP_B = \{x^B :\to s \mid s \in S, x \in B_s\}$.

Consider the set of equations $E = \{(t, t') \mid s \in S, t, t' \in T_{\Sigma(A+B),s} : eval_{A,s}(t) = eval_{A,s}(t')\} \cup \{(t, t') \mid s \in S, t, t' \in T_{\Sigma(A+B),s} : eval_{B,s}(t) = eval_{B,s}(t')\}$ over the term algebra $T_{\Sigma(A+B)}$ with $eval_i(x^i) = x$ for $x^i :\to s \in OP_i$, $i = A, B$. This results in a specification $SPEC = (\Sigma(A + B), E)$.

We then define the coproduct object of A and B by $A + B = T_{SPEC}|_\Sigma$ and the morphism families $i_{A,s} : A_s \to (A + B)_s : x \mapsto [x^A]$ and $i_{B,s} : B_s \to (A + B)_s : x \mapsto [x^B]$.

For morphisms $f : A \to X$ and $g : B \to X$, the induced morphism $[f, g] : A + B \to X$ is defined by

$$[f, g]_s([t]) = \begin{cases} op_X([f, g]_{s_1}([t_1]), & : t = op(t_1, \ldots, t_n), \\ \ldots, [f, g]_{s_n}([t_n])) & op : s_1 \ldots s_n \to s \in OP \\ c_X & : t = c, c :\to s \in OP \\ f_s(x) & : t = [x^A], x^A :\to s \in OP_A \\ g_s(x) & : t = [x^B], x^B :\to s \in OP_B \end{cases}.$$

This definition guarantees that $[f, g]$ preserves the operations and the uniqueness of $[f, g]$.

For $a \in A_s$, we have the result that $[f, g]_s(i_{A,s}(a)) = [f, g]_s([a^A]) = f_s(a)$ and, analogously, $[f, g]_s(i_{B,s}(b)) = g_s(b)$ for all $b \in B_s$; therefore $[f, g] \circ i_A = f$ and $[f, g] \circ i_B = g$. $\qquad \square$

The following lemma combines pushouts and binary coproducts in a category. It is used in the proof of the Parallelism Theorem (Theorem 5.18) and is called Butterfly Lemma in [Kre78] because the pushouts (1)–(3) below have the shape of a butterfly.

Lemma A.29 (Butterfly Lemma). *Consider a category with pushouts and binary coproducts. We then have:*

1. *If (1), (2), and (3) below are pushouts with $e_1 = d_1 \circ b_1$, $e_2 = d_2 \circ b_2$, and $c = d_1 \circ c_1 = d_2 \circ c_2$, then (4) is also a pushout.*
2. *Given that (4) is a pushout and given morphisms $f_1 : A_1 \to B_1$ and $f_2 : A_2 \to B_2$, then there exists a decomposition into diagrams (1)–(3) such that (1), (2), and (3) are pushouts with $e_1 = d_1 \circ b_1$, $e_2 = d_2 \circ b_2$, and $c = d_1 \circ c_1 = d_2 \circ c_2$:*

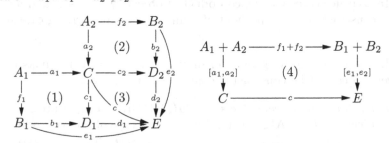

Proof.

1. Given the pushouts (1), (2), and (3) with $e_1 = d_1 \circ b_1$, $e_2 = d_2 \circ b_2$, and $c = d_1 \circ c_1 = d_2 \circ c_2$, consider an object X and morphisms $h : C \to X$ and $k : B_1 + B_2 \to X$ with $h \circ [a_1, a_2] = k \circ (f_1 + f_2)$:

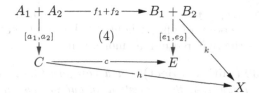

Comparing pushout (1) with the morphisms h and $k \circ i_{B_1}$, where $h \circ a_1 = h \circ [a_1, a_2] \circ i_{A_1} = k \circ (f_1 + f_2) \circ i_{A_2} = k \circ i_{B_1} \circ f_1$, we obtain a unique morphism $x_1 : D_1 \to X$, where $x_1 \circ c_1 = h$ and $x_1 \circ b_1 = k \circ i_{B_1}$. Analogously, we obtain from pushout (2) a unique morphism $x_2 : D_2 \to X$, where $x_2 \circ c_2 = h$ and $x_2 \circ b_2 = k \circ i_{B_2}$:

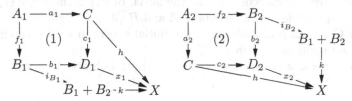

Now $x_1 \circ c_1 = h = x_2 \circ c_2$, and we obtain from pushout (3) a unique morphism $x : E \to X$, where $x \circ d_1 = x_1$ and $x \circ d_2 = x_2$.

From $x \circ e_1 = x \circ d_1 \circ b_1 = x_1 \circ b_1 = k$ and $x \circ e_2 = x \circ d_2 \circ b_2 = x_2 \circ b_2 = k$, it follows that $x \circ [e_1, e_2] = k$, and we have $x \circ c = x \circ d_2 \circ c_2 = x_2 \circ c_2 = h$. This means that x is the required unique morphism and (4) is a pushout.

2. Given the pushout (4) and f_1 and f_2, we define $a_1 = [a_1, a_2] \circ i_{A_1}$ and $a_2 = [a_1, a_2] \circ i_{A_2}$, and, analogously, $e_1 = [e_1, e_2] \circ i_{B_1}$ and $e_2 = [e_1, e_2] \circ i_{B_2}$. In the first step, we construct the pushouts (1) and (2) over f_1 and a_1 and over f_2 and a_2, respectively. Since $c \circ a_1 = c \circ [a_1, a_2] \circ i_{A_1} = [e_1, e_2] \circ (f_1 + f_2) \circ i_{A_1} = [e_1, e_2] \circ i_{B_1} \circ f_1 = e_1 \circ f_1$, we obtain from pushout (1) a unique morphism d_1, where $d_1 \circ b_1 = e_1$ and $d_1 \circ c_1 = c$. Analogously, we obtain from pushout (2) a morphism d_2, where $d_2 \circ b_2 = e_2$ and $d_2 \circ c_2 = c$. It remains to show that (3) is a pushout.

Given an object X and morphisms $h_1 : D_1 \to X$, $h_2 : D_2 \to X$, where $h_1 \circ c_1 = h_2 \circ c_2$, we have the following result for $k_1 = h_1 \circ b_1$ and $k_2 = h_2 \circ b_2$:
$k_1 \circ f_1 = h_1 \circ b_1 \circ f_1 = h_1 \circ c_1 \circ a_1$ and $k_2 \circ f_2 = h_2 \circ b_2 \circ f_2 = h_2 \circ c_2 \circ a_2$. Therefore $[k_1, k_2] \circ (f_1 + f_2) = h_1 \circ c_1 \circ [a_1, a_2]$. From pushout (4), we obtain a unique morphism $x : E \to X$, where $x \circ c = h_1 \circ c_1$ and $x \circ [e_1, e_2] = [k_1, k_2]$:

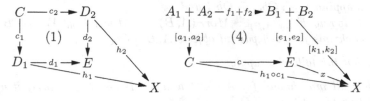

Because of the pushout (1), the morphism h_1 is unique with respect to k_1 and $h_1 \circ c_1$. Now we have $x \circ d_1 \circ c_1 = x \circ c = h \circ c_1$ and $x \circ d_1 \circ b_1 = $

$x \circ e_1 = x \circ [e_1, e_2] \circ i_{B_1} = [k_1, k_2] \circ i_{B_1} = k_1$, and therefore $x \circ d_1 = h_1$. Analogously, we obtain from pushout (2) the result that $x \circ d_2 = h_2$, and therefore x is the required unique morphism.   □

Definition A.30 (initial object). *In a category* **C**, *an object* I *is called initial if, for each object* A, *there exists a unique morphism* $i_A : I \to A$.

Example A.31 (initial objects).

- In **Sets**, the initial object is the empty set.
- In **Graphs** and **Graphs**$_{TG}$, the initial object is the empty graph.
- In **Alg(Σ)**, the initial object is the term algebra T_Σ.
- In a product category $A \times B$, the initial object is the tuple (I_1, I_2), where I_1, I_2 are the initial objects in A and B (if they exist).
- If **C** has an initial object I, the initial object in a slice category **C**\X is the unique morphism $I \to X$.
- In general, a coslice category has no initial object.

□

Remark A.32. The dual concept of an initial object is that of a final object, i.e. an object Z such that there exists a unique morphism $z_A : A \to Z$ for each object A. Each set Z with $card(Z) = 1$ is final in **Sets**, and each algebra Z in **Alg(Σ)** with $card(Z_s) = 1$ for all $s \in S$ is final in **Alg(Σ)** (see Definition B.11).

Initial objects are unique up to isomorphism.

A.6 Functors, Functor Categories, and Comma Categories

Functors are mappings between different categories which are compatible with composition and the identities. Together with natural transformations, this leads to the concept of functor categories. Another interesting construction for building new categories is that of comma categories.

Definition A.33 (functor). *Given two categories* **C** *and* **D**, *a functor* $F :$ **C** $\to$ **D** *is given by* $F = (F_{Ob}, F_{Mor})$, *with*

- *a mapping* $F_{Ob} : Ob_C \to Ob_D$ *and*
- *a mapping* $F_{Mor(A,B)} : Mor_C(A, B) \to Mor_D(F_{Ob}(A), F_{Ob}(B))$ *of the morphisms for each pair of objects* $A, B \in Ob_C$,

such that the following apply:

1. *For all morphisms* $f : A \to B$ *and* $g : B \to C \in Mor_C$, *it holds that* $F(g \circ f) = F(g) \circ F(f)$.
2. *For all objects* $A \in Ob_C$, *it holds that* $F(id_A) = id_{F(A)}$.

Remark A.34. For simplicity, we have left out the indices and have written $F(A)$ and $F(f)$ for both objects and morphisms.

To compare functors, natural transformations are used. Functors and natural transformations form a category, called a functor category.

Definition A.35 (natural transformation). *Given two categories* $\mathbf{C}$ *and* $\mathbf{D}$ *and functors* $F, G : \mathbf{C} \to \mathbf{D}$, *a* natural transformation $\alpha : F \Rightarrow G$ *is a family of morphisms* $\alpha = (\alpha_A)_{A \in Ob_{\mathbf{C}}}$ *with* $\alpha_A : F(A) \to G(A) \in Mor_{\mathbf{D}}$, *such that, for all morphisms* $f : A \to B \in Mor_{\mathbf{C}}$, *it holds that* $\alpha_B \circ F(f) = G(f) \circ \alpha_A$:

$$
\begin{array}{ccc}
F(A) & \xrightarrow{\ F(f)\ } & F(B) \\
\Big\downarrow{\alpha_A} & & \Big\downarrow{\alpha_B} \\
G(A) & \xrightarrow{\ G(f)\ } & G(B)
\end{array}
$$

Definition A.36 (functor category). *Given two categories* $\mathbf{C}$ *and* $\mathbf{D}$, *the functor category* $[\mathbf{C}, \mathbf{D}]$ *is defined by the class of all functors* $F : \mathbf{C} \to \mathbf{D}$ *as the objects, and by natural transformations as the morphisms. The composition of the natural transformations* $\alpha : F \Rightarrow G$ *and* $\beta : G \Rightarrow H$ *is the componentwise composition in* $\mathbf{D}$, *which means that* $\beta \circ \alpha = (\beta_A \circ \alpha_A)_{A \in Ob_{\mathbf{C}}}$, *and the identities are given by the identical natural transformations defined componentwise over the identities* $id_{F(A)} \in \mathbf{D}$.

Fact A.37 (constructions in functor categories).

- *In a functor category* $[\mathbf{C}, \mathbf{D}]$, *natural transformations are monomorphisms, epimorphisms, and isomorphisms if they are componentwise monomorphisms, epimorphisms, and isomorphisms, respectively, in* $\mathbf{D}$.
- *If the category* $\mathbf{D}$ *has pushouts, then pushouts can be constructed "pointwise" in a functor category* $[\mathbf{C}, \mathbf{D}]$ *as follows. Given functors* $F, G, H : \mathbf{C} \to \mathbf{D}$ *and natural transformations* $\alpha : F \to G$ *and* $\beta : F \to H$, *for every object* $A \in Ob_{\mathbf{C}}$ *we construct the pushout* (P_A) *below as* $H(A) \xrightarrow{\gamma_A} K_A \xleftarrow{\delta_A} G(A)$ *over* $H(A) \xleftarrow{\beta_A} F(A) \xrightarrow{\alpha_a} G(A)$ *in* $\mathbf{D}$. *Now we define the functor* $K : \mathbf{C} \to \mathbf{D}$ *by* $K(A) = K_A$ *for objects in* $\mathbf{C}$. *For a morphism* $f : A \to B \in Mor_{\mathbf{C}}$, *we obtain an induced morphism* $K(f)$ *from the pushout* (P_A) *in comparison with* $\gamma_B \circ H(f)$ *and* $\delta_B \circ G(f)$. K *is the pushout object in* $[\mathbf{C}, \mathbf{D}]$, *and* $(\gamma_A)_{A \in Ob_{\mathbf{C}}}$ *and* $(\delta_A)_{A \in Ob_{\mathbf{C}}}$ *are the required morphisms:*

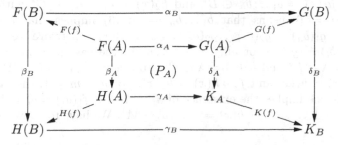

- *The construction of pullbacks is dual to the construction of pushouts if the underlying category $\mathbf{D}$ has pullbacks.*

Proof idea. It follows directly from the definition that a natural transformation is monomorphism, an epimorphism, or an isomorphism if it has that property componentwise in $\mathbf{D}$. The construction of pushouts in the functor category $[\mathbf{C}, \mathbf{D}]$ can be shown directly to satisfy the properties of pushouts in $[\mathbf{C}, \mathbf{D}]$ using the corresponding properties in $\mathbf{D}$. The result for pullbacks follows by duality. $\square$

In the following, we show that some explicit functors preserve pullbacks (along injective morphisms).

Lemma A.38 ($\square^*$ preserves pullbacks). *The free monoid functor $\square^*$: Sets $\rightarrow$ Sets preserves pullbacks, i.e., given a pullback (P) in Sets, then also (P^*) is also a pullback in Sets:*

$$
\begin{array}{ccc}
A \xrightarrow{\;f_1\;} B & \qquad & A^* \xrightarrow{\;f_1^*\;} B^* \\
\downarrow{f_2} \quad (P) \quad \downarrow{g_1} & \qquad & \downarrow{f_2^*} \quad (P^*) \quad \downarrow{g_1^*} \\
C \xrightarrow{\;g_2\;} D & \qquad & C^* \xrightarrow{\;g_2^*\;} D^*
\end{array}
$$

Proof. Given a pullback (P) in Sets, we have to show that (P^*) is also a pullback in Sets:

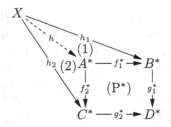

Given h_1, h_2, where (3) $g_1^* \circ h_1 = g_2^* \circ h_2$ we have to show that there exists a unique $h : X \rightarrow A^*$ such that (1) and (2) commute, i.e.

$$(4) \quad \forall x \in X : h_1(x) = f_1^* \circ h(x) \text{ and } h_2(x) = f_2^* \circ h(x).$$

Let $h_1(x) = b_1 \ldots b_n \in B^*$ and $h_2(x) = c_1 \ldots c_m \in C^*$ with $n, m \geq 0$, where $n = 0$ means that $b_1 \ldots b_n = \lambda$. (3) implies that $g_1^* \circ h_1(x) = g_1(b_1) \ldots g_1(b_n) = g_2(c_1) \ldots g_2(c_m) = g_2^* \circ h_2(x)$. Therefore we have $n = m$ and $g_1(b_i) = g_2(c_i)$ for all $i = 1, \ldots, n$. In the case $n = m = 0$, we have $h_1(x) = \lambda \in B^*$ and $h_2(x) = \lambda \in C^*$, and define $h(x) = \lambda \in A^*$, leading to $f_1^* \circ h(x) = h_1(x)$ and $f_2^* \circ h(x) = h_2(x)$. For $n = m \geq 1$, the fact that (P) is a pullback implies the existence of $a_i \in A$ with $f_1(a_i) = b_i$ and $f_2(a_i) = c_i$ for all $i = 1, \ldots, n$. Let $h(x) = a_1 \ldots a_n \in A^*$. We have to show (4):

$$f_1^* \circ h(x) = f_1^*(a_1 \ldots a_n) = f_1(a_1) \ldots f_1(a_n) = b_1 \ldots b_n = h_1(x) \text{ and}$$
$$f_2^* \circ h(x) = f_2^*(a_1 \ldots a_n) = f_2(a_1) \ldots f_2(a_n) = c_1 \ldots c_n = h_2(x).$$

It remains to show that h is unique. Let $h' : X \to A^*$ satisfy (4) with $h'(x) = a_1' \ldots a_m' \in A^*$.

Case 1. If $m \geq 1$, we have that:

1. $h_1(x) = f_1^* \circ h'(x) \Rightarrow f_1(a_1') \ldots f_1(a_m') = b_1 \ldots b_n \Rightarrow n = m$ and $f_1(a_i') = b_i$ $(i = 1, \ldots, n)$,
2. $h_2(x) = f_2^* \circ h'(x) \Rightarrow f_2(a_1') \ldots f_2(a_m') = c_1 \ldots c_n \Rightarrow f_2(a_i') = c_i$ $(i = 1, \ldots, n)$.

The uniqueness of the pullback (P) implies that $a_i' = a_i$ for $i = 1, \ldots, n$, and therefore $h'(x) = h(x)$.

Case 2. In the case $m = 0$, the commutativity of (1) implies that $h'(x) = \lambda = h(x)$. $\qquad\square$

Lemma A.39 ($\mathcal{P}$ preserves pullbacks). *The power set functor $\mathcal{P} : \mathbf{Sets} \to \mathbf{Sets}$ preserves pullbacks, i.e., given a pullback (P) in $\mathbf{Sets}$, then $(\mathcal{P}(P))$ is also a pullback in $\mathbf{Sets}$:*

$$
\begin{array}{ccc}
A & \xrightarrow{\pi_1} & B \\
{\scriptstyle \pi_2} \downarrow & (P) & \downarrow {\scriptstyle f_1} \\
C & \xrightarrow{f_2} & D
\end{array}
\qquad
\begin{array}{ccc}
\mathcal{P}(A) & \xrightarrow{\mathcal{P}(\pi_1)} & \mathcal{P}(B) \\
{\scriptstyle \mathcal{P}(\pi_2)} \downarrow & (\mathcal{P}(P)) & \downarrow {\scriptstyle \mathcal{P}(f_1)} \\
\mathcal{P}(C) & \xrightarrow{\mathcal{P}(f_2)} & \mathcal{P}(D)
\end{array}
$$

Proof. Given a pullback (P) in $\mathbf{Sets}$, we have to show that $(\mathcal{P}(P))$ is also a pullback in $\mathbf{Sets}$:

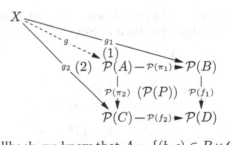

Since (P) is a pullback, we know that $A = \{(b, c) \in B \times C \mid f_1(b) = f_2(c)\}$, and the power set functor gives us $\mathcal{P}(f_1)(B') = f_1(B') \in \mathcal{P}(D)$ for all $B' \subseteq B$.

Given g_1 and g_2, where (3) $\mathcal{P}(f_1) \circ g_1 = \mathcal{P}(f_2) \circ g_2$, we have to show that there exists a unique $g : X \to \mathcal{P}(A)$ such that (1) and (2) commute, i.e.

(4) $X = \varnothing$ or $\forall x \in X : g_1(x) = \mathcal{P}(\pi_1) \circ g(x)$ and $g_2(x) = \mathcal{P}(\pi_2) \circ g(x)$.

For all $x \in X$, we define $g(x) = \{(b, c) \in A \mid b \in g_1(x), c \in g_2(x)\}$. This definition implies that $\mathcal{P}(\pi_1)(g(x)) \subseteq g_1(x)$, but we have to show that $\mathcal{P}(\pi_1)(g(x)) = g_1(x)$.

This is true for $g_1(x) = \varnothing$. For $g_1(x) \neq \varnothing$ and $b \in g_1(x)$, (3) implies that $g_2(x) \neq \varnothing$ and $\mathcal{P}(f_1) \circ g_1 = \mathcal{P}(f_2) \circ g_2$, i.e. $f_1(g_1(x)) = f_2(g_2(x))$. This means that $f_1(b) \in f_2(g_2(x))$, and therefore there exists a $c \in g_2(x)$ with $f_1(b) = f_2(c)$. It follows that $(b,c) \in A$ and $(b,c) \in g(x)$, and therefore $b \in \mathcal{P}(\pi_1)(g(x))$. This implies that $\mathcal{P}(\pi_1)(g(x)) = g_1(x)$. Similarly, we have $\mathcal{P}(\pi_2)(g(x)) = g_2(x)$ as required in (4).

It remains to show that g is unique. Let $g' : X \to \mathcal{P}(A)$ satisfy (4). For $g'(x) = \varnothing$, we have $g_1(x) = \varnothing$ and $g_2(x) = \varnothing$, and hence $g(x) = \varnothing$. Otherwise, for $(b,c) \in g'(x)$, we have from (4) the result that $b \in g_1(x)$ and $c \in g_2(x)$, and therefore $(b,c) \in g(x)$. This means that $g' = g$.   □

Lemma A.40 ($\square^\oplus$ preserves pullbacks along injective morphisms). *The free commutative monoid functor $\square^\oplus : \mathbf{Sets} \to \mathbf{Sets}$ preserves pullbacks along injective morphisms, i.e., given a pullback (P) in $\mathbf{Sets}$, where f_2 and g_1 are injective, then $(P^\oplus)$ is also a pullback in $\mathbf{Sets}$:*

$$
\begin{array}{ccc}
A \xrightarrow{\;f_1\;} B & \qquad & A^\oplus \xrightarrow{\;f_1^\oplus\;} B^\oplus \\
\downarrow{f_2} \quad (P) \quad \downarrow{g_1} & & \downarrow{f_2^\oplus} \quad (P^\oplus) \quad \downarrow{g_1^\oplus} \\
C \xrightarrow{\;g_2\;} D & & C^\oplus \xrightarrow{\;g_2^\oplus\;} D^\oplus
\end{array}
$$

Note that $\square^\oplus(A) = A^\oplus$ is the free commutative monoid over A, given by $A^\oplus = \{w \mid w = \sum\limits_{i=1}^{n} \lambda_i a_i$ in normal form, $\lambda_i \geq 0, a_i \in A, n \geq 0\}$, where "$w$ in normal form" means that $\lambda_i > 0$ and the a_i are pairwise distinct. On morphisms, $\square^\oplus(f) = f^\oplus$ is defined by $f^\oplus(\sum\limits_{i=1}^{n} \lambda_i a_i) = \sum\limits_{i=1}^{n} \lambda_i f(a_i)$ for $f : A \to B$.

Proof. Given a pullback (P) in $\mathbf{Sets}$, where g_1 and f_2 are injective, we have to show that $(P^\oplus)$ is also a pullback in $\mathbf{Sets}$:

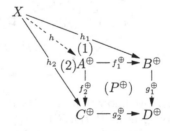

Given h_1, h_2, where

$$(3) \quad g_1^\oplus \circ h_1 = g_2^\oplus \circ h_2,$$

we have to show that there exists a unique $h : X \to A^\oplus$ such that (1) and (2) commute, i.e.

$$(4) \quad X = \varnothing \text{ or } \forall x \in X : h_1(x) = f_1^\oplus \circ h(x) \text{ and } h_2(x) = f_2^\oplus \circ h(x).$$

Let $h_1(x) = \sum\limits_{j=1}^{n} \lambda_j^1 b_j \in B^\oplus$ and $h_2(x) = \sum\limits_{i=1}^{m} \lambda_i^2 c_i \in C^\oplus$, in normal form, i.e. the b_j and c_i are pairwise distinct, and $\lambda_j^1 \neq o$ and $\lambda_i^2 \neq 0$, respectively. (3) implies that $g_1^\oplus \circ h_1(x) = \sum\limits_{j=1}^{n} \lambda_j^1 g_1(b_j) = \sum\limits_{i=1}^{m} \lambda_i^2 g_2(c_i) = g_2^\oplus \circ h_2(x)$. Since g_1 is injective, the $g_1(b_j)$ are pairwise distinct for $j = 1, \ldots, n$. Therefore $\sum\limits_{j=1}^{n} \lambda_j^1 g_1(b_j)$ is in normal form, and we have pairwise disjoint index sets I_j for $j = 1, \ldots, n$ with $\cup_{j=1}^{n} I_j = \{1, \ldots, m\}$ such that

$$(5) \quad \forall i \in I_j : g_1(b_j) = g_2(c_i) \text{ and } \lambda_j^1 = \sum_{i \in I_j} \lambda_i^2.$$

(5) and the fact that (P) is a pullback imply, for each pair (i, j) with $i \in I_j$, the existence of $a_{ij} \in A$ with $f_1(a_{ij}) = b_j$ and $f_2(a_{ij}) = c_i$.

Let $h(x) = \sum\limits_{j=1}^{n} \sum\limits_{i \in I_j} \lambda_i^2 a_{ij} \in A^\oplus$. We have to show the following, i.e. (4):

$$f_1^\oplus \circ h(x) = f_1^\oplus \left(\sum_{j=1}^{n} \sum_{i \in I_j} \lambda_i^2 a_{ij} \right) = \sum_{j=1}^{n} \sum_{i \in I_j} \lambda_i^2 f_1(a_{ij}) =$$

$$\sum_{j=1}^{n} \sum_{i \in I_j} \lambda_i^2 b_j = \sum_{j=1}^{n} \lambda_j^1 b_j = h_1(x)$$

and

$$f_2^\oplus \circ h(x) = f_2^\oplus \left(\sum_{j=1}^{n} \sum_{i \in I_j} \lambda_i^2 a_{ij} \right) = \sum_{j=1}^{n} \sum_{i \in I_j} \lambda_i^2 f_2(a_{ij}) =$$

$$\sum_{j=1}^{n} \sum_{i \in I_j} \lambda_i^2 c_i = \sum_{i=1}^{m} \lambda_i^2 c_i = h_2(x),$$

where $\sum\limits_{j=1}^{n} \sum\limits_{i \in I_j} \lambda_i^2 c_i = \sum\limits_{i=1}^{m} \lambda_i^2 c_i$, using $\cup_{j=1}^{n} I_j = \{1, \ldots, m\}$.

The uniqueness of h with respect to (4) follows from the injectivity of $f_2^\oplus$. In fact, we have f_2 injective $\Rightarrow f_2^\oplus$ injective, as we now show.

Let $f_2^\oplus(w) = f_2^\oplus(\sum\limits_{i=1}^{n} \lambda_i a_i) = f_2^\oplus(\sum\limits_{j=1}^{m} \lambda_j' a_j') = f_2^\oplus(w')$, with w and w' in normal form. It follows that $\sum\limits_{i=1}^{n} \lambda_i f_2(a_i) = \sum\limits_{j=1}^{m} \lambda_j' f_2(a_j')$ and, since f_2 is injective, the $f_2(a_i)$ are pairwise distinct, and also the $f_2(a_j')$. This means that $n = m$. Without loss of generality, let $f_2(a_i) = f_2(a_i')$. It follows that $\lambda_i = \lambda_i'$ and, since f_2 is injective, $a_i = a_i'$. Therefore we have $w = \sum\limits_{i=1}^{n} \lambda_i a_i = \sum\limits_{j=1}^{m} \lambda_j' a_j' = w'$, which means that $f_2^\oplus$ is injective. $\qquad\square$

In the following, we define comma categories and show under what conditions pushouts and pullbacks can be constructed.

Definition A.41 (comma category). *Given two functors $F : \mathbf{A} \to \mathbf{C}$ and $G : \mathbf{B} \to \mathbf{C}$ and an index set $\mathcal{I}$, the comma category $\mathbf{ComCat(F, G; \mathcal{I})}$ is defined by the class of all triples (A, B, op), with $A \in Ob_A$, $B \in Ob_B$, and $op = [op_i]_{i \in \mathcal{I}}$, where $op_i \in Mor_C(F(A), G(B))$, as objects; a morphism $f : (A, B, op) \to (A', B', op')$ in $\mathbf{ComCat(F, G; \mathcal{I})}$ is a pair $f = (f_A : A \to A', f_B : B \to B')$ of morphisms in $\mathbf{A}$ and $\mathbf{B}$ such that $G(f_B) \circ op_i = op'_i \circ F(f_A)$ for all $i \in \mathcal{I}$:*

$$
\begin{array}{ccc}
F(A) & \!-op_i\!\blacktriangleright & G(B) \\
\Big| & & \Big| \\
F(f_A) & = & G(f_B) \\
\Big\downarrow & & \Big\downarrow \\
F(A') & \!-op'_i\!\blacktriangleright & G(B')
\end{array}
$$

The composition of morphisms in $\mathbf{ComCat(F, G; \mathcal{I})}$ is defined component-wise, and identities are pairs of identities in the component categories $\mathbf{A}$ and $\mathbf{B}$.

Remark A.42. The short notation (F, G) for $\mathbf{ComCat(F, G; \mathcal{I})}$, where $|\mathcal{I}| = 1$, explains the name "comma category".

Note that we have $\mathbf{ComCat(F, G; \varnothing)} = \mathbf{A} \times \mathbf{B}$.

Fact A.43 (constructions in comma categories).

1. *In a comma category $\mathbf{ComCat(F, G; \mathcal{I})}$ with $F : \mathbf{A} \to \mathbf{C}$, $G : \mathbf{B} \to \mathbf{C}$, and an index set $\mathcal{I}$, morphisms are monomorphisms, epimorphisms and isomorphisms if they are componentwise monomorphisms, epimorphisms and isomorphisms, respectively, in $\mathbf{A}$ and $\mathbf{B}$.*

2. *If the categories $\mathbf{A}$ and $\mathbf{B}$ have pushouts and F preserves pushouts, then $\mathbf{ComCat(F, G; \mathcal{I})}$ has pushouts, which can be constructed componentwise.*

3. *If the categories $\mathbf{A}$ and $\mathbf{B}$ have pullbacks and G preserves pullbacks, then $\mathbf{ComCat(F, G; \mathcal{I})}$ has pullbacks, which can be constructed component-wise.*

Proof idea. All constructions can be done componentwise in $\mathbf{A}$ and $\mathbf{B}$ and then lifted to the comma category using the given properties. Note that these properties are sufficient, but in general are not necessary.

More precisely, we have the following pushout construction: given objects $X^j = (A^j, B^j, op^j)$ in $\mathbf{ComCat(F, G; \mathcal{I})}$ for $j = 0, 1, 2$ and morphisms $f^1 : X^0 \to X^1$ and $f^2 : X^0 \to X^2$, then the pushout object $X^3 = (A^3, B^3, op^3)$ is given by $A^3 = A^1 +_{A^0} A^2$ and $B^3 = B^1 +_{B^0} B^2$; $op_i^3 : F(A^3) \to G(B^3)$ for $i \in I$ is uniquely defined by the pushout properties of $F(A^3) = F(A^1) +_{F(A^0)} F(A^2)$ in $\mathbf{C}$. $\qquad\square$

A.7 Isomorphism and Equivalence of Categories

In the following, we define the isomorphism and equivalence of categories.

Definition A.44 (isomorphism of categories). *Two categories* **C** *and* **D** *are called* isomorphic, *written* $\mathbf{C} \cong \mathbf{D}$, *if there are functors* $F : \mathbf{C} \to \mathbf{D}$ *and* $G : \mathbf{D} \to \mathbf{C}$ *such that* $G \circ F = ID_{\mathbf{C}}$ *and* $F \circ G = ID_{\mathbf{D}}$, *where* $ID_{\mathbf{C}}$ *and* $ID_{\mathbf{D}}$ *are the identity functors on* **C** *and* **D**, *respectively.*

Remark A.45. Isomorphisms of categories can be considered as isomorphisms in the "category of all categories" **Cat**, where the objects are all categories and the morphisms are all functors. Note, however, that the collection of all categories is, in general, no longer a "proper" class in the sense of axiomatic set theory. For this reason, **Cat** is not a "proper" category.

Fact A.46 (isomorphic categories). *The category* **Graphs** *of graphs is isomorphic to the functor category* $[\mathcal{S}, \mathbf{Sets}]$, *where the "schema category"* $\mathcal{S}$ *is given by the schema* $\mathcal{S} : \cdot \rightrightarrows \cdot$.

Proof. Let us denote the objects amd morphisms of $\mathcal{S}$ by v, v', e, and e', i.e. $\mathcal{S} : v \underset{e'}{\overset{e}{\rightrightarrows}} v'$.

The functor $F : \mathbf{Graphs} \to [\mathcal{S}, \mathbf{Sets}]$ is given by the following:

1. For a graph $G = (V, E, s, t)$, let $F(G) : \mathcal{S} \to \mathbf{Sets}$, defined by $F(G)(v) = V$, $F(G)(v') = E$, $F(G)(e) = s$, and $F(G)(e') = t$.
2. For $f = (f_V, f_E)$, let $F(f) : F(G_1) \Rightarrow F(G_2)$ be a natural transformation defined by $F(f)(v) = f_V$ and $F(f)(v') = f_E$.

Vice versa, the functor $F^{-1} : [\mathcal{S}, \mathbf{Sets}]$ is given by the following:

1. For a functor $D : \mathcal{S} \to \mathbf{Sets}$, let $F^{-1}(D) = G = (V, E, s, t)$, where $V = D(v)$, $E = D(v')$, $s = D(e)$, and $t = D(e')$.
2. For a natural transformation $\alpha : D_1 \Rightarrow D_2$, let $f = (f_V, f_E) : F^{-1}(D_1) \to F^{-1}(D_2)$, defined by $f_V = \alpha(v) : D_1(v) \to D_2(v)$ and $f_E = \alpha(v') : D_1(v') \to D_2(v')$.

It is easy to verify that F and F^{-1} are functors satisfying $F^{-1} \circ F = Id_{catGraphs}$ and $F \circ F^{-1} = Id_{[\mathcal{S}, \mathbf{Sets}]}$, which implies that the categories **Graphs** and $[\mathbf{S}, \mathbf{Sets}]$ are isomorphic. $\square$

Definition A.47 (equivalence of categories). *Two categories* **C** *and* **D** *are called* equivalent, *written* $\mathbf{C} \equiv \mathbf{D}$, *if there are functors* $F : \mathbf{C} \to \mathbf{D}$ *and* $G : \mathbf{D} \to \mathbf{C}$ *and natural transformations* $\alpha : G \circ F \Rightarrow ID_{\mathbf{C}}$ *and* $\beta : F \circ G \Rightarrow ID_{\mathbf{D}}$ *that are componentwise isomorphisms, i.e.* $\alpha_A : G(F(A)) \overset{\sim}{\to} A$ *and* $\beta_B : F(G(B)) \overset{\sim}{\to} B$ *are isomorphisms for all* $A \in \mathbf{C}$ *and* $B \in \mathbf{D}$, *respectively.*

Remark A.48. If **C** and **D** are isomorphic or equivalent then all "categorical" properties of **C** are shared by **D**, and vice versa. If **C** and **D** are isomorphic, then we have a bijection between objects and between morphisms of **C** and **D**. If they are only equivalent, then there is only a bijection of the corresponding isomorphism classes of objects and morphisms of **C** and

D. However, the cardinalities of corresponding isomorphism classes may be different; for example all sets M with cardinality $|M| = n$ are represented by the set $M_n = \{0, \ldots, n - 1\}$. Taking the sets M_n ($n \in \mathbb{N}$) as objects and all functions between these sets as morphisms, we obtain a category $\mathbf{N}$, which is equivalent – but not isomorphic – to the category $\mathbf{FinSets}$ of all finite sets and functions between finite sets.

B

A Short Introduction to Signatures and Algebras

In this appendix, we give a short introduction to algebraic signatures and algebras, including terms and term evaluation, together with some illustrative examples. For a deeper introduction, see [EM85].

B.1 Algebraic Signatures

A signature can be considered on the one hand as a syntactical description of an algebra, and on the other hand as a formal description of the interface of a program. Algebraic signatures consist of sorts and operation symbols. In contrast to various kinds of logical signatures, they do not include predicate symbols.

Definition B.1 (algebraic signature). *An* algebraic signature $\Sigma = (S, OP)$, *or signature for short, consists of a set S of sorts and a family $OP = (OP_{w,s})_{(w,s) \in S^* \times S}$ of operation symbols.*

Remark B.2. For an operation symbol $op \in OP_{w,s}$, we write $op : w \to s$ or $op : s_1 \ldots s_n \to s$, where $w = s_1 \ldots s_n$. If $w = \lambda$, then $op :\to s$ is called a *constant symbol*.

As some basic examples, we present algebraic signatures for natural numbers, characters, and, based on characters, strings. We give these examples in a user-friendly notation as a list of sorts and operation symbols instead of in the set-theoretical notation.

Example B.3 (algebraic signatures).

- We describe the interface for natural numbers with our first signature. We have a sort *nat*, representing the numbers, a constant symbol *zero*, and operation symbols for a successor, an addition, and a multiplication operation:

$NAT =$
sorts :   nat
opns : $zero :\to nat$
$succ : nat \to nat$
$add : nat\ nat \to nat$
$mult : nat\ nat \to nat$

- The signature for characters is really simple; we have only a sort *char*, a constant *a*, and an operation symbol *next* implying something like an ordering on characters:

$CHAR =$
sorts :   char
opns : $a :\to char$
$next : char \to char$

- The signature for strings imports the signature for characters. This means that all sorts and operation symbols over characters can be used in the new signature. We define a new sort *string*, a constant for the empty string, and operations for the concatenation of two strings, for adding a character to a string, and for returning a character from a string:

Signature $STRING = CHAR+$
sorts :   string
opns : $empty :\to string$
$concat : string\ string \to string$
$ladd : char\ string \to string$
$first : string \to char$

$\square$

Finally, we present signature morphisms, which lead to the category **Sig** of signatures.

Definition B.4 (signature morphism). *Given signatures* $\Sigma = (S, OP)$ *and* $\Sigma' = (S', OP')$, *a signature morphism* $h : \Sigma \to \Sigma'$ *is a tuple of mappings* $h = (h_S : S \to S', h_{OP} : OP \to OP')$ *such that* $h_{OP}(f) : h_S(s_1) \dots h_S(s_n) \to h_S(s) \in OP'$ *for all* $f : s_1 \dots s_n \to s \in OP$.

Example B.5 (signature morphism). Consider the signatures NAT and $STRING$ from Example B.3. Then $h = (h_S, h_{OP}) : STRING \to NAT$, with $h_S(char) = h_S(string) = nat$, $h_{OP}(a) = h_{op}(empty) = zero$, $h_{OP}(next) = h_{OP}(first) = succ$, and $h_{OP}(concat) = h_{OP}(ladd) = add$, is a signature morphism. $\square$

Definition B.6 (category Sig). *Algebraic signatures (see Definition B.1) together with signature morphisms (see Definition B.4) define the category* **Sig** *of signatures.*

B.2 Algebras

An algebra is a semantical model of a signature and can be seen to represent an implementation. In this sense, an algebra implements the corresponding signature.

Definition B.7 (Σ-algebra). *For a given signature $\Sigma = (S, OP)$, a Σ-algebra $A = ((A_s)_{s \in S}, (op_A)_{op \in OP})$ is defined by*

- *for each sort $s \in S$, a set A_s, called the carrier set;*
- *for a constant symbol $c :\to s \in OP$, a constant $c_A \in A_s$;*
- *for each operation symbol $op : s_1 \ldots s_n \to s \in OP$, a mapping $op_A : A_{s_1} \times \ldots \times A_{s_n} \to A_s$.*

Many different algebras can implement the same signature, corresponding to different semantics. To analyze relations between algebras, we define homomorphisms.

Definition B.8 (homomorphism). *Given a signature $\Sigma = (S, OP)$ and Σ-algebras A and B, a homomorphism $h : A \to B$ is a family $h = (h_s)_{s \in S}$ of mappings $h_s : A_s \to B_s$ such that the following properties hold:*

- *for each constant symbol $c :\to s \in OP$, we have $h_s(c_A) = c_B$;*
- *for each operation symbol $op : s_1 \ldots s_n \to s \in OP$, it holds that $h_s(op_A(x_1, \ldots, x_n)) = op_B(h_{s_1}(x_1), \ldots, h_{s_n}(x_n))$ for all $x_i \in A_{s_i}$.*

Definition B.9 (category $\mathbf{Alg}(\Sigma)$). *Given a signature Σ, Σ-algebras and homomorphisms define the category $\mathbf{Alg}(\Sigma)$ of Σ-algebras.*

Example B.10 (algebras). Here, we present algebras for the signatures defined in Example B.3.

- The standard implementation of the signature NAT for natural numbers is the following algebra A:

$$A_{nat} = \mathbb{N}$$
$$zero_A = 0 \in A_{nat}$$
$$succ_A : A_{nat} \to A_{nat}$$
$$x \mapsto x + 1$$
$$add_A : A_{nat} \times A_{nat} \to A_{nat}$$
$$(x, y) \mapsto x + y$$
$$mult_A : A_{nat} \times A_{nat} \to A_{nat}$$
$$(x, y) \mapsto x \cdot y$$

- Since a signature gives us only the syntax, we can implement the signature NAT with a completely different algebra B, which describes operations on words that consist of the characters a, b, and c:

$$
\begin{aligned}
B_{nat} &= \{a, b, c\}^* \\
zero_B &= \lambda \in B_{nat} \\
succ_B &: B_{nat} \to B_{nat} \\
&\quad w \mapsto aw \\
add_B &: B_{nat} \times B_{nat} \to B_{nat} \\
&\quad (v, w) \mapsto vw \\
mult_B &: B_{nat} \times B_{nat} \to B_{nat} \\
&\quad (v, w) \mapsto v^n \text{ with } |w| = n
\end{aligned}
$$

- Now we can look for a homomorphism $h : A \to B$ or $g : B \to A$. Consider $h : A \to B$, $h_{nat} : A_{nat} \to B_{nat} : x \mapsto a^x$. The properties of a homomorphism can be easily verified. Indeed, this is the only homomorphism from A to B. Since h is not surjective, the two algebras are not isomorphic.

  In the other direction, $g : B \to A$, defined by $g_{nat} : B_{nat} \to A_{nat} : w \mapsto |w|$, is the only homomorphism, that exists.

- An implementation of the $CHAR$-algebra C can be defined as follows:

$$
\begin{aligned}
C_{char} &= \{a, \ldots, z, A, \ldots, Z, 0, 1, \ldots, 9\} \\
a_C &= A \in C_{char} \\
next_C &: C_{char} \to C_{char} \\
&\quad a \mapsto b, \ldots, z \mapsto A, A \mapsto B, \ldots, Y \mapsto Z, Z \mapsto 0, 0 \mapsto 1, \ldots, 9 \mapsto a
\end{aligned}
$$

- The $STRING$-algebra D is defined on the character part like the algebra C. Strings are words over characters, and we implement the remaining operations as follows:

$$
\begin{aligned}
D_{char} &= \{a, \ldots, z, A, \ldots, Z, 0, 1, \ldots, 9\} \\
D_{string} &= D_{char}^* \\
a_D &= A \in D_{char} \\
empty_D &= \lambda \in D_{string} \\
next_D &: D_{char} \to D_{char} \\
&\quad a \mapsto b, \ldots, z \mapsto A, A \mapsto B, \ldots, Y \mapsto Z, Z \mapsto 0, 0 \mapsto 1, \ldots, 9 \mapsto a \\
concat_D &: D_{string} \times D_{string} \to D_{string} \\
&\quad (s, t) \mapsto st \\
ladd_D &: D_{char} \times D_{string} \to D_{string} \\
&\quad (x, s) \mapsto xs \\
first_D &: D_{string} \to D_{char} \\
&\quad \lambda \mapsto A, s \mapsto s_1 \text{ with } s = s_1 \ldots s_n
\end{aligned}
$$

□

The *final algebra*, which we use for the attribution of an attributed type graph, is a special algebra.

Definition B.11 (final algebra). *Given a signature $\Sigma = (S, OP)$, the final Σ-algebra Z is defined by:*

- $Z_s = \{s\}$ *for each sort* $s \in S$;
- $c_Z = s \in Z_s$ *for a constant symbol* $c :\to s \in OP$;
- $op_Z : \{s_1\} \times \ldots \times \{s_n\} \to \{s\} : (s_1 \ldots s_n) \mapsto s$ *for each operation symbol* $op : s_1 \ldots s_n \to s \in OP$.

For an arbitrary Σ-algebra A, there is a unique homomorphism $z_A : A \to Z$ defined by $z_{A,s} : A_s \to \{s\} : x \mapsto s$ for all $s \in S$. This is the reason why Z is called the final algebra. In fact, it is the unique (up to isomorphism) final algebra in the category $\mathbf{Alg}(\Sigma)$.

Example B.12 (final $STRING$-algebra). As an example, we show the final algebra Z for the signature $STRING$ given in Example B.3. Z is defined as follows:

$$
\begin{aligned}
Z_{char} \quad &= \{char\} \\
Z_{string} \quad &= \{string\} \\
a_Z \quad &= char \in Z_{char} \\
empty_Z \quad &= string \in Z_{string} \\
next_Z \quad &: Z_{char} \to Z_{char} \\
&\quad char \mapsto char \\
concat_Z \quad &: Z_{string} \times Z_{string} \to Z_{string} \\
&\quad (string, string) \mapsto string \\
ladd \quad &: Z_{char} \times Z_{string} \to Z_{string} \\
&\quad (char, string) \mapsto string \\
first \quad &: Z_{string} \to Z_{char} \\
&\quad string \mapsto char
\end{aligned}
$$

$\square$

B.3 Terms and Term Evaluation

Terms with and without variables can be constructed over a signature Σ and evaluated in each Σ-algebra.

Definition B.13 (variables and terms). *Let* $\Sigma = (S, OP)$ *be a signature and* $X = (X_s)_{s \in S}$ *a family of sets, where each* X_s *is called the set of variables of sort* s. *We assume that these* X_s *are pairwise disjoint, and disjoint with* OP.

The family $T_\Sigma(X) = (T_{\Sigma,s}(X))_{s \in S}$ *of* terms (with variables) *is inductively defined by:*

- $x \in T_{\Sigma,s}(X)$ *for all* $x \in X_s$;
- $c \in T_{\Sigma,s}(X)$ *for all constants* $c :\to s \in OP$;
- $f(t_1, \ldots, t_n) \in T_{\Sigma,s}(X)$, *for each operation symbol* $f : s_1 \ldots s_n \to s \in OP$ *and all terms* $t_i \in T_{\Sigma,s_i}(X)$ *for* $i = 1, \ldots, n$.

The family $T_\Sigma = (T_{\Sigma,s})_{s \in S}$ *of* terms without variables, *also called ground terms, is defined for the empty sets* $X_s = \varnothing$ *for all* $s \in S$, *i.e.* $T_{\Sigma,s} = T_{\Sigma,s}(\varnothing)$.

Definition B.14 (evaluation of terms). *Let $\Sigma = (S, OP)$ be a signature with variables X, and let A be a Σ-algebra. The evaluation of the ground terms $eval_A : T_\Sigma \to A$ with $eval_A = (eval_{A,s} : T_{\Sigma,s} \to A_s)_{s \in S}$ is defined by:*

- *$eval_{A,s}(c) = c_A$ for all constants $c :\to s \in OP$;*
- *$eval_{A,s}(f(t_1, \ldots, t_n)) = f_A(eval_{A,s_1}(t_1), \ldots, eval_{A,s_n}(t_n))$ for all terms $f(t_1, \ldots, t_n) \in T_{\Sigma,s}$ and operation symbols $f : s_1 \ldots s_n \to s \in OP$.*

An assignment *$asg : X \to A$ is a family of assignment functions $asg_s : X_s \to A_s$ for all $s \in S$. The extended assignment $\overline{asg} : T_\Sigma(X) \to A$ of the assignment asg, where $\overline{asg} = (\overline{asg}_s : T_{\Sigma,s}(X) \to A_s)_{s \in S}$, is defined by:*

- *$\overline{asg}_s(x) = asg_s(x)$ for all $x \in X_s$;*
- *$\overline{asg}_s(c) = c_A$ for all constants $c :\to s \in OP$;*
- *$\overline{asg}_s(f(t_1, \ldots, t_n)) = f_A(\overline{asg}_{s_1}(t_1), \ldots, \overline{asg}_{s_n}(t_n))$ for all terms $f(t_1, \ldots, t_n) \in T_{\Sigma,s}(X)$ and operation symbols $f : s_1 \ldots s_n \to s \in OP$.*

Definition B.15 (term algebra $T_\Sigma(X)$). *The algebra $T_\Sigma(X) = ((T_{\Sigma,s}(X))_{s \in S}, (op_{T_\Sigma(X)})_{op \in OP})$, where the carriers sets consist of terms with variables, and with operations defined by*

- *$c_{T_\Sigma(X)} = c \in T_{\Sigma,s}(X)$ for all constants $c :\to s \in OP$,*
- *$f_{T_\Sigma(X)} : T_{\Sigma,s_1}(X) \times \ldots \times T_{\Sigma,s_n}(X) \to T_{\Sigma,s}(X); (t_1, \ldots, t_n) \mapsto f(t_1, \ldots, t_n)$ for all $f : s_1 \ldots s_n \to s \in OP$,*

is called the term algebra *over Σ and X.*

Fact B.16 (freeness of $T_\Sigma(X)$). *Let $\Sigma = (S, OP)$ be a signature with variables X, and let A and B be Σ-algebras. We then have the following:*

1. *If $asg : X \to A$ is an assignment, then $\overline{asg} : T_\Sigma(X) \to A$ is the unique Σ-homomorphism such that the following diagram commutes for all $s \in S$, where $u_s(x) = x$ for all $x \in X_s$:*

2. *$eval_A : T_\Sigma \to A$ is the unique Σ-homomorphism between T_Σ and A, i.e. T_Σ is an initial algebra.*
3. *Given a Σ-homomorphism $f : A \to B$, then $f \circ eval_A = eval_B$:*

4. *If $f : A \to B$ is a Σ-homomorphism, and $asg_A : X \to A$ and $asg_B : X \to B$ are assignments with $f \circ asg_A = asg_B$, then $f \circ \overline{asg}_A = \overline{asg}_B$.*

Proof. See Chapter 3 of [EM85].   □

C

Detailed Proofs

In this appendix, we present detailed proofs of some results which have been postponed from Parts II and III.

C.1 Completion of Proof of Fact 4.24

For the proof of Fact 4.24, it remains to show the following:

1. Strictness is preserved by POs.
2. Strictness is preserved by PBs.
3. The weak VK property is satisfied.

We know that $f : (SIG_1, E_1) \to (SIG_2, E_2) \in \mathcal{M}_{strict}$ iff f is injective and $f^{\#-1}(E_2) \subseteq E_1$.

1. Strictness is preserved by POs, i.e. if f_1 is strict, so is g_2:

$$(SIG_0, E_0) - f_1 \blacktriangleright (SIG_1, E_1)$$
$$\begin{array}{ccc} \big\downarrow f_2 & (1) & \big\downarrow g_1 \end{array}$$
$$(SIG_2, E_2) - g_2 \blacktriangleright (SIG_3, E_3)$$

Given that f_1 is strict, we know from Fact 4.19 that g_2 is injective. It remains to show that $g_2^{\#-1}(E_3) \subseteq E_2$. This is true for $E_3 = \varnothing$. Otherwise, let $e \in E_3$ and let $g_2^{\#-1}$ be defined for e; otherwise $g_2^{\#-1}(e) = \varnothing$ and we have finished. We have $E_3 = g_1^{\#}(E_1) \cup g_2^{\#}(E_2)$; therefore either $e \in g_2^{\#}(E_2)$, which implies $g_2^{\#-1}(e) \subseteq E_2$, or $e \in g_1^{\#}(E_1)$. In the second case, $e = g_1^{\#}(e_1)$ for some $e_1 \in E_1$. The requirement that $g_2^{\#-1}$ is defined for e implies that all operator symbols in e are in the image of g_1 and g_2. By the PO construction, all operator symbols in e must have preimages in SIG_0. Hence $f_1^{\#-1}(e_1)$ is defined and $e_1 = f_1^{\#}(e_0)$ for some $e_0 \in E_0$, because f_1 is strict. Finally, $e = g_1^{\#}(e_1) = g_1^{\#}(f_1^{\#}(e_0)) = g_2^{\#}(f_2^{\#}(e_0))$, and therefore $g_2^{\#-1}(e) = f_2^{\#}(e_0) \in E_2$ because $g_2^{\#}$ is injective. This means that $g_2^{\#-1}(E_3) \subseteq E_2$.

2. Strictness is preserved by PBs, i.e. if g_2 is strict, so is f_1.

   Given that g_2 is strict, we know from Fact 4.19 that f_1 is injective. Let $e_0 \in f_1^{\#-1}(E_1)$ for $e_0 \in Eqns(SIG_0)$. We have to show that $e_0 \in E_0$.

   By assumption, $e_1 = f_1^{\#}(e_0) \in E_1$. Since g_1 is a **Spec** morphism, we have $e_3 = g_1^{\#}(e_1) \in E_3$ and $e_3 = g_1^{\#}(f_1^{\#}(e_0)) = g_2^{\#}(f_2^{\#}(e_0))$. This means that $e_2 = f_2^{\#}(e_0) \in Eqns(SIG_2)$ and $g_2^{\#}(e_2) = e_3 \in E_3$, and, since g_2 is strict, $e_2 \in E_2$. Finally, $f_1^{\#}(e_0) \in E_1$ and $f_2^{\#}(e_0) = e_2 \in E_2$; therefore $e_0 \in f_1^{\#-1}(E_1) \cap f_2^{\#-1}(E_2)$ and, since (1) is a pullback, $e_0 \in E_0$.

3. The weak VK property is satisfied.

   Consider the following commutative cube, with $f_1 \in \mathcal{M}_{strict}$ and ($f_2 \in \mathcal{M}_{strict}$ or $h_1, h_2, h_3 \in \mathcal{M}_{strict}$):

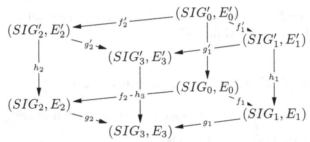

Part 1. If the bottom is a PO and all side faces are PBs, then the top is a PO.

This follows from Fact 4.19 for the signature component. It remains to show that $E_3' = g_1'^{\#}(E_1') \cup g_2'^{\#}(E_2')$. We know that $E_3 = g_1^{\#}(E_1) \cup g_2^{\#}(E_2)$.

For $e_3' \in E_3'$, we have $h_3^{\#}(e_3') \in E_3$. First, let $h_3^{\#}(e_3') \in g_1^{\#}(E_1)$, i.e. $h_3^{\#}(e_3') = g_1^{\#}(e_1)$ for $e_1 \in E_1$. The front right face is a pullback, and therefore there exists $e_1' \in E_1'$ with $h_1^{\#}(e_1') = e_1$ and $g_1'^{\#}(e_1') = e_3'$; therefore $e_3' \in g_1'^{\#}(E_1')$. In the case $h_3^{\#}(e_3') \in g_2^{\#}(E_2)$, we can conclude that $e_3' \in g_2'^{\#}(E_2')$.

Vice versa, for $e_3' \in g_1'^{\#}(E_1')$ we have $e_3' \in E_3'$ because $g_1'^{\#}(E_1') \subseteq E_3'$, using $g_1' \in$ **Spec**, and for $e_3' \in g_2'^{\#}(E_2')$ we have $e_3' \in E_3'$ using $g_2' \in$ **Spec**.

Part 2. If the bottom and the top are POs and the back faces are PBs, then the front faces are PBs.

This follows from Fact 4.19 for the signature component. It remains to show that $E_1' = h_1^{\#-1}(E_1) \cap g_1'^{\#-1}(E_3')$ and $E_2' = h_2^{\#-1}(E_2) \cap g_2'^{\#-1}(E_3')$.

For $e_1' \in E_1'$, since $h_1 \in$ **Spec**, we have $h_1^{\#}(e_1') \in E_1$, and therefore $e_1' \in h_1^{\#-1}(E_1)$. Analogously, since $g_1' \in$ **Spec**, we have $g_1'^{\#}(e_1') \in E_3'$, and therefore $e_1' \in g_1'^{\#-1}(E_3')$. Altogether, $e_1' \in h_1^{\#-1}(E_1) \cap g_1'^{\#-1}(E_3')$.

Vice versa, let $e_1' \in h_1^{\#-1}(E_1) \cap g_1'^{\#-1}(E_3')$. We have to show that $e_1' \in E_1'$. By assumption, f_2 or h_1 is strict; this implies that g_1' or h_1 is

strict, because strictness is preserved by pushouts and pullbacks. Therefore $g_1'^{\#-1}(E_3') \subseteq E_1'$ or $h_1^{\#-1}(E1) \subseteq E_1'$, which means that $e_1' \in E_1'$.
    It follows analogously that $E_2' = h_2^{\#-1}(E_2) \cap g_2'^{\#-1}(E_3')$.

$\square$

C.2 Proof of Lemma 6.25

To prove Lemma 6.25, we use the principle of Noether's induction concerning properties of terminating relations. We call a relation $> \subseteq M \times M$ *terminating* if there is no infinite chain $(m_i)_{i \in \mathbb{N}}$ with $m_i \in M$ and $m_i > m_{i+1}$.

Lemma C.1 (Noether's induction). *Given a terminating relation* $> \subseteq M \times M$ *and a property* $P : M \to \{true, false\}$ *then we have*

$$(\forall n \in M : (\forall k \in M : n > k \to P(k)) \to P(n)) \Rightarrow \forall m \in M : P(m).$$

Proof. Suppose that $\forall n \in M : (\forall k \in M : n > k \to P(k)) \to P(n)$ and that there is an $m_0 \in M : \neg P(m_0)$. We then have $\neg(\forall k \in M : m_0 > k \to P(k))$, i.e. there is an $m_1 \in M$ with $m_0 > m_1$ and $\neg P(m_1)$. Analogously, we have $\neg(\forall k \in M : m_1 > k \to P(k))$ and an element $m_2 \in M$ with $m_1 > m_2$ and $\neg P(m_2) \ldots$, leading to an infinite chain $m_0 > m_1 > m_2 \ldots$, which is a contradiction of $>$ being terminating. $\square$

Proof (of Lemma 6.25). Consider an adhesive HLR system AHS, which is terminating and locally confluent, i.e. the relation $\Rightarrow$ is terminating and locally confluent. We shall use this relation $\Rightarrow$ for $>$ and show, by Noether's induction for all graphs G, the following property $P(G)$: for transformations $H_1 \overset{*}{\Leftarrow} G \overset{*}{\Rightarrow} H_2$ there exist transformations $H_1 \overset{*}{\Rightarrow} G' \overset{*}{\Leftarrow} H_2$. Note that we use as the relation $>$ not the relation $\overset{*}{\Rightarrow}$, but only the relation $\Rightarrow$ of direct transformations.
    Given $H_1 \overset{*}{\Leftarrow} G \overset{*}{\Rightarrow} H_2$, we consider the following cases:
    Case 1. If $H_1 \overset{\sim}{=} G$, we have the diagram (1) below, which gives the confluence; here, $G \overset{0}{\Rightarrow} H_1$ means $G = H_1$ or $G \overset{\sim}{=} H_1$ (see Definition 5.2):

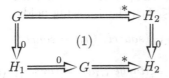

    Case 2. If $H_2 \overset{\sim}{=} G$, this is symmetric to case 1.
    Case 3. If $\neg(H_1 \overset{\sim}{=} G)$, $\neg(H_2 \overset{\sim}{=} G)$, we have transformations $H_1 \overset{*}{\Leftarrow} H_1' \Leftarrow G \Rightarrow H_2' \overset{*}{\Rightarrow} H_2$. Because of local confluence, there are an object G'' and transformations $H_1' \overset{*}{\Rightarrow} G'' \overset{*}{\Leftarrow} H_2'$.

We have $G \Rightarrow H_1'$; therefore, by the induction assumption, we have the property $P(H_1')$, i.e. for all transformations $K_1 \overset{*}{\Leftarrow} H_1' \overset{*}{\Rightarrow} K_1'$ there are transformations $K_1 \overset{*}{\Rightarrow} H_1'' \overset{*}{\Leftarrow} K_1'$. In our case, this means that for $H_1 \overset{*}{\Leftarrow} H_1' \overset{*}{\Rightarrow} G''$ there are transformations $H_1 \overset{*}{\Rightarrow} G_1 \overset{*}{\Leftarrow} G''$:

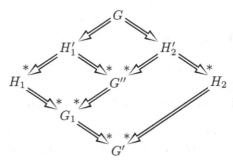

Moreover, we have $G \Rightarrow H_2'$, and hence, by the induction assumption, we have the property $P(H_2')$. This implies that for $G_1 \overset{*}{\Leftarrow} H_2' \overset{*}{\Rightarrow} H_2$ we obtain transformations $G_1 \overset{*}{\Rightarrow} G' \overset{*}{\Leftarrow} H_2$.

Altogether, we have $H_1 \overset{*}{\Rightarrow} G' \overset{*}{\Leftarrow} H_2$, which shows the confluence of $H_1 \overset{*}{\Leftarrow} G \overset{*}{\Rightarrow} H_2$. $\qquad\qquad\square$

C.3 Completion of Proof of Theorem 11.3

In this section, we show that the morphisms F and F^{-1} constructed in the proof of Theorem 11.3 are well defined, and that they are actually functors and isomorphisms.

C.3.1 Well-Definedness

We have to show that the morphisms F and F^{-1} are well defined.

1. $F(AG, t) = A$, where $AG = (G, D)$, is an $AGSIG(ATG)$-algebra.

We have to show that all operations are well defined. For all $e \in E_G^{TG} \subseteq S_E$ and $a \in A_e = t_{G,E_G}^{-1}(e) \subseteq E_G$, the following holds:

- $t_{G,V_G}(src_e^A(a)) = t_{G,V_G}(source_G(a)) = source_G^{TG}(t_{G,E_G}(a)) = source_G^{TG}(e)$,
- $t_{G,V_G}(tar_e^A(a)) = t_{G,V_G}(target_G(a)) = target_G^{TG}(t_{G,E_G}(a)) = target_G^{TG}(e)$.

Therefore we have $src_e^A(a) \in t_{G,V_G}^{-1}(source_G^{TG}(e)) = A_{source_G^{TG}(e)}$ and $tar_e^A(a) \in t_{G,V_G}^{-1}(target_G^{TG}(e)) = A_{target_G^{TG}(e)}$. This works analogously for $e \in E_{NA}^{TG} \subseteq S_E$ and $e \in E_{EA}^{TG} \subseteq S_E$. This means that the graph part of A is well defined.

For all $s \in S_D \backslash S_G$, we have $A_s = t_{D,s}^{-1}(s) = D_s$. Since $t : (G, D) \to (TG, Z)$ is a typing morphism with $V_D^{TG} = S_D'$ and $Z_s = \{s\}$, we have commutativity of (1) below for all $s \in S_D'$. It follows that $A_s = t_{G,V_D}^{-1}\{s\} = D_s = t_{D,s}^{-1}\{s\}$. Therefore all data operations are well defined (as they are in D).

$$
\begin{array}{ccc}
D_s & \xrightarrow{\ t_{D,s}\ } & \{s\} \\
\cup & (1) & \cup \\
V_D & \xrightarrow{\ t_{G,V_D}\ } & S_D'
\end{array}
$$

2. $F(f : (AG^1, t^1) \to (AG^2, t^2)) = h : A \to B$ with $F(AG^1, t^1) = A$ and $F(AG^2, t^2) = B$ is an algebra homomorphism.

For all $s \in S_G \cup S_D$ and $a \in A_s$, we have $h_s(a) \in B_s$, as shown in the following case distinctions:

1. $s \in V_i^{TG} \subseteq S_V$ for $i \in \{G, D\}$. Since $t_{G,V_i}^2(h_s(a)) = t_{G,V_i}^2(f_{G,V_i}(a)) = t_{G,V_i}^1(a) = s$, we have $h_s(a) \in t_{G,V_i}^{2\ -1}(s) = B_s$.
2. $e \in E_j^{TG} \subseteq S_E$ for $j \in \{G, NA, EA\}$. Since $t_{G,E_j}^2(h_e(a)) = t_{G,E_j}^2(f_{G,E_j}(a)) = t_{G,E_j}^1(a) = e$, we have $h_e(a) \in t_{G,E_j}^{2\ -1}(e) = B_e$.
3. $s \in S_D$. By construction, we have $A_s = D_s^1$, $B_s = D_s^2$, and $h_s = f_{D,s} : A_s \to B_s$.

It remains to show that h is a homomorphism. Since $h_D = f_D$, this is obviously true for the data part. For all $e \in E_G^{TG} \subseteq S_E$ and $a \in A_e = t_{G,E_G}^{-1}(e) \subseteq E_G$, we have

- $h_{source_G^{TG}(e)}(src_e^A(a)) = f_{V_G}(source_G^1(a)) = source_G^2(f_{E_G}(a)) = src_e^B(h_e(a))$,
- $h_{target_G^{TG}(e)}(tar_e^A(a)) = f_{V_G}(target_G^1(a)) = target_G^2(f_{E_G}(a)) = tar_e^B(h_e(a))$.

This can be shown analogously for $e \in E_{NA}^{TG} \subseteq S_E$ and $e \in E_{EA}^{TG} \subseteq S_E$. Therefore h is a homomorphism.

3. $F^{-1}(A) = (AG, t : AG \to ATG)$, where $AG = (G, D)$, is an attributed graph typed over ATG.

It is obvious that G is an E-graph. It holds that $\dot{\bigcup}_{s \in S_D'} D_s = \dot{\bigcup}_{s \in V_D^{TG}} A_s = V_D$. Thus, AG is an attributed graph.

t is well defined, since $t_{D,s}(a) = s = t_{V_D}(a)$ for $s \in S_D'$, $a \in A_s$. It then holds that $t^{-1}(s) = A_s$ for all $s \in S_D'$, and (1) commutes.

4. $F^{-1}(h : A \to B) = f : (AG^1, t^1) \to (AG^2, t^2)$ with $F^{-1}(A) = (AG^1, t^1)$ and $F^{-1}(B) = (AG^2, t^2)$ is a typed attributed graph morphism with $t_1 = t_2 \circ f$.

Obviously, f_D is an algebra homomorphism. We have to show that f_G preserves the source and target functions. For all $e \in E_G^{TG}$ and $a \in A_e$, we have

- $f_{G,V_G}(source_G^1(a)) = h_{source_G^{TG}(e)}(src_e^A(a)) = src_e^B(h_e(a)) = source_G^2(f_{G,E_G}(a))$,
- $f_{G,V_G}(target_G^1(a)) = h_{target_G^{TG}(e)}(tar_e^A(a)) = tar_e^B(h_e(a)) = target_G^2(f_{G,E_G}(a))$.

This holds analogously for all $e \in E_{NA}^{TG}$ and $e \in E_{EA}^{TG}$. The following diagram (2) commutes for each $s \in S_D'$, and therefore f_G is a graph morphism:

$$
\begin{array}{ccc}
D_s^1 & \xrightarrow{\quad f_{D_s}=h_s \quad} & D_s^2 \\
\cup & \quad (2) & \cup \\
\dot{\bigcup}_{s \in S_D'} D_s^1 & \xrightarrow{\quad f_{G,V_D}=(h_s)_{s \in S_D'} \quad} & \dot{\bigcup}_{s \in S_D'} D_s^2
\end{array}
$$

For $i \in \{G, D\}$, $s \in V_i^{TG}$, and $a \in A_s$, it follows that $t_{G,V_i}^1(a) = s = t_{G,V_i}^2(h_s(a)) = t_{G,V_i}^2(f_{G,V_i}(a))$. This holds for $j \in \{G, NA, EA\}$ and $e \in E_j^{TG}$ analogously. Since $t_D^1 = t_D^2 \circ f_D$ and since Z is the final algebra, it follows that $t_1 = t_2 \circ f$.

C.3.2 Functors

We show that F and F^{-1} are functors by verifying the necessary functor properties.

1. $F(g \circ f) = F(g) \circ F(f)$. Consider the following case distinctions:

1. $i \in \{G, D\}$, $s \in V_i^{TG} \subseteq S_V$, $a \in A_s$. We have $F(g \circ f)_s(a) = (g \circ f)_{G,V_i}(a) = g_{G,V_i} \circ f_{G,V_i}(a) = F(g)_s \circ F(f)_s(a)$.
2. $j \in \{G, NA, EA\}$, $e \in E_j^{TG} \subseteq S_E$, $a \in A_e$. We have $F(g \circ f)_e(a) = (g \circ f)_{G,E_j}(a) = g_{G,E_j} \circ f_{G,E_j}(a) = F(g)_e \circ F(f)_e(a)$.
3. $s \in S_D$. We have $F(g \circ f)_{D,s} = (g \circ f)_{D,s} = g_{D,s} \circ f_{D,s} = F(g)_{D,s} \circ F(f)_{D,s}$.

2. $F(id_{(AG,t)}) = id_{F(AG,t)}$. Consider the following case distinctions:

1. $i \in \{G, D\}$, $s \in V_i^{TG} \subseteq S_V$, $a \in A_s$. We have $F(id_{AG})_s(a) = id_{G,V_i}(a) = a = id_{A_s}(a)$.
2. $j \in \{G, NA, EA\}$, $e \in E_j^{TG} \subseteq S_E$, $a \in A_e$. We have $F(id_{AG})_e(a) = id_{G,E_j}(a) = a = id_{A_e}(a)$.
3. $s \in S_D$ We have $F(id_{AG})_s = id_{D,s}$.

3. $F^{-1}(g \circ h) = F^{-1}(g) \circ F^{-1}(h)$. Consider the following case distinctions:

1. $i \in \{G, D\}$, $s \in V_i^{TG} \subseteq S_V$, $a \in A_s$. We have $F^{-1}(g \circ h)_{G,V_i}(a) = (g \circ h)_s(a) = g_s \circ h_s(a) = F^{-1}(g)_{G,V_i} \circ F^{-1}(h)_{G,V_i}(a)$.
2. $j \in \{G, NA, EA\}$, $e \in E_j^{TG} \subseteq S_E$, $a \in A_e$. We have $F^{-1}(g \circ h)_{G,E_j}(a) = (g \circ h)_e(a) = g_e \circ h_e(a) = F^{-1}(g)_{G,E_j} \circ F^{-1}(h)_{G,E_j}(a)$.
3. $s \in S_D$. We have $F^{-1}(g \circ h)_{D,s} = (g \circ h)_s = g_s \circ h_s = F^{-1}(g)_{D,s} \circ F^{-1}(h)_{D,s}$.

4. $F^{-1}(id_A) = id_{F^{-1}(A)}$. Consider the following case distinctions:

1. $i \in \{G, D\}$, $s \in V_i^{TG} \subseteq S_V$, $a \in A_s$. We have $F^{-1}(id_A)_{G,V_i}(a) = id_{A_s}(a) = a = id_{G,V_i}(a)$.
2. $j \in \{G, NA, EA\}$, $e \in E_j^{TG} \subseteq S_E$, $a \in A_e$. We have $F^{-1}(id_A)_{G,E_j}(a) = id_{A_e}(a) = a = id_{G,E_j}(a)$.
3. $s \in S_D$. We have $F^{-1}(id_A)_{D,s} = id_{A,s} = id_{F^{-1}(A),D,s}$.

We conclude that F and F^{-1} fulfill the necessary properties and are therefore functors.

C.3.3 Isomorphism

Finally, we show the isomorphism of the categories considered by proving that $F^{-1} \circ F = ID_{AGraphs_{ATG}}$ and $F \circ F^{-1} = ID_{AGSIG(ATG)\text{-}Alg}$.

1. For an object (AG, t) in **AGraphs$_{ATG}$**, we show that, for the object $(AG', t') = F^{-1}(A) = F^{-1} \circ F(AG, t)$, it holds that $(AG, t) = (AG', t')$.

- For $i \in \{G, D\}$, we have $V_i' = \dot{\bigcup}_{s \in V_i^{TG}} A_s = \dot{\bigcup}_{s \in V_i^{TG}} t_{G,V_i}^{-1}(s) = V_i$.
- For $j \in \{G, NA, EA\}$, we have $E_j' = \dot{\bigcup}_{e \in E_j^{TG}} A_e = \dot{\bigcup}_{e \in E_j^{TG}} t_{G,E_j}^{-1}(e) = E_j$.
- For $e \in E_G^{TG}$ and $a \in E_G$ with $t_{G,E_G}(a) = e$, it holds that $source_G'(a) = src_e^A(a) = source_G(a)$ and $target_G'(a) = tar_e^A(a) = target_G(a)$, and analogously for $e \in E_{NA}^{TG}$ and $e \in E_{EA}^{TG}$.
- For $s \in S_D$, we have $D_s' = A_s = D_s$.
- For $op \in OP_D$, we have $op_{D'} = op_A = op_D$.
- For $i \in \{G, D\}$, $s \in V_i^{TG}$, and $a \in A_s$, it holds that $t_{G,V_i}'(a) = s = t_{G,V_i}(a)$.
- For $j \in \{G, NA, EA\}$, $e \in E_j^{TG}$, and $a \in A_e$, we have $t_{G,E_j}'(a) = e = t_{G,E_j}(a)$.
- $t_D' = t_D$ follows, since Z is the final algebra.

This means that $(AG, t) = (AG', t')$.

2. For a morphism $f : (AG^1, t^1) \to (AG^2, t^2)$ in **AGraphs$_{ATG}$**, we show that, for the morphism $f' = F^{-1}(h : A \to B) = F^{-1} \circ F(f)$, it holds that $f = f'$.

Consider the following case distinctions:

1. $i \in \{G, D\}$, $s \in V_i^{TG} \subseteq S_V$, $a \in A_s$. We have $f_{G,V_i}'(a) = h_s(a) = f_{G,V_i}(a)$.
2. $j \in \{G, NA, EA\}$, $e \in E_j^{TG} \subseteq S_E$, $a \in A_e$. We have $f_{G,E_j}'(a) = h_e(a) = f_{G,E_j}(a)$.
3. $s \in S_D$. We have $f_{D,s}' = h_s = f_{D,s}$.

Therefore $f = f'$.

3. For any algebra A in **AGSIG(ATG)-Alg**, we show that, for the object $A' = F(AG, t) = F \circ F^{-1}(A)$, it holds that $A = A'$.

- For $i \in \{G, D\}$ and $s \in V_i^{TG}$, we have $A_s' = t_{G,V_i}^{-1}(s) = A_s$.

- For $j \in \{G, NA, EA\}$ and $e \in E_j^{TG}$, we have $A'_e = t_{G,E_j}^{-1}(e) = A_e$.
- For $e \in E_G^{TG}$ and $a \in A_e$, it holds that $src_e^{A'}(a) = source_G(a) = src_e^A(a)$ and $tar_e^{A'}(a) = target_G(a) = tar_e^A(a)$, and analogously for $e \in E_{NA}^{TG}$ and $e \in E_{EA}^{TG}$.
- For $s \in S_D$, we have $A'_s = D_s = A_s$.
- For $op \in OP_D$, we have $op_{A'} = op_D = op_A$.

This means that $A = A'$.

4. For a morphism $h : A \to B$ in **AGSIG(ATG)-Alg**, we show that, for the morphism $h' = F(f) = F \circ F^{-1}(h)$, it holds that $h = h'$.

Consider the following case distinctions:

1. $i \in \{G, D\}$, $s \in V_i^{TG} \subseteq S_V$, $a \in A_s$. We have $h'_s(a) = f_{G,V_i}(a) = h_s(a)$.
2. $j \in \{G, NA, EA\}$, $e \in E_j^{TG} \subseteq S_E$, $a \in A_e$. We have $h'_e(a) = f_{G,E_j}(a) = h_e(a)$.
3. $s \in S_D$. We have $h'_s(a) = f_{D,s}(a) = h_s(a)$.

Therefore $h = h'$.

Altogether, the functors F and F^{-1} are isomorphisms, and therefore the categories **AGraphs$_{ATG}$** and **AGSIG(ATG)-Alg** are isomorphic. $\square$

C.4 Proof of Lemma 11.17

In this section, we show that the construction in Lemma 11.17 is well defined and is indeed an initial pushout over f, which means that the square constructed is a pushout with $b \in \mathcal{M}$ and the initiality property holds.

C.4.1 Well-Definedness

B is defined as the intersection of the subalgebras of A, and hence it is a subalgebra of A and therefore well defined.

For the algebra C, the data part is obviously well defined. For the graph part, we have to show that, for an operation $op : s' \to s \in OP_G$ and for a $c' \in C_{s'}$, we have $op_C(c') \in C_s$. If $s \in S_D$, we have $C_s = A_s$, and this is clear. Consider the case where $s \in S_G \backslash S_D$. Since $AGSIG$ is well structured we know also that $s' \in S_G \backslash S_D$.

Suppose there is a $c' \in C_{s'} = A'_{s'} \backslash f'_s(A_{s'}) \cup f_{s'}(B_{s'})$ such that $op_C(c') \notin C_s$. Since $C_s = A'_s \backslash f_s(A_s) \cup f_s(B_s)$, there is an $a \in A_s$ with $f_s(a) = op_C(c')$ and $a \notin B_s$. The following cases may occur:

1. $c' \in A'_{s'} \backslash f_s' A_{s'}$. In this case $a \in A_s^*$ follows from the first part of the definition of A_s^*. Therefore $A_s^* \subseteq B_s$ implies that $a \in B_s$, which is a contradiction.

2. $c' \in f_{s'}(B_{s'})$. In this case there is an $a' \in B_{s'} \subseteq A_{s'}$ with $f_{s'}(a') = g_{s'}(a') = c'$, and we have $f_s(a) = op_C(c') = op_C(g_{s'}(a')) = op_{A'}(f_{s'}(a')) = f_s(op_A(a'))$. Since $op_A(a') = op_B(a') \in B_s$ and $a \notin B_s$, we conclude that $a \neq op_A(a')$. Then $a \in A_s^* \subseteq B_s$ follows from the second part of the definition of A_s^*, which is a contradiction.

We conclude that, for every operation $op : s' \to s \in OP_G$ and $c' \in C_{s'}$, we have $op_C(c') \in C_s$. This means that C is well defined.

b and c are inclusions and g is a restriction of f, and therefore they are homomorphisms and the square commutes.

C.4.2 Pushout Property

Consider the following diagram with an object X and morphisms $l : C \to X$ and $k : A \to X$ such that $l \circ g = k \circ b$:

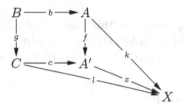

We have to show that there is a unique morphism $x : A' \to X$ with $x \circ c = l$ and $x \circ f = k$. We define $x_s : A_s' \to X_s$ by

$$x_s(a') = \begin{cases} l_s(a') & : & s \in S_D \\ k_s(a) & : & s \in S_G \backslash S_D, \exists a \in A_s : f_s(a) = a' \\ l_s(a') & : & \text{otherwise} \end{cases}$$

and prove that $x = (x_s)_{s \in S_G \cup S_D}$ is the required homomorphism.

First we show that all components x_s are well defined. For $s \in S_D$, we have the result that $A_s = B_s$, $A_s' = C_s$, $f_s = g_s$, and b_s and c_s are the identities. Therefore $x_s = l_s$ is well defined, $x_s \circ c_s = x_s = l_s$, and, for an $a \in A_s$, it holds that $x_s(f_s(a)) = l_s(f_s(a)) = l_s(g_s(a)) = k_s(b_s(a)) = k_s(a)$.

Consider $s \in S_G \backslash S_D$ and $a' \in A_s'$. The following cases can then occur:

1. $\exists a \in A_s : f_s(a) = a'$. We define $x_s(a') = k_s(a)$. This is well defined: if there is an $a_1 \in A_s$, $a_1 \neq a$ with $f_s(a_1) = f_s(a) = a'$, then we have $a_1, a \in A_s^* \subseteq B_s$ from the first part of the definition of A_s^*. It holds that $k_s(a) = k_s(b_s(a)) = l_s(g_s(a)) = l_s(f_s(a)) = l_s(a') = l_s(f_s(a_1)) = l_s(g_s(a_1)) = k_s(b_s(a_1)) = k_s(a_1)$.
2. $\nexists a \in A_s : f_s(a) = a'$. In this case $x_s(a') = l_s(a')$ is obviously well defined.

$x_s(f_s(a)) = k_s(a)$ holds by definition for all $a \in A_s$ with $s \in S_G \backslash S_D$. For $c' \in C_s \subseteq A_s'$, consider the following case distinctions:

1. $\exists a \in A_s : f_s(a) = c'$. In this case $c' \in f_s(B_s)$ from the definition of C_s. This means that there is an $a' \in B_s$ with $f_s(a') = c' = f_s(a)$. If $a = a'$, then it follows directly that $a \in B_s$; otherwise, $a \in A_s^* \subseteq B_s$, and $a \in B_s$ follows from the second part of the definition of A_s^*. We then have $x_s(c_s(c')) = x_s(c') = k_s(a) = k_s(b_s(a)) = l_s(g_s(a)) = l_s(f_s(a)) = l_s(c')$.
2. $\nexists a \in A_s : f_s(a) = c'$. In this case $x_s(c_s(c')) = x_s(c') = l_s(c')$ holds by definition.

Now we show that x is a homomorphism. The compatibility with operations in the data part follows from the fact that l is a homomorphism.

For an operation $op : s' \to s \in OP_G$, $s' \notin S_D$ follows from the well-structuredness of $AGSIG$. For $a' \in A'_{s'}$, we have to show that $x_s(op_{A'}(a')) = op_X(x_{s'}(a'))$, and we prove this for the following cases:

1. $\exists a \in A_{s'} : f_{s'}(a) = a'$. In this case we have $x_s(op_{A'}(a')) = x_s(op_{A'}(f_{s'}(a)))$ $= x_s(f_s(op_A(a))) = k_s(op_A(a)) = op_X(k_{s'}(a)) = op_X(x_{s'}(f_{s'}(a))) = op_X(x_{s'}(a'))$.
2. $\nexists a \in A_{s'} : f_{s'}(a) = a'$. In this case $a' \in C_{s'}$ follows from the definition of $C_{s'}$, and it holds that $x_s(op_{A'}(a')) = x_s(op_{A'}(c_{s'}(a'))) = x_s(c_s(op_C(a'))) = l_s(op_C(a')) = op_X(l_{s'}(a')) = op_X(x_{s'}(c_{s'}(a'))) = op_X(x_s(a'))$.

Therefore x is a homomorphism.

It remains to show that x is unique. Suppose that there is a homomorphism $\hat{x} : A' \to X$ with $\hat{x} \circ c = l$ and $\hat{x} \circ f = k$. Then $x_s(a') = \hat{x}_s(a')$ for each sort $s \in S_G \cup S_D$ and $a' \in A'_s$, as shown in the following case distinctions:

1. $s \in S_D$. Since $c_s = id_{C_s}$, we have $\hat{x}_s = \hat{x}_s \circ c_s = l_s = x_s$.
2. $s \in S_G \backslash S_D$, $\exists a \in A_s : f_s(a) = a'$. In this case it holds that $\hat{x}_s(a') = \hat{x}_s(f_s(a)) = k_s(a) = x_s(a')$.
3. $s \in S_G \backslash S_D$, $\nexists a \in A_s : f_s(a) = a'$. It follows that $a' \in C_s$, and then we have $\hat{x}_s(a') = \hat{x}_s(c_s(a')) = l_s(a') = x_s(a')$.

Hence it follows that $x = \hat{x}$, which means that x is unique.

C.4.3 Initial Pushout

Consider the pushout (2) below, with $d, e \in \mathcal{M}$. We have to show that there are morphisms $b^* : B \to D$ and $c^* : C \to E$ such that $d \circ b^* = b$, $e \circ c^* = c$, and (3) is a pushout:

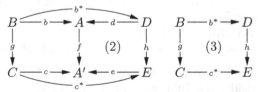

We define

$$c_s^*(c') = \begin{cases} e_s^{-1}(c_s(c')) & : \quad s \in S_D \\ e' & : \quad s \in S_G \backslash S_D, \exists e' \in E_s : e_s(e') = c_s(c') = c' \end{cases}.$$

We shall show that $c^* = (c_s^*)_{s \in S_G \cup S_D}$ is one of the required homomorphisms.

First, we show that c^* is well defined. For $s \in S_D$, e_s is an isomorphism; therefore the inverse morphism e^{-1} exists and, for each $c' \in C_s$, $e_s^{-1}(c_s(c')) = e_s^{-1}(c')$ is uniquely defined.

For $s \in S_G \backslash S_D$, we have to show that for each $c' \in C_s$ there is a unique $e' \in E_s$ such that $e_s(e') = c'$. Since e_s is injective, the uniqueness follows.

Suppose that there is a $c' \in C_s$ and no $e' \in E_s$ such that $e_s(e') = c'$. Since (2) is a pushout, e_s and f_s are jointly surjective. There is then an $a \in A_s$ with $f_s(a) = c'$. It follows that $a \in B_s$, from the construction of B and C. Now the following cases may occur:

1. $a \in A_s^*$, $\exists op : s' \to s \in OP_G$ $\exists a' \in A_{s'}' \backslash f_{s'}(A_{s'}) : f_s(a) = op_{A'}(a')$. Since (2) is a pushout, there is an $e_1 \in E_{s'}$ such that $e_{s'}(e_1) = a'$. It then holds that $e_s(op_E(e_1)) = op_{A'}(e_{s'}(e_1)) = op_{A'}(a') = f_s(a) = c'$. This is a contradiction; we have found an $e' = op_E(e_1) \in E_s$ with $e_s(e') = c'$.

2. $a \in A_s^*$, $\exists a' \in A_s, a \neq a' : f_s(a) = f_s(a')$. Since (2) is a pushout, we find elements $d_1, d_2 \in D_s$ with $d_s(d_1) = a$, $d_s(d_2) = a'$, and $h_s(d_1) = h_s(d_2)$. It then follows that $e_s(h_s(d_1)) = f_s(d_s(d_1)) = f_s(a) = c'$. This means that for $e' = h_s(d_1) \in E_s$ it holds that $e_s(e') = c'$, which is a contradiction.

3. $a \notin A_s^*$. Since $a \in B_s$ and B is the smallest subalgebra of A that contains A_s^*, there must be a chain of operations $op_i : s_i \to s_{i+1} \in OP_G$ and elements $a_i \in A_{s_i}$ for $i = 1, \ldots, n$ such that $a_1 \in A_{s_1}^*$ and $op_{i,A}(a_i) = a_{i+1}$ with $s_{n+1} = s$ and $a_{n+1} = a$. We have $s_1 \in S_G \backslash S_D$ because $AGSIG$ is well structured. Then $a_1 \in A_{s_1}^*$, and, from the proofs above in items 1 and 2, it follows that there is an $e_1 \in E_{s_1}$ such that $e_{s_1}(e_1) = f_{s_1}(a_1)$. We then have $c' = f_s(a) = f_s(op_{n,A}(\ldots(op_{1,A}(a_1)))) = op_{n,A'}(\ldots(op_{1,A'}(f_{s_1}(a_1)))) = op_{n,A'}(\ldots(op_{1,A'}(e_{s_1}(e_1)))) = e_s(op_{n,E}(\ldots(op_{1,E}(e_1))))$.

   For $e' = op_{n,E}(\ldots(op_{1,E}(e_1))) \in E_s$, it holds that $e_s(e') = c'$, which is a contradiction.

This means that c_s^* is well defined for each $s \in S_G \cup S_D$ and, obviously, $e_s \circ c_s^* = c_s$.

For the data part, it is clear that c^* is a homomorphism. For $op : s' \to s \in OP_G$, we have $s' \in S_G \backslash S_D$ since $AGSIG$ is well structured. It then holds for $c' \in C_{s'}$ that $e_s(op_E(c_{s'}^*(c'))) = op_{A'}(e_{s'}(c_{s'}^*(c'))) = op_{A'}(c_{s'}(c')) = c_s(op_C(c')) = e_s(c_s^*(op_C(c')))$. Since e_s is injective, $op_E(c_{s'}^*(c')) = c_s^*(op_C(c'))$ follows. Hence c^* is a homomorphism.

The square (2) above is a pushout along the $\mathcal{M}$-morphism d and therefore also a pullback. Comparing this pullback (2) with the morphisms b and $c^* \circ g$, we have $f \circ b = c \circ g = e \circ c^* \circ g$, and obtain the induced morphism $b^* : B \to D$ with $d \circ b^* = b$ and $h \circ b^* = c^* \circ g$.

It remains to show that (3) is a pushout. Consider the commutative cube (4) below. Since the bottom is the pushout (1) along the $\mathcal{M}$-morphism b, it is a VK square. We then have the following:

- the back left face is a pullback;
- the back right face, being a composition of pullbacks (since $d \in \mathcal{M}$), is a pullback;
- the front left face, being a composition of pullbacks (since $e \in \mathcal{M}$), is a pullback;
- the front right face, being the square (2), is a pullback.

From the VK square property, we conclude that the top, corresponding to square (3), is a pushout.

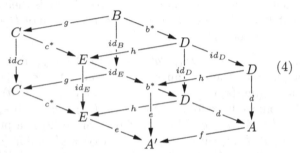

(4)

Altogether, this means that (1) is an initial pushout over $f : A \to A'$.　□

C.5 Proof of Theorem 13.12

In this section, we show that the following hold for the constructed morphism $type$:

1. $\overline{type} : AG \to \overline{ATG}$ is a well-defined AG-morphism.
2. $u_{ATG} \circ \overline{type} = type$.
3. For each AG-morphism $f : AG \to \overline{ATG}$ with $u_{ATG} \circ f = type$, we have $f = \overline{type}$.

1. We have to show that $\overline{type} : AG \to \overline{ATG}$ is a well-defined AG-morphism.

   (a) Well-definedness means that $\overline{type}_{E_i}(e_i) \in \overline{TG_{E_i}}$ for $i \in \{G, NA, EA\}$.

   i. For $\overline{type}_{E_G}(e_1) = (n_1, e'_1, n_2) \in \overline{TG_{E_G}}$, we have to show that $e'_1 \in TG_{E_G}$, $n_1 \in clan_I(src_G(e'_1))$, and $n_2 \in clan_I(tar_G(e'_1))$. From the definition of $\overline{type}_{E_G}$, we have

   $$e'_1 = type_{E_G}(e_1) \in TG_{E_G},$$
   $$n_1 = \overline{type}_{V_G}(s_{G_G}(e_1)) = type_{V_G}(s_{G_G}(e_1))$$
   $$\in clan_I(src_G \circ type_{E_G}(e_1)) = clan_I(src_G(e'_1)),$$
   $$n_2 = \overline{type}_{V_G}(t_{G_G}(e_1)) = type_{V_G}(t_{G_G}(e_1))$$
   $$\in clan_I(tar_G \circ type_{E_G}(e_1)) = clan_I(tar_G(e'_1)).$$

ii. For $\overline{type}_{E_{NA}}(e_2) = (n_1, e'_2, n_2) \in \overline{TG}_{E_{NA}}$, we have to show that $e'_2 \in TG_{E_{NA}}$, $n_1 \in clan_I(src_{NA}(e'_2))$, and $n_2 = tar_{NA}(e'_2)$. From the definition of $\overline{type}_{E_{NA}}$, we have

$$e'_2 = type_{E_{NA}}(e_2) \in TG_{E_{NA}},$$
$$n_1 = \overline{type}_{V_G}(s_{G_{NA}}(e_2)) = type_{V_G}(s_{G_{NA}}(e_2))$$
$$\in clan_I(src_{NA} \circ type_{E_{NA}}(e_2)) = clan_I(src_{NA}(e'_2)),$$
$$n_2 = \overline{type}_{V_D}(t_{G_{NA}}(e_2)) = type_{V_D}(t_{G_{NA}}(e_2))$$
$$= tar_{NA} \circ type_{E_{NA}}(e_2) = tar_{NA}(e'_2).$$

iii. For $\overline{type}_{E_{EA}}(e_3) = ((n_{11}, e''_3, n_{12}), e'_3, n_2) \in \overline{TG}_{E_{EA}}$, we have to show that $e'_3 \in TG_{E_{EA}}$, $e''_3 = src_{EA}(e'_3) \in TG_{E_G}$, $n_{11} \in clan_I(src_G(e''_3))$, $n_{12} \in clan_I(tar_G(e''_3))$, and $n_2 = tar_{EA}(e'_3) \in TG_{V_D}$. From the definition of $\overline{type}_{E_{EA}}$, we have

$$e'_3 = type_{E_{EA}}(e_3) \in TG_{E_{EA}},$$
$$(n_{11}, e''_3, n_{12}) = \overline{type}_{E_G}(s_{G_{EA}}(e_3)) \in \overline{TG}_{E_G}$$

according to step (i), where we have shown that $e''_3 = src_{EA}(e'_3)$, $n_{11} \in clan_I(src_G(e''_3))$, and $n_{12} \in clan_I(tar_G(e''_3))$, and

$$n_2 = \overline{type}_{V_D}(t_{G_{EA}}(e_3)) = type_{V_D}(t_{G_{EA}}(e_3))$$
$$= tar_{EA}(type_{E_{EA}}(e_3)) = tar_{EA}(e'_3).$$

(b) The AG-morphism property of $\overline{type} : AG \to \overline{ATG}$ requires us to show the following properties i–vii:

i. $\overline{type}_{V_D}(d) = s$ for $d \in D_s$ and $s \in S'_D$. This is true because the corresponding property holds for $type_{V_D}$, and $type_{V_D} = \overline{type}_{V_D}$.

ii. $\overline{type}_{V_G} \circ s_{G_G}(e_1) = \overline{src_G} \circ \overline{type}_{E_G}(e_1) \ \forall e_1 \in G_{E_G}$. From the definition of $\overline{type}_{E_G}$, we have $\overline{type}_{E_G}(e_1) = (n_1, e'_1, n_2)$ with

$$n_1 = \overline{type}_{V_G}(s_{G_G}(e_1)) \in TG_{V_G} \Rightarrow$$
$$\overline{src_G} \circ \overline{type}_{E_G}(e_1) = \overline{src_G}[(n_1, e'_1, n_2)] = n_1 = \overline{type}_{V_G}(s_{G_G}(e_1)).$$

iii. $\overline{type}_{V_G} \circ t_{G_G}(e_1) = \overline{tar_G} \circ \overline{type}_{E_G}(e_1) \ \forall e_1 \in G_{E_G}$. From the definition of $\overline{type}_{E_G}$, we have $\overline{type}_{E_G}(e_1) = (n_1, e'_1, n_2)$ with

$$n_1 = \overline{type}_{V_G}(t_{G_G}(e_1)) \in TG_{V_G} \Rightarrow$$
$$\overline{tar_G} \circ \overline{type}_{E_G}(e_1) = \overline{tar_G}[(n_1, e'_1, n_2)] = n_1 = \overline{type}_{V_G}(t_{G_G}(e_1)).$$

iv. $\overline{type}_{V_G} \circ s_{G_{NA}}(e_2) = \overline{src_{NA}} \circ \overline{type}_{E_{NA}}(e_2) \ \forall e_2 \in G_{E_{NA}}$. From the definition of $\overline{type}_{E_{NA}}$, we have $\overline{type}_{E_{NA}}(e_2) = (n_1, e'_2, n_2)$ with

$$n_1 = \overline{type}_{V_G}(s_{G_{NA}}(e_2)) \in TG_{V_G} \Rightarrow$$
$$\overline{src_{NA}} \circ \overline{type}_{E_{NA}}(e_2) = \overline{src_{NA}}[(n_1, e'_2, n_2)] = n_1 = \overline{type}_{V_G}(s_{G_{NA}}(e_2)).$$

v. $\overline{type}_{V_D} \circ t_{G_{NA}}(e_2) = \overline{tar_{NA}} \circ \overline{type}_{E_{NA}}(e_2) \ \forall e_2 \in G_{E_{NA}}$. From the definition of $\overline{type}_{E_{NA}}$, we have $\overline{type}_{E_{NA}}(e_2) = (n_1, e'_2, n_2)$ with

$$n_2 = \overline{type}_{V_D}(t_{G_{NA}}(e_2)) \in TG_{V_D} \Rightarrow$$
$$\overline{tar_{NA}} \circ \overline{type}_{E_{NA}}(e_2) = \overline{tar_{NA}}[(n_1, e'_2, n_2)] = n_2 = \overline{type}_{V_D}(t_{G_{NA}}(e_2)).$$

vi. $\overline{type}_{E_G} \circ s_{G_{EA}}(e_3) = \overline{src_{EA}} \circ \overline{type}_{E_{EA}}(e_3) \ \forall e_3 \in G_{E_{EA}}$. From the definition of $\overline{type}_{E_{EA}}$, we have $\overline{type}_{E_{EA}}(e_3) = ((n_{11}, e_3'', n_{12}), e_2', n_2)$ with

$$(n_{11}, e_3'', n_{12}) = \overline{type}_{E_G}(s_{G_{EA}}(e_3)) \Rightarrow$$
$$\overline{src_{EA}} \circ \overline{type}_{E_{EA}}(e_3) = \overline{src_{EA}}[((n_{11}, e_3'', n_{12}), e_3', n_2)] =$$
$$(n_{11}, e_3'', n_{12}) = \overline{type}_{E_G}(s_{G_{EA}}(e_3)).$$

vii. $\overline{type}_{V_D} \circ t_{G_{EA}}(e_3) = \overline{tar_{EA}} \circ \overline{type}_{E_{EA}}(e_3) \ \forall e_3 \in G_{E_{EA}}$. From the definition of $\overline{type}_{E_{EA}}$, we have $\overline{type}_{E_{EA}}(e_3) = ((n_{11}, e_3'', n_{12}), e_3', n_2)$ with

$$n_2 = \overline{type}_{V_D}(t_{G_{EA}}(e_3)) \Rightarrow$$
$$\overline{tar_{EA}} \circ \overline{type}_{E_{EA}}(e_3) = \overline{tar_{EA}}[((n_{11}, e_3'', n_{12}), e_3', n_2)] = n_2 =$$
$$\overline{type}_{V_D}(t_{G_{EA}}(e_3)).$$

2. We have to show that $u_{ATG} \circ \overline{type} = type$.

(a) $u_{ATG,V_G} \circ \overline{type}_{V_G} = \overline{type}_{V_G} = type_{V_G}$.

(b) $u_{ATG,V_D} \circ \overline{type}_{V_D} = \overline{type}_{V_D} = type_{V_D}$.

(c) For $\overline{type}_{E_G}(e_1) = (n_1, e_1', n_2) \in \overline{TG_{E_G}}$ with $e_1' = type_{E_G}(e_1)$, we have $u_{ATG,E_G} \circ \overline{type}_{E_G}(e_1) = u_{ATG,E_G}[(n_1, e_1', n_2)] = e_1' = type_{E_G}(e_1)$.

(d) For $\overline{type}_{E_{NA}}(e_2) = (n_1, e_2', n_2) \in \overline{TG_{E_{NA}}}$ with $e_2' = type_{E_{NA}}(e_2)$, we have $u_{ATG,E_{NA}} \circ \overline{type}_{E_{NA}}(e_2) = u_{ATG,E_{NA}}[(n_1, e_2', n_2)] = e_2' = type_{E_{NA}}(e_2)$.

(e) For $\overline{type}_{E_{EA}}(e_3) = ((n_{11}, e_3'', n_{12}), e_3', n_2) \in \overline{TG_{E_{EA}}}$ with $e_3' = type_{E_{EA}}(e_3)$, we have the result that $u_{ATG,E_{EA}} \circ \overline{type}_{E_{EA}}(e_3) = u_{ATG,E_{EA}}[(n_{11}, e_3'', n_{12})] = e_3' = type_{E_{EA}}(e_3)$.

(f) $u_{ATG,D} \circ \overline{type}_D = \overline{type}_D = type_D$.

3. Given an AG-morphism $f : AG \to \overline{ATG}$ with $u_{ATG} \circ f = type$, we have to show that $f = \overline{type}$, which is shown in (a)–(f) below.

(a) $f_{V_G} = u_{ATG,V_G} \circ f_{V_G} = type_{V_G} = \overline{type}_{V_G}$.

(b) $f_{V_D} = u_{ATG,V_D} \circ f_{V_D} = type_{V_D} = \overline{type}_{V_D}$.

(c) Let $f_{E_G}(e_1) = (n_1, e_1', n_2) \in \overline{TG_{E_G}}$. Now $type = u_{ATG} \circ f$ implies that $type_{E_G}(e_1) = u_{ATG,E_G} \circ f_{E_G}(e_1) = u_{ATG,E_1}[(n_1, e_1', n_2)] = e_1'$. The fact that f is an AG-morphism implies

$$\overline{type}_{V_G} \circ s_{G_G}(e_1) \overset{(a)}{=} f_{V_G} \circ s_{G_G}(e_1) =$$
$$\overline{src_G} \circ f_{E_G}(e_1) = \overline{src_G}[(n_1, e_1', n_2)] = n_1,$$

$$\overline{type}_{V_G} \circ t_{G_G}(e_1) \overset{(a)}{=} f_{V_G} \circ t_{G_G}(e_1) =$$
$$\overline{tar_G} \circ f_{E_G}(e_1) = \overline{tar_G}[(n_1, e_1', n_2)] = n_2$$
$$\overset{(*)}{\Rightarrow} \overline{type}_{E_G}(e_1) = (n_1, e_1', n_2) = f_{E_1}(e_1)$$
$$\Rightarrow f_{E_G} = \overline{type}_{E_G}.$$

(*) follows from the definition of $\overline{type}_{E_G}$.

(d) Let $f_{E_{NA}}(e_2) = (n_1, e_2', n_2) \in \overline{TG_{E_{NA}}}$. Now $type = u_{ATG} \circ f$ implies that $type_{E_{NA}}(e_2) = u_{ATG,E_{NA}} \circ f_{E_{NA}}(e_2) = u_{ATG,E_{NA}}[(n_1, e_2', n_2)] =$

e_2'. The fact that f is an AG-morphism implies

$$\overline{type}_{V_G}(s_{G_{NA}}(e_2)) = f_{V_G} \circ s_{G_{NA}}(e_2) =$$
$$\overline{src_{NA}} \circ f_{E_{NA}}(e_2) = \overline{src_{NA}}[(n_1, e_2', n_2)] = n_1,$$
$$\overline{type}_{V_D}(s_{G_{NA}}(e_2)) = f_{V_D} \circ t_{G_{NA}}(e_2) =$$
$$\overline{tar}_{NA} \circ f_{E_{NA}}(e_2) = \overline{tar}_{NA}[(n_1, e_2', n_2)] = n_2$$
$$\Rightarrow \overline{type}_{E_{NA}}(e_2) = (n_1, e_2', n_2) = f_{E_{NA}}(e_2)$$
$$\Rightarrow f_{E_{NA}} = \overline{type}_{E_{NA}}.$$

(e) Let $f_{E_{EA}}(e_3) = ((n_{11}, e_3'', n_{12}), e_3', n_2) \in \overline{TG}_{E_{EA}}$. Now $type = u_{ATG} \circ f$ implies that $type_{E_{EA}}(e_3) = u_{ATG, E_{EA}} \circ f_{E_{EA}}(e_3) = u_{ATG, E_{EA}}[((n_{11}, e_3'', n_{12}), e_3', n_2)] = e_3'$. The fact that f is an AG-morphism implies

$$\overline{type}_{E_G}(s_{G_{EA}}(e_3)) = f_{E_G} \circ s_{G_{EA}}(e_3) = \overline{src_{EA}} \circ f_{E_{EA}}(e_3) =$$
$$\overline{src_{EA}}[((n_{11}, e_3'', n_{12}), e_3', n_2)] = (n_{11}, e_3'', n_{12}),$$
$$\overline{type}_{V_D}(t_{G_{EA}}(e_3)) = f_{V_D} \circ t_{G_{EA}}(e_3) = \overline{tar}_{EA} \circ f_{E_{EA}}(e_3) =$$
$$\overline{tar}_{EA}[((n_{11}, e_3'', n_{12}), e_3', n_2)] = n_2$$
$$\Rightarrow \overline{type}_{E_{EA}}(e_3) = ((n_{11}, e_3'', n_{12}), e_3', n_2) = f_{E_{EA}}(e_3)$$
$$\Rightarrow f_{E_{EA}} = \overline{type}_{E_{EA}}.$$

(f) $f_D = u_{ATG, D} \circ f_D = type_D = \overline{type}_D$.

$\square$

C.6 Proof of Lemma 13.20

1. We have to show that (a) p_t is a concrete production and (b) p_t is unique. Let $R_{V_G}' = R_{V_G} \backslash r_{V_G}(K_{V_G})$.

(a) We show that t_L, t_K, and t_R are well-defined concrete ATGI-clan morphisms and fulfill the properties in Definition 13.16.

- From Fact 13.11 and the fact that $type_G$ is concrete, t_L and t_K are well-defined concrete ATGI-clan morphisms, and we have by definition, $t_K = t_L \circ l$. In addition, m is a match with respect to p and $(G, type_G)$, and therefore $t_L = type_G \circ m \leq type_L$ and, from Remark 13.15, we also have $t_K = t_L \circ l \leq type_L \circ l = type_K$.

- t_R is well defined: from Definition 13.18, we know that $t_{K, V_G}(x_1) = t_{K, V_G}(x_2)$ for $x_1, x_2 \in K_{V_G}$ with $r_{V_G}(x_1) = r_{V_G}(x_2)$.

- t_R fulfills the properties of a concrete ATGI-clan morphism in Definition 13.8:

  - (0), (4), (5), and (6) follow from $t_{R,X} = type_{R,X}$ for $X \in \{V_D, E_G, E_{NA}, E_{EA}, D\}$.

- For (1), we show $t_{R,V_G}(s_{G_G}(e_1)) \in clan_I(src_G(t_{R,G}(e_1)))$ using the properties of $type$.

   Case 1. If $s_{G_G}(e_1) \in R'_{V_G}$, we have, from Definition 13.16,
   $$t_{R,V_G}(s_{G_G}(e_1)) = type_{R,V_G}(s_{G_G}(e_1)) \in$$
   $$clan_I(src_G(type_{R,E_G}(e_1))) = clan_I(src_G(t_{R,E_G}(e_1))).$$

   Case 2. If $s_{G_G}(e_1) = r_{V_G}(v) \in r_{V_G}(K_{V_G})$, we have, using $t_K \leq type_K$, $type_R \circ r = type_K$, and Definition 13.8,
   $$t_{R,V_G}(s_{G_G}(e_1)) = t_{K,V_G}(v) \in clan_I(type_{K,V_G}(v)) =$$
   $$clan_I(type_{R,V_G}(r_{V_G}(v))) = clan_I(type_{R,V_G}(s_{G_G}(e_1))) \subseteq$$
   $$clan_I(src_G(type_{R,E_G}(e_1))) = clan_I(src_G(t_{R,E_G}(e_1))).$$

- (2) and (3) follow analogously.
- We show that t_R is concrete: $\forall x \in r_{V_G}(K_{V_G})$, $x = r_{V_G}(x')$: $t_{R,V_G}(x) = t_{K,V_G}(x') \notin A$, since t_K is concrete, and $\forall x \in R'_{V_G}$: $t_{R,V_G}(x) = type_{R,V_G}(x) \notin A$, since p is an abstract production.

  - All t_{N_i} are concrete by construction. Furthermore, $t_{N_i} \leq type_{N_i}$ and $t_{N_i} \circ n_i = t_L$ by construction.

(b) Given a concrete production $p_{t'}$ with concrete ATGI-clan morphisms $t' = (t'_L, t'_K, t'_R)$, where $t'_L = type_G \circ m = t_L$, then we have, from Definition 13.16,

  - $t'_K = t'_L \circ l = t_L \circ l = t_K$;
  - $\forall x \in R'_{V_G} : t'_{R,V_G}(x) = type_{R,V_G}(x) = t_{R,V_G}(x)$;
  - $\forall x \in r_{V_G}(K_{V_G}), \exists x' \in K_{V_G} : r_{V_G}(x') = x : t'_{R,V_G}(x) = t'_{K,V_G}(x') = t_{K,V_G}(x') = t_{R,V_G}(x)$;
  - $t'_{R,X} = type_{R,X} = t_{R,X}$ for $X \in \{V_D, E_G, E_{NA}, E_{EA}, D\}$, since $t'_R, t_R \leq type_R$.

This means that $t = t'$ and $r_t = r_{t'}$.

For $\overline{NAC}'$ of $p_{t'}$ and $\overline{NAC}$ of p_t, we have $\overline{NAC}' = \overline{NAC}$ because $\overline{NAC}'$ and $\overline{NAC}$ are uniquely determined by NAC and t'_L and by NAC and t_L, respectively, and we have $t'_L = t_L$. Therefore p_t is unique.

2. We have to show that m is a consistent match with respect to p_t and $(G, type_G)$.

   By assumption, m is a consistent match with respect to p and $(G, type_G)$, and we have $type_g \circ m = t_L$. It remains to show that m satisfies $\overline{NAC}$. Assume the contrary: There then is an $(N, n, t_N) \in \overline{NAC}$ that is not satisfied by m. This means that we have $i \in I$ and $(N_i, n_i, type_{N_i}) \in NAC$ with $N = N_i$, $n = n_i$, and $t_N \leq type_{N_i}$. There is then an AG-morphism $o : N \rightarrow G \in \mathcal{M}'$ with $o \circ n = m$ and $type_G \circ o = t_N$. Hence it follows that $type_G \circ o = t_N \leq type_{N_i}$, which means that m does not satisfy NAC. This is a contradiction.

   Therefore m is a consistent match with respect to p_t and $(G, type_G)$, and we can apply p_t to $(G, type_G)$ as defined in Definition 13.17. The result is a direct transformation $(G, type_G) \overset{p_t,m}{\Longrightarrow} (H, type_H)$. The explicit definition of $type_H$ follows from the construction of $type_H$ as the induced morphism of $type_D$ and t_R in **AGraphs**, and therefore it is well defined.

3. Given the abstract direct transformation $(G, type_G) \overset{p,m}{\Longrightarrow} (H', type_{H'})$ according to Definition 13.18 and the concrete direct transformation $(G, type_G) \overset{p_t,m}{\Longrightarrow} (H, type_H)$ constructed in step 2 of this proof, obviously we have $H = H'$ (or, at least, they are isomorphic and we can replace H' by H), since they are constructed as the same pushout in **AGraphs**.

We have to show that $type_H = type_{H'}$ from the definition of $type_H$ in step 2 and of $type_{H'}$ in Definition 13.18. For $X \in \{V_G, V_D, E_G, E_{NA}, E_{EA}, D\}$, the following holds:

- $\forall x \in r'_X(D_X), \exists x' \in D_X : x = r'_X(x') : type_{H,X}(x) = type_{D,X}(x') = type_{H',X}(x)$.
- $\forall x \in H_X \backslash r'_X(D_X) : type_{H,X}(x) = t_{R,X}(x'') = type_{R,X}(x'') = type_{H',X}(x)$ with $m'(x'') = x$.

Therefore $type_H = type_{H'}$.

$\square$

References

[AGG]   AGG. *The AGG Homebase*. URL: http://tfs.cs.tu-berlin.de/agg/.

[AHS90]   J. Adámek, H. Herrlich, and G. Strecker. *Abstract and Concrete Categories*. Wiley, New York, 1990.

[Bal00]   P. Baldan. *Modelling Concurrent Computations from Contextual Petri Nets to Graph Grammars*. Ph.D. thesis, University of Pisa, 2000.

[Bar02]   R. Bardohl. A Visual Environment for Visual Languages. *Science of Computer Programming*, 44(2):181–203, 2002.

[BE00]   R. Bardohl and H. Ehrig. Conceptual Model of the Graphical Editor GENGED for the Visual Definition of Visual Languages. In H. Ehrig, G. Engels, H.-J. Kreowski, and G. Rozenberg, editors, *Proceedings of TAGT 1998*, Lecture Notes in Computer Science, No. 1764, pages 252–266. Springer, 2000.

[BEd⁺03]   R. Bardohl, H. Ehrig, J. de Lara, O. Runge, G. Taentzer, and I. Weinhold. *Node Type Inheritance Concepts for Typed Graph Transformation*. Technical Report 2003/19, TU Berlin, 2003.

[BEdLT04] R. Bardohl, H. Ehrig, J. de Lara, and G. Taentzer. Integrating Meta-modelling Aspects with Graph Transformation for Efficient Visual Language Definition and Model Manipulation. In M. Wermelinger and T. Margaria, editors, *Proceedings of FASE 2004*, Lecture Notes in Computer Science, No. 2984, pages 214–228. Springer, 2004.

[BEU03]   B. Braatz, H. Ehrig, and M. Urbásek. Petri Net Transformations in the Petri Net Baukasten. In H. Ehrig, W. Reisig, G. Rozenberg, and H. Weber, editors, *Proceedings of PNTCS 2002*, Lecture Notes in Computer Science, No. 2472, pages 37–65. Springer, 2003.

[BFK00]   M.R. Berthold, I. Fischer, and M. Koch. *Attributed Graph Transformation with Partial Attribution*. Technical Report 2000-2, TU Berlin, March 2000.

[BJ97]   R. Brown and G. Janelidze. Van Kampen Theorems for Categories of Covering Morphisms in Lextensive Categories. *Journal of Pure and Applied Algebra*, 119:255–263, 1997.

[BK02]   P. Baldan and B. König. Approximating the Behaviour of Graph Transformation Systems. In A. Corradini, H. Ehrig, H.-J. Kreowski, and G. Rozenberg, editors, *Proceedings of ICGT 2002*, Lecture Notes in Computer Science, No. 2505, pages 14–29. Springer, 2002.

[BKPT05]   P. Bottoni, M. Koch, F. Parisi-Presicce, and G. Taentzer. Termination
of High-Level Replacement Units with Application to Model Transformation. In M. Minas, editor, *Proceedings of VLFM 2004, Electronic
Notes in Theoretical Computer Science*, Vol. 127(4), pages 71–86. Elsevier, 2005.

[BP02]   L. Baresi and M. Pezze. A Toolbox for Automating Visual Software
Engineering. In R. Kutsche and H. Weber, editors, *Proceedings of FASE
2002, Lecture Notes in Computer Science*, No. 2306, pages 189–202.
Springer, 2002.

[BST00]   P. Bottoni, A. Schürr, and G. Taentzer. Efficient Parsing of Visual Languages Based on Critical Pair Analysis and Contextual Layered Graph
Transformation. In *Proceedings of VL 2000*, pages 59–60. IEEE, 2000.

[CEKR02]   A. Corradini, H. Ehrig, H.-J. Kreowski, and G. Rozenberg, editors. *Proceedings of ICGT 2002, Lecture Notes in Computer Science*, No. 2505.
Springer, 2002.

[CL95]   I. Claßen and M. Löwe. Scheme Evolution in Object Oriented Models:
A Graph Transformation Approach. In M. Wirsing, editor, *Proceedings
of the Workshop on Formal Methods, ISCE 1995*, 1995.

[dLT04]   J. de Lara and G. Taentzer. Automated Model Transformation and its
Validation with AToM^3 and AGG. In A.F. Blackwell, K. Marriott, and
A. Shimojima, editors, *Proceedings of DIAGRAMS 2004, Lecture Notes
in Computer Science*, No. 2980, pages 182–198. Springer, 2004.

[dLV02a]   J. de Lara and H. Vangheluwe. ATOM^3: A Tool for Multi-Formalism
Modelling and Meta-Modelling. In R. Kutsche and H. Weber, edi-
tors, *Proceedings of FASE 2002, Lecture Notes in Computer Science*,
No. 2306, pages 174–188. Springer, 2002.

[dLV02b]   J. de Lara and H. Vangheluwe. Computer Aided Multi-Paradigm Modelling to Process Petri-Nets and Statecharts. In A. Corradini, H. Ehrig,
H.-J. Kreowski, and G. Rozenberg, editors, *Proceedings of ICGT 2002,
Lecture Notes in Computer Science*, No. 2505, pages 239–253. Springer,
2002.

[EE05]   H. Ehrig and K. Ehrig. Overview of Formal Concepts for Model Transformations Based on Typed Attributed Graph Transformation. In
G. Karsai and G. Taentzer, editors, *Proceedings of GraMoT 2005*, Electronic Notes in Theoretical Computer Science. Elsevier, 2005.

[EEdL$^+$05]   H. Ehrig, K. Ehrig, J. de Lara, G. Taentzer, D. Varró, and S. Varró-
Gyapay. Termination criteria for model transformation. In M. Cerioli,
editor, *Proceedings of FASE 2005, Lecture Notes in Computer Science*,
No. 3442, pages 49–63. Springer, 2005.

[EEHP04]   H. Ehrig, K. Ehrig, A. Habel, and K.-H. Pennemann. Constraints and
Application Conditions: From Graphs to High-Level Structures. In
H. Ehrig, G. Engels, F. Parisi-Presicce, and G. Rozenberg, editors, *Proceedings of ICGT 2004, Lecture Notes in Computer Science*, No. 3256,
pages 287–303. Springer, 2004. (Longer version to appear in Fundamenta Informaticae, 2005.)

[EEKR99]   H. Ehrig, G. Engels, H.-J. Kreowski, and G. Rozenberg, editors. *Handbook of Graph Grammars and Computing by Graph Transformation, Vol.
2: Applications, Languages and Tools*. World Scientific, Singapore, 1999.

[EEPR04]   H. Ehrig, G. Engels, F. Parisi-Presicce, and G. Rozenberg, editors. *Graph Transformations, Proceedings of ICGT 2004, Lecture Notes in Computer Science*, No. 3256. Springer, 2004.

[EEPT05]   H. Ehrig, K. Ehrig, U. Prange, and G. Taentzer. Formal Integration of Inheritance with Typed Attributed Graph Transformation for Efficient VL Definition and Model Manipulation. In *Proceedings of VL/HCC 2005*, pages 71–78. IEEE, 2005.

[EGP99]   H. Ehrig, M. Gajewsky, and F. Parisi-Presicce. High-Level Replacement Systems Applied to Algebraic Specifications and Petri Nets. In H. Ehrig, H.-J. Kreowski, U. Montanari, and G. Rozenberg, editors, *Handbook of Graph Grammars and Computing by Graph Transformation, Vol. 3:* Concurrency, Parallelism and Distribution, pages 341–399. World Scientific, 1999.

[EH86]   H. Ehrig and A. Habel. Graph Grammars with Application Conditions. In G. Rozenberg and A. Salomaa, editors, *The Book of L*, pages 87–100. Springer, 1986.

[EHKP91a]   H. Ehrig, A. Habel, H.-J. Kreowski, and F. Parisi-Presicce. From Graph Grammars to High Level Replacement Systems. In H. Ehrig, H.-J. Kreowski, and G. Rozenberg, editors, *Graph Grammars and Their Application to Computer Science, Lecture Notes in Computer Science*, No. 532, pages 269–291. Springer, 1991.

[EHKP91b]   H. Ehrig, A. Habel, H.-J. Kreowski, and F. Parisi-Presicce. Parallelism and Concurrency in High-Level Replacement Systems. *Mathematical Structures in Computer Science*, 1(3):361–404, 1991.

[EHPP04]   H. Ehrig, A. Habel, J. Padberg, and U. Prange. Adhesive High-Level Replacement Categories and Systems. In H. Ehrig, G. Engels, F. Parisi-Presicce, and G. Rozenberg, editors, *Proceedings of ICGT 2004, Lecture Notes in Computer Science*, No. 3256, pages 144–160. Springer, 2004. (Longer version to appear in Fundamenta Informaticae, 2005.)

[Ehr79]   H. Ehrig. Introduction to the Algebraic Theory of Graph Grammars (A Survey). In V. Claus, H. Ehrig, and G. Rozenberg, editors, *Graph Grammars and Their Application to Computer Science and Biology, Lecture Notes in Computer Science*, No. 73, pages 1–69. Springer, 1979.

[EK76]   H. Ehrig and H.-J. Kreowski. Parallelism of Manipulations in Multidimensional Information Structures. In A.W. Mazurkiewicz, editor, *Proceedings of MFCS 1976, Lecture Notes in Computer Science*, No. 45, pages 284–293. Springer, 1976.

[EK04]   H. Ehrig and B. König. Deriving Bisimulation Congruences in the DPO Approach to Graph Rewriting. In I. Walukiewicz, editor, *Proceedings of FOSSACS 2004, Lecture Notes in Computer Science*, No. 2987, pages 151–166. Springer, 2004.

[EKMR99]   H. Ehrig, H.-J. Kreowski, U. Montanari, and G. Rozenberg, editors. *Handbook of Graph Grammars and Computing by Graph Transformation, Vol. 3:* Concurrency, Parallelism and Distribution. World Scientific, Singapore, 1999.

[EM85]   H. Ehrig and B. Mahr. *Fundamentals of Algebraic Specification 1: Equations and Initial Semantics*, EATCS Monographs in Theoretical Computer Science, No. 6. Springer, Berlin Heidelberg, 1985.

[EM90]   H. Ehrig and B. Mahr. *Fundamentals of Algebraic Specification 2: Module Specifications and Constraints*, EATCS Monographs in Theoretical Computer Science, No. 21. Springer, Berlin Heidelberg, 1990.

[EMC⁺01]   H. Ehrig, B. Mahr, F. Cornelius, M. Große-Rhode, and P. Zeitz. *Mathematisch-strukturelle Grundlagen der Informatik*. Springer, Berlin Heidelberg, 2001.

[EPS73]   H. Ehrig, M. Pfender, and H.J. Schneider. Graph Grammars: an Algebraic Approach. In *Proceedings of FOCS 1973*, pages 167–180. IEEE, 1973.

[EPT04]   H. Ehrig, U. Prange, and G. Taentzer. Fundamental Theory for Typed Attributed Graph Transformation. In H. Ehrig, G. Engels, F. Parisi-Presicce, and G. Rozenberg, editors, *Proceedings of ICGT 2004, Lecture Notes in Computer Science*, No. 3256, pages 161–177. Springer, 2004. (Longer version to appear in Fundamenta Informaticae, 2005.)

[ER76]   H. Ehrig and B.K. Rosen. *Commutativity of Independent Transformations on Complex Objects*. Technical Report RC 6251, IBM Research, 1976.

[ERT99]   C. Ermel, M. Rudolf, and G. Taentzer. The AGG-Approach: Language and Tool Environment. In H. Ehrig, G. Engels, H.-J. Kreowski, and G. Rozenberg, editors, *Handbook of Graph Grammars and Computing by Graph Transformation, Vol. 2:* Applications, Languages and Tools, pages 551–603. World Scientific, 1999.

[FKTV99]   I. Fischer, M. Koch, G. Taentzer, and V. Volle. Distributed Graph Transformation with Application to Visual Design of Distributed Systems. In H. Ehrig, H.-J. Kreowski, U. Montanari, and G. Rozenberg, editors, *Handbook of Graph Grammars and Computing by Graph Transformation, Vol. 3: Concurrency, Parallelism and Distribution*, pages 269–340. World Scientific, 1999.

[FUJ]   FUJABA. *From UML to Java and Back Again: the FUJABA Homepage*. URL: http://www.fujaba.de.

[Gro]   Object Management Group. *UML Profile for Schedulability, Performance and Time*. URL: http://www.omg.org.

[GTV03]   *Proceedings of GT-VMT 2002, Electronic Notes in Theoretical Computer Science*, Vol. 72(3). Elsevier, 2003.

[GXL]   GXL. *Graph eXchange Language*. URL: http://www.gupro.de/GXL.

[Har87]   D. Harel. Statecharts: A Visual Formalism for Complex Systems. *Science of Computer Programming*, 8(3):231–274, 1987.

[HHT96]   A. Habel, R. Heckel, and G. Taentzer. Graph Grammars with Negative Application Conditions. *Fundamenta Informaticae*, 26(3/4):287–313, 1996.

[HHT02]   J.H. Hausmann, R. Heckel, and G. Taentzer. Detection of Conflicting Functional Requirements in a Use Case-Driven Approach. In *Proceedings of ICSE 2002*, pages 105–115. ACM, 2002.

[HKT02]   R. Heckel, J. Küster, and G. Taentzer. Confluence of Typed Attributed Graph Transformation Systems. In A. Corradini, H. Ehrig, H.-J. Kreowski, and G. Rozenberg, editors, *Proceedings of ICGT 2002, Lecture Notes in Computer Science*, No. 2505, pages 161–176. Springer, 2002.

[HP05]   A. Habel and K.-H. Pennemann. Nested Constraints and Application Conditions for High-Level Structures. In H.-J. Kreowski, U. Montanari,

F. Orejas, G. Rozenberg, and G. Taentzer, editors, *Formal Methods in Software and Systems Modeling*, Lecture Notes in Computer Science, No. 3393, pages 293–308. Springer, 2005.

[HW95]   R. Heckel and A. Wagner. Ensuring Consistency of Conditional Graph Rewriting – a Constructive Approach. In *Proceedings of SEGRAGRA 1995, Electronic Notes in Theoretical Computer Science*, Vol. 2. Elsevier, 1995.

[JR80]   D. Janssens and G. Rozenberg. On the structure of node-label-controlled graph languages. *Information Sciences*, 20(3):191–216, 1980.

[Kre78]   H.-J. Kreowski. *Manipulationen von Graphmanipulationen*. Ph.D. thesis, TU Berlin, 1978.

[Lam04]   L. Lambers. A New Version of GTXL: An Exchange Format for Graph Transformation Systems. In T. Mens, A. Schürr, and G. Taentzer, editors, *Proceedings of GraBaTs 2004, Electronic Notes in Theoretical Computer Science*, Vol. 127(1), pages 51–63. Elsevier, 2004.

[LKW93]   M. Löwe, M. Korff, and A. Wagner. An Algebraic Framework for the Transformation of Attributed Graphs. In M.R. Sleep, M.J. Plasmeijer, and M.C.J.D. van Eekelen, editors, *Term Graph Rewriting: Theory and Practice*, pages 185–199. Wiley, 1993.

[Löw90]   M. Löwe. *Extended Algebraic Graph Transformation*. Ph.D. thesis, TU Berlin, 1990.

[LS04]   S. Lack and P. Sobociński. Adhesive Categories. In I. Walukiewicz, editor, *Proceedings of FOSSACS 2004, Lecture Notes in Computer Science*, No. 2987, pages 273–288. Springer, 2004.

[LS05]   S. Lack and P. Sobociński. Adhesive and Quasiadhesive Categories. *Theoretical Informatics and Applications*, 39(3):511–545, 2005.

[Lyn96]   N. Lynch. *Distributed Algorithms*. Morgan Kaufmann, San Mateo, CA, 1996.

[Mac71]   S. MacLane. *Categories for the Working Mathematician*, Graduate Texts in Mathematics, No. 5. Springer, New York, 1971.

[Mil01]   R. Milner. Bigraphical Reactive Systems. In K. Guldstrand Larsen and M. Nielsen, editors, *Proceedings of CONCUR 2001, Lecture Notes in Computer Science*, No. 2154, pages 16–35. Springer, 2001.

[Min97]   M. Minas. Diagram Editing with Hypergraph Parser Support. In *Proceedings of VL 1997*, pages 230–237. IEEE, 1997.

[MM90]   J. Meseguer and U. Montanari. Petri Nets Are Monoids. *Information and Computation*, 88(2):105–155, 1990.

[MST02]   T. Mens, A. Schürr, and G. Taentzer, editors. *Proceedings of GraBaTs 2002, Electronic Notes in Theretical Computer Science*, Vol. 72(2). Elsevier, 2002.

[MST04]   T. Mens, A. Schürr, and G. Taentzer, editors. *Proceedings of GraBaTs 2004, Electronic Notes in Theoretical Computer Science*, Vol. 127(1). Elsevier, 2004.

[MTR04]   T. Mens, G. Taentzer, and O. Runge. Detecting Structural Refactoring Conflicts Using Critical Pair Analysis. In R. Heckel and T. Mens, editors, *Proceedings of SETra 2004, Electronic Notes in Theoretical Computer Science*, Vol. 127(3). Elsevier, 2004.

[Nag79]   M. Nagl. *Graph-Grammatiken. Theorie, Implementierung, Anwendungen*. Vieweg, Braunschweig, 1979.

[NRT92]   M. Nielsen, G. Rozenberg, and P. S. Thiagarajan. Elementary Transition
            Systems. *Theoretical Computer Science*, 96(1):3–33, 1992.
[Pad96]   J. Padberg. *Abstract Petri Nets: A Uniform Approach and Rule-Based
            Refinement.* Ph.D. thesis, TU Berlin, 1996.
[PER95]   J. Padberg, H. Ehrig, and L. Ribeiro. Algebraic High-Level Net Trans-
            formation Systems. *Mathematical Structures in Computer Science*,
            5(2):217–256, 1995.
[Plu93]   D. Plump. Hypergraph Rewriting: Critical Pairs and Undecidability of
            Confluence. In M.R. Sleep, M.J. Plasmeijer, and M.J.D. van Eekelen,
            editors, *Term Graph Rewriting: Theory and Practice*, pages 201–214.
            Wiley, 1993.
[Plu95]   D. Plump. On Termination of Graph Rewriting. In M. Nagl, editor,
            Proceedings of WG 1995, Lecture Notes in Computer Science, No. 1017,
            pages 88–100. Springer, 1995.
[PR69]   J.L. Pfaltz and A. Rosenfeld. Web Grammars. In D.E. Walker and L.M.
            Norton, editors, *Proceedings of IJCAI 1969*, pages 609–620. William
            Kaufmann, 1969.
[Pra71]   T.W. Pratt. Pair Grammars, Graph Languages and String-to-Graph
            Translations. *Journal of Computer and System Sciences*, 5(6):560–595,
            1971.
[Pra04]   U. Prange. *Confluence of Adhesive HLR Systems with Applications
            to Typed Attributed Graph Transformation Systems.* Technical Report
            2004/22, TU Berlin, 2004.
[Rao84]   J.C. Raoult. On Graph Rewriting. *Theoretical Computer Science*, 32:1–
            24, 1984.
[Rei85]   W. Reisig. *Petri Nets*, EATCS Monographs on Theoretical Computer
            Science, No. 4. Springer, Berlin, 1985.
[Ren04]   A. Rensink. Representing First-Order Logic Using Graphs. In H. Ehrig,
            G. Engels, F. Parisi-Presicce, and G. Rozenberg, editors, *Proceedings of
            ICGT 2004, Lecture Notes in Computer Science*, No. 3256, pages 319–
            335. Springer, 2004.
[RFW+04]   C. Raistrick, P. Francis, J. Wright, C. Carter, and I. Wilkie, editors.
            Model Driven Architecture with Executable UML. Cambridge University
            Press, 2004.
[Roz97]   G. Rozenberg, editor. *Handbook of Graph Grammars and Computing
            by Graph Transformation, Vol. 1:* Foundations. World Scientific, Singa-
            pore, 1997.
[RT05]   A. Rensink and G. Taentzer. Ensuring Structural Constraints in Graph-
            Based Models with Type Inheritance. In M. Cerioli, editor, *Proceedings
            of FASE 2005, Lecture Notes in Computer Science*, No. 3442, pages 64–
            79. Springer, 2005.
[Sch94]   A. Schürr. Specification of Graph Translators with Triple Graph Gram-
            mars. In E.W. Mayr, G. Schmidt, and G. Tinhofer, editors, *Proceedings
            of WG 1994, Lecture Notes in Computer Science*, No. 903, pages 151–
            163. Springer, 1994.
[Sch97]   A. Schürr. Programmed Graph Replacement Systems. In G. Rozen-
            berg, editor, *Handbook of Graph Grammars and Computing by Graph
            Transformation, Vol. 1:* Foundations, pages 479–546. World Scientific,
            1997.

[SET03]   *Proceedings of SETRA 2002, Electronic Notes in Theoretical Computer Science*, Vol. 72(4). Elsevier, 2003.

[Sob04]   P. Sobociński. *Deriving Process Congruences from Reaction Rules.* Ph.D. thesis, BRICS, 2004.

[SWZ99]   A. Schürr, A.J. Winter, and A. Zündorf. The PROGRES-Approach: Language and Environment. In H. Ehrig, G. Engels, H.-J. Kreowski, and G. Rozenberg, editors, *Handbook of Graph Grammars and Computing by Graph Transformation, Vol. 2:* Applications, Languages and Tools, pages 487–550. World Scientific, 1999.

[Tae01]   G. Taentzer. Towards Common Exchange Formats for Graphs and Graph Transformation Systems. In J. Padberg, editor, *Proceedings of UNIGRA 2001, Electronic Notes in Theoretical Computer Science*, Vol. 44(4), pages 1–13, 2001.

[Var04]   S. Varró-Gyapay. *Model Transformation from General Resource Models to Petri Nets Using Graph Transformation.* Technical Report 2004/19, TU Berlin, 2004.

[VP03]   D. Varró and A. Pataricza. VPM: A visual, precise and multilevel meta-modeling framework for describing mathematical domains and UML. *Journal on Software and Systems Modeling*, 2(3):187–210, 2003.

[VVP02]   D. Varró, G. Varró, and A. Pataricza. Designing the Automatic Transformation of Visual Languages. *Science of Computer Programming*, 44(2):205–227, 2002.

[Wol98]   D. Wolz. *Colimit Library for Graph Transformations and Algebraic Development Techniques.* Ph.D. thesis, TU Berlin, 1998.

Index

Monographs in Theoretical Computer Science · An EATCS Series

K. Jensen
Coloured Petri Nets
Basic Concepts, Analysis Methods
and Practical Use, Vol. 1
2nd ed.

K. Jensen
Coloured Petri Nets
Basic Concepts, *Analysis Methods*
and Practical Use, Vol. 2

K. Jensen
Coloured Petri Nets
Basic Concepts, Analysis Methods
and *Practical Use*, Vol. 3

A. Nait Abdallah
The Logic of Partial Information

Z. Fülöp, H. Vogler
Syntax-Directed Semantics
Formal Models Based
on Tree Transducers

A. de Luca, S. Varricchio
**Finiteness and Regularity
in Semigroups and Formal Languages**

E. Best, R. Devillers, M. Koutny
Petri Net Algebra

S.P. Demri, E.S. Orlowska
**Incomplete Information:
Structure, Inference, Complexity**

J.C.M. Baeten, C.A. Middelburg
Process Algebra with Timing

L.A. Hemaspaandra, L. Torenvliet
Theory of Semi-Feasible Algorithms

E. Fink, D. Wood
Restricted-Orientation Convexity

Zhou Chaochen, M.R. Hansen
Duration Calculus
A Formal Approach to Real-Time
Systems

M. Große-Rhode
**Semantic Integration
of Heterogeneous Software
Specifications**

H. Ehrig, K. Ehrig, U. Prange, G. Taentzer
**Fundamentals of Algebraic
Graph Transformation**

Texts in Theoretical Computer Science · An EATCS Series